Employment Law

Employment Law

James Holland LLB, PhD, Barrister
Professor of Employment Law, Associate Dean, Faculty of Law,
University of the West of England, Bristol

and

Stuart Burnett MA, LLM Barrister
Formerly Director of Operations, EEF Western
Visiting Lecturer, UWE, Bristol

OXFORD
UNIVERSITY PRESS

OXFORD
UNIVERSITY PRESS

Great Clarendon Street, Oxford OX2 6DP

Oxford University Press is a department of the University of Oxford.
It furthers the University's objective of excellence in research, scholarship,
and education by publishing worldwide in

Oxford New York

Auckland Cape Town Dar es Salaam Hong Kong Karachi
Kuala Lumpur Madrid Melbourne Mexico City Nairobi
New Delhi Shanghai Taipei Toronto

With offices in

Argentina Austria Brazil Chile Czech Republic France Greece
Guatemala Hungary Italy Japan South Korea Poland Portugal
Singapore Switzerland Thailand Turkey Ukraine Vietnam

Published in the United States
by Oxford University Press Inc., New York

First published Blackstone Press

British Library Cataloguing in Publication Data
Data available

Library of Congress Cataloging in Publication Data
Data available

ISBN 0-19-927730-3

1 3 5 7 9 10 8 6 4 2

Typeset by Newgen Imaging Systems (P) Ltd., Chennai, India
Printed in Great Britain
on acid-free paper by
Antony Rowe Ltd, Chippenham, Wiltshire

OUTLINE CONTENTS

DETAILED CONTENTS

PREFACE

This book is designed for use on the various Legal Practice Courses offered throughout the country. In writing the book we have tried to take into account the comments received from colleagues in other institutions concerning the particular needs of their courses as well as practitioners who also use the text, so that we hope we have at least pleased some of the people for some of the time. Each chapter deals with a specific area of employment law, but we have attempted throughout the text to show the overlap that exists between the common law and statutory rights and which pervades the subject so as to recreate the concerns that have to be foremost in a solicitor's mind when advising a client.

The book concentrates on what is usually termed 'individual employment law', touching on trade union matters only where they relate directly to this theme. Individual employment law nevertheless covers an extensive range of activities, so that we have sought to weight the chapters according to two main criteria: first, the need to address the concerns of both corporate and private clients; secondly, according to the workload of the courts and tribunals. Further, from our experience in lecturing on the LPC and previously on the Law Society Finals course, we have tried to identify the areas which cause students most concern and provide practical guidance on how these problems may be resolved.

The year 2004 has been another interesting one (along the lines of the Chinese curse 'may you live in interesting times'). More particularly, October 1st has proved to be an interesting date with the introduction of wide-sweeping reforms to the procedural aspects of unfair dismissal legislation. October 1st also saw changes to the law on disability discrimination, and the new Employment Tribunals (Constitution and Rules of Procedure) Regulations came into force. These regulations introduce (as from April 2005) prescribed forms for bringing claims (the ET1) and the novel idea of default judgments being made. Changes to time limits, fixed conciliation periods and how costs may be awarded will also prove 'interesting' for practitioners.

And once again we have the 'flared-trousers theory' in operation (revitalising an idea that was once out of fashion, then in, then out and now back in again) with the introduction of ERA 1996, s. 98A allowing employers to fail in their procedures but still argue this 'made no difference' to the fairness of the dismissal. In addition to this we have new regulations on religious discrimination and sexual orientation discrimination, together with developments in the so-called family-friendly provisions. The case law has also moved on at its usual pace as well with landmark decisions being handed down by the House of Lords in *Eastwood and another* v *Magnox Electric plc, Barber* v *Somerset County Council* and *Dunnachie* v *Kingston upon Hull City Council*.

At the time of writing we cannot be sure how all the new provisions will affect the practice of employment law; there will clearly be a settling-in period for employers, employees, and lawyers alike. This will apply on the shop floor in dealing with the new statutory dispute resolution procedures through to the employment tribunals themselves.

Employment law has always been a technically-challenging area of law; most of these changes appear to have made it more so. The original aims of what was then called the *industrial* tribunals system—to be speedy, informal, and accessible—now seem lost in the mists of time.

We would like to offer our thanks to the many people who have helped us with this and previous editions. At UWE, Bristol: to Tim Angell and Carol Crowdy for their help in ploughing through various drafts; to Dr Adrian Chandler for his advice and material relating to patents; and to our past students on the LPC. At the EEF: to practitioners and former colleagues for all their assistance and suggestions. We would also like to acknowledge the comments received from our colleagues in other LPC-provider institutions. We hope that we have incorporated the points raised.

During the last few years the Industrial Law Unit in the Faculty of Law conducted a survey of common practice within the top one hundred solicitors' firms concerning the drafting of confidentiality and restraint of trade clauses. References to this survey appear in **Chapters 7** and **8** under the title of 'the ILU Survey'. We would like to express our gratitude to all the firms who participated in that survey, many of which went well beyond merely supplying us with examples of their drafting practice. In particular, we would like to express our thanks to the following firms: Beaumont and Son, Charles Russell, Dawson & Co., Farrer & Co., Freshfields, Herbert Smith, Peter Carter-Ruck & Partners, Titmuss Sainer Dechert, Trowers & Hamlins and Watson, Farley & Williams.

Finally, our thanks to the publishers for their patience and encouragement and, specifically, to Rebecca Webb for all her help and advice.

The law is stated as at 1 October 2004.

James Holland
Stuart Burnett
Bristol

ABBREVIATIONS

ACAS	Advisory, Conciliation and Arbitration Service
art.	Article
Convention	European Convention on Human Rights
CRE	Commission for Racial Equality
DDA	Disability Discrimination Act 1995
DPA	Data Protection Act 1998
DRC	Disability Rights Commission
DTI	Department of Trade and Industry
EAT	Employment Appeal Tribunal
EC	European Community
ECJ	European Court of Justice
EDT	effective date of termination
EOC	Equal Opportunities Commission
EPA	Equal Pay Act 1970
EPCA	Employment Protection (Consolidation) Act 1978
ERA 1996	Employment Rights Act 1996
ERA 1999	Employment Relations Act 1999
ERDRA	Employment Rights (Dispute Resolution) Act 1998
ETA	Employment Tribunals Act 1996
ET Regs	Employment Tribunals (Constitution and Rules of Procedure) Regulations 2001
ET Rules	Employment Tribunals Rules of Procedure 2001
GMD	genuine material difference
GMF	genuine material factor
HRA 1998	Human Rights Act 1998
HSE	Health and Safety Executive
NDC	National Disability Council
NMWA 1998	National Minimum Wage Act 1998
para.	paragraph
PHI	permanent health insurance
PHR	pre-hearing review
PIDA	Public Interest Disclosure Act 1998
PTW Regs 2000	Part-time Workers (Prevention of Less Favourable Treatment) Regulations 2000
r.	rule
reg.	regulation
RRA	Race Relations Act 1976
s.	section
sch.	schedule
SDA	Sex Discrimination Act 1975

TULRCA	Trade Union and Labour Relations (Consolidation) Act 1992
TUPE	Transfer of Undertakings (Protection of Employment) Regulations 1981
TURERA	Trade Union Reform and Employment Rights Act 1993
UCTA 1977	Unfair Contract Terms Act 1977
WT Regs 1998	Working Time Regulations 1998

TABLE OF CASES

TABLE OF STATUTES

European legislation

International legislation

TABLE OF RULES AND REGULATIONS

European secondary legislation

1

Overview of employment law

1.1 Introduction

Employment law, on the whole, is not a conceptually difficult subject and a good dollop of analytical common sense can often work wonders. But instinct will not provide all the answers or the best advice. Employment law can be extremely detailed at times and a solicitor needs to grasp both the detail and the overall implications in order to give proper guidance to his or her client. The interrelationship between matters such as breach of contract and unfair dismissal, for instance, can cause some confusion to those new to the subject. Nevertheless, at its best employment law is logical, dynamic, interesting, and real. At its worst it resembles the M25: it all seems to have been built at the wrong time and in the wrong place, it grinds to a halt periodically for no apparent reason, it is frequently being dug up and expanded, and sometimes seems to go round in circles.

1.2 The topics covered in the book

These can be seen from the chapter headings. They centre on the substantive law, practice and procedure relating to the formation, operation, and termination of the contract of employment.

Collective employment law (i.e., the law concerning the rights, duties, and operations of trade unions) is not covered in this book except where it is necessary to explain the matters affecting individual rights.

1.3 The mixture of statutory and contractual rights

Modern employment law emerged out of a jumble of the Poor Laws, the history of Craftsmen's Guilds and Trade Unions, family law as applied to the behaviour of domestic servants and agricultural workers and, in the nineteenth century, the law of contract. By the 1960s one would find most employment texts set alongside contract textbooks, but, from the middle of that decade onwards, UK and European legislation has been the major driving force in the creation of employment rights and obligations.

Any questions raised in employment law may now involve: pure common law principles (mainly contractual); pure statutory principles; a combination of European Union and UK legislation and concepts; or a mixture of all the above. The lawyer who dabbles in employment law tends not to appreciate the detail (and often the conflict) involved in this mixture, so one of the recurrent themes in this book is to indicate the overlap between all these areas of law, but especially the key one of common law and statutory rules.

By way of a simple example, imagine that an employer has asked an employee to work at their Birmingham Factory instead of the Coventry site (these are about 20 miles apart) but she objects. Clearly, this problem centres on what the contract of employment says or means and one would hope that the dispute might be resolved by examining the contract to see whether there is a clause detailing when the employee can be required to work at different sites—a 'mobility' clause. If the contract is silent on the point, one would have to look at whether there are any implied terms which cover the situation and, in employment law, arguments on the use and range of 'implied terms' have kept many a lawyer's family from starving.

The contractual analysis does not reveal the whole picture, however. For instance, hidden in this simple order to move site may lurk questions of discrimination based on sex, race or disability, all involving a range of UK statutes and/or European Directives. And the position may become even more complicated if a dismissal results from the refusal of the employee to move to Birmingham.

Once dismissal has occurred (and even some resignations are deemed to amount to dismissals) the employee may have claims at common law and under statute. The most obvious common law claim is that of *wrongful dismissal*, which arises when a person is dismissed without notice or with inadequate notice and the employer had no contractually justifiable reasons for that action. The most obvious statutory claim is for *unfair dismissal* which is essentially based on two questions: (a) did the employer have a fair reason to dismiss; and (b) was that reason handled fairly (e.g., by use of proper procedures)? Many reports in newspapers or on television confuse wrongful and unfair dismissal, but they are quite different animals.

Thus the lawyer who thinks solely in terms of either common law or statutory rights may not cover all the potential claims (and there are other possibilities beyond those noted above). Equally, one needs to know where the issues will be determined. The main forum for employment disputes is that of the employment tribunals (known as industrial tribunals until August 1998), and they would have jurisdiction to determine nearly all the points raised in our example, though in contract-based matters they can only award a maximum of £25,000 and they would only have jurisdiction in the example above if a dismissal had occurred as they cannot entertain arguments about the operation of the contract while the employment relationship is still running. The ordinary courts, however, have some overlapping jurisdiction, so all the contractual claims could be decided there, but they could not hear any discrimination claims, nor the unfair dismissal action.

Figure 1.1 below sets out in diagrammatic form the various jurisdictions of the courts and tribunals. Employment tribunal practice and procedure is dealt with in **Chapter 13**.

1.4 A skeleton outline of the topics covered

1.4.1 Definition of 'employee'

Most of the rights and obligations dealt with in this book concern employers and employees; rights such as unfair dismissal, for instance, do not extend to independent contractors. The distinction is the same as you encountered at your academic stage of training in the law of torts (or obligations). Unfortunately, the term 'employee' has no workable statutory definition, so the analysis rests on a number of common law tests which explore the level of *control* a company has over an individual's work pattern, the extent to which the individual's

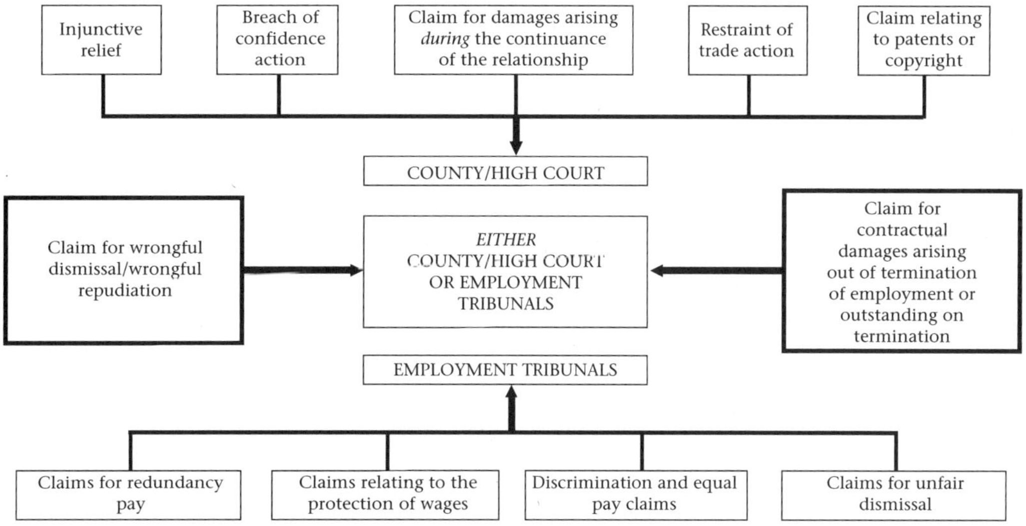

Figure 1.1 Jurisdictions of the courts and employment tribunals.

work is *integrated* into the main work of the company, whether there are *mutual obligations* present between the parties such as the payment of sick pay and the provision of personal service, and whether the individual in all the circumstances can be said to be *in business on their own account*.

However, modern work patterns have fudged the line between employees and independent contractors, e.g., one large company we know of has more people on site who are hired through employment agencies than it has full-time employees. Further, a great deal of EU-derived legislation does not make such a clear distinction between employees and other categories so that recent legislation has tended to define rights and obligations by reference to the more expansive term 'worker'. The question of who qualifies for employment rights (dealt with in **Chapter 2**) is therefore important in establishing rights but, will not concern most people as they will fall easily within the classification of 'employee'. When such problems do arise, however, they tend to centre on 'peripheral' workers such as those supplied by employment agencies and can often be extremely complicated matters.

1.4.2 The contract of employment

1.4.2.1 The form of the contract

We will deal in detail with the formation, contents, and operation of the contract in **Chapters 3** to **5**. Here we can say that a contract of employment is created like any other contract and may be made orally or in writing (or in any combination) and will be found in a mixture of express and implied terms. There is no standard format for such contracts and a solicitor should be wary of relying on general precedents that do not fit the circumstances of the case. There is a tolerated myth in employment law that each contract is negotiated on an individual basis with each employee. The reality is that most employees were simply given no option as to the contents of the contract, that many have never seen a written contract, that some think they have no contract (this applies to employers too), and that, if there are recognised trades unions in the company, they negotiated the terms of the contract (including those of non-members).

With this level of confusion over such a basic matter, it is hardly surprising, as we noted in passing above, that the employment contract is also riddled with *implied terms*. Very often these shape the contract; sometimes in a surprising way. Some, such as the duty of fidelity, cannot be excluded; others will stand unless express terms state the contrary.

1.4.2.2 Statutory intervention

There was a time when there was little statutory control over the *contents* of the contract. The first real intervention came in the 1960s with a document known as the *written statement*. The form of this statement is now prescribed by the Employment Rights Act 1996, s. 1 (ERA 1996). It is meant to provide a summary of the main contractual provisions. If an employer has not provided a contract containing all the matters which are meant to be included in the written statement he or she must provide a written statement to the employee within two months of their starting work. This is not the contract, though it can stand as very strong *prima facie* evidence of the contract and disputes regarding its alleged inaccuracies or its non-production can be referred to employment tribunals. Unfortunately, many employees have never seen one of these either.

More intervention has occurred recently covering matters such as the regulation of: the national minimum wage, maximum working hours, unauthorised deductions from wages, and the so-called 'family friendly' provisions. These are dealt with in **Chapter 4**.

1.4.2.3 The operation of the contract

Leaving aside questions of dismissal, the major concern of employees centres on how the contract is performed on a day-to-day basis. Problems will generally arise here relating to:

(a) what the terms are (a question of evidence); or

(b) what do those terms mean (a question of interpretation); or

(c) when can the employer change the terms (a question of law)?

As with our simple example above on mobility clauses, it is at this point that one first notices the real interplay between common law matters such as breach of contract and the other statutory rights and remedies. As we will explore in **Chapter 5** in particular, it is often best to approach this area by considering what the employee's response could be to any proposed interpretation or variation of the contractual terms. At one end the employee may simply put up with the employer's views, but there is a range of legal remedies which can be pursued such as seeking an injunction, suing for breach of contract or resigning and claiming wrongful and/or unfair dismissal.

1.4.3 Discrimination and equal pay

This topic is dealt with in **Chapter 6**.

Issues of sex, disability, race, or trade union membership discrimination may arise during recruitment, or in the operation of the contract or at termination.

It is unlawful to discriminate against anyone on the grounds of their sex, race, disability or marital status in recruitment, promotion, and access to benefits during employment, as well as in regard to dismissal. Discrimination on 'racial grounds' means in relation to colour, race, nationality, or ethnic or national origins. 'Disability' means a physical or mental impairment which is both substantial and has long-term effect. Trade union membership (or non-membership) discrimination is unlawful in terms of recruitment and there are special rules and penalties relating to selection for dismissal or action short of dismissal.

Discrimination may come in different forms: *direct* and *indirect* discrimination. Direct sex discrimination comes from an obvious act of treating the woman (usually) less favourably than a man. Indirect discrimination arises where the proportion of women (or a racial group) who can comply with a particular requirement or condition is considerably smaller than the proportion of men (or other racial groups) and it is to the person's detriment.

There are exceptions and defences to these general rules, e.g., that there is a genuine occupational qualification required (e.g., decency or authenticity points).

Enforcement is by means of application to an employment tribunal, which may make an order declaring the applicant's rights and award compensation.

1.4.4 Termination of the contract

The rights and remedies regarding termination at common law are dealt with in **Chapter 9** of this book; the statutory consequences are covered in **Chapters 10** and **11**. The central feature of **Chapter 9** is the concept of wrongful dismissal; **Chapter 10** deals with the most well-known aspect of employment law *viz* unfair dismissal; and **Chapter 11** deals with redundancy. We have hinted at how these topics interrelate in the text above.

A contract of employment can come to an end in a number of different ways:

(a) by agreement;

(b) by completion of a specific task;

(c) by expiry of a fixed-term;

(d) by automatic termination, e.g., frustration of the contract;

(e) by dismissal;

(f) by resignation.

1.4.4.1 Common law remedies

Dismissal and resignation are the most common forms of termination. In most cases either party may terminate the contract by giving adequate notice and, at common law, an employer can dismiss an employee for any reason. The only thing that matters to the common law is whether adequate notice was given. Notice periods are determined by the contract, subject to statutory minima which vary according to the length of service.

If the employer dismisses without giving adequate notice or payment in lieu of that notice, he or she may be in breach of contract. The claim is for what is termed a 'wrongful dismissal'. The employer is entitled to dismiss without notice (called a 'summary dismissal') only if the employee has committed a serious breach of the contract. Hence it is in both parties' interests to have the express terms clearly defined so that they know exactly where they stand on any given issue.

The amount of damages an employee will obtain is limited to what would have been earned during the notice period and is subject to the normal contractual rules—for example, the duty to mitigate loss.

If, on the other hand, the *employer* commits a serious breach of contract (e.g., the employer does not pay the employee) this will amount to a repudiation which the employee may accept as terminating the contract and resign. This is termed a 'wrongful repudiation' by the employer and means that the employee will be held to have been effectively dismissed. Damages are calculated in the same way as with a wrongful dismissal. The employee who does not resign and continues in employment may of course sue the employer for damages relating to any breach.

In limited cases one of the parties may obtain an injunction to prevent a breach of contract, e.g., to prevent a dismissal taking effect until contractual procedures have been followed. An order for specific performance will not be granted, however. The real importance of injunctions lies in actions for breach of confidence and restraint of trade.

In **Figure 1.2** you can see that where dismissal is with adequate notice there are no further common law consequences. Where dismissal is without notice (and that lack of notice

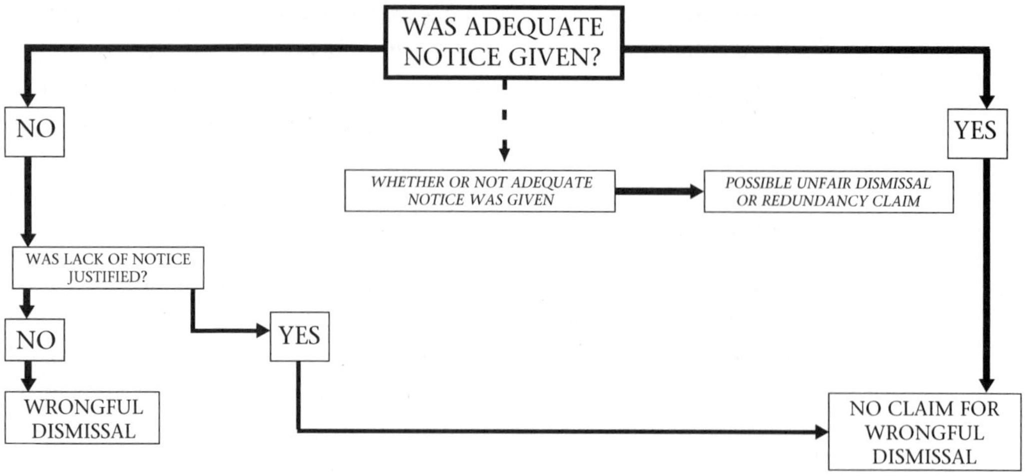

Figure 1.2 Dismissal with or without notice.

cannot be justified) the employee will be entitled to damages for wrongful dismissal. *Note, however, that in either case there may be statutory consequences such as a claim for unfair dismissal.*

1.4.4.2 Statutory remedies: unfair dismissal

'Unfair dismissal' is a technical term which has its own peculiar set of rules and procedures. Cases are heard exclusively in employment tribunals. Any claim must be presented within three months of what is termed the 'effective date of termination' (e.g., the end of the notice period).

Every employee is said to have the right not to be unfairly dismissed, but there are certain preliminary conditions to be met. First, the employee must qualify for the right. For instance, the right generally applies only to employees who have at least one year's continuous employment. Further, the employee must usually be aged below 65 or the 'normal retirement age' for that grade of employee in that company.

The employee must prove that he or she has been dismissed but, as with common law rights, a resignation may be deemed a dismissal if the employee resigned in the face of a serious breach by the employer. This is the same thing as wrongful repudiation but is called a 'constructive dismissal' in this setting.

'Fairness' is determined by a three-stage process. First, if there is any dispute on the matter an employee will have to prove they were, in law, dismissed, e.g., where there has been a resignation. Secondly, the burden is on the employer to show that the dismissal was for a 'fair reason'.

There are only five acceptable fair reasons: capability or qualifications; conduct; redundancy; statutory illegality; and 'some other substantial reason'. Dismissal for any other reason is unfair.

The third stage is to assess whether the fair reason was implemented fairly. The burden of proof here is neutral. Fairness is determined by three main factors:

- the definition contained in ERA 1996, s. 98(4) ('whether the dismissal is fair or unfair... (a) depends on whether in the circumstances (including the size and administrative resources of the employer's undertaking) the employer acted reasonably or unreasonably in treating... [the fair reason]... as a sufficient reason for dismissing the employee, and (b) shall be determined in accordance with equity and the substantial merits of the case');
- a vast amount of case law explaining the application of this definition in the setting of the tribunal's sense of industrial reality; and
- whether a fair procedure has been followed by the employer.

The primary remedies for unfair dismissal are reinstatement in the same job and re-engagement in a similar job. These are seldom ordered so that the main practical remedy is that of compensation.

Compensation is made up of two main elements—the basic and compensatory awards. They are assessed on different grounds *and the maximum figures are reviewed annually*, usually changing in February. The basic award is a fixed calculation, determined by reference to the age, length of service and earnings of the employee. The maximum basic award at the time of writing is £8,100. The compensatory award is based on what is just and equitable. It is calculated on nett payments. The maximum award is currently £55,000.

Both the basic award and the compensatory award may be subject to a number of deductions, e.g., in relation to contributory fault, *ex gratia* payments made, or failure to mitigate loss.

1.4.4.3 Statutory remedies: redundancy

Redundancy is a dismissal for a particular reason. That reason is that:

(a) the business has closed down; *or*

(b) the employee's particular place of work has closed down (even though other sites may still continue); *or*

(c) the requirement for employees to do that employee's particular work has ceased or diminished.

In effect, a redundancy arises where (without necessarily any fault on the employee's part) there is a surplus of labour. Where an employee is dismissed for redundancy there may be an entitlement to a statutory redundancy payment. This is calculated in the same way as the basic award for an unfair dismissal, i.e., according to age, length of service, and pay (again, to a maximum of £8,100). The contract may also entitle the employee to a contractual redundancy payment.

Redundancy is a fair *reason* for dismissal but, as with any other dismissal, if it is handled badly by the employer it may still constitute an unfair dismissal.

We can now consider an overview of the possible consequences of dismissal. You can see in **Figure 1.3** that, whatever the reason for dismissal, and whether adequate notice was given or not, the dismissal may yet be an unfair dismissal.

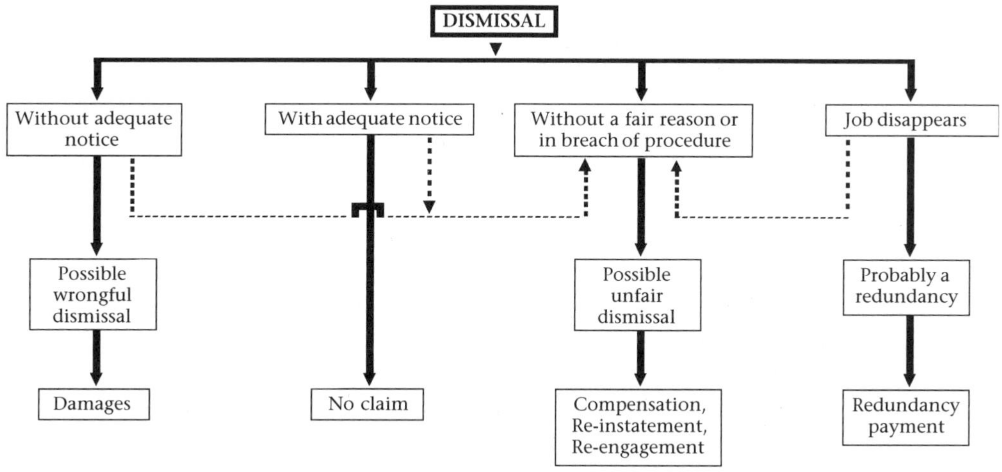

Figure 1.3 Possible consequences of dismissal.

The solicitor *must* be aware of this overview when giving advice to an employer. This applies at any stage: during the contract when the employer is issuing orders or varying terms of the contract, and also where a decision has been made to dismiss the employee.We have not included every possible consequence in the diagram, so matters such as discrimination must also be noted (there is no maximum figure for compensation in discrimination claims).

1.4.5 Takeovers and transfer of undertakings

This topic considers what happens to the employee's rights and duties when the ownership of the business changes (it is dealt with in **Chapter 12**). In many cases the transfer of ownership will be by share acquisition and this has no effect on the employee at all. However, where a business is transferred by other means (e.g., the business or part of it is sold), the position is that all the contractual and statutory rights concerning employees (except for pensions) will be automatically transferred as well. This will apply only where the transfer is a '*relevant transfer*', i.e., one in which:

(a) a business activity passes from one legal person to another;

(b) the unit transferred is a business or an identifiable part of a business.

Employees will maintain their contractual and statutory rights and obligations only if they are 'employed [by the transferor] immediately before the transfer', but the term 'immediately before' is now given a loose interpretation. In essence, therefore, employees employed as part of a transferred business can regard the transferee as having been their employer all along. Thus an employee who is dismissed at any time by the transferee can bring any contractual or statutory claims against the transferee.

Special rules apply where the employee is dismissed *because of the transfer*, either by the transferor in anticipation of the transfer or by the transferee after the sale. In such cases the employer can only rely on 'economic, technical or organisational reasons' affecting the workforce to justify the dismissal as a fair dismissal.

These ideas originated in and have been heavily influenced by EC Directives. They have proved to be the subject of much litigation and confusion.

1.4.6 Employment tribunal procedure

Chapter 13 examines employment tribunal procedure and the special rules that apply to actions for unfair dismissal and redundancy in particular. Employment tribunals operate in much the same way as the ordinary courts but there are peculiarities that can catch the unwary. They are not as informal as is commonly believed.

Settlement of cases is quite common practice.

1.4.7 Protecting the employer's interests

Chapters 7 and **8** concentrate on topics which do not fall within the jurisdiction of employment tribunals, *viz*, confidentiality and restraint of trade. These are technically complicated areas which require special attention. At one time employment lawyers very often did not deal with these topics at all, leaving them to Chancery specialists; but in the modern employment law context this is no longer the case as the advice given in relation to, say, a dismissal may have major repercussions on the efficacy of restraint or confidentiality clauses.

1.4.7.1 Confidentiality

During employment an employee owes his employer a fairly strict duty to maintain the secrecy of the employer's confidential information. Once the relationship has ended, however, only certain types of highly confidential information continue to receive protection. In **Chapter 7** we will see that a difficult balance has to be struck between the employer's trade secrets (which can be protected) and the employee's know-how (which cannot). The arguments (as with restraint of trade below) are usually set in the world of interim injunctions.

1.4.7.2 Restraint of trade

Employers are often anxious to guard against direct competition once employees have left the organisation. As well as seeking to protect their confidential information, employers may also wish to ensure that an ex-employee does not have the opportunity to exert influence over the employer's hard-earned trade connexions. Restraint clauses are used by all manner of businesses, from the small high-street hairdresser who wants to prevent the ex-stylist 'stealing' his clients, to the solicitor's firm which wishes to do the same as against the partner or assistant solicitor who has moved elsewhere, through to multi-national enterprises. In all cases the restraint is presumed to be void unless it passes a test of reasonableness as between the parties in terms of the time covered by the restraint, the area affected, and the market in which the business operates.

Restraint clauses take three main forms: *non-competition* restraints which prevent the ex-employee working in that industry or at least working for named competitors; *non-dealing* restraints which prevent ex-employees accepting business from, or conducting business with, former clients; and *non-solicitation* restraints which prevent ex-employees actually initiating contact with former clients. In all cases enforcement will be granted to the minimum level needed to protect the employer's legitimate interests. The aim is to protect against *unfair* competition, not competition *per se*.

1.5 The institutions

There are three main arenas in which employment law issues are settled:

(a) *At the workplace between employers and employees, or their trade unions*
This always gets extensive publicity in the media and the image is usually one of constant warfare. The reality is that, in general, major battle-lines are not drawn here on a day-to-day basis. The image of the 1960s, with pointless strikes and poor industrial relations, has long ceased to be reality. There are certainly disputes, usually connected with annual pay awards, but employers and employees are not locked in constant turmoil.

(b) *In the ordinary courts*
It is a key point that we will be dealing with *contracts* of employment, and thus the normal law of contract plays a vital role in our considerations. Anything which centres on breach of contract is primarily, and often exclusively, the province of the county court or High Court and not that of employment tribunals, e.g., restraint of trade.

(c) *In employment tribunals*
These bodies were set up to deal with employment law problems and their jurisdiction is immense. Most commonly they will hear unfair dismissal, redundancy, and discrimination cases. An appeal from the decision of an employment tribunal lies

with the Employment Appeal Tribunal (almost exclusively on a point of law only) and from there to the Court of Appeal.

In addition to all this there are other institutions which are relevant to this book and need to be noted specifically here.

1.5.1 ACAS

The Advisory, Conciliation and Arbitration Service (ACAS) seeks to promote improvements in industrial relations, e.g.:

(a) as regards collective matters in relation to the settlement of trade disputes, e.g., by arranging arbitration;
(b) to give employers, employers' associations, workers and trade unions advice on matters of industrial relations;
(c) to provide 'good practice' codes (e.g., relating to disciplinary procedures) which are not legally binding on parties but are admissible as evidence of good industrial practice; and
(d) to promote the settlement of any complaint presented to employment tribunals, e.g., for unfair dismissal.

ACAS may now charge for its services.

ACAS now has a new function as regards unfair dismissal complaints: that of offering litigants the option of arbitration instead of going to an employment tribunal (see **10.12.2** below).

1.5.2 EOC, CRE, and DRC

The Equal Opportunities Commission (EOC) seeks to eliminate discrimination on the grounds of sex or marital status. The Commission attempts to do this by means of research, advice, codes of practice and by providing assistance to individuals in proceedings, or by instituting its own proceedings, e.g., in the face of discriminatory advertisements, or formal investigations. It has recently been held to have sufficient locus to bring judicial review actions.

The Commission for Racial Equality (CRE) performs the same functions as the EOC in relation to equality of opportunity for racial groups. A new Disability Rights Commission was established under the Disability Rights Commission Act 1999 but all three bodies are due to merge into a single commission for equality and human rights. A white paper was published in May 2004 but it is unlikely that the single body will be established before late 2006. .

1.6 European influences

Employment law has been one of the most active areas of European legislation. Thus matters such as free movement of workers, rights to receive particulars of employment, equal pay, transfers of undertakings and redundancy consultations have all been the subject of Treaties, Regulations or Directives of the EU.

The effect of all this is four-fold:

(a) Some legislation is directly enforceable by individuals against the state or other individuals, i.e., they can enforce rights such as equal pay under art. 141 (formerly 119),

EC Treaty, by reference to the EC legislation itself. The EC legislation may therefore be cited and relied upon in any action (having direct applicability and direct effect).

(b) Other forms of EC legislation do not have direct applicability; though in limited cases they may have *direct effect*, which will amount to much the same thing. In the case of *Faccini Dori* v *Recreb srl* [1995] ECR I-3325, the full court of the ECJ addressed the issue of the *horizontal* direct effect of Directives, i.e., the applicability of Directives, outside any enacting national legislation, to legal persons (individuals and companies) suing other legal persons. The *Faccini Dori* case made it quite clear that Directives did not have direct horizontal effect. So, all employees in the *private sector* who seek to sue their employer must rely either on the wording of the UK legislation *simpliciter* or sue the UK Government under the *Francovich* principles (*Francovich* v *Italian Republic* [1995] ICR 722). Most Directives, however, do have *vertical direct effect*, so if the employee is employed by the State he or she may be able to rely on the wording of the Directive itself. It is therefore quite possible to have different rights ascribed to different groups of employees by reason only of who they work for.

(c) Where UK legislation has been implemented to comply with EC legislation it may be interpreted in a very purposive manner. That is, the statutory interpretation techniques used by the courts and their willingness to read the UK legislation so as to comply with the *spirit* of the EC enactment means that a purely literal approach to such UK legislation is unsafe even when the words are unambiguous in themselves. This is known as giving the Directive *indirect effect*.

(d) The influence of the Court of Justice of the European Communities and its general lack of a doctrine of binding precedent means that many areas are still in a state of flux.

Following the ratification of the Treaty of Amsterdam by all Member States of the EU in 1999, most of the Article numbers originally found in the Treaty of Rome 1957 have been changed. Thus, art. 119 has now become art. 141 EC Treaty. We will only refer to both the old and new numbers where the context demands it.

1.7 The Human Rights Act 1998 and employment law

In the general part of the LPC you will already have dealt with the key issues of incorporation of the European Convention on Human Rights via the 1998 Act. You will have seen that:

(a) All legislation, whenever enacted, must be interpreted in such a way as to comply with the rights granted under the Convention: HRA 1998, s. 3(1).

(b) But, in all cases, unless the UK legislation can be interpreted so as to comply with Convention rights, an Act of Parliament still takes precedence over Convention rights. This means that the *validity* of primary legislation is beyond judicial control. The same will be true of secondary legislation. However, even before the introduction of the HRA 1998, secondary legislation which was *ultra vires* its parent Act could be struck down by the normal process of judicial review. That principle can also be applied when human rights issues are involved unless the primary legislation prevents removal of the incompatibility between the legislation and human rights principles: s. 3(2)(c) and s. 6(2)(b), i.e., the incompatibility lies in the primary legislation itself. For these purposes primary legislation includes commencement orders and orders which amend primary legislation: HRA 1998, s. 21(1).

(c) All courts and tribunals must take into account the jurisprudence of the Convention, which means the decisions of the European Court of Human Rights, whenever a Convention right arises (HRA 1998, s. 2). However, UK courts are not bound to apply the decisions of the European Court. Equally, the doctrine of *stare decisis* is modified in that domestic binding precedents which are now found to conflict with Convention rights may be ignored.

(d) Certain courts (but not employment tribunals or the EAT) have the right to declare primary and secondary legislation incompatible with Convention Rights: HRA 1998, s. 4. A declaration of incompatibility only allows judges to scrutinise legislation. Such a declaration does not affect the validity of primary legislation, nor does it affect secondary legislation (subject to our comments above in (b)). Neither is the declaration directed at the litigants, so the case in hand is not affected by the declaration; it has no legal effect and is simply a 'warning shot' aimed at Parliament.

(e) There is no system of sending references (akin to art. 234, EC Treaty) to the European Court so that there is a possibility of conflict between the UK courts' interpretation of the Convention and that of the European Court (to which a 'victim' can still apply after exhausting the UK system).

(f) All public authorities must act in a way which is compatible with Convention rights: HRA 1998, s. 6. 'Public authority' includes 'any person certain of whose functions are functions of a public nature'; s. 6(3)(b). This includes courts and tribunals.

(g) Certain rights have not been incorporated e.g., art. 13 of the Convention.

(h) The areas which are likely to impact on employment law are detailed below at **1.7.3**.

If British courts follow the general pattern seen in decisions of the European Court of Human Rights on employment-related matters then the HRA 1998 is not likely to have a major, widesweeping impact on employment law. Many issues which fall within the ambit of the Convention are already covered in some detail by UK and European Legislation, though there is always the possibility that British courts will take a more inventive role than the Strasbourg court.

1.7.1 Which employers are affected?

Action may be taken directly against a 'public authority' under the HRA 1998, s. 6 claiming a breach of Convention rights; with ordinary employers an employee would have to persuade a court that, in analysing a cause of action, existing legislation or judicial precedents should be read in the light of Convention rights. Thus there is a distinction between 'vertical' and 'horizontal' effect akin to the application of Directives in EU Law.

The term 'public authority' has not been defined in the Act but will obviously include bodies such as local authorities. This still begs the question whether all activities undertaken by a public authority are caught by s. 6 or only those which are clearly a 'public function'. It was confirmed in parliamentary debates that the definition of 'public authority' in s. 6 was intended to apply to public bodies even when acting as employers (which is not a public function *per se*). Following *Pepper* v *Hart* [1993] AC 593 on the use of Hansard this may well settle any argument on s. 6 for employment purposes so that employees of public bodies will have a direct cause of action against their employers, whereas employees of private organisations will have to take the more circuitous route.

However, the Act does recognise that there will be hybrid bodies (e.g., privatised utilities, the BBC and professional bodies) who exercise both private and public functions. In relation to hybrid bodies s. 6(5) states that, '. . . a person is not a public authority by virtue of subsection (3)(b) if the nature of the act is private'.

At the time of writing, there is considerable debate as to whether employment matters should be classified as public or private functions. It may well be that some such activities (e.g., health and safety matters) are classified as public whilst general employment matters are private.

1.7.1.1 Victim

A person can only rely on Convention rights against a public authority where they fall within the definition of 'victim' (HRA 1998, s.7(7)). This generally means that the claimant must be a person who is directly affected by the alleged breach and prevents representative actions (e.g., by trade unions) except for very limited situations.

Proceedings against public authorities must be brought within one year of the act complained of.

1.7.2 Rights directly relevant to employment

1.7.2.1 Forced/compulsory labour, under art. 4 of the Convention

No forced labour claim has succeeded in Strasbourg to date, and speculations that working conditions, long hours and compulsory overtime amount to such a breach are not convincing. The employment relationship is a contractual one which both parties can terminate and, even within the relationship, existing legislation on working time, harassment etc. cover these areas adequately.

1.7.2.2 Freedom to join or not to join trade unions, under art. 11 of the Convention

Article 11 establishes the right to peaceful assembly and to freedom of association with others, including the right to form and join a trade union. Domestic law on this topic is already well-developed and this article is unlikely to have a major impact on employment law.

1.7.3 Other rights (indirectly) relevant to employment

1.7.3.1 Fair and public hearing, under art. 6 of the Convention

This is the most frequently-invoked article of the Convention. It states that '. . . everyone is entitled to a fair and public hearing within a reasonable time by an independent and impartial tribunal established by law'. Clearly this exists in the procedures adopted by the courts and employment tribunals. Some arguments have been raised that internal disciplinary proceedings are caught by this provision but these appear to be speculation for its own sake as any such decision can be 'reviewed' in a tribunal or court.

What is not so clear-cut is whether the lack of legal help/representation in tribunals might breach this article (see for instance *Airey* v *Ireland* (1979) 2 EHRR 305) or even the fact that some rights (e.g., unfair dismissal and redundancy) require qualification periods. As regards the latter point Convention jurisprudence shows (e.g., in cases dealing with limitation periods such as *Stubbings* v *United Kingdom* (1996) 23 EHRR 213) that the argument will centre on whether the qualification period is part of the substantive right to claim, say, unfair dismissal (in which case interference is unlikely) or whether it is a procedural 'add on'. ERA 1996, s. 94(1) states that an employee has the right not to be unfairly dismissed which looks like a bare declaration of the right with any qualifying period being an add on, but s. 94(2) makes subsection (1) subject to a range of sections including s. 108 which sets out the qualification. The point is therefore quite well-balanced.

The question of tribunals hearing cases involving their paymasters and what constitutes a public hearing have already caused some consternation and brought about changes in procedure. And on the commercial side, Part 25 of the Civil Procedure Rules was clearly drafted with art. 6 in mind, but the question of how interim injunctions and search orders operate may still occupy the attention of the courts. Whether the proposed ACAS arbitration scheme may breach art. 6 (in that the participating parties must waive their rights to a trial) is one of those issues still under debate. We would suggest that, as the new scheme is a voluntary one, it is unlikely that art. 6 would be breached.

1.7.3.2 Respect for private and family life, home and correspondence, under art. 8 of the Convention

This does raise the thorny problem of employers monitoring staff by use of devices such as CCTV, drug testing, interceptions of e-mails, and the keeping of personnel records. There exists plenty of case law and legislation covering matters such as access to medical information and data protection, but less on monitoring employees (though see *Halford* v *United Kingdom* [1997] IRLR 471 on telephone interceptions). We can reasonably expect developments in this area (see for example, **7.9.4** on monitoring communications).

The Privy Council was recently faced with an interesting problem on the question of art. 8 in *Whitefield* v *General Medical Council* [2002] UKPC 62, [2003] IRLR 39, where a doctor with a serious history of alcohol problems was required by the General Medical Council to abstain absolutely from alcohol, to submit to random breath, blood, and urine tests, and to attend Alcoholics Anonymous. The doctor argued that together or individually these amounted to a breach of art. 8 as the conditions interfered with the right to respect for his private life. His argument was rejected on the basis that there was no authority to support the proposition that a ban on the consumption of alcohol is, *per se*, a breach of art. 8 and that he could still socialise without consuming alcohol. Further, even if these actions were a breach of art. 8(1) the conditions were lawfully imposed in the circumstances under art. 8(2) which allows for the interference in private life in limited circumstances such as the protection of health or morals. This also applied to the compulsory medical tests, which have been held to be in breach of art. 8 in other jurisdictions and circumstances.

On the facts, one has little difficulty with the analysis in *Whitefield.* Whether it gives birth to a whole range of arguments determining just how far bans by (public authority) employers on employees' 'out of work' activities will be held acceptable without breaching art. 8 (e.g., bans on smoking or taking part in dangerous sports) is more debatable.

The impact of the Human Rights Act 1998 on unfair dismissal was considered by the Court of Appeal in *X* v *Y* [2004] EWCA Civ 662.

1.7.3.3 Freedom of thought, conscience and religion, under art. 9 of the Convention

The UK already has legislation covering religious activities e.g., Race Relations Act 1976 and aspects relating to working on Sundays in the ERA 1996. Arguments centring on employees taking time off for religious holidays have been lodged under indirect discrimination claims. Under art. 9 there is possibly some scope for further argument where the employer disregards the employee's religious beliefs, but claims based on religious holidays have failed in Strasbourg (see, for instance, *Ahmad* v *UK* [1982] 4 EHRR 126).

On 27 June 2000 the Council of Europe Committee of Ministers adopted Protocol 12 to the European Convention which provides for a general prohibition on discrimination. The protocol has been open for signatures as from 4 November 2000.

1.7.3.4 Freedom of expression, under art. 10 of the Convention

This article includes the right to receive and impart information and ideas without interference, subject to restrictions which are necessary in a democratic society. Matters such as the law of defamation, the Public Interest Disclosure Act 1998 and the duty of confidentiality already cover many aspects raised here (see **Chapters 7** and **8** below). The extent to which 'expression' extends to matters like dress codes has been the subject of speculation, though there is nothing in the Convention case law to support this.

1.7.3.5 Non-discrimination, under art. 14 of the Convention

This is not a free-standing right but relates to the provisions of the Convention itself *viz* it only prohibits discrimination in the enjoyment of one or other of the rights guaranteed by the Convention. The new Protocol 12 modifies this position.

1.8 The internet and other sources

There are numerous sites on the Internet which now give access to a wide range of information on employment law. We cannot list all of those here, but a useful starting point is: *www.emplaw.co.uk* which is a portal to a whole host of relevant sites; *www.employment-appeals.gov.uk* for the EAT; *www.dti.gov.uk* for the Department of Trade and Industry; *www.acas.org.uk* for ACAS; and *www.legislation.hmso.gov.uk/acts.htm* for recent statutes and statutory instruments.

The best practitioners' text is *Harvey on Industrial Relations and Employment Law* (London: Butterworths) and, amongst the many journals in this field, the *IDS Brief* (Income Data Services Ltd) stands out as being informative and up to date.

2

Definition of 'employee'

2.1 Introduction

This chapter examines how the presence of an employment relationship is determined, what factors should be considered in making that determination, and what are the possible consequences of the classification.

The relevance of these questions is that they will determine:

(a) who is *responsible* for matters such as liability for tax and National Insurance contributions, injury in the workplace and damage caused to others;

(b) what contractual *rights* the company has in controlling the activities of the worker;

(c) what specific *statutory rights* the worker has acquired, such as unfair dismissal compensation, redundancy pay, maternity rights and so on.

Thus the first, and most basic, problem confronting anyone dealing with employment law is: 'How does one determine whether a worker is an employee or self-employed (i.e., an independent contractor)?' Few of the statutes covering the working environment relate to the self-employed. Legislation relating to sex and race discrimination together with health and safety matters has general application, but most of the statutory rights refer only to employees. As will be seen, the mere fact that the parties reach agreement on their respective status is not the determining feature.

This chapter will adopt the following structure:

(a) The tests for an employment relationship.

(b) The benefits and pitfalls of each type of relationship.

(c) Types of employee.

(d) Vicarious liability.

(e) The new statutory meaning of 'Worker'.

To most employment lawyers this area has usually been of general background relevance only. However, the basic questions raised here have begun to surface more frequently.

Some employers, recognising the increased protection the law now gives to 'permanent' or 'core' employees (whether full-time or part-time), have sought to create a second tier of temporary or 'peripheral' workers with fewer rights. Sometimes this involves an attempt to categorise them as independent contractors and not employees at all, or to devise fictions such as 'zero hours' contracts. These tests of employment status are therefore currently a very live issue. It is also the case, however, that both EU and Government policy is moving towards doing away with the distinction between employees and independent contractors. It is increasingly common to find the term 'worker' appearing in Directives and statutes concerned with employment rights. Indeed, ERA 1999, s. 23 specifically confers upon the Secretary of State by order the power to extend statutory employment rights to workers other than employees.

We will therefore first examine the practicalities of the classic distinctions of employees and independent contractors and then look at the effect of the new classification of 'worker' used in modern legislation.

2.2 The tests for an employment relationship

Various tests have been developed over the years to answer what appears to be a very simple question—how to define the term 'employee'. There is a statutory definition contained in ERA 1996, s. 230(1) but it has been deliberately left vague. It states that an 'employee' means an individual who has entered into or works under a contract of employment—which in turn is defined as a contract of service or of apprenticeship. This is less than helpful but sums up the approach of the courts *viz*, if it looks like a duck and quacks like a duck, it is a duck. Other (more legal) tests exist, as described below.

Note: to avoid confusion between the noun 'worker' and the new legally-defined statute-protected 'Worker' we have used the inelegant term 'workman' to describe the non-statutory kind. For brevity, the term also applies to women.

2.2.1 The control test

The problems associated with defining the term 'employee' or, in older terminology, 'servant' have been with us for centuries, arising long before the application of contract terminology to the employment relationship. The assessment of the presence and extent of responsibilities closely followed the analytical line as to whether the putative employer had 'control' over what the individual did and the manner in which it was done. This seemed a natural path to take. The greater the degree of control, the more likely it was that there was a contract *of* service rather than a contract *for* services; that the person was a servant rather than an independent contractor or agent. The employee sells his labour; the contractor sells a product.

The courts are concerned here to find who it is that determines the operation of the contract; who exercises the discretion? This is achieved by what may be termed a *'Who, what, where, when and how' test*. That is to say:

(a) *Who*

To what extent does the 'employer' control who does the work? The contract of employment is a contract of *personal* service, so if the workman can delegate the task or send replacements this essential element of personal service will be missing. This point was strongly emphasised in *Ready Mixed Concrete (South East) Ltd* v *Minister of Pensions and National Insurance* [1968] 2 QB 497, which held that a lorry driver (who had to obey a wide range of company rules) was nevertheless an independent contractor because, *inter alia*, he could, with the company's consent, arrange for a substitute driver to do his job instead. This analysis was affirmed in another 'driver' case (*Express and Echo Publications Ltd* v *Tanton* [1999] ICR 693), where the Court of Appeal went further in stating that it was established on the authorities that where a person who works for another is not required to perform his service personally, then *as a matter of law* the relationship between the worker and the person for whom he works is not that of employer and employee. This, it must be said seems to overstate the position and, indeed, the President of the EAT took the opportunity in *MacFarlane* v *Glasgow City Council* [2001] IRLR 7 to state that a limited power of delegation was not inconsistent with a contract of service, so that a gymnastics instructor working on a casual basis for the Council was held to be an employee even though she could send a substitute teacher, because here the substitute had to be from the list of instructors as approved by the Council, and the Council itself organised the replacements and paid them directly (which just shows how *all* factors have to be taken into account, because the 'approved list' element was also present in *Ready Mixed Concrete* but not the direct payment point).

(b) *What*
Does the 'employer' control what work is done, e.g., the order in which jobs are undertaken?

(c) *Where*
What control does the 'employer' have over the place of work? If work is done at home or on the workman's own business premises, this will point away from an employment relationship.

(d) *When*
A similar point to 'where' which relates to the hours worked.

(e) *How*
Can the 'employer' control how the work is to be performed? With skilled workmen it becomes unrealistic to suppose that control can be exercised here. In truth, though, the courts have approached this by asking, does the 'employer' have the *right* to control activities, rather than asking whether control is *physically* exercised.

The control test is still used widely today, though usually in combination with other tests. In *Motorola Ltd* v *Davidson & Melville Craig Group* [2001] IRLR 4, for instance, Davidson brought a claim against Motorola for unfair dismissal. Motorola defended this by claiming he was not employed by them. He had worked for Motorola as an agency worker supplied by the Melville Craig Group (MCG). MCG did not just send any agency worker to Motorola; Motorola had to agree the service of each worker and selection from MCG's list was subject to very specific requirements. Davidson's terms and conditions were set down by MCG, but he worked directly under the instructions of Motorola and was treated the same as any full-time employee. He used Motorola tools, wore their uniform, and took holidays only with their permission. He worked exclusively at Motorola for just over two years, though he could have refused to work without being in breach of any contract with Motorola itself and MCG could have assigned him elsewhere without Motorola's permission.

The argument before the EAT was based solely on the control test and came down to whether one should emphasise legal control or practical control. On balance, and with an eye on the fact that MCG did not even know Motorola had disciplined and then dismissed Davidson, the EAT held that the employer was Motorola.

2.2.2 The integration test

The integration test developed to cope with the problems of controlling *how* a job is to be done. 'Integration' was never accurately defined and the test only ever really applied to fringe occupations. The formula applied was: If the workman was fully integrated into—'a part and parcel of'—the enterprise then there was likely to be a contract of service. This meant investigating whether the workman took part in administrative duties, management decisions or undertook other tasks. If some degree of mutuality was present, with the 'employer' providing benefits such as holiday pay, this would tend to indicate a contract *of* service. However, where a person performed only a single task, usually for only a short time, this raised the presumption of a contract *for* services.

2.2.3 Economic reality test

The control test and the integration test tend now to be subsumed into a more general balancing exercise which goes by various names—the economic reality test, the mixed test, and the multiple test. The question of who is or is not an employee is generally one of fact, not law (except in the interpretation of written contracts).

This economic reality test recognises that it is the *combination and balance* of features and the degree of emphasis that matters more than one simple checklist. So the modern approach demands that all the factors for and against the presence of an employment relationship are put into balance. Two key questions are then posed. These are:

(a) *Are these workmen in business on their own account?*
Here one looks to the financial risk and input of capital as regards equipment and varying profits. Any company, when set against an individual, will obviously have injected more capital and have taken more sizeable financial risks, so the emphasis has to be on the level provided by the workman: Is it higher than one would normally expect from an employee? This entrepreneurial aspect of the test was emphasised in one of the key cases in this area, *viz Ready Mixed Concrete* v *Minister of Pensions* (see **2.2.1**) as regards lorry drivers. If a workman is in business on his or her own account not only will he or she have some chance of increasing his or her profits (a pieceworker could claim the same), but he or she will also be at some *risk* of losing money.

(b) *Is there a mutual obligation to provide work and perform tasks as directed?*
Here one looks to matters such as the provision of sick and holiday pay, set hours and whether workmen doing the same tasks are usually classed as employees. This aspect of mutuality was emphasised in *Nethermere of St Neots* v *Gardiner and Taverna* [1984] ICR 612, where homeworkers, who largely regulated their own workload, were nevertheless found to be employees on the basis that in many respects they were treated the same (and did the same type of work) as their full-time equivalents.

The tests above are the guiding forms of analysis adopted by the courts, but in the end the exercise is one of balancing these features. As the Court of Appeal has stated in *Hall (Inspector of Taxes)* v *Lorimer* [1992] ICR 739, although one needs to compile a detailed checklist the court must evaluate the overall effect of that detail.

2.2.4 Labels and descriptions

It may be thought that, in a contractual setting such as this, what the parties call themselves would be determinative. However, the history of this area is littered with cases where one or other party attempts to avoid liability with the use of such devices, and so the relationship is analysed under an objective test: the label is just one factor to take into account. For instance, in *Young and Woods* v *West* [1980] IRLR 201, West opted to be called self-employed although doing the same work as ordinary employees. The Inland Revenue treated him as self-employed, and all would have been well, but the company declared redundancies and, as a self-employed worker, West was not entiled to any compensation. He therefore claimed that, in reality, he was an employee all along. The Court of Appeal eventually agreed (though they also referred the matter to the Inland Revenue as regards past tax bills).

Mere labels therefore do not carry much weight, but how the contract is expressed—the written terms defining duties, etc.—is a factor which is being used more widely to determine the workman's status. Thus, in *Express and Echo Publications Ltd* v *Tanton* (above), the Court of Appeal noted that one should look first at the terms of the agreement and then consider whether any of those terms are inherently inconsistent with the existence of a contract of employment. If there is an inherently inconsistent term, such as clear arrangements for the provision of substitute workers on a commercial footing (i.e., a clause showing personal service is not important), the term is more likely to mean that this is not an employment relationship; if there is no inconsistency one must still look at the balance of all the terms.

It should also be stressed that the mere fact that an external body, such as the Inland Revenue, classes a workman as one thing or another, is only marginally important for employment law purposes.

2.2.5 Irreducible minima?

You may gather from all this (and the point is reinforced below when we look at *types* of employees) that this area is in something of a mess. The courts are constantly trying to find some overriding factors which can be used to determine all situations—often referred to as the *irreducible minima* which go to make an employment relationship—but it is the search for the Holy Grail. Nevertheless, the main modern contenders are as follows:

(a) The question of who exercises *control* in terms of *procedures*, e.g., the *right* to control as seen in *Ready Mixed Concrete* (above); or the presence or absence of grievance and disciplinary procedures, as seen in *Montgomery* v *Johnson Underwood Ltd* [2001] EWCA Civ 318; [2001] IRLR 269 (below at **2.4.7**).

(b) The question of who exercises *control* in terms of the requirement of *personal service/the right to delegate*, as seen in *Ready Mixed Concrete*, *Motorola Ltd* v *Davidson* and *Tanton*, and as more recently re-explained in *MacFarlane* v *Glasgow City Council* (all noted above).

(c) The question of whether there is *mutuality of obligation* in terms of:
   (i) commitment, as evidenced in the presence of sick pay schemes, holiday arrangements, etc.—*Nethermere* (above, and at **2.4.5** below);
   (ii) some form of continuing consideration, as with the use of a retainer—*Clark* v *Oxfordshire Health Authority* [1998] IRLR 125 (see below at **2.4.6**); or
   (iii) some binding commitment, or express or implied guarantee of work and guarantee of service—see *Carmichael* v *National Power plc* [2000] IRLR 43, HL (below at **2.4.6**) and *McMeechan* v *Secretary of State for Employment* [1997] ICR 549 (below at **2.4.7**).

(d) As noted in **2.2.4** above, what the parties actually *agree*. Although not determinative, if the parties expressly negative mutuality of obligation, e.g., they agree that there is no obligation to provide work or to accept any work offered, and that the relationship is *ad hoc* and causal, then, short of finding this to be a sham, the courts will have the devil's own job to say that a casual worker (even a regular one) was employed on some form of global contract: *Stevedoring & Haulage Services Ltd* v *Fuller* [2001] EWCA Civ 651; [2001] IRLR 627. However, this case (in which a docker working 'on many more days on than not' for a number of years was held not to be an employee), although attempting to promulgate the use of a pure contractual analysis, in reality raises more issues than it solves regarding the balance of express terms, implied terms, labels and evidence of conduct.

2.2.6 Noting the basis of the question

The decisions in this area are not always consistent, but it is often useful to ask why the court had to make its judgment. If the matter is a simple question of money, e.g., tax liability, the court tends to take a very detached and analytical stance. If, however, the question is one of responsibility for safety as was the case in *Lane* v *Shire Roofing Co. (Oxford) Ltd* [1995] IRLR 493, one may find the Court of Appeal stretching definitions to their limit to prise the workman into the category of 'employee'. The grey area arises when the question of establishing status relates to the acquisition of rights (e.g., unfair dismissal); and, as noted above, perhaps this is the very area most likely to give rise to problems in the future.

The arguments on tax liability relate, of course, to the advantages gained by being self-employed in terms of deductions, etc. that can be made in assessing a person's yearly income. Most people are employees and so subject to the PAYE scheme, which allows for little or no leeway in the calculation of tax liability. The rules on National Insurance contributions differ according to status as well. The most recent controversy on 'employee' status and tax liability has arisen in the area of 'service providers', i.e., a person who operates a business or is engaged through an agency but works so regularly (often exclusively) for one company (e.g., providing IT services) that he or she looks to all the world like an employee. A new Inland Revenue scheme, commonly referred to as IR35, now creates a presumption that, under certain conditions, such people are deemed to be employees rather than self-employed.

2.3 The benefits and pitfalls of each type of relationship

Advantages to a company of hiring independent contractors

(a) That the company will not have to take on the administrative difficulties of tax, National Insurance, including the costs of the employer's contributions, or statutory sick pay.

(b) That the company is unlikely to be vicariously liable for the actions of the workmen (see **2.5** below).

(c) That a *notionally* lower duty as to safety is owed to independent contractors at common law under the tort of

Advantages to workmen of being independent contractors

(a) The workman will be able to register under Schedule D for tax purposes, gaining benefits of claiming expenses, etc.

(b) The workman will be free to undertake work from other sources without gaining permission from the 'employer'.

(c) The workman can determine his or her own pattern of work to fit in with personal commitments or other jobs.

negligence if not under the Health and Safety at Work Act 1974.

(d) That the company does not have to issue written statements of terms and conditions (under ERA 1996, s. 1—see **Chapter 3**)

(e) That the company is not responsible for the provision of training or the payment of training levies.

(f) That the company owes no duty to deal with trade unions as regards collective bargaining, redundancy consultation, or the provision of office facilities or time off.

(g) That the company will be dealing with commercial operators and so the contracts formed, the terms and conditions, will be viewed by courts in that setting. The company can thus hire groups of employees for specific tasks for short periods of time only.

(h) That the company cannot be liable for unfair dismissal or redundancy.

Advantages to a company of hiring employees

(a) The contract of employment requires *personal* service. The employer has made the judgment as to the make-up of its workmen.

(b) The employer maintains a higher level of control over employees, particularly where the company wishes the workmen to perform tasks on the periphery of the 'job description'.

(c) This control can be emphasised by the use of disciplinary procedures and sanctions.

(d) The contract is viewed as containing a much higher degree of loyalty and good faith via the device of implied terms (see **Chapter 5**).

(e) Unfair dismissal actions, etc. on the whole will cost less than the termination of a commercial contract. Furthermore, actions short of dismissal can be taken more easily under a contract of employment's disciplinary procedures.

(f) The company does not have to pay VAT.

(d) The workman may hire others to undertake the work.

(e) The workman is often free to choose where the work will be done.

(f) The workman may be able to negotiate better contractual terms than the equivalent employee.

(g) Work completed ahead of time will mean that the workman may move on to other tasks or even obtain a completion bonus.

Advantages to workmen of being classed as employees

(a) Minimal financial input and risk.

(b) Fringe benefits, e.g., company cars and accommodation.

(c) Membership of company sick pay and pension schemes.

(d) The payment of holiday pay.

(e) Greater job security in terms of increased potential for capital investment.

(f) Greater job security in terms of statutory rights, e.g., unfair dismissal.

(g) The ability to demand more money for the performance of additional tasks not defined in the contract through trade union negotiation.

(h) The employer must indemnify the employee for expenses and liabilities occasioned in the course of employment.

2.4 Types of employee

Although the position of most workmen will never lead to litigation, specific occupations still cause problems. In the past three decades, and particularly in the last few years, the questions raised above have grown in importance with the advent of different patterns of work following company restructuring in the 1980s, the move towards establishing small businesses and the massive increase in the numbers of women joining the workforce, mainly through a variety of forms of part-time jobs (e.g., temporary work, casual work, job-share schemes, and homeworking). It is fast becoming the norm to encounter employment relationships which do not fit the standard full-time pattern. This is mainly due to the pressures placed on employers to cut costs, even during the course of some commercial contracts, and the consequent reluctance to take on permanent full-time staff at the cost of immediate flexibility of operation.

2.4.1 Crown servants

Crown servants are those individuals employed under or for a Government department or any body exercising Crown functions, e.g., civil servants.Traditionally, Crown servants have not been classed as 'employees' but have had protection against unfair dismissal. Under TULRCA 1992, s. 273, Crown servants have now gained employee status, and even those employed in the armed services have acquired certain employment rights under the ERA 1996, s. 192 and sch. 2, para. 16.

2.4.2 Directors and shareholders

Directors will not be classed as employees unless there is a contract of employment to that effect. In many cases, however, a director's duty as a fiduciary will create a greater burden of responsibility and accountability than if there were a contract of employment. The appointment of directors as employees is subject to various controls under the Companies Act 1985. There is, however, no rule of law which prevents even a controlling shareholder from being held to be an employee too—it is a question of fact and, in some cases, public policy: *Secretary of State for Trade and Industry* v *Bottrill* [1999] IRLR 326.

2.4.3 Consultants

Consultants may be classed as employees if they become sufficiently integrated into the business—and note the IR35 scheme above.

2.4.4 Part-timers

Under common law no real distinction has ever been made between full-time and part-time employees. Part-time employees will, for instance, owe duties of fidelity and confidentiality and will be covered by the law on intellectual property rights (e.g., patents). And although the courts have become increasingly aware that the standard expected of part-time employees (especially where restrictions are imposed on their activities) must inevitably be less than that expected of full-timers, the residual elements of the duties will nevertheless be present.

Neither, since 1994, does the epithet of 'part-time' affect a person's statutory rights (see below at **10.3.2**). As the amount of work taken diminishes, however, there may be problems as to status—as with those who work at home or who are casual workers.

The ERA 1999, ss. 19–21, implemented the Part-time Workers Directive (97/81/EC) and gave the Secretary of State powers to make regulations and codes of practice on part-timers with the aim of eliminating discrimination and developing more flexible work patterns. Those regulations are now in force under the Part-time Workers (Prevention of Less Favourable Treatment) Regulations 2000 (SI 2000/1551) and are dealt with in **Chapter 6**.

2.4.5 Homeworkers

Once a workman is removed from the normal workplace, he or she gains some measure of independence as to 'control'. The more the workman can exercise discretion as to workload, timing and organisation of work, the more he or she is likely to be an independent contractor. However, as was seen in *Nethermere of St Neots* v *Gardiner and Taverna* [1984] ICR 612, if these workmen are treated in much the same way as full-time employees and gain benefits as to holiday entitlements, sick pay, etc., they are more likely to be employees.

In *Nethermere* the company manufactured boys' trousers. They employed full-time staff in their factory and a number of homeworkers. The applicants were part-time homeworkers. Taverna had previously worked in the factory as an employee. Both had worked with the company since the late 1970s. They sewed trouser flaps and pockets using machines provided by the company. There were no fixed hours of work; but they usually worked four to five hours a day. They were paid weekly by piece-rate. They filled out time sheets and received daily deliveries. They were not obliged to accept any particular quantity of work. There arose a dispute over holiday payments, as a consequence of which the arrangement came to an end. The workmen claimed they were unfairly dismissed. The company argued they were self-employed. The Court of Appeal held that there was sufficient mutuality of obligations for the relationship to constitute a contract of employment. Although the traditional use of homeworkers has now declined, the points raised here will take on a greater significance as more and more people work from home utilising information technology as the means of performing their jobs.

2.4.6 Casuals

Presently, the two most litigated areas on the definition of 'employee' relate to casuals and employment agency staff.

In certain industries, e.g., catering or agriculture, it is quite common for staff to be employed casually or seasonally. Some are employed on a regular basis, others from time to time according to demand. The more regular the 'employment', the more the workers look like employees: but what does it take before an employment relationship is triggered by this regular contact? In one of the major cases in this area (*O'Kelly* v *Trusthouse Forte* [1983] ICR 728) the Court of Appeal held that some staff who worked exclusively for the hotel chain for an average of 31 hours per week, were paid weekly and received holiday pay and incentive bonuses, were still not employees because they were not compelled to take work if it was offered to them and did not receive sick pay or belong to the company pension scheme. They were deemed to be in business on their own account.

O'Kelly highlights the problem: it may well be the case that on each occasion when the workman is hired by the company there is a contract of employment for a day, a week, a month or even longer, but such intermittent periods would be unlikely to form such a cohesive whole that there could be said to be an overall employment relationship continuing during the off-periods. Without such continuity of employment the workman would not gain access to many statutory employment rights, such as redundancy payments. The rights could be present only if one could find some form of 'global' contract, spanning the gap between the periods of engagement; and to establish that one needs to find that there is sufficient mutuality of obligation between company and workman during that slack time so as to override any view that these putative employees are simply people in business on their own account.

How can such mutuality be found? One needs to find some express or implied term that work would be provided and performed when reasonably required. Thus, in *Clark* v *Oxfordshire Health Authority* [1998] IRLR 125, bank nurses were found to be employees on the basis that they were paid a retainer during the off-period; on the other hand, in *Carmichael* v *National Power plc* [2000] IRLR 43, the House of Lords held that power station tour guides who worked as much as 25 hours per week, were paid an hourly rate, given training and wore company uniforms, were not employees because their letters of appointment stated that they worked on an 'as required basis' and they were not paid between engagements.

These cases are, however, far from satisfactory in providing practical solutions which a solicitor can put in place for his or her client. First, it should be noted that on each occasion the putative employee provides his or her service, the primary tests used above (control, etc.) determine whether *that particular contract* is a contract of employment or not. If it is, and that employment goes on for long enough, the employee will gain various statutory employment rights anyway (e.g., generally a year for unfair dismissal). Secondly, even if the contractual periods are for short bursts, that does not mean there *cannot* be an employment relationship. The cases have not properly explored whether these contract periods could be melded together under the rules on establishing continuity of employment so that, even with a number of short-duration contracts, statutory rights might be acquired (see below at **5.3** for the rules on continuity). Thus, we would suggest that the focus should be on whether the established rules of continuity apply and not on the nebulous problem of whether there is a 'global contract' covering the off-periods. We would submit that the existence of any global contract can be determined by the purely contractual analysis of whether there is continuing consideration during those off-periods (as in *Clark*). One should not need to go beyond that contractual analysis and explore the vague topic of 'mutuality'.

2.4.7 Temp Agency workers

Employment bureaux exist to supply workmen to client companies as temporary workers—or 'temps' as they are often called. The bureaux enter into contracts with both the workman and the client company. These bureaux are colloquially known as 'employment agencies', though this tag has a particular meaning in law, referring to recruitment consultants ('headhunters'). The difference is that 'headhunters' are forbidden from paying the workman; their money is made from finders' fees. Our interest lies with the status of 'temps' so we shall continue to refer to employment agencies (because the older cases do) and make it clear where we are specifically referring only to recruitment consultants.

For many years, temps were not regarded as employees of either the employment or their clients. Their position was said to be *sui generis*: *Ironmonger* v *Morvfield Ltd* [1988] IRLR 461. This analysis changed following the Court of Appeal decision in *McMeechan* v *Secretary of State for Employment* [1997] ICR 549. Here the workman was suing for unpaid wages due on his final engagement with the agency. As the agency became insolvent his claim was against the Secretary of State (see **12.8.3.2** for why this is so), but such liability would exist only if the workman had been an employee of the agency. The Court of

Appeal determined that he was an employee, despite the fact that the agency contract described him as 'self-employed'. This was because, although the *general agreement* (what is often termed 'being on the books') did not amount to an employment contract, the *specific contract* (i.e., the day-to-day one) did on the balance of facts. So, it was now clear that an agency worker *could* have a contract of employment, though that still depended upon examining all the key points laid out in **2.2** *above*. *McMeechan* does not mean that agency workers always have contracts of employment; they may be independent contractors on the facts (as was the case in *Montgomery* v *Johnson Underwood Ltd* (see **2.2.5** above). But, if there is a contract of employment, the key question became (on the variety of facts available): with whom?

The problem is that there is a tri-partite agreement: the agency 'takes on' the workman; the agency sends the workman to a client company; the workman works under the general rules of the agency but under the specific rules and directions (control?) of the client company; the client company pays the agency a fee, and the agency pays the workman an agreed sum. Is the contract of employment between the workman and the agency, the workman and the client company—or is there no contract of employment at all? We have seen that *McMeechan* established that there could be a contract between workman and agency; *Motorola Ltd* v *Davidson and Melville Craig Group* (see above for facts at **2.2.1**) held that there could be a contract between workman and the client company (where there was strong evidence of control). In *Franks* v *Reuters Ltd* [2003] EWCA Civ 417, [2003] IRLR 423 the Court of Appeal felt that the employment tribunal had paid too much attention to the idea of mutuality of obligations and not enough to the evidence: in particular to the length of uninterrupted service involved (nearly six years). Their Lordships indicated that a contract of employment (between the workman and the client company) could be implied in such circumstances but remitted the case for a new hearing. This line has been developed in *Dacas* v *Brook Street Bureau (UK) Ltd* [2004] EWCA Civ 217, [2004] IRLR 358. Mrs Dacas was a cleaner registered with the employment agency Brook Street Bureau. Their agreement stated that the relationship 'shall not give rise to a contract of employment between Brook Street and the temporary worker, or the temporary worker and the client.' Brook Street had a contract with Wandsworth Borough Council for the provision of agency staff at various of the council's establishments. For a number of years, Mrs Dacas worked exclusively at a hostel, 8.30 am to 5.30 pm five days a week on a rota system, for the long-term care of people with mental health problems run by the council. The council, through the management at the hostel, exercised day-to-day control over her and supplied her with cleaning materials, equipment and an overall.

The agency set her rate of pay and paid her wages out of the payments made to them by the council for supplying her services. The agency was responsible for deducting PAYE and national insurance contributions, issuing payslips and for the performance of statutory obligations in relation to holiday and sick pay. Mrs Dacas booked her holidays and notified any sickness absence through the agency.

Following an altercation between Mrs Dacas and a visitor to the hostel, the council asked that she be withdrawn from the contract and the agency complied. Brook Street informed her that no further work would be found for her. Mrs Dacas then presented a complaint of unfair dismissal on the basis that she was an employee either of the agency or of the council. The tribunal held she was employed by no one. The EAT held she was employed by the agency but not by the council. The majority of the Court of Appeal held that she was *not* employed by the agency: Brook Street was under no obligation to provide Mrs Dacas with work, and she was under no obligation to accept any work offered by Brook Street. Nor did Brook Street exercise any relevant day to day control over her or her work.

But the Court did hold she was employed by the Council, and the express wording of her contract with Brook Street as to status did not override this. Even though the obligations and the power to dismiss were not contained in an express contract between Mrs Dacas and the Council, the fact that the obligations were contained in express contracts made between Mrs Dacas and Brook Street and between Brook Street and the Council did not prevent them from being read across the triangular arrangements into an implied contract and taking effect as implied mutual obligations as between Mrs Dacas and the Council.

Thus, once a tribunal finds there is some irreducible minima of mutuality of obligations between the workman and the client company together with some level of control exercised by the client company, it is likely that there is a contract of employment established between the workman and client company. Unfortunately for Mrs Dacas, she had not cross-appealed against the EAT's decision that she was not employed by the Council, and was now out of time, so we are left with a decision from which Mrs Dacas derived no benefit.

In April 2004 new regulations came into force which affect how both employment businesses (the new term for employment agencies) and employment agencies (the term for recruitment consultants) operate: see Conduct of Employment Agencies and Employment Businesses Regulations 2003 SI 2003/3319. There are separate regulations covering workmen who operate as limited companies and the specialist Nursing Agencies. 'Temps' are now known as 'work-seekers'.

The Regulations lay out detailed rules on the provision of contractual documents as between all parties, including statements on whether the work-seeker is to be an employee of the employment business or is working under a contract for services. The details of these documents are outside the scope of this text but the key question as to the determination of status is not clarified in the Regulations. It would appear that the Regulations were meant to exclude the client company from the employment issues, but this is not borne out by the Regulations themselves. Thus, if the agreement states that the work-seeker is not an employee of the employment business the existing case law (in particular the *Dacas* case above) appears to be the best guideline we have on whether or not the client company (called the 'hirer' in the Regulations) can be classified as the work-seeker's employer.

The EU Council of Ministers failed to reach agreement in 2003 regarding the proposed new Directive on the rights of agency workers, which had been designed to afford agency workers the same rights as permanent workers.

2.4.8 Employees on fixed-term contracts

Employers sometimes use the device of a fixed-term contract to define the length of an acknowledged employment contract. There is nothing untoward here and the term may be of short (e.g., months) or long (years) duration. When the time expires there are no further consequences at common law, though (as will be seen in **Chapter 6** and **Chapter 10**) the non-renewal of a fixed-term contract will constitute a dismissal for statutory purposes such as unfair dismissal. Whether the non-renewal *actually is* an unfair dismissal is a separate question.

2.4.9 Apprentices

Apprentices are a *sui generis* category of employees. The purpose of an apprenticeship is primarily that of training so that, although most of the normal rules will cover them, there are some key differences from ordinary contracts, e.g., there are restrictions on how the contract can be terminated. The so-called 'Modern Apprenticeship Agreement' is another of the tri-partite schemes (between the individual, the 'employer' and the local training organisation). In *Whiteley* v *Marton Electrical Ltd* [2003] IRLR 197 the EAT had treated this the same as a traditional apprenticeship, the contract being between the 'employer' and the apprentice. However, in *Thorpe* v *Dul* [2003] ICR 1556 another division of the EAT considered *Whiteley* but remitted a similar case to the tribunal, apparently deciding that it was wrong to treat a modern apprenticeship as akin to a traditional one. We can only say that we may be in the same position as we were with agency workers before the Court of Appeal applied a common sense approach in *Dacas* (above).

2.4.10 Employees employed for the completion of a specific task

Employees may be employed for a specific task, e.g., a research assignment or building project. This does not in itself generally affect their status as employees, but the contract is discharged by performance when the task is complete. A dismissal during the course of performance of the task will be treated like any other dismissal.

2.4.11 Employees of unincorporated associations

The issue here is simply: 'Whom do such employees sue?' The answer has been provided by the EAT in *Affleck* v *Newcastle MIND* [1999] IRLR 405: one member of the committee should be named as respondent, in his own right and on behalf of all the other members of the committee. Any compensation should be awarded against all those on the committee at the relevant time.

2.4.12 Posted workers

There are three situations to consider here: (a) workers temporarily working in Great Britain; (b) workers temporarily working abroad; and (c) workers whose work pattern takes them across international boundaries. Points (a) and (b) are covered by the Posting of Workers Directive (96/71/EC), implemented by the ERA 1999, s. 32. This requires that where a Member State has certain minimum terms and conditions of employment (see **3.4.3.1** below), these must apply to workers posted temporarily by their employer to work in that state. The contract may allow for greater benefits. It does not matter for these purposes whether the organisation posting the worker is from a Member State or not.

2.4.13 Voluntary workers

Many people work on a voluntary basis (e.g., for charities); this does not make them employees. In *South East Sheffield Citizens Advice Bureau* v *Grayson* [2004] IRLR 353 the EAT held that an unpaid CAB volunteer was not an employee (for the purposes of Discrimination legislation), even when paid expenses and even where the CAB would be liable to indemnify the person against negligence claims, as there was no mutuality present.

2.5 Vicarious liability

An employer may be vicariously liable for the actions of employees where those actions were undertaken by the employee 'in the course of employment' and not, in the magical phrase 'on a frolic of his own'. The traditional test has been that if the employee is performing a task which falls within the general expectations of the contract but is performing it in an unauthorised manner, the employer is still likely to be held vicariously liable. Obviously, the employer is liable for any wrongful acts which have been authorised. In *Lister and others* v *Helsey Hall Ltd* [2001] UKHL 22; [2001] IRLR 472, however, the House of Lords adopted a broader test: were the employee's acts and the nature of his duties closely connected? Using this test (which is similar to that used in discrimination cases, see below a **6.5.3**), their Lordships held that an employer (operating a children's residential school) was vicariously liable for the sexual assaults on boys in the school committed by an employee-warden. The Court of Appeal, utilising the old test, had held that there was no vicarious liability because the act had not been committed in the course of employment.

If this test is satisfied, the employer will be liable for any personal injury or other damage caused by the employee. This principle can even apply where the injured person is another employee.

2.6 The new statutory meaning of 'worker'

As we noted above, employment rights are often now defined as extending to 'workers' rather than merely employees. The genuinely self-employed will still not fall within this definition, but 'worker' covers a wider range of people than 'employee'. For instance, the definition to be found in the Working Time Regulations 1998 (dealing with the regulation of hours of work, holidays etc., see **Chapter 4**) and the Part-time Workers (Prevention of Less Favourable Treatment) Regulations 2000 is the same (see **Chapter 6**). The definition includes anyone who has entered into, or works under, a contract of employment and any other contract 'whereby the individual undertakes to do or perform personally any work or services for another party to the contract whose status is not by virtue of the contract that of a client or customer of any profession or business undertaking carried on by the individual', e.g., agency workers and homeworkers.

Cases are beginning to filter through on the meaning of this new term. In *Edmonds* v *Lawson, Pardoe & Del Fabro* [2000] IRLR 391, the Court of Appeal held that a pupil barrister was not a 'worker' for the purpose of the National Minimum Wage Act 1998. The Northern Ireland Court of Appeal, however, extended equal pay protection (under EU law) to employment tribunal chairmen (who are statutory office-holders), classifying them as 'workers' by reference to EU legislation on equal pay and freedom of movement: *Perceval-Price* v *Department of Economic Development* [2000] IRLR 380. The EAT have also held that 'labour-only subcontractors' in the building industry who worked exclusively for one employer and undertook to provide personal service were not 'in business on their own account' and were 'workers' for the purpose of the Working Time Regulations (and so entitled to holiday pay): *Byrne Brothers (Farmwork) Ltd* v *Baird* [2002] IRLR 96. On the other hand, sub-postmasters (who were not employees even under pre-WTRegs case law) are apparently neither employees nor workers: *Commissioners of Inland Revenue* v *Post Office Ltd* [2003] IRLR 199. Bricklayers have received special attention in 2004 from the Court of Appeal where a group of subcontractors was classified as 'workers' for the purposes of the Working Time Regulations in *Redrow Homes (Yorkshire) Ltd* v *Wright* [2004] EWCA Civ 469; [2004] IRLR 720, largely because the contract involved an obligation to carry out work personally. This decision follows similar reasoning seen in the EAT recently as regards joiners and (another group of) bricklayers.

3 Formation of the contract

3.1 Introduction

The role played by the contract of employment is central to understanding all aspects of employment law. For many years the contract of employment was, with few exceptions, the sole determinant of all issues within the employment relationship; all rights, obligations and remedies were exclusively contractual. Today, many features of that relationship are determined by statutory provisions, e.g., rights to claim unfair dismissal and redundancy. However, these features have not supplanted contractual theories but have been annexed to the basic contractual points, so that many issues discussed in this book require an understanding of both contractual and statutory matters.

The next two chapters describe briefly where a solicitor may discover the contractual terms. **Chapter 5** will examine what may be done with those terms. In dealing with any employment question the first port of call has to be the contract itself as made up from the express and implied terms. It is nevertheless an unfortunate feature of employment law practice that, whereas a solicitor may regard the contract as the first port of call, the employer-client tends to regard it as 'any port in a storm', often arguing *ex post facto*, and without evidence, that the contract justifies the action taken.

We can start with the fact that the ordinary rules of contract apply to contracts of employment. All the classic offer and acceptance points, the need for consideration, etc., can be seen at work here. However, there are also specially formulated rules which apply only to employment contracts, e.g., principles of fidelity and rules of procedure. These rules have arisen for three main reasons:

(a) Employers and employees have traditionally shown complete indifference to recording accurately, or even understanding, the terms of their agreements so that someone has had to iron out the basic requirements (i.e., the courts and tribunals).

(b) Employment contracts generally last for an indefinite term and therefore rules have had to be created to allow the contract to change and develop with time.

(c) Employment contracts were born out of feudal and criminal law concerns. The feudal notions stretch back to legislation in the fourteenth century (1348) which set limits on the movement of labourers and on wage increases. And it was not until late in the nineteenth century that actions such as disobedience to lawful orders on the part of an employee ceased to be criminal offences. When judges had to analyse the structure of the contract of employment it was hardly surprising, then, to find that they drew upon many of the old and established feudal notions of service. This history has influenced the judicial view of the employment relationship, especially as regards notions of loyalty and commitment to the enterprise.

These three factors have meant that the strict rules of contract have often had to be bent a little in order to make sense in the employment setting. This 'bending' can cause problems because it leaves some uncertainty as to when distortion can occur. One of the aims of this chapter and, in particular, **Chapter 5** will be to give some structure to this uncertainty.

Some commonly used concepts will inevitably be vague, and much of this can be seen in the extensive use of *implied terms* to determine the scope and intentions of the contract of employment, e.g., the requirement that the parties owe each other a duty of mutual trust and confidence. The device of implying a term is used in the same way as with ordinary commercial contracts (e.g., 'officious bystander' test), but the range of questions posed—from whether sick pay is due to the extent that an employee is expected to perform work outside the strict terms of the contract—means that a great deal of judicial inventiveness is evident, and has been necessary, over the years.

This chapter will adopt the following structure:

(a) The needs of the client.

(b) Types of contract.

(c) Sources of terms.

(d) Written statements of terms and conditions.

(e) The process of incorporation of terms.

(f) The role of trade unions in the employment relationship.

3.2 The needs of the client

The most obvious need is to obtain the best terms possible. The employee will look primarily at remuneration and benefits; the employer's concerns may be wider, stretching to matters of protecting confidentiality, rights to inventions, flexibility of operations, etc. As with any contract there is a bargain to be struck. However, this tends to give the impression of detailed haggling over terms when the reality for the vast majority of employees is quite different.

When drafting or analysing a contract of employment you will need to consider the size and resources of the administration, the requirements of the business and the market in which it operates, the types of employees involved and the resulting industrial relations consequences of any action.

3.2.1 Needs of the employee–client

Many contracts will be the subject of long-standing agreements with trade unions so that the individual has no say in the basic format of the contract. And even when the individual does negotiate a specific contract, or negotiates certain aspects of it, e.g., pay or holiday rights, employers still effectively dictate the *form* of the contract. Thus, if involved at all, solicitors will most likely be asked to advise employees or trade unions on the structure and content of the contract, on any legal requirements, and on any pitfalls to the proposals.

If the individual employee does seek advice at the formation stage, his or her concerns will tend to centre on the *meaning and scope* of stated or unstated obligations and take the form of the following type of questions:

(a) How is pay calculated, especially regarding things such as commission rates?

(b) How are other benefits (perks) calculated?

(c) What, if any, are the requirements to be moved to other sites?

(d) What, if any, are the requirements as to overtime?

(e) What are the notice requirements?

(f) What are the pension and sickness benefit rights?

(g) What happens if I leave? Can I take a job elsewhere in the same line of business?

All these points are addressed in **Chapters 4, 5,** and **9**.

3.2.2 Needs of the employer–client

Employers will tend to be more concerned with establishing to their satisfaction matters such as the employee's duties, flexibility of operations and rights to vary the contract. But even here, many employers rely on their personnel departments or on antiquated standard forms which have not been altered in years (but should have been). A further problem is that the contract may be made orally or in writing (or in any combination). Many employees in this country have never seen written evidence of their contract. Thus the scope for imprecision and misunderstanding is great.

Consequently, the more control that can be exercised by the solicitor at these early stages the better; from the wording of any advertisement through to the final offer letter. If such control is possible the solicitor should be briefed clearly on points such as:

(a) Does the employer wish to hire an employee, or would an independent contractor be better suited to the needs of the business (see **Chapter 2**)?

(b) If an employee is needed, what is to be the job description and what degree of flexibility do you want from the post?

(c) Is the advertisement, appointment or promotion in any way discriminatory (see **Chapter 6**)?

(d) What are the needs of the business in terms of working patterns, e.g., shift work, job-sharing, overtime, mobility clauses (see **Chapter 5** in particular)?

(e) Is there a special need to protect business secrets, e.g., by use of confidentiality or restraint of trade clauses (see **Chapters 7** and **8**)?

(f) What does the client want in terms of disciplinary and dismissal procedures (see **Chapters 9** and **10** in particular)?

(g) The need, if any, for any special requirements such as compulsory medical examinations, smoking bans and outlawing the introduction of computer disks to the workplace (this sort of term appears in an increasing number of contracts, e.g., on oil-rig platforms, where the presence of computer viruses could prove disastrous or even fatal).

3.3 Types of contract

Chapter 2 dealt with problems as to *status* (e.g., whether casual workers can be classed as employees). In this chapter we are concerned only with proven employees and the *contractual terms* themselves. Thus when we talk of 'types' of contract here we are referring to the variations in drafting styles necessary to meet specific organisational needs. The structure of employment contracts can vary tremendously, from the kind whose complexity could justify inclusion in a Tolkien novel to the rather prosaic 'I said he could start work on Monday'.

Where an employer wishes to employ workers who do not fall within the traditional definition of full-time permanent workers, each *type* of worker will require special attention in the drafting of contractual terms. Issues as to formation of contract do not vary as between these different types of workers but any standard contractual terms will obviously have to be modified to take account of the employee's status in the organisation. If the employer requires distinctive provisions or working arrangements for these employees then the contract needs to reflect this explicitly.

For instance, one might have a director with an employment contract who is still classed as a part-time employee. Thus, if this is the employer's aim, the question of hours to be worked should be spelled out in the contract. Again, if the employment is to terminate on the happening of a specific event (e.g., where the employee has been taken on to install a new computer network) it is necessary to explain that the contract is for a specific task and will terminate on the completion of that task; otherwise the contract could be interpreted as being open-ended so that other work might have to be found or notice of termination would need to be given.

3.3.1 Limited-term contracts

Most employment contracts are open-ended (i.e., for an indefinite term). They are usually terminated by one or other party giving notice (see **Chapter 9** for more detail). However, contracts may be made to last for a fixed term (say, six months) or for the completion of a particular task. Employees may be employed on a seasonal basis or to cover work for a short period (e.g., agricultural workers or shop assistants working specifically for the Christmas period). Employees may also be employed to cover for maternity or sick leave or for a specific project, e.g., setting up a new database. The arrival of the agreed date, or the completion of the task, terminates the contract automatically and there are no further consequences at common law (though the position is different as regards statutory remedies such as unfair dismissal). These forms of contract are collectively known as *limited-term contracts*, the most common of which is the *fixed-term* contract. Both expressions appear in the legislation, though *limited-term* is wider and includes both fixed-term and specific-task contracts (see sch. 2, para. 3(18) of Fixed-term Employees (Prevention of Less Favourable Treatment) Regulations SI 2002/2034, inserting new ERA 1996, s. 235 (2A) and (2B)).

The certainty that a limited-term contract possesses also brings with it a degree of inflexibility, for the contract cannot be terminated except by passage of time or the completion of the task. Therefore most limited-term contracts will contain a clause permitting the contract to be terminated before expiry in the case of gross misconduct by the employee. It is also possible, strange as it sounds, to have a limited-term contract which allows for termination by either party giving notice *for any reason* to take effect before the set finish date.

3.4 Sources of terms

Employment contracts are frequently a nightmare in practice. Except in the larger and better-organised companies, the discovery of the precise up-to-date terms would tax even the skills of Indiana Jones on a good day.

Terms of employment are derived from a number of sources. The most obvious is that of a written contract. Unfortunately many employees have never seen a written contract and, even if they have, it was probably issued in 1990, no one can find a copy, and there is no firm evidence that it has been changed in the intervening years. Your client, employer or employee, will tell you that it has been altered several times, but proving this fact tends to be somewhat perplexing. Your employer-client will also justify his understanding of the terms with phrases such as: 'We've always done it that way'; 'They (the employees) all knew about it'; 'We definitely agreed that with the union sometime'; 'I would have said that in the interview'; 'I didn't think to ask—it's obvious isn't it?'; and, from the heart, 'I haven't got time for legal technicalities—I've a business to run'.

You may therefore be faced with two equally unpalatable situations—a total lack of evidence or a wealth of jumbled evidence. If there is no clear evidence you will have to extract some kind of pattern from general working practice (judges and tribunal chairmen simply love this one!). The plausibility of this evidence might therefore depend upon your advocacy skills. On the other hand, if there is a wealth of evidence you will have to create some sort of priority, working from both the evidential strength of the documents, statements, etc. and from the chronology. You must be prepared to accept, in even the best-organised companies, that many 'rules' will still not appear in writing and that relevant dates of changes in practice are lost in the mists of time.

The range of source material can be extensive. You must be aware of the possible existence of:

(a) written terms;
(b) orally agreed terms;
(c) written statements (under ERA 1996, s. 1—see **3.5** below);
(d) itemised pay statements;
(e) collective agreements reached with trade unions;
(f) national and local agreements of the industry concluded between employers' associations and trade unions;
(g) works' rules and staff handbooks;
(h) custom and practice;
(i) job descriptions;
(j) job advertisements;
(k) related documents, e.g., disciplinary arrangements, grievance procedures, health and safety policies, pension booklets;
(l) a vast range of implied terms derived from the facts of the relationship, from the common law and from statute; and
(m) EC legislation, e.g., Treaties and Directives.

We shall examine these sources below. One 'source' deserves a special mention at this point: the written statement, under ERA 1996, s. 1. This is something of a sheep in wolf 's clothing. As we shall see in **3.5**, written statements must be given to every employee (including agency workers) within two months of starting work; they act as summaries of the contractual terms. These documents are not, strictly, a source of contractual terms but they are nevertheless important enough to warrant particular attention.

3.4.1 The parties

In many, if not most, cases there will be three parties involved in setting the contractual terms: the employer, the employee, and trade unions. The law works on the basis that each employee has an individual contract with the employer, but most contracts have been the subject of a collective agreement between an employer and trade union, the terms of the agreement then being translated into individuals' contracts (which may have been varied from time to time, as with an annual pay rise—see **3.6** below). Not all terms of an employer-trade union agreement are capable of being applied to individual workers; they may relate only to how the employer and trade union conduct themselves. In such cases (such as union recognition agreements) the terms do not translate into the employee's contract.

3.4.2 The express terms

As may have been gathered, employment contracts are treated with far less respect by the parties than are other contracts; many only exist as oral agreements. To quote Sam Goldwyn, the result is that, when it comes to a dispute, these oral contracts are often not worth the paper they are written on.

So 'express terms' are not necessarily the same as 'written terms'. Express terms may be found in oral statements and in a variety of documents. Thus the most reliable source would be a written contract. There you would expect to find a wide range of terms which we shall explore in **Chapter 5**, e.g., payment, hours of work and notice requirements.

There may be many other different terms, e.g., as to the maintenance of confidentiality. Equally, the contract does not have to detail every aspect of the contract so that (as with pension scheme details) reference may be made to other documents. These documents should have been given to the employee, or at least have been available for inspection at, say, the personnel department.

3.4.2.1 Works' rules, employment policy statements, and staff handbooks

These documents can present particular difficulties. They usually take the form of booklets, or notices posted on boards, containing rules of practice or behaviour in the workplace. Most tend to be nothing more than codes of conduct and are significant only because their breach might *indicate* incompetence or misconduct. They are not strictly terms of the contract. But if these rules are expressly or impliedly incorporated in the contract, or can be used to make sense of a bald statement in the contract, they may have become as much a term as any other statement, despite the fact that they probably have been imposed unilaterally.

Where an employee has signed a document which acknowledges the binding effect of the works' rules then the rules will become a term of the contract. But even without a signature, if the employer has given reasonable notice of the rules and their importance they are most likely to be classed as terms. Much will depend on the availability of the rules (e.g., handed out or displayed in a prominent place) and whether they were treated by the employer as important. The trick lies in distinguishing on the facts between a mere *policy* and an obligatory term: *Grant* v *South West Trains Ltd* (C-249/96) [1998] IRLR 188 (equal opportunities policy not incorporated); and is really a question of intention to create legal relations.

The arguments in this area are therefore purely contractual, but the question of incorporation is not always straightforward and even tribunal chairmen can approach the topic from quite different presumptions as to what is required to incorporate 'rules' which are not clearly stated as express contractual terms (see the problems relating to disciplinary procedures raised in **Chapters 9** and **10**, for instance). Certainly, the more precise the policy's terms and the more it ties in with obvious contractual terms, the more likely incorporation has been effected.

3.4.2.2 Orally agreed terms

Oral statements have the same status as written documents. Their disadvantage is one of proof. Where there is a conflict between written and oral evidence clearly the document will have the edge. But statements made at interview, for instance, have been allowed to stand in the face of apparently contradictory written evidence. Thus, say two site engineers have been instructed to transfer from the company's Bristol plant to Coventry. Both have refused, claiming this to be outside their contractual obligations. They tell you that when they commenced work in 1994 they were given a written contract of employment which stated they would be required to work on any site in the UK 'at the discretion of Grime Ltd'. However, before agreeing to sign the contract they were assured by the personnel director that their work would be limited to the Bristol area.

The written contract will be taken as binding unless evidence can be adduced to prove otherwise. The oral assurance will suffice if it can be proven, either as a collateral contract or as an overriding oral undertaking (this was so in the case on which this example is based: *Hawker Siddeley Power Engineering Ltd* v *Rump* [1979] IRLR 425). You can imagine that the question of proof could be an obstacle but, if proven, the contract would be that the employees are not required to move. With these sorts of cases in mind some employers now make use of 'entire agreement' clauses which specify that no other material or representations except those contained in the contract may amount to a contractual term: see *White* v *Bristol Rugby Club* [2002] IRLR 204 for such an example.

3.4.2.3 Custom and practice

Terms may be found by reference to established custom, though this has always been a debatable area and its use is not common today. To have effect the custom cannot be inconsistent with express terms or statutory rights. But, if a custom is reasonable, certain (i.e., can be stated precisely) and well-known in the company and has been treated *consistently* as a term in the past (see *Quinn* v *Calder Industrial Materials Ltd* [1996] IRLR 126), it may be classed as a term of the contract. The employee's ignorance of the custom is not a valid point if 'everyone else' in the company or industry knew about it.

3.4.2.4 Proof of terms

You will have gathered from the above that this is not always a simple exercise, and often there is conflicting evidence. Further, in interpreting the contract the general rule, of course, is that the use of evidence as to what the parties said or did *after* the contract was made is not permitted. In reality, however, tribunals have tended to take such evidence where nothing else is available. In *Dunlop Tyres Ltd* v *Blows* [2001] EWCA Civ 1032; [2001] IRLR 629, the Court of Appeal effectively acknowledged this practice when faced with a very ambiguous agreement on the level of pay to be made for working on bank holidays. Their Lordships admitted evidence of the position before and after the date of the relevant agreement, on the basis that 'the absence of any change of practice would be a clear indication that the parties . . . intended no change in the contractual terms'. It should be stressed, however, that this case rested on a very ambiguous agreement reached some 30 years before the case itself.

3.4.3 Implied terms

A word of caution is needed regarding implied terms: in the employment setting the courts frequently operate from a set of long-established presumptions. Many of these presumptions can look rather strange because they are feudal in their origin. But the basic rules for implying terms will normally apply. Thus, in keeping with general contractual theory, terms will only be implied where they are *necessary* for the business efficacy of the contract, not simply because it would be *reasonable* so to imply them (*Liverpool* v *Irwin* [1977] AC 239). However, once a term has been found to be necessary to the contract the court will then determine the limits of that term within reasonable parameters. The idea is to make the contract workable, no more than that; and the courts will certainly avoid *writing* the contract for the parties.

A full discussion of the importance of implied terms in contracts of employment will take place in **Chapters 4** and **5**. An implied term has the same force as an express term and may even be used to resolve conflicts between express terms. However, implied terms will give way to any inconsistent express statement. The range of terms is not fixed. Implied terms will include the following:

The duties incumbent on the employer	*The duties incumbent on the employee*
The duty to pay.	A duty to act in good faith.
A limited duty to provide work.	The duty to obey lawful orders.
Duties relating to the health and safety of employees.	A duty to provide personal service.
A duty of mutual trust and confidence.	The duty to exercise reasonable skill and care.
A duty to provide proper information to employees.	The duty to take care of the employer's property.

3.4.3.1 Terms implied by law

Terms may be implied by law. For instance, the courts have created a term that employers and employees must show the other party mutual trust and confidence. Such terms are often called 'legal incidents' of the relationship and do not depend upon the intentions of the parties. Many are a matter of common sense, e.g.:

(a) a duty to act honestly;

(b) a duty on the employee's part to cooperate and obey lawful orders;

(c) a duty on the employee's part to provide faithful service, e.g., not to disclose the employer's confidential information;

(d) a duty on the employee's part not to take bribes or make secret profits from the position;

(e) a reciprocal duty of mutual trust and confidence (which is something of a minefield to define precisely—see **Chapter 5**);

(f) a duty on the employer's part not to act capriciously in operating express terms (e.g., disciplinary rules);

(g) a duty on the employee's part to be adaptable as the contract changes over time.

Others have been worked out over the years to deal with more specific situations, e.g.:

(h) that there is no *presumption* whether contractual sick pay will or will not be payable;

(i) that there is no rule that the parties will act *reasonably* towards each other;

(j) that the employer will ensure the reasonable safety of the employee at work;

(k) that the employer is usually under no duty to provide references.

Equally, statutes have created similar irrebuttable points. Thus, for example, non-discrimination clauses relating to sex and race are automatically included in any contract, whatever the terms may say. Clauses which seek to oust the jurisdiction of the court will be void. And the duties may take a more positive form in requiring compulsory insurance for employees or in the creation of employers' liability for the provision of defective equipment.

In the case of workers posted overseas (see **2.4.12** above) the minimum terms and conditions which must be applied to such workers as set out in Directive 96/71 are: maximum work periods and minimum rest periods; minimum paid holidays; minimum rates of pay; regulations on hiring out workers; health and safety matters; protective measures regarding pregnancy; and equal treatment between men and women.

3.4.3.2 Terms implied in fact

Terms may also be implied from the particular conduct of the parties and by examining the parties' presumed intentions. Custom and practice is one example; documents not expressly included in the contract but used frequently by the parties may be another.

The two devices used by the courts (which will be familiar from studies of contract law) are those of the 'business efficacy test' and the 'officious bystander'. Conduct subsequent to the original agreement should be treated with caution unless it shows some form of estoppel varying the original terms. It can be useful to show what the parties *seem* to have left unstated at the outset.

So, with our example above (at **3.4.2.2**) regarding the transfer of employees from Bristol to Coventry there would be scope for arguing that an implied term, arising from the *nature* of their work (they were site engineers) or custom and working practice over the last few years might exist requiring the men to move.

Of course, all this fails if there is a clear, express term to the contrary; though, even here, there is the possibility of arguing for a move under the duty to cooperate if the distance is, say, within reasonable commuting distance.

The key rule therefore has to be: would the parties have agreed to such a term if the problem had been posed to them at the outset of the contract, and is such a term necessary to make the contract work?

3.5 Statements of terms and conditions

3.5.1 The right

Most employees have the right, under ERA 1996, s. 1, to receive from their employer a statement of initial employment particulars (usually called a *written statement* of their terms and conditions). These particulars must be issued not later than *two months* after the beginning of employment. The necessary contents are detailed below. This s. 1 statement largely complies with the Proof of Employment Directive 91/533.

It needs to be stressed, however, that this written statement is *not* the contract. Rather it is very strong *prima facie* evidence of the terms. It is like an MOT certificate: it tells you what the contract/vehicle looks like at a particular moment—it is no guarantee of the real condition of the contract/vehicle or its 'roadworthiness'. Employment tribunals and courts will accept such evidence only if there is nothing in the contract proper to contradict it. Thus written or oral evidence of agreed terms, express or implied, will all prevail over a written statement. For example, in *Robertson* v *British Gas* [1983] ICR 351, the employee's letter of appointment gave details of an incentive bonus agreed with the union. The employers subsequently withdrew from the agreement with the union and ceased paying the bonus. The employee sued for the arrears of pay. The mere withdrawal from the agreement with the union did not alter the employee's contract and a written statement permitting withdrawal from the agreement as a contractual right was held to be ineffective in altering the terms of the original agreement.

Nor does this fundamental point alter simply because the employee has signed the written statement as a receipt (as in *System Floors (UK) Ltd* v *Daniel* [1982] ICR 54) or has continued in employment after it has been issued without objection. Signing a written statement *as a contract of employment*, however, will bind the employee.

Nevertheless, a written statement may be the only documentary evidence and an employee may have a hard job convincing a court or tribunal that a document, issued by the employer, does not accurately reflect the contractual agreement.

The qualifying period for this right is one month (ERA 1996, s. 198) and a qualifying employee is entitled to the statement even where the employment ends before the period of two months in case they need to make a claim against the employer and need to refer to the statement in evidence. Many employees who were previously excluded from this right, e.g., those employed for less than eight hours a week, and those working wholly or mainly outside Great Britain, now have the right to receive a written statement. Also, in keeping with logic, those employees who have received a document containing express terms detailing the particulars required under ERA 1996, s. 1, do not have to be given a s. 1 statement (ERA 1996, s. 7A).

Written statements are a useful way of informing employees of the general terms of the contract. They are no substitute for a properly-drafted contract. Despite all this, many employees have never seen a written statement of terms (or a written contract).

3.5.2 The contents

Under ERA 1996, ss. 1–7 the written statement must contain:

(a) the names of the employer and employee;
(b) the date when the employment began;
(c) the date on which the employee's period of continuous employment began (usually the same as the start date but work with another employer might be included);
(d) the scale, rate, and method of calculating remuneration;
(e) the pay intervals (e.g., weekly);
(f) terms and conditions of hours of work;
(g) holiday entitlements;
(h) sickness and incapacity details and entitlements;
(i) pension scheme details;
(j) notice entitlement;
(k) job title or brief description of the work;
(l) if the job is not permanent, the period for which it is meant to last, including any fixed term;
(m) the expected place of work and address of the employer;
(n) any collective agreements affecting the employment, including things such as national agreements;
(o) details of any work abroad lasting more than one month;
(p) a note specifying any grievance and disciplinary rules applicable to the employee.

If there are no details to enter under any of these heads, e.g., there is no sick pay payable, this must be so stated (s. 2).

The statement may be given in instalments but certain matters must be given in a *single document*, namely: names of the parties; start date and dating of continuous employment; method of calculating payment and pay intervals; hours of work; holiday entitlement; job title; and place of work. The statement may, exceptionally, refer to other documents to which the employee has reasonable access in respect of terms relating to sickness, incapacity, notice periods, collective agreements, disciplinary rules and procedures, and pensions.

Where a change occurs to any of the provisions mentioned above then, under s. 4, the employer must notify the employee of such changes at the earliest opportunity (and not later than a month after the change).

3.5.3 Enforcement

Originally, in 1963, it was a criminal offence not to issue written statements but now, should the employer fail to comply with the requirements of ERA 1996, ss. 1 to 7, ss. 11 and 12 allow reference to be made to an employment tribunal. Where no particulars have been issued concerning any matter falling within s. 1, or the particulars are said to be inaccurate, the tribunal may determine what the parties have actually agreed and so what should have appeared in the statement.

However, this is almost a right without a remedy because the tribunal will not make the contract for the parties, it will not insert a term; it will simply *record* what the evidence reveals had been agreed by the parties. The tribunal will look first for evidence of express terms and then implied terms, and will also look at how the contract has actually been performed. Thus in *Mears* v *Safecar Security Ltd* [1982] IRLR 183, the fact that employees asking for details on sick pay had not previously been paid any sick pay was damning to the question posed under s. 11.

There is uncertainty as to what is the correct approach when there is no evidence of the terms whatsoever. Should the tribunal then invent something? In *Mears* it was suggested, *obiter*, that this would be acceptable. But the Court of Appeal in *Eagland* v *British Telecommunications plc* [1992] IRLR 323 re-affirmed the rule that the tribunal should not make the contract. Thus, if the relevant term *should* have appeared in the statement then the tribunal may have to make some form of ruling; if the term in question is not one specifically covered by the s. 1 statement the tribunal should leave well alone.

Under EA 2002, s. 38 tribunals have acquired additional powers. If an employee:

- makes a claim under one of the jurisdictions set out in sch. 5 to the Act (an extensive list including an unfair dismissal claim, a redundancy payments claim, an action for breach of contract, a discrimination claim, and a minimum wages claim); and
- finds in favour of the employee in respect of that claim; and
- finds that the employer was also in breach of ERA 1996, s. 1 or s. 4(1) at the time the claim was made,

then the tribunal must make an award to reflect this unless there are exceptional circumstances which would make this unjust or inequitable. If the tribunal has made no award regarding the triggering claim it must award the employee two weeks' pay and may award four weeks' pay. If the tribunal has made an award regarding the triggering claim the tribunal must increase the award by two weeks' pay and may increase it by four weeks' pay.

A 'week's pay' is statutorily defined in Chapter 2 of Part 14 ERA 1996 and is increased annually. At the time of writing it is £270 per week (or lower if the employee is not paid this much).

3.5.4 Written statements on sunday working

The classic written statement has a sibling. Under ERA 1996, s. 42(1), where a person becomes a shop or betting worker he or she must receive (within two months of starting) a written statement in a prescribed form detailing rights to 'opt out' of Sunday working by giving three months' notice to do so. If the employer fails to provide this statement the employee need only give one month's notice of opting out.

This right applies to new and existing shop and betting workers, but does not apply to those employed only to work on Sunday.

3.6 The process of incorporation of terms

From the text above it will have become clear that there is rarely *one single* document constituting the contract of employment. It should also be clear that the contract of employment is not immutable; that because it deals with a continuing relationship it is subject to express and implied change.

Many terms are *incorporated in the contract by reference*. Such incorporation may occur through notification or working practice but the best insurance is that of the written contract. Equally, sometimes it might be better to leave things such as 'works' rules' on the level of non-contractual conditions. For instance, a policy on smoking at work (e.g., only in designated areas) might be more easily converted (in terms of legal consequences) to a ban on smoking if the original policy carried no contractual weight.

The most common problem of incorporation, however, relates to collective agreements. An agreement between an employer and a trade union does not in itself form part of an employee's contract. If the terms are vague (e.g., that both parties will seek to promote industrial harmony), or if the terms can relate only to collective matters (i.e., how disputes are to be settled between employers and trade unions) they *cannot* form part of an individual's contract. The courts are aware, however, that these documents must not be read too literally, but rather according to their industrial setting: *Adams* v *British Airways plc* [1996] IRLR 574.

Incorporation is not an automatic process. Even if there are parts of the agreement which are capable of being applied to the individual, unless they are specifically incorporated into the employee's contract neither the employer nor the individual employee is bound by them.

Membership or non-membership of the trade union is not the issue here. All employees' contracts *may* be determined by collective agreements. The most common method by which this will happen is by express incorporation, e.g., a clause that states the employee's contract is 'subject to the collective agreements for the time being in force between' the employer and trade union. The second method is by *custom*, where the practice is so well-established that it has clearly become part of each employee's contract (what has been termed 'tacitly embodied' in the contract—see **3.4.2.3** above). The third method is by implication in fact. A fourth, but less common, method is by arguing that the union had ostensible or implied authority to bind the members. We would only comment that reliance on anything other than express incorporation is a dangerous game, though if the idea of *custom* is accompanied by general acquiescence on the part of the employees (as was seen in *Henry* v *London General Transport Services Ltd* [2002] IRLR 472 (CA)) then employees will have great difficulty saying at a later date (here, two years after the agreement was reached) that the collective agreement was not incorporated.

3.7 The role of trade unions in the employment relationship

Collective agreements may adopt different guises. The most obvious form of collective agreement is that conducted between an employer and the trade union in the company. But there may also be local-level agreements relating to a group of companies or an industry, and there may be national agreements along the same lines, e.g., as between employers' federations and trade union groups. In such negotiations it is common to find agreements on minimum levels of conditions (e.g., as to holiday entitlements) which would apply to the member companies or trade unions.

Agreements between trade unions and employers are not legally binding even as between these parties unless they are in writing and expressly state that they are legally binding: TULRCA 1992, s. 179.

The role and impact of trade unions, however, goes much wider than this. Although many matters concerning trade unions are outside the scope of this book it is worth noting the following:

(a) trade union rights depend largely on the trade union being 'independent' (i.e., not within an employer's control) and, more importantly, 'recognised' for bargaining purposes by the employer;

(b) those rights will include such matters as being consulted when redundancies are being made and being consulted when a business is being transferred.

These matters will be discussed further in **Chapters 11** and **12**.

Furthermore:

(c) trade unions may be sued in respect of tortious actions, usually those arising out of industrial disputes;

(d) trade unions may be joined in actions brought by employees against employers, e.g., in unfair dismissal claims where the union has brought industrial pressure to dismiss the employee (for instance, where the employee has refused to join the union);

(e) union members have specific rights concerning exclusion from trade union membership.

Lastly, it is worth noting that although the traditional representation of industrial relations in this country has been one of confrontation and lack of cooperation, this is not a fair general picture. As a solicitor acting for a company, your approach to trade unions can be a constructive one of partnership on many occasions. The same is true for employers if you represent workers.

More importantly, when considering employment law issues it would be short-sighted to think only in legal terms. The industrial relations consequences need to be accounted for too. Thus, as you will see, it may be lawful to dismiss striking employees (sometimes without any legal repercussions), but few solicitors would advocate such action apart from in extreme circumstances. An employment contract is not a one-off event like a commercial contract; the participants usually have to continue working with each other when the dispute is over and businesses normally work best when there is cooperation rather than confrontation.

4

Statutory controls on the contents of the contract

4.1 Introduction

At the start of this book we commented on the often haphazard growth of employment law. Most of it grew out of the law of contract, itself mostly developed during the nineteenth century to reflect the preoccupation of the age with *laissez-faire* and the freedom of the parties to agree whatever terms they liked.

Much of the law that fills this book reflects a recognition by the courts of the practical reality that employer and employee are not equal partners. Most job-seekers have the stark choice of accepting the job as the employer offers it or looking elsewhere, and therefore need some protection in an unequal bargaining position. This explains the ever-growing list of common-law implied terms that we shall examine in **Chapter 5**.

Statute law used to confine itself generally to termination of the contract of employment (unfair dismissal in **Chapter 10**; redundancy in **Chapter 11**; takeovers in **Chapter 12**), and to certain specific areas which cover employment as one among several areas of human activity (discrimination in **Chapter 6**; health and safety, which is outside the scope of this book).

That position has now changed dramatically. In the National Minimum Wage Act 1998 (in this chapter, NMWA 1998) and the Working Time Regulations 1998 (WTRegs 1998), we have for the first time (except for war-time and in specific occupations) a statutory control of the two most basic elements of the contract of employment: how much employees are paid and how long they can be required to work in return. This chapter therefore examines the limitations that statute now imposes on the freedom of employer and employee to decide the terms of the contract. As well as NMWA 1998 and WTRegs 1998 we shall consider briefly some other topics, especially the 'family-friendly' measures introduced by the Employment Relations Act 1999 (ERA 1999) and the Employment Act 2002 (EA 2002). Solicitors need to know that these rights exist, but the complicated rules governing them and the detailed statutory instruments lie outside the scope of this book. The matters to be looked at are:

(a) National minimum wage.

(b) Working time.

(c) The protection of wages.

(d) Work on Sundays.

(e) Maternity rights.

(f) Paternity and adoption leave.

(g) Parental leave.

(h) Time off for dependants.

(i) Flexible working.

Perhaps we should note before we start on the detail that this is not a comprehensive list of statutory controls on the content of the contract of employment. There are quite a few other matters that space will not permit us to discuss—including tax and social security, statutory sick pay and also the complex subject of pensions, despite the existence now of the European Occupational Pensions Directive 2003/41/EC.

4.2 The national minimum wage

The national minimum wage (NMW) stands at £4.85 per hour from 1 October 2004. The basis of the law is set out in NMWA 1998, but this is then expanded by several sets of regulations, the most important of which are the National Minimum Wage Regulations 1999 (NMWRegs 1999). While the basic principles of NMW are quite simple, the special rules to govern exceptional cases are complex and a guidance booklet published by the Department of Trade and Industry runs to some 112 pages including some worked examples. We shall therefore examine in brief outline:

(a) who is entitled to NMW;

(b) how the entitlement is calculated;

(c) administration of NMW and the remedy for infringements.

4.2.1 The scope of NMW

Under NMWA 1998, s. 54(3), the entitlement to the NMW belongs to *workers*, a broader term than merely *employees*, and the definition reproduces that used in WTRegs 1998. This seems to reflect the general approach of the present Government of widening the scope of employment protection to include many who would previously have been regarded as self-employed. Workers are both those working under a contract of employment (i.e., employees) and also those working under some other contract to perform personal work or services except for those who are genuinely clients or customers of professions or businesses. In *Wolstenholme* v *Post Office Ltd* [2003] ICR 546 the EAT held that sub-postmasters and postmistresses were not workers because their contracts were not personal but allowed them the choice whether to do the work themselves, and in *Edmonds* v *Lawson* [2000] ICR 567 the Court of Appeal held that a pupil barrister was not a worker either. There have also been cases about this definition in relation to other statutes where it appears—see, e.g., **6.9.1.1** below.

The broad scope of the statutory definition is then restricted by NMWRegs, reg. 12. Apprentices under the age of 19 are excluded, as are apprentices under the age of 26 during the first year of their apprenticeship. There are two lower rates for workers under 21: £3.00 per hour for those aged 16 and 17; £4.10 per hour for those aged 18 to 20. The latter rate also applies to those over 21 during the first six months of their employment if they are undergoing defined training.

There is no exclusion of those over retirement age, and both agency workers and homeworkers are included. The only significant exclusions are those working outside the United Kingdom (NMWA 1998, s. 1(2)), certain workers in family businesses (reg. 2(2) and (3)) and those undergoing work experience as trainees on certain Government schemes or as a compulsory element in undergraduate courses (reg. 12(5) and (8)).

4.2.2 Calculation of the entitlement

For most people, most of the time, the calculation of their NMW entitlement is straightforward: the number of hours worked × £4.85 or the lower figure where it applies. The time that qualifies for NMW has been interpreted broadly. Time that a night watchman spent on the employer's premises counted as working time, although he was permitted to sleep, according to the Court of Session in *Scottbridge Construction Ltd* v *Wright* [2003] IRLR 21. Time spent training or travelling on the employer's business counts too, as does time spent at home waiting to answer the telephone on the employer's night-time service—*British Nursing Association* v *Inland Revenue* [2002] EWCA Civ 494, [2003] ICR 19.

There is a more complex case where the worker is not paid by the hour but by reference to output and the employer does not control the length of working time. An example is traditional 'piecework', although this is now much less common in industry than was the case a generation or two ago. The rules here are set out in the National Minimum Wage Regulations 1999 (Amendment) Regulations 2004, which require the employer to test workers to determine the 'mean hourly output rate' and to pay accordingly from 1 October 2004, allowing workers 120 per cent of that rate from 6 April 2005. For factory-based employment this is now quite rare and these cases are relatively few, but payment by the piece is still normal for most home-work.

There is another set of rules governing the case of workers paid an annual salary in return for annual hours. The practical problem here is that some such people may be paid a standard amount at regular weekly or monthly intervals, but if their hours of work during those periods vary they may receive less than NMW per hour actually worked in some reference periods and more in others. However, most salaried employees (including manual workers on annualised hours arrangements) are probably paid sufficiently more than NMW that this will also be a relatively rare problem. See regs 21–23 for the detail.

The next question is how to decide whether the worker is actually being paid the NMW, and which payments can be offset against the employer's liability.

Most money payments made by the employer count. Payments in kind do not (reg. 9) and neither do payments not in the nature of wages (reg. 8). There are some more detailed rules in regs 30–35. Thus, for example, by reg. 31(1)(e), tips in a restaurant given by customers but passed on by the employer count against the employer's liability only if paid through the payroll; payments not through the payroll are additional to NMW and any payments made direct by customers to staff are not payments *by the employer*. By reg. 31(1)(c), premium payments made to workers in return for working unsocial hours do not count if identifiable as additional payments. Thus it seems that the employer who simply pays people £5.00 an hour for work on a Saturday has met NMW; but another employer whose conditions of employment specify time-and-a-half for Saturdays has not met NMW if paying the same cash amount, because the balance when premium is excluded is less than £4.85.

4.2.3 Administration and enforcement

An early draft of NMWRegs required employers to issue all employees with regular statements about NMW, but that was abandoned in the final version. Now the sole administrative obligation on employers is to keep records 'sufficient to establish' that a worker is receiving NMW, and the record for each employee must consist of a single document which is retained for three years. For employees paid substantially more than NMW, this obligation presumably requires very little. Workers are entitled to inspect the employer's record concerning themselves.

The fundamental point about enforcement of NMW is that it is made a contractual right of every worker: NMWA 1998, s. 17. All the usual civil remedies for breach of contract then apply (see **5.8** below), and it becomes the minimum for other statutory rights—see **10.13.2**.

There is provision under NMWA 1998 for the appointment of 'officers' to ensure enforcement of NMW. Generally this means the Inland Revenue, but powers also belong to the agricultural wages inspectors. It is an offence for an employer to pay less than NMW or to fail to keep adequate records, and the officers are entitled to bring prosecutions.

Any employee who takes steps to secure payment of NMW is protected against suffering any detriment for doing so—NMWA 1998, s. 23. Furthermore NMWA 1998, s. 25 adds a new s. 104A to ERA 1996, so that two new sets of circumstances are added to the list where dismissal is automatically unfair. First, it is automatically unfair to dismiss an employee for seeking to be paid NMW (whether or not in the event that attempt succeeds) or as a consequence of a prosecution of the employer. Secondly, it is automatically unfair to dismiss an employee as a means of avoiding paying NMW.

4.3 The Working Time Regulations 1998

4.3.1 The origin of the regulations

The WTRegs 1998 are the implementation in Great Britain of the European Working Time Directive 93/104/EC of 23 November 1993. The Directive was adopted under art. 138 of the Treaty of Rome, as amended by the Amsterdam Treaty (previously art. 118a), the article that permits qualified majority voting on matters concerned with the health and safety of workers.

The original form of WTRegs 1998 was amended by regulations in 1999, which removed many of the uncertainties. There have been other amendments since. There are several instances of 'copy-out' of Eurospeak and some scope for uncertainty still exists.

In *Gibson* v *East Riding of Yorkshire Council* [2000] ICR 890, the Court of Appeal held that art. 7 of the Directive (dealing with annual leave as in WTRegs, reg. 13—see **4.3.9** below) was insufficiently precise to be capable of direct enforcement against an emanation of the state.

There has been pressure from various quarters for revision of the current Directive, especially, for example, to provide some curtailment of the provisions for opt-out from the 48-hour week discussed at **4.3.4** below. As we go to press a period set by the European Commission for 'social dialogue' about revisions is still continuing.

4.3.2 The form of the regulations

For anyone involved in categorising legal materials, WTRegs 1998 represent something of a novelty. Previously employment law and the law about health and safety were largely separate topics, and practitioners were able to claim expertise in one while admitting to massive ignorance of the other. In particular, individual remedies in the employment tribunals and enforcement by the Health and Safety Executive (HSE) have had little overlap.

That distinction is blurred in WTRegs 1998. As we shall see there are six substantive rules. The first two are limits: the 48-hour week and restrictions on nightshift. Subject to the precise rules we shall consider shortly, employers must not exceed them, and any who are found by HSE inspectors to have done so risk prosecution. By contrast the remaining four (daily and weekly rest, rest breaks, and annual leave) are entitlements. Individuals denied them can bring a complaint in the employment tribunal; but where employees forgo the entitlement and choose not to complain, the employer has done nothing wrong.

4.3.3 Scope of the regulations and some definitions

As we noted at **4.2.1** above, both NMWA 1998 and WTRegs give rights to *workers*, a broader term than merely *employees*. In relation to WTRegs, this reproduces the wording of the Directive, but also seems to reflect the trend to include in employment protection many who would previously have been regarded as self-employed. The definition in reg. 2 provides that workers are both those working under a contract of employment (i.e., employees) and also those working under some other contract to perform personal work or services except for those who are genuinely clients or customers of professions or businesses. Thus in *Redrow Homes (Yorkshire) Ltd* v *Wright* [2004] EWCA Civ 469, [2004] IRLR 720 it was held that bricklayers engaged as sub-contractors qualified as workers under this rule because they were obliged to perform work personally.

Most of the rules apply to workers of all ages, but there are a few stricter rules that apply only to those over minimum school leaving age but under 18, described in some guidance issued by the Department of Trade and Industry as 'adolescent workers'. The rules do not apply to children: so a paper-boy was not entitled to paid annual leave—*Addison* v *Ashby* [2003] ICR 667.

Various parts of the Regulations are subject to specific exceptions, often picking up derogations available in the Directive. In addition it is possible for employers and trade unions or other employee representatives to agree to *modify or exclude* many of the Regulations, subject to certain restrictions in some cases. The original general exclusions have largely been removed by subsequent amendments, especially the Working Time (Amendment) Regulations 2003. Mobile transport workers are now generally covered by regulations specific to particular modes of transport as too are doctors in training. The only remaining general exception is the armed services, the police and some civil protection services under reg. 18.

'Working time' is defined so as to include expressly most kinds of work experience, but more generally as time which meets the following three tests:

(a) the worker is working;

(b) the worker is at the employer's disposal; and

(c) the worker is carrying out his activity or duties.

There is some scope for speculation here. We had assumed from a classical British approach to the interpretation of a statute that *all three* elements of the definition must be satisfied for time to count as working time. Thus time while the worker is on standby would generally not count, as (a) and (c) are not satisfied, even if (b) is satisfied. The ECJ, construing the wording of the Directive in *Sindicato de Médicos de Asistencia Pública (SIMAP)* v *Conselleriá de Sanidad y Consumo de la Generalidad Valenciana* (Case C-303/98) [2001] ICR 1116, took a more purposive approach. Working time and rest periods are mutually exclusive within the scheme of the Directive, the objective of which is to grant workers minimum periods of rest. Thus doctors on call are at work if required to be present and available at the workplace, but not if they are merely required to be contactable at all times but not necessarily at the health centre.

Application of the same principle to the other main area of doubt, time when the worker is travelling on the employer's business, might suggest that the critical question will be whether the mode of travel allows the worker to rest or not. There is obviously much opportunity for argument, e.g., about the difficulty of sleeping given the restricted leg-room provided by airline economy class! The three elements of the definition may still need to be applied with some care in each case.

4.3.4 The 48-hour week

By reg. 4, workers must not work on average more than 48 hours a week. The average is normally calculated over a period of 17 weeks, which can be a fixed period if so agreed between employer and worker, but by default is the last 17 weeks. In certain defined cases it can be longer—up to 26 weeks—and up to a year if some justification exists and the employer so agrees with employee representatives.

Workers who agree to work more than 48 hours may continue to do so. The original rules about formalities of such agreements were deleted by the 1999 amendments to WTRegs, except that notice to terminate the agreement cannot exceed three months.

Employees have the choice whether to sign the opt-out. In *Barber* v *RJB Mining (UK) Ltd* [1999] ICR 679, the EAT held that reg. 4(1) had the effect of prohibiting employers from requiring employees to work more than 48 hours.

Managing executives and others *with autonomous decision-taking powers*, family workers and clergy are excluded from the 48-hour rule under reg. 20 on the basis that their working time is not measured or predetermined or can be fixed by the worker concerned. The terms we have emphasised are undefined. There is an extension of the exclusion under the 1999 amendments, so that, if only part of the worker's time is unmeasured, not predetermined or fixed by the worker, the exclusion covers that part.

4.3.5 Nightshift

There is a complicated definition in reg. 2(1) of night work and, by reference to it, of what constitutes a night worker. On the face of the definitions, it might seem that a worker is only a night worker if working at least three hours a day during night time on a *majority* of the days of work, i.e., presumably more than half. This ignores the crucial element in the regulation, 'without prejudice to the generality' of the expression, 'as a normal course'. Thus in *R* v *Attorney-General for Northern Ireland, ex parte Burns* [1999] IRLR 315, the High Court in Northern Ireland held that three hours of night work per shift had only to be a *regular feature* of the worker's pattern of working time.

Workers who fall within the statutory definition of a night worker must not work more than eight hours on average per 24-hour period (reg. 6(1)). Again there is a 17-week reference period subject to some possibilities of variation. In the case of those whose work involves *special hazards or heavy physical or mental strain* (terms that are simply copied out of the Directive), the eight-hour limit applies under reg. 6(7) to each nightshift and not to an average. The only definition supplied by the Regulations for the crucial terms is that they are to be understood by reference to an agreement between employer and worker representatives or to the risk assessment the employer carries out as part of normal health and safety management.

Those undertaking night work must be given the opportunity under reg. 7 of a free health assessment before doing so and at intervals thereafter. The form of the health assessment is not specified but it does not seem to extend necessarily to a medical examination by a doctor. Slightly more stringent requirements exist in the case of adolescent workers. The employer's obligation appears to be limited to ensuring that workers have the opportunity of a health assessment and not that they avail themselves of it.

4.3.6 Daily rest

In principle, adult workers are entitled to 11 consecutive hours rest in each 24-hour period, and adolescent workers to 12 hours (reg. 10). There are various flexibilities about the operation of the rules for adults (mostly under regs 21 and 22) but the broad principle is that workers whose daily rest is not strictly in accordance with reg. 10 should have some *compensatory rest* instead (reg. 24). This term is undefined, but it seems that a commonsense approach will be taken.

4.3.7 Weekly rest

Adult workers are entitled to one day off each week under reg. 11 and adolescent workers to two days off. Again there is some flexibility about the way weekly rest is arranged for adults, subject to the same principle of compensatory rest as for daily rest. In addition there is specific provision under reg. 11(2) enabling an employer to provide two days a fortnight as an alternative arrangement for adults.

The 24-hour weekly rest under reg. 11 and the 11-hour daily rest under reg. 10 are separate and additional to each other. However, despite some suggestions to the contrary, it does not seem that they must necessarily be consecutive so as to provide an obligatory 35-hour break for every shift rota.

4.3.8 Rest breaks

Adult workers are entitled under reg. 12 to a rest break of at least 20 minutes if their daily working time exceeds six hours. There is no requirement for the break to be paid. Flexibility about the rule again depends on compensatory rest.

The rule about adolescent workers is stricter. Their break is a minimum of 30 minutes if daily working time exceeds four and a half hours. There is much less flexibility. Furthermore, if the adolescent has more than one job, daily working time must be aggregated across the jobs to determine entitlement to a break. There is no explanation of how employers are to obtain the information to operate this rule.

4.3.9 Annual leave

Workers are entitled under reg. 13 to four weeks' paid leave annually. Under the Working Time (Amendment) Regulations 2001, the entitlement runs from the start of employment, an earlier rule requiring three months' service having been declared unlawful by the ECJ in *R (BECTU)* v *Secretary of State for Trade and Industry* [2001] ICR 1152. The employer cannot require a worker to accept pay in lieu.

Elsewhere in Europe statutory annual leave is often additional to the equivalent of our bank holidays. That is not the case here, and paid leave on the customary eight days of holiday in England and Wales or in Scotland can therefore go towards meeting the employee's entitlement under the Regulations, a provision the Trades Union Congress described in August 2002 as a loop-hole in the law, which the Government has apparently now agreed to remove.

There are rules in reg. 16 about the calculation of payment for annual leave, which are broadly the same as for all other statutory purposes (see ERA 1996, ss. 220–229). There are also rules in reg. 15 about the notices employer and worker can serve on each other as to when leave can and cannot be taken. Some of these rules may cause practical difficulties in that they conflict with established practices in many workplaces.

There has been rather more litigation about this aspect of WT Regs 1998 than about the rest. In *Kigass Aero Components Ltd* v *Brown* [2002] IRLR 312, the EAT held that an employee who was off work long-term sick could choose to give notice to take holiday even although he would not otherwise have been at work. There has been a long-running debate whether it is possible for the employer to pay a 'rolled-up' rate of pay inclusive of holiday pay and then not to pay separately for holidays. The current rule from *Caulfield* v *Marshalls Clay*

Products Ltd [2004] EWCA Civ 422, [2004] IRLR 564 seems to be that it is possible in England and Wales, subject to safeguards, but the Court of Appeal noted that this decision conflicts with the position in Scotland according to *MPB Structures Ltd* v *Munro* [2003] ScotCS 90, [2004] ICR 430. They therefore referred the matter to the ECJ, which had shortly before been asked some similar but differently expressed questions by the employment tribunal in Leeds.

4.3.10 Enforcement and remedies

We noted at **4.3.2** above that the first two of the items we have just been discussing are limits enforced by inspection by HSE and possible criminal prosecution, while the remaining four are entitlements enforceable by individual claim in the employment tribunal.

HSE inspectors do not enforce the limits by any rigorous policing of employers. Indeed *The Health and Safety Practitioner* of September 1998 quotes HSE as saying it lacks the resources to enforce the Regulations effectively. The likelihood is that the employer's records of hours actually worked, for example, come to be inspected only if there is an HSE investigation for some other reason, perhaps because of an accident where tiredness through long hours may have been a factor.

As regards the four entitlements, reg. 30 sets out the procedure for a worker to complain to an employment tribunal. The claim must be presented within three months of the alleged denial of the right concerned. If the tribunal finds the claim well-founded it must make a declaration to that effect and may make an award of compensation of an amount to reflect both the degree of the employer's fault and the amount of the worker's loss.

4.4 Protection of wages

Subject to the minimum set under NMWA 1998, it is for the parties to set the level of pay under the contract. Nevertheless, whatever level they set, Part II of the ERA 1996 provides that employers may not make deductions from employees' wages other than those required by statute and those that meet specified conditions. The rules, still often referred to as from the Wages Act 1986, although that is now consolidated into ERA 1996, are (broadly speaking) that either employees must expressly authorise the deduction or they must be subject to the deduction under some term of the contract which the employer has confirmed in writing. We shall see in **5.8** that there is sometimes an overlap between this rule and that giving employees a remedy in the employment tribunals for breaches of contract.

4.4.1 The meaning of 'wages'

Wages are defined in s. 27 of ERA 1996. Under s. 27(1), the term includes any fee, bonus, commission, holiday pay or other emolument referable to the employment, whether payable under the contract or otherwise. It also includes various payments made as a result of employment tribunal orders, statutory guarantee payments, statutory sick pay, and statutory maternity pay.

By s. 27(2), the following are *excluded* from the definition:

(a) advances of wages as a loan;

(b) expenses payments (even where the employee makes a profit from the expenses: *London Borough of Southwark* v *O'Brien* [1996] IRLR 420);

(c) pensions or other retirement provisions;

(d) redundancy payments;

(e) payments made to the employee in another capacity.

By s. 27(5), benefits in kind are also excluded except where they consist of vouchers or the equivalent with a fixed monetary value.

The inclusion by s. 27(1) of certain non-contractual matters is enlarged in s. 27(3) by specific reference to non-contractual bonuses. The test seems to be that discretionary commission or similar payments may be included if it is the reasonable expectation of the parties that they will be paid: *Kent Management Service* v *Butterfield* [1992] ICR 272.

The breadth of this definition is obvious. It includes almost any payment made by the employer to the employee *qua* employee. Thus, tips paid to waiters by customers in cash are never the property of the employer and therefore do not count as remuneration; tips paid by cheque or credit card, initially to the employer, become the employer's property and therefore *are* remuneration from the employer: *Nerva* v *R.L. & G. Ltd* [1997] ICR 11. About the only item that has been held to fall outside the definition is *pay in lieu of notice*, which of course has been regarded by the law as liquidated damages for breach of contract rather than as a payment referable to the employment. However, it took a decision of the House of Lords (*Delaney* v *Staples* [1992] ICR 483) finally to exclude payments in lieu of notice, by holding that payments in lieu relate to termination of the employment and not to the provision of services under the employment.

4.4.2 Permitted deductions

The circumstances in which employers may make deductions from wages are set out in ss. 13 and 14 of ERA 1996. Employers are similarly only permitted under ss. 15 and 16 to receive payments from employees in the same circumstances. There are four broad categories:

(a) *Deductions authorised or required by statute*. Examples might be the collection of income tax or maintenance payments under a court order.

(b) *Deductions provided for by a term of the employee's contract of employment* where either that term is already recorded in writing to the employee, or the employer has previously notified the employee of it in writing. The deduction must also be justified on its facts, however.

(c) *Deductions expressly authorised in writing by the employee*. Examples might be payments to a pension scheme or a savings plan, or recovery in instalments of the cost of initial purchase of working clothes.

(d) *Deductions in retail employment* for the recovery of cash shortages or stock deficiencies, subject to specific controls including a limit to the deduction of 10 per cent of gross pay: see ERA 1996, ss. 17 to 22.

Various exceptional cases are set out in s. 14 as excluded from the general ban on deductions. Two cases are of some importance, but each belongs to an area of the law where there are restrictions from other sources:

(a) Deductions are excluded from the section if made by the employer to recover an *overpayment of wages or expenses*. However, such overpayments may still be subject to the ordinary law of mistake under the law of contract and employers often experience great difficulty in recovering overpayments, especially if the employee has in good faith spent the money. Furthermore, in *Murray* v *Strathclyde Regional Council* [1992] IRLR 396, the EAT cast considerable doubt on the scope of the statutory exception by restricting it to deductions and overpayments relating to the same pay period. Since such circumstances can arise only very rarely, there must be some uncertainty whether the case was correctly decided.

(b) A deduction cannot be questioned under these provisions if made *because the employee is taking part in a strike or other industrial action: Sunderland Polytechnic* v *Evans* [1993] ICR 392.

4.4.3 Remedies for unlawful deductions from wages

If the employee has suffered an unauthorised deduction from wages, the remedy provided by ERA 1996, s. 23 is by way of a claim in an employment tribunal. The claim must be presented within three months of the making of the deduction complained of, or (where there has been a series of similar deductions) within three months of the most recent deduction. In this instance there seems to be no limit on the retrospective period the employment tribunal may examine: *Reid* v *Camphill Engravers* [1990] ICR 435.

The employment tribunal is given little discretion as to its award if it finds the claim well-founded. It is bound to make a declaration to that effect, and also to order the employer to reimburse the money improperly deducted or received, subject only to a possible reduction of the full amount if there has been a partial authorisation or repayment: ss. 24 and 25.

4.4.4 Practical uses of the remedy in the employment tribunals

This topic may seem an obscure possibility. It is not. In practice, about a fifth of all claims recently brought to the employment tribunals fall under this jurisdiction and we shall discuss it further at **5.7.5** below.

The point is that there is no jurisdiction for the employment tribunals to deal with alleged breaches of contract concerning current employees. The only such jurisdiction concerns people whose employment has ended. So if an employee wishes to complain about an alleged breach of contract the case must be brought in the courts, with consequently higher costs than are incurred in the tribunals. If the same claim can be presented as an alleged deduction from wages, the tribunal has jurisdiction and this possibility may be attractive to the employee.

An example may help. Suppose the issue is a dispute about the calculation of a bonus. Maybe a group of people in a sales office are paid a bonus based on sales of the company's products. When the company starts export sales the employer bases calculation of the bonus on home sales (which is all there has been until now), but the sales staff argue that it has always been based on total sales. Both sides argue that their case is a continuation of past practice and there is logic behind both contentions, depending whether the bonus was originally intended to reward the effort of the staff concerned or to reflect the success of the enterprise. The legal issue is one of construction of the rules of the bonus scheme, wherever they are to be found, whether in writing or not. An employment tribunal cannot entertain a case of construction of the contract of employment in respect of current employees, but the amount at stake for a small group of people does not seem to warrant litigation in the courts. So the employees, through their trade union perhaps, present their case to the tribunal as an alleged unlawful deduction from wages. Their bonus, they argue, should properly be based on the total sales of the company and the employer has unlawfully *deducted* the part which represents export sales. Now, when it is presented in this way, the tribunal acquires jurisdiction to adjudicate on the issue, which is legally precisely the same as it would have been in the court—construction of the contract of employment.

With a little ingenuity many contractual issues can be presented in an alternative form like this. As we shall see at **5.7** there are other ways of dealing with such issues; the relative merits of this against the others are considered at **5.8**.

4.5 Sunday working for shop and betting workers

4.5.1 The right

Under ERA 1996, Part IV, special statutory rights have been created covering employees who may be asked to work on Sundays. The legislation is somewhat convoluted but, in essence, seeks to provide shop and betting workers with the right not to work on Sundays if they so wish. The following points may be noted by way of summary:

(a) The definition of 'shop worker' in s. 232 extends beyond sales assistants to cover employees such as clerical workers, security staff and cleaners. The definition of 'betting worker' in s. 233 covers work 'which consists of or includes dealing with betting transactions' at a track and 'work in a licensed betting office . . . open for use for the effecting of betting transactions'.

(b) Employees employed to work only on Sundays are not covered by the Act.

(c) Existing shop workers (as at 25 August 1994) and existing betting workers (as at 2 January 1995) are covered provided their contracts do not, and may not, require them to work on Sundays—these are termed 'protected workers'.

(d) Any shop or betting worker who is or may be required under the contract to work on Sunday may give three months' written notice of 'opting-out' (hence 'opted-out employees'). During that notice period he or she may be required to work on Sunday.

(e) Employees may also give 'opting-in' notice, expressly agreeing to work Sundays or a particular Sunday—and, indeed, may opt in or out as the whim takes them.

(f) Questions of age, length of service or hours worked are irrelevant for qualification for these rights.

4.5.2 Written statements

As we noted at **3.5.4** above, new shop and betting workers are entitled to receive a written statement in a prescribed form summarising their right to opt out of Sunday work.

4.5.3 Remedies

Both protected and opted-out workers (in the meanings defined above) have the right to complain to an employment tribunal if they suffer any detriment by reason of refusing to work on Sundays or a particular Sunday (ERA 1996, s. 45). We shall note at **10.8.7.3** below that they have a similar protection against dismissal or selection for redundancy for the same reason.

4.6 Maternity rights

There has been much recent attention by the legislators on the balance between work and family life. Thus ERA 1999 established several 'Family-Friendly Policies,' as they had been described in an earlier White Paper. Two of them were new, derived from the Parental Leave Directive 96/34/EC and are discussed in detail in **4.8** and **4.9** below. Then EA 2002 introduced several more rights by further amendment to ERA 1996, and we shall consider them in **4.7** and **4.10**. Some employers go beyond the statutory requirements, e.g., by providing work-based crèche facilities. By contrast, provisions relating to pregnancy and childbirth are of much longer standing, dating back originally to the Employment Protection Act 1975, although now much amended—including amendments from ERA 1999 and EA 2002 and associated statutory instruments. There are four matters to consider:

(a) time off with pay for ante-natal care;
(b) protection against dismissal because of pregnancy;
(c) maternity leave; and
(d) maternity pay.

The fourth of those rights is found in the Social Security Act 1986; the remaining three in ERA 1996, as amended. The main impact of the amendments is on maternity leave, where the old law has extensively been simplified. We shall also note in **Chapter 6** that any detriment suffered by a woman because of her pregnancy is likely to constitute unlawful sex discrimination and this point is of particular importance in relation to protection against dismissal. The employer also has special responsibilities for the health and safety of pregnant women, especially in relation to risk assessment, but such matters lie outside the scope of this book.

4.6.1 Time off with pay for ante-natal care

By s. 55 of ERA 1996, every pregnant employee is entitled to time off with pay for ante-natal appointments she is medically advised to attend. There is no qualifying service and no limit to the time off.

4.6.2 Protection against dismissal because of pregnancy

By s. 99 of ERA 1996, almost any dismissal because of pregnancy or childbirth is automatically unfair and there is no service qualification. The employer is not permitted to dismiss an employee even if her pregnancy makes her incapable of doing her usual job. Indeed, if her incapability is because of some statutory restriction relating to pregnancy, childbirth or breastfeeding or some similar recommendation of a code of practice, she is to be treated under ERA 1996, s. 66 as suspended from work and she is entitled to be paid.

The scope of the statutory protection afforded to pregnant women is now very wide, mostly because women have succesfully argued that any detriment suffered because of pregnancy or childbirth is unlawful discrimination on grounds of sex. We shall therefore return to this topic at **6.5.6** below.

4.6.3 Maternity leave

Until the amendments under ERA 1999, the rules on maternity leave had become very complicated. We now find in sch. 4 of ERA 1999 a complete replacement of Part VIII of ERA 1996, and in particular new ss. 71 to 75 setting out the structure of maternity leave. In addition we need to take account of the Maternity and Parental Leave etc. Regulations 1999

(MPL Regs 1999) as amended in 2002 which enlarge on the statutory framework. There are three kinds of maternity leave:

(a) ordinary maternity leave;

(b) compulsory maternity leave; and

(c) additional maternity leave.

We shall examine each of them in turn and then consider the right not to suffer detriment on account of exercising any of them.

4.6.3.1 Ordinary maternity leave

Ordinary maternity leave is covered by ERA 1996, s. 71 as amended. All pregnant employees, regardless of length of service, are entitled to a 26-week period of leave. The contract of employment subsists throughout this absence and the employee continues to benefit from her terms and conditions of employment except for remuneration. MPL Regs, reg. 9 defines remuneration for this purpose as wages or salary. Thus the employee is entitled to all fringe benefits during the leave period, a position that was generally thought to exist before but was never clearly set out.

The start of the ordinary maternity leave period is a matter over which the employee has some choice but it cannot start earlier than the beginning of the eleventh week before the expected week of childbirth (EWC). If childbirth occurs early, ordinary leave starts at once. Childbirth includes a live birth and a stillbirth or miscarriage after 24 weeks of pregnancy.

The employee returns to work after ordinary maternity leave with that whole period of absence counting for seniority and pension purposes. The right to return is to the job in which she was employed before her absence on terms and conditions not less favourable than those which would have applied if she had not been absent. There are special provisions in MPL Regs, reg. 10 covering the position if the employee becomes redundant during maternity leave, ordinary or additional.

No later than the 15th week before EWC, or as soon as reasonably practicable, she must tell the employer that she is pregnant, what her EWC is (by means of a medical certificate if the employee so requests) and when she wishes to start her leave (in writing if her employer so requests). Under the 2002 amendments the employer must respond, notifying her of the date when her maternity leave will end.

A woman returning to work after ordinary maternity leave does not need to give notice of her return unless she wishes to return early, in which case she must give her employer 28 days' notice of her intended return date. Failure to do so will allow the employer to postpone her return so as to obtain 21 days' notice.

4.6.3.2 Compulsory maternity leave

Under ERA 1996, s. 72 as amended, the employer is not permitted to allow the employee to work during the compulsory maternity leave period which is the two weeks following the baby's birth. This provision implements the health and safety requirement in the Pregnant Workers Directive.

4.6.3.3 Additional maternity leave

Under ERA 1996, s. 73, employees whose service with the employer is 26 weeks or more at the 14th week before EWC are entitled to additional maternity leave. This is the right to return up to 26 weeks after the birth. Additional maternity leave follows on after ordinary maternity leave.

The employee's contract of employment continues to subsist throughout the period of additional maternity leave as during ordinary leave. However, the rights and duties of the parties during additional leave are much reduced. There is no right to remuneration or to fringe benefits. Under MPL Regs 1999, reg. 17(1), the only terms of the contract that apply for the benefit of the employee are the right to notice, the right to redundancy pay, access to disciplinary or grievance procedures and the employer's implied obligation of trust and confidence. On the other hand, she is bound only by the implied obligation of good faith and by any express terms about termination, disclosure of confidential information, acceptance of gifts and her participation in any business.

Under MPL Regs, reg. 18, the employee is entitled to return after additional maternity leave to the same job or, if it is not reasonably practicable for the employer to permit her to do that, to a job which is both *suitable* for her and *appropriate for her to do in the circumstances*. The words we have emphasised are undefined and so we await clarification from cases. In any event, however, her terms and conditions of employment are to be the same as would have applied to her if she had not been absent. Her seniority on the day she returns is to be the same as it was when she started the additional leave. Thus the period of additional leave, unlike ordinary leave, does not count towards continuity of service in relation to any contractual right, e.g., service-related holidays. It counts under ERA 1996, s. 212 towards continuity for statutory purposes.

The employee is required to give no notice of her intention to return if she returns at the end of the 26-week period but must give 28 days' notice of an intention to return early (reg. 11). A statement of her intention to return at all can be required by the employer in a prescribed written form, in which event the woman must reply in writing (reg. 12).

4.6.3.4 The right not to suffer detriment

Under s. 47C, which ERA 1999 inserts into ERA 1996, an employee who is subjected by her employer to any detriment because of pregnancy, childbirth or maternity, or because she exercised her right to maternity leave, can bring a claim to the employment tribunal. If she succeeds, the tribunal can award compensation of an amount it considers just and equitable in the circumstances having regard to the employee's loss.

4.6.4 Maternity pay

Statutory maternity pay is payable for a 26-week period. For the first 6 weeks it is at the rate of 90 per cent of normal weekly earnings. For the remaining 20 weeks it is either 90 per cent of normal weekly earnings or a prescribed rate which is reviewed annually and has stood since April 2004 at £102.80 per week, whichever of those is lower. It is usually a straightforward administrative matter that causes few problems. In *Gillespie* v *Northern Health Board* [1996] ICR 498, the ECJ rejected the argument that full pay was due during maternity leave.

4.7 Paternity and adoption leave

Both these rights arise under EA 2002 which amends ERA 1996 by adding new sections that we shall identify shortly. In both cases the statutory provision acts as little more than an enabling measure for delegated legislation and both are governed by the Paternity and Adoption Leave Regulations 2002 (PALRegs 2002), which came into effect on 8 December 2002, so that the rights could start to operate on 6 April 2003. There are also other more detailed sets of regulations, mostly dealing with pay. We shall give only an outline.

4.7.1 Paternity leave

The statutory basis of this right is ss. 80A and 80B of ERA 1996. For an employee to be eligible for paternity leave, three tests must be satisfied.

(a) The employee must have at least 26 weeks service at the start of the 14th week before EWC, or in the case of an adoption at the end of the week in which the adopter is matched with the child.

(b) The employee must be the father of the child or married to or the partner (of either sex) of the child's mother or adopter. (So women may be eligible for paternity leave.)

(c) The employee must have or expect to have responsibility for the upbringing of the child.

Employees can take either one or two consecutive weeks of paternity leave. It can be taken at any time from the birth or placement up to 56 days later (or up to 56 days from EWC in the case of a premature birth). They must give the employer notice of the intention to take paternity leave by the 15th week before EWC in the case of a birth or no later than 7 days after being told of being matched in the case of adoption. If it is not reasonably practical to give that amount of notice, they must give notice as soon as reasonably practical.

The rate of statutory paternity pay is the same as the later rate (after the first 6 weeks) of statutory maternity pay—see **4.6.4** above.

4.7.2 Adoption leave

The statutory basis of this right is ss. 75A and 75B of ERA 1996. The rules in many ways mirror those for maternity leave. Where a couple adopts, either but not both can take adoption leave. The other may be able to take paternity leave. Where there is a single adopter, it is that person who may take adoption leave and the partner may be able to take paternity leave.

In order to be eligible for adoption leave, the employee must have at least 26 weeks service at the end of the week of notification of being matched with the child. The employee must notify the employer of the intention to take adoption leave within seven days of that notification, or as soon as is reasonably practicable if that is not reasonably practicable. The employer must respond, informing the employee of the date adoption leave will end. Ordinary adoption leave lasts for 26 weeks and additional adoption leave for a further 26 weeks.

The employee must give 28 days notice of an intention to return early from adoption leave.

Statutory adoption pay is payable for 26 weeks and its rate is the same as the later rate (after the first six weeks) of statutory maternity pay—see **4.6.4** above.

4.8 Parental leave

The next 'family friendly' right we need to consider derives from Directive 96/34/EC and is provided for in ERA 1996, s. 76, as amended by ERA 1999, sch. 4. It gives both parents a right to unpaid time off during the first five years of a child's life, or the first five years after adoption.

4.8.1 The form of the Directive

The Parental Leave Directive 96/34/EC was one of the measures agreed by the other Member States of the EU at a time when the United Kingdom remained outside the 'Social

Chapter' of the Maastricht Treaty. After the Labour Government decided to abandon the 'opt-out' there was a further Directive 97/75/EC which simply extended the 1996 Directive to the United Kingdom.

The 1996 Directive was the means of giving statutory force to an agreement reached between European trade unions and employers' organisations (the 'social partners') through the process of negotiation known as social dialogue. It is much more common elsewhere in Europe than in the United Kingdom for collective agreements to be given some sort of legal force so that they then apply to more employees and employers than just the original signatories. In this case the Directive expressly encouraged the social partners at local level to agree voluntary arrangements which could become an alternative to the law in defined workplaces. Such a process is virtually unknown in this country, and there is no legal basis for it to be built upon. However, MPL Regs provide in reg. 16 for voluntary arrangements to be agreed as an alternative to the detailed default provisions in sch. 2. The difficulty of any such arrangement is the provision in reg. 21 that employees may not treat statutory and contractual rights as cumulative, but may choose whichever is better in any particular regard. We do not yet know whether this rule might enable an employee, in a case where a voluntary arrangement exists, to argue that some particular provision in the voluntary arrangement fails to satisfy the minimum terms of the Directive, and that sch. 2 is therefore still relevant. Few employers will want to become test cases. Furthermore the first addition to the default provisions that any employee representative will seek is some kind of payment for parental leave, and most employers will wish to resist that. In practice, therefore, voluntary arrangements are unlikely to become common for the time being. For the remainder of this section we shall concentrate on the default provisions.

4.8.2 Qualification for the right

The right to take parental leave applies to all employees with service of one year or more if they have responsibility for a child. Parental responsibility is defined by reference either to the provisions of the Children Act 1989, or to registration as a child's father.

Under ERA 1996, s. 76(5) (inserted by ERA 1999, sch. 4), the regulations implementing parental leave may specify things that are to be taken as done for the purpose of caring for a child. Such rules would limit the circumstances in which parental leave can be taken. There is no such provision in MPL Regs 1999. Consequently employees do not have to justify a request to take parental leave by reference to the circumstances.

4.8.3 The right

Each qualifying employee may take parental leave up to a total of 13 weeks for each child. Thus each parent of twins may take up to 26 weeks. Under the default provisions the leave cannot be taken in blocks shorter than a week, nor for more than four weeks in any year (sch. 2, paras 7 and 8).

The right normally expires on the child's fifth birthday. Where the child is adopted it expires on the fifth anniversary of the adoption, or the child's 18th birthday, whichever is earlier. If the child is disabled (defined by reference to entitlement to a disability living allowance), the maximum leave is 18 weeks instead of 13, the right expires on the child's 18th birthday, and in this instance the default provisions do not apply the rule about minimum blocks of a week; the minimum is a day.

The employee's rights during parental leave are exactly the same as those concerning additional maternity leave—see **4.6.3.3** above. The right to return at the end of it is to the same job if the leave is four weeks or less. If leave exceeds four weeks, or it is added on to additional maternity leave, the right to return is the same as after additional maternity leave.

4.8.4 Notices and administration

Under the default provisions, the employee is normally required to give the employer 21 days' notice of an intention to take parental leave. The employer may delay the leave for up to six months if the business would unduly be disrupted and an alternative time is offered. The expiry of the right that we discussed above will be delayed to cover this postponement if necessary. The employer is entitled to ask for evidence of the employee's entitlement, but not of course for any explanation of the circumstances of the particular request.

Fathers wanting to take parental leave at the time of a birth are required to give 21 days' notice of the expected week of childbirth and of the required length of leave. They are then entitled to take the leave whenever the birth actually occurs and the employer cannot postpone it. There is a similar provision covering both parents in relation to an expected adoption.

The employee's right is to a *total* of 13 weeks' leave in relation to each child. Thus an employee who changes jobs after taking eight weeks of leave in the first two years of a child's life enjoys no entitlement during the next year, having not yet achieved the necessary service in the new job, but thereafter has a right to five more weeks in the period up to the child's fifth birthday. There is no obligation on the first employer to pass any records to the second, and monitoring of this rule may therefore cause problems.

4.8.5 Remedies

The right not to suffer any detriment and to present a claim to an employment tribunal under s. 47C of ERA 1996 (considered in relation to maternity rights at **4.6.3.4** above) also applies to parental leave. Under ERA 1996, s. 80, claims can also be presented of unreasonable postponement of parental leave.

4.9 Time off for dependants

The third and last of the family friendly provisions that we are considering is also a result of the Parental Leave Directive 96/34/EC. Unlike parental leave, it is not subject to regulations but is set out in detail in ERA 1999, which inserts a new s. 57A into ERA 1996. The requirement in the Directive is *for time off work for urgent family reasons*; in the UK version this has become *time off for dependants*, which is probably significantly broader in its scope. The time off is unpaid.

4.9.1 Circumstances when the right arises

There are two aspects to the statutory definition of the circumstances when employees have a right to time off for dependants. First, there is the question of who is a dependant; and, secondly, there is the question of when the right arises in relation to those dependants.

A dependant is defined in s. 57A(3), (4) and (5) as:

(a) a spouse;

(b) a child;

(c) a parent;

(d) anyone else living in the same household except as employee, tenant etc.;

(e) *for certain purposes only*, anyone else who 'reasonably relies on the employee' for that help.

The circumstances are defined in precise terms in s. 57A(1). In outline, the employee must need the time off to take action related to any of the following events concerning a dependant:

(a) where any of the above dependants falls ill or is injured or assaulted, or where a dependant in categories (a) to (d) above gives birth;

(b) arranging care in relation to illness or injury—all dependants;

(c) death—(a) to (d) only;

(d) unexpected disruption or termination of arrangements for care—all dependants;

(e) unexpected incidents at school, only in relation to a child—(b).

The circumstances are thus quite tightly defined. For example, the right relates to making arrangements for the provision of care, but not to provision of care by employees themselves.

4.9.2 Time off

The statutory right is to unpaid time off. There is no stated limit to the amount of time, beyond the reference to *a reasonable amount* of time off in ERA 1996, s. 57A. In *Qua* v *John Ford Morrison* [2003] ICR 482, the EAT held that time off was permitted for urgent reasons such as dealing with a child who has fallen ill unexpectedly, but not regular relapses from a known underlying condition. Reasonableness related to the employee's needs and her compliance with conditions about notification to the employer; not disruption or inconvenience caused to the employer's business. In many employments, there is already a contractual right to paid time off in defined circumstances like bereavement or childbirth, but the duration is usually defined. There is no statutory reference to the interrelationship of two such rights and they therefore exist independently.

4.9.3 Notices and administration

The whole purpose of these provisions is to enable employees to deal with emergencies. There can therefore be no requirement on employees to give advance notice. They are, however, required to tell the employer the reason for the absence as soon as reasonably practicable and, unless the explanation is only being given on return to work, to state how long the absence is expected to last.

Despite the strict statutory definition of the circumstances in which the right arises, there is nothing in s. 57A to give the employer any right to demand evidence of the employee's entitlement. This is a strange omission, and it may be that the employment tribunals will nevertheless accept that employers need evidence of some kind to know whether the right exists at all.

4.9.4 Remedies

Under ERA 1996, s. 57B (inserted by ERA 1999), an employee can present a claim to an employment tribunal of being refused time off for a dependant and the tribunal may award compensation.

Perhaps of greater practical significance is the addition of this right to the list of those in connection with which dismissal is automatically unfair under ERA 1999, s. 99 (see **10.8.7** below). This could cause employers a lot of difficulty in dealing with absenteeism. Employees with a poor attendance record are sometimes warned and are told that further unauthorised absence will lead to dismissal. If further absence occurs, but is in fact covered by s. 57A, it will automatically be unfair for the employer to dismiss.

4.10 Flexible working

The last of the 'family friendly' rights we need to consider is the right of the employee to ask the employer for a variation of contract of employment in order to care for young or disabled children. It exists as s. 80F of ERA 1996, inserted by EA 2002, and is supplemented by two sets of regulations issued in 2002. It took effect in April 2003. Permitted requests are for changes in hours of work, place of work, or time of work.

To be eligible to make such a request employees must satisfy the following criteria.

(a) They must have 26 weeks service when making the request.

(b) The child must not be more than 6 years old, 18 if disabled, 2 weeks after the request is made.

(c) The employee must have or expect to have responsibility for the child's upbringing.

(d) The request must be to enable the employee to care for the child.

(e) The employee must be the mother, father, guardian, adopter or foster parent of the child, or alternatively married to or the partner of such a person.

(f) The employee must not have made another application to work flexibly within the preceding 12 months.

The application must be made in writing and the employer must consider it seriously. The grounds on which it may be refused are set out in detail—to summarise, they are grounds of cost, detrimental consequences, effect on other staff, or planned structural changes.

An employee who is refused unreasonably or whose employer does not properly consider the request can present a claim to the employment tribunal. The tribunal can order the employer to reconsider the request and can award compensation up to a maximum of 8 weeks pay, subject to the usual statutory maximum of £270 per week.

4.11 Self-test questions

1. A 19-year old student friend had been earning some extra money by working in a bar on Friday evenings from 7.30 to about 11.45. He has just started an additional job working in a shop on Saturday mornings from 8.00 to 1.00 pm. He gets no break and is paid £30 for five hours' work. Your friend tells you that he understands that other people get

time-and-a-half for Saturdays. The shop manager told him that as a part-time worker he is not entitled to holidays.

Your friend is fed up with feeling tired when he goes to play football on Saturday afternoon, feels he is being exploited for a poor rate of pay, and wonders if there is anything you can do to help. Do you think the shop has broken any of the rules set out in this chapter?

2. An employer has until now paid at the rate of time-and-a-half for Saturday overtime. Recently the employer announced that such additional costs made the company uncompetitive compared with others overseas and gave three months' notice that weekend overtime would henceforth be paid at time-and-a-quarter. The trade union objected on behalf of the employees but the employer was adamant that the change was necessary and the trade union responded that its members would not work overtime on that basis. In fact, the employer did not require any overtime for several weeks after the expiry of the three months, but then a request was made and several people agreed to work on a Saturday. There is some suggestion that one or two expressly asked their supervisor about payment and he replied evasively, saying that payment would be sorted out later. They were in fact paid at time-and-a-quarter. Their trade union now asks whether that payment can be challenged in the tribunals. Could you use the 'deductions from wages' jurisdiction?

5

Operation of the contract

5.1 Introduction

This chapter examines how the contract of employment operates on a day-to-day basis. The sort of questions asked by employers and employees alike tend to be:

(a) Which terms usually appear in a contract?

(b) Does the law place limitations on how those terms can be used by either party?

(c) How may those terms be varied over the course of time?

(d) What are the legal rules for resolving disputes as to the content or implementation of those terms?

(e) What are the rights and duties regarding the payment of wages?

In attempting to answer these points this chapter will concentrate on the common law position and will adopt the following structure:

(a) The usual terms (express and implied) and how they are used.

(b) Qualifying for employment rights.

(c) Management decisions and employees' responses.

(d) Methods of resolving disputes, short of termination of contract.

(e) Breach: summary of sanctions and enforcement.

(f) Civil remedies for breach of contract.

(g) Deductions versus breach of contract.

(h) Example of an employment contract.

5.2 The usual terms and how they are used

We saw in **Chapters 3** and **4** that the contract is made up of express, implied and statutory terms. We have set out below the *most commonly-occurring express terms* you would find in a contract, together with commentary on their purpose, scope and operation. Some additional terms encountered in contracts will also be noted. Many of the express terms listed below correlate to the information that must be provided under the written statement detailed in **Chapter 3**. Indeed, many contracts contain no more than the basic requirements (some even fail in this aim) and, in practice, it is often quite difficult to ascertain whether you are dealing with a written statement or a rather terse contract of employment. In any case, the shoddy document might be the only real evidence of terms available to you. Do not expect the heights of drafting when dealing with many companies.

Having looked at express terms, we will then consider the implied terms, arising from common law and from statute. There is no fixed list of implied terms and some will be more applicable to a particular contract than others.

STANDARD EXPRESS TERMS	IMPLIED TERMS
(a) The names of the parties.	*The duties incumbent on the employer*
(b) Job title.	(a) The duty to pay.
(c) Commencement date.	(b) A limited duty to provide work.
(d) The expiry date of a fixed-term contract	(c) Duties relating to health and safety.
(e) Pay.	(d) The duty of mutual trust and confidence.
(f) Hours of work.	(e) A duty to provide proper information to employees.
(g) Place of work.	
(h) The sick pay scheme, if any.	
(i) Holiday entitlement.	*The duties incumbent on the employee*
(j) Pension scheme.	(a) A duty to act in good faith.
(k) Notice requirements.	(b) The duty to obey lawful orders.
(l) Dedication to enterprise clause.	(c) A duty to provide personal service.
(m) Disciplinary/grievance procedures.	(d) The duty to exercise reasonable skill and care.
(n) Confidentiality clause.	
(o) Intellectual property protection.	(e) The duty to take care of the employer's property.
(p) Restraint of trade clause.	
(q) Details of other benefits.	
(r) Any 'contracting out' clause.	

Figure 5.1 Common terms of the contract.

5.2.1 Express terms

The extent of such terms, reached orally or in writing, will vary a great deal. The style of drafting is also quite variable, especially with the more complicated terms such as confidentiality and restraint of trade clauses. Therefore we have not provided 'model' clauses because these will change with the needs of the client and, more importantly, this is a matter for your course rather than this book. We have attached an example of a working contract taken from practice. We had considered using a contract which we considered to be an example of good practice, but in the end decided that a faulty contract might provide more help (and realism). This appears at the end of the chapter together with commentary so that you can see some of the clauses *in situ*.

As noted in **Chapter 3**, in reality employees rarely negotiate their own terms; the contract is either in a standard form or has been the subject of negotiations with trade unions. The common terms will be:

(a) The names of the parties.

(b) *Job title* and general statement of duties.
The wider this is drafted the more built-in flexibility there is for the employer (e.g., 'clerk/typist and receptionist' allows for mobility between tasks). However, if there is ever a dispute as to performance of duties, or if the employer needs to declare the employee redundant, then an expansive list of duties may prove problematic (e.g., the job of clerk/typist might have disappeared but not that of receptionist).

(c) When the *commencement date* occurred.
This is important in establishing the employee's continuity of employment, the timing of which may affect rights to claim, *inter alia*, unfair dismissal compensation, redundancy payments, maternity rights and pension rights (for details see **5.3** below).

(d) The *expiry date* of a fixed-term contract.
We noted these and other forms of limited-term contracts above at **3.3.1**.

(e) *Pay*.
Always an essential ingredient and an apparently simple point, but if payment is determined by piece-work, commission, or is variable according to the shift pattern worked then these points need to be spelled out clearly. The application of minimum pay levels under the National Minimum Wage Act 1998 was dealt with at **4.2** above.

Included in the general description of 'pay' one might also find other benefits—'perks' and bonuses—such as company cars, accommodation, 'golden handshakes', share option agreements, private health insurance schemes, and discretionary performance-related payments. The range is extensive and, especially in relation to senior employees, quite inventive. The motivation behind these is often one of tax-avoidance.

(f) *Hours of work*, including a statement as to the status of overtime, i.e., is overtime compulsory or merely voluntary and how is payment calculated?
The number of hours worked by employees together with patterns of working (e.g., shift systems, part-time, flexitime, 'annualised hours') vary enormously but working patterns for many workers are now subject to specific constraints (see above at **4.3**).

(g) *Place of work*.
The employer's business may have more than one site. If the employer wishes to be able to move the employee from place to place it is advisable to spell this out. Equally, the employer may wish to show that the employee is only expected to work in Southampton even though there are sites in London and Plymouth (see **Chapter 11** on how this relates to redundancies in a particular place of work).

(h) *The sick pay scheme*, if any.
Many employees are not entitled to payments during sickness absences other than those provided by the state. Thus statutory sick pay entitlements will be administered by the employer, but this is usually much more limited than a company sick pay scheme (e.g., nothing is payable for the first 3 days' illness and payment is limited to 28 weeks at a fixed rate). The employer is under no duty to provide company sick pay, and even where such schemes do exist there is often a sliding scale of payments, e.g., no sick pay until the employee has worked for one year, one month's entitlement for service between one and three years, and so on.

(i) *Holiday entitlement*.
This area has traditionally been the domain of pure contract law. However, the Working Time Regulations now lay down established patterns of holiday entitlement for many workers. For those workers not covered by the Regulations, this area is still governed by the express and implied terms of the contract.

(j) *Pension scheme* arrangements, if any.
Such details will relate to any schemes operating outside the state provisions. An employer is not bound to operate a company pension scheme and an employee is not bound to join it. There are a number of different schemes available, e.g., final salary schemes and money-purchase schemes. Details are outside the scope of this book.

(k) *Notice* requirements.
This will detail what length of notice to terminate the contract is due from each party. The amount will often vary according to length of service, though there are certain *statutory minima* required under ERA 1996, s. 86 (see **5.2.3** below and **Chapter 9**). Employers may also wish to insert a term that *payment*

in lieu of notice may be given by the employer. Payment in lieu simply means that the employer makes a money payment equivalent to the sum the employee would have earned during the notice period. If calculated correctly the sum equates to any damages the employee might have been awarded for the failure actually to give notice. The employer can choose to do this even if there is no clause in the contract allowing for such action. However, although no further damages will fall due, giving a payment in lieu when there is no term to that effect is technically a breach of contract and, as will be seen, this may negate any restraint of trade clause in the contract (see **8.9**). The disadvantage to having such a clause is that it becomes an agreed contractual liability and so tax will certainly be deducted.

Notice clauses can take a variety of forms. The notice due from one party does not have to be the same as from the other, and there is no standard term which one could expect to occur in every industry. In general, American companies tend to favour short notice periods and British companies have tended to favour longer terms (e.g., one or two years for senior executives). Moreover, with senior employees a whole host of ingenious devices may be found, often designed to minimise tax liabilities. One increasingly common term is the 'garden leave' clause—a mechanism which attempts to use notice provisions to overcome some of the problems of restraint of trade clauses (see **8.10** for details).

Some employers use a clause which requires an employee to forfeit part of their final salary or holiday pay if the employee fails to give adequate notice. In *Giraud* v *Smith* [2000] IRLR 763, Kay J held that such clauses would have to constitute a genuine pre-estimate of loss in order to stand—otherwise they amounted to penalty clauses. Oddly enough, the Working Time Regulations (see **Chapter 4**) do permit such deductions provided *some* payment is still made: *Witley & District Men's Club* v *Mackay* [2001] IRLR 595, EAT, so different analyses apply depending on how the claim is framed.

(l) *Dedication to enterprise clause*, sometimes called a 'whole time and attention clause'. This clause states the limitations under which an employee can undertake other work for a different employer, either during or after working hours. The clause, especially with senior employees, may also impose a duty to inform on colleagues' misdeeds.

(m) *Disciplinary/grievance procedures*.
Procedures have always been very important in employment law disputes; now they are even more so. Until the implementation of EA 2002, ss. 31 to 40 by the Employment Act 2002 (Dispute Resolution) Regulations SI 2004/752, employers were relatively free to devise their own procedures. The employer's conduct in, say, an unfair dismissal action would then be judged against his own published disciplinary procedure (or lack of one) in determining the fairness of any dismissal. But, apart from guidelines issued by ACAS, there was no standard minimum procedure. Nor was an employee expected to follow any grievance procedure before resigning in order to claim that the employer's conduct was so intolerable as to constitute a repudiation of the contract. That has now changed. ACAS still issues guidelines and companies will still have their own disciplinary and grievance procedures but, whatever the position, the new statutory procedures apply. This is an extremely important and wide-reaching change in employment law and we shall deal with these in more detail at **5.3** below. The ACAS Guidelines can be found on the ACAS web site at http://www.acas.org.uk/.

In this context we should note which types of disciplinary and grievance procedures may be discovered in an ordinary company other than the statutory ones:

(i) agreed 'collective agreement' schemes

(ii) contractual schemes: which will be viewed in addition to the statutory procedures and in the light of the ACAS Guidelines. Larger companies will still be expected to have procedures which reflect their size and resources. Consequently these documents can run to many pages and be quite elaborate. They are rarely contained in the contract itself and instead should be referred to in the contract and set out in a separate document.

The following terms will occur more frequently, though not exclusively, in contracts for senior employees, sales people and research and development staff:

(n) *Confidentiality clause.*

During the currency of the contract an employer's 'secrets' will be protected by the implied terms relating to confidentiality and fidelity (see below at **5.2.2** and **Chapter 7**). However, an express term can serve to detail the nature of the confidential information and also serve as a warning to employees. Without such a clause there may be circumstances where junior employees who come into contact with confidential information are not bound by any duty of confidence because this was not made obvious to them.

Confidentiality clauses are also frequently drafted to protect against the use or disclosure of information once the relationship has terminated. It is a matter of some debate whether such clauses are effective and we will deal with this point extensively in **Chapter 7**. For the moment we can say that it is advisable to insert properly-drafted clauses of this nature in the contract; certainly as regards employees who are likely to handle confidential information.

(o) *Intellectual property clause.*

This clause seeks to detail ownership of copyright, designs and inventions made by the employee during the working relationship. Such clauses cannot overturn certain statutory definitions, e.g., Patents Act 1977, s. 39, which defines the circumstances where the employer will gain rights to any invention made by the employee (see **Chapter 7**).

(p) *Restraint of trade clause.*

Such clauses endeavour to prevent an employee working in a particular job or industry for a set time, and usually within a defined area, after the contract has ended. The effect of restraint clauses is therefore far more dramatic than any confidentiality clause. Many employers seek to rely on both types of clause in order to protect against disclosure of secrets and/or to prevent the former employee poaching the employer's trade connections. The presumption with restraint of trade clauses is that they are void unless:

(i) they seek to protect a *legitimate interest;* and

(ii) they are shown to be *reasonable* by reference to time, area and the market setting. See **Chapter 8** for details.

The following terms, which may apply to all staff, occur occasionally but are useful:

(q) *A right to search employees.*

Companies wishing to protect against the removal of confidential documents or, more generally, against the removal of stock, are advised to insert such a clause. There will be no general implied term to this effect and there may well now be human rights implications under art. 8 of the European Convention on Human Rights. We would suggest that the same degree of caution should be applied to searching employees' offices and desks, even though, technically, these are the employer's property.

(r) *A right to demand employees undergo medical examinations on request.*
As will be seen in **Chapter 7** (at **7.9.2**), a term will not be implied which forces an employee to submit to a medical examination. An express term is necessary and often very useful. Indeed it has become common practice in some industries (e.g., oil exploration) for the employer to have the contractual right to demand that employees undertake regular drug tests. This is defended on the grounds of health and safety; but many employers would like to see this sort of term extended to all kinds of employees. Again, art. 8 of the European Convention on Human Rights needs to be considered here (see *Whitefield* v *General Medical Council* at **1.7.3.2** above).

(s) *Suspension clause.*
This gives the employer the right to suspend an employee (i) with pay, or (ii) without pay as part of disciplinary proceedings or sanctions. It should occur in the disciplinary details (see (m) above). There will be no right for an employer to suspend without pay in the absence of such a clause, and any prolonged suspension with pay may be a breach of contract even with such powers in the contract as it may strike at the mutual trust of the relationship.

(t) *Lay-off and guarantee clauses.*
If an employer 'lays off' the employee (i.e., sends him or her home without pay because there is a shortage of work) this will constitute a breach of contract and may eventually be deemed a redundancy. Many industries therefore have specific rates of pay relating to short-time working, termed 'guarantee payments'. There are statutory guarantee payments as well which will operate as a minimum (at the time of writing, £17.80 per day to a maximum of five days in any three-month period).

(u) *Variation clause.*
As we will see below, although the unilateral variation of a contract by the employer is not unknown there may be complex legal consequences (see **5.5.2.1**). Some employers therefore incorporate an express term allowing for the power to vary the contract (usually in stated circumstances). Such clauses are viewed with great suspicion by the courts and tribunals.

(v) *Maternity leave.*
Some employers offer maternity rights which are more beneficial to the employee than the bare statutory rights (see **Chapter 4** above).

5.2.2 Implied terms

Employment contracts are rarely thought out by the parties. The exact terms of contracts are often difficult to locate or are silent on many aspects. There is therefore great scope for implying terms; for instance, 'Is sick pay payable?', 'Is there a limit on overtime hours that may be worked?', 'Can the employee be asked to work at different sites?'.

The various methods of implying terms were noted in **Chapter 3** (by law, under the 'officious by stander' test, by custom and by statute). In line with general contractual theory, terms will be implied only where they are *necessary* for the business efficacy of the contract, not simply because it would be *reasonable* so to imply them. However, once a term has been found to be necessary to the contract the court will then determine the limits of that term within reasonable parameters. Thus it may be found reasonable to imply a term that an employee will work at a variety of sites operated by the employer; it may, however, be unreasonable to include the Birmingham site where the employee normally works in Oxford.

The courts and tribunals are not afraid of implying terms, either to give a purposive interpretation to the contract or on the basis of *general* employment practice rather than by detailed analysis of the negotiations, etc. entered into by the specific parties. These general points, however, centre on how the parties would be expected to behave, e.g., to act in good faith; the courts and tribunals are more wary of accepting arguments of 'common practice' or 'general working practice' within a company without firm evidence of the fact. The generally-established implied terms as to duties owed are set out below.

5.2.2.1 The duties incumbent on the employer

(a) The duty to *pay* the employee the agreed remuneration for being ready and willing to work. There is no general duty actually to supply work, though there are exceptional cases here (see (b) below).

The major statutory controls on pay are the Employment Rights Act 1996, Part II, Protection of Wages (which concerns the right for employers to make deductions from pay) and the National Minimum Wage Act 1998. Various other pieces of legislation also outlaw discriminatory pay schemes (e.g., the Equal Pay Act 1970).

Particular problems have nevertheless arisen over:

(i) *Sick pay*.

In addition to statutory sick pay rights the vast majority of employees will be subject to some form of contractual sick pay arrangement. But if there is no written or oral evidence of this then the right to payment becomes an issue. The Court of Appeal has stated that there is no presumption either way, in *Mears* v *Safecar Security Ltd* [1982] ICR 626 (sick pay not due on the facts). One would thus have to look at all factors such as custom and practice within the company and even the seniority of the employee. If there is a term as to sick pay its duration is limited to that stated in the contract or for a reasonable period: *Howman* v *Blyth* [1983] ICR 416. It is not uncommon for employers to exclude certain types of illness from the sick pay scheme: e.g., those relating to the employee's own misconduct or generated by some activities outside work.

Where sick pay schemes exist they usually take the form of offering full pay for, say, three months and then maybe half-pay for the same period (most schemes require a qualifying period of employment). Some employers go beyond this and offer their employees membership of permanent health insurance (PHI) schemes (i.e., schemes drawn up by health insurance companies and offered at preferential rates to companies). Unfortunately, the wording of the sick pay scheme and that of the PHI scheme sometimes do not correlate. For instance, the PHI scheme may provide generous terms and payments (e.g., long-term incapacity payments continuing until retirement), whereas the contractual scheme will usually be framed more narrowly and allow for dismissal of incapacitated employees after (say) six months' absence. The case law (*Aspden* v *Webbs Poultry & Meat Group (Holdings) Ltd* [1996] IRLR 521; *Adin* v *Sedco Forex International Resources Ltd* [1997] IRLR 280; *Bainbridge* v *Circuit Foil UK Ltd* [1997] ICR 541; *Brompton* v *AOC International Ltd and UNUM Ltd* [1997] IRLR 639) has shown that the courts may adjudge, on the wording of the various documents or by implication of terms, that the employer's contractual scheme has to give way to these more beneficial insurance provisions. Oddly enough, the reverse was the case in *Jowitt* v *Pioneer Technology (UK) Ltd* [2003] EWCA 411, [2003] IRLR 356. Here the contractual scheme was more beneficial to the employee than the PHI: the former allowed for payments for long-term disability until retirement age, the latter limited this to cases where no other occupation could be undertaken. The insurance company felt the employee could undertake other work and so withdrew payments to the employer; the employer then withdrew payments to the employee. The employee succeeded in his argument that, as the limiting term in the PHI agreement between the insurance company and the employer had not been expressly incorporated into the contractual sick pay scheme, he could rely on the contractual scheme.

One important consequence of these cases is that, as Staughton LJ states *obiter* in *Brompton*, there was 'a good deal to be said for' the view expressed by Sedley J in *Aspden* that in these circumstances a term should be implied to the effect that the employer would not terminate the contract so as to deny the employee of his or her rights under the PHI scheme (at least not without having inserted some power to do so in the PHI agreement or having to pay a great deal in damages). A dismissal for good cause or a genuine redundancy will not be covered by this new implied term: *Hill* v *General Accident Fire & Life Assurance Corporation plc* [1998] IRLR 641 (see further at **10.9.2.3**).

(ii) *Share purchase option schemes*.
The problem is the same as with PHI schemes: what happens to the option to purchase when the contract is terminated? In *Levett* v *Biotrace International plc* [1999] IRLR 375, the contract included an option for the employee to purchase shares in the company. The right lapsed in the event of the employee being dismissed following disciplinary procedure (it is quite common to find such terms in contracts of employment, whereby the option lapses on termination). Here, however, the employee had been summarily dismissed in breach of the disciplinary procedure. The Court of Appeal held that he was still entitled to exercise his option; the employers were not entitled to deprive the employee of his rights by relying on their own breach of contract.

Equally, wording the scheme so that employers have an 'absolute discretion' on dismissal to reduce any share option has been held not to entitle the employer to reduce it to nil: *Mallone* v *BPB Industries plc* [2002] EWCA Civ 126, [2002] ICR 1045. This is particularly interesting because, as we will see when we come to consider how each party reacts to demands made by the other (see **5.4** below), this was the first real acknowledgement by the Court of Appeal of a power to limit managerial discretion based not merely on the technicalities of 'collateral' contracts or on the presence of dishonesty, bad faith or perversity but rather on 'irrationality'.

(b) A limited duty to *provide work*. Traditionally, only in exceptional cases will there be a duty to provide work. The most significant example occurs where the lack of work leads to an effective wage reduction, as where pay is related to commission or piece-work. A time when this is likely to be an issue is when the employee has been given notice of dismissal and not provided with work (or pay in lieu) during that time: see *Devonald* v *Rosser* [1906] KB 728.

Where lack of work might have a damaging effect on reputation (e.g., in the case of actors, television personalities, or perhaps even senior business executives) there is the possibility of arguing breach of contract. And where the employer deliberately refuses to allow the employee to work for no good contractual reason, the possibility of arguing a repudiatory breach of contract becomes stronger: *Breach* v *Epsylon Industries* [1976] ICR 316.

Although the above propositions have been established law for some time, the Court of Appeal decision in *William Hill Organisation Ltd* v *Tucker* [1998] IRLR 313 has confirmed that there will be cases where a right to work exists (and changing social attitudes may mean the list is wider than previously thought). The case is detailed at **8.10** below and concerned the doctrine of restraint of trade. The key point here is that their Lordships, on the facts, held that the employee, a senior dealer in the fixed odds compiling department, had not just a right to receive wages but also a right to perform his work. As in many a bad Dracula film, it seems this area was not dead, only undead, and consequently may yet be revived (darkness permitting).

(c) A duty to *indemnify* the employee regarding expenses necessarily incurred in the course of employment. Obviously this extends to expenses such as hotel and travel costs; it may also extend to covering the employee's legal costs, but only to those relating to actions undertaken during employment.

(d) Duties relating to *safety*. In *Wilsons and Clyde Coal* v *English* [1938] AC 57, these duties were said to relate to the provision of safe fellow employees, equipment, premises and the system of work. There are also statutory duties relating to defective equipment and compulsory insurance in addition to the responsibilities created by the Health and Safety at Work etc. Act 1974 which impose criminal liabilities in this field.

There is a vast body of case law and statutory authority on duties of health and safety. More recent developments, however, have caused employers concern. The Management of Health and Safety Regulations 1992 require employers to carry out risk assessments for both physical and mental hazards at work. To this has been added case law developing the implied terms relating to psychological damage arising out of stress at work. In *Walker* v *Northumberland County Council* [1995] ICR 702 the employer's duty of care was extended to cover lack of attention in dealing with the workload of an (already distressed) employee (for more detail see **9.10.1.3** below).

The area of health and safety duties is certainly one of developing importance. The *Walker* case has had an impact on personal injury litigation, and other areas of working activity are generating new duties. One such relates to smoking in the workplace and its effect on non-smokers. In *Waltons & Morse* v *Dorrington* [1997] IRLR 488, for instance, the EAT held that an employer 'will provide and monitor for his employees, so far as is reasonably practicable, a working environment which is reasonably suitable for the performance by them of their contractual duties'. Moreover, this duty is not restricted to smoke-filled offices; the formulation extends to incorporate most aspects of the working environment.

What is not clear as yet is the exact balance to be struck between express terms of the contract (e.g., those requiring excessive working hours) and the emergence of this implied term under *Walker*. The earlier case of *Johnstone* v *Bloomsbury Health Authority* [1991] IRLR 118 (concerning health workers) was settled before the substantive issues could be debated, but at interlocutory stage there was an indication in the Court of Appeal that the express term on working hours was limited by the implied terms as to health and safety. There is also an overlap here with disability discrimination law where the disability relates to psychological illness (see, particularly, **Chapter 6**).

(e) The duty of *mutual trust and confidence*. This is a rather nebulous duty and much of the case law has arisen in the context of unfair dismissal claims based on constructive dismissals (see **Chapter 10**). Just as employees have found that duties of obedience and loyalty can be vastly extended beyond the perceived agreement by implied terms, so too is an employer bound by an element of reciprocity. Thus there will be a serious breach of the duty of mutual trust (and so of the contract) if the employer victimises the employee, acts capriciously towards the employee, fails to allow *some* employees (e.g., part-timers) access to benefits, maliciously undermines an employee's authority in front of subordinates, harasses the employee and so on. The list is open-ended and the use of this duty as a sort of 'default rule' in the governing of employment relationships has been endorsed by the House of Lords in *Malik and Mahmud* v *Bank of Credit and Commerce International SA (in compulsory liquidation)* [1997] ICR 606. In *French* v *Barclays Bank plc* [1998] IRLR 646, the Court of Appeal applied such principles to the case where an employee had been directed to move across country within the organisation and had been granted a discretionary relocation bridging loan by his employer which was then withdrawn when the employee had difficulty selling his house. The employee was forced to sell his house at a lower value than anticipated and so sued for breach of contract in respect of the shortfall. He succeeded on the grounds that the bank had breached the duty of mutual trust by seeking to change the arrangement once the employee had relied upon it.

We shall see more of this in operation in **Chapter 10**; we should stress, however, that this is not a duty to act reasonably, only a duty to give fair treatment under the terms of the contract. What the courts are looking for is to establish a breach of contract which makes further continuance of the relationship impossible. This will not always be the same as a finding of unreasonableness; especially if express terms allow the employer to take that particular action. Indeed, in *Johnson* v *Unysis Ltd* [2001] UKHL 13; [2001] ICR 480 (dealt with at **9.10.1.1** below), the House of Lords did not see the duty of mutual trust as an overarching legal principle which might be used to control the wording of express contractual provisions (at least in relation to cases on termination of the contract). Thus it may seem unreasonable to move employees across the country every two or three years, but it is less likely to constitute a breach if a mobility clause has been incorporated in the contract. Matters such as a right to harass or discriminate cannot of course form part of an express term.

The issue of an employer's (bad faith) motives, what constitutes a lawful order, and the boundaries of mutual trust and confidence was explored in *Macari* v *Celtic Football and Athletic Club Ltd* [1999] IRLR 787. Following the takeover of Celtic, the new managing director sought to enforce the strict terms of the incumbent manager's contract relating to residence within 45 miles of the club and absences from the club. He also excluded the manager (Macari) from board meetings, which Macari had previously attended. Exchanges over a period of months eventually led to Macari's dismissal. Macari sued for breach of contract as he had been dismissed without notice or payment in lieu contrary to the express terms of the contract. Macari claimed the employers had acted in bad faith in dismissing him.

The Court of Session, Inner House (equivalent to the Court of Appeal) held that the issue of bad faith motive was irrelevant provided the orders themselves were lawful, i.e., within the terms of the contract, even if such conduct had been proven (which, on the facts, it had not). The Court did find that the employers had breached the duty of mutual trust, both by excluding Macari from board meetings and by the general conduct of the managing director in not communicating with Macari, given Macari's position within the organisation. This would have entitled

Macari to treat this as a repudiation, leave and sue for damages. However, as Macari had remained and continued to draw his salary this breach by the employer did not excuse his failure to comply with the terms of the contract in ignoring the employer's lawful and legitimate instructions—a sort of 'if you stay you obey' interpretation. The Court therefore decided that the employers were not in breach of contract. Lord Caplan did, however, profer the view that certain bad faith instructions could amount to a breach, e.g., those designed to embarrass or harm the employee (though there would seem to be quite an overlap here with the general duty of mutual trust).

What is clear from all this is that the area of bad faith and the ambit of the duty of mutual trust and confidence is still open to a wide range of arguments and applications and that the 'pure contract' approach seen above is at some variance with the analysis of the same topic employed in unfair dismissal cases (see **Chapter 10** below). *Macari* is also worth reading just for one sentence, *viz* 'The Lord Ordinary assoilzied the defenders . . .', which apparently means to release from liability (or purgatory).

(f) A limited duty to *provide proper information* to employees regarding matters affecting rights under the contract. This implied term arises out of the decision of the House of Lords in *Scally* v *Southern Health and Social Services Board* [1991] ICR 771, where new employees were not informed of their rights to enhance their years of pension entitlement. This case effectively gave legal force to what is good practice anyway; but it did not create a universal rule regarding the provision of information. In *University of Nottingham* v *Eyett and the Pensions Ombudsman* [1999] IRLR 87, for instance, the High Court did not find as an implied term a duty for an employer to inform an employee taking voluntary early retirement that if he had waited a month he would have received a higher pension owing to the operation of the annual pay rise. The employer had not set out to mislead the employee but had merely implemented its general policy of offering no advice to employees on retirement provisions (see also *Outram* v *Academy Plastics Ltd* [2000] IRLR 499 (CA) to the same effect). In *Scally*, Lord Bridge had stated that a positive term of this nature would only be implied when the contract had not been negotiated with the individual employee, the particular term required the employee to take some action to avail himself of the right and the employee could not reasonably be expected to be aware of the term without notice.

Further limitations have now been put on the term by the Court of Appeal. In *Lennon v Commissioner of Police of the Metropolis* [2004] EWCA Civ 130; [2004] IRLR 385 the Court acknowledged the existence of liability where the employer voluntarily assumed responsibility for providing information (and negligently misstated it) but distinguished this from implying a term that the employer owed any *positive* duty to provide information. Thus, *Scally* is looking more and more like a flash in the pan.

(g) One may also imply a term of *affording employees a reasonable opportunity to obtain redress of grievances*. This emerged in an unreserved decision of the EAT in *W. A. Goold (Pearmak) Ltd* v *McConnell* [1995] IRLR 516. The logic is simple: the s. 1 written statement demands that employers should inform employees to whom they may apply to redress an employment grievance; Parliament must therefore have intended this to be a sign of good industrial practice. It must therefore be an implied term that procedures are in place to allow for speedy redress of grievances. Failure to do so will therefore be a breach of contract—in this case a breach serious enough to justify the employees leaving and claiming that they had been constructively dismissed.

There are three points worth commenting upon: first, it is not clear whether the grievance in question must be made in good faith; secondly, it must be said that if all aspects of the written statement, or all good industrial relations practices were transformed into implied terms with such ease, there would be some raised eyebrows amongst employment law practitioners. Finally, the area of grievance procedures has been changed radically by the implementation of EA 2002 (see **5.4**).

5.2.2.2 The duties incumbent on the employee

(a) A duty to act in *good faith*. This is a wide and undefined duty which relates to the loyalty and fidelity that can be expected of an employee. This duty has had a major bearing on matters such as confidentiality, spare-time working, employees competing with their employer, and pre-1977 patent law. Its operation can be seen in the following examples:

(i) A duty *not to disrupt* the employer's business interests: *Secretary of State for Employment* v *ASLEF* [1972] 2 QB 455. This case concerned workers observing their contracts to the letter under a 'work-to-rule'. The disruption that followed was held to be a breach of contract. It appears therefore that the employees were held to be in breach of contract because they had observed the terms of the contract to the letter. Why this should be so is explained at **5.5.3** below.

(ii) A duty of *honesty*. This incorporates actions beyond simple theft or fraud. In *Sinclair* v *Neighbour* [1967] 2 QB 279, a betting shop manager habitually left IOUs in the till, though he always repaid them. He was expressly forbidden to do this, but he continued. The summary dismissal was held to be justified. It was said that a breach occurred where further continuance of the relationship would prove impossible. That was the case here. Again, in *Denco Ltd* v *Joinson* [1991] ICR 172, the use of an unauthorised password to gain access to a computer was found to constitute gross misconduct, analogous to dishonesty.

(iii) A duty to *account for secret profits: Boston Deep Sea Fishing and Ice Co.* v *Ansell* (1888) 39 ChD 339. Most cases involve high-ranking employees taking bribes, or who have undisclosed interests which affect the employment relationship. Strictly speaking, however, this duty extends to such things as the gift from a client of a bottle of whisky at Christmas time.

Note: Points (i) to (iii) do not mean that the employment relationship is a fiduciary relationship (except in the case of certain employees such as directors). As was noted in *Nottingham University* v *Fishel* [2000] IRLR 471, an employee's duty of fidelity requires the employee to take the employer's interests into account; it does not require the employee to act in the employer's interests. In *Fishel* this meant that the head of the university's infertility unit was not under a fiduciary duty in respect of the work he did abroad (and the money earned), but he was liable to account for the money earned from work done by other university employees.

(iv) A duty to *disclose misdeeds*. There is no obligation to incriminate oneself: *Bell* v *Lever Bros* [1932] AC 161. When asked direct questions, however, there is a duty not to mislead. An intermediate area exists here under the provisions of the Rehabilitation of Offenders Act 1974. In general, this Act allows certain criminal convictions to be 'spent' after an appropriate length of time so that they do not have to be declared. What has also developed recently is the idea that there is a duty, at least incumbent on senior management whose responsibilities are affected by the actions, to notify the employer of serious breaches by fellow employees even when that involves self-incrimination: *Sybron Corp.* v *Rochem Ltd* [1983] ICR 801. This 'duty to rat' may often be made explicit or extended by the express terms. Thus in *Fishel*, although it was held that there was no *implied* term requiring the employee to inform the employer of his extra-university activities, there was a valid *express* clause to this effect. The High Court decision of *Item Software (UK) Ltd* v *Fassihi* [2003] EWHC 3116; 2003] IRLR 769 added two interesting points to this discussion: first, that a senior employee involved in negotiations on behalf of his employer owed a duty to the employer to disclose factors which could affect the negotiations (including his own attempts to sabotage those negotiations!); secondly, that the activities in *Bell* v *Lever Bros* were held not to be fraudulent, and where fraud was present (as here) the *Bell* v *Lever Bros* principle could not apply, so there was a duty to self-incriminate. This is in keeping with other High Court decisions (e.g., *Horcal* v *Gatland* [1983] IRLR 459—with *obiter* agreement in the Court of Appeal—and more recently (again *obiter*) *Tesco Stores* v *Pook* [2004] IRLR 618) that senior employees may well owe a duty to incriminate themselves, their positions being treated as akin to fiduciaries.

(v) A duty not to disclose *confidential information: Thomas Marshall (Exporters) Ltd* v *Guinle* [1978] ICR 905. This duty arises during the course of the relationship and, in some cases, will continue to operate after its termination: *Faccenda Chicken* v *Fowler* [1986] ICR 297 (see **Chapter 7** for details).

(vi) A duty to surrender *inventions*. Sections 39 to 43 of the Patents Act 1977 deal with this point extensively. As regards most employees any invention arising out of the employee's *normal duties* will belong to the employer: *Harris's Patent* [1985] RPC 19 (see **Chapter 7**).

(vii) A duty *not to compete* with the employer: *Hivac Ltd* v *Park Royal Scientific Instruments Ltd* [1946] Ch 169. This duty relates to actions during the currency of the contract and corresponds with 'whole time and attention' express terms. Competition cannot be prevented once the contract has been determined, subject to a valid restraint of trade clause.

(b) The duty to *obey lawful orders*. This is an essential element in the relationship. The nomenclature begs the question as to what is a lawful order. 'Lawful' in the employment context means 'contractually justified'; such orders do not necessarily have to be reasonable as well (see, for instance, *Cresswell* v *Board of Inland Revenue* [1984] ICR 508 and **5.5.1** below).

(c) A duty to provide *personal service* and to be ready and willing to work. Things such as taking part in a strike or other industrial action will generally amount to a breach. This will allow the employer either to withhold some or all of the wages due, or even to accept the employee's repudiation by dismissing him (see **5.5.4.6**). Illness is not a breach of this duty and, once the employee has recovered, the employer will be in breach if (subject to any express term in the contract) he insists on the employee delaying the return to work in order to undergo an examination by the company doctor and not paying the employee during that period: *Beveridge* v *KLM UK Ltd* [2000] IRLR 765.

(d) The duty to exercise *reasonable skill and care: Janata Bank* v *Ahmed* [1981] ICR 791.

(e) The duty to *take care* of the employer's property. Negligence in allowing property in the employee's care to be stolen has fallen within this heading. There are obvious limits: losing the company cat has been held to be an insufficient ground to justify dismissal.
Interestingly, there is no corresponding duty placed on the employer to safeguard the employee's property.

5.2.3 Automatically imposed terms

As we saw in **Chapter 4**, terms may also be imposed by statute. For example, terms relating to sex discrimination and equal pay will automatically become part of the contract and cannot be evaded even by express agreement (see **Chapter 6**). The most important of these terms, for present purposes, relates to notice periods. There are requirements for the provision of minimum periods of notice laid down in ERA 1996, s. 86. *The contractual periods may be longer, but not shorter.* They operate on a sliding scale; the greater the length of service, the greater the minimum notice entitlement. The maximum statutory minimum allowed under s. 86 is 12 weeks' notice (see **Chapter 9** for a fuller explanation).

5.2.4 Statutory dispute resolution procedures

In 5.3 below we will examine the new statutory dispute resolution procedures, which came into force on 1 October 2004 (see The Employment Act 2002 (Dispute Resolution) Regulations SI 2004/752 and The Employment Act 2002 (Commencement No. 6 and Transitional Provision) Order SI 2004/1717). The procedures relate to a wide range of disputes and claims, including some we have encountered already (e.g., disputes about payment of the national minimum wage) and claims we will encounter in later chapters (especially unfair dismissal). **This is an important point to note: it is tempting to think that these new procedures relate only to unfair dismissal claims, but they may arise in relation to equal pay claims, discrimination claims and many others.**

The Regulations enact EA 2002, ss. 31–40. Section 30, EA 2002, which would have created a new imposed term that 'every contract shall have effect to require the employer and employee to comply' with the procedures has not been implemented and this provision will be reviewed in 2006. This means that these new procedures, although packing a hefty financial and procedural thump, are not an automatically imposed term. In turn, this means that, whereas they are relevant to claims placed before an employment tribunal, they do have any force as regards claims covering the same cause of action in a county court or High Court (e.g., for breach of the employment contract).

The sometimes incomprehensible technical complexities will have little appeal to employers or employees (and probably tribunals). It seems to the authors that the government has taken a sledgehammer to crack a nut. The procedures were introduced to deal with simple situations but their excessive detail brings to mind the immortal line in The Italian Job (where they are testing the explosive on a van): 'You were only supposed to blow the bloody doors off'.

5.3 The new statutory procedures

As noted at **5.2.1(m)** above, the new statutory procedures operate as a statutory floor of rights and duties—default procedures. The purpose behind introducing these procedures is to prevent both employers and employees from acting precipitously when a dispute arises. Now, a failure by an employee to comply with the relevant steps will mean that any award may be reduced and, in some cases, that a claim cannot be brought at all until key steps have been followed; a failure to comply on the part of the employer who dismisses an employee will mean that the dismissal is automatically unfair (we will deal with the effects of non-compliance as regards unfair dismissal in **Chapter 10**). In this section we will outline the procedures and explain when they will apply.

5.3.1 The statutory dismissal and disciplinary procedures

These procedures (referred to here as 'D&DPs') are set out in EA 2002, sch. 2. They are not revolutionary in their expectations of reasonable behaviour, but their operational complexities may catch out many employers and employees. There is a **standard** procedure for dealing with cases where the employer is contemplating dismissal or taking 'relevant disciplinary action' against an employee. There are three key steps to this procedure. There is also a **'modified procedure'** for dealing with *some* cases of gross misconduct. There are two steps to this procedure. Finally, there are **general requirements** applicable to both forms of procedure. We will deal with those first, but we must also note here that a 'meeting' held for the purposes of the D&DPs is a hearing for the purposes of s. 13(4) and (5) of the Employment Relations Act 1999 (c. 26). As we shall see when we look at unfair dismissal, this means that there is a right, under s. 10 of that Act, for an employee to be accompanied at these hearings.

5.3.1.1 The general requirements

These are contained in EA 2002, Part 3, sch. 2 and are quite straightforward.

Timetable	Each step and action under the procedure must be taken without unreasonable delay.
Meetings	(1) Timing and location of meetings must be reasonable. (2) Meetings must be conducted in a manner that enables both employer and employee to explain their cases. (3) In the case of appeal meetings which are not the first meeting, the employer should, as far as is reasonably practicable, be represented by a more senior manager than attended the first meeting (unless the most senior manager attended that meeting).

Figure 5.2 The general requirements.

There will undoubtedly be some exploration in future cases of what is meant by terms such as 'unreasonable delay' and 'reasonably practicable' but these must largely be questions of fact.

5.3.1.2 The standard dismissal and disciplinary procedure.

This is contained in EA 2002 Part 1, Chapter 1, sch. 2. It applies to all cases where the employer is contemplating dismissing the employee (**for any reason**) or taking 'relevant disciplinary action' against the employee. A 'relevant disciplinary action' is defined in SI 2004/752, reg. 2(1) as an 'action, short of dismissal, which the employer asserts to be based wholly or mainly on the employee's **conduct or capability**, other than suspension on full pay or the issuing of warnings (whether oral or written)' (*emphasis added*). The exclusion of suspension on full pay is understandable as this is used by employers as a holding operation while investigations take place and is not per se a breach of contract (suspension without pay will fall within the procedures). The exclusion of 'warnings' may seem a little strange as this is the most common form of disciplinary action. This exclusion was the subject of debate in the consultation process and was inserted so as not to overburden small employers by allowing for a range of ordinary workplace procedures to be used before the statutory ones start to have effect. Given that the spirit of the D&DP is one of reasonable action, this is not altogether convincing. Nevertheless, where an employer is contemplating merely issuing a warning the D&DP is not applicable. One presumes that if the employer is contemplating issuing a warning, but may perhaps be thinking of dismissal as an alternative, then the D&DPs will still apply.

The standard D&DP is as follows:

Step 1: statement of grounds for action and invitation to meeting	(1) The employer must set out in writing the employee's alleged conduct or characteristics, or other circumstances, which lead him to contemplate dismissing or taking disciplinary action against the employee. (2) The employer must send the statement or a copy of it to the employee and invite the employee to attend a meeting to discuss the matter.
Step 2: meeting	(1) The meeting must take place before action is taken, except in the case where the disciplinary action consists of suspension. (2) The meeting must not take place unless— (a) the employer has informed the employee what the basis was for including in the statement under paragraph 1(1) the ground or grounds given in it, and (b) the employee has had a reasonable opportunity to consider his response to that information. (3) The employee must take all reasonable steps to attend the meeting. (4) After the meeting, the employer must inform the employee of his decision and notify him of the right to appeal against the decision if he is not satisfied with it.
Step 3: appeal	(1) If the employee does wish to appeal, he must inform the employer. (2) If the employee informs the employer of his wish to appeal, the employer must invite him to attend a further meeting. (3) The employee must take all reasonable steps to attend the meeting. (4) The appeal meeting need not take place before the dismissal or disciplinary action takes effect. (5) After the appeal meeting, the employer must inform the employee of his final decision.

Figure 5.3 The standard D&DP.

Note that the decision whether to appeal or not lies with the employee.

5.3.1.3 The modified dismissal and disciplinary procedure.

This is contained in EA 2002, Part 1, Chapter 2, sch. 2. The modified procedure becomes relevant only when an employer dismisses an employee summarily (i.e., without notice—'on the spot') for gross misconduct. The employer must be entitled to dismiss without notice by reason of the conduct and the dismissal must take place as soon as the employer becomes aware of the misconduct or immediately afterwards, and it must be reasonable for the employer to dismiss without making further enquiries (sometimes described as cases where investigations would be 'futile' e.g., where the employer has just witnessed the employee assaulting a customer). The procedure is as follows:

Step 1: statement of grounds for action	The employer must— (a) set out in writing— (i) the employee's alleged misconduct which has led to the dismissal, (ii) what the basis was for thinking at the time of the dismissal that the employee was guilty of the alleged misconduct, and (iii) the employee's right to appeal against dismissal, and (b) send the statement or a copy of it to the employee.
Step 2: appeal	(1) If the employee does wish to appeal, he must inform the employer. (2) If the employee informs the employer of his wish to appeal, the employer must invite him to attend a meeting. (3) The employee must take all reasonable steps to attend the meeting. (4) After the appeal meeting, the employer must inform the employee of his final decision.

Figure 5.4 The Modified D&DP.

The modified procedure will clearly not apply in many cases. Not every instance of gross misconduct is covered; only those where the employer responds immediately to the incident.

5.3.1.4 When the D&DPs do not apply

Under reg. 4, the D&DPs will not apply to a mixed bag of cases mainly centred on where the employer makes 'collective dismissals' (e.g., redundancies). This provision was inserted because in such cases the individual characteristics of the employee are usually irrelevant to the decision to dismiss.

Exclusions under reg. 4 SI 2004/752
(a) where the employee belongs to a category of employees who are all dismissed and then all offered re-engagement on new terms; (b) where there is a collective redundancy of 20 or more employees and a duty to consult and inform representatives arises (but for redundancies affecting fewer than 20 employees, or where the redundancies will take effect in a period longer than 90 days, the statutory procedures will still apply—see **Chapter 11**); (c) where at the time of the employee's dismissal he is taking part in some form of industrial action (there are complicated rules regarding exactly which actions are covered); (d) where the employer's business suddenly ceases to function, because of an event unforeseen by the employer, with the result that it is impractical for him to employ any employees; (e) where it has become illegal for the employee to continue in his job; or (f) where the employee is one to whom a dismissal procedures agreement designated by an order under ERA 1996 s. 110 Act applies at the date of dismissal. This covers specific and detailed collective agreements incorporated into the employees' contracts.

Figure 5.5 When the D&DPs do not apply.

The non-application of the D&DPs does not mean the employer is free to ignore procedures altogether: the ACAS guidelines on discipline and dismissal are still relevant as are the contractual provisions. The difference is that the consequences of failing to follow the D&DPs do not apply. We should also note here that the term 'dismissal' does not include constructive dismissals. Instead, the employee will need to follow either the standard or modified grievance procedure (see below) if he or she wishes to make a tribunal claim relating to the constructive dismissal.

5.3.1.5 Circumstances in which the parties are treated as complying with the D&DPs

There will be instances where one or other party is deemed to have complied with the requirements. These fall into two categories: the first, under reg. 5, covers technical points where other procedures interrupt the D&DP; the second, under reg. 11, where one party's behaviour makes continuance impossible or it is not reasonably practicable to continue. In such cases, the 'innocent' party is relieved of responsibility but the 'guilty' party may be penalised in any award made. See **Figure 5.6** overleaf.

5.3.1.6 Consequences of failures in the D&DPs

Where the procedures cannot be started or completed because of the actions of one party the failure of the procedures will be attributed to that party (e.g., the person harassing the other party). However, the two procedures (covering 'dismissal' and 'relevant disciplinary action') have to be viewed separately as regards the consequences:

(a) *Dismissal:*

- Where a dismissal has occurred and the failure in the D&DP is down to the **employer** this will mean that any dismissal will be an 'automatically unfair dismissal'. We will explain the significance of this in the context of **Chapter 10**.

Under reg. 5 SI 2004/752	Under reg. 11 SI 2004/752
(a) where the procedures have started but the employee claims 'interim relief'; (b) where the employee has appealed under an 'appropriate procedure'. *Both (a) and (b) are very specialist situations and are not expanded upon here.*	(a) that either party has reasonable grounds to believe that commencing the procedure or complying with the subsequent requirement would result in a significant threat to himself, his property, any other person or the property of any other person; (b) that either party has been subjected to harassment and has reasonable grounds to believe that commencing the procedure or complying with the subsequent requirement would result in his being subjected to further harassment; or (c) it is not practicable for the party to commence the procedure or comply with the subsequent requirement within a reasonable period.

Figure 5.6 Where the parties are treated as complying with the D&DPs.

- The failure is also relevant to a range of possible claims listed in EA 2002, sch. 3. These are:
  - — Section 2 Equal Pay Act 1970
  - — Section 63 Sex Discrimination Act 1975
  - — Section 54 Race Relations Act 1976
  - — Section 146 Trade Union and Labour Relations (Consolidation) Act 1992
  - — Paragraph 156 of Schedule A1 to that Act
  - — Section 8 Disability Discrimination Act 1995
  - — Section 17A Disability Discrimination Act 1995
  - — Section 23 Employment Rights Act 1996 (unauthorised deductions and payments)
  - — Section 48 of that Act (detriment in employment)
  - — Section 111 of that Act (unfair dismissal)
  - — Section 163 of that Act (redundancy payments)
  - — Section 24 of the National Minimum Wage Act 1998
  - — The Employment Tribunal Extension of Jurisdiction (England and Wales) Order 1994 (SI 1994/1623) (breach of employment contract and termination) and 1994 (SI 1994/1624) (corresponding provision for Scotland)
  - — Reg 30 Working Time Regulations 1998 (SI 1998/1833) (breach of regulations)
  - — Reg 32 Transnational Information and Consultation of Employees Regulations 1999 (SI 1999/3323)
  - — Reg 28 Employment Equality (Sexual Orientation) Regulations 2003
  - — Reg 28 Employment Equality (Religion or Belief) Regulations 2003

Under ERA 1996, s. 31 the failure by the employer can be used by the employee to obtain extra compensation in 'Schedule 3' claims. On the other hand, if the failure is down to the employee, compensation can be reduced. The details are covered at **10.13.5 and 10.13.6.** Perhaps surprisingly, some actions are missing. Thus, issues relating to less favourable treatment of part-time workers (see SI 2000/1551) and those on limited-term contracts (see SI 2002/2034) are not included in Schedule 3. This means that employees can bring claims relating to these matters without going through the statutory dispute resolution procedures.

(b) *Relevant disciplinary action:*

- A failure by the employer in operating the D&DP does not give rise to a cause of action in itself. However, as with 'dismissal', a tribunal may award extra compensation in successful 'Schedule 3' claims arising from the disciplinary action. For example, say the employee is subject to disciplinary action and is demoted: she may have a claim for unlawful deduction of wages arising from the lower salary or even a sex discrimination claim. If she is successful in either or both of these claims she may obtain a further award related to the employer's failure to operate the D&DP properly.

We have tried to represent all this in **figures 5.7 and 5.8** below.

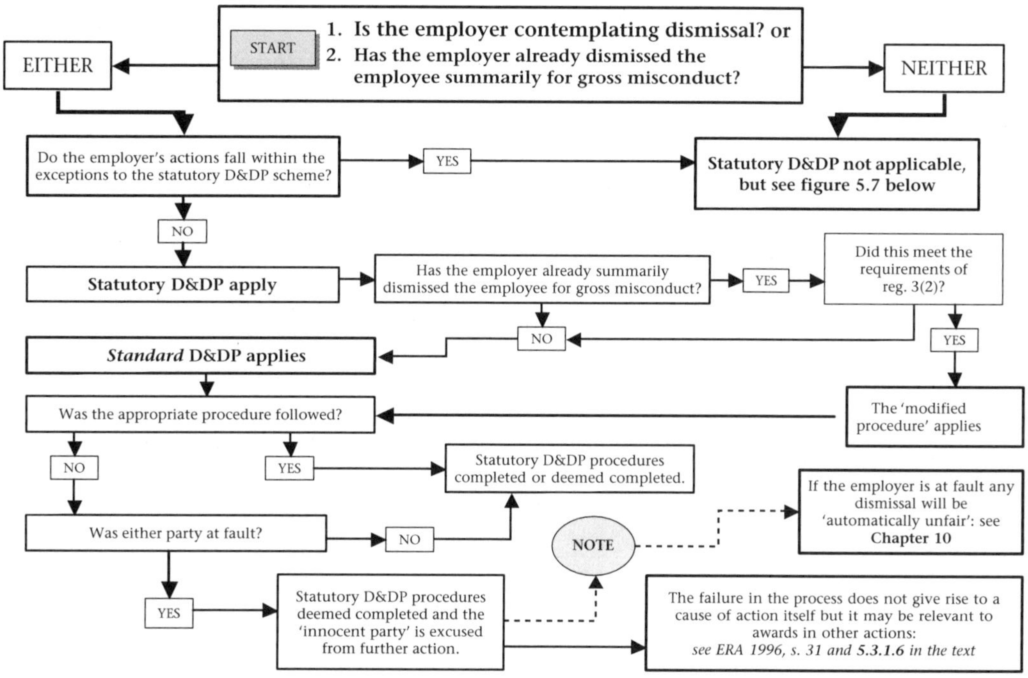

Figure 5.7 Dismissal and the Statutory D&DP.

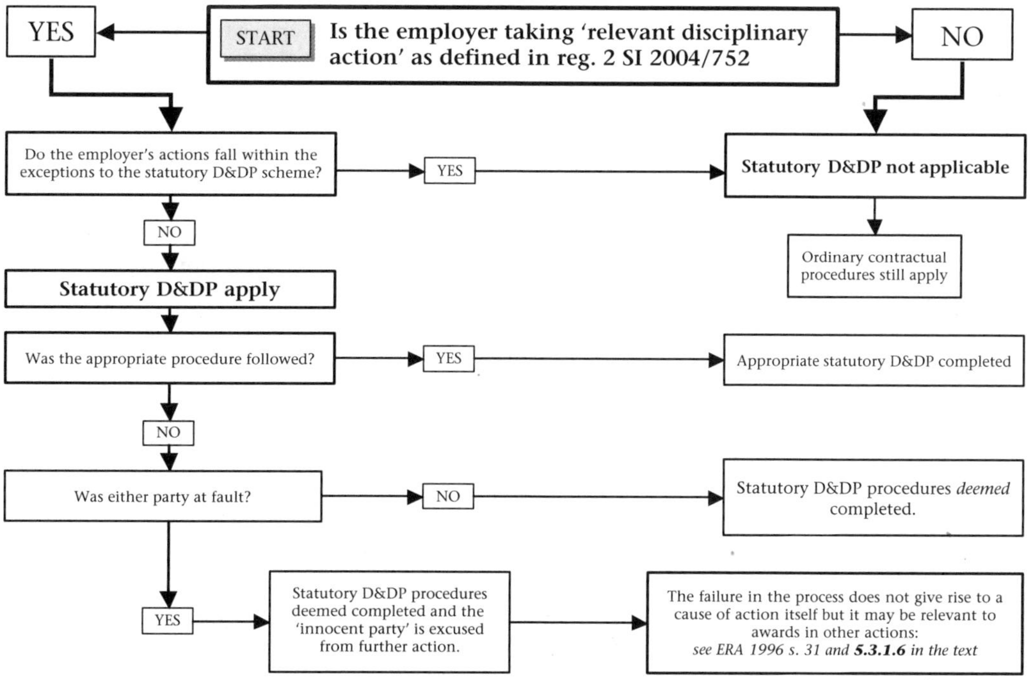

Figure 5.8 Disciplinary action and the statutory D&DP.

5.3.2 The statutory grievance procedures

As with D&DPs, there is a standard procedure containing three stages and a '**modified procedure**' containing two. The general requirements also apply here, as do the definitions of 'meetings'. A 'grievance' is defined in regs 2(1) and 6, SI 2004/752 as meaning:

- 'a complaint by an employee about action which his employer has taken or is contemplating taking in relation to him' and which
- 'could form the basis of a complaint by an employee to an employment tribunal under a jurisdiction listed in Schedule 3 or 4, or could do so if the action took place' (sch. 4 is almost identical to sch. 3 but includes claims for breach of contract in employment tribunals).

Under reg. 2(1) 'action' includes 'omission'. It is not clear, however, whether the actions of other employees can be deemed the actions of the employer (though the DTI guidance notes assume that the actions of fellow employees fall within the procedures if the conditions for vicarious liability are present).

The rules governing Grievance Procedures are formulated slightly different from those on D&DPs in that, in addition to the penalties that may be imposed by a tribunal where one party is at fault, there are also 'admissibility' requirements. These are rules which prevent a tribunal hearing some cases until the procedures have been complied with in whole or in part. There are further elaborate rules on extending the limitation periods where grievance procedures are relevant. We shall cover these points below.

5.3.2.1 The standard grievance procedure

This is contained in EA 2002, Part 2, Chapter 1, sch. 2.

Step 1: statement of grievance	The employee must set out the grievance in writing and send the statement or a copy of it to the employer.
Step 2: meeting	(1) The employer must invite the employee to attend a meeting to discuss the grievance. (2) The meeting must not take place unless— (a) the employee has informed the employer what the basis for the grievance was when he made the statement under paragraph 6,and (b) the employer has had a reasonable opportunity to consider his response to that information. (3) The employee must take all reasonable steps to attend the meeting. (4) After the meeting, the employer must inform the employee of his decision as to his response to the grievance and notify him of the right to appeal against the decision if he is not satisfied with it.
Step 3: appeal	(1) If the employee does wish to appeal, he must inform the employer. (2) If the employee informs the employer of his wish to appeal, the employer must invite him to attend a further meeting. (3) The employee must take all reasonable steps to attend the meeting. (4) After the appeal meeting, the employer must inform the employee of his final decision.

Figure 5.9 The standard statutory grievance procedure.

There is nothing surprising here: it just requires an employee who has a grievance to follow a simple procedure and for the employer to respond accordingly. The standard grievance procedure applies to cases where the employee wishes to complain about action taken in relation to him, for example, that the employer has given him a final warning, demoted him or changed the terms of his contract.

5.3.2.2 The modified grievance procedure

This is contained in EA 2002, Part 2, Chapter 2 sch. 2. It only comes into play where:

- the employee has ceased to be employed by the employer, **and**
- either the employer was unaware of the grievance before employment ceased, or was so aware but the standard procedure had not been commenced or had not been completed before the last day of the employee's employment; **and**
- the parties must have agreed in writing that the modified, rather than the standard, grievance procedure shall apply. The agreement has to be specific to each case and a clause in the contract allowing for this to happen will be inoperative: reg. 6(3)(c).

Unless all the conditions are satisfied the standard grievance procedure applies. The idea behind the 'modified' procedure is that it should only apply to cases where the parties have expressly agreed that it would be pointless to follow the standard procedure, including attendance at meetings, where there is no ongoing employment relationship and the parties have no interest in following the procedures. This will therefore not arise in many instances but may be relevant where the employee is attempting to pursue a constructive (unfair) dismissal claim (see **Chapter 10** on this).

Step 1: statement of grievance	The employee must— (a) set out in writing— (i) the grievance, and (ii) the basis for it, and (b) send the statement or a copy of it to the employer.
Step 2: response	The employer must set out his response in writing and send the statement or a copy of it to the employee.

Figure 5.9a The modified statutory grievance procedure.

5.3.2.3 When the statutory grievance procedures do not apply

Under reg. 6 neither of the grievance procedures applies where:

- the employee has ceased to be employed by the employer, neither procedure has been commenced, and since the employee ceased to be employed it has ceased to be reasonably practicable for him to issue a statement of grievance: reg. 6(4).
- where the grievance is that the employer has dismissed or is contemplating dismissing the employee: reg. 6(5); or
- where the grievance is that the employer has taken or is contemplating taking relevant disciplinary action against the employee **unless** one of the reasons for the grievance is a reason mentioned in reg. 7(1) (see **5.3.2.4** below): reg. 6(6).

5.3.2.4 Circumstances in which the parties are treated as complying with the Statutory Grievance Procedures

There are a number of cases where either or both parties are treated as having complied with the requirements. The importance of this is that the 'innocent' party is deemed to have played their part so that no adverse consequences flow from their later conduct. The first of these 'deemed compliance' elements is common to D&DPs and Grievance Procedures, namely, reg. 11 (concerning harassment etc) and is not repeated here. In addition to reg. 11, regs 7 and 9 apply (see **Figure 5.9b** below).

Additionally, under reg. 8, where the standard grievance procedure is the applicable statutory procedure, the employee has ceased to be employed by the employer, the

reg. 7	reg. 9
Although reg. 6(6) disapplies both of the grievance procedures as specified above, they will apply if one of the reasons for the grievance is a reason mentioned in regulation 7(1). These are: (a) that the relevant disciplinary action amounted to or, if it took place, would amount to unlawful discrimination, or (b) that the grounds on which the employer took the action or is contemplating taking it were or are unrelated to the grounds on which he asserted that he took the action or is asserting that he is contemplating taking it. However, the parties are treated as having complied with the grievance procedure in full as long as the employee writes to the employer setting out his grievance (a step 1 statement) before the appeal meeting under the applicable dismissal and disciplinary procedure. This is said to give the parties a chance to address the grievance directly in the context of the dismissal and disciplinary procedure.	Where an 'appropriate representative' of the employee has written to the employer setting out the grievance on behalf of at least two employees. This is designed to allow grievances to be dealt with collectively where more than oneemployee has the same grievance. An 'appropriate representative' is an official of an independent trade union recognised by the employer for the purpose of collective bargaining or an employee of that employer who was elected or appointed to represent employees and has authority to do so under an established procedure to resolve grievances

Figure 5.9b Parties are treated as complying with the statutory grievance procedures.

grievance statement has been issued, and since the end of his employment it has ceased to be reasonably practicable for the employee, or his employer, to comply with the procedure, the parties shall be treated as having complied with the outstanding parts of the procedure **provided** the employer responds to the grievance in writing and it is not reasonably practicable to have a meeting (e.g., where the employee has moved to another part of the country or found another job). Finally, in some industries, employers and trade unions have jointly developed sophisticated dispute resolution procedures. These schemes may allow the employee to raise a grievance with this joint body: reg. 10. At this stage you may feel we are entering the world of the surreal.

5.3.2.5 Consequences of failures in the statutory grievance procedures

In itself, a failure by the employer to follow the relevant statutory grievance procedures does not create a cause of action. However, as with D&DPs, should the employee make a successful claim for, amongst others, discrimination, protection of wages or unfair dismissal claim (the full list is set out in sch. 4 ERA 1996), the employer's failure as regards the Statutory Grievance Procedure may lead to extra compensation being awarded against him in the lead action.

Should the fault lie with the employee, ERA 1996 s. 32 states that he will be prevented from pursuing any claim listed in sch. 4 (which includes unfair dismissal and thereby includes such a claim arising from a constructive dismissal) until the procedures have been complied with or treated as having been complied with. For example, say an employee suffers a deduction in wages. He cannot now simply resign and claim constructive dismissal without issuing step 1 of the relevant procedure. Section 32 effectively creates a 'cooling-off' period in that, even where procedures have started, a claim may not be brought within 28 days. So as not to prejudice employees bringing a claim within the relevant limitation period (three months in the case of unfair dismissal) there are further provisions allowing tribunals to extend these periods in prescribed circumstances.

5.3.2.6 Discrimination questionnaires and whistleblowing

There is a potential overlap between a grievance and these two issues which we should mention now.

(a) *Discrimination questionnaires*. As we shall see in **Chapter 6** an employee is permitted to pose certain questions to an employer in order to ascertain whether discrimination has taken place (e.g., on comparisons of pay for an equal pay claim). These questions do not constitute a grievance (see reg. 14).

(b) *Whistleblowing*. There are detailed provisions on whether an employee can make a 'protected disclosure' to various bodies concerning his employer's alleged wrongdoing. It is up to the employee to decide whether, faced with the employer's actions, to decide whether to pursue a grievance (if indeed it falls within the definition noted at **5.3.2** above) or to make a protected disclosure.

5.3.2.7 Overlapping claims

In the real world of industry and commerce disciplinary and grievance issues often become intertwined. An employer may start disciplinary action only for the employee to lodge a grievance about the same matter, or the way the procedure is being handled, or about something else. As a summary, we should note that:

(i) Where there has been a dismissal or the employer is contemplating dismissing, the statutory D&DPs apply. The employee should make use of the appeal procedure within the D&DP. Reg. 6(5) makes the grievance procedures irrelevant here. But note that 'constructive dismissals' (resignations which are deemed to be dismissals because of the employer's conduct) fall under the grievance procedures and are excluded from the D&DPs. We will return to this in **Chapter 10**.

(ii) Where the issue is that of 'relevant disciplinary action' again the D&DPs apply and the employee should follow his part of the procedure. However, if the regs 6(6) and 7(1) become relevant then the employee must complete Step 1 of the statutory grievance procedure. This will occur when the employee believes the disciplinary action is discriminatory or being undertaken for an ulterior motive. The employer would be advised here to suspend the operation of the D&DP in order to hear the grievance.

5.4 Qualifying for employment rights

Employment rights do not necessarily apply automatically to all employees. For example:

(a) unfair dismissal and redundancy rights do not usually accrue until the employee has acquired some 'continuity of employment' with that employer (see **10.3** below);

(b) the right to claim the statutory minimum period of notice on dismissal usually requires one month's continuous employment;

The detailed rules governing continuity are found in ERA 1996 ss. 210–219 and in the Employment Protection (Continuity of Employment) Regulations 1996 (SI 1996/3147), and whereas employers and employees can agree *contractual* variations to the rules, these agreements cannot affect the *statutory* rights: *Secretary of State for Employment* v *Globe Elastic Thread Co. Ltd* [1979] ICR 706 HL, and *Collison* v *British Broadcasting Corporation* [1998] IRLR 238, EAT.

It is unfortunately not uncommon for solicitors to advise on the merits of, say, an unfair dismissal case, without determining the basic qualification rights first. Thus solicitors need to establish:

(a) what rights are being claimed and whether the worker actually is an 'employee' or, in some cases such as under the Working Time Regulations, a qualifying 'worker';

(b) exactly when the employment began;

(c) exactly when it ended;

(d) any breaks in that employment; and

(e) especially if there has been a dismissal, whether the reason falls under the continuity exceptions so that no time qualification is required.

Some of the basic questions in computing continuity are:

(a) *Who must prove continuity?* Continuity of employment and the calculation of lengths of continuous employment are rebuttable presumptions. The basic presumption of continuity is set out in s. 210(5) of the ERA 1996: 'A person's employment during any period shall, unless the contrary is shown, be presumed to have been continuous.' In *Nicoll* v *Nocorrode Ltd* [1981] ICR 348, the EAT held that if it is unclear whether the employee had worked the necessary number of qualifying weeks, the employee need only show some weeks count and then the burden shifts to the employer to disprove continuity.

(b) *When does continuity start and finish?* Sections 211–213 detail the start and finish dates for calculating continuity as beginning on the day on which the employee starts work, and ending with the 'effective date of termination' for unfair dismissal purposes (called the 'relevant date' in redundancies). Any service before the age of 18 does not count for redundancy purposes (but does for unfair dismissal).

(c) *Which weeks count towards continuity?* Under s. 212(1), any week during the whole or part of which an employee's relations with his employer are governed by a contract of employment counts in computing the employee's period of employment, e.g., in *Colley* v *Corkindale* [1995] ICR 965 the employee only worked for five and a half hours every alternate Friday; she nevertheless qualified to bring an unfair dismissal claim because the court found that there was one contract governing the intervening periods between actual work. However, this must be distinguished from the case of regular but *separate* contracts: see *Hellyer Bros* v *McLeod* [1987] ICR 526, where trawlermen employed for separate sea voyages did not gain continuity of employment.

(d) *What happens with maternity leave?* The basic rules of continuity apply in such situations: see the Maternity and Parental Leave etc. Regulations 1999, SI 1999/3312 and the detailed explanation given in **4.6.4** above.

(e) *What happens when there is no contract?* The basic rule is that if there is no contract then continuity is broken. A good illustration of this is *Booth* v *United States of America* [1999] IRLR 16, where the US Government deliberately dismissed employees in the UK just short of the qualifying period for unfair dismissal (then, two years) but gave them the option to re-apply for their old jobs. This dismissal and re-engagement broke the continuity of employment.

(f) *Can continuity be preserved even when there is no contract?* In limited circumstances, yes. The position is governed by s. 212(3), which states that certain weeks *will* count in computing the employee's period of employment even though the employee appears not to have a contract with the employer. These are very odd and highly technical provisions which occasionally cause problems in practice. The weeks which count are those weeks during the whole or part of which an employee is:

(i) incapable of work in consequence of sickness or injury. Note here that if the employee has not been dismissed the contract will have continued as normal. The point of this provision is that if an employee has been absent because of illness, has been dismissed and then is re-employed at a future date, those weeks during which he was not employed may still count towards continuity provided the gap between dismissal and re-engagement was no more than 26 weeks;

(ii) absent from work on account of a temporary cessation of work. There is no definition of 'temporary'—it is a question of fact. How both parties regarded the absence would be cogent evidence, but, if necessary, one must use hindsight rather than intent to establish just how temporary it was. In *Ford* v *Warwickshire County Council* [1982] ICR 520 (a case concerning continuity of employment for part-time teachers employed only during each term and not for the school holidays), 'temporary' was said to mean 'transient'—which might exclude seasonal workers. In that case Lord Diplock also favoured a strictly mathematical approach in calculating length of service, though the Court of Appeal, in *Flack* v *Kodak Ltd* [1986] ICR 775, preferred a 'broad brush' approach, i.e., was the absence 'short' in relation to the overall employment relationship. Taking a job in the interim is not fatal to a claim of continuity (*Thompson* v *Bristol Channel Ship Repairers and Engineers Ltd* (1970) 5 ITR 85, CA) but is unlikely to cover the situation where an employee moves to a new employer, fails to settle, and quickly moves back to his old job. A 'cessation' has been defined in *Fitzgerald* v *Hall Russell & Co. Ltd* [1970] AC 984, HL: it refers to a cessation of the employee's work (not the employer's business). Thus, there was no temporary cessation in *Booth* v *USA* (above) because the work still remained;

(iii) absent from work in circumstances such that, by arrangement or custom, he is regarded as continuing in the employment of his employer for any purpose. That agreement or custom must exist when the absence begins: *Todd* v *Sun Ventilating Co. Ltd* [1976] IRLR 4. Equally, the mere fact that the parties might have discussed terms and conditions on which the employee might return did not amount to an implied arrangement: *McEwen* v *Brentwood & Ongar Conservative Association* (EAT 399/96, unreported). The reason for the absence appears immaterial (e.g., personal reasons, employee on 'reserve list' to be called-on when necessary: *Puttick* v *John Wright & Sons (Blackwell) Ltd* [1972] ICR 457).

This area has re-emerged from the shadows over the question of 'career breaks'. In *Curr* v *Marks & Spencer plc* [2002] EWCA Cic 1852, [2003] ICR 443 the Court of Appeal held that an agreed career break (here, a 'child break scheme') did not preserve continuity on the facts because there was no evidence of mutual agreement *regarding the issue of continuity*. In other words, the agreement to take the break was not enough; one needed direct evidence on the matter of continuity, e.g., an express agreement or perhaps the continuation of contractual benefits such as pension scheme arrangements.

(g) *Can some weeks which do not count still not break continuity?* The most common example arises in the case of industrial disputes. Under s. 212, if during the week, or any part of the week, the employee takes part in a strike action then the week cannot count towards calculating the total period of continuous employment but this does not break continuity.

(h) *What happens if an employee is made redundant and then re-employed at a later date?* Section 214 states that the continuity of a period of employment is broken and then re-starts afresh as regards redundancy pay entitlements only where a redundancy payment has previously been paid to the employee.

(i) *What happens when there is a change of employer?* If the employee leaves to join another company then continuity is generally broken unless that company is an associated company, or the absence and return can be classed as a temporary cessation. Where the employer changes identity the likelihood is that continuity will be maintained with the new employer (see **Chapter 12** below).

As you will see in later chapters, some rights arise immediately on employment so that no qualification period is necessary, e.g., the rights relating to discrimination on grounds of sex, race, disability, or trade union membership, 'protective awards' in redundancies, and time off for ante-natal care.

5.5 Management decisions and employees' responses

It is quite common for an employee to ask for legal advice along the lines of, 'They've told me I have to take on a different job. Can they do that?'; the context being perhaps an order to change shifts, take a pay cut, change duties, move to another site and so on. The pragmatic advice might be unpalatable: 'No, but are you prepared to fight?'

The corresponding question from the employer might be, 'We need to cut costs: can we change the system of working?'. There is a practical angle here too: what will the employer do in the face of individual or collective resistance? Is the employer willing to venture into brinkmanship, e.g., threatening to dismiss in the face of refusal to cooperate? It is therefore vital to know what the contract allows, whether that is legally permissible in itself, and how the terms might be open to both expansion and alteration.

In deciding on the balance between these two views you need to keep in mind all the points detailed above on express and implied terms.

5.5.1 Lawful orders

A 'lawful order' is one which is permitted under the contract, derived from the express terms, the implied terms or a mixture of both. Should the employee fail to obey this order he or she will be in breach of contract. If the breach is serious the employer will be entitled to dismiss the employee without notice. Equally, employers can only demand that lawful orders be obeyed. An employee is free to disregard anything which falls outside the scope of contract.

As with ordinary contracts, therefore, the courts *could* have adopted the view that the parties are restricted to the originally agreed express terms (with limited help from implied terms) and bound by nothing else. But this view does not hold true for three main reasons:

(a) Most employment contracts are for an indefinite period, terminable by notice. They may therefore last a considerable length of time. Like language, they need to be dynamic or they become useless; thus they do not fit easily with the static models of one-off or short-term contracts for goods or services. Both the exact terms and the method of working will inevitably change during that time and some account of this must be allowed for.

(b) Employment contracts are made up from a variety of sources, many of them not reduced to writing, so that certainty and proof is always a problem.

(c) The employment contract stands in the wider setting of the *employment relationship* so that the range of implied terms is more extensive than with most contracts and includes matters such as loyalty and mutual trust (matters you do not get when you hire a plumber, for instance, to fix your central heating—if indeed you manage to get the plumber in the first place).

5.5.2 The employer's handling of the contract

The employer generally has the economic bargaining power to insert terms which best serve the employer's interests. Further, it is the employer who issues orders under the contract. Both these points engender a high level of managerial prerogative. What curbs are placed on managerial prerogative?

5.5.2.1 The legitimacy of terms

There are now *statutory limitations* which make certain terms in contracts of employment illegal or ineffective. For example, those terms:

(a) which seek to license various forms of discrimination; or
(b) which offend against the principle of equal pay; or
(c) which attempt to diminish employee-inventors' rights; or
(d) which seek generally to contract out of statutory rights (such as unfair dismissal or redundancy); or
(e) which seek to exclude liability for negligence which causes death or personal injury; or
(f) which offend against safety legislation; or
(g) which are illegal in themselves, such as instructions to undertake criminal activities.

Away from these statutory concerns, however, there are few cases which have addressed the issue as to the *type* of terms acceptable in an employment contract. Thus, *prima facie*, employers are free to insert any terms they wish and the parties can construct any form of reasonable or unreasonable contract (restraint of trade clauses providing the rare example of common law interference: see **Chapter 8**). And express terms generally take precedence over implied terms. We use the word 'generally' because it is not clear whether terms 'implied by law' (sometimes referred to as legal incidents of the relationship), e.g., the duty of mutual trust and confidence, can be expunged by express terms. In *Johnstone* v *Bloomsbury Health Authority* [1991] IRLR 118, for instance, the Court of Appeal held that an express term requiring health workers to be 'available' for 48 hours over and above their normal 40-hour week could not stand in the face of the implied term to protect the employees' health and safety (see **5.2.2.1(d)** above). However, to do this the court had to find that the express term did not create an absolute duty (only a discretionary one as to requests for overtime), and because the term was equivocal the implied term had not been overridden. If the term had created an absolute duty of absurd overtime hours the court would have faced a more difficult question. In contrast to this problem of 'basic obligations', terms implied in fact (i.e., under the officious bystander test) cannot stand against contradictory express terms.

Judicial moderation of all this has had little focus. The concept of public policy might be invoked to overcome express terms, or the uncertainty of the term or, more recently, the implying of a term that contractual rights must be implemented on reasonable grounds.

PROBLEM

An employer encounters financial difficulties. The written contract is a complicated document, laden with detailed clauses, which sets out a very generous sick pay scheme. The employer decides to reduce the benefits substantially. The union objects on behalf of its members. The employer points to page 5 of the contract, where the final clause reads: 'The employer reserves the power to alter, amend, withdraw, terminate or revoke any term in this contract for any reason by giving one calendar month's notice.' The union has come to you for advice on the legality of this action.

ANSWER

The arguments available to you are multiple. You may seek to challenge the drafting of the term. For instance, you could argue that it is uncertain because of its width or seek to rely on *contra proferentem* interpretations (which is becoming a favoured method: see *Bainbridge* v *Circuit Foil UK Ltd* [1997] ICR 541). You could argue that such a clause permits only minor changes to be made (a point conceded by counsel and accepted by the EAT in *United Association for the Protection of Trade* v *Kilburn* (LEXIS transcript, EAT 787/84). You might seek to argue that such a clause can only be implemented in good faith and inherently requires renegotiation rather than mere unilateral change. Arguing from basic contractual principles you could claim that the court should try to avoid a construction which effectively destroys the aim of the contract or which produces absurd consequences. Similarly you might argue that reliance on this term *in this particular way* constitutes a breach of mutual trust and confidence; that such a term can be exercised only where it is reasonable in all the circumstances so as not to damage the employment relationship irrevocably. In all these cases, however, you are on uncertain ground; the express terms clearly outflank you so that on a literal reading of the contract the odds are against your client on the strict wording.

Cases in this area are now becoming more common. In *Airlie* v *City of Edinburgh District Council* [1996] IRLR 516, a majority of the EAT held that a bonus scheme payable under a collective agreement (which had been incorporated into the individual contracts) *was* open to variation by the employers on the proper construction of its wording (e.g., 'the scheme ... may be altered at the request of either side after consultation ...'). The employers had consulted, failed to reach an agreement, and acted accordingly. In *Candler* v *ICL System Services* (1996, unreported), based on the then Wages Act 1986 (now ERA 1996, Part II), the EAT held against the employer on the wording of the clause, but did not question the efficacy of the clause itself. The employer lost again in *Glendale Managed Services Ltd* v *Graham* [2003] EWCA Civ 773, [2003] IRLR 465 when they decided not to adhere to a nationally agreed pay rise. The employers argued that this national agreement was stated to be 'normally paid' to the employees but they had the power to withdraw it as the contract said the rate of pay would be the national rate 'as adopted by the Authority from time to time'; they had chosen not to adopt it. True, said the Court of Appeal, but only with sufficient notice so as not to breach mutual trust.

The employer will therefore argue that the clause is valid because: (i) it is an express term; and (ii) it simply reflects managerial prerogatives. The employee's arguments are more nebulous but the main ones must be: (i) to attack the wording itself on a *contra proferentem* basis; (ii) to argue that such a clause changes the nature of the contract itself and is therefore void.

We have also seen that in the cases concerning PHI schemes and share option agreements (**5.2.2.1** above) the courts have become more inventive in limiting the use of discretionary powers in the contract. A further step in this direction was taken in *Jenvey* v *Australian Broadcasting Corporation* [2002] EWHC 927, [2002] IRLR 520. Here, an employee fell into dispute with his employer over his contractual terms. He was dismissed shortly afterwards. The employment tribunal found that there was a redundancy situation on the facts, but that the actual reason for dismissal was the 'assertion of a statutory right' and therefore automatically unfair (see **10.8.7.1** below for details). They had to make an award based on this reason and, at the time of the hearing, an unfair dismissal award was subject to a cap of £12,000. This would have been fine except that the employee's contract incorporated a contractual redundancy scheme, which meant that if he had been dismissed for redundancy, he would have had a contractual claim of £58,000. By the tribunal's justified finding of an automatically unfair reason for dismissal the employee had effectively been deprived of the contractual redundancy package.

The employee had wisely reserved his right to bring a breach of contract claim in the High Court. He was estopped from claiming that the reason for his dismissal was redundancy and so brought a claim that there was a breach of the implied term on use of discretion in that the employer had decided to dismiss for redundancy and could not then be allowed (without good cause as noted above) to dismiss for some other or no reason, even though notice had been given. Elias J agreed with this and awarded damages for the contractual redundancy package.

Unfortunately (from the viewpoint of looking for clear guidance), there are also signs that this embracing of a wide-ranging implied term of the abuse of discretion may not be welcomed in all quarters. In the Privy Council case *Reda* v *Flag Ltd* [2002] UKPC 38, [2002] IRLR 747, their Lordships were clear that implied terms must give way to clear express terms so that a power to dismiss without cause contained in the contract was a power to dismiss for any cause or none and could not be limited by implied terms, even where the employer had dismissed in order to exclude the employees from the benefits of a share option plan whilst offering such benefits to other employees; nor was there any need to imply a term that reasonable notice had to be given. The employer's decisions, at least on the facts, were commercially justifiable as the employees' contracts only had a few weeks to run (and would not be renewed) and the employers wanted to introduce the share options to its employees as an incentive. Whether this case (especially given its peculiar facts) bucks the trend described in *Jenvey* and in other cases noted above remains to be seen.

Judicial interference is therefore still somewhat unpredictable and has tended to focus more on the *use* of terms rather than their innate legitimacy. This is illustrated by the *obiter* comments of Lord Woolf MR in *Wandsworth LBC* v *D'Silva* [1998] IRLR 193 that with such terms:

(a) clear language is required to reserve to one party an unusual power of this sort;
(b) the court is unlikely to favour an interpretation which does more than enable the employer to vary contractual provisions with which the employer is required to comply (i.e., the outlawing of major changes to substantive rights);
(c) the courts should avoid constructions which produce unreasonable results.

It is certainly the case that arguments based on *implying* a power of unilateral variation are, to use the words of Fraser in *Dad's Army*, doomed: *Hayes* v *Securities and Facilities Division* [2001] IRLR 81, CA.

5.5.2.2 Reasonable use of terms

At the beginning of the nineteenth century employers held a position of feudal dominance over their employees (servants). Early nineteenth-century cases, where servants were lawfully dismissed for refusing to work through their lunch hour, or where a woman visited her sick mother in her own time contrary to her master's instructions, determined that practically *any* order given by an employer was lawful. Constraints on how employers use the terms of the contract began to emerge in mid-nineteenth-century case law, so that from a position where the terms 'servitude' and 'service' were almost inseparable there emerged judgments which placed limitations on the employer's discretionary powers. However, it is still a well-established axiom that an employer does not have to act *fairly: Western Excavating (ECC) Ltd* v *Sharp* [1978] ICR 221 and, more recently, *McLory* v *Post Office* [1992] ICR 758. The fact that your client works for (or is) the worst employer in the city does not, in itself, matter in law.

Nevertheless, despite the avowed intentions of the EAT and the Court of Appeal that fairness is not a matter for contractual relationships, the rudiments of managerial prerogative constraints can be detected. As with so many of the recent developments of contractual theory, most of the examples have arisen in unfair dismissal cases, especially those centring round the concept of constructive dismissal. In *Cawley* v *South Wales Electricity Board* [1985] IRLR 89, for instance, the employer utilised the disciplinary procedure (technically within the contractual bounds) to demote an employee. The EAT decided nevertheless that this was an *excessive* use of the contractual power and found a breach of contract. Again, in *Woods* v *WM Service (Peterborough) Ltd* [1981] ICR 666, it was stated that 'employers will not, without reasonable and proper cause, conduct themselves in a manner calculated or likely to destroy or seriously damage the relationship of confidence and trust between employer and employee'.

There is thus a 'scale of reasonableness'. The *reasonable* use of legitimate terms (including ones that the employee does not like) carries with it no potential for breach. Neither does the *unreasonable* use of terms in itself constitute a breach. A court might concur with your employee-client's refusal to obey these orders, but you could not be certain of this (and see **5.5.3** on 'employee adaptability' below). The employer's action needs to lie somewhere over the half-way line of the reasonableness scale, heading toward the capricious use of power and the extreme end of unreasonableness, before a breach will have occurred and your client, in law at least, can legitimately choose to refuse to obey the order. The further over the half-way line the more serious (repudiatory) the breach and, as you will see, the more the employee may have to decide whether to accept the repudiation, resign and claim damages—or simply put up with it.

Further, the basic contractual approach means that reasonableness relates to the operation of the employment relationship and not to the individual's needs. Your client may well have just started a family and find it impossible to move job from Bristol to Coventry at the employer's request. That is not the issue; the issue is whether it is permissible to demand the move under the contract and how that demand is handled, e.g., the amount of notice given. Thus the only clear guideline is that in order to challenge the legitimacy of the clearly expressed terms one must find unconscionability rather than mere unreasonableness: see *Spafax* v *Harrison and Taylor* [1980] IRLR 442. The employee's arguments on the use of stated contractual powers will thus have to fix on:

(a) the employer's reliance on terms in bad faith (subject to the comments in *Macari*, noted above at **5.2.2.1**);

(b) the employer's dishonest, irrational or perverse use of discretionary powers;

(c) the employer's reliance on terms contrary to the practice of that workplace or, in some cases, the industry as a whole;

(d) the employer's failure to give reasonable notice regarding such things as the implementation of mobility clauses;

(e) the possibility of indirect discrimination (see **5.5.2.3** below).

A word of caution is needed here. What constitutes a lawful order falls to be decided in two quite different arenas. As a pure contractual matter (where a declaration, injunction, or damages are sought) that arena is the county court or High Court. There is a tradition for tying the rules of contracts of employment to ordinary contracts here and so things like the employee's individual needs tend to be put to one side.

But matters of contract can arise in the setting of employment tribunals; both as separ-ate issues and as adjuncts of unfair dismissal actions, redundancy claims, etc. (see **5.7**). With one eye on contractual principles, the tribunals and the EAT are not averse to implying terms which look far more like imposing a standard of reasonableness. Interestingly, in a pure contractual setting, we saw above (at **5.2.2.1 (a) (ii)**) that the Court of Appeal appears to be moving more towards an analysis based on irrationality/ unreasonableness too: see *Mallone* v *BPB Industries plc*.

Students often raise the question whether legislation relating to exclusion clauses and 'unfair terms' is relevant here. The usual answer given is no, because, with the exception of excluding liability for death or personal injury, the Unfair Contract Terms Act 1977 and the Unfair Terms in Consumer Contract Regulations 1999 (SI 1999/2083) generally apply only to businesses dealing with other businesses (on standard terms) or with consumers in defined circumstances, but this may be about to change. First, in the High Court decision of *Brigden* v *American Express Bank Ltd* [2000] IRLR 94, Morland J held that UCTA 1977 was capable of applying to the employment relationship, although it was not applied on the facts.

Secondly, the Unfair Terms in Consumer Contracts Regulations 1994 (revoked by the 1999 Regulations) specifically excluded employment contracts from their ambit; the 1999 Regulations are silent on this. It has to be said, however, that on the definitions given in these enactments it is stretching matters quite a bit to fit 'employee' into the definition of 'consumer' in UCTA, s. 12, or 'employer' into 'seller or supplier' in the 1999 Regulations. As you will remember from the law of contract, however, even if UCTA 1977 could be applied to the employment contract one must still distinguish whether the clause in question excludes or restricts liability or actually defines the actual rights and liabilities. If falling within the latter, a clause will not be covered by UCTA. This is the line most frequently used at the moment when such issues arise: see, for instance, *Peninsula Business Services Ltd* v *Sweeney* [2004] IRLR 49. Further, the Directive from which the Regulations are derived (93/13/EC) specifically excludes employment contracts (in the Recitals) from the ambit of the Directive. Consequently, it seems unlikely that this opens an avenue for employees to challenge the efficacy of employment terms.

5.5.2.3 Discriminatory clauses

The Court of Appeal decision in *Meade-Hill and National Union of Civil and Public Servants* v *British Council* [1995] IRLR 478 has brought into play the question of discrimination and the use of mobility (and similar) clauses. Here, the contract stated that employees above a certain grade 'shall serve in such parts of the United Kingdom . . . as the Council may at its discretion require . . .'. The Council planned to move its headquarters from London to Manchester. Mrs Meade-Hill objected. The Court of Appeal found that the proportion of women who could comply with the mobility clause was considerably smaller than the proportion of men who could comply. The clause was therefore indirectly discriminatory unless the employer could justify the clause in relation to the position held by the employee, irrespective of her sex.

The appraisal of all contractual provisions against 'non-discrimination' criteria has become increasingly important, and the sophistication of the analysis involved can easily trap the unwary. Employers need to be able to justify imposing changes in working patterns such as moving employees from part-time to full-time employment. In *London Underground Ltd* v *Edwards (No. 2)* [1998] IRLR 364, CA, for instance, the contractual issue focused on a change in shift patterns for train operators. The change was agreed with the relevant unions and, out of an affected workforce of 2,044, Ms Edwards was the only person unable to comply with the new system. Her problem centred on child care provisions as a single parent. The change in contractual terms was found by the EAT to constitute indirect discrimination. The problem lay in deciding whether a 'considerably smaller' proportion of women than men could comply with the change. Ms Edwards may have been the only person affected, so that statistically this reasoning looks weak, but there were only 21 female train operators—a figure which makes comparison statistically unreliable. The EAT thus found that 'The disproportionate impact of the condition may be assessed by looking both at the picture as it was at the time, and as it may be, had the small pool of women been larger and statistically significant'. Further, on the facts, the employer could not justify the change in the light of its business arrangements as set against Ms Edwards' personal circumstances. The Court of Appeal agreed with the EAT's approach.

Such clauses, or variations on the general theme, appear in many contracts. Employers will now need to show objective reasons why such clauses are necessary rather than merely relying on the fact that the clause was lifted from a precedent book and looked useful.

5.5.2.4 Discretionary payment clauses

As we noted at **5.2.1(e)** above, pay is often built up from a range of different elements. Anyone in sales will be quite used to the idea of receiving a low basic salary, with most of their earnings being derived from commission payments; manual workers often work on a piece-rate system. Equally, employers may operate a 'bonus scheme' which, at its base, will include a simple Christmas bonus payment, but which may extend to much more complicated arrangements. If the bonus can be calculated on a mathematical basis it is no different from commission or piece-rate; but sometimes there is an element of discretion built in to preserve management powers or in the hope of avoiding tax. Here, both the wording of the discretionary payment clause and the exercise of that discretion are open to argument. Employers tend to believe that the use of the word 'discretion' means absolute freedom; the case law shows otherwise.

In *Clark* v *BET* [1997] IRLR 348, for instance, the High Court held that a clause stating pay rises would be 'reviewed annually and be increased by such amount if any as the board shall at its absolute discretion decide' meant that the board must review on the basis of good faith. In *Clark* v *Nomura International plc* [2000] IRLR 766 the High Court again held that a bonus payment (of some £1.35 million) had been withheld in breach of contract. The phrase in question here was that the discretionary bonus scheme '... is not guaranteed in any way, and is dependent upon individual performance ...'. The employer argued that 'individual performance' was not just a mathematical calculation of business obtained but also included matters such as conduct (which they said was not satisfactory) and motivation for the future (which was irrelevant as they had dismissed the employee). On this basis they had awarded no bonus. The High Court held that the grounds given by the employer, which seemed to centre on the employer's personal and professional dislike of the employee, were unacceptable; that no reasonable employer faced with the business generated by the employee would have awarded a nil bonus. The discretion had been exercised irrationally. Again, note the analysis in *Mallone* v *BPB Industries plc* as regards the withdrawal of discretionary share options.

There is always room, however, for the well-drafted express term. Thus, in *Peninsula Business Services Ltd* v *Sweeney* the rules of a commission scheme stated clearly that no commission was payable if the employee was not in the company's employment at the relevant date. When Sweeney resigned part of his claim against his former employer related to £20,000 in earned commission. The EAT refused his claim on the pure contractual grounds that the employee had signed up to this term.

5.5.3 Stretching the contract—employee adaptability

If the employer must adhere to an honest use of the contract the same is certainly true for the employee. This will mean that as well as observing instructions given under the express terms of the contract, the employee is expected to be flexible in the observance of those terms. At its very basic level this is a duty to observe the contract reasonably, or at least not to disrupt the enterprise; it has also been described as a more positive duty of cooperation. The most famous example of this arose in *Secretary of State for Employment* v *ASLEF* [1972] 2 QB 455. As part of an industrial dispute the employees decided to 'work-to-rule', i.e., to observe the absolute letter of the contract. This meant that extensive safety checks were undertaken, no leeway was allowed on manning levels, etc., and disruption to the rail network followed.

Under the ill-fated and now defunct Industrial Relations Act 1971, these activities constituted 'industrial action' only if they were in breach of contract. If they were industrial action then the Secretary of State could order a 'cooling off' period. The question was, could the strict observance of the contract constitute a breach of that contract? The Court of Appeal decided that it could because the purpose behind the strict observance was to cause disruption. There was an implied duty not to cause disruption. The duty was also described as the more burdensome 'duty to promote the commercial interests of the employer'. In *British Telecommunications plc* v *Ticehurst* [1992] ICR 383, the Court of Appeal further classified the withdrawal of goodwill (as part of industrial action) as a breach of contract (see also *Sim* v *Rotherham Metropolitan Borough Council* [1986] IRLR 391 on the level of duties owed by professional employees (here, schoolteachers)).

Much of the development in this area relates yet again to claims of constructive dismissal. Perhaps the clearest statement of 'employee adaptability' came in *Cresswell* v *Board of Inland Revenue* [1984] ICR 508. The employers sought to change the method of working by the introduction of computers. The employees objected, at least on the grounds that the acquisition of new skills should bring with it extra pay. The issue was whether the alteration in how the job was done could be enforced as a lawful order, or whether this was beyond the scope of the contract. It was held that employees are expected to be adaptable in performing their duties. If the change is merely as to *how* the job was done, rather than a change to the job content itself, modern employees are expected to respond favourably.

Many cases have centred on employee mobility. In *White* v *Reflecting Roadstuds Ltd* [1991] ICR 733, an *express term* reserved to the employer the power to transfer employees to alternative work on grounds of business efficiency. White was not the best of employees and his performance affected the work of others in his team. He was transferred to a lower-paid job. This was held not to be in breach. One key factor was that the transfer correlated to the aims stated in the contract, i.e., it was for business efficiency. But there is no general requirement for any transfer to be made on reasonable operational grounds.

Subject to the possibility of arguing indirect discrimination, express mobility clauses therefore tend to be left alone by the courts provided they are clear and unambiguous: see the redundancy case of *Rank Xerox Ltd* v *Churchill* [1988] IRLR 280. Reasonableness, say the courts, is not the issue; only some form of abuse of discretion will overturn the express term (e.g., moving the employee around the country every month so that performance of the contract becomes practically impossible). This does, however, sometimes seem like trying to distinguish a Hun from a Visigoth.

If a mobility term is not clear, or is missing, there is still room for implication. Thus, if the job is of the kind where mobility might be expected (i.e., it is quite common for employees to move around in the industry, such as construction workers), or the individual employee has moved during employment, a term will be implied easily. In any other case a term might still be implied (see the constructive dismissal case of *United Bank Ltd* v *Akhtar* [1989] IRLR 507—junior employee told to move from Leeds to Birmingham at six days' notice) provided:

(a) the transfer is not actuated by malice;

(b) reasonable notice is given; and

(c) the employer does not effectively frustrate the employee's attempt to perform the contract.

But even then, the transfer is commonly limited to within commuting distance: *Courtaulds Northern Spinning Ltd* v *Sibson* [1988] ICR 451 (a heavy goods driver whose place of work was really only a starting and finishing point).

There are limits to adaptability. First, the contract may be stretched, but there comes a breaking point—usually some abuse of discretion. Secondly, *pay* has nearly always been sacrosanct; it takes a clear term permitting a cut in wages (as in *White* v *Reflecting Roadstuds*) and no apparent abuse of that right to overcome this. There are, however, conflicting decisions of the EAT on whether the use of an express term to alter working patterns, which has an indirect adverse affect on wages or hours worked (e.g., because of changes in shift patterns), constitutes a breach of contract. In view of the comments and caveats in *White* v *Reflecting Roadstuds* and *United Bank* v *Akthar*, it is respectfully submitted that such indirect effects should not be deemed a breach of contract. However, cases dealing with reductions in pay which do not have surach clear terms (however small and however economically justified) invariably class these as a breach of contract: see *Burdett-Coutts* v *Hertfordshire County Council* [1984] IRLR 91 and *Rigby* v *Ferodo* [1988] ICR 29, below. In *Cantor Fitzgerald International* v *Callaghan* [1999] IRLR 234, the Court of Appeal affirmed this approach but noted that a *deliberate* denial of the obligation to pay agreed salary should be contrasted with a failure to pay owing to some temporary fault in equipment, accounting error or simple mistake. These are technically breaches of contract but certainly not serious breaches. Further, there are statutory rights to consider as well under ERA 1996, Part II, Protection of Wages (see **Chapter 4**).

Lastly, the court or tribunal may also choose to interpret a wide clause quite narrowly, almost using the *contra proferentem* idea. For instance, in *Haden* v *Cowen* [1982] IRLR 314, the Court of Appeal took a common phrase 'the employee is required to undertake, at the discretion of the company, any and all duties which reasonably fall within the scope of his capabilities' and restricted the range of additional duties to those which would normally fall within the employee's job as a quantity surveyor.

5.5.4 Variation of contract and reorganisations

Under strict contract theory a contract cannot be varied unilaterally. It can be varied by agreement, either by individual agreement or through the use of collective agreements, notably where a contract is subject to 'alteration from time to time agreed with XYZ union'. The most familiar example is the annual pay increase. Consideration should also be present, although courts have paid little genuine attention to this (though see *Lee* v *GEC Plessey Telecommunications* [1993] IRLR 383 in holding that continuing to work for a company constituted consideration for an enhanced redundancy payments scheme).

Thus, if an employer seeks to change the rate of pay or the place of work, or to insert a new restraint of trade clause, the employee is not bound in law to accept such an alteration unless the instruction is lawful, i.e., contractually justified.

Business reorganisation is the area where the real question of employee adaptability arises. The employer either clearly seeks to change the terms of the contract, or argues that the proposed changes in working practice fall within the general ambit of the contract anyway. These situations may come about in a number of ways:

(a) The employer argues that the contract is clear. In this case any opposing argument must rest on the legitimacy of the terms themselves: see **5.5.2.1** above.

(b) The employer argues that, although the express terms do not sanction the change, the implied terms (derived from adaptability or custom and practice) allow for the change: see *ASLEF*.

(c) The employer argues that there is still no real change to the job, only a change in *how* the job is done: see *Cresswell* v *BIR*.

(d) The employer simply imposes the terms, offering no argument apart from economic necessity: see *Rigby* v *Ferodo*, below.

(e) The employer accepts that there is a breach but presents the argument of 'accept the change or be sacked'.

(f) The employer formally terminates the contract and offers new contracts with different terms (see below, **5.5.4.5**).

To consider the full impact of all this it is best to look to the possible actions that **employees** may take in response and their consequences. The overall position can be seen in **Figure 5.10**. Although in this chapter we are dealing only with *contractual* rights and remedies, it is worth noting here that a serious breach of contract (such as a unilateral reduction in pay) will not always amount to an unfair dismissal if the employee is dismissed for refusing to accept the change (see **Chapter 10**, at **10.9.6** on the topic of business reorganisations constituting 'some other substantial reason' as a fair reason for dismissal).

Figure 5.10 looks daunting at first sight but shows that out of one simple question there are numerous factors to consider. Do not therefore be put off by the complexity; in the following text we will break this diagram down and examine each particular consequence. The overall picture will then make more sense.

Note that **Figure 5.10** takes into account both the common law claims (wrongful dismissal, wrongful repudiation, injunctions and damages) and also the statutory claim of unfair dismissal. Changes in contractual terms may well lead to resignation or dismissal and such occurrences carry statutory consequences as well as contractual ones. As we are concerned in this chapter only with the common law position, we can simplify the discussion for the moment by ignoring the statutory consequences noted on the left of the diagrams. In discussing the various consequences we will repeat the whole diagram but highlight only the parts relevant to the particular issues.

5.5.4.1 The employee stays in the job and agrees to the change

Most employees cannot afford to lose their job (whether on principle or by default) so it may well be that they are effectively forced to continue in their employment. They may simply put up with the change or they make take some form of legal action.

If the employee specifically agrees to, or acquiesces in, the alteration it will be deemed a legitimate change in the terms of the contract. This is illustrated in **Figure 5.10**. However, where a change in terms *does not have immediate effect* on a particular employee, e.g., as to retirement ages or the right to move employees from one site to another, there is now the strong possibility that silence on that employee's part will not constitute acquiescence or agreement. In *Jones* v *Associated Tunnelling Co. Ltd* [1981] IRLR 477, the EAT stated that mere failure to object to a matter which had no immediate practical effect did not imply assent. The matter may lie dormant for a number of years, so that the employee is like a Cold War 'sleeper' whose problems will emerge long after the change was thought to have been implemented. Such was the case in *Anglia Regional Co-operative Society* v *O'Donnell*

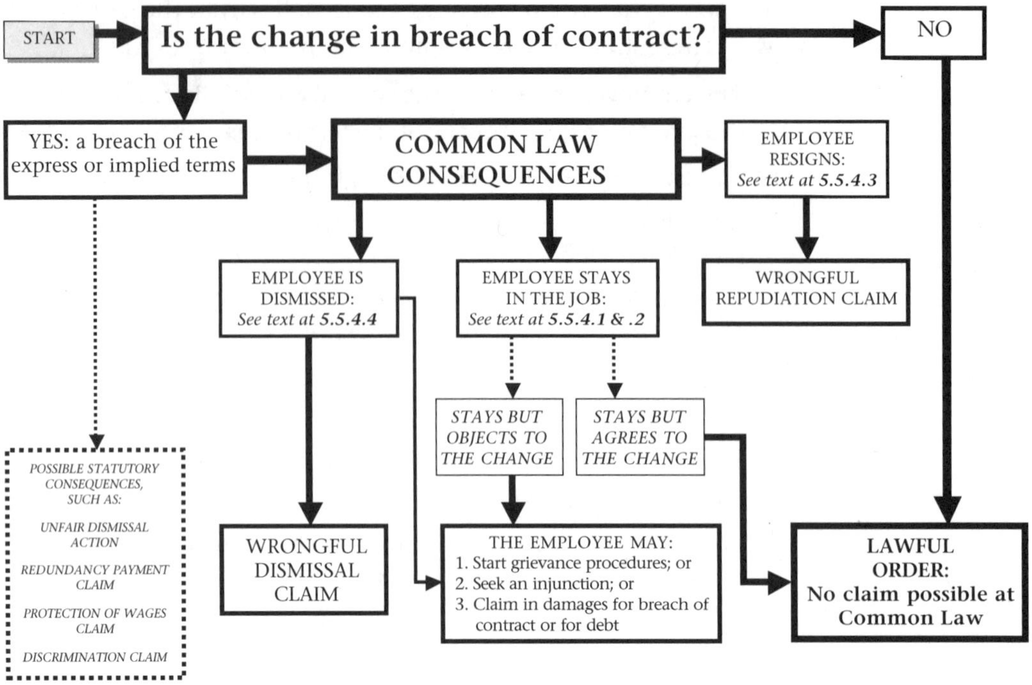

Figure 5.10 Possible consequences of variation of the contract.

(1994, unreported, EAT 655/91) where an employer's assumption that an employee's silence on the imposition of a mobility clause in 1987 was found to be unfounded when tested in 1992. The EAT has confirmed this approach in *Aparau* v *Iceland Frozen Foods plc* [1996] IRLR 119. Thus an employer may well have to decide whether to risk this course or take the equally risky alternative of terminating the contracts and re-engaging the employees on the modified terms. The second course brings with it clarity at the cost of possible wrongful and unfair dismissal claims (see **5.5.4.5**, below).

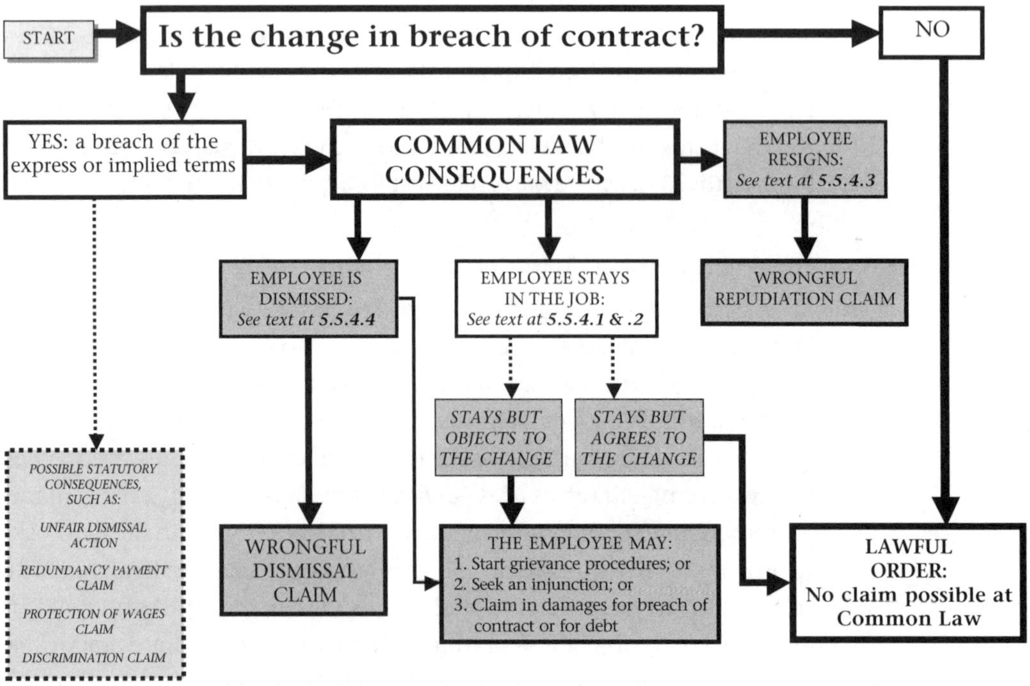

Figure 5.11 The employee stays and agrees to the change.

5.5.4.2 The employee stays in the job and objects to the change

It is difficult for employees to take this course of action where they are not supported by a trade union. Nevertheless, it is possible for an employee to continue to work for an employer whilst arguing that the change is unlawful. Silent objection is not enough (except possibly with the dangerous technical arguments of 'lack of immediate effect' noted above).

In the face of more immediate changes and certainly if they relate to pay, however, the employees would have to do something to demonstrate their opposition; their objections would have to take on substance or be deemed acquiescence. One practical option is simply to refuse to comply with the new terms. Obviously this has to relate to changes in things such as duties (pay, for instance, would be beyond the employee's control). The employee would then bring matters to a head and the employer would have to decide on the efficacy of any response, including disciplinary measures and dismissal.

Another option is to make use of the grievance procedures. As we saw at **5.4** there are now statutory grievance procedures which operate as a minimum standard. Company schemes may go beyond the level expected in the statutory scheme but the parties must comply with the statutory scheme or risk the consequences. For the employee this may mean that if he or she is at fault and eventually resigns because of the changes imposed by the employer, they will be unable, for instance, to claim constructive dismissal unless the statutory procedures have been followed. The employer at fault may find that should the employee claim unfair dismissal, discrimination or any other matter listed in ERA 1996, any sch. 4 award may be increased by the failure to follow the statutory grievance procedures.

An employee may also seek a *declaration or an injunction* to prevent an unlawful variation or, wider, disciplinary and dismissal proceedings. It has long been established in employment law that, apart from exceptional cases, specific performance will not be ordered; but an injunction which restrains a breach of contract (remarkably similar in effect at times) can be ordered. More than a simple breach is required to obtain an injunction (however serious the breach) because damages would be an adequate remedy.

This means that dismissed employee will not be able to obtain an order for *specific performance* to regain employment; though it is feasible that a court would grant an interim injunction requiring the dismissal not to take effect *unless and until* the employer had complied with the contractual terms (e.g., disciplinary procedures).

It has become more common for an employee to seek a declaration and/or to invoke injunctive relief prior to dismissal (see, for example, *Rigby* v *Ferodo*, where a declaration on the legality of the variation was sought as well as damages); and the principles are constantly being tested. Normally injunctions will be granted only where there is still trust and confidence between the parties: *Powell* v *Brent London Borough Council* [1988] ICR 176. This requires an examination of the employer's attitude, the nature of the work, fellow employees and the effect on the employer's operations— some cases have asked if the contract is still 'workable'.

Injunctions can thus be granted to restrain dismissals which do not comply with binding contractual procedures: *Dietmann* v *Brent London Borough Council* [1988] ICR 842. But, as the remedy is discretionary, there is no guarantee of effectiveness.

An application can be under Part 24, Civil Procedure Rules to determine a question of law or the construction of a document. A final determination of the whole action may be made provided questions of fact are not at issue: see *Jones* v *Gwent County Council* [1992] IRLR 521. *This option is not included in the diagrams* (for further explanation see **Chapter 9**, at **9.10.6.3**).

Finally, an employee may object and sue for damages: *Rigby* v *Ferodo* [1988] ICR 29. The employer sought to implement, for good economic reasons, a wage cut of 5 per cent. The employees not unnaturally objected; their union did not accept the change. Eventually the employer imposed the wage cut. The employees did not resign, nor were they dismissed. Instead they continued to voice their objections and, after six months, sued their employer for the lost 5 per cent. The House of Lords held that they were entitled to recover the lost money as the employer's unilateral variation of the contract constituted a repudiation which the employees had neither affirmed in continuing to work nor accepted as repudiatory by resigning.

One would not argue with the principle of this case. However, four points deserve attention:

(i) The employers did not contend that Rigby had accepted the change, because Rigby's objections were made obvious.

(ii) The employers did not argue that the change was lawful; their argument was the more technical one that the contract had been effectively automatically terminated by their announcement and that the employees could not therefore recover any more than their contractual notice period by way of damages (12 weeks here).

(iii) The employers were sloppy in their response to the objections. They might have dismissed the employees and offered them re-engagement on new terms.

(iv) The level of damages was easy to assess on the facts. If the change in terms centred on working practice, as in our example about hours of work, damages would be more difficult to assess (e.g., loss of commission); there might not even be a quantifiable loss.

The full range of options open to an employee can be seen in **Figure 5.12**.

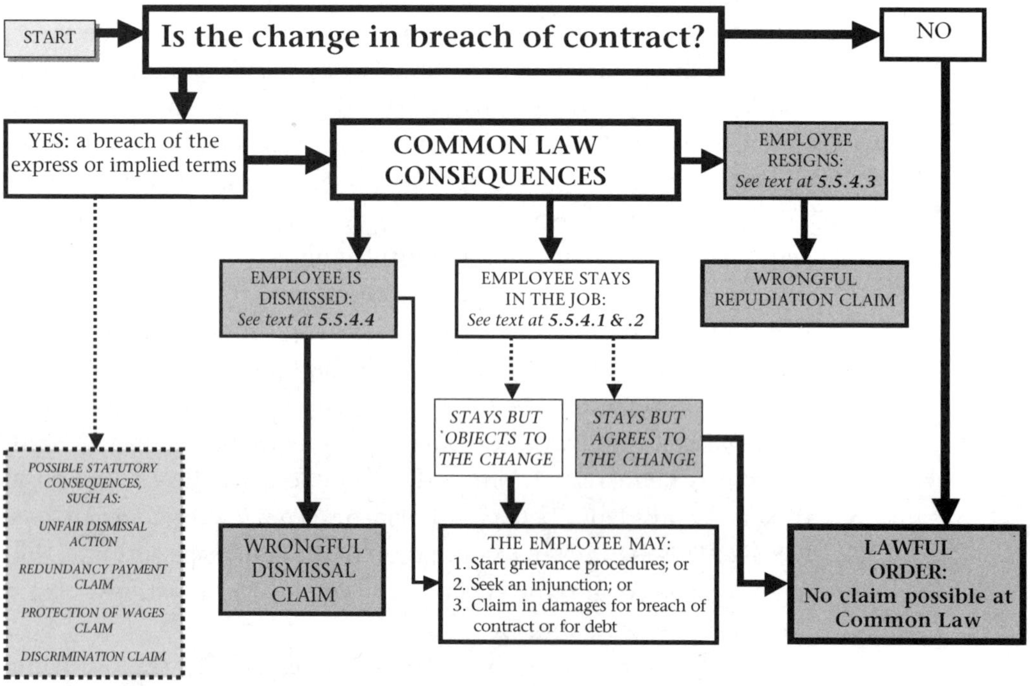

Figure 5.12 The employee stays and agrees to the change.

5.5.4.3 The employee refuses to accept the new terms and resigns

If the employer's actions constitute a *repudiation* of the contract the employee can lawfully accept the repudiation by resigning and sue for damages. This action is strictly termed a *wrongful repudiation* claim but is sometimes referred to as 'constructive dismissal'. The term 'constructive dismissal' really belongs to claims for unfair dismissal but both terms describe the situation where an employee resigns in response to a serious breach of contract by the employer and this resignation is classed as a dismissal. The consequences flowing from an employee's resignation can be see in **Figure 5.13**.

There is common analytical ground in determining what constitutes a wrongful repudiation and a constructive dismissal. The sorts of acts (there is an extensive range) that may be classified as repudiatory range from a failure to pay wages through to a series of minor but cumulative breaches (for a fuller list see **9.8.2** below). In all cases the employer must have committed a serious breach of the contract. If the employee gets this wrong he or she will have simply resigned and, indeed, will be in breach himself for not giving contractual notice. Another mistake employees frequently make in this area is to wait too long before resigning (often because they are trying to find another job first). If the employee does not act promptly enough he or she will at some stage be deemed to have affirmed the change in terms. This would mean that the employee was no longer entitled to resign and, by doing so, is again in breach. The length of time an employee may wait depends upon the seriousness of the change in terms, how immediate their effect is and whether he or she maintained some form of objection.

However, there now exists a clear distinction here between common law claims and statutory claims relating to resignations. We have noted at **5.3** that the introduction of the statutory grievance procedures means an employee will have to have complied with these before an employment tribunal will entertain a claim for constructive (unfair) dismissal. No such limitation exists as regards claims for wrongful repudiation in the county court or the High Court as EA 2002, s. 32 is only concerned with employment tribunal claims.

Damages for wrongful repudiation are limited to the amount the employee would have received had they been given their contractual notice.

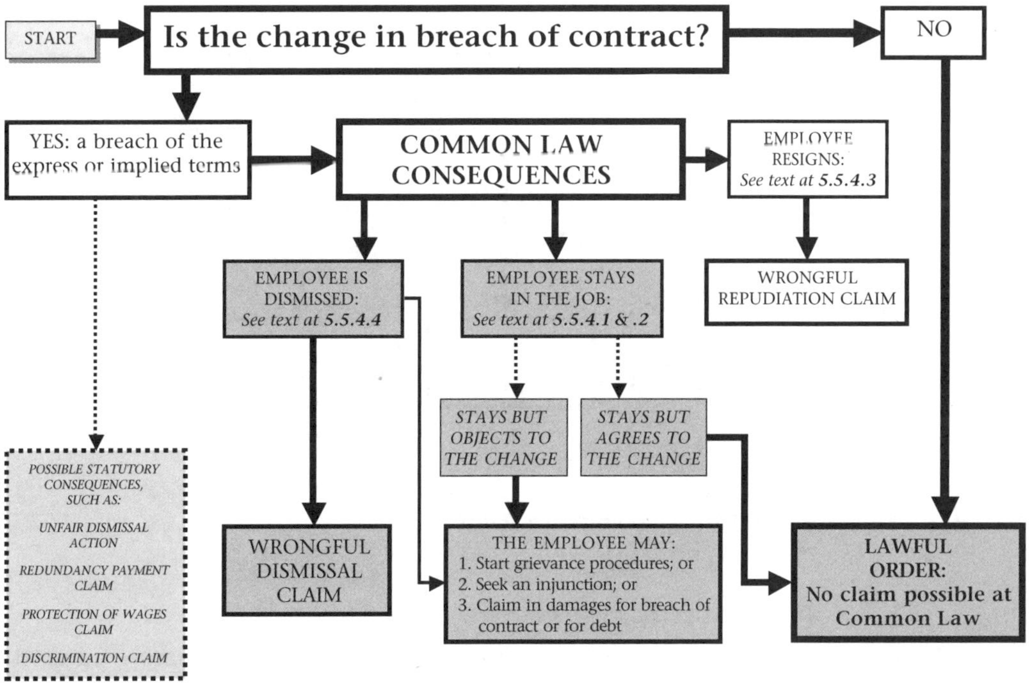

Figure 5.13 The employee resigns.

5.5.4.4 The employee is dismissed

The employer might take direct action when met with a refusal to accept the order and dismiss the employee. If the dismissal is with adequate notice or payment in lieu of notice the employee has no further contractual claim. If the dismissal is without adequate notice there will be a potential claim for wrongful dismissal. In assessing the amount due as part of pay in lieu of notice account might have to be taken of fringe benefits and commission payments.

But remember that the courts are only concerned with the *contractual right* to dismiss summarily, so that the employer's business reasons for the change are irrelevant here. The question is whether the employee has seriously breached the contract by not giving adequate notice. Note, in **Figure 5.14**, that we have included the possibility of a dismissed employee claiming damages/debt or seeking an injunction. The damages/debt aspect here will relate to any outstanding claims that the employee may have (e.g., for past failures to pay wages). Injunctions will rarely be granted once dismissal has occurred unless the dismissal was clearly in breach of a contractual procedure—and even then the best an employee can hope for is an injunction restraining the dismissal until the procedures have been adhered to (see **9.10.6.2** below).

Whether or not the employee is given notice, he or she might also claim unfair dismissal. In such a case the employer is likely to argue business reorganisation as a defence to this action (see **Chapter 10**). Again, the rules regarding D&DPs do not apply to common law claims in the ordinary courts.

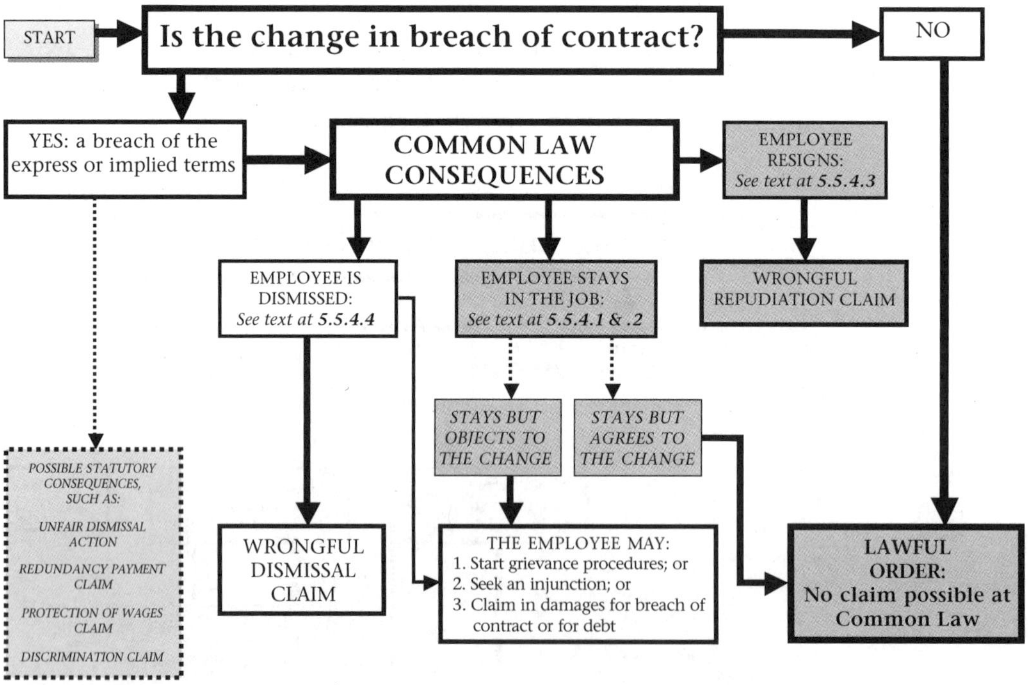

Figure 5.14 The employee is dismissed.

5.5.4.5 The employee is dismissed and then re-engaged

As noted above, dismissal provides a clear way of terminating the existing agreement. The points noted in **5.5.4.4** on the giving of notice apply here too. The notice must be unequivocal. Merely announcing the change (as in *Rigby* v *Ferodo*) will not be sufficient. If the termination is clear the employee will then be deemed to have accepted the new contract by continuing to work after the set date.

Contractually speaking, the employer gains an advantage with this option. But from an industrial relations angle this may prove disastrous; the loss of goodwill may rebound at a later stage on the employer. Equally, employees working out a notice period will most likely feel disaffected and work poorly; the alternative of paying in lieu of notice being an expensive tactic.

Employees dismissed in these circumstances may also have a claim for unfair dismissal even if they are re-engaged immediately.

5.5.4.6 Duty to consult with trade unions

You will see below in **Chapter 11** at **11.4.2** that where dismissals arise by reason of redundancy the employer has both a duty to consult with the individual employee and, where 20 or more employees are being made redundant, a separate duty of collective consultation with employee representatives. In *GMB* v *Man Truck & Bus Ltd* [2000] IRLR 636 and *Scottish Premier Meat Ltd* v *Burns* [2000] IRLR 639, the EAT held that this duty of collective consultation applied not only to standard redundancies but also to dismissals arising out of restructuring. In *GMB* the employer sought to impose a change in terms by dismissing the employees and immediately re-engaging them on less favourable terms. The employer argued that the duty to consult under the TULRCA 1992, s. 188 did not apply to such 'technical' dismissals, but the EAT disagreed. This imposes quite a different burden on employers who seek to 'strong arm' the imposition of new terms (though note that the duty only kicks in where there are 20 or more affected employees).

5.5.4.7 The employee objects but the trade union agrees

Although in law contracts of employment are made between employer and the individual employee, the reality for about 70 per cent of employees is that the terms are negotiated by the employer and trade unions (known as collective agreements). Collective agreements are virtually never enforceable between employers and trade unions but the agreed terms may be incorporated in the individual contracts and so be binding as between *employer and employee*—if the express or implied terms of the contract allow for such incorporation: *Marley* v *Forward Trust Group Ltd* [1986] ICR 891. If the contract is silent on the point then custom and practice may still lead to the same decision, but incorporation is not an automatic process.

Any new agreement between employer and trade union will therefore vary the terms of the individual's contract provided the collective agreement is incorporated into the individual's contract. Membership or non-membership of the union is immaterial. If an individual whose contract already incorporates such an agreement objects to the change, therefore, he or she must make that objection clear; otherwise the general presumption is that the change has been accepted. And if the right to vary the contract according to terms incorporated by collective agreements is expressly stated in the contract, the employee will have no option (subject to such considerations as arguing indirect discrimination) but to accept the change.

It is also worth noting here that if the employer or trade union unilaterally withdraws from an existing collective agreement this has no effect upon the employee's terms unless the employee consents to the change: *Robertson* v *British Gas Corporation* [1983] IRLR 302; the change of terms is treated exactly the same as with any other variation.

5.5.4.8 The employees take industrial action

Industrial action takes many forms. The most obvious is the strike. Others exist: working to rule, go-slows, overtime bans and so on. The employer and employees will therefore be in a power struggle. We have not included this in our summary diagram simply because the variety of consequences are too dependent upon the employer's response to the action.

For instance, as a general rule most forms of industrial action will constitute a breach (usually a serious breach) of contract so that the points detailed above in **5.5.4.4** will apply. However, in some cases there may be industrial action without a breach of contract; the two are no longer interdependent (they were when *ASLEF*—noted above at **5.5.3**—was decided). What seems to be the determining factor is whether the employees' actions are intended to disrupt the business for industrial relations purposes. Thus in *Power Packing Casemakers* v *Faust* [1983] QB 471, the refusal to work non-contractual overtime amounted to industrial action, though it was probably not a breach of contract on the facts. In response to industrial action the employer may therefore:

(a) dismiss the employees, with or without notice. A strike will usually amount to repudiation entitling the employer to dismiss without notice, though a one-day strike would probably not allow for such an extreme response. Equally, other industrial action whereby most of the duties were being performed would be treated the same. But any form of industrial action which is a breach would entitle the employer to dismiss *with notice*;

(b) refuse to accept the deficient performance and send the employees home, withholding pay, as in *Cresswell* v *Board of Inland Revenue*;

(c) accept their partial performance but withhold wages equivalent to the time lost (see below);

(d) sue the employees for damages. The employee is liable only for the loss for which he or she is responsible. This can be difficult to calculate (at least with workers not directly involved in production) and is a rarely-used response, hence the significance of withholding payments.

The response of withholding pay is often used where the industrial action is sporadic or set for one day every week, or aimed at fulfilling only the non-contentious part of the contract. Such was the case in *British Telecommunications plc* v *Ticehurst* [1992] ICR 383. Here, a long-standing dispute had developed into a 'rolling campaign of strategic strikes'. The employees refused to sign an undertaking to work normally and were told to leave the premises. Their claim for wages during this period was based on the fact that they were prepared to work, though not to comply with all the terms. The Court of Appeal held that the employer could legitimately refuse to pay for this partial performance (see also *Miles* v *Wakefield Metropolitan District Council* [1987] ICR 368 and *Wiluszynski* v *Tower Hamlets LBC* [1989] IRLR 259).

Just to add to the complications, *an employee dismissed whilst taking part in industrial action may also lose any right to claim unfair dismissal* (see **Chapter 10**).

5.6 Methods of resolving disputes, short of termination of contract

If at all possible, both parties should seek to resolve differences before any termination occurs. The most obvious method is by consultation and negotiation, leading eventually to agreement.

If *employers* wish, for instance, to instigate changes they are advised to consider the practical consequences as well as the legal ones. Thus:

(a) consider the effect on the individuals in terms of future loyalty and performance;

(b) consider the effect on any relationship with trade unions;

(c) consider whether this change, if challenged, would lead to an injunction being granted or to claims for wrongful or unfair dismissal;

(d) take into account the possibility that the change may be indirectly discriminatory. Look at the effect on employees, consider whether alternatives or additional facilities are possible and be prepared to justify the change;

(e) get any agreement in writing with effect from the proposed date of change. Consider the effect of 'sleepers' in the organisation. Do not presume that simply because a change has been implemented it is legally effective;

(f) do not forget disciplinary procedures;

(g) if the change is necessary to the business it is probably worth paying for—make the change part of the annual pay negotiations thus avoiding all the problems of unilateral variation.

From the *employee's perspective* any action tends to be in response to proposed changes. Again, however, the practical and legal consequences need to be considered:

(a) consider whether the change is worth fighting in terms of job security, promotion prospects and so on;

(b) do not resign hastily;

(c) make use of the grievance procedure;

(d) do not assume that silence equals valid opposition;

(e) consider applying for declarations or injunctions;

(f) make use of any trade union representation.

5.7 Breach: summary of sanctions and enforcement

Most of the substantive content of the following points has been made in the text at various stages. We have added this section merely to recap.

The employer is in breach

In response to a breach by the employer the employee may:

(a) accept the order or change as being lawful;

(b) instigate grievance procedures;

(c) seek a declaration as to the meaning of the contract;

(d) seek an injunction to prevent a breach;

(e) remain in employment but claim damages for any loss sustained;

(f) resign and claim for wrongful repudiation (though this will only prove successful if the employer's breach was serious);

(g) claim damages for wrongful dismissal, if dismissed without adequate notice;

(h) claim in a debt action;

(i) claim that the change constitutes indirect discrimination.

The employee is in breach

In response to a breach by the employee the employer may:

(a) discipline the employee (e.g., downgrading, refusal to promote, or provision of a warning). One should note the significance of D&DPs here;

(b) dismiss the employee with notice;

(c) dismiss the employee without notice (though this is justifiable only in the face of a serious breach);

(d) sue the employee for any loss attributable to his or her actions (though quantifying the amount can be difficult);

(e) seek an injunction to prevent disclosure of confidential information or to enforce a restraint of trade clause (as regards ex-employees).

In addition, we should also note that in the case of a resignation in the face of a wrongful repudiation or a wrongful dismissal, any restraint of trade clause in the contract will be inoperative, however reasonable the clause may be: *General Billposting Co. Ltd* v *Atkinson* [1909] AC 118 (see **Chapter 8**).

5.8 Civil remedies for breach of contract

Aside from questions involving National Minimum Wage issues (see **4.2** above) or equal pay and discrimination issues, rates of pay are a purely contractual matter. If the employee alleges a breach of contract there are several (potentially overlapping) possible courses of action.

5.8.1 In the civil courts

Most obviously, a breach of the contract of employment can be pursued like any other breach in the courts, either the High Court or a county court. Perhaps, for example, the employee understood at interview that a greater bonus was to be paid than has in fact been received. The sum involved may be unlikely to justify the expense of litigation, especially where the chance of success is poor because of the evidential difficulty of showing a clear promise. Furthermore, such litigation by an individual will not be conducive to good future working relationships. So such a remedy is really only feasible if a trade union takes the case on behalf of a number of employees in the same position, e.g., *Burdett-Coutts* v *Hertfordshire County Council* [1984] IRLR 91. The same analysis applies if the action is framed as a debt.

5.8.2 In the employment tribunal by claiming a constructive dismissal

It is open to an employee who has not been paid according to the contract of employment to resign, argue constructive dismissal and to present a complaint of unfair dismissal to the employment tribunal. The employee must usually have one year's continuous employment with the employer in order to qualify to bring such an action. Any substantial underpayment by the employer may well give good grounds for resignation, provided of course that the underpayment was in breach of contract. Failure to give a pay increase at an annual review is unlikely to constitute a breach: *Murco Petroleum* v *Forge* [1987] ICR 282. However, reinstatement of the employee is not guaranteed even if the complaint succeeds; and the employee consequently runs a real risk of losing everything—the sum not paid and also the job. This mechanism for bringing such an issue within employment tribunal jurisdiction is dangerous territory.

5.8.3 In the employment tribunal by arguing discrimination

If the employee is able to show for instance, that another employee of the opposite sex or of a different racial background received some benefit denied to him or her, this may be a means of bringing a claim for underpayment within the employment tribunal jurisdiction. For the purposes of the claim it may be sufficient to imagine a 'notional other employee' rather than an actual example: see **Chapter 6**.

5.8.4 Action short of dismissal

Related to a discrimination action is the position where an employer subjects an employee to a detriment after the employee has sought to enforce some statutory right, e.g., where the employee has sought to enforce some of the rights noted in **Chapter 4** or has made a 'protected disclosure' against the employer in the light of the employer's unlawful behaviour. The range of actions which receive special protection is given in **10.11** below. The relevance here is that if the employee's actions fall within this list and the employer responds by, e.g., demoting him, then, as well as any of the remedies noted in this chapter there may be further remedies under Part V of the ERA 1996.

5.8.5 In the employment tribunal for breach of contract

The Employment Tribunals Extension of Jurisdiction Order 1994 restricts the tribunal jurisdiction to a claim which **'arises or is outstanding on the termination of the employee's employment'**. It could not therefore be used, for example, by current employees wishing to challenge the amount of wages paid to them, nor for claiming a breach of a compromise agreement concluded after termination: see *Miller Bros* v *Johnston* [2002] ICR 744. The maximum that can be claimed in the employment tribunal is £25,000 and the following categories of claim are specifically excluded:

(a) personal injuries;
(b) claims relating to the provision of living accommodation;
(c) intellectual property rights (e.g., rights to an invention);
(d) restrictive covenants (e.g., confidentiality agreements).

The phrase 'arises or is outstanding on the termination . . .' clearly excludes claims arising during the contract; but what are its boundaries? Three EAT decisions have explored this. In *Universe Foods Ltd* v *Wallbank* (1996, unreported, EAT) it was held that an 'amicable' dismissal settlement which went unpaid fell within the ambit of the phrase. In *Hendricks* v *Lewden Metal Products Ltd* (1996, unreported, EAT), however, an employee failed in her claim for unpaid sick leave dating back some four years from termination as she had never taken any legal action relating to the non-payments during the currency of the contract. The claim for these payments was thus held not to be 'outstanding' on termination. We are in some agreement with the editors of the *IDS Brief* that this logic is questionable. In *Miller Brothers & Butler* v *Johnston*, although negotiations for an agreement settling outstanding claims had commenced prior to the termination date of Johnston's employment, the settlement itself had not been concluded until afterwards. When the employee sought to enforce the agreement in the tribunal the EAT held (in line with *Capek* v *Lincolnshire CC* [2000] ICR 878) that the tribunal had not had jurisdiction to hear the claim as the claim was not outstanding *'on termination'*. The phrase 'arising or is outstanding . . . etc' meant that an actual date had to be fixed, not a process, and so the date of the agreement art. 3(c) of the 1994 Order had to be interpreted as applying only to claims which were either outstanding on the termination of employment or arose on termination in a purely temporal sense. The tribunal has no jurisdiction on misrepresentation claims: *Lakin* v *British Steel Engineering Ltd* (2000, EAT 183/99, unreported), though an argument based on a collateral contract is within the tribunal's general jurisdiction.

This jurisdiction is therefore of limited application, and some claims are still actionable only in the civil courts. A novel aspect is that an employer is permitted to counterclaim against the employee for breach of contract, subject to the same restrictions noted above, but only if the employee has first brought a claim *under this jurisdiction*. Employees vulnerable to counterclaims may therefore prefer to bring their claims by a different method. For example, an employee not paid outstanding holiday pay on dismissal for alleged theft will be better advised to bring a protection of wages claim than to risk an employer's counterclaim for the proceeds of the alleged theft.

The time limit for presenting the claim is three months from the Effective Date of Termination or last date worked.

5.8.6 In the employment tribunal by arguing unlawful deduction from wages

Part II of ERA 1996, a consolidation of the Wages Act 1986, forbids employers making deductions from employees' wages except where the employee has expressly authorised the deduction according to rules described above at **4.4**. Wages are defined quite broadly.

This provision raises the possibility that, if the employee wishes to challenge an underpayment of wages, it may be better to portray it as an *unlawful deduction* rather than as a breach of contract. This technique will bring the claim *even for a current employee* into the jurisdiction of the employment tribunal.

5.9 Deductions versus breaches of contract

The overlap between pure contractual claims and those relating to deductions led, in the early days of the Wages Act 1986, to different philosophies of approach. There was one body of opinion that suggested that a dispute about the terms of the contract ought to be addressed in the courts as an alleged breach of contract and that deductions could only be challenged where the contractual entitlement was already well-established or was not in dispute. The interpretation is difficult to justify against the clear inclusion in the definition of wages under s. 27 of non-contractual matters.

The matter was finally resolved in the case we have already considered in discussing pay in lieu of notice, *viz, Delaney* v *Staples* [1992] ICR 483. The employee in that case complained on the termination of employment about various unlawful deductions which were in fact non-payments. Although the House of Lords' decision excluded the nonpayment of pay in lieu of notice from the definition in s. 27, the House of Lords also impli-citly approved the judgment of the Court of Appeal ([1991] ICR 331) that non-payment of commission and accrued holiday pay *could* properly be classified as deductions from wages.

This case also appears to support the view in *Alsop* v *Star Vehicle Contracts* [1990] ICR 378 (despite the opposite final result) that there is no essential illogicality in imagining a deduction as becoming steadily larger and larger until it completely removes an element of pay that is arguably a contractual entitlement.

Indeed, in *Davies* v *Hotpoint Ltd* [1994] IRLR 538 the EAT further held that a *reduction* in pay (here, a unilateral reduction of guaranteed wages) constituted a *deduction* for these purposes. Why this should be so is not explained clearly in the case but the decision seems to be a logical extension of the points made above. If this decision is followed it effectively appends the principles seen in *Rigby* v *Ferodo* to the jurisdiction of employment tribunals.

All these cases were decided before the employment tribunals were given their limited jurisdiction to hear claims for breach of contract. There is now some overlap between that jurisdiction and the protection of wages legislation in ERA 1996, Part II. Solicitors will wish to exercise some care in deciding whether to pursue a possible breach of contract claim under one jurisdiction or the other, or both. Some relevant differences are listed below.

Protection of Wages	Breach of Contract
Unlawful deductions brought under ERA 1996, s. 23.	Under the Employment Tribunals Extension of Jurisdiction Order 1994, and ETA 1996, s. 3.
(a) Available to current employees.	(a) Only available on termination of employment.
(b) No counterclaim permitted—except that the employer may make deductions in retail employment for cash shortages and stock deficiencies.	(b) An employer's counterclaim is possible. and is a self-contained cause of action which can survive the failure, withdrawal or settlement of the employee's initial claim: *Patel* v *RCMS Ltd* [1999] IRLR 161.
(c) No limit to amount of claim.	(c) Claim limited to a maximum of £25,000.
(d) Claims regarding payment in lieu of notice excluded.	(d) Includes claims for payment in lieu of notice.
(e) There exist statutory exceptions, e.g., loans, expenses, compensation for loss of office.	(e) A narrower set of statutory exceptions exist, e.g., those claims relating to intellectual property rights.
(f) Errors of computation are excluded (though 'errors' are narrowly construed: *Morgan* v *West Glamorgan CC* [1995] IRLR 68).	(f) The test is the factual one of whether a breach has occurred and the employer's intentions are irrelevant.

Note: None of the above affects an employee's right to bring a claim in a county or High Court for breach of contract or debt during the term of the contract or on, or after, termination.

5.10 Example of an employment contract

We noted at the start of this chapter that we intended to include an employment contract by way of example of industrial practice. We have chosen to include a contract that is deficient in a number of respects so that we can make some specific comments on it. Because each LPC will develop its own methods of examining drafting and interpretation, and because there is no such thing as a 'model contract' to cover all situations, we must emphasise that this contract is **not** an example of good practice. Our comments in **5.9.2** are placed after the text of the contract in order for you to determine, as you read the contract, what are its strengths and weaknesses.

This is a copy of a real contract drafted in 1992 which was still in use until recently. Only the names, as they say, have been changed to protect the innocent.

5.10.1 The contract of employment

AN AGREEMENT made on [4th October 1992]

BETWEEN [MONTANA AND MARINO LTD] WHOSE REGISTERED OFFICE IS SITUATED AT [221B QUARTER BACK LANE, BRISTOL]
AND
[MS VICKY LOMBARDI] OF 113, ALLESLEY OLD ROAD, CLIFTON, BRISTOL IN THE COUNTY OF AVON

WHEREBY IT IS MUTUALLY AGREED AS FOLLOWS

1. SAVE where a contrary intention appears the following terms shall hereinafter have the following meanings:

    (a) 'the Company' shall mean [Montana and Marino Ltd]

    (b) the 'Employee' shall mean Ms Vicky Lombardi

2. The Company shall employ the Employee and the Employee shall serve the Company or any of its subsidiaries in the capacity as

   Secretary, Grade A4

   or in any other such capacity as the Company may reasonably require upon the terms and conditions hereinafter appearing. For the purpose of this employment the Employee shall reside in such place in the United Kingdom as the Company may reasonably require. The Employee shall be entitled to receive payment towards the expenses resulting from any change in residence required by the Company as set out in scales of terms and conditions laid out in the document 'Removal expenses' which may be amended from time to time. A copy of this document is available from the personnel department.
3. The Company shall pay the Employee a salary of £10,000 per annum to be paid monthly in arrears together with such expenses or allowances as may be approved. The Company shall in each calendar year review the remuneration hereunder payable to the Employee and any increase in such remuneration shall be notified to the Employee in writing and shall be substituted for the sum specified above and shall be payable as from the date specified in such notification. It is also recognised that the Employee will from time to time be required to work beyond normal working hours. Where the Employee at the date hereof or at any date hereafter is classified by the Company as being below Job Grade 6 the Employee will be paid subject to the conditions in force at that time for any overtime worked. Where the Employee at the date hereof or at any date hereafter is classified by the Company as being in a Grade 6 Job or higher his salary is deemed to include a supplement in respect of overtime and no further entitlement is due.
4. This agreement shall be deemed to have commenced on the First day of November 1992 and unless previously determined in accordance with Clause 12 of this agreement or by mutual agreement shall continue until determined by either party giving to the other One month's notice in writing expiring at any time ALWAYS PROVIDED that the period of employment shall terminate in any event on the last day of the month during which the Employee, if male, attains the age of 65 or, if female, attains the age of 60.
5. EMPLOYEES who wish to publish papers give addresses or lectures or engage in discussions on professional or technical subjects connected with their work must first seek and obtain the written consent of the Company.
6. DURING the period of his employment hereunder the Employee shall join and shall be entitled to the benefits of membership of such Pension Scheme as may be provided by the Company for the benefit of the Employee. The Employee shall contribute to such scheme in accordance with the scale of contributions from time to time in force and conform to and be bound by the rules and regulations thereof.
7. DURING his period of employment hereunder the Employee shall perform such duties and carry out such instructions and directions within the scope of his employment hereunder as from time to time may be given to him by the Company and shall obey and conform to all the general orders service regulations and notices from time to time issued by the Company and shall in all respects use his best endeavours to assist in carrying on the duties of the business of the Company in the most economical and profitable way and diligently and faithfully serve the Company and protect its interests in all things to the best of his ability and judgment.
8. DURING his period of employment hereunder the Employee shall devote the whole of his time and attention during ordinary business hours to his duties with the Company and shall not without the consent in writing of the Company previously obtained be in any way engaged in any other trade or business on his own account or with or on behalf of any other person.
9. THE Employee shall not whether during the continuance of his employment hereunder or at any time hereafter without the consent in writing of the Company previously obtained either directly or indirectly divulge or make known to any person any information relating to the business customers methods processes or secrets of the Company which may have come to his knowledge at any time during his service with the Company. Information relating to the business customers methods processes or secrets of any third party possessed by the Company and information in respect of which the Company is under an obligation of confidence towards any third party shall be deemed to be a secret of the Company for this purpose. All instructions drawings notes and memoranda relating to the said business customers methods processes or secrets made by the Employee or coming

into his possession during his said service shall be the exclusive property of the Company and the Employee shall use his best endeavours to prevent the publication or disclosure of any such information or documents.

10. THE Employee shall forthwith communicate to the Company every improvement, invention, discovery, design, Trade Mark or specification which he may devise during the continuance of his employment hereunder whether capable of legal protection or not and which might be used in connection with or relate to the business of the Company or any articles manufactured or dealt with in any of the processes or methods employed by the Company or any tools or machines or plant used by the Company. The Company will ensure that the Company and its professional advisers keep confidential all details of any invention which the Employee simultaneously claims belongs to him until either those details have entered the public domain, or it has been established that the invention belongs to the Company or the Employee releases the Company from its obligation to ensure the maintenance of confidentiality. Every such improvement, invention, discovery, design, Trade Mark or specification shall, except insofar as it may be deemed by statute to belong to the Employee, become the sole and absolute property of the Company. The Employee at any time whether during his period of employment hereunder or thereafter when required by the Company and at the Company's expense shall do and execute all acts deeds and things which may be required to enable the Company to obtain the fullest benefit and advantage from every such improvement, design, discovery, Trade Mark or specification (including the copyright in any design data in whatever form or specification) not deemed by statute to belong to the Employee.

11. THE Employee shall be entitled to such payments in respect of periods of service during which he is incapacitated due to illness or accident and to such holidays on such terms as are specified in instructions from time to time by the Company.

12. IF during his period of employment hereunder the Employee shall be guilty of any misconduct (including misconduct of a personal nature likely in any way to affect the carrying out of his duties hereunder) or of any breach or neglect of the terms of this Agreement or of the duties from time to time assigned to him the Company may without previous notice or payment in lieu of notice terminate his employment hereunder and in such circumstances he shall be paid the remuneration due to him hereunder down to the date of such termination and no more.

13. THE Employee shall not for one year after his employment hereunder ceases either on his own account or for any other person solicit or interfere with or endeavour to entice away from the Company any person who shall have been a customer of the Company during the Employee's period of service provided that this restriction shall only apply:

    (i) with respect of business of the type on which the Employee was employed

    (ii) to customers other than those introduced to the Company by the Employee at the beginning of his said employment.

14. ALL notices and other documents required to be served or given pursuant to this Agreement shall be deemed:

    (i) to be duly served upon the Employee if left for him or sent by prepaid registered post to him at his address last known to the Company

    (ii) to be duly served upon or given to the Company if served or given to the Company at its registered office

and all notices and other documents sent by post shall be deemed to have been delivered and served at the time at which they would be delivered in the ordinary course of post.

AS WITNESS the hand of an authorised official of the Company and the hand of the Employee the day and year first above written

SIGNED
for and on behalf of the Company: ....

in the presence of: ....

SIGNED by the above named: ....

5.10.2 Comments

5.10.2.1 General comments on style

This document will not win any 'Good English' prizes. Presumably the draftsman had rushed headlong from an intensive course in conveyancing and probate gobbledygook. The purpose of this contract seems to be that it should sound legal; certainly most employees and employers would not understand half of it—though they might be suitably impressed by this and maybe this is what your client wants. There is the risk that the more legalistic the contract appears, the more a court or tribunal will interpret it accordingly, offering little leeway for the employer to argue that the real meaning of any clause 'was common knowledge'.

Apart from the language it is also difficult to see why this contract should be used for a secretary. The intellectual property clause (clause 10) and the restraint of trade clause (clause 13) are hardly relevant to this position and clearly reflect the use of one general contract designed to meet the needs of all kinds of employees. Such blanket coverage is not desirable and may have adverse effects as we shall note below (or should it be hereunder?).

Punctuation also appears to be a variable theme. With one eye on nineteenth-century approaches there is generally no punctuation, but then in clause 10 it appears from nowhere. Why? Lastly, the agreement was drafted in 1992. It had not been updated and suffered from this both in style and detail. The agreement was reached in advance of starting work, which is fine, but the date 'deemed' to be the starting date is in fact a Sunday. Presumably a secretary would have no reason to start work on a Sunday and so this is likely to be mere carelessness. If the employee actually contractually started work before November that earlier date will in fact be the start date. The document also fails to meet the requirements of an ERA 1996, s. 1 written statement (even in the form required in 1992).

5.10.2.2 Some specific clauses

Clause 2 begins in a standard way with a job grading. The grading system has in fact changed since 1992 and there is documentary evidence to show regrading. The phrase 'or in any other such capacity' is very wide; it was meant to mean 'in any other capacity at that grade' which would make more sense—especially if at some time the employer claims the job is redundant. But why a secretary must reside in a required place is puzzling. If this is a limitation on living within so many miles of the site then such terms usually only apply to employees who might be called upon urgently. If it is a disguised 'mobility' clause, again this is most odd for a secretary.

Clause 3 is simply convoluted. The grade A4 is below grade 6 so the secretary is entitled to overtime payments.

Clause 4 was generous in its notice period in 1992, but now falls short of ERA 1996, s. 86 requirements. The different ages of retirement for men and women are discriminatory.

Clause 5 is irrelevant to this employee and again shows the use of a standard clause. Likewise *Clause 10* (intellectual property rights) is general waffle.

Clause 9 concerns confidentiality and may be relevant to a secretary (though we will see in **Chapter 7** that it may be ineffective anyway once employment has finished); *Clause 13* is a restraint of trade clause. It is totally inappropriate to the status of the employee and would fail.

Clause 12 concerns gross misconduct but never specifies what is meant by this.

6

Discrimination and equal pay

6.1 Introduction and sources

In this chapter we look at unlawful discrimination—on grounds of race, sex, disability, part-time or other 'atypical' work, or trade union membership—and at the closely connected matter of equal pay.

6.1.1 Statutory sources

6.1.1.1 Race Relations Act 1976

Racial discrimination was the first category of discrimination to be outlawed in this country. The original statute of 1965 is now incorporated into the Race Relations Act (RRA) 1976. Our task in understanding discrimination is greatly simplified by the fact that RRA 1976 adopts exactly the same definitions of discrimination as the Sex Discrimination Act (SDA) 1975. The scope of RRA 1976 is much broader than employment alone but we shall be concerned with only that aspect.

6.1.1.2 Sex Discrimination Act 1975

This statute outlaws discrimination based on sex or married status. It was enacted in 1975 so as to be brought into effect at the same time as the final stage of phased implementation of the Equal Pay Act (EPA) 1970. The two statutes are therefore complementary: EPA 1970 deals with pay, while SDA 1975 deals with other matters, especially non-contractual ones. Both statutes are drafted in terms of a woman who is discriminated against in comparison with a man, but make it plain that the opposite comparison is equally valid. Like RRA 1976, SDA 1975 covers employment but also other possible areas of discrimination.

6.1.1.3 Part-time Workers (Prevention of Less Favourable Treatment) Regulations 2000 (SI 2000/1551)

Until recently it was generally held to be unlawful discrimination under SDA 1975 to treat part-time workers less favourably than those working full time. (Statistical evidence showed there was a higher proportion of women workers than men who wanted to work part time.) Now in compliance with the European Directive we have separate regulations with the above cumbersome title, which we shall refer to as PTW Regs 2000. The importance of the new rules is that they are based on a different comparison: the part-time worker must show less favourable treatment than is given to a comparable full-time worker, on a pro rata basis if appropriate, and the sex of either is irrelevant. (Note that these regulations have themselves since been amended by the regulations covering fixed-term workers mentioned at **6.1.1.8** below.)

6.1.1.4 Equal Pay Act 1970

This statute requires that men and women receive the same pay and other heads of remuneration if doing similar or equivalent work. The original 1970 version was found to be inadequate to satisfy a European Directive and is now subject to the Equal Pay (Amendment) Regulations 1983. Unlike RRA 1976 and SDA 1975, EPA 1970 deals only with employment.

6.1.1.5 Disability Discrimination Act 1995

On 2 December 1996 a new category of unlawful discrimination was added to the list: discrimination on grounds of a person's disability. Like RRA 1976 and SDA 1975, the scope of the Disability Discrimination Act (DDA) 1995 is wider than employment alone. It also covers provision of goods and services, occupation of premises, education, and transport. We shall consider only the employment aspects.

There are some similarities between the approach of DDA 1995 and the common elements of RRA 1976 and SDA 1975, but also some important differences.

6.1.1.6 Trade Union and Labour Relations (Consolidation) Act 1992

It is generally unlawful for the employer to treat trade union members less favourably than non-members, or the reverse. It is also unlawful to penalise those who take part in trade union activities.

6.1.1.7 The Human Rights Act 1998

As we noted at **1.7** above, the Human Rights Act 1998 (HRA 1998) came into force in England on 2 October 2000. Opinions differ about the long-term impact of its incorporation into UK law of the European Declaration on Human Rights. We suggested in the earlier chapter that the direct and immediate effect on employment law is very limited, especially outside public authorities, and we therefore intend to say very little about it in the present chapter. It is worth noting, however, that some believe that the law on discrimination and that on human rights generally will become more intertwined. Thus, for example, we may expect to see HRA 1998 leading to yet more expansion of the frontiers of the kind we discuss at **6.5.7** below.

6.1.1.8 Other kinds of 'atypical work'

There has been increasing attention recently, both from UK law and from Brussels, on the special problems of 'atypical' workers—those employed other than on a permanent, full-time contract with an employer. We have just encountered one result, dealing with part-time workers, at **6.1.1.3** above, but that was a special case in that they had long received some protection through SDA 1975. The next group to receive statutory protection consists of those employed on a fixed-term basis. The Fixed-Term Employees (Prevention of Less Favourable Treatment) Regulations 2002—which implement the European Fixed Term Work Directive (99/70/EC)—took effect on 1 October 2002. It is now unlawful to treat a fixed-term employee less favourably than a comparable permanent employee, unless the less favourable treatment can be justified objectively. Less favourable treatment may arise in relation to terms and conditions of employment (including pay and pensions) or if the fixed-term employee is subjected to some other detriment. Fixed-term employees also have the right to be informed by their employer of available permanent vacancies. Such rules are somewhat specialist and we intend to say no more in this Chapter.

6.1.1.9 Discrimination on grounds of religion and sexual orientation

As we state the law in this edition of this book these are the two newest heads of statutorily prohibited discrimination. Hitherto it had occasionally been possible to define a religious group in terms of race so as to bring discrimination against that group within RRA 1976, and there was a long saga we shall mention briefly at **6.5.9** of unsuccessful attempts to bring discrimination on grounds of sexual orientation within SDA 1975. Both sets of cases are now only of historical interest.

The Employment Equality (Religion or Belief) Regulations 2003 took effect on 2 December 2003. The structure is similar to RRA 1976 and SDA 1975. Discrimination is forbidden on grounds of religion, religious belief or similar philosophical belief, or a perception of that belief. There seem to have been few cases so far but there is much scope for speculation about the scope of that definition, which appears, e.g., to exclude atheism.

The Employment Equality (Sexual Orientation) Regulations 2003 took effect on 1 December 2003. They too follow the familiar structure and prohibit discrimination on the grounds of sexual orientation to the same sex, the opposite sex or both sexes. Again, the alleged discriminator's perception is included as an unlawful ground of discrimination.

6.1.2 Evidence in particular cases

There has been a large increase recently in the number of cases brought to the employment tribunals alleging unlawful discrimination: from just over 4,000 in 1993–94 to well over 21,000 in 2001–2, although the number has fallen a little since then. A few have been spectacularly successful for the applicants—for example, female army officers forced to resign when pregnant or policewomen subjected to sexual harassment—whether as a result of tribunal hearings or in out-of-tribunal settlements.

In practice only a small minority of cases are of this kind. A great many involve very little law, and a lot of difficulty with the evidence.

Suppose, for example, that a client comes to you complaining of having been discriminated against. Maybe the client is a woman who has been rejected in an application for promotion in favour of a man, or an Asian applicant for a job who knows that only whites were short-listed for interview. You ask some preliminary questions and may well find that you are drawn to one of the following two views:

(a) The unfavourable treatment received may well have been discriminatory on grounds of race or sex, although you may have reservations about the client's ability to prove it. The employer has perhaps already been challenged directly by the client and claims reasons that have nothing to do with race or sex. Sometimes you may establish that a junior member of management involved in making the choice has said something foolish that helps your case.

(b) Alternatively, the client may have been turned down because of a lack of merit but disagrees with the employer's assessment.

We suggested at the start of this book that a little common sense often works wonders in understanding employment law. Nowhere is that more so than in relation to discrimination. More cases in this subject rest on straightforward analysis of the facts and on the quality of the evidence than on complicated principles distilled from the cases, a view supported by the EAT in *Stewart* v *Cleveland Guest (Engineering) Ltd* [1996] ICR 535. We shall return to the evidential difficulties a little later in the chapter.

Inevitably, though, some cases become more complicated. From the point of view of those trying to understand the topic, it is perhaps unfortunate that the following factors get in the way of the simplicity we have mentioned.

6.1.3 Non-statutory sources

6.1.3.1 A European dimension

The principle of equal pay for men and women is contained in art. 141 of the Treaty of Rome, the treaty which established the European Community. It is directly enforceable in the courts of the UK. The elimination of discrimination, especially on grounds of sex, has since become one of the major strands of European social policy and the original Treaty provision is now supplemented by several Directives. The most important are:

The Equal Pay Directive 75/117/EEC;

The Equal Treatment Directives 76/207/EEC and 2000/78/EC;

The Directive on Reversal of the Burden of Proof 97/80/EC;

The Race Discrimination Directive 2000/43/EC.

As in so many other areas of the law, the Directives establish general principles that then have to be expanded in domestic legislation. Early versions of the UK statutes contained restrictions and limitations that did not appear in the Treaty or Directives. As we shall see shortly, in some cases these have been held by the ECJ to be a legitimate setting of procedural rules by the member state; in other cases they have been held not to comply with the relevant European requirement. Where an individual has a choice of bringing a case either under UK legislation or directly under European law (either because the Treaty provision is directly enforceable or because, e.g., a Directive may be directly enforceable against an emanation of the state), there has sometimes been an advantage in the latter route because it circumvents the restrictions. Many such restrictions have progressively been removed, often as we shall see by new UK regulations following ECJ decisions, and the difference is not as great as it used to be, but new possibilities for imaginative use of European law may of course still arise.

The only one of the Directives mentioned above that is not yet fully implemented in this country is the later Equal Treatment Directive 2000/78/EC. It gave rise to the two sets of regulations about discrimination on grounds of religion and sexual orientation that were mentioned at **6.1.1.9** above, and in due course it will lead to implementation of regulations about discrimination on grounds of age but domestic legislation on that matter is not required until 2 December 2006. The much longer period for implementation recognises that this is a more complex matter than most other kinds of discrimination, raising difficult issues of national retirement policy. In some circumstances, discrimination on grounds of age is not prohibited, e.g., under art. 6(1) (c) it is possible to fix a maximum age for recruitment based on the training requirements of a particular job. The latest press reports suggest that draft legislation will be laid before Parliament before the end of 2004 to take effect on 1 October 2006.

6.1.3.2 Codes of practice

Both RRA 1976 and SDA 1975 are to be interpreted by the tribunals having regard to codes of practice. The code on racial discrimination was issued by the CRE and came into force in 1984, and that about sex discrimination by the EOC in 1985. In 2003 a new code came into force on equal pay, issued by the EOC under SDA 1975. Both bodies have a statutory authority to issue codes which can be used in the employment tribunals as evidence of good practice. All three codes recommend practices by employers that go well beyond anything contained in the statutes. Revisions are currently under discussion, as is a proposal to replace CRE, EOC and DRC (see **6.9.1.1** below) with a single body, provisionally called the Commission for Equality and Human Rights (CEHR).

While RRA 1976 and SDA 1975 are each supported by one code of practice, DDA 1995 already has one code, one book of guidance issued under statutory authority and two statutory instruments. Much of this complexity arises from a basic problem. Whether an employee is male or female, or from a different ethnic group from a comparator is usually a straightforward matter of fact. Whether the same person ought to be protected as disabled is much more a matter of judgment, and the guidance, for example, is entirely concerned with this definition.

6.1.3.3 Maternity rights

Under ERA 1996, as we noted in **4.6** above, women enjoy certain rights in relation to maternity, especially a right to maternity pay, a right to maternity leave and a special protection against dismissal because of pregnancy. All these rights are precisely defined, but cases outside the statutory restrictions have sometimes been brought under SDA 1975 or under the European rules, on the basis that anything dealing with limiting women's rights in relation to maternity is inevitably discriminatory, since men do not (often!) become pregnant.

The interrelationship of maternity rights and sex discrimination law can become a complex topic. Men are not permitted to bring complaints of sex discrimination on the basis of provisions made for women about pregnancy or maternity (SDA 1975, s. 2(2)) but women can usually complain that any action taken against them because of pregnancy is by definition action that would not have been taken against a man.

6.1.4 The content of the chapter

The remainder of this chapter is set out to reflect the observation made above that many cases in practice depend more on the evidence than on difficult points of law. We shall cover the law quite briefly:

(a) The meaning of discrimination under RRA 1976 and SDA 1975.
(b) Scope of RRA 1976.
(c) Scope of SDA 1975.
(d) Circumstances in which such discrimination arises.
(e) Remedies in relation to sex and racial discrimination.
(f) Equal pay.
(g) Remedies in relation to equal pay.
(h) Disability discrimination.
(i) Trade union membership and activities.

6.2 The meaning of discrimination

Discrimination is defined by both RRA 1976 and SDA 1975 as taking three forms:

(a) direct discrimination;
(b) indirect discrimination;
(c) victimisation.

6.2.1 Direct discrimination

Direct discrimination consists of treating one person (in this context meaning either an employee or an applicant for a job) less favourably than another, and doing so because of the person's race or sex: RRA 1976, s. 1(1)(a); SDA 1975, ss. 1(1)(a) and 3(1)(a). Examples might be the following:

(a) When recruiting to fill a vacant job, the employer short-lists a white candidate for interview while a black candidate with equivalent qualifications is not called for interview.

(b) The employer promotes a man to a supervisory post when a woman is apparently better suited to the job.

The employer's intention is immaterial. The test is not the employer's motive but the objective fact of less favourable treatment, viewed from the perspective of the applicant's reasonable perception. Some early cases where the courts ignored minor differences in treatment on the basis of the maxim *de minimis non curat lex* are no longer reliable. Almost any less favourable treatment falls within the definition, provided that the applicant can show that some detriment resulted—see *Shamoon* v *Chief Constable of the Royal Ulster Constabulary* [2003] UKHL 11, [2003] ICR 337.

There is an important difference between direct discrimination and indirect discrimination. In the latter it is possible for the employer to argue that an otherwise discriminatory act is justified by the requirements of the job. There is no such argument in relation to direct discrimination.

A particularly topical and also troublesome kind of direct discrimination is harassment, especially *sexual harassment*. This expression has passed into popular parlance, rather incongruously very often in the mispronunciation adopted for comic effect in the television serial 'Some Mothers Do 'ave 'em'—the dictionary shows harass as rhyming with embarrass rather than morass. It is generally used to denote unwanted sexual attention towards one employee from another, or occasionally from the employer. It qualifies as direct discrimination because it consists of less favourable treatment because of the employee's sex. The range of conduct covered by the term is enormous: from criminal acts to seemingly trivial remarks. The topic will be mentioned again at **6.5.5** below. *Racial harassment* has the equivalent meaning of attention from one employee to another based on some kind of racial prejudice: see especially **6.5.3** below.

6.2.2 Indirect discrimination

The definition of indirect discrimination has unfortunately recently become rather complicated. It used to be simpler as, originally, the definitions in s. 1(1)(b) of RRA 1976 and both s. 1(1)(b) and s. 3(1)(b) of SDA 1976 were identical. Then, in order to comply with the Burden of Proof Directive 97/80/EC, the definitions in SDA 1976 were changed by the Sex Discrimination (Indirect Discrimination and Burden of Proof) Regulations 2001. So the precise similarity was lost and we could no longer assume that subsequent cases about one statute necessarily applied to the other. It seemed that order would be restored when the definition in RRA was going to be amended using at least some of the same words as SDA (with effect from 19 July 2003) by the Race Relations Act 1976 (Amendment) Regulations 2003, so as to comply with the Race Directive 2000/43/EC. Sadly, real life is not so straightforward. As the amendment was made by regulations under the European Communities Act 1972, it could only cover matters strictly required by the Directive. But whereas RRA 1976 covers (as we shall see shortly in **6.3**) discrimination on grounds of colour, race, nationality or ethnic or national origins, the Directive is narrower and relates only to racial or ethnic origin. So the absurd result is that we now have three different definitions—one under SDA 1975 as amended; a second, using the earlier wording of RRA 1976 for all four kinds of discrimination; but also a third (with some similarities to the first) which is an additional definition for race and ethnic origin alone under the amendments to RRA 1976. The authors decline to speculate about the parliamentary drafters' ability to organise a party in a brewery.

In order to try to make the best of that nonsense, we shall begin with the definition under SDA 1975 s. 1(2)(b) which probably also applies, subject to some adjustment, to half of RRA 1976. Indirect discrimination means applying to a woman some provision, criterion, or practice which meets three tests:

(a) it is to the detriment of a considerably larger proportion of women than men;

(b) it cannot be shown to be justifiable irrespective of sex; and

(c) it is to the woman's detriment.

An example may help in understanding that rule.

EXAMPLE

Suppose the employer operates a system of flexible working hours but insists that everyone must start at or before 9.00 a.m. Statistics can probably be produced to show that more women than men have the responsibility of getting children to school and are unable to meet that requirement, so suffering a detriment. Maybe a 9.30 a.m. start would accommodate women with childcare responsibilities. It will be for the employer to show some justification for the 9.00 rule.

The new and additional rule under RRA 1976 in relation to race and ethnic origin also uses the expression *provision, criterion or practice*, but speaks of a *disadvantage* rather than a *detriment*. The difference may seem unlikely to have much significance, but the lack of any reference to proportions may mean that statistical evidence becomes less important than in the example above. The rule under RRA then replaces the employer's justification under (b) above with a requirement to show that the *provision, criterion or practice* was *a proportionate means of achieving a legitimate aim*. This may lead to some very different interpretations.

The old rule under RRA 1976 which is all that exists in relation to colour and nationality, defines indirect discrimination as the application of a *requirement or condition* to all employees, so that a *considerably smaller proportion* of employees from one sex or racial group can comply, which is to the detriment of the claimant employee and which the employer cannot justify.

It will be seen that the old rule is narrower than the more recent amendments. For example, the old rule depended on a *requirement or condition* imposed on job applicants or employees and a mere *practice* by the employer was not enough even if it had discriminatory results. The new rules expressly include practices. Yet the cases all arise from the old definition, and it will be necessary to view some of the following remarks with caution where the new rules plainly differ.

The person concerned must actually have suffered a *detriment*. It is not enough that the condition is theoretically capable of being discriminatory—see *De Souza* v *Automobile Association* [1986] ICR 514, CA.

The proportion of those in the applicant's group able to comply with the condition must be *considerably smaller* than the proportion of the rest of the population who can do so. Those words must be given an ordinary, straightforward meaning: there is no specific statistical test to be applied: *Perera* v *Civil Service Commission* [1983] ICR 428. Despite that apparent simplicity, the words often cause difficulty, especially where there are various ways of presenting the statistics. In *London Underground Ltd* v *Edwards* [1995] ICR 574, the employee was a female single parent employed as a train operator. She was unable to work a new duty roster because of her family responsibility. The employment tribunal had found indirect discrimination on the ground that amongst train operators a smaller proportion of female single parents could cope with the new roster than male single parents. The EAT held that this selective statistical analysis was not permitted: comparison had to be between all male train operators and all female train operators. However, the second employment tribunal found such small numbers of female train operators that simple statistical comparison was impossible. In deciding that indirect discrimination had occurred, they relied in part on the statistics and in part on 'common knowledge that females are more likely to be single parents and caring for a child than males'. In *London Underground Ltd* v *Edwards (No. 2)* [1998] IRLR 364, the Court of Appeal approved that reasoning and suggested that analysis of statistics needed to be flexible and not purely mechanistic. A difference of 4.8 per cent as in this case might often show a less than *considerably smaller* proportion, but there was a necessary 'area of flexibility (or margin of appreciation)'.

The flexible approach recommended by the Court of Appeal in *Edwards (No. 2)* was reflected, albeit with no express reference, in guidance on the use of statistics set out by the EAT in *Harvest Town Circle Ltd* v *Rutherford* [2002] ICR 123. There were some cases where on the statistics a disparate impact was obvious. In less obvious cases, the tribunal would have to look at more than one form of comparison—numbers as well as proportions, both disadvantaged and non-disadvantaged groups, and even the respective proportions in the disadvantaged groups expressed as a ratio of each other. This may reduce the clever statistical manipulation that seemed to be invited in some earlier cases. Under the new rule in RRA 1976 it may be possible to show a disadvantage without any statistics.

The employer can resist on the basis that the condition is *justifiable*. The burden of proof lies on the employer, and in *Hampson* v *Department of Education and Science* [1989] ICR 179 the Court of Appeal held that this required some objective balance between the discriminatory effect of the condition and the reasonable needs of the employer who applies it.

For several years there was a continuing uncertainty, now we hope resolved, concerning a 1985 statutory instrument that increased the service qualification to complain of unfair dismissal from one year to two, a rule that no longer applies. In *R* v *Secretary of State for Employment, ex parte Seymour-Smith* [1995] ICR 889, the Court of Appeal held that the change had an indirectly discriminatory effect against women because statistics showed a considerable difference in the distribution of service as between men and women in the working population. Many commentators felt that the amount of the difference was less than considerable. The House of Lords—[1997] ICR 371—referred that question and others to the ECJ, who effectively ruled that it was a matter for the national court to decide—[1999] ICR 447. Eventually, in *R* v *Secretary of State for Employment, ex parte Seymour-Smith (No. 2)* [2000] ICR 244, the House of Lords avoided that issue (although it still split their Lordships three to two) because they also found that the Secretary of State at the time had shown that the order was objectively justified as suitable to achieve a legitimate aim of encouraging employment.

Under SDA 1975, s. 66 as amended in 1996, the award of compensation by the tribunal is restricted if the employer proves that the indirect discrimination was unintentional. However, in *London Underground Ltd* v *Edwards* (see above) it was held that this defence did not mean that the employer was only liable for the results of discrimination deliberately applied *against the applicant*. In that case the employment tribunal was entitled to infer that the new roster was introduced with knowledge of its unfavourable consequences for the applicant as a single parent and an intention to produce those consequences could be inferred. A similar logic was applied in *J. H. Walker Ltd* v *Hussain* [1996] ICR 291. A rule about when holidays could be taken affected the religious observance of Muslim employees: compensation was awarded.

6.2.3 Victimisation

The third kind of discrimination is victimisation, which is defined as less favourable treatment of an employee by reason that the person has taken some kind of action under RRA 1976, or SDA 1975 or EPA 1970, or has been involved in such action.

The House of Lords redefined victimisation in *Nagarajan* v *London Regional Transport* [1999] ICR 877. The applicant was an Indian who had previously made several successful complaints of racial discrimination against the same (or a closely associated) employer, and now alleged that his latest rejection for two vacancies was victimisation. The employment tribunal found in his favour, mostly by inference: the interviewers had been 'consciously or unconsciously' influenced by their knowledge of the previous complaints. Both EAT and the Court of Appeal found that the process of inferring victimisation from unexplained events was insufficient to meet the necessary tests but the majority in the House of Lords disagreed. Motive was irrelevant and it was the objective fact that mattered, as with direct and indirect discrimination. In *Chief Constable of West Yorkshire* v *Khan* [2001] UKHL 48; [2001] ICR 1065, the House of Lords stressed the importance of applying the statutory language, 'by reason that': substitution of a 'but for' test was not good enough. The employer was entitled to protect itself by declining to provide Mr Khan with a reference while proceedings on a complaint of discrimination continued. Such less favourable treatment was not victimisation.

6.2.4 Employees and others

We have noted elsewhere in this book the growing tendency to extend employment rights to *workers*, a broader term than employees, and one which includes various people who are not employed under conventional contracts of employment. Thus, for example, the most recent extension of discrimination law gives rights to part-time workers and not only employees.

The older measures against discrimination use the term *employee*, but there are express provisions in SDA 1975, s. 9 and RRA 1976, s. 7 which perhaps anticipate the modern trend and prohibit discriminatory acts by principals against contract workers. In *MHC Consulting Services Ltd* v *Tansell* [2000] ICR 789, also reported as *Abbey Life Assurance Co. Ltd* v *Tansell* [2000] IRLR 387, the Court of Appeal interpreted a very similar rule under DDA 1995, s. 12. It included a relationship where there was no direct link between the principal and the contract worker, but only one through an intermediate contractor.

6.2.5 Positive discrimination

A question that is often asked is whether an employer can discriminate positively, i.e., in favour of one sex or a particular racial group that may be under-represented at the workplace generally or in particular groups. Generally speaking, to discriminate *in favour* of one person is to discriminate *against* another, and the employer is given no protection against a complaint by the second. There are very limited exceptions to be found in RRA 1976, ss. 35 and 37–38, and in SDA 1975, ss. 47–48. Employers may discriminate positively to the extent of providing specialist training to remedy underrepresentation and of encouraging people in under-represented groups to apply for jobs, but no more.

The position has been different elsewhere in Europe. There has been a string of ECJ decisions, for example, about the validity under European law of German rules permitting positive discrimination. In *Marschall* v *Land Nordrhein-Westfalen* (C–409/95) [1998] IRLR 39, the ECJ permitted positive discrimination in favour of women if subject to a safeguard protecting the interests of an individual equally qualified male. Without such a safeguard, a rule of positive discrimination cannot be operated—*Abrahamsson* v *Fogelqvist* C–407/98 [2000] IRLR 732. In a Dutch case, *Lommers* v *Minister van Landbouw, Natuurbeheer en Visserij* (Case C-476/99) [2002] IRLR 430, the ECJ held that the Directive did not preclude a scheme giving women preferential access over men to subsidised nursery places for their children, provided that it gave special treatment to men who cared for children by themselves.

6.3 Scope of RRA 1976

The definition of 'racial grounds' is found in s. 3 of RRA 1976. Discrimination is unlawful if on grounds of:

(a) colour;
(b) race;
(c) nationality; or
(d) ethnic or national origins.

There are few cases in which that definition causes problems or uncertainty. 'National origins' has been held to refer to race rather than citizenship: *Tejani* v *Peterborough Superintendent Registrar* [1986] IRLR 502. An 'ethnic group' has been held to be broader than race alone and may include any community with a shared history and culture. Sikhs and Jews satisfy the definition; Rastafarians do not, because they are defined by religion alone: *Crown Suppliers* v *Dawkins* [1993] ICR 517. This point has of course lost its significance since the implementation of the regulations on religious discrimination mentioned at **6.1.1.9**. Language alone (e.g., restricting employment to speakers of Welsh) does not define an ethnic group: *Gwynedd County Council* v *Jones* [1986] ICR 833.

The exceptions to RRA 1976 are set out in s. 5(2) and are very limited. They cover circumstances where being a member of a particular racial group is a genuine occupational qualification for a job in one of the following cases:

(a) actors/actresses or other entertainers;
(b) artists' and photographers' models;
(c) waiters/waitresses or other workers in public restaurants, etc. with a setting requiring a particular race for authenticity;
(d) those providing welfare services to a particular racial group.

There is also an exception under s. 35 to allow the employer to provide special services such as training or welfare to specific racial groups. Lessons in English would be a good example.

6.4 Scope of SDA 1975

6.4.1 Discrimination prohibited by SDA 1975

The SDA 1975 makes unlawful by s. 1 any discrimination on the basis of a person's sex, a relatively straightforward provision. The statutory rules are expressed in terms of a woman who is less favourably treated than a man, but s. 2(1) states that they apply equally the other way round.

An identical set of provisions in s. 3 makes unlawful any discrimination against married people in comparison with single people. In this case the reverse does not apply. It has been assumed that this permits employers to treat married employees more favourably, e.g., by giving them a better reimbursement of relocation expenses than single employees, but that interpretation is now open to some doubt. As we shall see at **6.5.9** the regulations about discrimination on grounds of sexual orientation mean that it is not lawful to treat less favourably those in same-sex relationships where marriage is not possible.

6.4.2 Exception from SDA 1975

There are limited exceptions, establishing circumstances in which acts that would otherwise constitute unlawful discrimination are permitted:

(a) where the essential nature of the job requires a person of one sex rather than the other, including dramatic performances, but excluding physical strength or stamina;

(b) where decency or privacy requires it, e.g., a changing room attendant; or if providing personal services like welfare or education;

(c) in domestic service involving close personal contact and in single-sex hospitals and prisons;

(d) if living accommodation is provided and cannot reasonably be equipped to provide separately for both sexes;

(e) if the job involves work in a country (e.g., Saudi Arabia) where the law or custom requires one sex rather than the other;

(f) in relation to any payment (which is covered by EPA 1970 instead);

(g) if consisting of provisions for death or retirement. This is a particularly complicated area which we shall consider as a separate matter at **6.4.3** below.

An exemption from SDA 1975 in respect of those employing five or fewer employees was repealed in 1986 and the Act now applies to all employers regardless of number of employees.

6.4.3 Provisions for death or retirement

This topic is partly covered by SDA 1975 and partly by EPA 1970, but the difference is unimportant; if it is not one it is the other, and there is no middle ground excluded entirely.

By s. 6(4) of SDA 1975, provisions for death or retirement are excluded, but subject to such a wide exception that in practice the scope of the exclusion is small. In *Marshall* v *Southampton and South West Hampshire Area Health Authority (Teaching)* [1986] ICR 335, the ECJ held that it was contrary to a European Directive to require women to retire at an earlier age than men. The Sex Discrimination Act 1986 was introduced in consequence and amended s. 6 of SDA 1975.

The discriminatory provisions of many occupational pensions schemes were examined by the ECJ in *Barber* v *Guardian Royal Exchange Assurance Group* [1990] ICR 616. It was held that pension benefits were a part of pay under art. 119 (now art. 141) and therefore subject to a strict rule of equality, whatever exclusion appeared in the UK statute. The judgment was delivered on 17 May 1990 and provided that equality should run from that date.

The time limitation in the *Barber* decision was unclear. Did it refer to pensions paid from that date, or to service after it or to something else? The question was answered clearly by the ECJ (after having been covered in a Protocol attached to the Maastricht Treaty of the EC) in *Ten Oever* v *Stichting Bedrijfspensioenfonds* [1995] ICR 74 and some subsequent cases. It required equality in respect of *service* after 17 May 1990.

That case did not exhaust the questions raised by the underlying principle of the *Barber* decision that pensions were an element of pay subject to art. 141 and cases continue to arise, both in the UK and at the ECJ. For example, in *Quirk* v *Burton Hospitals NHS Trust* [2002] EWCA Civ 149, [2002] ICR 602, it was held that benefits on early retirement after 17 May 1990 had to be equal in respect of service after that date but could differentiate between the sexes in relation to earlier service. See also **6.5.7** below about the right of access to pension schemes for part-time workers.

6.5 The circumstances in which discrimination may arise

6.5.1 Guidance from codes of practice

There are various stages in the employment relationship where discrimination may occur, and these are listed in the codes of practice, especially the EOC code on sex discrimination. The codes are primarily directed to employers with the intention of encouraging positive steps to eliminate discrimination, especially through the establishment of equal opportunity policies. They may, however, sometimes be of use to solicitors preparing a case for an individual client.

6.5.1.1 Advertisements for jobs

There is a specific prohibition of discriminatory advertising in s. 29 of RRA 1976 and s. 38 of SDA 1975. This is particularly a problem under SDA 1975, since words like 'waiter' or 'stewardess' as well as 'he' and 'she' are taken as indicating an intention to discriminate. However, only the EOC can bring proceedings to enforce s. 38 of SDA 1975.

6.5.1.2 Recruitment

Both codes urge employers to adopt recruitment practices that will avoid unintentional discrimination. Close contacts between employers and single-sex schools, advertising in publications which some racial groups are unlikely to read, and recruitment by word of mouth from existing employees may all produce discriminatory results. However, breach of the codes does not provide a ground of complaint without evidence of such results—*Lord Chancellor* v *Coker* [2001] EWCA Civ 1756, [2002] ICR 321.

6.5.1.3 Selection methods

Whilst both codes refer to this matter, the code on race relations makes a particular point about language difficulties. Complicated application forms or aptitude tests that require a higher standard of English than is necessary for the job probably constitute unlawful indirect discrimination.

6.5.1.4 Opportunities in employment

There are references in the codes to opportunities for promotion, transfer, and training, and also to provision of benefits, facilities, and services. It is also suggested that grievance and disciplinary procedures can easily be operated in a discriminatory way, probably quite unintentionally.

6.5.1.5 Dismissal

There is no separate category of unfair dismissal to cover discriminatory reasons for dismissal, but (as we shall see in **Chapter 10**) such reasons can increase the amount of compensation that might otherwise be awarded. This includes discriminatory selection for redundancy, as mentioned in **Chapter 11**. See **6.5.6** below, however, for specific rules about pregnancy-related dismissals.

6.5.1.6 Post-dismissal

A long argument whether the employment provisions of RRA 1976 or SDA 1975 could still apply after employment was ended has been resolved in *Rhys-Harper* v *Relaxion Group plc* [2003] UKHL 33, [2003] IRLR 484. Thus, e.g., a refusal by an employer on discriminatory grounds to supply a reference to a former employee would fall within the relevant statute.

6.5.2 Pressure to discriminate

There are specific provisions (in RRA 1976, ss. 30 and 31, and in SDA 1975, ss. 39 and 40) making it unlawful for anyone, including one employee, to instruct another to discriminate or to put pressure on another to discriminate. Only the CRE and EOC may enforce these provisions.

6.5.3 Vicarious liability

It is expressly provided by s. 32 of RRA 1976 and by s. 41 of SDA 1975 that if a discriminatory act is done by an employee in the course of employment, *both* employer and employee may be liable. This is particularly of importance in relation to sexual harassment: *Strathclyde Regional Council* v *Porcelli* [1986] ICR 564. It is a defence for the employer to have taken reasonable steps to prevent the discrimination, but this is not limited to steps that would have succeeded in achieving that result—*Canniffe* v *East Riding of Yorkshire Council* [2000] IRLR 555.

Until recently it seemed that the question of whether an act was done by an employee in the course of employment was to be answered using the standard test for vicarious liability from the law of tort that we encountered at **2.5** above. Thus, for example, in *Irving and Irving* v *Post Office* [1987] IRLR 289, a postman wrote a racially abusive remark ('Go back to Jamaica, Sambo') on the back of an envelope addressed to one of his neighbours. The Court of Appeal held that the misconduct formed no part of his duties and could not be classified as merely a means of performing them. Therefore the employer was not liable for the racial harassment.

That approach to harassment of an employee was comprehensively rejected by the Court of Appeal, perhaps not before time, in *Jones* v *Tower Boot Co. Ltd* [1997] ICR 254. A 16-year-old mixed-race employee had been subjected to verbal abuse and to physical assault that extended to whipping and deliberate branding with a hot screwdriver. A majority of the EAT had felt bound by *Irving* to hold that these were independent wrongs, committed outside the course of employment and for which the fellow employees (but not the employer) were liable. Waite LJ suggested that the rules of vicarious liability might have been relevant in *Irving* (presumably because the injured party was not an employee), but could not be used to evade employer responsibility in a case like this. The words 'in the course of employment' must be given their ordinary meaning by the employment tribunal, acting as an industrial jury.

The extent to which activity outside work falls within the definition of 'in the course of employment' is a fine point, and the *Tower Boot* decision probably represents a watershed. The Court of Appeal held earlier in *Waters* v *Commissioner of Police of the Metropolis* [1997] ICR 1073 that the employer was not liable when a woman police constable was sexually assaulted by a male colleague while both were off duty, but more recently, in *Chief Constable of Lincolnshire Police* v *Stubbs* [1999] ICR 547, that incidents in a pub immediately after work fell within the definition. It is difficult to reconcile these two decisions, especially since the incidents in the first were rather more serious than the second, except on the basis of a changing attitude to employers' responsibilities. (Other parts of the Court of Appeal decision in *Waters* were subsequently overturned by the House of Lords—[2000] ICR 1064—but the complaint under SDA 1975 was not appealed.)

Despite the extension of the employer's liability for discrimination, there are still cases where the employer can use the defence of having taken reasonable steps and where the individual employee remains liable, e.g., *Yeboah* v *Crofton* [2002] EWCA Civ 794, [2002] IRLR 634.

6.5.4 Employees working under illegal contracts

We shall see at **10.3.6.1** below that employees whose contracts are tainted by illegality, usually tax evasion, may have no right to complain of unfair dismissal. A less strict approach is taken under discrimination law. In *Leighton* v *Michael* [1995] ICR 1091, a woman worked in a fish and chip shop without paying tax or National Insurance contributions. The majority in the EAT acknowledged that she could not complain of unfair dismissal, a right that depended on the existence of a contract untainted by illegality, but held that her right to complain under SDA 1975 rested on a statutory protection independent of the contract. The EAT decision was approved by the Court of Appeal in *Hall* v *Woolston Hall Leisure Ltd* [2000] IRLR 578. A different result ensued when the EAT held that the conduct of the employee, an asylum seeker, was 'causative of the illegality' in *Vakante* v *Governing Body of Addey and Stanhope School (No. 2)* [2004] ICR 279.

6.5.5 Sexual harassment

As we noted at **6.2.1**, one example of direct sex discrimination is the conduct known as sexual harassment, and racial harassment is the equivalent. Until very recently harassment was not defined in any statute, but a definition has now been introduced into RRA 1976 by the Race Relations Act 1976 (Amendment) Regulations 2003 and a broadly similar definition to SDA 1975. Both definitions are required by recent European Directives. Harassment is defined in RRA as unwanted conduct which has the purpose or effect of violating another person's dignity or creating an intimidating, hostile, degrading, humiliating, or offensive environment for that person. There is no requirement for an intention to harass; if the conduct is unwanted and its effect is as described, it is unlawful. We do not expect that this new definition will in practice make a great deal of difference to the established definition in *Wardman* v *Carpenter Farrar* [1993] IRLR 374, where the EAT borrowed from a European code of practice:

> Sexual harassment means 'unwanted conduct of a sexual nature, or other conduct based on sex affecting the dignity of women and men at work.' This can include unwelcome physical, verbal or non-verbal conduct.

That definition was applied by the EAT in *British Telecommunications plc* v *Williams* [1997] IRLR 668 where they go on to note that the conduct which constitutes sexual harassment is itself gender-specific, so that there is no necessity to look for a male comparator.

Employers often find it difficult to deal with sexual harassment for at least four very practical reasons:

(a) The term covers a very wide range of conduct, ranging from criminal acts, possibly as serious as rape, to seemingly trivial remarks, the sexual overtones of which can only be understood by the recipient concerned and in all the surrounding circumstances. The usual pattern of a man harassing a woman is not invariable. Like other kinds of misconduct, there is no one disciplinary sanction appropriate for all incidents of sexual harassment, regardless of seriousness.

(b) Those perpetrating sexual harassment rarely commit the outrageous or major offences. Typically they go just one small step beyond that which the victim will tolerate. So the employer will often be faced with the seemingly trivial.

(c) Victims are typically reluctant to complain, and put up with unwelcome attention for a long time. When it eventually becomes unbearable, they expect instant remedial action from the employer, so as to remove them from contact with the perpetrator.

(d) Perpetrators often claim to have believed that their attentions were welcomed. Sometimes such a claim is ludicrous; in other cases it is plausible. If the perpetrator was genuinely unaware that the victim found the attention objectionable, no disciplinary offence can be said to have been committed until the perpetrator is put on notice of that fact. This is a special kind of warning.

The cases—such as *Strathclyde Regional Council* v *Porcelli* [1986] ICR 564—generally take a very supportive view of victims of sexual harassment, recognising that it may make their working lives intolerable. The particular finding in *British Telecom* v *Williams* above is perhaps a surprising exception. Miss Williams alleged that the male manager interviewing her had been sexually aroused. The employment tribunal found as a fact that he was not, but nevetheless found that she had suffered sexual harassment. They were imprecise about the detail of what had happened, beyond describing the interview as sexually intimidating. The EAT criticised the vagueness of the tribunal decision and went on to find that, as the tribunal had rejected all Miss Williams' specific allegations, there was no basis to find that she had been harassed. In doing so they appear to have concentrated more on what the manager did or did not do than on Miss Williams' reaction. We respectfully suggest that this approach would not meet the new definition.

An approach much more attuned to the victim's feelings was adopted by the EAT in *Reed* v *Stedman* [1999] IRLR 299. If a victim had made it clear that she found particular conduct unwelcome, continuation of such conduct constituted harassment, even if some might regard her as being unduly sensitive. By contrast, there were some kinds of conduct that, unless expressly invited, could generally be described as unwelcome. We must assume that the new definition is likely to increase the willingness of the tribunals to find harassment proved. In *Thomas* v *Robinson* [2003] IRLR 7, where the alleged harassment consisted of the use of racially abusive language, the EAT emphasised that the tribunal had to satisfy itself on two counts: that the language had in fact been used, and that the victim thereby suffered a detriment. They could not take the second element for granted.

Authorities about dismissal of perpetrators are limited to employment tribunal cases and seem to underestimate the difficulty for the employer of treating both parties fairly. Advice to employers is therefore not easy to give but might include the following:

(a) Encourage victims to complain informally and in confidence at an early stage. It was suggested in *Insitu Cleaning* v *Heads* [1995] IRLR 4 that this may best be done by means of a separate grievance procedure.

(b) Ensure that the confidence is respected, that support is given and that some action is seen to be taken, as the victim may otherwise have good grounds to resign and to claim constructive dismissal.

(c) Be careful about suspension of the alleged perpetrator, especially if the complaint of harassment appears ill-founded and/or if there are other temporary solutions like transfer to another department to avoid contact with the victim. In *Gogay* v *Hertfordshire County Council* [2000] IRLR 703, a care worker in a children's home was suspended following allegations of sexual abuse by a disturbed child and this led to clinical depression. The Court of Appeal held that the employers were in breach of the implied duty of trust and confidence.

(d) In any disciplinary proceedings, ensure that the perpetrator's rights are respected and that fair treatment results, recognising the need for some warning except when gross misconduct has occurred.

(e) Encourage complaints early enough that action can be taken before relationships have deteriorated to the point where victim and perpetrator cannot safely be left to work together.

f) ensure e'ees generally aware sexual harassment will be viewed seriously.

(f) Ensure that employees generally are aware that sexual harassment will be viewed seriously.

6.5.6 Pregnancy-related dismissal

We noted at **4.6.2** above that by s. 99 of ERA 1996, dismissal of a woman because of pregnancy or childbirth is almost always unfair, so that the remedies we shall consider in **Chapter 10** are available. Such a dismissal is also likely to be direct sex discrimination, so that the woman also has rights under SDA 1975 and/or European law. The importance of this alternative right of action is that compensation for unfair dismissal is subject to a statutory maximum, while compensation for sex discrimination is unlimited. Furthermore, discrimination law covers forms of less favourable treatment other than dismissal as in *Busch* v *Klinikum Neustadt GmbH* C-320/01 [2003] IRLR 625.

In *Webb* v *EMO Air Cargo (UK) Ltd* [1994] ICR 727, the ECJ ruled on questions referred by the House of Lords. A woman employee was recruited to fill a vacancy created when another employee was on maternity leave and then was herself found to be pregnant. The replacement was dismissed and had too little service to complain of unfair dismissal under the law as it then existed. She complained of sex discrimination on the ground that an equivalent man would not have been dismissed; the employer justified the dismissal on the ground that a man would indeed have been dismissed if he had for any reason become incapable of fulfilling the whole purpose of the contract—to remain at work during the maternity leave. In an important judgment the ECJ ruled that, because a male replacement could not have become incapable of fulfilling the contract in the same circumstances, the dismissal was by definition unlawful sex discrimination. This approach has now been confirmed by the House of Lords on the return of *Webb* from the ECJ (*Webb* v *EMO Air Cargo (UK) Ltd (No. 2)* [1995] ICR 1021). Their Lordships noted, however (as the ECJ had done before them), that:

> It does not necessarily follow that pregnancy would be a relevant circumstance in the situation where the woman is denied employment for a fixed period in the future during the whole of which her pregnancy would make her unavailable for work, nor in the situation where after engagement for such a period the discovery of her pregnancy leads to cancellation of the engagement.
>
> (Per Lord Keith of Kinkel at p. 1027C.)

In *Caruana* v *Manchester Airport plc* [1996] IRLR 378, the EAT declined to interpret Lord Keith's reservation as making an exception of a fixed-term contract when the employee was not unavailable for the *whole* of its period.

During pregnancy and childbirth, women thus enjoy a very high level of protection, and there is an obvious question of how long it lasts. The ECJ laid down a rule in *Brown* v *Rentokil Ltd* [1998] ICR 790, which was followed by the Court of Appeal in *Halfpenny* v *IGE Systems Ltd* [1999] ICR 834. The House of Lords overruled the *Halfpenny* decision at [2001] ICR 73, but not on this point. There are two distinct phases. Dismissal (or indeed any other action) in relation to sickness that starts during pregnancy or maternity leave and results from pregnancy is sex discrimination and automatically unfair. Once the baby has been born and the woman has returned to work after her maternity leave, she must be treated like any other employee. Thus, for example, if her attendance record is unsatisfactory, she can fairly be dismissed for incapability (see **Chapter 10**) provided that a man with comparable absence would be treated similarly. This rule apparently includes conditions caused by pregnancy or childbirth, provided that sickness starts after the return to work. In *Caledonia Bureau Investment & Property* v *Caffrey* [1998] ICR 603, the applicant's post-natal depression started during her maternity leave. Her dismissal after she was due to return to work was therefore related to maternity and unfair.

6.5.7 Transsexuals

Under the Sex Discrimination (Gender Reassignment) Regulations 1999, a new s. 2A was added to SDA 1975. This section created a new category of discrimination to cover any person undergoing gender reassignment, who is intending to do so or who has done so. This additional category is subject to all the other provisions of SDA 1975 that we have been considering.

The Government was forced to make those regulations by the decision of the ECJ in *P* v *S* [1996] ICR 795 that the Equal Treatment Directive applied to discrimination on the basis of gender reassignment as well as discrimination on the basis of sex alone. This cut across the conventional view of United Kingdom law that a person's sex is fixed at birth as recorded on the birth certificate and cannot be changed. A convenient distinction was drawn by the EAT in *Chessington World of Adventures* v *Reed* [1998] ICR 97 between *sex* which is unchangeable from birth and *gender* which is capable of *reassignment*. Later the European Court of Human Rights held in *Goodwin* v *United Kingdom* [2002] IRLR 664 that there was a breach of both Art. 8 and Art. 12 of the European Convention on Human Rights when a male to female transsexual was denied the opportunity to marry a man. In *KB* v *National Health Service Pensions Agency* (Case C-117/01) [2004] ICR 781 the ECJ held that Art. 141 EC precluded domestic legislation which breached the rule from *Goodwin* by denying a female to male transsexual the opportunity to marry a woman and therefore denying him part of her pay, namely her pension.

More recently the House of Lords held in *Chief Constable of the West Yorkshire Police* v *A* [2004] UKHL 21, [2004] ICR 806 that a post-operative male to female transsexual had unlawfully been discriminated against when (prior to the 1999 regulations) rejected for appointment as a police constable on the ground of a supposedly genuine occupational qualification—the requirement to undertake intimate personal searches of women. After the operation it was no longer possible in the context of employment to regard her as other than female. So the exception for genuine occupational qualifications is henceforth likely to be interpreted very narrowly indeed.

In relation to a very practical matter the Court of Appeal took a more pragmatic view in *Croft* v *Royal Mail Group plc* [2003] EWCA Civ 1045, [2003] ICR 1425. It was necessary to be sensitive about the provision of toilet facilities before the operation, and the employment tribunal had not erred in accepting a compromise put forward by the employer.

6.5.8 Part-time workers

Until 2000 part-time workers obtained some protection under SDA 1975 on the basis of the argument we have already mentioned at **2.4.4** above and at **6.2.2** that there are significantly more women than men among the part-time workforce. Consequently any rule or practice that treats part-time employees less favourably than full-time employees (without justification—something very difficult to establish) is indirectly discriminatory on grounds of sex. The key case that established that rule in the ECJ was *Bilka Kaufhaus GmbH* v *Weber von Hartz* [1987] ICR 110. In this country it was followed by *R* v *Secretary of State for Employment, ex parte Equal Opportunities Commission* [1994] ICR 317, which extended the rule to statutory rights such as the right to complain of unfair dismissal.

Now the PTW Regs 2000 (see **6.1.1.3** above) have provided a statutory basis of protection. The regulations bring into force the Part-time Workers Directive (97/81/EC), which incorporates a 'framework agreement' between European trade unions and employers' associations.

Part-time workers have the right under PTW Regs 2000 not to be treated less favourably than their employer treats a comparable full-time worker. There thus needs to be a comparison with a full-time worker, defined generally as one who is employed by the same employer under the same type of contract, engaged in the same or broadly similar work and working or based at the same establishment as the part-time worker. This language is reminiscent of the kind of comparison involved in cases under EPA 1970 (see **6.7** below). Its scope was explored by the Court of Appeal in *Mathews* v *Kent and Medway Towns Fire Authority* [2004] EWCA Civ 844, [2004] IRLR 697. They held that part-time ('retained') firefighters could not claim the same pension provision as full-time firefighters because they were not employed on the same or broadly similar work. The part-timers did not engage in 'measurable additional functions' besides fighting fires, a perhaps surprisingly strict approach in view of the statutory inclusion of the word 'broadly'. However the Court was less strict in deciding whether the two groups were employed under the same type of contract and overruled the finding of the EAT that they were not. Part-timers should receive a pro rata benefit unless that is inappropriate.

Workers can complain to an employment tribunal if the employer treats them less favourably, or dismisses them or subjects them to a detriment for a reason related to the exercise of rights under the regulations. There is a defence available to the employer if the unfavourable treatment can be justified on objective grounds. Compensation can be awarded but does not include injury to feelings.

A new head of discrimination unrelated to the law on sex discrimination is thus created by the Regulations and it is based on a comparison between a part-time and a full-time worker, who may be of the same sex. The initial surge of over 10,500 complaints to the employment tribunals during 2000–01 after the Regulations came into force, most of them about the pensions rights of part-timers, has not been maintained since. While ERA 1999, s. 20 made provision for the issue of codes of practice about part-time work, none has yet been produced.

6.5.9 Sexual orientation

Until 2003 there was a long history of unsuccessful attempts by homosexuals to secure protection against discrimination by arguing that sexual orientation falls within a broad definition of sex under SDA 1975, especially when interpreted to accord with HRA 1998 or the Equal Treatment Directive. The cases about 'gays in the military' were some of the best known. The House of Lords confirmed in *Macdonald* v *Ministry of Defence* [2003] UKHL 34, [2003] ICR 937, where a former officer in the Royal Air Force had been forced to resign in 1997 after admitting that he was homosexual, that such discrimination did not breach SDA 1975. The statute would apply only if less favourable treatment was accorded to a male homosexual than would have been accorded to a female homosexual. Such cases are now relevant only to allegedly discriminatory acts or omissions prior to 1 December 2003.

Since that date any such discrimination is made unlawful by the Employment Equality (Sexual Orientation) Regulations 2003, the terms of which were described at **6.1.1.9** above. As we go to press we are unaware of any significant complaints brought under the new rules. The one relevant case is *R (Amicus)* v *Secretary of State for Trade and Industry* [2004] EWHC 860 (Admin), [2004] IRLR 430 where a group of trade unions sought judicial review of the regulations on the ground that they were an inadequate transposition of the Directive, especially as regards the scope of the exception for 'genuine occupational requirements'. Richards J rejected the application. He accepted that the regulations had to strike a balance between the right of individuals not to suffer discrimination on the grounds of sexual orientation and the right of others to manifest their religious belief, and in doing so indicated that the meaning of the exception must be construed narrowly.

6.6 Remedies in relation to discrimination

A claim of unlawful discrimination in employment can be made only to the employment tribunals. Enforcement in other fields is generally to the county court. There are certain respects in which the procedure in these tribunal cases is slightly different from others.

6.6.1 Employment tribunal procedure

The claim in the tribunal must be presented within three months of the act complained of, although the tribunals have a discretion to extend this period if they think it just and equitable to do so: RRA 1976, ss. 54 and 68; SDA 1975, ss. 63 and 76. (See also **Chapter 13**.)

There are specific provisions under s. 66 of RRA 1976 and s. 75 of SDA 1975 for the CRE and EOC respectively to provide assistance to applicants in pursuing cases, especially if:

(a) the case raises a question of principle;

(b) it is unreasonable to expect the applicant to act alone;

(c) any other special consideration applies.

Applicants are also permitted, either before or after starting tribunal proceedings, to serve on the employer a questionnaire in a prescribed form, inviting the employer to comment on the applicant's version of events and asking specific questions. The employer is not obliged to reply, but any reply sent or the absence of a reply is admissible as evidence in the tribunal. This questions procedure can be very useful in assembling statistical evidence in support of a claim.

Conciliation officers from ACAS automatically receive copies of tribunal paperwork and attempt to reach settlements. In most ACAS regions certain conciliation officers are designated as having special responsibility for discrimination cases.

6.6.2 The burden of proof

Proving discrimination is often a problem. Your client, perhaps an Asian woman, may have been turned down for a job for which she seemed well qualified but which was in fact given to a white male. When challenged, the employer says that the man had better personal qualities. Maybe there is an element of truth in the employer's statement; indeed some other white males may have been rejected. But you doubt it was the full story. Under the usual rule of law that 'those who assert must prove', where do you start with the difficult task of getting into the employer's mind to find the real reason for rejection? Was the true reason direct race or sex discrimination, or were the 'personal qualities' so closely related to traditional white culture as to be indirectly discriminatory?

As we shall see shortly the courts have long been sympathetic to the difficult task faced by a complainant in such circumstances, but it has been made simpler by an amendment under regulations of 2001 that inserts a new s. 63A into SDA 1975 so as to implement the Burden of Proof Directive. A similar amendment has been made to RRA 1976 by 2003 regulations, at least in relation to complaints of discrimination on grounds of race or ethnic or national origins and complaints of harassment brought from 19 July 2003. Where the applicant proves facts from which the tribunal could conclude, in the absence of an adequate explanation, that the employer has committed an act of unlawful discrimination or harassment, it is then for the employer to prove otherwise.

The new rule was examined in *Barton* v *Investec Henderson Crosthwaite Securities Ltd* [2003] ICR 1205 where the EAT produced a 12-point list of steps for employment tribunals to consider. In essence, recognising that it is unusual to find any direct evidence of discrimination, the applicant is to be required to produce evidence from which the tribunal *could* conclude that discrimination has occurred. This could include any evasive reply to a questionnaire and reference to a code of practice but the tribunal must establish there is prima facie evidence of a link between less favourable treatment and the difference of sex and not merely two unrelated events—*University of Huddersfield* v *Wolff* [2004] IRLR 534. The burden of proof then moves to the respondent who has to prove on the balance of probabilities that the treatment received was in no sense on the ground of sex (or race, as the case may be). The Court of Appeal adopted a similar approach in the case that became the leading authority prior to the 2001 amendments, *King* v *Great Britain China Centre* [1992] ICR 516, although they disliked the idea of a shifting burden of proof.

In *Chamberlin Solicitors* v *Emokpae* [2004] IRLR 592 the EAT suggested replacing 'in no sense on the ground of' by 'not significantly influenced by' and this may leave some uncertainty how far minor influences can be disregarded. As we noted at **6.2.1** the rule *de minimis non curat lex* is not usually applied in relation to discrimination.

Statistical evidence can be a very effective way of satisfying this initial requirement: *West Midlands PTE* v *Singh* [1988] IRLR 186. If the case is about promotion, for example, evidence of a substantially different racial balance (or balance of the sexes) between the group from which selection is made and the group of those selected will require the employer to produce a detailed innocent justification. This is why the questions procedure can be so useful. If the employer is unable to supply statistical evidence, that itself may be evidence of having failed to meet the recommendation of the code of practice concerning ethnic monitoring.

It is usually essential to have concrete evidence of less favourable treatment. Sometimes it is possible to produce a comparison with an actual person of the opposite sex or a different racial group, but in *Balamoody* v *United Kingdom Central Council for Nursing, Midwifery and Health Visiting* [2001] EWCA Civ 2097, [2002] ICR 646, the Court of Appeal accepted that it would often be impossible to do so and that a hypothetical comparator would suffice. By contrast, in *Zafar* v *Glasgow City Council* [1998] IRLR 36, the House of Lords rejected a comparison with treatment that might have been expected from a hypothetical reasonable employer. The *Zafar* case was also important for approving *King*, above, and the guidance it gave about evidence of unlawful discrimination. The employment tribunal was not *bound* to draw an inference of unlawful discrimination from the absence of an adequate explana-tion by the employer for less favourable treatment. They should draw such inferences from *all* the surrounding facts as they considered proper. It is, however, essential that the employment tribunal draws its inferences from findings of primary fact and not just from evidence that is not taken to a conclusion, as the Court of Appeal emphasised in *Anya* v *University of Oxford* [2001] EWCA Civ 405; [2001] ICR 847. An employer may behave unreas-onably or dismiss unfairly in circumstances that involve no unlawful discrimination.

An exception to the requirement for an actual comparison occurs if the treatment complained of was 'gender-specific' or race-specific, i.e., if it can be shown to have been meted out *because of* the complainant's sex or race. This exception was expressly approved, albeit *obiter*, by the Court of Appeal in *Sidhu* v *Aerospace Composite Technology Ltd* [2000] ICR 602.

6.6.3 Compensation to be awarded

Compensation to be awarded in the event of a successful claim of discrimination is to be calculated by the tribunal as an amount that is just and equitable to reflect the loss suffered by the applicant. There is a complex rule about the award of compensation for indirect discrimination. At one time there was no compensation if the employer could show that the discrimination was unintentional. Under the Sex Discrimination and Equal Pay (Miscellaneous Amendments) Regulations 1996, compensation for indirect discrimination is restricted to cases where the tribunal considers it would not be just and equitable to grant one or both of the other possible remedies alone—a declaration or a recommendation of action by the employer. Otherwise the rules are the same as for awards of damages in the county court, and damages for injury to feelings are often awarded. There have been some large awards for injury to feelings, but the Court of Appeal has now held in *Vento* v *Chief Constable of West Yorkshire Police* [2002] EWCA Civ 1871, [2003] ICR 318 that there should be three broad bands: between £15,000 and £25,000 for the most serious cases involving a lengthy campaign of discriminatory harassment; between £5,000 and £15,000 for serious cases not meriting an award in the highest band; and between £500 and £5,000 for less serious cases, such as an isolated or one-off act of discrimination. In *Sheriff* v *Klyne Tugs (Lowestoft)* [1999] ICR 1170 CA, it was held that psychiatric illness brought on by harassment was an additional head of damages beyond injury to feelings and in *Laing Ltd* v *Essa* [2004] EWCA Civ 2, [2004] ICR 746 it was confirmed that the test was one of causation rather than foreseeability.

Originally, the rule under both RRA 1976 and SDA 1975 was that the compensation that could be awarded in cases of unlawful discrimination was subject to the same limit as for unfair dismissal. Then in *Marshall* v *Southampton and South West Hampshire Health Authority (No. 2)* [1993] ICR 893, it was held that a limit was inconsistent with European law. The Government was obliged to amend SDA 1975 accordingly, but decided to amend RRA 1976 too, preserving the symmetry we noted above. Compensation is therefore now unlimited.

6.7 Equal pay

The EPA 1970 establishes the principle that women should receive the same pay as men. Like SDA 1975, EPA 1970 states in s. 1(13) that the converse comparison is equally valid, but it is expressed throughout in terms of giving a woman equality of treatment with a man.

Under s. 1(1) of EPA 1970, every woman's contract of employment is deemed to include an equality clause, unless one already exists, and s. 1(2) explains what this means. The following is a simplification:

Each term of the woman's contract is to be no less favourable than a man's in the same employment if:

(a) she is employed on like work to his; or

(b) she is employed on work rated as equivalent to his under a job evaluation scheme; or

(c) (if neither (a) or (b) applies) her work is of equal value to his,

unless the difference can be justified on the basis of a genuine material factor other than the difference of sex.

The two paragraphs (a) and (b) above both derive from the original 1970 version of EPA; paragraph (c) was added by the Equal Pay (Amendment) Regulations 1983 in order that the 1970 statute was brought into compliance with the Equal Treatment Directive. There are some significant differences between the conditions attached to (a) and (b), and those attached to (c). It is therefore convenient to examine the detailed application of s. 1(2) in three parts:

(a) general remarks about all equality clauses;

(b) equal pay for like work and work rated as equivalent;

(c) equal pay for work of equal value.

Despite more than a quarter-century of operation of EPA 1970, national statistics on pay for women and men in a wide variety of occupations still show a substantial 'gender gap' and both the EOC and Government ministers have expressed determination to eradicate or at least to reduce it. The 2003 Code of Practice mentioned at **6.1.3.2** above is part of the process. Under the Employment Act 2002 the questionnaire procedure (as described in **6.6.1** above) is extended to equal pay claims. The topic may therefore soon acquire renewed importance.

6.7.1 General remarks about equality clauses

The mechanism by which equal pay is achieved is *contractual* and s. 1(2) allows for both the case where a term in a woman's contract is inferior to the equivalent term in a man's, and that where a term in the man's contract is wholly absent from the woman's. So, once the existence of an equality clause is established by any of the three comparisons, it can be enforced like any other contractual term. The parties may not contract out of the effect of EPA 1970: SDA 1975, s. 77(3).

The scope of s. 1(2) includes all contractual terms and not only pay or remuneration. The only significant exception is that preventing men from claiming any statutory restriction on the employment of women or any benefit related to pregnancy or childbirth: EPA 1970, s. 6(1). Non-contractual differences may of course fall within SDA 1975.

Every case must be brought on the basis of a specific *comparison*: it is not possible for a woman to use EPA 1970 to seek an assessment of a fair rate of pay apart from a comparison with a man: *Pointon* v *University of Sussex* [1979] IRLR 119. (We shall adopt the same practice as EPA 1970 of describing a case brought by a woman in comparison with a man; the reverse comparison could equally well be made, but it is not possible for any comparison to be brought with another employee of the same sex.)

The comparison must be made with a man *in the same employment*. This normally means a man employed by the same employer or by an associated employer at the same establishment. However, it also includes other establishments where the same terms and conditions of employment are applied: EPA 1970, s. 1(6). The rule was broad enough to permit a comparison between two Scottish local authorities, although they acted independently of each other, in *South Ayrshire Council* v *Morton* [2002] ICR 956, Court of Session.

It has been held that EPA 1970 requires a comparison with a man employed contemporaneously, but that art. 141 of the Treaty of Rome does not: *Macarthys* v *Smith* [1979] ICR 785, CA; [1980] ICR 672 on reference to ECJ; and [1980] ICR 672, CA, now permitting the woman to compare herself with her *predecessor* in the job. In *Diocese of Hallam Trustee* v *Connaughton* [1996] ICR 860, the EAT allowed a woman to compare herself with her *successor*, but some commentators doubt whether that is generally permitted. Often the employer has to pay more to recruit a new employee than was paid to a predecessor, irrespective of the sex of the two people.

The equality clause operates in relation to *each individual term* of the woman's contract. It is therefore no defence for the employer to argue that, taken overall, the woman is treated as favourably as the man, and that a benefit in one term must be offset against a detriment in another: *Hayward* v *Cammell Laird* [1988] ICR 464.

(Both of the above two points must be read in conjunction with the explanation at **6.7.2** and **6.7.3** below about genuine material factors, which may provide the employer with a defence in such cases.)

There is a partial exception in s. 6 of EPA 1970 in respect of *pensions*. However, in consequence of the recent cases on this aspect already discussed at **6.4.3** above, it seems that these provisions are largely inoperative, since European law circumvents most of the restrictions in UK law.

6.7.2 Equal pay for like work and work rated as equivalent

'Like work' is defined in s. 1(4) of EPA 1970. There are two steps:

(a) the man's and woman's work must be the same or broadly similar; and

(b) differences between their work must not be of practical importance.

The consideration whether the man and the woman are doing like work is a practical one, with the emphasis on what is actually done rather than what the contract might in theory require, e.g., *Shields* v *Coomes* [1978] IRLR 263.

'Work rated as equivalent' is defined in s. 1(5) of EPA 1970 to mean jobs that have been given an equal value as a result of an evaluation of those jobs under various headings. This is of course a reference to the technique usually referred to in business and industry as *job evaluation*, but not every such scheme is included. Examples are given of the kinds of headings envisaged: effort, skill, and decision. The statutory definition requires that the job evaluation should involve an *analytical process* and not merely a comparison of the whole job. Some schemes in use in business (e.g., 'paired comparisons') are of this latter type and do not satisfy the statutory definition: *Bromley* v *Quick* [1988] IRLR 249.

The scheme itself must be *non-discriminatory*. For example, there must not be excessive emphasis on the physical strength required.

Under either of these two possibilities of equal pay for like work or equal pay for work rated as equivalent, it is possible for the employer to escape the effect of the equality clause if it can be shown that a *genuine material difference* (GMD) exists between the woman's case and the man's. It must be other than the difference of sex.

Employers have a variety of reasons for paying one person differently from another, e.g., skill or experience, length of service, qualifications, grading. The problem arises when any such factor has a disproportionate effect on men and on women, because it will not fall within the definition of a GMD if it is tainted by indirect discrimination. In *Ministry of Defence* v *Armstrong* [2004] IRLR 672 the EAT reviewed leading cases in the ECJ and concluded that the definition of indirect discrimination for purposes of EPA 1970 was broader than that under SDA 1975. In that case a difference in pay between two groups of retired army officers now serving in recruiting offices showed an obvious and recognisable form of sex discrimination in the pay structure. Nevertheless the EAT also confirmed in *Health & Safety Executive* v *Cadman* [2004] IRLR 29 that length of service remained a valid GMD for which the employer does not have to provide special justification. The important tests are:

(a) the GMD must not be a reflection of the difference of sex; and

(b) it must actually exist in the two individual cases being compared.

However, it would go beyond the statutory provision if the employer were to be required to produce some *objective justification* for the GMD—see *Strathclyde Regional Council* v *Wallace* [1998] ICR 205.

A possible GMD that has caused difficulty occurs when the employer pays more in order to attract a particular person into employment than is paid to an existing employee. In *Rainey* v *Greater Glasgow Health Board* [1987] ICR 129, it was held that market forces could indeed be a GMD. However, market forces will not be a sufficient GMD if in truth they represent discrimination on historical grounds of sex: see *Ratcliffe* v *North Yorkshire County Council* [1995] IRLR 439.

One other example that has caused difficulty is the practice of 'red-circling' a particular employee's rate of pay when he is perhaps down-graded and is allowed to keep his old rate for some period of time. Is this a GMD to prevent a woman in the same job from claiming equal pay with the red-circled man? The answer from a string of cases is that it depends on the reason for the historical anomaly. If it was not the result of any past discrimination, a GMD probably exists: *Methven* v *Cow Industrial Polymers* [1980] ICR 463. If it is a method of perpetuating past discrimination, no GMD exists: *Snoxell and Davies* v *Vauxhall Motors* [1977] ICR 700.

6.7.3 Equal pay for work of equal value

The third possible comparison a woman can introduce is with a man who is not doing the same work and whose work has not been rated as equivalent, but who is claimed to be doing work of equal value. The fact that she is in a job where there are men doing the same job or work rated as equivalent does not prevent her from finding another man with whom to make this different comparison: *Pickstone* v *Freemans* [1988] ICR 697.

If such a claim is made to the employment tribunal, the question whether the jobs are indeed of equal value can be referred to an independent expert. This has usually been a tortuous procedure which we shall examine in very brief outline in **6.8**.

The operation of an equality clause established by this third possibility is subject to an escape clause rather wider than that in relation to cases brought under (a) or (b). Here a genuine material factor (GMF) *may* be the kind of closely restricted GMD we considered above: EPA 1970, s. 1(3)(b). There is little guidance from the cases so far on what may be included in GMF that is excluded from GMD. In *Enderby* v *Frenchay Health Authority* [1994] ICR 112, doubt was expressed by ECJ as to whether market forces constituted a sufficient GMF under art. 141 of the Treaty of Rome to justify a difference in pay between speech therapists and pharmacists.

6.8 Remedies in relation to equal pay

An employee or former employee may present a claim to the employment tribunal that the equality clause in the contract of employment is being contravened: EPA 1970, s. 2(1). There is a little used provision in s. 2(1A) that enables an employer to seek clarification from the tribunal of the meaning of an equality clause: this is a rare example of the opportunity for an employer to initiate tribunal proceedings.

The ECJ and then the House of Lords considered whether the procedural rules in EPA 1970 complied with art. 141 EC Treaty in *Preston* v *Wolverhampton NHS Trust*, respectively (Case C-78/98) [2000] ICR 961 and (No 2) [2001] UKHL/5, [2002] ICR 217. The rule in s. 2(4) that requires an employee to bring a complaint while still employed or within six months of the ending of employment was held to comply with art. 141 in that it was for the member state to regulate such procedural matters. In the same case, a rule limiting the arrears of pay that could be claimed to two years was held to breach the principle of equivalence and consequently not to comply with art. 141. As a result, the Equal Pay Act 1970 (Amendment) Regulations 2003 were passed and the arrears recoverable are now limited to six years like any other action for breach of contract. However, retrospective claims for up to 20 years are permitted if the employer has concealed necessary information for the claim to be brought, and retrospective claims about pension schemes can go back to 8 April 1976, the date of the ECJ judgment in *Defrenne* v *Sabena* (Case 43/75) [1976] ICR 547.

The burden of proof rests with the applicant in cases brought under the provisions dealing with like work and work rated as equivalent, although there is a suggestion in the '*Danfoss*' case [1989] IRLR 532 that this may conflict with the Equal Pay Directive. However, as with sex discrimination, the evidential burden quickly shifts to the employer to explain if a *prima facie* case of unequal treatment is established.

The procedure in cases brought under the equal value provisions in paragraph (c) of EPA 1970, s. 1(2) is currently undergoing some change. Originally the tribunal could reject the claim if they found there were no reasonable grounds to determine that jobs were of equal value or they could refer the question to an independent expert. The procedure was almost unimaginably complicated and lasted many months. Very few claims went the full distance. In 1996 an attempt was made to simplify the process and reference to the independent expert was no longer mandatory; the tribunal had the power to make a decision themselves.

Now as we go to press the Equal Pay Act 1970 (Amendment) Regulations 2004 and the Employment Tribunals (Constitution and Rules of Procedure) (Amendment) Regulations 2004 have just been published to come into force on 1 October 2004. Again the employment tribunal can choose to determine the question of equal value itself rather than appoint an independent expert to prepare a report. In a case where a job evaluation study has ascribed different values to the work of the claimant and the comparator, the tribunal must conclude that the work is not of equal value unless it has reasonable grounds for suspecting that the study was itself discriminatory or otherwise unreliable. The procedural regulations amend the new 2004 rules of procedure that we shall discuss in **Chapter 13** by adding a new sch. 6 which provides new case management powers for tribunals and also aims to simplify further the rules of procedure so as to speed up equal value claims. An indicative timetable for equal value hearings is set out in an annex. It is possible that these changes will reduce the enormous costs these cases have generally involved until now, and solicitors will not find them such a rarity. Most practitioners currently have no experience of the procedure.

6.9 Disability discrimination

As we noted at the start of the chapter, DDA 1995 adds an additional category of unlawful discrimination. The decided cases show that we must have regard not only to the provisions of the statute, but also to the code, the guidance and the statutory regulations.

There are some significant differences between the framework of DDA 1995 and that of RRA 1976 or SDA 1975. The aspects we shall need to cover, albeit briefly, are these:

(a) the scope of DDA 1995;

(b) the meaning of discrimination under DDA 1995;

(c) the employer's duty to make 'reasonable adjustments';

(d) remedies.

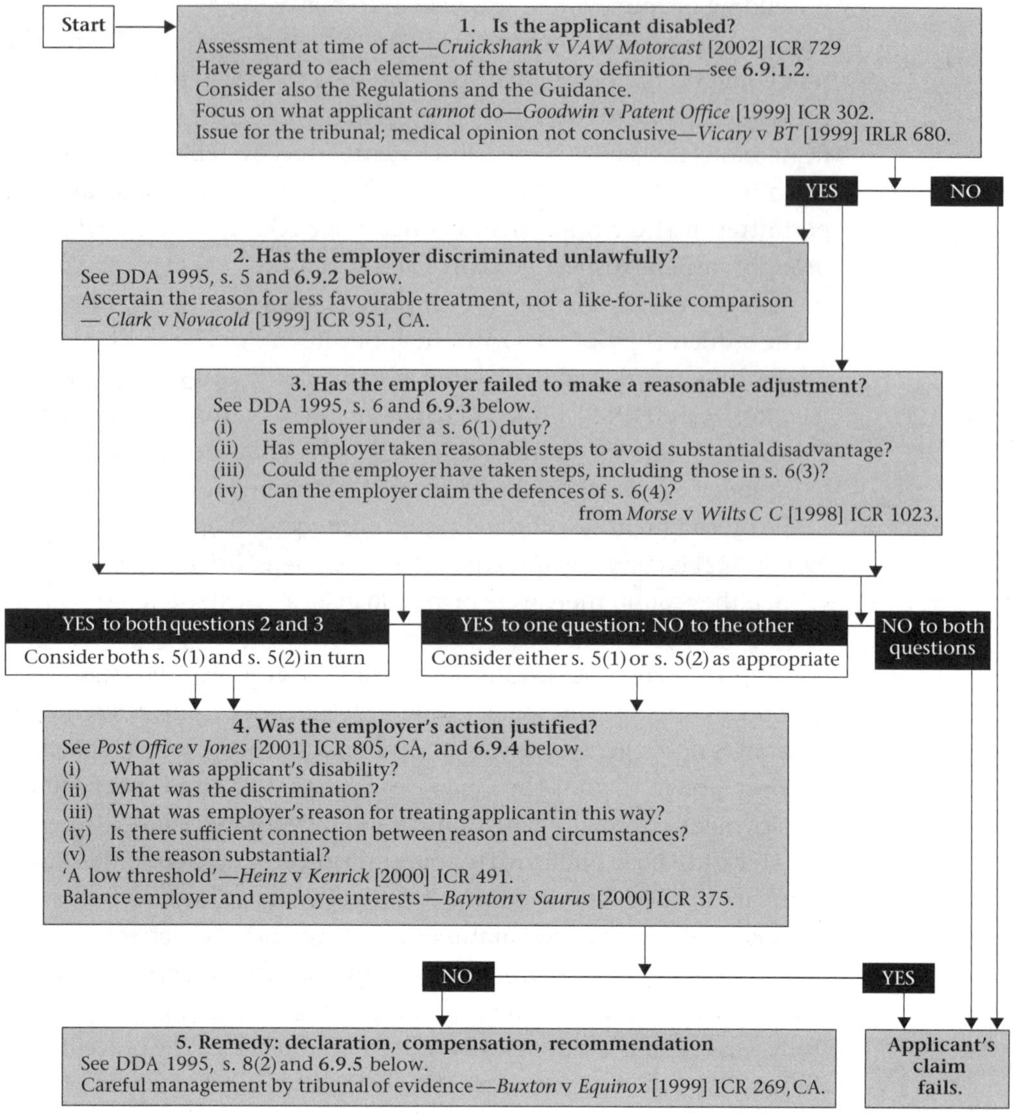

Figure 6.1 Key questions under DDA 1995.

It seemed to take a long while after the employment aspects of DDA 1995 were brought into effect for many significant cases to reach the EAT and the higher courts, so that we were forced to rely on the statutory provisions alone. Now, however, there are quite a few decided cases, several of them taking the trouble to set out a sequence of questions that need to be addressed in interpreting the statutory language.

Some readers may find it helpful to have the five key questions and the tests under each of them set out in the form of **Figure 6.1**. Inevitably it summarises very briefly the material in the text. The algorithm makes plain that there are two possible ways for a worker to establish unlawful discrimination under DDA 1995, one using s. 5 and the other s. 6.

6.9.1 The scope of DDA 1995

6.9.1.1 Differences between the scope of DDA 1995 and the other rules

Since we have already considered the scope of RRA 1976 and SDA 1975, a convenient starting point in defining the scope of DDA 1995 is to note some main points of difference. We shall then move on to look at the statutory definition of disability.

(a) While both RRA 1976 and SDA 1975 apply to all employers irrespective of the number employed, there was a specific exclusion under DDA 1995 for those employing fewer than 15 but it was removed from 1 October 2004 by the Disability Discrimination Act 1995 (Amendment) Regulations 2003.

(b) Subject to the point we mentioned at **6.2.4** above, both RRA 1976 and SDA 1975 apply (in relation to the aspects that concern us) only to job applicants and to employees. By contrast, DDA 1995 expressly applies to anyone subject to a contract personally to do any work. It therefore includes the self-employed and other sub-contractors—see *Burton* v *Higham* [2003] IRLR 257, but not ex-employees—*Jones* v *3M Healthcare Ltd* [2002] ICR 341.

(c) We noted that SDA 1975 speaks of a comparison brought by a woman with a man, but applies equally to one brought by a man with a woman. There is a similarly reciprocal approach in RRA 1976: a member of any racial group could complain of discrimination compared with a member of any other group. The comparison under DDA 1995 is in one direction only: a disabled person can complain of being discriminated against, but a non-disabled person cannot. So the employer is permitted to discriminate 'positively'—i.e., in favour of disabled people.

(d) While the CRE and EOC, the two statutory bodies set up under the other two statutes, have played an important role in their enforcement, the statutory body originally set up under DDA 1995, the National Disability Council, was purely advisory and had no such function. Under the Disability Rights Commission Act 1999, the Disability Rights Commission (DRC) now has a range of powers and functions much closer to those of CRE and EOC.

(e) We noted certain exceptions under RRA 1976 and SDA 1975 where the nature of the job required a particular kind of person. There are no equivalent exceptions under DDA 1995. The only exception remaining after 1 October 2004 is the armed forces.

6.9.1.2 The meaning of 'disabled'

Under s. 1 of DDA 1995 a person is defined as disabled who

> ... has a physical or mental impairment which has a substantial and long-term adverse effect on his ability to carry out normal day-to-day activities.

Each element of that definition merits closer attention.

(a) The impairment may be *physical or mental*. The conventional view of disability probably emphasises physical disability, but DDA 1995 also protects those with recognised mental illnesses and those with learning difficulties.

(b) The effect must be *substantial*. This term is further defined in the guidance issued under s. 2 as meaning more than minor or trivial. That is undoubtedly a lower threshold than might have been expected from the use of the term 'substantial' on its own. In *Kapadia* v *London Borough of Lambeth* [2000] IRLR 699 the Court of Appeal held that uncontested medical evidence on the degree of effect is generally conclusive. In *Woodrup* v *London Borough of Southwark* [2002] EWCA Civ 1716, [2003] IRLR 111, the applicant claimed she was disabled under the rule in para. 6(1) of sch. 1 that requires a condition to be assessed as if medical treatment were not being given. The Court of Appeal supported the rejection by the employment tribunal of that contention on the ground that she had produced no medical evidence in support. However, the EAT, in *Vicary* v *British Telecommunications plc*

[1999] IRLR 680 and in *Abadeh* v *British Telecommunications plc* [2001] ICR 156, has emphasised that it is a matter of fact for the employment tribunal to decide, and medical evidence must not usurp the tribunal's function.

(c) The effect must be *long-term*. This is also further defined in the guidance as meaning likely to last for 12 months or more, or for the rest of the person's life. Furthermore, past disability also brings the person within the definition. So, those once qualifying as disabled remain protected by DDA 1995 for the rest of their lives. According to the EAT in *Cruickshank* v *VAW Motorcast Ltd* [2002] ICR 729, the material time at which the assessment whether someone is disabled is to be made is the time of the alleged discriminatory act. However they also held in *Greenwood* v *British Airways plc* [1999] ICR 969, that in deciding whether the effect is long-term the employment tribunal is entitled to take into account adverse effects *up to and including the employment tribunal hearing*. This decision seems to make it impossible for the employer, having only the information available at the time, to know whether the person is disabled or not.

(d) The effect must be on *normal day-to-day activities*. A person is not regarded as disabled if suffering an impairment which merely limits exceptionally strenuous activities or only specific kinds of job. However, this does not exclude impairments such as an asthmatic response which may be aggravated by specialist work—*Cruickshank* as above.

(e) The Disability Discrimination (Meaning of Disability) Regulations 1996 list some *specific exclusions*. Not many statutory instruments manage to link kleptomania, hayfever, and body piercing. Pub quiz enthusiasts might take note! However, the exclusions are interpreted narrowly: thus addiction to alcohol is excluded, but depression is not, even if there is a causal link with alcoholism—*Power* v *Panasonic Ltd* [2003] IRLR 151.

The combined effect of those elements of the definition has been to include many more people than most practitioners would probably have expected. In particular, the tribunals have taken a broad approach to depression and other mental illnesses, so that many employers have found themselves defending complaints of unfair dismissal against applicants they had never regarded as disabled. In *Goodwin* v *The Patent Office* [1999] ICR 302, the applicant was a paranoid schizophrenic but managed to care for himself, largely satisfactorily, at home. The employment tribunal had held that the effect of his impairment was not substantial and he was consequently not disabled. The EAT disagreed and in doing so gave lengthy and detailed guidance for the tribunals on how to approach the question of whether an applicant is disabled. The proper approach was to focus on things G could not do or could only do with difficulty and not merely on things he could do, an approach also adopted in *Leonard* v *Southern Derbyshire Chamber of Commerce* [2001] IRLR 19.

6.9.2 The meaning of discrimination

The definitions of discrimination under DDA 1995 have been extended by the Disability Discrimination Act 1995 (Amendment) Regulations 2003 with effect from 1 October 2004, implementing Directive 2000/78. The main two categories in DDA 1995, s. 5(1) and s. 5(2) are unchanged, as is the definition of victimisation in s. 55, but we shall add a few words about the new concepts of direct discrimination and harassment.

The definition of direct discrimination under s. 5(1) is similar to that of direct discrimination under the other two statutes: treating a disabled person less favourably than others who are not disabled and in this case doing so for a reason related to the person's disability. As we noted at **6.2.1**, the employer's intention is irrelevant under RRA 1976 and SDA

1975, and it is the objective fact of less favourable treatment that matters. The position under DDA 1995 is more complex.

We shall consider below at **6.9.3** the employer's duty to make reasonable adjustments. Under s. 6(6) the duty does not arise if the employer neither knows of the employee's disability nor could reasonably be expected to know of it. There is no such exception under s. 5(1). In an early case, *O'Neill* v *Symm & Co. Ltd* [1998] ICR 481, the EAT ignored that omission and held that the employers' dismissal of Miss O'Neill was not unlawful discrimination under DDA 1995. The employers knew only that she suffered from a viral illness and not (as subsequently emerged) that it was more serious, so that she was in fact disabled. In *H. J. Heinz Co. Ltd* v *Kenrick* [2000] ICR 491 the EAT reviewed that decision in the light of the judgment of the Court of Appeal in *Clark* v *Novacold* [1999] ICR 951 and effectively decided it was wrong: the test was objective and not subjective. The employer dismissed Mr Kenrick for excessive absence and therefore clearly knew of his symptoms; it was immaterial that a medical diagnosis of chronic fatigue syndrome only came later.

Another area of difficulty is the proper comparison. In *Clark* v *Novacold* [1999] ICR 951, Mr Clark was dismissed for long-term sickness absence and his incapability resulted from a disability. Should he be compared with a non-disabled person with comparable absence or with someone who because not disabled had not been absent? Perhaps surprisingly, the EAT took the first of those options, but the case was then appealed. The Court of Appeal contrasted the language of DDA 1995 with RRA 1976 and SDA 1975 and concluded that it did not require the same like-for-like comparison, a conclusion later approved by the House of Lords in *Archibald* v *Fife Country Council* [2004] UKHL 32, [2004] IRLR 651—see below. Others without C's disability would not have been absent to the same extent and would not have been dismissed. So his treatment was less favourable. (The case was remitted to the employment tribunal to examine the issue of justification which we shall discuss below.)

An aspect of DDA 1995 with no parallel in the other kinds of discrimination is the employer's duty under s. 6 to make reasonable adjustments to accommodate the disabled person. By s. 5(2), failure to make a reasonable adjustment is also discrimination.

Direct discrimination is defined as less favourable treatment on the ground of (rather than merely related to) a person's disability, and there is no defence of justification. Harassment is defined as subjecting a disabled person to unwanted conduct which has the purpose or effect of violating their dignity or creating an intimidating, hostile, degrading, humiliating, or offensive environment.

6.9.3 The employer's duty to make reasonable adjustments

The duty to make reasonable adjustments appears in s. 6(1) of DDA 1995. The employer is required to take steps that are reasonable in all the circumstances to prevent a disabled person from being placed at a substantial disadvantage compared with others.

Further explanation of the kinds of steps that are envisaged is provided. In s. 6(3) there is a list of examples which includes making adjustments to premises, altering working hours, providing an interpreter and much else. In s. 6(4) there is a list of factors that may be taken into account in deciding whether a particular step is reasonable. Both lists are then subject to much further expansion in the code of practice.

The list in s. 6(2) of circumstances in which adjustments have to be made does not include dismissal. In *Clark* v *Novacold* [1999] ICR 951, the Court of Appeal ruled that the duty therefore does not apply to a dismissal, but *does* apply to events prior to dismissal, thereby distinguishing the decision of the EAT in *Morse* v *Wiltshire County Council* [1998] ICR 1023, which concerned an adjustment to criteria for selection for redundancy. The opposite view of the EAT, that s. 6 duties *do* extend to dismissal, must therefore be ignored, but the remainder of their decision in *Morse* remains valid. The significance is that they used the opportunity to set out sequential steps for employment tribunals to examine in such cases: first to ask whether a duty arises to make adjustments; then to ask whether the employer has taken any such steps; then to ask whether the employer could reasonably have taken any steps; at the same time considering the mitigating factors for employers under s. 6(4); and only finally to ask whether any failure by the employer was justified, although that last step is now removed by the 2004 amendments. In asking those questions there is nothing to prevent the tribunal from substituting its own judgment for that of the employer. Those tests were referred to in *Prison Service* v *Beart* [2003] EWCA Civ 119, [2003] ICR 1068, where the Court of Appeal accepted the need for the employer to consider reasonableness, but not necessarily to have followed the *Morse* steps sequentially.

Just as the meaning of 'disabled' under DDA 1995 is much wider than the conventional view of physical disability, so it is important not to think of adjustments as limited to physical steps such as providing wheelchair access. In *Archibald* v *Fife County Council* [2004] UKHL 32, [2004] IRLR 651 the applicant was left almost unable to walk by complications from minor surgery and could not carry out her duties as a roadsweeper. The House of Lords held that the duty to make adjustments was triggered when the employee was put at a substantial disadvantage because her disability made it impossible for her to perform the main or essential function of her job, and she was therefore at risk of dismissal, a risk that would not have arisen for a non-disabled employee. The employer had investigated transferring her to a different job (which the code of practice requires), but their Lordships felt it was insufficient for this to be on the basis of merely giving her the opportunity to participate in competitive interviews.

The amendments from 1 October 2004 require the employer to make adjustments in any 'provision, criterion or practice' concerning employment, promotion, transfer, training, or any other benefit that places a disabled person at a substantial disadvantage.

The employer is not required to make adjustments in connection with any disability he did not know about and could not reasonably be expected to know about—s. 6(6). The scope of that exception was examined by the EAT in *Ridout* v *TC Group* [1998] IRLR 628. Morison J held that the employer was not put under any duty to undertake extensive enquiries of a job applicant about the suitability of an interview room, merely because of the mention on an application form of a rare form of epilepsy that in fact made her sensitive to bright light. This is very much a decision on the particular facts and the EAT upheld the employment tribunal. It may be dangerous for employers to assume that they do not need to react to more obvious indications of disability or to investigate further.

The duty to make adjustments applies to job-related matters. In *Kenny* v *Hampshire Constabulary* [1999] ICR 27 the applicant needed personal help to use the toilet and this was held to fall outside s. 6.

6.9.4 Justification by the employer

An act that would otherwise constitute discrimination under s. 5(1) ceases to do so if the employer can show that it is *justified*. This term is defined in DDA 1995 as meaning a reason that is both *material to the circumstances of the particular case* and *substantial*. The code of practice gives some examples. Failure to appoint a person with a disfiguring skin condition to a job that involves modelling cosmetics, for example, is said to satisfy both parts of the definition of 'justified'. Not to appoint the same person to a clerical post because other employees or customers might feel uncomfortable is unlikely to be a substantial reason. It will be recalled that under RRA 1976 and SDA 1975 justification applies only to indirect discrimination; here it applies to direct discrimination.

In the early days of DDA 1995, tribunals seemed reluctant to accept employers' arguments of justification. However, as the more recent cases we have discussed make it relat-ively easier for workers to establish that they are disabled, or that treatment they have received is discriminatory, so the balance seems to have shifted in the employer's favour about what constitutes justification. In *H. J. Heinz Co. Ltd* v *Kenrick* [2000] ICR 491, Lindsay J described the statutory test as a very low threshold. The Court of Appeal quoted his comment without disapproval in *Post Office* v *Jones* [2001] EWCA Civ 558; [2001] ICR 805. Here the employee was a delivery driver who became diabetic, and the justification depended on medical evidence of the risks presented by an insulin-requiring driver. The Court of Appeal ruled that the function of the employment tribunal was merely to assess the employer's reasoning against the statutory definition and not to substitute their own view, even if presented with conflicting medical evidence. Arden LJ set out the sequence of questions we noted in **Figure 6.1** above. This may involve the presentation at the tribunal hearing of expert evidence not available to the employer at the time—see *Surrey Police* v *Marshall* [2002] IRLR 843.

In *Baynton* v *Saurus General Engineers Ltd* [2000] ICR 375, the EAT suggested justification required a 'balancing exercise' between the interests of the employer and the disabled employee. In the particular case, the fact that the disabled employee was unable to do his job was insufficient, as the employers had not warned him of the risk of dismissal or found out the up-to-date medical position before dismissing him.

As we noted in **Figure 6.1**, discrimination is defined in two ways: straightforward less favourable treatment under s. 5 (1) and failure to make a reasonable adjustment under s. 5(2). The defence of justification has hitherto applied to both. The Court of Appeal held in *Collins* v *Royal National Theatre Board* [2004] EWCA Civ 144, [2004] IRLR 395 that the tests in *Jones* also applied to both. However, the defence of justification is removed from s. 5(2) discrimination by the 2004 amendments. Even in relation to discrimination under s. 5(1), less favourable treatment, in any case where an adjustment was required but not made, the tribunal must consider an argument of justification by asking what the position would have been if the employer had made the adjustment—s. 5(5) and *Nottinghamshire County Council* v *Meikle* [2004] EWCA Civ 859, [2004] IRLR 703.

6.9.5 Remedies under DDA 1995

The remedy for any infringement of the employment provisions of DDA 1995 is by way of a claim in the employment tribunal, which must be brought within three months of the act complained of. If the tribunal finds the complaint well founded, it must use such of the following remedies as it considers just and equitable:

(a) a declaration of the rights of the claimant and the employer;

(b) an award of compensation, with no statutory limit, and including an award for injury to feelings; and

(c) a recommendation of action the employer should take to alleviate the claimant's problem.

According to the EAT in *Buxton* v *Equinox Design Ltd* [1999] ICR 269, the assessment of compensation in disability discrimination cases may require careful management by the tribunal and medical evidence of the applicant's prognosis. If the tribunal issues a recommendation and the employer fails without justification to comply, the amount of compensation may be increased.

The overlap with dismissal actions is dealt with in **Chapter 10** (particularly at **10.9.2.4**).

6.10 Trade union membership and activities

The fourth of the four heads of unlawful discrimination we identified at the start of the chapter was that on the basis of trade union membership or activities. This is on the fringe of the topics covered in this book, since it consists of individual rights related to collective employment law. The following is therefore only a very brief outline of the relevant statutory provisions, all of them taken from TULRCA 1992.

By s. 137 of the Act, it is unlawful to discriminate in making offers of employment on the basis of:

(a) trade union membership or non-membership; or

(b) willingness to become a trade union member.

By s. 144, it is unlawful to take any action short of dismissal against an individual employee for the purpose of:

(a) stopping the employee from being a trade union member;

(b) stopping the employee from taking part in trade union activities;

(c) forcing the employee to join some trade union; or

(d) forcing the employee to join a particular trade union.

The scope of this section is much narrower than the definition of discrimination at **6.2** above under RRA 1976 or SDA 1975, or even that at **6.9.2** under DDA 1995. It clearly includes the employer's intention. The action must be direct and must be for the *purpose* of deterring or forcing. Action for some other purpose which happens to affect unionists and non-unionists in a discriminatory way is not included, and neither is action taken against the union rather than against the individual.

By s. 152, any dismissal where the main reason is the employee's trade union membership, non-membership or participation in activities is automatically unfair. (See **Chapter 10** for a fuller explanation.) Particularly heavy penalties follow for the employer. Furthermore, it is possible for the employee apparently dismissed for such reasons to seek an order continuing the employment until a tribunal hearing can be held about the fairness of dismissal—see s. 161, 'interim relief'.

By s. 153, it is unfair to select an employee for dismissal for redundancy on the basis of trade union membership, non-membership or activities. See **Chapter 11**.

Claims about all these matters must be presented to the employment tribunal within three months of the allegedly discriminatory act or of the dismissal. The tribunal may only prolong that period if satisfied that it was 'not reasonably practicable' for the claim to be presented in time—see **Chapter 13**.

6.11 Self-test questions

1. The Department for Work and Pensions has a dress code under which all staff are required to dress 'in a professional and businesslike way'. Men are required to wear a collar and tie but women merely 'to dress appropriately and to a similar standard'. The code goes on to ban denim clothing, lycra leggings, shorts, cropped tops, trainers, and baseball caps.

Matthew Thompson, an administrative assistant whose work does not bring him face-to-face with the public, objects to the rule about collar and tie and brings to the employment tribunal a claim of direct sex discrimination. What factors should decide whether he succeeds?

2. What are the key elements that define whether someone is disabled under DDA 1995?

7

Protecting business secrets

7.1 Introduction

7.1.1 Summary of Chapters seven and eight

The next two chapters deal with the complex topics of confidentiality and restraint of trade. We have given these areas separate chapters, but often the issues blend together. The following is therefore a general summary of the main subjects covered:

(a) Questions of protecting *confidential information* can arise both during the employment relationship and afterwards; the *restraint of trade doctrine* applies only to ex-employees. The remedy for an alleged breach (of either type of duty) is by way of a claim for damages in the ordinary courts, usually accompanied by an application for injunctive relief. **Employment tribunals have no jurisdiction over confidentiality or restraint matters.**

(b) The duty of confidentiality is concerned with protecting information which is central to the employer's business, the use or disclosure of which would cause harm to the employer.

(c) Once employment has been terminated the employer's confidential information may still be protected by the implied duty of fidelity which will continue even though the relationship has ended.

(d) But, confidential information will generally be protected only if it can be classified as a trade secret. There is no one common definition of 'trade secret' that can be applied to all organisations.

(e) What cannot be protected is the employee's 'know-how' acquired during his or her employment and which he or she wishes to use in another employment.

(f) There is some debate as to whether an express term of confidentiality or a restraint of trade clause can extend protection to information which falls outside the definition of trade secret.

(g) An ex-employee may be prevented from using or disclosing his ex-employer's confidential information for a defined limited period or for ever depending upon the nature of the information.

(h) A restraint of trade clause seeks to prevent unfair competition from ex-employees by restricting their activities after termination of the contract.

(i) Restraint clauses are presumed to be void unless they are reasonable. Reasonableness depends upon the employer showing that there was a 'legitimate interest' to protect (e.g., customer contacts) and that the wording of the clause is reasonable as between the parties in terms of the length of the restraint, area covered, the status of the employee, and the general market conditions.

(j) Restraint clauses are usually concerned with preventing the ex-employee making use of his or her customer contacts made when he or she was employed by the former employer, but such clauses can be used to prevent the dissemination of the employer's information by precluding the ex-employee from operating within the same field of business. It is therefore possible for a contract to contain an implied duty of fidelity relating to confidential information, an express term on the same subject, and have a restraint clause which seeks to do the same thing.

(k) Restraint clauses come in varying degrees of severity e.g., *non-competition clauses* seek to prevent the ex-employee working in a particular industry for a defined period, whereas *non-solicitation clauses* only seek to prevent the ex-employee approaching clients of the former employer. The more Draconian the clause the stricter the test of reasonableness applied by the courts.

7.1.2 Introductory comments on confidentiality

This chapter deals with the protection of information. Every business, from the small backstreet engineering company to the large multi-national, will generate business secrets of some nature. These may take the simple form of customer lists, discount concessions, or manufacturing know-how. Equally, the information may take the form of formulae, inventions, secret recipes, or technical data and drawings. All these items are at least *capable* of attracting the protection of the law. The size and importance of the company is not the determining feature; nor will the perceived value of the information be conclusive of any classification of secrecy. The problems of protecting confidential information are quite real. Recent research has shown that over 65 per cent of professionals have admitted to having stolen commercially-sensitive information, and departing employees often take with them e-mail lists, customer lists and technical specifications. Computer misuse is a particular problem today.

Anyone claiming that another has breached their confidence must show three things:

(a) that the law would class the information as possessing the necessary quality of confidence about it; and

(b) that the information was imparted in circumstances which conveyed an obligation of confidence; and

(c) that there was unauthorised use of that information.

Rights to confidentiality are more nebulous than patent rights, design rights or copyright; often the information is intangible, proof of breach is not always straightforward and remedies may be difficult to enforce effectively. The information does not have to be contained in a document but it must have an identifiable source.

This chapter will therefore adopt the following lines:

(a) How will a duty of confidentiality arise?

(b) What makes information confidential?

(c) The duty owed by employees.

(d) The duty owed by former employees.

(e) The case law.

(f) Remedies for breach of confidence.

(g) Intellectual property rights.

(h) The employee's right to confidentiality.

(i) References.

7.2 How will a duty of confidentiality arise?

Mere receipt of information is not enough to generate a duty of confidentiality. The recipient of the information must accept or realise that the information is to be treated as confidential before any duty will be imputed to him or her. This is tested objectively.

Employees are caught by such a duty. Employers are concerned to prevent *disclosures* by employees to third parties (usually trade rivals) and, in the event of unauthorised disclosures occurring, to prevent the further *use* of the information. Thus third parties may also be caught by the duty of confidentiality.

There are two principal ways in which an employee will acquire a duty of confidentiality:

(a) by way of an *express term* inserted in the contract; or

(b) because the range of *implied terms* may supplement (or stand in the place of) the express terms.

7.2.1 Express terms of the contract

Employers use two key express terms to protect confidential information: *confidentiality clauses* and *restraint of trade clause*. As noted in **7.1.1** they are different animals. A confidentiality clause only seeks to prevent the use or disclosure of information, e.g., 'The employee shall not either during his appointment or at any time for two years after its termination: disclose to any person(s) (except those authorised by the Company to know or as otherwise authorised by law); use for his own purposes or for any purposes other than those of the Company any information of a confidential or secret nature which may be made known to the employee by the Company or any customer or supplier of the Company or which may be learned by the employee during his employment, including, in particular, information which relates to: (a) research and development; (b) technical programmes, technical data and operations; (c) manufacturing formulae, processes and techniques; (d) customers' details and specific requirements. Saving that, in all cases, this list of confidential items is not to be treated as closed or exhaustive of the employee's duties'.

A restraint clause seeks to prohibit the employee working (in some capacity) for another employer, e.g., '*Non-Dealing with Clients*: For a period of 12 months after termination of the Employment, the Employee shall not directly or indirectly (and whether on his own account or for any other person, firm, company, or organisation) deal with any person, firm company or organisation who or which at any time during the preceding 12 months shall have been a client customer of, or a person or company in the habit of dealing with, or any person or company who has been in negotiations with, the Company, and with whom or which the Employee has had direct dealings or personal contact as part of the Employment so as to harm the goodwill of the Company or any other Group company or so as to compete with the Company or any other Group Company'.

Many contracts include a confidentiality clause of some form; often of great detail and length. Employers can therefore set out in clear terms what the responsibilities of the employee are as regards information gained in the course of employment. They should be advised to do so. In a number of cases employees have been held free to use information because the contract did not make the confidentiality point clear. For instance, in *United Indigo Chemical Co. Ltd* v *Robinson* (1932) 49 RPC 178, an injunction to restrain a former employee from using 'secret processes' learned during employment was refused on the grounds that access to the information was freely available within the company and the employee had never been told that what he had learned was to be regarded as confidential.

Although the law will usually imply obligations necessary for the protection of confidential information the inclusion of an express clause is recommended as an additional precaution. Certainly one would expect such clauses to appear in contracts with scientific, research, technical and other skilled or professional employees. The advantages of the inclusion of an express term are:

(a) it makes obvious to a court the employer's 'subjective' assessment regarding the importance of confidentiality;

(b) in borderline situations it may be that a clear policy will convince a court that certain information deserves to be labelled 'confidential';

(c) such clauses serve as a warning to employees;

(d) a negative formulation of the duty (i.e., that disclosure will constitute a breach) may serve as the basis for an injunction.

As we will see below, information may be protected even without the use of an express term. On the question whether the 'belt and braces' policy of inserting an express term should be held against the employer when the wording is deficient, the courts have not maintained consistency. Thus, in some cases deficiencies in drafting have been treated with leniency; though there is always the potential drawback that in spelling out the confidentiality of certain information any omissions will not be covered: *Thomas Marshall (Exporters) Ltd* v *Guinle* [1978] ICR 905 and *Triplex* v *Scorah* [1938] Ch 211. In these cases, however, the courts still felt free to supplement inadequate express terms with wider implied duties. It would be unwise to rely on this.

7.2.2 Implied terms of the contract

The existence of a duty of confidentiality is treated as axiomatic in the employment relationship because a violation of confidence is a breach of the duty of fidelity or good faith which is an intrinsic part of every employee's contract. Indeed, the courts treat this so seriously that even the *possibility* of a breach of confidence may prevent employees being permitted to work for others in their spare time: *Hivac Ltd* v *Park Royal Scientific Instruments Ltd* [1946] Ch 169. And, as seen in *Thomas Marshall* v *Guinle*, implied terms relating to fidelity and good faith will be implied very easily: they are effectively a 'fall-back' for missing or badly drafted express terms.

The implied duty is usually expressed as a *negative* responsibility, i.e., a duty not to use or disclose confidential information acquired during the course of employment (*Thomas Marshall* v *Guinle*), not to make unauthorised copies of documents (*Robb* v *Green* [1895] 2 QB 315), nor deliberately to memorise documents for further use after the relationship has ended (*Johnson & Bloy* v *Wolstenholme Rink plc and Fallon* [1987] IRLR 499).

The compass of the duty is also said to expand with the level of seniority of the employee. Such a statement can mislead, however, for most employees who would be likely to come in contact with confidential information will be expected to behave in a similar manner. It is unrealistic to think of 'fidelity' and 'super fidelity' in the abstract. To say that a financial manager owes a greater duty of fidelity than a manual worker is a statement of the obvious because of the level of information available to each, and to this extent therefore the duty of confidentiality does indeed vary with status. But to say that a senior researcher owes a substantially (or even measurably) higher level of confidentiality than that expected of a junior researcher working on the same project is to create a distinction without any real difference. What may change is the degree of *positive* duties expected of different types of employees (see **7.4.3** below).

The duty of confidentiality owed by an employee whilst the contract subsists is now different in nature from that owed by former employees. The case of *Faccenda Chicken* v *Fowler* [1986] ICR 297 drew a clear distinction between the responsibilities owed by present and former employees. It was said in *Faccenda* that the only implied term which continues after the contract has ended is that the employee must still respect the employer's *trade secrets* to the same extent as when the contract subsisted; other confidential information will not be protected and, indeed, (*obiter*) *cannot* be protected by an express term either. We will return to this below in **7.6**.

7.3 What makes information confidential?

Anyone seeking an injunction to restrain the use or disclosure of confidential information will be called upon to specify the secrecy element; to give clear particulars of the information. It will not suffice for an employer merely to say that there is *some* confidential information in need of protection. In *Thomas Marshall* v *Guinle* (**7.2.1.1** above), Megarry V-C also noted that something which is public property and public knowledge cannot be confidential.

So there is a prerequisite that the information must not be in the public domain already. There are *five* additional elements to be identified:

(a) Does the employer believe that the information is of a kind whereby disclosure would harm the business? What amount of effort or expediture has been expended by the employer in developing the information? What is the value of the information to the employer and to any competitor?

(b) Does the employer believe the information is secret, i.e., that it has not become public knowledge?

(c) Are these reasonable beliefs? For instance, what has the employer done to protect the secrecy of the information? How widely is the information disseminated within the organisation? How easily can the information be acquired or duplicated by others?

(d) The information must be judged in the light of the usage and practices of the particular industry or trade.

(e) The maintenance of secrecy must not offend the public interest.

7.3.1 What kind of information is capable of attracting protection?

The range is extensive. The list would include chemical formulae; customer lists; sales figures; drawings; industrial designs; fashion designs; details of an invention currently under development; information contained in computer programs; computer access codes; discount concessions given to customers; delivery route plans; research papers; financial and other reports; and, of course, state official secrets. All of these items and more are *capable* of being classed as confidential. The information may be of a technical, commercial or even personal nature, but it should have what has been termed a 'basic quality of inaccessibility' about it. The mere fact that other companies are willing to pay for the information in question does not, however, mean the information is confidential: *Potters-Ballotini* v *Weston-Baker* [1977] RPC 202.

Equally, confidential information does not have to be *novel* to draw protection. It is the *security* of secrets that matters, not inventiveness. Thus a company has the right to protect all information which relates to the running of a business provided the company has not already made the information public knowledge.

Whilst the employment relationship continues the employer can rely heavily on the duty of fidelity to ensure that secrets are protected. The grade of that information (trade secret or merely confidential) does not really matter. The employee will be expected to observe the duty of confidentiality in either case unless the employer takes no steps to preserve the confidentiality of information or takes inadequate steps to inform employees that they are under such a duty.

7.3.2 What is expected of the employer?

An employer can exercise a great degree of control in this area. Reliance on the implied terms is probably safe in most situations during employment, though it will not guarantee safety (where, for example, security is so lax as to show lack of interest). So even during the currency of the employment relationship an employer is well advised to:

(a) ensure that employees are informed as to their duty in respect of confidential information;

(b) ensure that any changes in company policy, the status or responsibility of the employee, or changes in access to information, are made clear to the employee;

(c) restrict access to information which the employer believes is confidential;

(d) detail in writing any information which might not normally be classified as confidential in that industry but which the employer has special reason to regard as such.

On this last point, any classification should not be too restrictive; a detailed and closed list might be deemed to exclude other information. Some companies issue a detailed explanation of what was meant by 'confidential information'; in each case the list is declared as not being exhaustive as a definition. As regards the ability of employers to monitor employees' communications, see **7.8.4** below.

7.3.3 Information in the public domain

Once information is in the public domain it is no longer confidential and so not protectable. This general statement is subject to a number of explanatory caveats. Megarry V-C was anxious to point out in *Thomas Marshall* v *Guinle*, for instance, that just because an item has been constructed from *materials* which themselves are in the public domain does not mean the *preparatory information* fails the confidentiality test, for the ingenuity in constructing the finished item may be the confidential information, not the final product *per se*. The fact that competitors or others might eventually ascertain how and why the information was used to produce an item, e.g., the basis for combining certain features, does not destroy confidentiality—at least in the meantime: see *Weir Pumps Ltd* v *CML Pumps Ltd* [1984] FSR 33. The specific 'secret', its unique attributes, must be capable of being precisely identified (see also **7.7** below).

During the currency of the contract, therefore, an employee will not be free to disclose information even if it has entered the public domain, provided there is still an element of confidentiality attached to the processes behind the product or service. The confidentiality might, for instance, be founded on the reason why certain microchips were rejected rather than why one was chosen. But the duty of fidelity is so fundamental to the employment relationship that it is not understating the position to say that the employee will be bound by practically any confidence *during* the operation of the contract.

7.3.4 The springboard doctrine

Inextricably tied in with the 'public domain' point is the springboard doctrine. The term 'springboard' highlights the fact that the design of something may be as important as its features. The doctrine was the brainchild of Roxburgh J in *Terrapin Ltd* v *Builders' Supply Co (Hayes) Ltd* [1960] RPC 128. The springboard doctrine is used by the courts in two ways:

(a) Where an individual is making use of information which he or she has taken (effectively stolen) from the former employer. In *Roger Bullivant* v *Ellis* [1987] ICR 464, an employee (managing director) resigned his employment and launched a competing business. He took with him various documents containing technical and commercial information, including trade secrets and a card index of customers. There is no doubt about the secrecy of the information in such instances. The fact that the lists *could* have been compiled legitimately from other sources was deemed irrelevant. In this sense the courts use the term to denote the length that any injunction should last, which will be until the ex-employee has ceased to gain any advantage from the information. The basis for the claim is the breach of confidence (not merely any breach of contract) by the employee during the currency of the contract. This breach continues to have an effect even after termination and can therefore form the basis of a claim for damages and injunctive relief.

(b) When the information has entered the public domain but the *background knowledge* of the product or process gives the employee an advantage or headstart over those who also have access to that publicised information. Here the employee will not be allowed to take advantage of such an edge to take the appropriate short cuts in development of the product. In such cases the idea of 'springboard' is very difficult to apply in practice.

A 'springboard injunction' can thus operate even if there is no express contractual clause preventing use or disclosure, particularly as regards (a) above. Neither does it matter that the information is not of a highly confidential nature or even that the information is no longer confidential (though this will be a factor when an interim injunction is being sought: *Sun Valley Foods Ltd* v *John Philip Vincent* [2000] FSR 825), for it is the unfair advantage gained by the ex-employee that is the key feature.

7.3.5 The maintenance of secrecy must not offend the public interest

7.3.5.1 What is the public interest?

In *Gartside* v *Outram* (1857) 26 LJ Ch 113 at p. 114, Sir Wiliam Page Wood V-C declared that 'There is no confidence as to the disclosure of iniquity'. Under the common law, therefore an employee was not acting in breach of confidence by disclosing the employer's wrongdoings as such disclosures were in the public interest: *Lion Laboratories Ltd* v *Evans* [1984] 2 All ER 417. The case law shows that disclosure had to be made to the appropriate bodies, usually the police, regulatory and professional bodies or even Royal Commissions (newspapers have been occasionally accepted but with criticism: *Initial Services Ltd* v *Putterill* [1968] 1 QB 396).

The defence of public interest disclosure has been applied to all types of information and many different activities; the employer's criminal behaviour has not been a pre-requisite.

The defence has, however, not extended to the 'public good', e.g., disclosing the suppression of the apocryphal everlasting lightbulb.

7.3.5.2 The Public Interest Disclosure Act 1998

This Act affords special protection for 'whistle-blowers' in defined circumstances. The Act is convoluted at best, but its aim is to give protection to workers (not just employees, but also independent contractors and third-party contractors) who disclose specified forms of information using the procedures laid out in the Act. That protection focuses on providing rights to workers in cases of action short of dismissal being taken against them as well as dismissal itself following their disclosure of information. We will return to the dismissal aspect more fully in **Chapter 10** (at **10.8.7.3**).

Our concern here is to note the types of information that fall within the Act and the procedures to be utilised in order to gain protection. Strictly speaking, the Act does not deal with the question whether a relevant disclosure is a breach of confidence, but it must be assumed that the effect of this Act will be to re-define this area.

The information disclosed

The Public Interest Disclosure Act (PIDA) 1998 creates a new s. 43B to the ERA 1996. Section 43B provides that for a worker to gain protection:

(a) the disclosure in question must be a 'qualifying disclosure';

(b) the worker must have followed the correct procedure on disclosure; and

(c) the worker must have suffered a detriment or have been dismissed as a result of all this (see **10.8.7.3** on the last point).

A 'qualifying disclosure' means one that, in the reasonable belief of the worker, tends to show one or more of the following (occurring anywhere in the world):

(a) that a criminal offence has been committed or is likely to be so;

(b) that a person has failed, is failing or is likely to fail to comply with any legal obligation to which he or she is subject. In *Parkins* v *Sodexho Ltd* [2002] IRLR 109, the EAT held that the idea of a 'legal obligation' was not limited to statutory obligations and could encompass complaints made by the employee that the contract had been breached. The decision, however, was not given with the greatest conviction ('We find it difficult to define the spirit of this sort of legislation or to be confident that we know about it, but it certainly comes within the letter of the provision, on a literal interpretation.') and we await further analysis of this dubious line of argument;

(c) that a miscarriage of justice has occurred or is likely to occur;

(d) that the health or safety of any individual has been, is being or is likely to be endangered;

(e) that the environment has been, is being or is likely to be damaged;

(f) that information tending to show any matter falling within any of the above has been, is being or is likely to be deliberately concealed.

Note that the standard is the reasonable belief of the worker, but the protection does not apply where the worker commits a criminal offence in making the disclosure. Reasonable belief is judged against the standards of good faith. Although an employee can be mistaken but still act in good faith (what the Americans call the 'pure heart but empty head test'), where there is a predominant ulterior motive for making the disclosure this may destroy the element of good faith: *Street* v *Derbyshire Unemployed Workers Centre* [2004] EWCA Civ 964, [2004] I.R.L.R. 687 (e.g., personal antagonism).

The procedures

The Act sets out the ways in which a disclosure may be made in order to gain protection. These are:

(a) disclosures to the worker's employer or other responsible person: s. 43C, ERA 1996;

(b) disclosures made in the course of obtaining legal advice: s. 43D;

(c) disclosures to a Minister of the Crown, under s. 43E, where the worker's employer is an individual appointed under any enactment by a Minister of the Crown;

(d) disclosures to a 'prescribed person': s. 43F. The list of prescribed persons is set out in the Public Interest Disclosure (Prescribed Persons) Order 1999, SI 1999/1549 and includes people such as the Information Commissioner, the Civil Aviation Authority, the Environment Agency and the Health and Safety Executive.

Additionally, where the worker cannot follow the above procedural lines of communication, disclosures made in good faith and without personal gain (except as provided for under an enactment) will be permitted to other people:

(a) in 'other cases' which fall within the guidelines laid out in s. 43G. Essentially these are instances where the worker reasonably believes that the employer will subject them to a detriment if they follow the procedure noted in s. 43C; or where there is no 'prescribed person' and the worker reasonably believes that evidence may be concealed or destroyed; or where disclosures have been made to the relevant people before. The reasonableness of the worker's actions are decided by reference to matters such as the seriousness of the relevant failure, whether the disclosure is made in breach of the duty of confidentiality, etc.

(b) in cases of 'exceptionally serious' breaches: s. 43H. The bypassing of the noted procedures is again allowed where the worker acts in good faith and without personal gain. In determining the reasonableness of the worker's actions, it is specifically provided that regard must be had to the identity of the person to whom the disclosure was made, i.e., as with the common law before, merely running to the press without thought is frowned upon.

Once a whistle-blowing worker has complied with the above requirements, he or she will gain protection from a dismissal related to the disclosure, etc., as set out in **10.8.7.3** below. It is worth noting here, however, that s. 43J of ERA 1996 provides that any term in the worker's contract which purports to prevent any worker from making a protected disclosure (i.e., a gagging clause) will be void. We should also note here that there may be cases where the employee has to decide whether to utilise these procedures or the statutory grievance procedures described in **Chapter 5**. In such a case, it is up to the employee, faced with the employer's actions, to decide whether to pursue a grievance (if indeed it falls within the definition noted at **5.3.2** above) or to make a protected disclosure. Where the employee is thinking both about the employer's practice and also about the effect on his individual position (and so contemplating tribunal action) it is likely that the employee would pursue the grievance procedures.

7.3.5.3 Anonymity of accusers

In a closely-related area, the High Court has held that an employee who is dismissed owing to allegations made to the employer by a third party is entitled to know the identity of any anonymous informant and to see details of the allegations: *A* v *B Ltd* [1997] IRLR 405. This decision extends the guidelines laid down by the EAT in *Linfood Cash & Carry Ltd* v *Thomson* [1989] ICR 518, which sought to allow the accused as fair a hearing as possible in such circumstances. However, this development may well have the effect both of enhancing the accused's chances to respond *and* of discouraging informants, thereby making management's task more difficult. The onus, however, still lies on the accused to convince the High Court to order the release of such information on the grounds of the possibility of defamation.

7.4 The duty owed by employees

As we have seen, the identification of the employee's duties is a fairly straightforward exercise. Closely linked with the duty of confidentiality are the rules covering the soliciting of clients and customers for the employee's own purposes. Again, reasonably clear guidelines can be offered as to employees working for rival firms or generally 'moonlighting', during or after the relationship. We have noted these anti-competition aspects in **Chapter 5** and will return to them in **Chapter 8**. For the moment we can say that an employee will be forbidden from competing with the employer during the currency of the contract if harm is likely to be occasioned.

What follows is therefore an examination of what is expected of the employee as regards the use of information: how is the employee's duty formulated? We shall explore the following:

(a) What level of information is protected.

(b) The role of honesty.

(c) The positive duty to disclose details about oneself and others.

7.4.1 What level of information is protected?

The general extent of this topic has been discussed at **7.3** above. To this we add one further question: can trivia be the subject of a duty of confidentiality? One would think not; though defining trivia might prove difficult. So the fact that the company chairman has a cat called Henry or budgerigar called Bertie is hardly deserving of protection. However, information need not be complex in order to attract protection. As was noted in *Coco* v *Clark (A. N.) (Engineers) Ltd* [1969] RPC 41, the simpler the idea the more likely it is to require protection. In the same case, however, Megarry J also noted that 'equity ought not to be invoked to protect trivial tittle-tattle, however confidential'.

Unfortunately, the assessment of 'trivia', like one's grasp of 'general knowledge' in a game of Trivial Pursuit, is subjective—the 'How come you always get the easy questions?' approach. In different contexts information may be trivial or important. What biscuits the chairman has with his tea strikes a chord of irrelevancy, unless the information reveals that the company produces biscuits and these are either 'test' biscuits or biscuits from another manufacturer. And when pieces of information are put together the sum might be greatly more significant than the parts—the individual pieces of the jigsaw might now reveal a discernible picture.

The safest presumption to make, therefore, is that during the currency of the contract any doubt is likely to be decided in favour of the employer. In reality, this is not so much a question of confidentiality as one of fidelity. If there is doubt, then company documentation which seeks to define more precisely what is confidential is an advisable precaution.

7.4.2 The role of honesty

An employee is expected to act with honesty. With regard to confidentiality the most obvious example of this is that the employee will not be permitted to copy or memorise confidential documents for use after the contract ends. Companies often include such a term demanding 'delivery up' of such items as books, records, computer software, memoranda, lists and other documents relating to the business of the company on termination of the contract.

Thus, copying and deliberately memorising lists (see *Roger Bullivant* v *Ellis* at **7.3.4**) have been held to be actions which restrict the employee's use of that information. In the area of unfair dismissal, cases such as *Denco Ltd* v *Joinson* [1991] ICR 172 show the importance that the courts place on the gaining of access to confidential information. The employee was a trade union shop steward who gained access to computer files using another employee's identity code and password. The employee claimed this was an accidental, isolated incident. The information would have been of use to the trade union in negotiations. This was found to constitute gross misconduct, analogous to dishonesty. The EAT held that it was irrelevant that the employers had not proven the purpose of access was for illegitimate reasons.

However, the employer's casual or careless approach to the information will mean that the employer may be deprived of protection. To ensure protection from the courts, therefore, any express term should specifically include a phrase to impose a duty of confidentiality on employees who receive information from whatever source and by whatever means. There should be specific reference made to this in disciplinary procedures. In *Denco* v *Joinson* the EAT stated that there should be clear indications placed in areas of restricted access or alongside computers to the same effect.

7.4.3 To what extent the duty requires positive action on the part of the employee

As well as the duty *not to disclose* confidential information, an employee (at least a senior employee) also owes a positive duty to surrender information relevant to the relationship, e.g., where an employee detects patterns in the market which might have an adverse or beneficial effect on the employer's business: see *Sanders* v *Parry* [1967] 1 WLR 753, *Industrial Development Consultants* v *Cooley* [1972] 1 WLR 443 and *General Nutritions Ltd* v *Yates, The Times*, 5 June 1981. In *MacMillan Inc.* v *Bishopsgate Investment Trust plc* [1993] 1 WLR 1372, however, this general duty was limited to information obtained *in the course of employment*. The Court of Appeal held that the employer did not have a right to demand a copy of a transcript of evidence given by the employee to liquidators under s. 236 of the Insolvency Act 1986 as the information (although obtained in the employment relationship) was not *provided* by the employee in the course of his employment.

The ILU Survey (referred to in the Preface) did not reveal a common pattern in this area. Some draft precedents did indeed include a duty to surrender information gained in the course of employment, but most contracts (if dealing with positive duties at all) focused on a term requiring the employee to do all that was reasonable to *prevent* disclosures. This clause is, of course, aimed mainly at those in managerial positions.

But the idea of positive duties becomes more problematic when it involves self-incrimination. In the absence of fraud there is no duty to volunteer information regarding the employee's own misconduct: *Bell* v *Lever Brothers* [1932] AC 161. However, in *Swain* v *West (Butchers) Ltd* [1936] 3 All ER 261, it was held that employees were under a duty to notify their employer of the misconduct of their fellow employees. When these two principles were combined in the case of *Sybron Corp.* v *Rochem* [1983] ICR 801, the finding was that there is a duty, at least incumbent on senior management whose responsibilities are affected by the actions, to notify the employer of serious breaches by fellow employees even when that involves selfincrimination (as was the case here).

In this context one should also note the limited effects of the Rehabilitation of Offenders Act 1974 regarding statements of 'spent' convictions.

7.5 The duty owed by former employees

Most disclosures or use of information are likely to occur once the employee has left the company. It is here that the real battle lines are drawn. The courts are wary of imposing the same level of duty on former employees as is placed on existing employees. Partly this is because once the employee has left then any fetters placed on the exercise of that person's skill, expertise, technical competence or general ability to earn a living could be disastrous to the employee (see also **Chapter 8**).

This is a complex area, and one which demands that the practitioner makes a number of judgment calls, often based on commercial or scientific practices. Many LPC students find that 'flow charts' can at least help to reduce some of the problems and so we have tried in **Figure 7.1** to map out the basic analytical structures employed by practitioners. This diagram shows you the overall pattern of analysis, but we shall repeat the diagram with highlighted sections to accompany the relevant text.

The key questions we need to address are:

- Does it matter how the contract came to an end?
- What sort of information is protectable? In particular, can an employer prevent an employee making use of the employee's own skill and knowledge acquired during his employment?

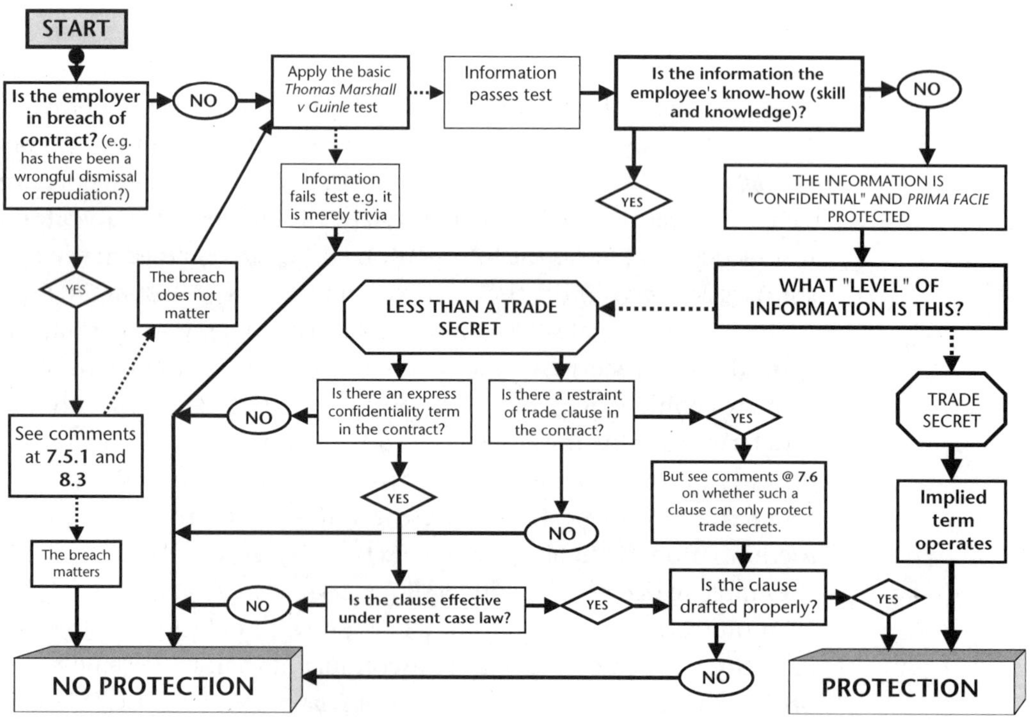

Figure 7.1 Diagrammatic summary.

- If the information is protectable, does this mean that all confidential information gains protection or are there further limitations?
- What is the protection offered by the law (i.e., what are the remedies for breach of confidence)?

7.5.1 The importance of how the contract came to an end

In some instances ex-employees may be relieved of any post-termination duties owed to their former employer. The most obvious instance as regards confidentiality is where the employer puts the information into the public domain. The next most common method occurs when the employer wrongfully dismisses the employee or wrongfully repudiates the contract of employment. Wrongful dismissal will be dealt with in depth in **Chapter 9**. For the moment, we can say that a *wrongful dismissal* occurs where the employer terminates the contract without giving the employee due notice; a *wrongful repudiation* occurs where the employer breaches the contract and the employee resigns as a consequence.

However, although case law on the efficacy of restraint of trade clauses established this idea as long ago as 1909 (see **8.3** below), there has been no direct authority on whether a wrongful dismissal or wrongful repudiation affects the validity of either the implied term or any express term of *confidentiality*, and practitioners have been divided on this one. The only case to comment on the topic of confidentiality has been *Campbell* v *Frisbee* [2002] EWCA Civ 1374, [2003] ICR 141, where, on an appeal based on an application for summary judgment, Lightman J had to decide whether an express confidentiality term survived a repudiatory breach (here, an alleged assault by the model, Naomi Campbell) on her ex-personal assistant. Their relationship, however, was one of a contract *for* services so any comments on the position of employees had to be *obiter*. Lightman J held: (a) that Ms Campbell's confidentiality regarding her private life was a form of property and this could not be destroyed by a repudiatory breach; (b) *(obiter)* the same would apply to employment relationships had this been one (an observation itself based on *obiter* statements in a Court of Appeal case on restraint of trade, *Rock Refrigeration Ltd* v *Jones* [1997] ICR 938).

Ms Frisbee's appeal from this decision to the Court of Appeal was successful, but only on the ground that the issue of law involved was not suitable for summary determination under Part 24 CPR. However, Lord Phillips MR also commented, again *obiter*, (at [22]) that,

> We do not believe that the effect on duties of confidence assumed under contract when the contract in question is wrongfully repudiated is clearly established. While we do not consider that it is likely that Miss Frisbee will establish that Lightman J erred in his conclusions in a manner detrimental to her case, it cannot be said that she has no reasonable prospect of success on the issue.

We have argued in previous editions of this book that a serious breach of contract by the employer *should* invalidate both express confidentiality terms (for the same reasons that restraint clauses are so affected) and the implied term of confidentiality (because this is based on the implied term of 'good faith' which has its roots in equity), but, for the moment at least, these cumulative *obiter* comments present the strongest authority we have on the matter—and they essentially say, we are wrong.

The highlighted boxes in **Figure 7.2** illustrate the place of this argument in the overall structure. The dotted lines denote the different consequences. You can see that if there has been no breach or the case law makes the breach irrelevant, the next step in the analysis is to apply the *Thomas Marshall* v *Guinle* test noted above at **7.2.1** and **7.2.2**.

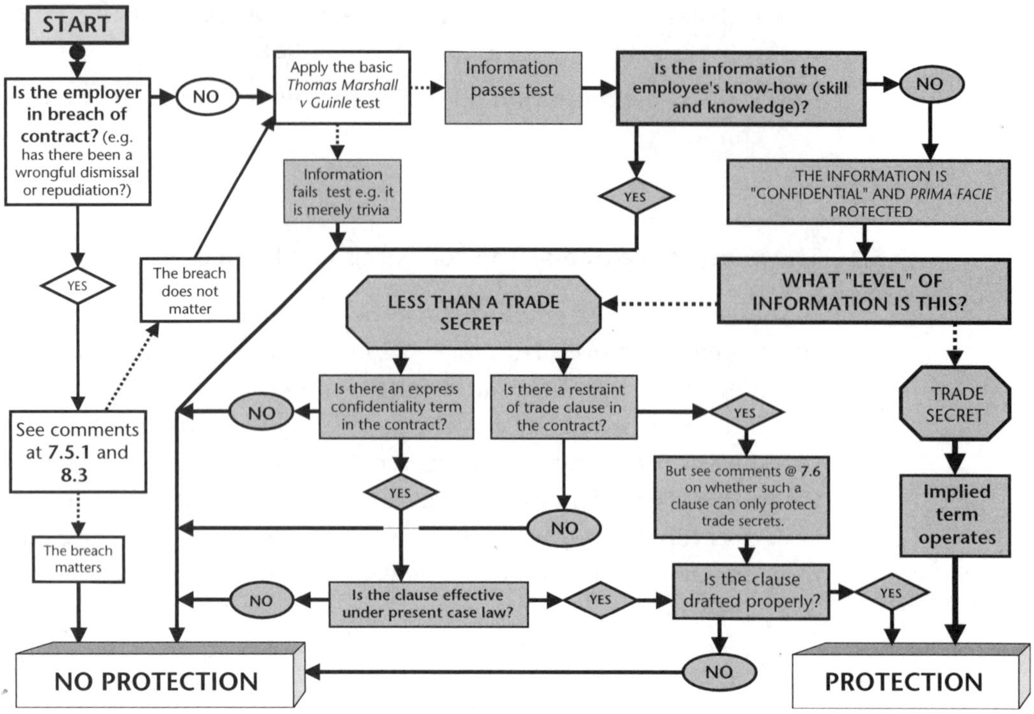

Figure 7.2 Effect of termination on the duty of confidentiality.

7.5.2 Information: the basic protection

The *Thomas Marshall* v *Guinle* test is essentially a simple one, requiring us to determine whether or not the employer has done something which shows the information is confidential and that it is not already in the public domain. **Figure 7.3** takes us down that simple analysis, but then leads us to the very vexed question of whether the information is in reality the employee's 'know-how'. Again, the highlighted boxes in illustrate the place of this argument in the overall structure.

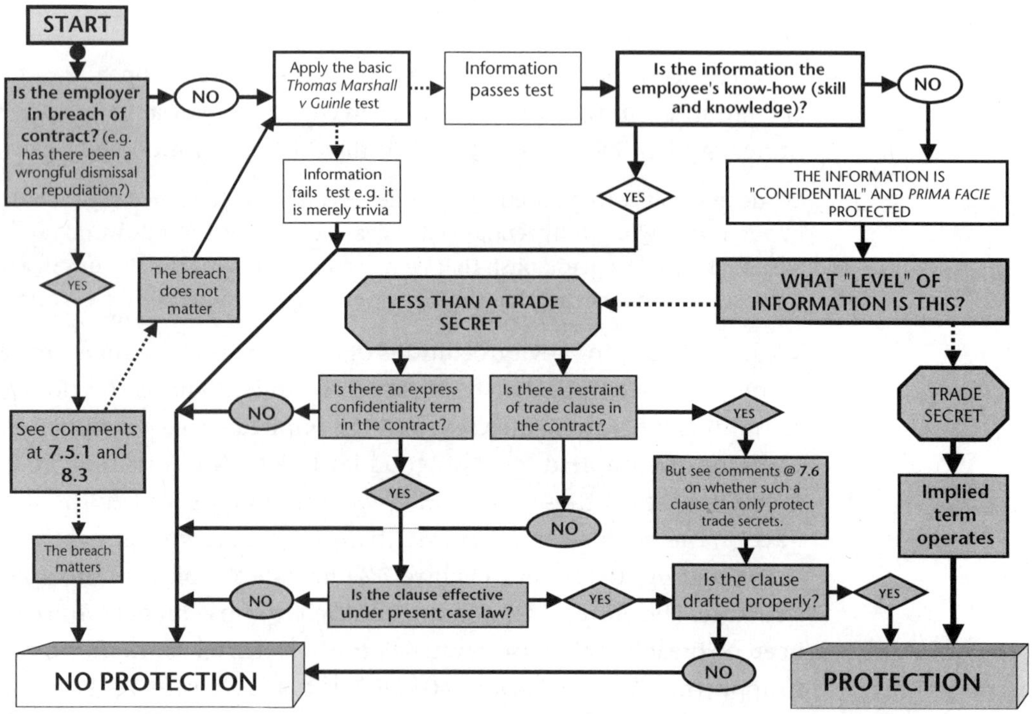

Figure 7.3 What sort of information is protectable?

7.5.3 Information: distinguishing employees' know-how

Exactly what information will constitute an employee's 'know-how' (otherwise referred to as the employee's 'skill and knowledge'), as opposed to the employer's confidential information, is a difficult judgment call even for experienced practitioners. We would suggest that, in essence, *technical information* is likely to belong to the employer whereas *the technique* of performing the job belongs to the employee.

In *FSS Travel and Leisure Systems Ltd* v *Johnson* [1998] IRLR 382 (a restraint of trade case based on the protection of confidential information), for instance, the Court of Appeal again confirmed that the exercise of an employee's skill, experience, know-how and general knowledge cannot be controlled by a former employer. This will apply whether that employer is claiming the information is a trade secret or under an express confidentiality clause. Indeed, the *FSS Travel* case shows how difficult the line between know-how and confidential information can be to draw sometimes. Here the company was seeking to show that, as the ex-employee programmer knew that a program could be run to produce a certain effect (e.g., to obtain credit card bookings), the knowledge of this *design solution* could be applied in competitors' systems so that mere disclosure of the solution could be damaging to the company. Thus, it was not the detailed knowledge of the 2,852 programs that was at issue but the knowledge of what the programmes could achieve by way of problem-solving. The company's claim failed; this was skill and knowledge.

Although the cases cannot be said to describe clear tests, certain features can be discovered in order to identify employees' know-how. Anything which relates to general methods of performing the company's business rather than information related to particular negotiations or transactions is likely to be classed as know-how. Equally, knowledge which is not 'readily separable' from the employee's general knowledge and which is 'inevitably', 'necessarily', or 'naturally' acquired in the course of employment will also be know-how. Thus, methods of working and industrial practices will be more difficult than facts and figures to label as one or the other. In *Ocular Science Ltd* v *Aspect Vision Care Ltd* [1997] RPC 289 at 370 Laddie J. put it this way:

> ... [F]or public policy reasons, an employee is entitled to use and put at the disposal of new employers all his acquired skill and knowledge. That is so, no matter where he acquired that skill and knowledge and whether it is secret or was so at the time he acquired it. Where the employer's right to restrain misuse of his confidential information collides with the public policy, it is the latter which prevails. The critical question is how to distinguish information, which can be treated as an employee's acquired skill and knowledge from that which is not.

One final point here: something does not become part of the employee's know-how merely because he or she has copied or memorised the information. In *PSM International plc* v *Whitehouse* [1992] IRLR 279 the Court of Appeal noted that there was a difference between the typical confidential information cases which involved using or disclosing information, and those of the 'copying and taking' variety (such as *Robb* v *Green* and *Roger Bullivant* v *Ellis*) where the information in question takes a more tangible form and could be protected under the springboard doctrine. It was suggested that the 'springboard doctrine' (see above at **7.3.4**) could be used as *an alternative method* of protecting information which did not qualify as a trade secret. In line with this the Court of Appeal has confirmed that information which is carried away in the employee's head does not automatically belong to the employee (*Johnson & Bloy* v *Wolstenholme Rink PLC and Fallon* [1987] IRLR 499). Nor does ownership of the information depend on whether the information was or was not learned with the deliberate intent to misuse. Even where the employee has memorised information without any thought of misuse it is an objective test whether that information belongs to the employer or not: *SBJ Stephenson* v *Mandy* [2000] IRLR 233. You can see from **Figure 7.3** above that, if the information can be classed as something other than the employee's know-how one must still ask what *level* of information is it? For even if the information is 'confidential', not all types of confidential information will be protected.

7.5.4 Levels of information: defining trade secrets

An employer will gain the protection of the law for all information which is either a *trade secret eo nomine* (by that name) or *information akin to a trade secret*. That protection arises from the continuing nature of the implied duty of good faith/fidelity which is present in all employment relationships and which is deemed to run on even after the contract has been terminated. This is shown in **Figure 7.4**.

Until the case of *Faccenda Chicken* v *Fowler* [1986] ICR 297 the term 'trade secret' simply meant anything that was not the employee's know-how. Use of this 'know-how' could not—and still cannot—restrict the activities of former employees; but anything which was not part of an employee's know-how was referred to as the employer's 'trade secret' and *prima facie* could be protected. That was the traditional distinction. However, as we shall see in more detail below, in *Faccenda Chicken* Neill LJ created a further distinction, dividing an employer's confidential information into two categories: (a) trade secrets, which could be protected by the implied term of good faith; and (b) information which, though confidential, was not important enough to be classed as a trade secret and so not protected by the implied term.

Neill LJ sought to identify what would make information a 'trade secret'. He listed the following points as a general guide:

(a) *The nature of the employment*—where 'confidential' material is habitually handled by the employee this may impose a high obligation of confidentiality.

(b) *The nature of the information itself*—a limited circulation list for the information may indicate a higher level of secrecy.

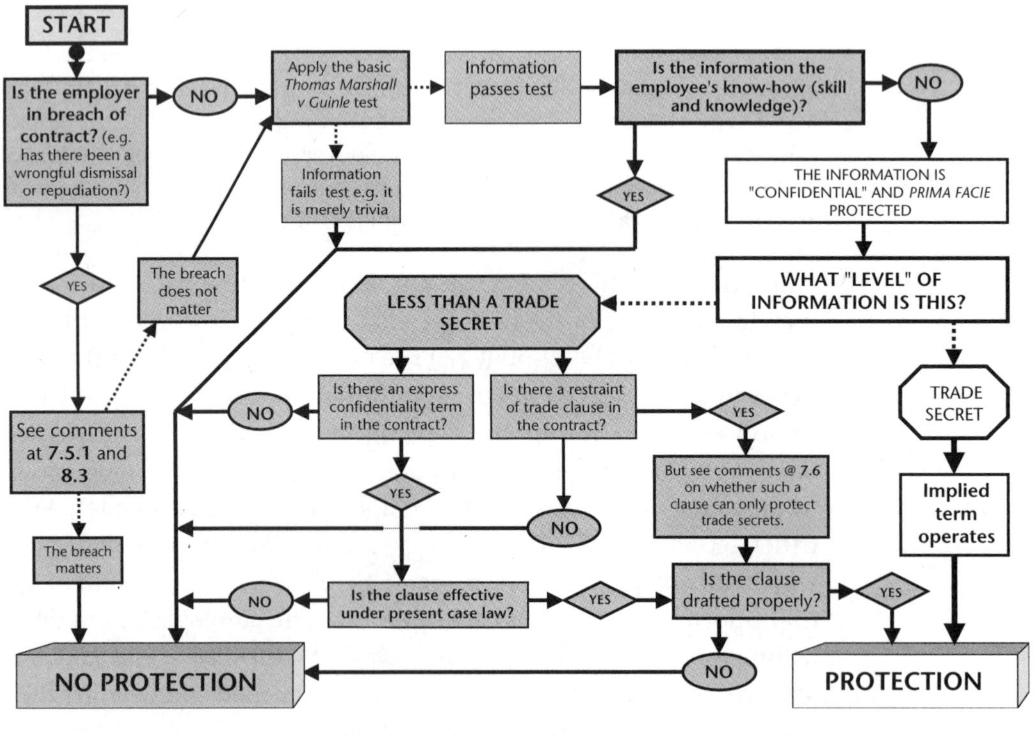

Figure 7.4 Trade secrets and the implied term of good faith.

(c) *Whether the employer impressed on the employee the confidentiality of the information.*

(d) *Whether the relevant information can be easily isolated from other information which the employee is free to use or disclose.*

The courts have obviously become wary of making the criteria too restrictive in deciding what information should be classed as a trade secret. Equally, the mere designation of information as either 'confidential' or as a 'trade secret' does not determine the matter; though in borderline cases it may be persuasive. The information must also have passed the *Thomas Marshall* v *Guinle* [1978] ICR 905 basic test (see **7.3**).

As Neill LJ noted, it is impossible to provide a definitive list of trade secrets or their equivalent. Secret processes of manufacture provide obvious examples, but innumerable other pieces of information are *capable* of being trade secrets. With a heavy defensive *caveat* our suggestions for classification are:

(a) The information must provide a competitive edge so that disclosure would cause significant harm to the employer.

(b) The information must be inaccessible to the rest of the industry.

(c) There must be proof that serious attempts have been made to limit and safeguard the dissemination of the material within the company.

(d) The 'pure and applied research' cases tend to cause fewer problems so that it is reasonably safe to give the tag of trade secret to:

  (i) inventions (patentable and not patentable);

  (ii) technical or design data and specifications;

  (iii) specific technical processes of construction and manufacture;

  (iv) test performance figures for a new product;

  (v) chemical and other formulae;

  (vi) craft secrets;

  (vii) secret recipes.

(e) Which business secrets are the equivalent of trade secrets is a more difficult question. The names and commercial preferences of customers, for instance, can obviously amount to sensitive information and, in some cases, might be so highly confidential and useful to a business as to amount to a trade secret. That commercial information might be as deserving of the same level of protection offered to more traditional 'scientific' trade secrets was a principle recognised in *Lansing Linde Ltd* v *Kerr* [1991] 1 All ER 418. There, for instance, Butler-Sloss LJ commented that the term 'trade secret' has to be 'interpreted in the wider context of highly confidential information of a non-technical or non-scientific nature'. With that in mind, we offer the following points as to what business secrets may amount to trade secrets:

  (i) manufacturer's 'know-how' (as distinct from the employee's know-how). By this we mean the *particular applications* of technology unique to that company and which are not part of public knowledge. This might extend to things such as specific and detailed 'quality control' procedures developed by the company;

  (ii) customer lists when connected to things such as discount or purchasing policies and which are not otherwise available. Although customer pricing lists were not protected in *Faccenda*, this should not be taken as a rule of universal application because (as was noted by Staughton LJ's in *Lansing Linde* v *Kerr* and again in *Frayling Furniture Ltd* v *Premier Upholstery Ltd* (1998, unreported, ChD) and in *SBJ Stephenson* v *Mandy* the importance of these lists and their relative secrecy may matter a great deal to particular companies' business;

(iii) operative tenders and quotations which have not been published;

(iv) detailed plans for expansion and market projections;

(v) computer software containing novel features;

(vi) access codes for computers and secure areas.

7.5.5 Levels of information: other confidential information

Neill LJ's guidelines for determining whether information meets the test of being a trade secret are used widely; but there was a more controversial aspect to his Lordship's judgment. Neill LJ also decided that information which ranked lower than a trade secret not only failed to gain the protection of the implied term but also could not be protected by the use of an express confidentiality clause. His Lordship then speculated that such information might be protectable by means of a restraint of trade clause. There was no express confidentiality term in *Faccenda Chicken* so, strictly, this point is *obiter*. Nevertheless, as you will see, this aspect of the case has caused problems.

The question of how to deal with information which is confidential but does not rank as a trade secret is a complicated one, but it lies at the heart of how practitioners deal with matters of confidentiality, both from a litigation and drafting perspective. To best explain this, therefore, instead of going straight to the next diagram we have laid out the text in section **7.6** in the following order:

- Description of *Faccenda Chicken* v *Fowler*.
- The case law since *Faccenda Chicken*.
- The practical effects.

The relevant diagrams (**Figures 7.5 and 7.6**) appear after this discussion.

7.6 *Faccenda Chicken* v *Fowler*

Fowler was employed as a sales manager for the company. He established a system of selling fresh chickens from refrigerated vans and subsequently resigned to set up a similar business which would compete with Faccenda Chicken. He took a number of Faccenda's employees with him. It was alleged that Fowler and the others had used and disclosed information, derived from Faccenda's operations, in their new business. The information related to delivery routes, customers' addresses, delivery times, and pricing policy. Faccenda sought an injunction to prevent the use and disclosure of this information.

7.6.1 *Faccenda Chicken* in the High Court

Goulding J (after a 39-day trial) refused the injunction. He stated, 'In my view information acquired by an employee in the course of his service, *and not the subject of any relevant express agreement*, may fall as regards confidence into any of three classes' (emphasis added for reasons noted below). His classification was:

Category 1: Trivia and information easily accessible from public sources (e.g., a published patent specification). This information cannot be protected.

Category 2: Information which the employee must treat as confidential during employment but 'which once learned necessarily remains in the servant's head and becomes part of his skill and knowledge'. On leaving employment the employee can make use of this knowledge. The only form of protection open to the employer is a non-competition restraint of trade clause.

Category 3: Specific trade secrets, which are automatically protected for their life-span by the implied term of fidelity or good faith.

Goulding J held that the information in this case fell into category 2. As it did not make it into the trade secrets category and there was no restraint of trade or express confidentiality clause in the contracts of employment, the information was not protected. This looks fairly straightforward, but the apparent simplicity hides some problems.

(a) *The first problem.*

Goulding J's category 2 clearly recognises that there may be information which stands above trivia [category 1], but below trade secrets [category 3] and yet which is still specific enough to the operation of the business that its disclosure might cause harm to the employer (e.g., some pricing or discount policies). But Goulding J rather paints the picture that all such information will fall within an employee's know-how so that the employee can always make use of this category 2 information. His Lordship does, however, add the rider: 'If an employer wants to protect information of this kind, he can do so by express stipulation restraining the servant from competing with him . . . after termination of employment.'

We would respectfully suggest that this is an over-simplification because it implies that, provided the employee can remember the information, it is automatically part of his know-how and if he cannot remember it then it does not matter because he cannot make use of it anyway—subject to copying it, which has always been forbidden. This is superficially attractive but, as we noted in **7.5.3**, some information may fall short of being a trade secret yet still not be the employee's skill and knowledge. So, if there is information in category 2 other than an employee's know-how, is this simply unprotected, or can an employer rely on some form of express term to protect it? Goulding J is silent on this, but the cases he cites rather indicate that there is indeed a distinction between technical information which might be learned but which still belongs to the employer and information which is acquired *and* which becomes part of an employee's know-how (technique).

(b) *The second problem.*

If Goulding J's category 2 information only covers employee know-how, it seems very odd that he feels the employer has the right to restrict the employee's use of this information at all, since know-how belongs to the employee. In support of this analysis, however, Goulding J cited *Printers & Finishers Ltd* v *Holloway* [1965] 1 WLR 1, where Cross J said that, 'if [the employer] is right in thinking that there are features . . . which can fairly be described as trade secrets and which the employees will inevitably carry away with in their heads . . .' then the proper course is to impose a restraint of trade clause. This appears to support Goulding J's analysis but there is a key point: as we noted at **7.5.4**, prior to *Faccenda* the term 'trade secret' was used very loosely by the courts to describe: (a) information which was beyond trivia and was not an employee's skill and knowledge; **and** (b) high-level information which one would recognise as justifying the term 'trade secret'—sometimes referred to in the reports as 'trade secrets in the strictest sense'. In *Printers & Finishers Ltd* v *Holloway* Cross J used the terminology in both ways. What he also said is that, 'If the information in question can fairly be regarded as a separate part of the employee's stock of knowledge which a man of ordinary honesty and intelligence would recognise to be the property of the old employer, and not his own to do as he likes with, then the court, if it thinks there is a danger of the information being used by the ex-employee to the detriment of the old employer will do what it can to prevent that result by granting an injunction. Thus an ex-employee will be restrained from using or disclosing a chemical formula or a list of customers which he has committed to memory'.

On the facts, Cross J appears to have classified the information as the employee's know-how and so refused the injunction. But this analysis clearly recognises that some information, even though learned by the employee, remains the property of the old employer and does not become the employee's know-how.

(c) *The third problem.*

Both Cross and Goulding JJ envisaged a situation where the employer might impose some form of express post-termination covenant which would restrict an employee from making use of information. There are rather contradictory statements as to whether this covenant could be applied to know-how. As noted above, we would submit it is difficult to see how that could be justified. But could such a covenant be workable? We know that trivia cannot be protected at all, and that trade secrets (in the strictest sense) receive automatic protection under the continuing duty of fidelity/good faith. So, this leaves the runt of category 2 information: information of a lower priority than trade secrets; higher than trivia, *but separate from know-how*.

What sort of covenant could be used to protect such information? Here we have another problem with terminology as the cases use different phrases: (a) restrictive covenants; (b) covenants restricting the employee's field of activity; (c) express terms/agreements; and (d) restraint of trade clauses. Goulding J, for instance, uses phrases (c) and (d) interchangeably. We would suggest that the only term which could be relied upon to prevent an employee using or disclosing information which was not a trade secret (in the strictest sense) would be a confidentiality clause. We say this because you will see that restraint of trade clauses are quite Draconian in nature. At one level or another they seek to prevent an employee continuing to work in a particular industry. To permit such a blunderbuss to be used to protect lower-level information is rather heavy-handed. Further, the cases which have allowed a restraint of trade clause to be used to protect confidential information have all centred on high-level information/trade secrets.

There are therefore three possible options as to what Goulding J meant in his judgment:

- That lower-level information *and* skill and knowledge could be protected by a non-competition restraint. This would encounter the 'circular argument' problem noted above;
- That skill and knowledge was not protectable (thus recognising the existing case law) *but that* lower-level information could be protected by a non-competition restraint;
- That lower-level information could be protected by *express agreement* which would certainly include a restraint clause but might also extend to an express confidentiality clause.

7.6.2 *Faccenda Chicken* in the Court of Appeal

In the Court of Appeal, Neill LJ gave the only judgment. His Lordship had some important things to say about defining a 'trade secret' (noted above at **7.5.4**). As to the case, Neill LJ confirmed the decision of Goulding J on the facts but analysed the legal position slightly differently:

(a) The duty of confidentiality owed in employment relationships is based purely on contractual, not equitable, principles;

(b) 'In the absence of any express term, the obligations of the employee in respect of the use and disclosure of information are the subject of implied terms';

(c) The implied term of fidelity or good faith continuing after employment has ended is narrower in its scope that that owed during employment

(d) The obligation of fidelity applies only to trade secrets and other information which is of a sufficiently high degree of confidentiality as to amount to a trade secret. It does not extend to information which is confidential only in the sense that an unauthorised disclosure of such information to a third party while the employment subsisted would be a clear breach of the duty of good faith.

Although put slightly differently, none of this *prima facie* conflicts with Goulding J's reasoning. However, instead of there being three categories of information the Court of Appeal effectively divided information into:

(a) *trade secrets* and things akin to trade secrets (as per Goulding J's category 3). These are deemed protectable; and

(b) *everything else*, ranging from trivia through skill and knowledge and onto the borders of trade secrets (combining Goulding J's category 1 and 2). These are deemed unprotectable.

Point (a) does not present a problem (except for the practical difficulty in actually defining 'trade secrets' for different industries). The problem relates to point (b) and begins to surface when Neill LJ addresses the efficacy of express terms (which, as we have noted, is an *obiter* point). Neill LJ expressly disagreed with Goulding J's analysis on the efficacy of express terms [1986] ICR 310E. His Lordship did not explicitly deal with the question of employees' know-how. Instead, his Lordship took another stance, *viz*, that the case law was clear that a restraint of trade clause would not be upheld unless the information in question was a trade secret or equivalent. Thus, a non-competition restraint clause could not protect Goulding J's category 2 information because it could only apply to trade secrets and category 2 was, by definition, information which falls short of being a trade secret. This is the same argument we have noted as regards know-how and therefore we would respectfully agree with this analysis; but with three important *caveats*:

1. The first point concerns the terminology used by Neill LJ: his Lordship did not actually say that a 'restraint of trade' would be of no use; the term he used was 'a restrictive covenant'. From the context it seems likely that his Lordship meant 'restraint of trade' but the term 'restrictive covenant' is wide enough to encompass an express confidentiality clause of the sort seen in **7.2.1** above. This confusion of terminology is carried through in later cases but the two types of clause perform different functions. To equate confidentiality clauses with Draconian restraint of trade clauses appears to be overkill. Certainly, the two principal cases cited by Neill LJ do not support this, *viz*,: *Printers & Finishers Ltd* v *Holloway* [1965] 1 WLR 1 and *Worsley (E.) & Co. Ltd* v *Cooper* [1939] 1 All ER 290.

We also noted above that one of the principles ventured by Neill LJ was that: 'In the absence of any express term, the obligations of the employee in respect of the use and disclosure of information are the subject of implied terms'. It might well be that that this is simply a general introductory description of the 'restrictive covenant' point. What has confused practitioners, however, is, again, whether this sentence permits or outlaws *express confidentiality clauses*. Shortly after the case the common view was that the language used by Neill LJ made express confidentiality clauses obsolete, but, as we shall see shortly, that is no longer the view generally held.

2. Goulding J's category 2 is a huge mixed band, and some of the information included in this band will fall only just short of being a trade secret. To the extent that Neill LJ sought to make ineffective an express confidentiality clause which related to such high-level information on the margins of trade secrets, we would have to respectfully disagree with his Lordship. The division of information into trade secret (protectable) and other information (ranging from trivia through skill and knowledge and onto high-level information) seems over-simplistic and the authorities cited (e.g., *Herbert Morris Ltd* v *Saxelby* [1916] 1 AC 688) do not support this analysis.

3. If the information is a trade secret it is protected by the implied term of confidentiality anyway so express terms are irrelevant. It is certainly true that a restraint of trade clause is easier to police than an injunction based on confidentiality, but, that aside, the two perform the same function. Thus, what Neill LJ is suggesting is that the already-protected trade secret should be protected (again?) by use of a restraint of trade clause. This seems very odd.

7.6.3 The case law since *Faccenda Chicken*

Most of the points dealt with in *Faccenda* are not controversial, and it has been accepted as the leading authority by all levels of court (though the issue has not been reviewed directly by the House of Lords). However, the question as to the validity of express confidentiality clauses has provoked some debate. It is fair to say that the cases subsequent to *Faccenda* have not cleared the air.

The first key case was *Balston Ltd* v *Headline Filters Ltd* [1987] FSR 330 (though see also Harman J in *Systems Reliability Holdings plc* v *Smith* [1990] IRLR 377). In *Balston* Scott J offered a new interpretation of Neill LJ's judgment. He pointed out that when Neill LJ indicated that 'a restrictive covenant will not be enforced unless . . . [the information] . . . is a trade secret . . .' the implied term already protected trade secrets, so any express term would be superfluous. From this Scott J concluded that when Neill LJ speculated about how lower-level information might be protected at all, he must have been contemplating the protection of information falling short of 'trade secret' by express restrictive covenant—which one has to say does not seem to quite fit the words chosen by Neill LJ. In as much as this gives blessing to express confidentiality clauses (and the contractual provision in question in *Balston* was such a clause) most practitioners would welcome this. If, however, it means that information of a lower level than trade secret could be protected by a restraint of trade clause, we have raised doubts on this already because this reasoning merely goes round in circles. The other slightly confusing point in the judgment is that Scott J tested the *reasonableness* of the confidentiality clause as against restraint of trade principles. As we shall see in **Chapter 8**, restraint of trade clauses face a presumption that they are void unless reasonable—such analysis had not been applied to confidentiality clauses before *Balston*.

In *Roger Bullivant* v *Ellis* [1987] ICR 464 (see **7.3.4** above) Nourse LJ (who had also appeared in *Faccenda*) stated, somewhat Delphically (at 473E): 'What is now clear [referring to *Faccenda Chicken*], **at all events in cases where there is no express agreement between the parties**, is that confidential information whose misuse is actionable at the suit of the employer may fall into one of two distinct classes' (emphasis added). Unfortunately, it is not obvious whether the emphasised portion means that express confidentiality clauses are workable and effective or that an employer would have to resort to a restraint of trade clause.

In *Mont* v *Mills* [1993] IRLR 172 the Court of Appeal again came tantalisingly close to commenting specifically on this point. This case concerned a restraint of trade clause but the legitimate interest to be protected was that of confidential information. Simon Brown LJ noted that once employment ends, 'All that is left is a residual duty of confidentiality in respect of the employer's trade secrets' (at 177). This looks fairly clear but Glidewell LJ added: 'The employee remains, however, under a continuing but limited obligation not to disclose the trade secrets of *or use information confidential* to his former employer to the detriment of the previous employer' (at 178, emphasis added).

In *Poly Lina Ltd* v *Finch* [1995] FSR 751 His Honour Judge Phelan distinguished *Faccenda Chicken* on the grounds that, *inter alia*, the company was relying on an express confidentiality clause. This was perhaps the first case to clearly recognise the *obiter* standing of Neill LJ's words in *Faccenda* on the use of express terms. However, in *Lancashire Fires Ltd* v *S.A. Lyons & Company Ltd* [1996] FSR 629 Sir Thomas Bingham MR (*obiter*) believed that Goulding J's reference to gaining protection by use of an *express agreement* must relate to the use of *restraint of trade clauses* to protect information and that consequently there really was no difference between what Goulding J had said in *Faccenda* and what Cross J had said in *Printers & Finishers Ltd* v *Holloway*—both were saying that trade secrets could be protected by a restraint of trade clause. With respect, this does not get us anywhere, as Scott J indicated in *Balston*—trade secrets already gain the protection of the implied term so any express term is redundant.

More recently, in *Poeton Industries Limited* v *Horton* [2000] ICR 1208, the Court of Appeal had to decide upon the level of confidentiality involved in a highly technical process of electroplating. The Court referred to the classification used by both Goulding J and Neill LJ in *Faccenda*. Morritt LJ's reasoning drew heavily on Goulding J's system. In doing so, Morritt LJ gave detailed consideration as to whether the information fell within the 'trade secrets' category and decided it did not (using Neill LJ's method of determining what is a trade secret—see above at **7.5.4**). His Lordship concluded: 'If my assumption that the information came within *[Goulding J's category of lower-level information]* is right then *[the company]* might have protected themselves by covenant or patent . . .'. Again, the *type* of covenant required is not made clear.

We really should not be in this position where we do not know whether an express confidentiality clause or a restraint of trade clause can or cannot protect information once the employment contract has ended. As we noted in **7.5.4**, what the courts have concentrated on instead is extending the boundaries of what is meant by 'trade secret' to bring more commercial information within the protection of the implied term of good faith.

If we look at all this in diagrammatic form, **Figures 7.5 and 7.6** below demonstrate the analytical pathways. You will see that, whether one is dealing with have an express confidentiality clause or a restraint of trade clause based on the preservation of confidence (or both), and even if it is accepted that these clauses can protect information, which is less than a trade secret, one must still look to the actual drafting of the clauses (especially in the case of restraint terms) to see whether they do in fact provide the protection sought.

7.6.4 The practical effects of *Faccenda Chicken* and drafting strategies

7.6.4.1 Practical effects

There are probably no fewer than *six* ways of classifying information:

(a) *trade secrets*, which will gain automatic protection by the continuing effect of the implied term;

(b) *high-level confidential information*; so high-level that it is equivalent to a trade secret and protected by the implied term;

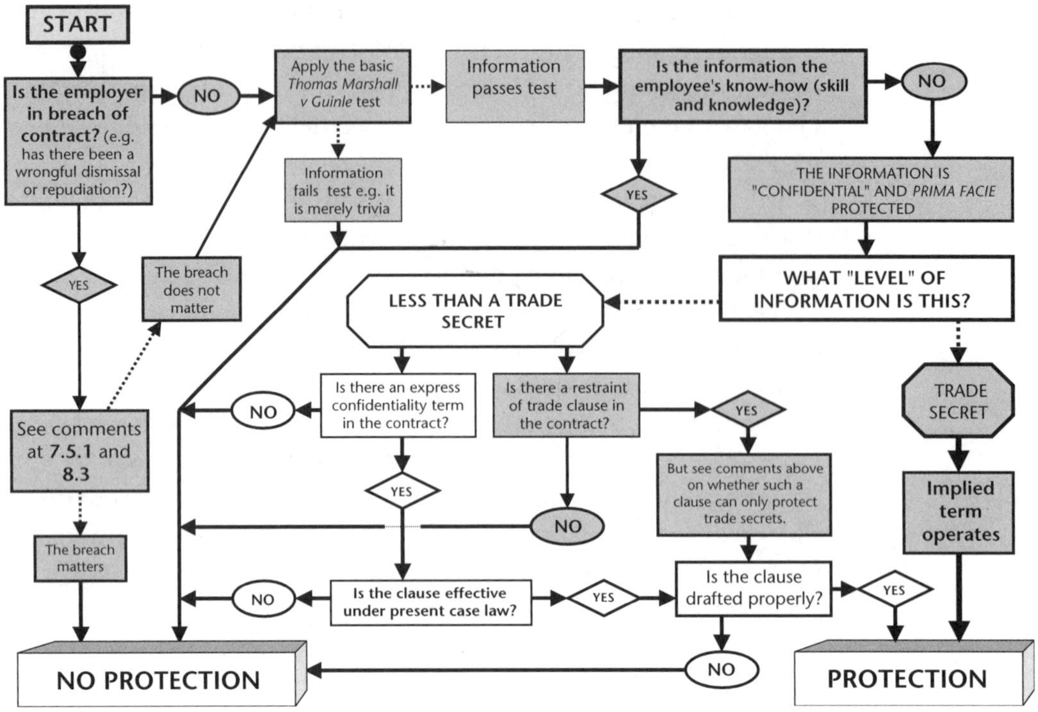

Figure 7.5 Protecting lower-level information by use of an express term.

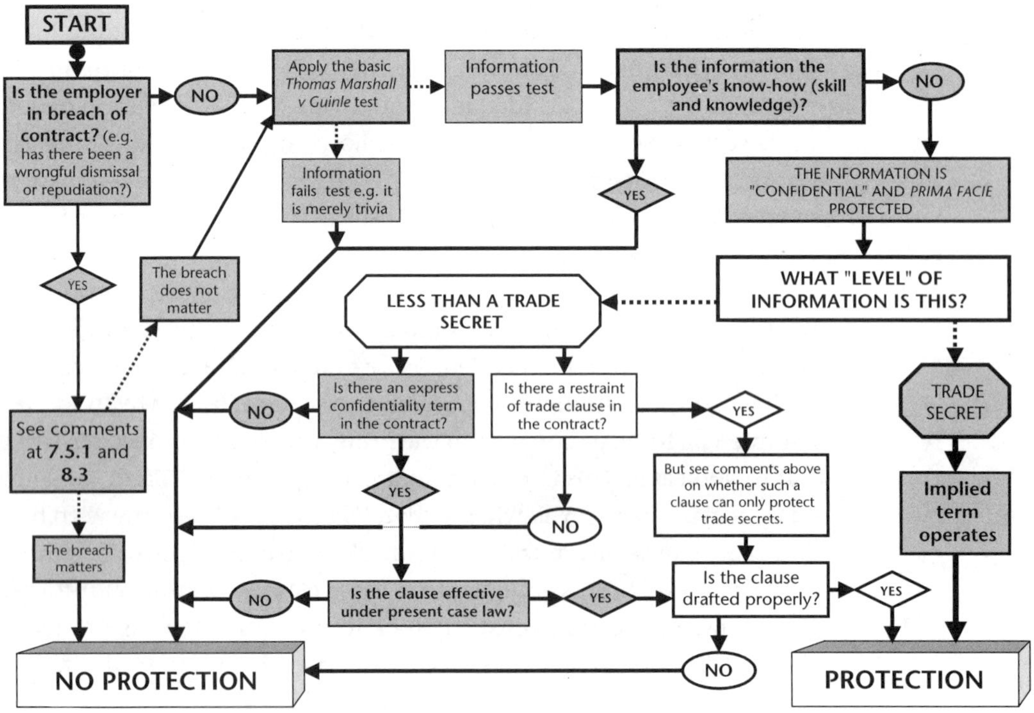

Figure 7.6 Protecting lower-level information by use of a restraint clause.

(c) *confidential information,* falling short of such protection but which may be the subject of a reasonable restrictive covenant (either a confidentiality clause or restraint of trade clause);

(d) *copied or memorised information* which will be protected by the springboard doctrine because it involves a breach of fidelity occurring *during* the relationship;

Information clearly protected under Faccenda Trade secrets. High-level confidential information.	*Information possibly protected under Faccenda* Lower-level confidential information, by means of an effective restraint of trade clause.

Information protected under other cases Copied or memorised information.	*Information arguably protected* Lower-level confidential information, by means of an express confidentiality clause.	*Information never protected* Skill and knowledge. Trivia.

Figure 7.7 Levels of protection afforded to information.

(e) *skill and knowledge*, which inevitably becomes part of the employee's experience and cannot be protected.

(f) *trivia*, which, except in rare cases, cannot be protected.

The *level of protection* afforded to each type of information can be seen in **Figure 7.7**.

That all things in life were so clear!

7.6.4.2 Drafting practice

The decision in *Faccenda Chicken* means that there is *prima facie* little value in inserting a clause in the contract which seeks to protect information once the relationship has ended. The implied term will protect trade secrets (or their equivalent) and nothing else can be covered. An express clause might nevertheless achieve two things: first, it may help to determine whether particular information could be regarded by the courts as attaining the level of trade secrets; secondly, it may deter employees.

Alternatively, we would say that the inclusion of an express term is vital in order to give information which is not automatically protected by the implied term any chance of being safeguarded. Express terms may appear in two forms: (a) as part of the contract itself; and (b) as part of a termination agreement. We shall cover specific points relating to the latter in **Chapter 8**.

The key point as regards drafting practice, however, is that *even if Faccenda Chicken is correct* there is a great deal to gain and very little to lose by inserting such a clause. For, if *Faccenda Chicken* is right, the clause will be ignored; but if *Faccenda Chicken* is wrong and the draftsman has not inserted such a clause, then protection will be lost for all but 'trade secrets'. The full 'belt and braces' approach, of course, demands the use of a restraint of trade clause as well.

Thus, if your client asks whether a former employee can be stopped from disclosing some lower-level confidential information your answer might have to be: 'Possibly not'. But turn the point around. If you wish to give your client any chance of protection in the future you will need to insert an express confidentiality clause and/or a restraint of trade clause. In a slightly different context the Court of Appeal recently affirmed this approach. In *Brooks* v *Olyslager OMS (UK) Ltd* [1998] IRLR 590 the employer and employee reached a compromise agreement concerning the employee's resignation. The employee later told an investment banker a few 'home truths' about the operation of his former employer's business concerning the management style and financial stability of the company. The company heard about this and refused to pay the balance of the agreement, claiming there should be an implied term in the agreement that the employee would not disclose information of a sufficiently high degree of confidentiality as to amount to a trade secret. The Court of Appeal refused to do this, both on the grounds of fact and law; on the latter point because the information did not fall into the category of trade secret, merely being information concerning the reason for the employee's resignation and matters which might be seen as detrimental to the company. An express term may still, on the facts, not have saved the day; but it would have provided a fighting chance.

Perhaps the most secure line to take is that anything which is not clearly part of an employee's know-how should be included in an express confidentiality term. Materials such as general research data, details of drawings, costings, accounting information, customers' credit ratings, the contents of forthcoming catalogues, company-produced quality maintenance manuals (if not already a trade secret), restricted circulation memos and minute of meetings, problems encountered in the development of a product or reasons why certain matters were rejected, and personnel records such as salary packages would therefore seem appropriate to this category. One might also include in this clause any item which may only be debatable as a trade secret (e.g., customer lists or sales strategies).

The confidentiality precedents supplied in the ILU Survey did not limit themselves to the protection of trade secrets; most made reference to 'trade secrets and other confidential information' and then went on to define that information (these definitions in turn being open to modification according to the specific needs of the client). Earlier ILU surveys, which looked at the terms which actually appear in company's contracts (rather than solicitors' precedents) found some evidence of a change in drafting after the *Faccenda Chicken* decision; references to information other than trade secrets being omitted.

7.6.5 Precedents

The ILU Survey revealed a fair degree of commonality in the definitions of confidential information being protected. As noted above, most precedents included a general ban on the use or disclosure of trade secrets or other confidential information and then provided a (non-exhaustive) list of examples. In addition to the items mentioned above, common items were: customer requirements; trade arrangements; marketing strategies; mark-ups; the affairs of clients; expansion plans; the movements of senior employees; litigation in progress; potential customer lists; and various terms on computer information.

Most draft precedents included a specific clause on the 'delivery up' of documents, papers, computer disks, etc. on the termination of employment. And a number included prohibitions on writing papers, giving lectures, etc. *during* employment without the express permission of management.

7.7 Remedies for breach of confidence

Any unauthorised disclosure of information during the currency of the contract is likely to amount to a breach of contract; a serious one if the effect is to cause harm to the enterprise (potential or actual). Disciplinary action may result. Realistically, however, these responses strike at the symptom and not the cause. What the employer requires is the prevention of use or disclosure of the information and to recover any lost profit.

Many judges have commented that the duty of confidentiality is of minimal value to an employer because of the difficulty of enforcement. The alternative sometimes suggested by the courts is for employers to rely more on the insertion of a restraint of trade clause which will prevent the employee from working in the industry. But while it is true that restraint clauses are generally a more effective means of impeding ex-employees, they are not a panacea because (i) it is likely that such clauses can only protect trade secrets anyway and (ii) they are far more likely to fail for lack of reasonableness than any confidentiality clause.

Thus the first 'remedy' is prevention: insert both confidentiality and restraint of trade clauses in order to protect confidential information. Failing prevention, the remedies available for breach of the duty will include:

Permanent remedies	*Interim remedies*
Injunction.	Interim injunction.
Delivery up or destruction of documents.	Order for delivery up of documents.
Damages.	Search order (formerly called an *Anton Piller* order).
An account of profits.	
Declaration as to confidentiality.	

To this list the Civil Procedure Rules have added: interim declarations (r. 25(1)(b)); pre-action disclosures (r. 31.16); and summary judgments (under Part 24), now obtainable by both claimant and defendant.

Note: To avoid repetition, injunctions are disussed in **Chapter 8** regarding confidentiality and restraint of trade (at **8.11**) and more generally in **Chapter 9** (at **9.10**).

However, it is useful to note here the comments of Laddie J. in the *Ocular Science* case on drafting Statements of Case (p. 359). These show that the claimant must be able to provide full and proper particulars of all the confidential information in question. The defendant must know what breach is being alleged; it is not enough to rely on a loose contention that a 'package' of information is confidential.

With this burden placed on the claimant it also follows that the claimant should not be obstructed in establishing the evidence. Thus, it is also possible for the claimant to obtain a disclosure order requiring the employee to give up the names and addresses of business contacts, irrespective of whether those contacts had been made before or after termination of employment. When it comes to lists of post-termination contacts, however, the defendant's own confidentiality is in need of *prima facie* protection. The best way to achieve this is by way of undertakings from the defendant's solicitor as to use of that information: *Intelec Systems Ltd* v *Grech-Cini* [1999] 4 All ER 11.

7.7.1 The parties

The employer may well join the new employer as a third party, but there are difficulties attached to this. First, this will inevitably slow things down. Secondly, one of the factors the court takes into account in awarding an injunction (see **8.11** below) is the ability of the defendant to pay any damages that might be awarded at trial; the joining of a company with all its resources is therefore disadvantageous to the applicant. Thirdly, there is the question of proving that the new employer received the information knowing of the breach or at least turning a blind eye to its potential. In *Thomas* v *Pearce* [2000] FSR 718 the Court of Appeal made it clear that the test is one of honesty not reasonableness.

7.7.2 Springboard injunctions

In some cases an employer may be able to obtain an injunction even where the information is not a trade secret, nor is it protected by an term of the contract: see above at **7.3.4**.

7.7.3 Defences

Aside from arguing that the information is simply not confidential at all, the two main defences are: (a) publication; and (b) just cause. We touched on publication at **7.3.3** above regarding 'the public domain'. 'Just cause' was covered at **7.3.5** above in the discussions on public interest.

Some further points need to made on publication. Although publication destroys confidentiality, the law is unclear on two key aspects:

(a) The degree of publication necessary. The case law shows (notably *Attorney-General* v *Guardian Newspapers Ltd (No. 2)* [1988] 3 All ER 545 (CA)—the *Spycatcher* case) that partial publication may not destroy confidentiality as long as the information retains the 'basic attributes of inaccessibility' i.e., it is not *generally* available to the public.

(b) Whether publication by the defendant destroys confidentiality. The answer to this may seem to be an obvious 'no' as the defendant should not profit from his or her own wrong (see *Speed Seal Products Ltd* v *Paddington* [1986] 1 All ER 91), but Lord Goff in *Spycatcher* expressed the view that once disclosed, by whatever means, the information was no longer confidential. This would affect the calculation of damages aspect (i.e., dating the termination of the duty), though the defendant would still probably be bound by the springboard doctrine.

7.8 Intellectual property rights

7.8.1 Ownership of inventions

Intellectual property is a generic title which covers such things as patents, copyright, trade marks and design rights. The common denominator is that each right to some extent prevents others from reproducing or imitating the particular subject matter without the prior approval of the owner. By way of example we can only hope here to outline relevant points on the ownership of inventions and patent rights.

A patent is a grant of a monopoly by the state for a limited period of time (currently 20 years) to inventors enabling them to prevent unauthorised use of an invention. A patent protects the physical embodiment of an invention which must be: novel, inventive (i.e., not obvious), capable of industrial application, and not excluded from patentability by the Patents Act 1977 (e.g., offensive). The Patents Act 1977 applies to inventions made after 1 June 1978. The basic presumption in s. 39 is that if an employee can prove that he or she made the invention he or she will possess rights to ownership and/or compensation. But an invention made by an employee will belong to the *employer* if:

(a) it was made in the course of the *normal duties* of the employee; or

(b) in the course of duties falling outside his normal duties, but as part of *duties specifically assigned* to him; or

(c) the invention was made in the course of the duties of the employee and, at the time of making the invention, because of the nature of his duties and the particular responsibilities arising from the nature of his duties, he had *a special obligation* to further the interests of the employer's undertaking.

7.8.1.1 Normal duties

It is probable that 'normal duties' refer to those duties commonly performed by the employee (i.e., standard, everyday duties) rather than all of those duties which might happen to fall within the contract. But inventions made outside normal working hours do not automatically fall outside the scope of an employee's duties: *Peart's Patent* (SRIS O/209/87), e.g., the employee may be provided with facilities to work at home.

Implied terms may also have to be accounted for (e.g., fidelity). In *Harris's Patent* [1985] IRLR 232, however, the implied duties were held to be co-extensive with and did not go beyond the express contractual duties. Here, the court was not unduly influenced by job titles but preferred to 'lift the veil' to establish detailed facts. Harris's primary duty was to sell valves and use his specialist knowledge to deal with problems experienced by customers of his employers. He had no research laboratory and never undertook creative design activity. Nor did he attend board meetings even when, as manager, his department was under discussion. Whenever major design problems arose they were referred to the licensors of the employers. The court decided that, as the employers never took it upon themselves to solve design problems in the valves, it could not have been part of Harris's *normal* duties to provide solutions to these problems. Thus implied terms will reflect more 'how' the job is done rather than 'what' the job is.

The second case in this area, *Greater Glasgow Health Board's Application* [1996] RPC 207, confirmed the *Harris* approach. Here a Dr Montgomery, a junior registrar employee of the Health Board, invented an optical spacing device while he was at home. He had clinical responsibilities in his department, was expected to do some teaching and to 'avail himself of the facilities provided' for research. He was not contracted to research and he said his greatest responsibility might be to organise the Christmas party. Jacob J held that the doctor's job was to treat patients so the invention had nothing to do with the carrying out of his duties under s. 39(1)(a) of the Patents Act 1977. His invention might be a useful accessory to his contracted work but it was not really part of it. Just because an employee applies his mind to a problem does not mean *ipso facto* it is part of his duties to invent diagnostic devices.

7.8.1.2 Specifically assigned duties

Duties which are 'specifically assigned' refer to:

(a) other duties within the employee's contract of employment which the employer directs the employee to perform on an *ad hoc* basis, e.g., temporary reassignments; and

(b) duties which fall outside the employee's contract of employment at the time of their assignment, e.g., additional work or separate contracts to perform a particular task.

7.8.1.3 Invention reasonably expected

Under the Patents Act 1977, s. 39(1)(a), an employer must also show that an invention was 'reasonably ... expected to result' from the performance of the employee's normal or specifically assigned duties before the employer may own the invention. But do the words 'an invention' in s. 39(1)(a) refer to *the* invention which is the subject of the dispute, a broader class of invention, or any expected invention? In *Harris* the court concluded that the first possibility was too narrow, whilst the third by-passed the connection between the invention and the performance of the employee's duties. Falconer J preferred the middle ground as it encompassed any invention: '... which achieves, or contributes to achieving, whatever was the aim or object to which the employees's efforts in carrying out those duties were directed ... that is to say, such an invention as that made though not necessarily the precise invention actually made'. Therefore, there must be a logical connection between the invention and the performance of the contractual duties.

7.8.1.4 Special obligation

Where the employee's status within his or her employer's business creates a *special obligation* to further the interests of the employer then the invention will belong to the employer. This obligation might arise where the employee represented the *alter ego* of his or her employer, occupied a position very high in the management structure (see *Staeng Limited's Patents* [1996] RPC 183), or was an employee-consultant being paid a high salary to invent. Middle management will thus normally be exempt from the strictures of this subsection: see *Harris's Patent*. And even where a special obligation is established, the invention must still arise 'in the course of the duties of the employee'.

7.8.1.5 Contracting out of the Patents Act?

Section 42(2) of the 1977 Act declares any contractual provisions unenforceable to the extent that they diminish employees' rights under the Act. Aside from outlawing crude assertions that all inventions belong to the employer this section also effectively proscribes the use of pre-assignment clauses, definitions of 'normal duties' which encompass a duty to invent which is not borne out by the facts, and the unwarranted creation of 'special obligations' for all manner of employees. Thus the practice most commonly advoc-ated is to insert a rather meaningless blanket pre-assignment clause such as 'all employee's inventions belong to your employer [X company], subject to s. 39(1) of the Patents Act 1977'.

It is preferable, however, for the contract of employment to spell out clearly the wording of s. 39 (perhaps with appropriate explanations where the language of the Parliamentary draftsman is too obscure for a clear understanding by the average employee).

7.8.2 Compensation

Once it has been established that the employee *made* the invention, but that it is nevertheless owned by his employer, s. 40 compensation may be available to the employee. The section requires the fulfilment of three main (and onerous) conditions:

(a) the invention must be patented;

(b) the patent must be of 'outstanding benefit' (described once as a 'real humdinger of a winner' and varying with the size of the company: *British Steel plc's Patent* [1992] RPC 117);

(c) it is just that the employee obtain compensation from the employer.

Alternatively, if the *employee* owns the invention but rights have been assigned, or an exclusive licence has been given, to the employer, s. 40(2) provides a limited opportunity for the employee to claim compensation; amongst other things, the employee must show that the benefit derived by the employee from any contract of assignment is inadequate in relation to the benefit derived by the employer from the patent.

7.9 The employee's right to confidentiality

In addition to the human rights implications noted at **1.5** above, there are four main areas to note here:

(a) The Data Protection Act 1998.

(b) The Access to Medical Reports Act 1988.

(c) The provision of references.

(d) The interception of communications

7.9.1 The Data Protection Act 1998

This Act (as amended by the Freedom of Information Act 2000) implements Data Protection Directive (95/46/EC) and came into force on 1 March 2000. The aim of this Act is the same as its (repealed) 1984 predecessor—to allow employees access to data held on them by 'data controllers' (i.e., their employer)—but this Act extends protection to paper-based records. Employees have the right to challenge inaccuracies and claim compensation for any ensuing loss. The 1998 Act has been implemented through various regulations and there are transitional provisions operating from 24 October 2001 to 23 October 2007 (see sch. 8). The Office of the Information Commissioner has issued guidance notes and a draft Code of Practice: see the website on www.informationcommissioner.gov.uk.

7.9.1.1 Outline of the provisions

At the heart of the Data Protection Act (DPA) 1998 lie eight principles around which the Act is structured, enforced and interpreted (see sch. 1). There is an obligation on all data users to observe these principles, e.g., that the information shall be processed fairly and lawfully; that 'personal data' (a term which includes expressions of opinions) shall be accurate and, where necessary, kept up to date; that personal data shall not be kept for longer than is necessary; that unauthorised processing shall be guarded against; and (a new principle) that personal data should not be transferred outside the EC unless that recipient country has adequate levels of data protection. The Act also confers on the Information Commissioner extensive powers of enforcement, so that any failure to comply with the provisions may lead to criminal liability.

7.9.1.2 The meaning of 'data'

In addition to material covered by the 1984 Act (basically computer-based information) the 1998 Act extends the meaning of 'data' to information which is 'recorded as part of a relevant filing system or with the intention that it should form part of a relevant filing system', e.g., personal files (s. 1(1)(c)). A 'relevant filing system' is defined at s. 1(1) as:

> any set of information relating to individuals to the extent that, although the information is not processed by means of equipment operating automatically in response to instructions given for that purpose, the set is structured, whether by reference to individuals or by reference to criteria relating to individuals, in such a way that specific information relating to a particular individual is readily accessible.

In the case of *Durant* v *Financial Services Authority* [2003] EWCA Civ 1746 the Court of Appeal considered the meanings of 'data' and 'relevant filing system'.

(a) Data

The Court of Appeal first analysed how data 'relate to' an individual and concluded they do so if they are: 'information that affects [a person's] privacy, whether in his personal or family life, business or professional capacity'. The Court held that this will include information which is biographical in a significant sense. It must go beyond the mere recording of the individual's involvement in a matter or an event which has no personal connotations. The Information Commissioner concludes (see web site for guidance on the Act and this case) that this means that, 'Simply because an individual's name appears on a document, the information contained in that document will not necessarily be personal data about the named individual.' The Information Commissioner gives examples of personal data: information about the medical history of an individual, an individual's salary details, information concerning an individual's tax liabilities, information comprising an individual's bank statements, and information about individuals' spending preferences.

(b) Relevant filing system

The Court of Appeal gave a narrower meaning to 'relevant filing system' than many had thought to be the case. It is limited to a system:

> '(i) in which the files forming part of it are structured or referenced in such a way as to clearly indicate at the outset of the search whether specific information capable of amounting to

personal data of an individual requesting it under section 7 is held within the system and, if so, in which file or files it is held; and

(ii) which has, as part of its own structure or referencing mechanism, a sufficiently sophisticated and detailed means of readily indicating whether and where in an individual file or files specific criteria or information about the applicant can be readily located.'

This means that not all manual filing systems are covered by the Act: only manual filing systems broadly equivalent to computerised systems in ready accessibility are within the system of data protection. The Information Commissioner's web site provides a number of working examples.

7.9.1.3 Accessible records

The question of 'relevant filing systems' does not arise in relation to *accessible records*, so that in such cases, rights of access are much wider. Section 68 defines this term as:

(a) a health record;

(b) certain educational records (set out in sch. 11); and

(c) certain public records (set out in sch. 12).

A 'health record' is one which consists of information relating to the physical or mental health of an individual which has been made by or on behalf of a health professional in connection with the care of that individual. 'Health professional' is defined in s. 69.

7.9.1.4 Sensitive personal data

This term covers racial or ethnic origin, political opinions, religious beliefs, trade union membership, physical and mental health, the employee's sexual life, and the commission of an offence or proceedings relating to an offence (s. 2). There are specific *additional* restrictions placed on the processing of such information (see sch. 3). So, for instance, the employee must have agreed to the processing of this information and it must be necessary for the performance of rights and obligations, legal proceedings, administration of justice (e.g., attachment orders), or monitoring equal opportunities. Problems are beginning to surface here with regard to the standing of 'sickness absence' records by employers.

7.9.1.5 Employees' rights

An employee, as a 'data subject', has certain rights under the Act (see generally ss. 7–15). These can be broadly categorised as:

(a) the right to be informed, in response to a written request, that personal data about him or her is being processed;

(b) the right of access (on payment of a fee) to personal data held by the employer. This must be communicated in an 'intelligible form';

(c) the right to apply to a county court or to the High Court to have inaccurate data corrected or deleted;

(d) the right, in certain cases, to be informed of the logic involved in computerised decision-making;

(e) the right to compensation for damage caused by any breach of the Act as well as in certain cases of distress;

(f) the right to complain to the Commissioner that the principles of the Act have been broken.

Section 7 allows certain information or parts of it not to be disclosed if information relating to another individual would be revealed, and sch. 7 lays out the exemptions relating to the general rights, e.g., in relation to references supplied by the employer, data processed in connection with proposed redundancies, company takeovers, or negotiations on pay increases.

7.9.1.6 Contractual and other obligations

Under s. 56 employers (or prospective employers in the case of recruitment) commit a criminal offence if they seek to require an employee or third party to supply them with certain records (i.e., emanating from certain data controllers (e.g., a chief officer of police) and relating mainly to criminal convictions) unless required by an enactment or by showing that, in the circumstances, this was justified as being in the public interest.

Under s. 57 any term or condition of a contract is void in so far as it requires an employee to supply any record which has been obtained by the employee under s. 7 and which consists of the information contained in any health record as defined by s. 68(2): see **7.8.1.3** above.

7.9.1.7 Effect on the Access to Medical Records Act 1990

The 1990 Act dealt with paper-based health records compiled after November 1991 and applied to a whole range of individuals, not just employees. The DPA 1998 repeals the sections in the 1990 Act covering access by 'patients' (in our case, employees) and amalgamates those rules into the DPA itself. It was always debatable whether the 1990 Act applied at all to records held by a company's medical department; there is still the potential for such argument under the definition of *accessible records* (see above).

7.9.2 The Access to Medical Reports Act 1988

Under the provisions of this Act a person may apply to gain access to medical reports relating to that person which are to be, or have been, supplied by a medical practitioner for employment or insurance purposes. The administrative consequences of this Act fall to a great extent on the employer; and the employee may seek access to the report(s) at several stages in the process—an employee's statutory 'right of inspection and veto'.

7.9.2.1 The basic right

The Access to Medical Reports Act 1988 does not apply to medical reports prepared before 1 January 1989.

An employer may request a medical report concerning an employee at any time. To fall within the Act the medical report must be for 'employment purposes', but no distinction is drawn in the Act between employees and prospective employees; or for that matter with those undertaking a contract *for* services. The Act allows an employee or prospective employee to withhold consent to a medical report being sought. This will apply whatever the contract states. Further, under s. 3 the employer seeking a medical report *cannot* do so unless the employee has been notified of this right *and* the employee notifies the employer that consent is given. Any notification by the employer must inform the employee of the relevant rights which apply at various stages in the procedure. These are noted below.

The report itself can relate to physical or mental health matters. Perhaps more importantly it also allows the employee the right in most cases to see the report and, to a limited extent, challenge it. The major effect of this is that employees will be allowed to correct inaccuracies that may be present in any report (provided the medical practitioner so agrees). The right to withhold consent is a fine theoretical right but, in the end, of less practical significance than it first appears because the employer will still have to make a decision (e.g., to employ or even to dismiss) on the evidence available. And what the Act does not permit is the suppression of *particular* items of information by the employee.

7.9.2.2 Outline of the Act's provision

The 1988 Act concerns reports made by 'medical practitioners' as defined in the Medical Act 1983. The Act defines a medical report as one 'prepared by a medical [practitioner] who is or has been responsible for the *clinical care of the individual*' (emphasis added). Thus the Act seems to be aimed at the employee's general practitioner, consultant or psychiatrist who has treated the employee on a continuing basis. Company doctors appear to be exempt from the Act unless there is this element of continuity present in providing 'care' (as defined in s. 2(1)).

The employee must also be notified of his or her various rights, e.g., that there is the right to withhold consent, a right of inspection, and a right to request that amendments be made before submission of the report. Equally, information may be withheld by the medical practitioner from the employee where disclosure would be likely to cause serious harm to that individual or others, or would be likely to reveal information about another person, or the identity of the supplier of the information. This last point does not apply where the affected individual has given consent or is a health professional involved in the care of the employee.

7.9.2.3 The effect on employers

Aside from the detailed administrative requirements, the 1988 Act does not effect changes to the law of confidentiality. But neither does the Act create extra rights of protection from dismissal, etc. Thus, although an individual may obtain an order securing compliance with the terms of the Act (s. 8), there is no separate right of damages.

The employer must treat the information in confidence but can act on it in the same way as any other information, e.g., looking at alternative work, dismissal, etc.

7.9.2.4 Requesting medical examinations

Where the request relates to prospective employees there are few restraints placed on employers, save the practical one of deterring employees who might object to the examination. The reporting medical practitioner will owe a duty of care to the prospective employee to produce an accurate assessment. But as regards existing employees, express terms allowing an employer to demand a medical examination and report are necessary. Such a clause will still be subject to the provisions of the 1988 Act. It would seem extremely unlikely that a refusal by an employee to consent to the release of the report could be construed as misconduct which might justify a dismissal; although an employee's refusal to submit to *any* medical examination where there is justifiable concern, or a valid dispute, as to suitability to perform the job may be held to constitute misconduct.

There is, however, no implied duty to participate in medical examinations: *Bliss* v *South East Thames Regional Health Authority* [1987] ICR 700, though exceptions might occur where there is a justifiable need for a report, e.g., following an accident. Mandatory medical examinations may also, in some cases, be a breach of human rights (see **1.8** above).

7.9.2.5 Testing employees

It is estimated that about 8 per cent of the workforce in Britain are subject to some form of drug testing. On blood and urine, the ECHR has determined that individuals have the right not to be subjected to such testing but these cases did not arise in the employment context. As regards alcohol and drug policies, in the non-ECHR case of *South West Trains* v

Ireland (EAT/0783/01, 2002, unreported) an employment tribunal found the dismissal of a train guard who tested positively in a random drugs test to be unfair because they felt there was insufficient evidence that his ability to carry out his duties had been compromised, given that the policy was surely based on safety rather than morality. The EAT set aside the decision holding that the tribunal had substituted its own view for that of the respondent, and had ignored medical evidence of the applicant being unfit to work on the day in question.

What Art. 8 ECHR might have added to this analysis is unclear but a fairly conservative view has emerged from two cases that have considered Art. 8 to date. In *O'Flynn* v *Airlinks The Airport Coach Company Limited* [2002] Emp LR 1217 the applicant was dismissed after testing positive for cannabis in a random drugs test. The dismissal took place before the Act came into force, so Art. 8 could not be relied on in any event. However, the EAT considered whether the Convention would have made any difference and concluded that it would not. They said that they had difficulty seeing how the zero-tolerance policy operated by the employer interfered with the employee's right to a private life, save to the extent that she could not report for duty with drugs in her system. In any event, they would have held any interference to have been justified under Art. 8(2) for public safety reasons, given that she could be called upon to serve hot drinks on moving coaches.

The Privy Council have strengthened this approach with *Whitefield* v *General Medical Council* [2003] IRLR 39 where a general practitioner appealed against conditions imposed on his registration by the Health Committee of the General Medical Council. These conditions included complete abstention from alcohol at all times and submitting to random blood and breath tests. He argued that these restrictions were disproportionate to the object to be achieved and deprived him of the enjoyment of social drinking on family occasions contrary to his rights under Art. 8(1). The Privy Council rejected his appeal and took the view that there was no authority supporting a view that an absolute ban on alcohol infringed a right to private family life and rather chastely reminded him that he was free to enjoy a social life with non-alcoholic drinks. They also held that any interference would have been permissible under Art. 8(2) in any event, for public safety reasons.

7.9.2.6 Employee's declarations

As we noted above in **7.4.3**, there is no generally applicable implied obligation for employees to volunteer information about their activities. Nor will prospective employees be under any duty other than that of not misrepresenting their position. This will include, in some cases, information concerning spent criminal convictions under the Rehabilitation of Offenders Act 1974. However, where employees have been asked direct questions at an interview, on an application form, or during the course of their employment, they will come under a duty not to mislead or be fraudulent. As an alternative, or in addition to, seeking a medical report more companies are therefore making use of questionnaires on health matters. Apart from questions which may be discriminatory (direct or indirect) there is no legal bar as such on this type of investigation though again we may have to take account of human rights' issues.

If an employee is taken on under false pretences this may well justify a later dismissal when the concealment is discovered. This principle applies to concealment of physical or mental illness, at least where such illness affects the job: *O'Brien* v *Prudential Assurance Co. Ltd* [1979] IRLR 140.

7.9.3 References

7.9.3.1 The common law position

At common law an employer is not obliged to provide references; though specific rules of bodies created under statute (e.g., financial institutions) may mean that an employer is bound to do so and these rules may require the inclusion of specific information so that any failure may amount to a breach of contract between the employer and employee: *TSB Bank plc* v *Harris* [2000] IRLR 157. The general common law rule is also subject to the law on discrimination. Thus the provision of defective references (or even the refusal to give references) because an employee has previously brought a sex discrimination claim against the employer may amount to discrimination under Equal Treatment Directive 76/207: *Coote* v *Granada Hospitality Ltd* (Case C-185/97) [1998] IRLR 656 (ECJ). And here, the EAT was prepared to stretch the words in the SDA 1975, s. 6(2) ('a woman employed by him') to include *ex-employees* (see [1999] IRLR 942). At present, however, because of a Court of Appeal decision (*Adekeye* v *The Post Office (No. 2)* [1997] IRLR 105), this same inventiveness does not apply to a race discrimination claim even though the wording in the RRA 1976 is to the same effect.

Employers will owe the *recipient* of references a duty of care under the principles of negligent misstatement. It is quite common, and good practice, for a new employer to make any offer of employment subject to the receipt of satisfactory references; the meaning of 'satisfactory' is essentially a subjective one: *Wishart* v *National Association of Citizens Advice Bureaux* [1990] IRLR 393.

The *employee* will have an action against the employer who provides faulty references for defamation and malicious falsehood; though not for breach of confidentiality, if permission for full disclosure has been given. References are therefore subject to qualified privilege and the key point, in defamation or malicious falsehood, will be the presence or absence of malice.

An employee also has a cause of action in negligence against the employer for any failure to use reasonable skill and care in the provision of references: *Spring* v *Guardian Assurance plc* [1994] ICR 596. This House of Lords' decision has caused employers some consternation. The Court of Appeal has now added a gloss, and further problems, to this area. In *Bartholomew* v *London Borough of Hackney* [1999] IRLR 246 the Court dealt with the position where references were provided which detailed (beyond the information actually requested) that the employee had left Hackney after disciplinary action had been taken against him, this action only ceasing when the employee had agreed to voluntary severance. The reference did not give a full explanation of the position (e.g., that the employee had been counter-claiming race discrimination). Although finding against the employee on the facts, the Court indicated that the mere accuracy of a reference is not enough to provide protection to an employer; what is required is a broader test of 'fairness'—although the reference need not be comprehensive, it must not give an unfair overall impression of the employee.

One aspect of 'fairness' is that if employers provide negative information on employees they will be at risk if the employees have not had the opportunity to comment on these complaints. Thus, in *Cox* v *Sun Alliance Life Ltd* [2001] EWCA Civ 649; [2001] IRLR 448, an ex-employee succeeded in his claim against his former employer on facts very similar to *Bartholomew*, because whereas in *Bartholomew* it was held that the statements did not ultimately give a false impression, here the references were seriously inaccurate and the allegations cited had never been put to the ex-employee.

7.9.3.2 Effect of Data Protection Act 1998

Schedule 7 of the DPA 1998 (dealing with exemptions from the provisions of s. 7) lays out certain rules as regards access to references. References given in confidence by the data controller (the employer) relating to the employee are exempt from the provisions of s. 7 if given for the purposes of education and training, the appointment to any office, or the provision of services.

Employees may therefore gain access to references given by previous employers if held on their present employer's files, but as the author's identity would be revealed by such an investigation this access seems to fall within the exceptions to s. 7 so that the ex-employer's permission would most likely have to be gained first.

7.9.4 The interception of communications

Many employees now have access to computers as part of their work. The development of e-mails and the growth of the Internet have begun to cause problems for employers in terms of monitoring with whom their employees are communicating, and what they are saying. The issues involve abuse of company time and facilities, employees accessing pornographic Internet sites, confidential information being disclosed through e-mails, etc., and (in this great age of constant quality-control) the need for employers to standardise or regulate telephone and written communications. The more employers intercept such communications the more they open themselves to problems of infringement of privacy (see *Halford* v *United Kingdom* [1997] IRLR 471, regarding the tapping of telephone calls without prior warning).

7.9.4.1 Surveillance

It is estimated that about 80 per cent of all employees are subject to monitoring or surveillance of some form in the workplace. Surveillance may take many forms, given the wide availability and low cost of employee monitoring technology. No distinction is made in the various pieces of legislation between systematic monitoring and occasional monitoring. There is also some indication that disciplinary proceedings/dismissals for breaches of e-mail and internet policies now outnumber proceedings for breaches of health and safety regulations, dishonesty and theft.

The starting point for any analysis of the legality of this now has to be Art. 8(1) ECHR (incorporated into UK law by the Human Rights Act 1998) which states that: 'Everyone has the right to respect for his private and family life, his home and his correspondence'. Article 8 rights were extended to the workplace in *Niemietz* v *Germany* (1992) 16 EHRR 97 (search of a lawyer's office), where the ECHR stated that the term 'private life' does not exclude professional and business activities.

Although (debatably) the Human Rights Act 1998 only applies cases involving 'public authorities', courts and tribunals are also public authorities within the Act so that, in reaching any decision, they must operate within the Convention (see **Chapter 1** above). Art. 8 may therefore be used indirectly in relation to the acts of a private employer (or, debatably against a public authority undertaking a private act as per HRA 1998), s. 6(5).

Halford v *United Kingdom* also established the idea of the 'reasonable expectation of privacy' at the workplace. American authorities would indicate that 'reasonable expectation' includes both a **subjective** expectation which is **objectively** reasonable. This leaves open the question whether an employer can remove the 'reasonable expectation of privacy'. In *Halford* this was not an issue as there was no waiver/warning but the cases dealing with contracting-out regarding the related Articles, 9 and 10 ECHR, strongly suggest that workers may 'opt-out' or be deemed to have opted-out of the protection of Convention rights in the employment context.

7.9.4.2 The statutory framework on accessing information

Interception of communications occurs when the contents of the communication can be read by a third party. The Regulation of Investigatory Powers Act 2000 (RIPA) governs the interception of communications over both public and private networks (if attached to a public system). It creates criminal liability and a civil tort of unlawful interception.

Under these regulations it is unlawful for a person, without authority, intentionally to intercept a communication in the course of its transmission by means of the postal service or public telecommunications system. The employer may monitor communications **and not be in breach where:**

- The employee has consented; or
- The employer has reasonable grounds to so believe; or
- The employer does other acts which comply with RIPA.

Monitoring of traffic data is not covered by RIPA. Instead, this is covered by the Telecommunications (Lawful Business Practice) (Interception of Communications) Regulations 2000 (LBP Regs). These regulations authorise monitoring and recording of all communications (telephone or e-mail) *without consent*:

- to ensure compliance with regulatory practices, e.g. Financial Services Authority requirements;
- to ensure standards of service are maintained, e.g. in call centres, to prevent or detect crime;
- to protect the communications system—this includes guarding against unauthorised use and potential viruses;
- to determine the relevance of the communication to the employer's business, i.e., picking up relevant messages when someone is away from work.

The monitoring should be limited to cases where it is necessary and relevant to the employer's business needs (thus *obviously* private communications do not fall within the permission to monitor, etc). The LBP Regs require businesses to make all reasonable efforts to inform users of possible interception (there is no requirement to get consent). However, the LBP Regs also allow employers to monitor (but not record) for the purpose of determining whether the communications are relevant to the system controller's business (and thus open up employees' e-mail accounts).

The Information Commissioner's Code of Practice, *Monitoring at work: an employer's guide,* states that any monitoring of e-mails should only be undertaken where: the advantage to the business outweighs the intrusion into the workers' affairs; employers carry out an impact assessment of the risk they are trying to avert; workers are told they are being monitored; information discovered through monitoring is only used for the purpose for which the monitoring was carried out; the information discovered is kept secure; employers are careful when monitoring personal communications such as emails which are clearly personal; employers only undertake covert monitoring in the rarest circumstances where it is used for the prevention or detection of crime.

Further, the Information Commissioner's guidance indicates that the employer should only undertake acts such as monitoring where there is a clear problem which needs to be examined. The theme throughout the Codes is transparency. If monitoring takes place, then save in exceptional circumstances the employer should ensure that employees know what is being done, how it is being done and the reasons for it.

The Information Commissioner has also issued a wide range of Codes covering matters such as the use of CCTV cameras in the workplace.

7.9.4.3 Storage of information

This is covered by the Data Protection Act 1998 as detailed above.

A combined 'self-test' question covering the topics raised in this chapter and the next will appear at the end of Chapter 8.

8

Restraint of trade

8.1 Introduction

Employers are often anxious to guard against direct competition from former employees. They may wish to ensure that an employee does not have the opportunity to utilise any confidential information or exert influence over the employer's trade connections. The only sure way to guarantee this is to remove them from the marketplace for a limited period of time, and the only way to do this is by means of a restraint of trade clause. Restraint of trade clauses seek to prevent an employee from working in a particular field. Such clauses curtail the employee's opportunity to gain employment and are so subject to stringent analysis, justification resting solely on the prevention of *unfair* competition.

In this chapter we will examine the doctrine of restraint of trade under the following general headings:

(a) What constitutes a restraint of trade?

(b) Importance of how the contract was terminated.

(c) How reasonableness is determined: legitimate interests.

(d) How reasonableness is determined: reasonableness of drafting.

(e) Drafting and interpretation.

(f) Implied restraints.

(g) Restraints during employment.

(h) Preparatory actions.

(i) Garden leave.

(j) Injunctions.

8.2 What constitutes a restraint of trade?

8.2.1 Definition

A restraint clause is an anti-competition clause. The archetypal restraint clause seeks to prevent an employee, for a specific length of time, usually within a defined geographical area, setting up in a competing business, working for another employer, or soliciting former trade connections once the employment relationship has come to an end.

When faced with such a clause the courts will presume the restraint to be *void* unless the employer can show it is reasonable. First the court will be concerned to ensure that the employer is seeking to protect a 'legitimate interest'. Once this has been established the restraint clause is then subjected to a more particular and extensive analysis based on the actual wording of the clause. Reasonableness will be judged as at the date when the restriction was imposed. There are four grounds to be considered in determining reasonableness:

(a) reasonableness in terms of the '*market*' in which the parties are operating and the appropriateness in relation to that employee;

(b) reasonableness in terms of *time*;

(c) reasonableness in terms of *area* covered;

(d) *public policy*.

A major caveat is necessary: each case turns very much on its facts. One cannot say that a one-year restraint, for instance, will always be reasonable or that a worldwide restraint is automatically unreasonable. Indeed, in *Dairy Crest Ltd* v *Pigott* [1989] ICR 92, the Court of Appeal made it clear that even authorities concerning the same trade (here a milkman) were not to be regarded as binding precedents.

One theme emphasised by nearly all participants in the ILU Survey of solicitors' firms (noted in the Preface) was that the reliance on standard terms, without seeking to modify them according to the client's needs, was a particularly disastrous form of practice in this area. Thus it has been said that the client who demands to be given a standard clause is misguided and the solicitor who provides one is a fool.

8.2.2 Types of restraint

The basic rule is that an employer cannot be protected from competition *per se*, only from *unfair competition*. Given that there is no set formula for a successful restraint clause they come in many different forms and with varying degrees of severity according to the employer's perceived needs. The most common types of restraint are:

(a) *non-competition restraints* (i.e., preventing the employee working in that industry as a whole, or at least with named competitors);

(b) *non-dealing restraints* (i.e., preventing employees accepting business from or conducting business with former clients or specifically named former clients);

(c) *non-solicitation restraints* (i.e., preventing employees actually initiating contact with former clients, though not barring the employee from dealing with such clients who transfer their business without solicitation);

(d) *non-poaching restraints* (i.e., preventing the employee from soliciting former colleagues to join him in the new venture).

Non-competition and, to a lesser extent, non-dealing clauses may effectively preclude a former employee from operating in a particular field of commerce or industry. They are therefore viewed with great suspicion by the courts. And 'non-dealing/competition' restraints, in particular, may affect third party rights. For instance, even if a trade connection prefers to take his or her business to the employee in the new job rather than continue dealing with the employer, any action by the employee may still constitute a breach of contract (see *John Michael Design plc* v *Cooke* [1987] ICR 445).

Non-solicitation clauses are usually less dramatic in their effect and, in many cases, procure a more sympathetic reception from the courts; though this does not necessarily ensure their success. We will deal with non-solicitation clauses later as a separate topic (see **8.5.4** below).

8.2.2.1 Termination agreements

Although most restraint clauses arise under the ordinary terms of the contract, some will be found in termination agreements negotiated with departing employees (usually senior employees). This will occur where the contract is silent on the point or the employer feels that the clause needs updating in the circumstances. Confidentiality agreements may appear here too. Obviously, the employer will have to pay for the inclusion of such restrictions, but the clauses themselves will be treated in the same way as those arising in the employment contract.

If a covenant is introduced for the first time at this stage, or an existing one is varied, any monies paid may be subject to tax.

8.2.3 Which type of restraint to choose

Many employers will wish you to draft a clause that would make a pact with the devil look like an attractive alternative. For the most part this should be resisted if only because a clause which seeks to restrain an employee more than is necessary will fail on this ground alone. Therefore, one should ask what level of protection is necessary to protect those interests, starting with non-solicitation clauses and moving on to non-dealing and then non-competition clauses. It may well be that the employer's interests can only be protected adequately by a full non-competition clause because a non-solicitation clause would be ineffective and a non-dealing clause impossible to police properly in that trade; but you need to be sure.

Lastly, it must be acknowledged that tactics may play a part here. Your client may insist upon a non-competition clause in order simply to scare off ex-employees. If so, you need (in writing) to advise that the clause is likely to fail. Equally, from the employee's perspective, one might accept the imposition of a Draconian clause on the basis that it will never stand up in court so why worry about it! Whatever the ethical points here, both tactics carry dangers. These dangers may be summarised as follows:

8.2.3.1 From the employer's perspective

(a) Such a wide clause may well alienate an otherwise loyal employee.

(b) The opportunity to draft a potentially workable clause may be lost.

8.2.3.2 From the employee's perspective

(a) The court may find a way to 'blue-pencil' (i.e., edit) the clause so that a clause, assumed to be unlawful, becomes binding.

(b) The court may narrow the ambit of wide-ranging phrases (e.g., restrict the term 'business' to a particular aspect of the company's business) even though the strict meaning of the words might not allow for this and, in doing so, catch the unwary employee who has agreed to the clause believing it meant something else.

(c) Precedent, or at least *stare decisis*, is treated with caution in this area. Even the same clause (appearing in slightly different circumstances) may not be treated with consistency.

On points (a) and (b), see **8.6** *below.*

8.2.3.3 Usual approach

As we have said, all firms taking part in the ILU Survey emphasised the need for 'bespoke' clauses for each client. Examples from industry, derived from previous surveys, however, show that the most common restraint clause incorporates *all* the various forms of restraint. This may well be necessary in order to cover all eventualities; but there is a

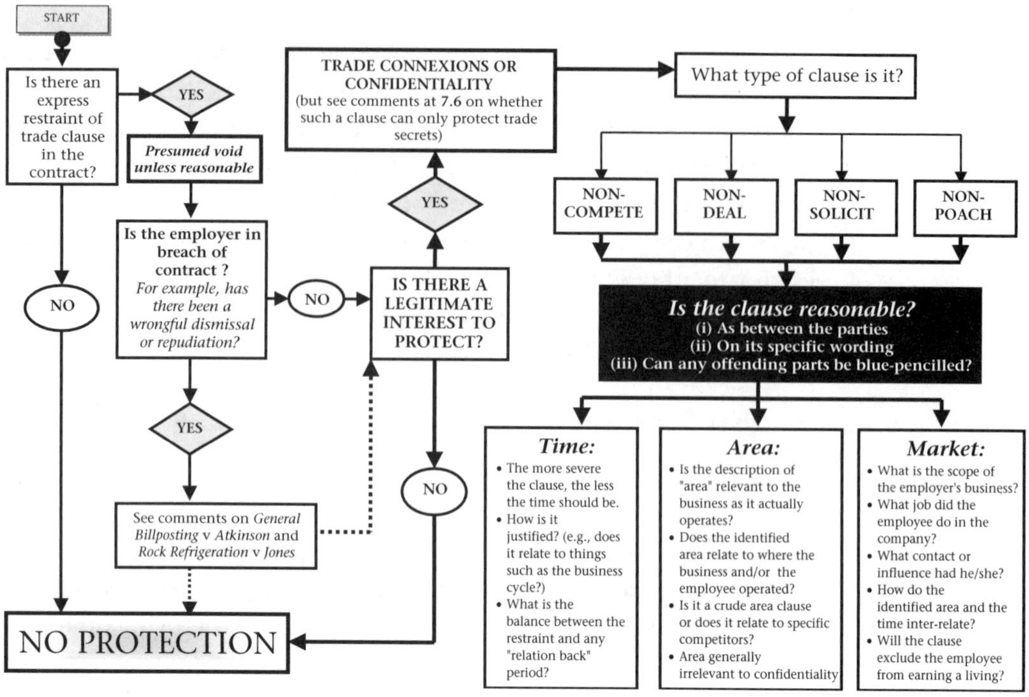

Figure 8.1 Diagrammatic summary.

danger here that, unless there is a distinction drawn between the clauses (e.g., how long each type of restraint lasts), the court may find all the clauses invalid.

As with Confidentiality in **Chapter 7** we have tried in **Figure 8.1**, to map out the basic analytical structures employed by practitioners as regards restraint of trade. This diagram shows you the overall pattern of analysis. As this is a simpler structure than Confidentiality, we shall not repeat the diagram throughout the chapter, but will refer back to it at times.

You can see from **Figure 8.1** that one starts from the presumption that any restraint is void unless reasonable and then, as with Confidentiality, the first key question is to establish how the contract came to an end.

8.3 The importance of how the contract was terminated

8.3.1 Wrongful dismissal

At common law an employer can terminate the contract for any reason provided the proper notice is given. In such a case there is no breach of contract and the restraint clause will survive the termination of the relationship. However, if the dismissal constitutes a wrongful dismissal this will amount to a repudiation by the employer and all contractual duties will cease. This will mean that the employer cannot rely on any post-termination covenants. This principle, as applied to restraint clauses, was established by the House of Lords in *General Billposting Co. Ltd* v *Atkinson* [1909] AC 118. It has a major impact on all we have discussed.

An employer who fails to give proper notice under the contract is only open to damages equivalent to the amount that should have been paid or worked in the first place. However, if restraint clauses fall by reason of the wrongful dismissal then all protection against 'competition' has gone.

As noted in 7.7.2 above, there is no case law authority on whether *General Billposting* applies to express or implied confidentiality clauses. It was submitted that the principle should be so applied. The principles of *General Billposting* do not apply, however, to unfair dismissals; only to wrongful dismissal or wrongful repudiation cases. Whether they might apply to a finding by a tribunal that an employee was constructively dismissed, and that dismissal was also unfair, is open to question but there seems no good reason why this should not be so.

Some contracts contain a statement that the restraint clause will be effective no matter how the contract came to an end (i.e., even in the face of a wrongful dismissal). These clauses recount the restraint and add that it will be binding, e.g., 'after termination of the employment *however that comes about and whether lawful or not*' (emphasis added), or 'following termination for whatever reason'. For some time it was unclear whether such clauses could effectively sidestep the decision in *General Billposting*. In *Briggs* v *Oates* [1990] ICR 473, the answer given was 'no'. *General Billposting* was taken as applying to contracts even when clauses such as those noted above were included. This was confirmed in *Living Design (Home Improvements) Ltd* v *Davidson* [1994] IRLR 69. Despite this, most draft precedents in the ILU Survey contained such phrasing.

Once it was established that such 'howsoever terminated' clauses were ineffective, the next issue was whether their inclusion made the whole restraint void simply because they sought to overcome *General Billposting*. The final word has gone to the Court of Appeal in *Rock Refrigeration Ltd* v *Jones* [1997] ICR 938 which reviewed the authorities and implicitly agreed with an earlier Court of Appeal decision, *Coral (UK) Ltd* v *Richardson* (1995, unreported). In *Rock Refrigeration* there appears to have been no wrongful dismissal, so the issue was simply whether the presence of a 'howsoever occasioned' clause made the restraint inherently bad. The Court of Appeal thought not. However, the Court also took time to take a little side-swipe at *General Billposting*. Both Simon Brown and Philips LJJ (*obiter*) questioned whether *General Billposting* accorded with current legal principle in the light of the House of Lords' decision in *Photo Productions Ltd* v *Securicor Transport Ltd* [1980] AC 827 regarding the effect of a fundamental breach on exclusion clauses. Their Lordships' point was that if, as in *Photo Productions*, an exclusion clause can survive a fundamental breach of contract, then why cannot a restraint clause be treated the same way? There has been no judicial reaction to this suggestion.

8.3.2 Justifiable dismissal

A dismissal without notice or with inadequate notice may still be a lawful dismissal if there is a contractually justifiable reason. A justifiable dismissal represents the employer accepting the repudiation of the contract by the employee. The employer is therefore still able to rely on the restraint covenants.

8.3.3 Resignation by the employee

If the employee resigns without giving notice, in the face of repudiatory conduct by the employer, he or she will have accepted the repudiation so that the restraint clause will cease to have any effect, as with a wrongful dismissal. If the employee gives notice, however, it seems that this will preserve the restraint clause: *Normalec* v *Britton* [1983] FSR 318.

8.3.4 Dismissal with payment in lieu of notice

In *Rex Stewart Jeffries Parker Ginsberg Ltd* v *Parker* [1988] IRLR 483 the Court of Appeal dealt with the situation where the contract of employment contained a non-solicitation clause of 18 months' duration. The employee was dismissed with six months' wages in lieu of notice. He then acted in breach of the non-solicitation clause. The employer sought to enforce the clause. The court held that the principle of *General Billposting* v *Atkinson* (**8.3.1**, above) did not apply here because the contract specifically allowed for payment in lieu of notice. It would seem to follow then that, if the contract does not allow for payment in lieu, such a method of terminating the contract (whilst making any wrongful dismissal claim somewhat pointless) may have the side-effect of invalidating any restraint clause.

The Court of Appeal has recently classified the failure to pay in lieu of notice as a debt, rather than a wrongful dismissal, where there is an express payment in lieu clause in the contract: *Abrahams* v *Performing Rights Society* [1995] IRLR 486. This is discussed below at **9.10.3**. Athough the court made reference to *Rex Stewart*, no comment was made as to whether this re-classification affected the continuing validity of restraint clauses.

8.3.5 Transfer of the business

As will be seen in **Chapter 12**, when a business is transferred existing employment rights are generally transferred as well. In *Morris Angel & Son Ltd* v *Hollande* [1993] IRLR 169, the question raised was whether a restraint of trade clause was subject to this rule. The Court of Appeal decided that a restraint clause entered into by the transferor company and the employee could be enforced by the transferee (purchaser) of the business. This is an area which begs further examination. In *Morris Angel* v *Hollande* the employee's contract was terminated very soon after the transfer so that the 'inherited restraint' related directly to contacts, etc. gained by the employee in the *transferor's* business. But what if there was a gap of one year: should the restraint apply to the *transferee's* contacts or should it still include those of the transferor? What if the employee was employed by the transferor selling computer hardware but is now employed by the transferee selling office furniture? When will the restraint (if not replaced) either become stale or unreasonable?

As will be seen in **Chapter 12**, there are uncertainties regarding contractual rights on the transfer of a business. Some clarification has come by way of two cases. *British Fuels Ltd* v *Baxendale; Wilson* v *St Helens Borough Council* [1998] ICR 387, and *Credit Suisse First Boston (Europe) Ltd* v *Lister* [1998] IRLR 700, CA. The general rule is that any alteration to an employee's contractual rights is invalid if the reason for the alteration relates to the transfer of the business. The first combined case is of more general application and is dealt with in depth in **Chapter 12** at **12.6.3.2**. It is appropriate to deal with the *Lister* case now. Here, a business was taken over and new terms (some better than before, some worse) were introduced by the transferee. One disadvantageous change to the employee was the replacement of a 12-month non-solicitation clause with a three month non-solicitation clause and a three month non-competition clause. The Court of Appeal held that, as these changes were detrimental to the employee and were as a result of the transfer, they were invalid (despite the fact that, on balance, the employee's position after all the changes, including monetary payments, was at least neutral).

8.4 Legitimate interests

As you can see from **Figure 8.1**, at the heart of all that follows is the notion that the employer must be seeking to protect a legitimate proprietary (business) interest. The restraint must afford adequate, but no more than adequate, protection to the employer's interest. Justification is recognised as arising only in 'legitimate interests'. It is legitimate to:

(a) seek to prevent the potential disclosure of confidential information;

(b) seek to prevent the employee making use of the employer's trade connections.

These are the standard touchstones, though a court can always recognise other legitimate interests: see *Office Angels Ltd* v *Rainer-Thomas and O'Connor* [1991] IRLR 214 and *Dawnay, Day & Co. Ltd* v *De Braconier D'Alphen* [1997] IRLR 442. It should also be noted here that a contract of employment may contain a confidentiality term (implied and, more debatably, express) *and* a restraint of trade clause, the justification for each often overlapping the other.

8.4.1 Legitimate interest: preventing the potential disclosure of confidential information

Irrespective of any express or implied confidentiality terms, a restraint clause may still serve as a warning to employees and offer a form of protection that is more easily enforceable. A breach of the restraint clause (e.g., working in that industry) is more easily detectable and policed than the mere act of disclosing information. As Cross J stated in *Printers & Finishers Ltd* v *Holloway* [1965] 1 WLR 1, at p. 6, employers faced with this problem should 'exact covenants from their employees restricting their field of activity after they have left their employment' rather than ask 'the courts to extend general equitable doctrine to prevent breaking of confidences beyond all reasonable bounds'. However, there is no bar on the insertion of both restraint and confidentiality clauses side by side.

It follows that there must exist confidential information capable of being protected, and in need of protection, in order to justify any restraint. There is a problem here as to whether that information has to be a trade secret or be merely confidential in order to attract the courts' protection. The position is not clear because the courts use the terms 'trade secret' and 'confidential information' quite interchangeably. And, as we noted in **Chapter 7**, even the formulation of what is or is not a trade secret is fraught with difficulties. One should start with the presumption that a restraint clause justified on the basis of protecting information should relate to the protection of *trade secrets* only (though the ILU Surveys show that this is not reflected in drafting practice).

8.4.2 Legitimate interest: preventing the employee making use of the employer's trade connections

8.4.2.1 Trade connections: what are they?

There are a number of aspects hidden in the term 'trade connections'. There are categories to which the term clearly applies, *viz*:

(a) the employer's customers and clients;

(b) the employer's suppliers.

There are categories where the application is likely to be made, *viz*:

(c) existing senior company employees.

And there are categories where the application is more debatable, *viz*:

(d) the employee's previous client base;

(e) customers who no longer deal with the employer;

(f) future potential customers.

8.4.2.2 Trade connections: customers, clients, and suppliers

These categories are sometimes referred to as the employer's 'goodwill' because they sum up the range of the employer's contacts and therefore the operational value of the business. This goodwill is a major part of the company's worth and therefore an obvious legitimate interest to be protected. Most cases will be concerned with these types of trade connections, but there is no need to consider the class closed and other 'contacts' such as the company's accountants or management consultants might in exceptional cases also be considered under this heading. A solicitor's clients are treated no differently here from, say, a milkman's customers; the professional connection with those clients does not carry with it some form of implied restraint of trade: *Wallace Bogan & Co.* v *Cove* [1997] IRLR 453.

8.4.2.3 Trade connections: existing employees

Recruiting another employer's employees is not unlawful provided those employees are not induced to breach their existing contracts. The corollary to this is: can an employer regard existing employees as 'legitimate interests' capable of being covered by a restraint? If existing employees can be regarded as legitimate interests, a clause which seeks to prevent an ex-employee soliciting former colleagues should stand or fall on the same tests as with any other trade connection or (and probably more justifiably) the protection of trade secrets. This line of reasoning has been seen in *Kores Manufacturing Co. Ltd* v *Kolok Manufacturing Co. Ltd* [1959] Ch 108, where two companies entered into an agreement that neither would, without the consent of the other, employ anyone who had been an employee of the other company during the previous five years. As well as this restraint being rejected on grounds of public policy, the clause also fell foul of the reasonableness test in relation to the employees affected (manual workers).

In recent years the validity of clauses which seek to prevent employees poaching their former colleagues has been the subject of intense debate in various Court of Appeal interlocutory (now interim) judgments. *Hanover Insurance Brokers Ltd* v *Schapiro* [1994] IRLR 82 appeared to invalidate such clauses on the basis that 'staff are not an asset of the company like apples or pears or other stock in trade'; but the clause in question was drawn too widely anyway as it included employees who might join the company after the potential poacher's departure. Thus in *Ingham* v *ABC Contract Services Ltd* (1993, unreported, LEXIS transcript) another Court of Appeal held that employers have a right to maintain a stable workforce (but *Hanover* was not cited here). And in *Alliance Paper Group plc* v *Prestwick* [1996] IRLR 25, injunctive relief was granted in relation to employees of a 'senior capacity'. In *Dawnay, Day & Co. Ltd* v *De Braconier D'Alphen* [1997] IRLR 442, the Court of Appeal reviewed these interim judgments. The Court held that an employer did have a legitimate interest in maintaining a stable workforce within the limits of reasonableness, but added that 'it does not always follow that this will always be the case'. On this basis, it is suggested that any non-poaching clause can relate only to employees who were former colleagues, and probably only to those of senior status, though, like many 'rules' in this field, this is not a certainty (see, for instance, *SBJ Stephenson* v *Mandy* [2000] IRLR 233 where Bell J allowed a clause which protected against the poaching of all staff on the basis that the prime assets of the company—an insurance brokerage—were its staff).

The ILU Survey clearly shows that most firms retain a clause relating to the poaching of former colleagues. The majority of these refer to 'senior employees' or similar descriptions (e.g., 'skilled employees' as defined in the contract). Some extend this category to employees above a certain (defined) level of seniority or pay, or those who have to report to the Board, or those with whom the employee has had direct contact (or combinations of these), or to those who are also similarly covered by a restraint clause. A small percentage gave more limited definitions of 'forbidden employees'; mainly those whose work involved the handling of confidential information or who had influence over customers.

8.4.2.4 Trade connections: the employee's previous client base

The employee may have legitimately brought to the business useful connections which he or she now wishes to carry forward to the next employment. To what extent have these connections become the 'property' of the employer? In *M & S Drapers* v *Reynolds* [1956] 3 All ER 814 (concerning a salesman), the Court of Appeal viewed such contacts as belonging to the employee. In contrast to this, in *Hanover Insurance Brokers Ltd* v *Schapiro* the former employee—a *senior* employee—was offered no such sympathy. The legitimacy of inserting an express clause in the contract to counter such possibilities, akin to partnership agreements, does not appear to have been reviewed by the courts.

8.4.2.5 Trade connections: past and future customers

In *Hinton & Higgs (UK) Ltd* v *Murphy and Valentine* [1989] IRLR 519, a clause attempting to restrain contact with the employer's 'previous or present' connections was declaredun reasonable because of the ambit of the words 'previous clients' (though Lord Dervaird did not rule unreasonable as such any restraint relating to customers with whom the employee had had no contact). An employer cannot, however, guard against the employee's contact with potential future customers of the employer (*Konski* v *Peet* [1915] 1 Ch 530) unless the departing employee has made some initial contact with the customer before leaving: *Rex Stewart Jeffries Parker Ginsberg Ltd* v *Parker* [1988] IRLR 483.

Complications will arise, however, when the employer and customer are merely at the stage of negotiating potential contracts. In *International Consulting Services (UK) Ltd* v *Hart* [2000] IRLR 227 the High Court held that, in principle, such trade connections could be protected even where the employee's contact with the customer was unconnected with those negotiations and fell outside the 'relation back' period in the contract of 12 months; the employee having been in a central and influential position within the company.

8.5 How is reasonableness determined?

Once the presence of a legitimate interest has been shown the question of reasonableness has to be tackled. The traditional dimensions to be measured in restraint cases have been those of *time and area*. Although the unreasonableness of either factor by itself may invalidate the restraint, the factors do overlap a great deal. Thus a restraint that is too wide in geographical terms will generally fail, but it may be saved if the time limitation is short. Likewise, a lengthy restraint may be valid especially where the geographical limitation is not extensive.

In the text below we have analysed the concept of 'reasonableness' in relation to the headings of:

(a) the market setting;

(b) time; and

(c) area.

Under the headings of 'time' and 'area' we have applied 'reasonableness' to each of the accepted legitimate interests, *viz* protection of confidential information and trade connections. Specific case examples are referred to, but it should be stressed that this is an area of shifting sands, even setting aside the introduction of public policy concepts. The same general test applies to both trade secrets and connections: *are the employer's interests in such jeopardy or open to such exploitation from the employee that the restraint can be justified?* Recent authorities have again stressed the need for employers to show harm or potential harm: in *Jack Allen (Sales and Service) Ltd* v *Smith* [1999] IRLR 19 a restraint injunction seeking to protect confidential information was refused where the employee joined the workforce of the main supplier, since the supplier would obviously know all the details relating to supplying the employer in the first place.

8.5.1 Width of the clause: reasonableness in terms of the 'market setting'

In every case the court has to relate the restraint to the market setting of the company and the individual in question. Thus we need to find out what both the employer and employee were concerned with: what is the scope of the employer's activities and what was the employee employed to do? However reasonable the clause itself may look, however much it might fit a desirable precedent, if the clause is not directly relevant it will be doomed.

It is not reasonableness as an abstract concept that matters but rather reasonableness in relation to the *particular* contract of employment.

8.5.1.1 The scope of the employer's business

The *nature* of the employer's operations has a significant bearing on the width of the geographical restraint; anything from a part of a city to the world as a whole (compare a local electrical goods shop with Comet or Dixons). The 'scope' of the employer's business will also relate to the range of products or services in which the employer deals, and even the siting of competitors. The effects of a standard clause would be different, for instance, when dealing with a butcher's business, a finance company, an estate agency, or a national frozen foods company. Or what if a range of products is made and the employee was only ever concerned with one product? For instance, in *Marley Tile Co. Ltd* v *Johnson* [1982] IRLR 75, the clause in question sought to restrain the employee from soliciting, canvassing or dealing with customers of the employer for a period of one year. The restraint related to customers falling within any area in which the employee had worked during the year prior to leaving. In that year the employee had worked mainly in Devon, but several months before leaving he had worked in Cornwall. This meant that the possible number of customers covered by the clause was in the region of 2,500. The restraint was held to be void because of the size of the area covered, the number of customers covered, and the range of the class of products produced by Marley Tile (see also *Commercial Plastics Ltd* v *Vincent* [1965] 1 QB 623).

One question charged with danger here is: would it make a difference if the business was located in the centre of London as opposed to a provincial town such as Taunton? In both instances a two-mile restraint might, in the abstract, appear reasonable. But those two miles may well cover many more customers in the heart of London than in Taunton. Paradoxically, the whole market for the service might be wiped out in Taunton whilst not being significantly affected in London; more so if the business is that of selling farming equipment. Thus, the question only begs further investigation of the employer's business interests and how realistic the restraint is in relation to those interests. Further, business methods have changed substantially from the nineteenth century, where the conventional analysis of restraint clauses originated. More and more, the notion of preventing the maintenance of direct physical contact through a restraint clause represents only a preliminary stage of the analysis. For continued contact and influence may be exerted by means of telephone, advertisement, fax, internet or letter as well as by personal proximity. One can be situated in London and still *deal* with customers in Bristol, for instance. The courts therefore have to examine other factors in the arguments relating to the width of geographical boundaries.

It becomes open to the courts to say, as regards many modern businesses, that a United Kingdom, European Union, or even worldwide ban could be appropriate or, in the alternative, that a defined restraint of say 10 miles (other than perhaps a non-solicitation restraint) would in fact be pointless. Thus in *Office Angels Ltd* v *Rainer-Thomas and O'Connor*, regarding an employment agency, a clause which sought to prevent the employee engaging in or undertaking the trade or business of an employment agency within an area of 1.2 square miles from the relevant branch was held void. The clause did not seem over-demanding but, again, client contact was generally made by telephone. The actual siting of any rival office was largely irrelevant.

Perhaps as a reflection of modern business, or the make-up of their client base, most draft clauses appearing in the ILU Survey were drafted with a specified geographic area in mind (usually the UK). Obviously these were open to contraction or expansion in the final application; but few firms used as their template the idea of 'radius' from the employer's business. Such measurements would be more applicable to small businesses such as hairdressers, butchers, etc. where the catchment area is defined by the siting of the business. The use of 'radius' is not applicable to many other types of business today.

However, one case of importance to solicitors is *Hollis* v *Stocks* [2000] IRLR 712, where the Court of Appeal upheld a one-year, 10-mile radius non-competition clause against an assistant solicitor which also forbade the solicitor representing any clients at specified police stations and a named Magistrates' Court. The Court of Appeal interpreted the phrase 'work within 10 miles from the firm's office' to mean 'to work as a solicitor' and, looking at the geography of the East Midlands, the proximity of large towns not covered by the restraint, and the general work of the solicitor's practice, held that the clause was reasonable.

In summary, the employer must therefore be able to show a functional correspondence between the area circumscribed by the restriction and the area particularly associated with the employee's former place of work. It may very well be the case, for instance, that a non-solicitation clause would be the highest level of protection acceptable.

8.5.1.2 The status of the employee

At its simplest level the employer needs to be able to justify the fact that the position held by the employee warrants the imposition of a restraint. Junior employees may get more gentle treatment from the courts than their seniors. In *Spafax Ltd* v *Harrison and Taylor* [1980] IRLR 442, however, seniority was the undoing of a branch manager/salesman facing a two-year restraint. The case is also of interest in that it focused on the effect of the clause in relation to the employee by looking at what the clause allowed the employee to continue doing rather than concentrating on what was forbidden. In other words, the court considered whether the clause acted to prevent unfair competition or sterilise activities. Thus care should be taken when dealing with employees who have gained expertise in a particular field to the exclusion of all else. If the restraint effectively prevents them working within that field it is likely to fall foul of the test for reasonableness.

In *Systems Reliability Holdings plc* v *Smith* [1990] IRLR 377, Smith was employed by ECS as a computer engineer. In 1989 he was dismissed for misconduct. He owned 1.6 per cent of the company's shares. ECS was bought out by Systems Reliability Holdings and Smith received £247,000 for the shares from the purchaser. The share sale agreement contained a restraint. Smith then set up a rival business supplying computer services and approached former customers. Harman J upheld the worldwide ban because that is where the company's business lay, and a computer engineer could work in Tokyo, Seoul, Paris or many cities in the United States. The ban reflected modern business conditions.

EXAMPLE

Your client is a salesman in the drapery trade. His contract contains a nonsolicitation clause set to last for five years and applicable to the employer's connections who had been customers during the three years prior to termination. He wants to know whether he is likely to be restrained from working for a rival company.

This is based on the case of *M & S Drapers* v *Reynolds* [1956] 3 All ER 814. The Court of Appeal refused the restraint, partly on the grounds that the employee did not hold a position which warranted such a restriction.

8.5.1.3 The level of contact between the employee and the trade connection

Here we ask:

(a) does the employee have to have had *contact* with the trade connection before a restraint is valid and, if so,

(b) what level of contact is necessary?

To answer the first point: the long-standing approach has been that contact is necessary. Usually this has meant *physical contact*, but repeated indirect contact can change this. Managers of butchers' shops, solicitors' clerks, milk roundsmen who are known to the customers, tailors and others *who procure business without direct contact* have been held to fall within the ambit of restraint clauses. This is because frequency of contact coupled with some degree of attachment can generate reliance and influence; even more so with doctors, dentists, vets or accountants. The closer the contact and the more reliant on the employee the customer/supplier becomes the more justifiable the restraint: *Scorer* v *Seymour Johns* [1966] 1 WLR 1419 and *Office Angels Ltd* v *Rainer-Thomas and O'Connor* [1991] IRLR 214. What is more debatable is whether an employee's *reputation* can be considered as a trade connection (and therefore a legitimate interest) because mere personal attributes cannot be the subject of a restraint. Thus, in *Cantor Fitzgerald (UK) Ltd* v *Wallace* [1992] IRLR 215 an 'inter-dealer broker' who acted as a go-between with clients was not caught by a restraint clause, though the court also found that the company did not actually have any *clients* as such. In *Austin Knight (UK) Ltd* v *Hinds* [1994] FSR 52 Vinelott J noted that it was possible that influence might exist via *reputation* (at least in a business operating in a tightly-knit market) although on the facts would not infer such influence. It is suggested that, if any form of restraint is permissible, it is most likely to be that of preventing solicitation of existing clients, rather than a general ban on acting within the general field of, say, financial services.

On the whole, however, it would be unwise for an employer to rely on merely proving *some form* of contact. One must also look at the degree of *influence* that could be exerted by the employee: see *Herbert Morris Ltd* v *Saxelby*. A looser test of 'mere contact' has occasionally found favour (e.g., *Marley Tile* v *Johnson* [1982] IRLR 75) but recently the courts have again placed the analysis on influence (*Hinton & Higgs (UK) Ltd* v *Murphy and Valentine* [1989] IRLR 519). The argument runs: it is not just customer *contact* that matters; for many employees come into contact with customers without exerting influence; it is influence which counts. Obviously, the more a trade connection deals with a particular employee the more likely it is that influence will arise. But even when influence is present, one has to judge the significance and commercial reality of that influence. In analysing the degree of influence the court must set the 'employer's hold' over the customer against the type of contact the customer has with the employee (the level of reliance), the seniority of the employee, the nature of the goods or services, and the frequency of contact.

EXAMPLE

The owner of a hairdresser's business is tired of losing staff to rivals. She particularly values the work of the new stylist, and the receptionist who gets on very well with customers. She wants to know, in principle, whether she can impose a restraint of trade clause.

Receptionists may well have as much contact with a customer as the person cutting or styling hair. They will come into contact with all customers, but the degree of influence is infinitely less than is likely with the particular stylist and, though a restraint might prove to be effective, the argument favours the employee. But if we move to the stylist there appears far greater justification for the imposition of a restraint clause. So now, if that stylist sets up in business a short distance away it is arguable that some customers may well follow (see *Marion White Ltd* v *Francis* [1972] 3 All ER 857). However, it is equally arguable that the customer's allegiance is to the employer-hairdresser because of reputation, level of service, the inconvenience of change or whatever. If *influence* is missing the clause is less justifiable, unless there are other factors present such as deceit: *East* v *Maurer* [1991] 1 WLR 461.

Hairdressers have long occupied the minds of judges in this area. In *Steiner (UK) Ltd* v *Spray* (1993, unreported, LEXIS transcript) the Court of Appeal was again concerned with this trade. Affirming the test of *influence* the court approved a non-competition clause on the basis that a ban on solicitation was irrelevant in this business and that non-dealing was impossible to police. Their Lordships were, however, influenced by the fact that the clause covered an area of only three-eighths of a mile for six months. In the ILU Survey the emphasis on 'contact' as an integral element in justifying the restraint was almost universal. Occasionally, *influence* was mentioned specifically.

8.5.1.4 Contact: relationship with employee's past dealings

In practice, both non-dealing and non-solicitation restraints tend to relate the restraint to contacts which the employee made during some period prior to termination. For instance, a clause which seeks to restrain an employee from dealing with customers or suppliers of the company for 12 months from termination will frequently contain a 'relation back' phrase such as:

> who are at the date of termination of the employment and who shall have been at any time in the preceding 12 months a customer of . . . the Company and with whom the employee has had direct dealings or personal contact as part of that employment.

The relation back period of prior dealings/contact tends to be either of six or 12 months relation back from termination. However, like many cases in this area, this is not a golden rule. For instance, we noted in *Hinton & Higgs* v *Murphy and Valentine* (see **8.4.2.5** above) that lack of *any* contact might not be disastrous. In a similar (but, we would submit, more defensible) vein the Court of Appeal, in *Dentmaster (UK) Ltd* v *Kent* [1997] IRLR 636, did not declare void a non-solicitation clause which related to customers the employee had dealt with, but which placed no pre-termination time limit on the contact (i.e., the contact could have been made a number of years before termination). Their Lordships were, however, influenced by two things:

(a) the restraint only applied to persons who had actually been customers of the company within six months prior to termination (i.e., 'live' customers); and
(b) the short period of restraint being sought (six months), so that the overall tenor of the clause was one of reasonableness.

8.5.2 Width of the clause: reasonableness in terms of time

8.5.2.1 Time in relation to confidential information

The aspect of 'time' is of vital importance in relation to the protection of confidential information. The restraint can last no longer than the projected useful life of that information. An obvious difference lies in the considerations applied to ex-employees of organisations famed for their 'secret recipes' and those, say, in the fashion industry, where the secrecy of next season's designs has a limited lifespan. It may be reasonable in the former case to impose a lifetime ban; in the latter case, probably no more than a few months.

Highly technical information will probably have a short lifespan, both because of the speed at which technology changes and also because an employee could not retain enough detail of the information for too long. This second point will be of no significance, of course, if the employee has copied or specifically memorised data; a breach of fidelity will have occurred. Thus the designer of a new compact disc player, for instance, is an ideal target for poaching by rival firms; but the confidentiality of the information may have a lifespan of only six months. The confidentiality of a low technology 'secret recipe' may last forever. As with confidentiality clauses, the majority of firms in the ILU Survey delineate the restraint according to the lifetime of the information.

It must also be the case that different employees, or at least groups of employees, will have access to varying levels and types of confidential information. Thus, a restraint clause applied without variation to all employees is likely to fall foul of the reasonableness test because a one-year restraint, whilst reasonable in relation to the head of computer design, may be too great when applied even to a computer programmer or a technician.

8.5.2.2 Time in relation to trade connections

A more relaxed attitude to lengthy or unlimited restraints has been taken by the courts in relation to trade connections: *Fitch* v *Dewes* [1921] 2 AC 158—a solicitor's managing clerk who interviewed about half of the firm's clients prevented from practising within seven miles of Tamworth Town Hall for an unlimited time. But this does not set a general pattern. Before a restraint runs its course any advantage gained by the former employee will begin to fade. Knowledge of the market will become out of date and, more importantly, connections will be lost. With this in mind, Jessel MR suggested in *Middleton* v *Brown* (1878) 47 LJ Ch 411, at p. 413, that the duration of the restraint should be limited to the time it takes for a replacement employee to demonstrate his effectiveness to customers. In truth this does nothing more than give effect to the adage 'out of sight, out of mind'; how soon will any hold that the employee had over trade connections cease, or at least be weakened sufficiently?

It is suggested that any time limit must be justifiable both in relation to the 'replacement employee' idea coupled with an investigation into the *cycle* of the employer's business, i.e., how often contracts are renewed or repeat customer contact expected. Thus if a firm of accountants, say, is in contact with clients only every twelve months, a restraint lasting at least this long would appear justifiable before the ex-employee's influence could be said to have been eradicated.

8.5.3 Width of the clause: reasonableness in terms of area covered

The key point here is that the size of the area is related more to density of population than mere acreage. It is thus an oversimplification to state that the wider the area the more likely it will be unreasonable; although it is a convenient rule of thumb.

Both United Kingdom and worldwide bans have succeeded. In *Littlewoods Organisation Ltd* v *Harris* [1976] ICR 516, a director concerned with mail order catalogues was restrained from employment within the UK for one year. *Under Water Welders and Repairers Ltd* v *Street and Longhorne* [1968] RPC 498, concerned a diver under a three-year worldwide restraint. But these examples should be treated with some caution and, with the increase in national and multi-national companies, the problems as to which area is to be covered by the restraint will be ever-increasing.

8.5.3.1 Area in relation to confidential information

Where the justification for a restraint rests on the protection of information, its geographical ambit may have to be very wide. After all, information knows no real boundaries. A piece of information may be just as useful to an employer in Aberdeen as in Penzance, whereas, as we shall see, trade connections may be more geographically limited.

Thus, the general 'market' in which the employer operates is a justifiable 'area'; and that area might these days be the UK, Europe, or even worldwide.

The restraint based on protecting confidential information is most likely to be aimed at preventing competitors from benefiting from the employee's expertise. It is permissible to limit a restraint to named competitors or competitors within a defined area: *Littlewoods Organisation Ltd* v *Harris* [1977] 1 WLR 1472. Here the restraint was designed to protect business secrets, those being the fashion designs for the following year's mail order catalogue. Harris was in a senior position and had access to confidential information. The restraint was for one year. The clause was drafted to prevent Harris working for Littlewoods' major rival, Great Universal Stores (GUS). Harris left Littlewoods and went to work for GUS. The clause (which was effectively worldwide in its scope) was construed as applying only to the UK (because that was the only place where Littlewoods and GUS were rivals) and only to the type of business in which GUS competed with Littlewoods. With these limitations (and debatable interpretations) the clause was held to be enforceable.

The *Littlewoods* case also illustrates the point that the courts will not adopt a strict literal interpretation of the clause where a more generous interpretation appears reasonable. For instance, in *Turner* v *Commonwealth & British Minerals Ltd* [2000] IRLR 114, the restraint was worded so as to apply to geographical areas which fell within the company's influence but in which the employees had not worked. The clause might have failed on the same analysis as *Marley Tile* v *Johnson* (see above at **8.5.1.1**) but the Court of Appeal construed the clause as only applying to those areas in which the employees *had* worked, thereby saving the restraint.

8.5.3.2 Area in relation to trade connections

The reasonableness of geographical restraints in relation to trade connections is more problematic. Non-dealing or non-competition clauses are crude devices. And, as we have discussed, the justification for the protection of trade connections is based on the fact that employees can exert influence over these connections. In time, that influence will wane; but how far should the geographical restraint extend in the meantime?

To answer this the courts must do two things: first, they must survey the actual width of the employer's operations; secondly, they must determine whether the restriction effectively negates the former employee's potential *influence* over the company's connections. On the first point, for instance, if a company operates only in Coventry, a restraint extending to Newcastle would go beyond what is necessary. This form of analysis works very well with localised businesses. Note also the comments on 'radius' restraints at **8.5.1.1** above.

When the employer's business is less localised the definition of a reasonable area has to rest on the factual point of understanding the employer's business and the appropriateness to the employee. It can no longer be the case that merely because the employer operates across the whole UK, the restraint should also cover such an area. The clause should relate to the siting of the employer's competitors and/or the employee's activities.

8.5.4 Non-solicitation covenants and trade connections

The general rules described above apply equally to non-solicitation covenants as to non-dealing and non-competition clauses. We have separated out this area only because it brings with it some extra matters for consideration. Non-solicitation clauses relate to the protection of trade connections. The time qualification in the restraint will therefore be germane, though the question of the area covered is usually irrelevant. Oddly enough, there appears to be no case where a non-solicitation clause has been held void purely on the grounds of its duration; but this does not negate the need for the employer to show it is reasonable on the facts.

8.5.4.1 What constitutes solicitation?

Solicitation involves action by the employee: the enticing or active attraction of connections away from the former employer. The terms 'soliciting' and 'enticing' have not, however, been defined authoritatively and the circumstances in which, for example, an employee's notifying clients that he or she is about to leave and join another company/set up in business will constitute soliciting are not altogether clear. We would suggest that anything which seems to carry an invitation to defect, rather than merely provide information, will amount to soliciting. Certainly, being approached by a former customer of the employer is not solicitation; and to prevent this activity the employer will need to have inserted a non-dealing clause.

Apart from the more obvious act of contacting connections directly and overtly it is also probable that *indirect* approaches such as advertising in newspapers and trade journals will constitute solicitation. If the solicitation clause has a geographical limit the issue of advertising material which spills over into the forbidden zone could present a problem. There appears to be no direct case law on this point, though in *Cullard* v *Taylor* (1887) 3 TLR 698, a solicitor restrained from operating within a particular area who sent letters to clients residing in the area was held to be in breach of the restraint; and New Zealand authority (*Sweeney* v *Astle* (1923) 42 NZLR 1198) indicates that advertising which spills over into the protected area so that customers become aware of the employee's position will be outlawed. If such is the position then the question of time constraint becomes particularly important if the clause is to be seen as reasonable rather than punitive.

8.5.4.2 Which connections are covered?

These need to be capable of identification. The conclusive factor will then be whether the clause is protecting against influence being exerted by the former employee. Thus in *Gledhow Autoparts* v *Delaney* [1965] 1 WLR 1366, the clause sought to restrict the activities of a salesman. The clause prohibited solicitation 'within the districts in which the traveller operated'. Many of the customers had no contact with the employee. The clause was therefore wider than necessary and void (see also *Marley Tile Co. Ltd* v *Johnson* [1982] IRLR 75).

The comments on prior contact noted above at **8.5.1.4** apply equally here and are not repeated.

We should also note again that if a clause is otherwise reasonable it will not be deemed unreasonable simply because the employer's connections state they are unlikely to continue doing business with the employer anyway: see *John Michael Design plc* v *Cooke* [1987] ICR 445.

8.5.5 Public policy considerations

Strictly speaking, the whole doctrine of restraint of trade is based on the concept of public interest; the balancing of an individual's liberty with principles of freedom of contract. Courts can therefore 'fall back' on pronouncements of public interest or public policy in order to strike out clauses which, though reasonable perhaps as between the parties, offend some vague judgment as to what is acceptable.

One thing which is certain about public policy is that it is not immutable. The perceived needs of society vary from decade to decade so that no firm rules can be laid down. Nothing that has been said in this Chapter, therefore, can guarantee that a specific form of wording carries with it magical qualities of immunity. As a starting point, however:

(a) If the restraint has passed the tests of legitimate interest as well as temporal and spatial reasonableness it will fall on the employee to prove that it is nevertheless contrary to public policy: *Herbert Morris* v *Saxelby*.

(b) It will not be contrary to public policy simply on the grounds that the employee's interests are more adversely affected than the employer's interests are protected. Except in the extreme cases, where the employee is prevented from working at all, the effect on the employee is not really a consideration addressed by the courts. The test is not based on the *balancing* of interests: *Allied Dunbar (Frank Weisenger) Ltd* v *Weisenger* [1988] IRLR 60.

(c) It was suggested in *Faccenda Chicken* v *Fowler* that the use to which an employee puts confidential information may have an effect on the court's approach to the protection sought, e.g., seeking to earn a living is viewed as potentially warranting protection but merely *selling* the information will lose the court's favour.

Other examples of courts invoking 'public policy' to strike out clauses include: *Bull* v *Pitney-Bowes* [1967] 1 WLR 273, where a pension scheme contained a clause stating that if a retired employee entered into any form of competition with the employer that employee's pension rights would be affected; and *Kores Manufacturing Co. Ltd* v *Kolok Manufacturing Co. Ltd* [1959] Ch 108.

But public policy does not always damn restraint clauses. Thus in *Bridge* v *Deacons* [1984] AC 705 the Privy Council perceived the value of restraint clauses as providing a means whereby the young can replace the old. And in *Kerr* v *Morris* [1987] Ch 90 the Court of Appeal did not agree that doctors in general practice formed a special class which were exempt from the applications of restraint of trade clauses.

It would also appear that a defective restraint cannot be saved by the fact that during the time it should have applied the employee also received some post-termination payments: *TSC Europe (UK) Ltd* v *Massey* [1999] IRLR 22, ChD.

8.6 Drafting and interpretation

8.6.1 The problems in giving meaning to the clause

The basic premise is that an employer stands or falls by what is written in the restraint clause. Here is a typical restraint clause:

Non-competition
For a period of 6 months after termination of the Employment, the Employee shall not (whether directly or indirectly) be engaged or interested whether as principal, servant, agent, consultant or otherwise in any trade or business which by virtue of its location competes with any trade or business being carried on in the United Kingdom at the date of termination of the Employment by the Company and in which trade or business the Employee has been involved as part of his Employment.

It does not make for light reading, partly because the tradition of not using punctuation (which died out elsewhere in legal documents years ago) still rears its ugly head in this area. Further, the clause often makes no sense at all when actually applied to the employer and employee, because it has simply been lifted from a book of precedents. It is therefore advisable to make the meaning of any clause as clear as possible. Phrases such as 'engage', or 'undertake' or 'carry on a business' are somewhat flexible expressions which may bear a different meaning in a given context. A solicitor must make sure the context fits. If the contract is silent or ambiguous on a particular point it will most likely be construed against the employer. One of the most recent examples appeared in *WAC Ltd* v *Whillock* [1990] IRLR 23, where the clause in question prohibited a shareholder from carrying on a business in competition *personally* but was silent about taking on a directorship or becoming an employee of a competitor. The shareholder was therefore entitled to become a director.

As a matter of drafting practice, therefore, it is imperative that any restraint clause actually reflects (without necessarily specifying) both a legitimate interest *and* the relevance of that clause to the employee's work. The easiest clauses to draft are those which prohibit actions on a sweeping basis. They are equally the most dangerous clauses because they cannot hope to cover all eventualities. Even an immaculately-worded contract which contains only one general clause intended to cover the entire workforce will probably be drafted too widely to cover specific situations or will not be appropriate to grades of employees (see also **8.6.2** below).

Thus some draftsmen adopt a style of maintaining one general contractual term containing a large quantity of bracketed alternatives within clauses, or even of alternative clauses for each grade of employee. The inappropriate alternatives are then struck out for each individual. It is also common to find extensive definition sections in the text.

8.6.1.1 Narrowly drafted clauses

Clauses which are narrowly drafted will generally not be read as protecting wider interests. The courts will not write words into a clause to make it effective. If an interest needs protecting the restraint clause must be drafted to achieve this. At its simplest, this will mean that a non-solicitation clause will fail to prevent employees dealing with customers *who contact them*.

8.6.1.2 Construing wide wording

Courts may choose to read wide wording in a restricted way so as to make it workable. Given what has already been said, it might be thought that an extremely literal interpretation would be applied to the wording of such clauses. This is not always so. Sometimes the courts have limited the application of any restraint, however widely worded, to the employer's actual business interests. Thus in *Home Counties Dairies Ltd* v *Skilton* [1970] 1 WLR 526, the prohibition on an employee-milkman from serving or selling 'milk or dairy produce' to any customers of his former employer could have meant that the employee would be unable even to sell cheese in a grocer's shop. The Court of Appeal took a less fanciful interpretation, limiting the clause to 'the same type of business as the employer's'. The clause was therefore valid in this form. And in *Business Seating (Renovations) Ltd* v *Broad* [1989] ICR 713 a non-solicitation clause failed to say what the '*business* of any customers or clients' actually was. The court interpreted the clause by reference to other clauses in the contract to define the business as that of the repair and renovation of office furniture; but the court could simply have struck out the clause for ambiguity. Indeed, this is exactly what happened in *Mont (J. A.) (UK)* v *Mills* [1993] IRLR 173. The clause was again too general and did not attempt to focus on the need to protect confidential information; its defects were not a 'mere want of accuracy of expression'. It is advisable to define the 'business' involved, especially in multi-product companies.

Recently, some level of unspoken disagreement has emerged in the Court of Appeal as to the most appropriate style of interpretation to be used. *Mont* v *Mills*, in particular, took the stance that an employer should be bound by the words used (Glidewell, Beldam, and Simon Brown LJJ). This approach was specifically approved by Sedley and Simon Brown LJJ (perhaps not surprisingly) in *Wincanton* v *Cranny & SDM European Transport Ltd* [2000] IRLR 716. Here the non-competition restraint referred to being employed 'in any . . . with any business carried on by' Wincanton. Wincanton had a number of parts to their business. Cranny was only involved in one area and the Court of Appeal refused to read the clause as being limited to that one area. In *Hanover* v *Schapiro*, however, the court had adopted a far more purposive approach (Dillon and Nolan LJJ). But again, in *Ingham* v *ABC Contract Services*, another court expressed favour for binding the employer to the language chosen (Russell and Leggatt LJJ) and we saw above, in *Turner* v *Commonwealth & British Minerals Ltd* (at **8.5.3.1**) and *Hollis* v *Stocks* (at **8.5.1.1**), that judges are not bound to take a literal view of restraint clauses. *Scully UK Ltd* v *Lee* [1998] IRLR 259 (Sir Richard Scott V-C, Aldous and Potter LJJ) stated a preference for a purposive approach, but tended to adopt a fairly *contra proferentem* view of the employer's argument. Here, the clause in question read:

> The employee shall not . . . be engaged . . . as an employee . . . in . . . *any business* involving the manufacture supply installing modification servicing advertising or otherwise dealing in overspill prevention or tank gauging equipment or without prejudice to the foregoing *any other business which competes with any business carried on by the Company* . . . (Italicised words added for emphasis here.)

The question was, what was the effect of the italicised words? The employee argued that the clause sought to prevent him working not just for competitors but across other industries which might use overspill prevention equipment. The employer argued that the phrase 'any other competing business . . .' explained the limitations of the clause. The Court held that the use of the term 'any business' was too wide and went beyond reasonable protection; it was not apparent that the parties intended the clause to be limited to competing business. It is not surprising that their Lordships, in all cases, have expressed the need for a full hearing of a case to resolve what is a fundamental divergence of principle.

So should the employer make clear the interests for which protection is sought, e.g., in an introductory section? At first sight this appears to be good drafting practice. However, the draftsman may be caught on the horns of a dilemma. In *Office Angels Ltd* v *Rainer-Thomas and O'Connor*, Sir Christopher Slade indicated that where the restraint clause does not specifically state the interest which the covenant is intended to protect the court can look at the wording and the general circumstances to ascertain the parties' intentions. But where the covenant *does* state the interest the employer 'is not, in my opinion, entitled thereafter to seek to justify the covenant by reference to some separate and additional interest which has not been specified'. The introductory words in this case referred to the 'clients of the company' and safeguarding 'the company's goodwill'. The words did not preclude the employees from contacting the pool of temporary workers whom they had known in their work in the employment agency; the restraint could apply only to the employer-clients. Thus spelling out the legitimate interest gains the advantage of definition and certainty, but runs the risk of limitation. Many firms in the ILU Survey used the device of an introductory 'acknowledgement' clause stating that the employee was aware of the significance of information held or contacts made and the harm that might befall the business.

What the courts will not tolerate from the ex-employee are 'colourable evasions'—minor and meaningless alterations of status on the behalf of the employee (e.g., a change in job title) made simply to avoid the exact wording of the restraint. An employee who argues that acting as an assistant to, say, an architect, is not in breach of a restraint which forbids him 'carrying on that profession', will see little sympathy from the courts. Setting up a limited company under which to continue in the same trade will also count as a colourable evasion: *Gilford Motors* v *Horne* [1933] Ch 935.

8.6.2 Severance and 'blue-pencilling'

The courts have no general power to re-write a restraint to make it reasonable. They may give some interpretation to the wording, but it is not the courts' function to make contracts. What they have long accepted, however, is the idea of editing the clause—or applying the infamous blue pencil.

'Blue-pencilling' means that the courts may, within limitations, remove words or sentences which are felt to make the clause unreasonable. The remaining part of the clause is then allowed to stand and be effective. In *Sadler* v *Imperial Life Assurance of Canada* [1988] IRLR 388, three conditions were stated as necessary for severance (or 'blue-pencilling') to occur:

(a) that the unenforceable provisions could be removed without the need to add to or modify the remaining part;

(b) the remaining terms continued to be supported by adequate consideration; and

(c) the removal of the words did not change the character of the clause, i.e., make the contract substantially different from that which was originally agreed.

In truth this will occur most often when there are separate clauses: one clause may be struck out leaving the other (narrower) clause operative. Where the restraint stands as a single clause it is more difficult to sever parts so as to allow the remainder still to make sense grammatically and be considered reasonable. It is for these reasons that restraint clauses are sometimes structured so that wider clauses are accompanied by narrower *independent* promises—what has sometimes been called the 'shopping list' approach. The limitations in all cases are that the court cannot add words and the extant part of the clause must make grammatical and legal sense. Effectively, the severed promise must be quite independent from the remainder of the restraint. Few companies seem to adopt this approach other than by dividing up competition, dealing and solicitation, although one 'shopping list' example we have seen ran to two pages of close type.

A final clause stating that each undertaking is a separate and distinct undertaking and the invalidity or unenforceability of any part of any of them shall not affect the validity or enforceability of the remainder can prove useful. Indeed, in the ILU Survey such clauses appeared in nearly all draft contracts.

It is therefore impossible to rely on the notion of severance saving a bad clause, e.g., by removing irrelevant references to 'Associated Companies'. What is not tolerated is a clause which states that it will be effective 'so far as the law allows': *Davies* v *Davies* (1887) 36 ChD 359.

8.6.3 When is reasonableness determined?

The reasonableness of a clause is determined by looking at the point when it was entered into: *Gledhow Autoparts* v *Delaney*, **8.5.4.2** above. Promotions and changes in job titles, which effectively involve new contracts, could therefore have an effect on the reasonableness of any clause unless the new contract terms take this into account. It is common practice, therefore, to draft clauses which refer to events at the point of termination, such as the prevention of solicitation of customers 'who have been customers of the employer during the last 12 months prior to termination'.

One worrying aspect of *Gledhow Autoparts*, however, was that the Court of Appeal also contrasted the length of notice due (two weeks) with the length of the restraint (three years). The court's view was that it was unreasonable that an employee of only a few weeks' standing could receive only two weeks' notice and yet be subject to a lengthy restraint. Whatever the validity of the reasoning in this case, if this was applied as a universal determinant of reasonableness it would mean that *nearly all* restraint clauses would be unreasonable.

8.7 Implied and indirect restraints

Stenhouse Australia Ltd v *Phillips* [1974] 1 All ER 117 provides a good example of such terms. The clause required the employee to pay to his former employer, for five years, half the commission emanating from deals struck with any of the former employer's customers. By another name this was a restraint clause. In *Sadler* v *Imperial Life Assurance of Canada* (**8.6.2**), the employee was entitled under the contract to receive commission on life policies even after ceasing employment. However, the contract also stated that if he entered into competition with his former employer in a way defined in the contract by reference to competition *during* employment then this commission would cease to be payable. He entered into such competition and the employers refused to pay the commission. The clause was held to be an indirect restraint of trade clause and it was void as being drawn too widely.

Thus, in *Marshall* v *NM Financial Management Ltd* [1997] IRLR 449, where a contract stipulated that commission should be payable to an employee after termination only if the employee did not enter into competition with the former employer, this was held to be an unreasonable restraint of trade. That was not so on similar facts in *Peninsula Business Services* v *Sweeney* (2003, unreported, EAT 1096/02), the key difference being that here the employee merely lost his outstanding commission on termination; the loss was not tied in to his entering another company's employ. Most of the argument in *Marshall* centred on the issues raised in **8.6.2** above regarding severance. Because of the drafting of the clause, simple severance of the restraint from the commission aspect was quite difficult. The court achieved severance, however, on the basis that the agreement was in substance one of establishing a right to commission, and that the form should not frustrate that substance. Quite inventive, really.

Thus it is open to the courts to deem any clause which is considered to affect seriously an employee's chances of gaining employment as being in restraint of trade. Such might be the case even with confidentiality clauses if the prevention of disclosure relates to such a narrow market that the maintenance of secrecy itself means that the employee is prevented from working.

8.8 Restraints during employment

When will an existing employee be prevented from competing with the employer's business? We saw in **Chapter 5 (5.2.2.2)** that an employee should not put himself in a position which will generate a conflict of interest. Traditionally one would apply a test of 'servile incident' to clauses which operated during the currency of the contract (e.g., the width of a 'whole time and attention' clause), whilst reserving the application of restraint of trade doctrine to actions occurring *after* the termination of the contract. Following cases such as *Schroeder (A) Music Publishing Co. Ltd* v *Macaulay* [1974] 1 WLR 1308 and *Davis (Clifford) Management Ltd* v *WEA Records Ltd* [1975] 1 WLR 61, however, there has developed a thesis that one should apply the restraint of trade doctrine to terms relevant to the currency of the employment contract (see *Electrolux* v *Hudson* [1977] FSR 312). This is despite the fact that all the leading cases have not been concerned with employment law at all, but rather with commercial contracts (and most recently relating to exclusive contracts for 'exploited' songwriter-performers).

There are important analytical distinctions between the two types of term. First, courts are reluctant even today to upset express terms relating to the operation of the contract, e.g., terms relating to hours, pay, etc. At the same time, courts have always subjected restraint clauses to a detailed and rigorous analysis. Secondly, an express term relating to the currency of the contract is presumed valid unless shown otherwise; restraint clauses are presumed to be void. Thus both restraint of trade and servile incidents may be based upon the same *common rule* of preventing undue restrictions on personal liberty, but one should be clear as to which is being used.

The notion of restraint *during* employment may, however, apply where the effect of a term is effectively to tie the employee to that employment or to sterilise the employee's skills. As was explained in *Lapthorne* v *Eurofi Ltd* [2001] EWCA Civ 993, if such restraints on activities *during* employment are only those which are incidental and normal to the positive commercial arrangements at which the contract aims, even though those ties exclude all dealings with others, there is probably no restraint of trade within the meaning of the doctrine and no question of reasonableness arises. *Lapthorne* concerned a consultant accountant providing services, during the currency of the contract with his employer, to companies other than the employer's clients. The Court of Appeal decided that it was clear, at the time that the contract was formed, that the parties had anticipated that the employee would not work exclusively for the employer. The terms that aimed to prevent Lapthorne from providing general accountancy services to others while he was engaged by Eurofi, and subsequently, were drafted too widely to protect E's legitimate interests and to be reasonable; therefore the covenants were in restraint of trade. We would only comment here that this is still not a mainstream employer–employee relationship case and does not in itself mean that the doctrine of restraint is relevant to restrictions imposed on employees taking on extra-work activities during the currency of an employment contract.

8.8.1 Express terms

These usually appear in the form of 'whole time and attention'. Frequently they state as their justification the prevention of competition. An express term can indeed limit the activities of employees undertaken in their spare time. Any restriction the employer imposes on the employee will not deprive the employee of earning any livelihood and therefore will most likely be tolerated by the courts. At least this should hold true with full-time workers; contracts with part-time workers or consultants may well be viewed in a different light—the light of servile incidents or restraint of trade. If the *Schroeder* approach has a part to play in employment law, it is most likely to be applicable as regards these employees.

As noted in **Chapter 5**, a serious breach of such an express term will allow the employer to dismiss summarily the employee or to claim for damages.

8.8.2 Implied terms

In the absence of an express term the employee (at least senior employees) will still be bound under the duty of fidelity to use the employer's time for the employer's purposes, i.e., not to pursue other activities during working hours—at least if those activities are in competition with the employer, cause harm to the employer's interests, e.g., by divulging (or having the potential to divulge) confidential information (see *Hivac Ltd* v *Park Royal Scientific Instruments Ltd* [1946] Ch 169), or cause harm to the relationship (e.g., by undertaking work which adversely affects the proper fulfilment of the employment contract).

It follows that some low-ranking staff will have greater freedom as to the use of their spare time and cannot be so easily limited: *Nova Plastics Ltd* v *Froggatt* [1982] IRLR 146 (odd-job man not in breach when working for a competitor in his spare time). Proof of real or potential harm to the employer would be necessary for any restriction to have effect.

8.9 Employees' actions before termination

If an employee is planning to resign and set up in business, he or she will have made some preparations. Any business venture will need some planning. If the employee uses the employer's time and facilities to do this then this action will constitute a breach of contract: *Wessex Dairies Ltd* v *Smith* [1935] 2 KB 80, where the employee milkman (on his last day of employment) set about informing customers of his plans to set up in business on his own account.

More recently, adjustments have been made to the latitude allowed to enterprising employees. In *Laughton* v *Bapp Industrial Supplies* [1986] IRLR 245, the two employees wrote to their employer's clients informing them of their intention to set up in business on their own account and asking for product lists, price lists and general terms. They were summarily dismissed when this was discovered by the employers. The EAT held that their actions did not amount to a breach of fidelity; their actions were *merely preparatory*. The position would have been different if they had used the employers' time and equipment; or even if there had been express terms forbidding such action. Again, in *Balston Ltd* v *Headline Filters Ltd* [1987] FSR 330, a director's *intentions* to set up in a competing business were held not to be a breach of fiduciary duty or breach of fidelity; neither were his actions which were undertaken during his notice period but at a time when he had been released from his duties. But in *Marshall* v *Industrial Systems & Control Ltd* [1992] IRLR 294, the employee was in breach when he formed concrete plans with a fellow employee to steal away the business of the employer's best client. And again, in *Adamson* v *B&L Cleaning Services Ltd* [1995] IRLR 193 the EAT found the dismissal of a foreman to be fair when he had sought to tender for a contract in competition with his employer. This was a breach of fidelity and distinguishable from *Laughton* v *Bapp*.

These cases tended to focus on acts of preparation as distinct from substantive actions. What is not entirely clear, however, is whether potentially harmful acts such as soliciting customers, suppliers or even fellow employees, *pursued in the employee's own time*, will constitute a breach of fidelity. There are indications (see *Thomas Marshall* v *Guinle* [1978] ICR 905, at p. 925 and *Hivac Ltd* v *Park Royal Scientific Instruments Ltd* [1946] Ch 169, at p. 178) that the answer would be that a breach has occurred. Certainly this should be the case where the contract contains a 'dedication to enterprise' clause.

If the employee is simply planning to leave the company to join another (e.g., attending interviews), it follows from the above discussion that this will not constitute any breach of fidelity. Care must be taken here to distinguish preparatory acts, such as attending interviews, from acts such as copying confidential information or memorising data. In *Sanders* v *Parry* [1967] 1 WLR 753, for instance, an assistant solicitor agreed with one of his principal's clients to resign and set up in business, in premises provided by the client, taking with him the client's business. Havers J commented that the employee was 'knowingly, deliberately and secretly acting, setting out to do something which would inevitably inflict great harm on his principal'. Thus, such actions will constitute a breach of contract and may render the employee subject to an injunction.

8.10 Garden leave

The rather graphic term 'garden leave' refers to attempts to hold the employee (who usually wishes to terminate the contract) to his or her notice period. The idea is that the employee will not be forced to work during that notice period but may stay at home (in the garden!) and still be paid. If successful, the effect of such a clause is that it operates as some form of restraint as the employee cannot work for any competitor during this time because of the employee's continuing duty of fidelity. Contacts and confidential information thus become less and less useful. Injunctions have been granted to this effect. Such relief is discretionary.

The most well-known instance arose in *Evening Standard Co. Ltd* v *Henderson* [1987] ICR 588. Henderson was the production manager for an evening newspaper. His notice period was 12 months. He sought to leave to work for a rival newspaper, giving only two months' notice. The company sought to put him on garden leave. As noted in **Chapter 5**, courts do not grant injunctions to compel specific performance of the contract; an employee cannot be forced to work for an employer, nor can an employer be forced to employ someone. Nevertheless in this case an injunction was granted because the company was not seeking to compel Henderson to continue working as such, nor was the company refusing him the right to work, nor would it be seeking damages from him for not working.

In *Provident Financial Group plc* v *Hayward* [1989] ICR 160, the employee (the financial director) gave six months' notice as required by this contract. After working for two months he agreed to take four months' pay on the understanding that (i) he did not work elsewhere during this time (i.e., he took garden leave); and (ii) he maintained confidentiality for a period of two years. He sought work with another estate agent and his ex-employer sought an injunction to prevent him doing so. The Court of Appeal held that the injunction should be refused. The key point in granting an injunction is whether breaching an 'anti-competition' clause materially and adversely affects the employer. Here, on the facts, it was found that the employer's position would not be seriously affected by Hayward's actions.

This area took another twist in *GFI Group Inc* v *Eaglestone* [1994] IRLR 119 where a successful foreign exchange options broker sought to work for a competitor during an agreed 20-week notice period (where he was on garden leave). The High Court believed that the 20-week period was arbitrary and not specifically designed to protect the employer's interests; and given that other employees on only four-week notice periods had already joined the rival company the restriction was fairly meaningless. The garden leave was reduced to 13 weeks by the court (although had it not been for the other ex-employees the court would apparently have held to the full term).

Oddly enough, most of the arguments on garden leave have not developed out of express clauses of this nature, though one such was the subject of debate in *Eurobrokers Ltd* v *Rabey* [1995] IRLR 206. Here, the employee (a money broker) resigned and the employers sought to bind him to an express six-month garden leave clause. He declined to observe this and an injunction was granted enforcing the period. The court noted that the employer had expended a great deal of money in developing contacts for the employee and that this period represented a reasonable time for the employer to cement new relations with those customers. Nearly all firms in the ILU Survey included such a clause in their draft precedents, at least as regards senior employees who may be under extensive notice periods.

However, all this may yet change. In *William Hill Organisation Ltd* v *Tucker* [1998] IRLR 313, the Court of Appeal refused to grant a 'garden leave' injunction where there was no express term allowing for this, holding that the employer was under an obligation to let this senior employee perform his job, not just receive his wages (which is a little odd given that the employee actually wanted to leave his job to work elsewhere). This part of the judgment seems to revive long-dead arguments on whether an employee has the right to work (see **5.2.2.1(b)** above). However, on a 'belt and braces' approach it is advisable for an employer to include both a garden leave clause and a payment in lieu clause in the contract.

The case did not end there. Morritt LJ went on to comment that in the case of a garden leave injunction being sought, 'it had to be justified on similar grounds to those necessary to the validity of the employee's restraint covenant in restraint of trade . . .'. The same point was made again by Morritt LJ in *Symbian Ltd* v *Christenson* [2001] IRLR 77. This case contains an additional problem, however. Here, at first instance, Sir Richard Scott V-C held that during garden leave periods an employee no longer owed a duty of good faith or fidelity to his employer. If this were so, employers might well find themselves in some difficulty, with 'employees' on garden leave being free to disclose confidential information. At best, employers would need to have such duties spelt out as applying to garden leave periods. Unfortunately, the Court of Appeal did not have to, and did not, deal directly with these rather controversial comments. The days of using garden leave clauses to overcome some of the drafting difficulties of restraint clauses may well have disappeared with these cases.

Where an employer seeks to enforce both a garden leave clause and a restraint clause there is a persuasive argument that the overall effect might be unreasonable. Some contracts therefore specify that if the garden leave is enforced the restraint will be reduced accordingly. Following the Court of Appeal decision in *Crédit Suisse Asset Management Ltd* v *Armstrong* [1996] IRLR 450, however, we now know that (except in extreme cases) there is no juridical basis for such a set-off. The Court also confirmed its powers in deciding on the permissible length of garden leave clauses in any particular case.

8.11 Injunctions

Though a claimant may have a remedy of damages as of right (see **7.7** above regarding remedies in general), there exists the additional or alternative discretionary remedy of an injunction. However, if damages will compensate the claimant fully an injunction will not be granted. Neither will the court grant an injunction which amounts to an order for specific performance.

8.11.1 Basic rules

Injunctions come in two forms: interim (pending a full hearing of the issues) and final (granted at the conclusion of the full action). In either case they may be limited in duration or perpetual in their effect. The granting of injunctions is a discretionary remedy. The key section of the Civil Procedure Rules is Part 25.

As far as employment matters are concerned interim injunctions have the greater prominence. Despite the fact that the interim injunction really does not decide the merits of the case at all, the granting of such injunctions can effectively determine the issue. For instance, if the lifespan of a restraint of trade clause is one year it is unlikely that the full action will be heard before its expiry. Thus where an employer is faced with an employee or former employee who is about to divulge confidential information, breach copyright, destroy the novelty of a patentable invention and so forth, the effectiveness of an injunction can come into play. Even in advance of any breach it is possible to obtain a *quia timet* (because he fears) injunction.

Almost inevitably, where an interim injunction is granted the claimant will have to undertake to pay any damages due should the final action determine that the injunction was not justified. In some cases the court will require proof that this undertaking can be honoured. It is also possible for a defendant to seek to avoid the full implications of an interim injunction by offering to the applicant or the court an undertaking in relation to some or all of the relief sought.

8.11.2 *American Cyanamid* v *Ethicon*

The decision of the House of Lords in the patent case of *American Cyanamid Co.* v *Ethicon Ltd* [1975] AC 396 established the position as regards *with notice* applications for prohibitory injunctions. In these cases evidence is normally given by witness statement, to the exclusion of cross-examination. The employer does not have to show a *prima facie* case to obtain an injunction preventing, for example, the breach of a restraint of trade or confidentiality clause. Rather, the test is whether:

(a) there is a serious issue to be tried at the full hearing; and

(b) if there is, whether the 'balance of convenience' favours the granting of the injunction. This aspect has been described as a shorthand phrase for 'the balance of the risk of doing an injustice' or 'the balance of hardship'. The primary factor in deciding this question is whether damages at trial would be a sufficient remedy. If they would be, this negates the need for an injunction. However, damages are often not an adequate remedy in this area as (especially in confidentiality cases) once the 'cat is out of the bag' the injury caused may well be uncompensatable in monetary terms. Equally, if the defendant is unlikely to be able to pay any damages awarded this points towards an injunction being granted—and if the applicant cannot give a cross-undertaking on damages this makes the granting of an injunction less likely.

In *Lawrence David* v *Ashton* [1989] ICR 123, the Court of Appeal stated that the *American Cyanamid* principles will *normally* apply to restraint of trade and confidentiality cases. The court will then seek to make an order for a speedy trial of the full action, usually on the application of the defendant. If, however, a speedy trial is not possible the judge is placed in something of a dilemma: to tie down the employee for a lengthy period so that long-term employment prospects might be adversely and seriously affected; or to allow the employee to continue working for the competitor so that, even if the restraint is finally found to be valid, the employer's remedy is purely a Pyrrhic one. In such instances (as was noted specifically in *Lansing Linde Ltd* v *Kerr* [1991] ICR 428 by the Court of Appeal), the judge at the interim hearing may have to investigate the substantive merits of the case in order to decide whether or not to grant the injunction. Thus, if the full action cannot be tried before the period of the restraint has expired (or almost expired), the court's decision could for most practical purposes effectively determine the issue at the interim stage. Equally, there is little point in granting an interim injunction concerning confidential information where there can be no further material damage to the employer.

As a basic approach, therefore, if a speedy trial is not possible a judge will have to consider, in a limited way because of the availability of evidence, the actual merits of the case. Indeed, in *Series 5 Software Ltd* v *Philip Clarke* [1996] FSR 273 Laddie J made the point that assessing the merits of the case was not in itself contrary to the spirit or intentions of *American Cyanamid*. Laddie J reviewed the authorities in depth and concluded that Lord Diplock in *American Cyanamid* had not intended to exclude consideration of the strength of the parties' cases; what was intended was that the court should not at this stage attempt to resolve difficult issues of fact or law. Thus it is necessary that a clear view of the evidence adduced can be gained by the judge without great debate before the relative strengths can be considered. The application of the *American Cyanamid* principles, as modified by *Series 5*, remains the position as regards interim injunctions applications based on restraint of trade clauses relating to the protection of trade connexions. With applications relating to the protection of confidential information (based on the implied term, any operative express terms or any restraint justified by the protection of information) matters have taken a different route because of the impact of the Human Rights Act 1998.

8.11.3 Impact of the Human Rights Act 1998

Article 10 ECHR states:

> 1. Everyone has the right to freedom of expression. This right shall include freedom to hold opinions and to receive and impart information an ideas without interference by public authority. . . .
> 2. The exercise of these freedoms, since it carries with it duties and responsibilities, may be subject to such formalities, conditions, restrictions or penalties as are prescribed by law and are necessary in a democratic society . . . for the protection of the reputation or the rights of others, *for preventing the disclosure of information received in confidence* . . . . . [emphasis added]

In cases involving the publication of material concerning others, therefore, this article (via the Human Rights Act) has to be considered. In terms of the granting of interim injunctions, the procedural method of dealing with this is set out in s. 12(3) HRA 1998 which states: 'No [relief affecting the exercise of a Convention right to freedom of expression] is to be granted so as to restrain publication before trial unless the court is satisfied that the applicant is likely to establish that publication should not be allowed.'

High-profile case law has sprung up in this area (sometimes involving the potential conflict between art. 10 and art. 8—respect for private and family life): see, for instance, *Douglas* v *Hello! Ltd* [2001] QB 967, on the infamous wedding photos of the Douglas's; *A* v *B (a company)* [2002] EWCA Civ 337, [2002] 3 WLR 542 on the sexual exploits of a footballer; *Venables* v *News Group Newspapers Ltd* [2001] Fam 430, on the identities of the killers of James Bulger and the more technically biased case of *Imutran Ltd* v *Uncaged Campaigns Ltd* [2001] 2 All ER 385, where a group campaigning for the cessation of animal experiments sought to publish confidential information belonging to a pharmaceutical company. These cases have generally been concerned with the freedom of the press or the protection of reputation. None of the cases had to consider, as part of the *ratio*, what was meant by the phrase in s. 12(3): 'the applicant is likely to establish that publication should not be allowed'. That problem fell to the Court of Appeal in *Cream Holdings Ltd* v *Banerjee* [2003] EWCA Civ 103, [2003] 2 All ER 318. As Sedley LJ puts it: how likely is 'likely'? The Court of Appeal held that the word 'likely' means '*a real prospect of success, convincingly established*'—a standard higher than that expected under *American Cyanamid* but lower than the notion of 'more probable than not'. 'Real prospect' here means 'not fanciful' rather than 'on the cards'.

As was noted in *Cream Holdings*, however, this test is just the first step; it is still open to the court to decide on the merits available to it whether to grant or refuse the injunction (indeed, in *Cream Holdings* itself the Court of Appeal was divided on the application issue). Simon Brown LJ put it this way: 'That is not, of course, to say that, whenever the [likely to succeed] test is satisfied, the court will grant interlocutory relief [sic] . . . . Often the court will not think it right to exercise that discretion in favour of prior restraint unless it is indeed satisfied that the claim will more probably than not succeed at trial' (at [61]). This is because, as Simon Brown LJ further commented (at [56]) on the move away from the original *American Cyanamid* principles, 'there will indeed be a number of claims for injunctive relief which will now fail when earlier they would have succeeded; they will fail because the court is required by s. 12(3) actually to consider the merits . . . .'.

It is possible that human rights issues may arise in an employment context and trigger a s. 12(3) analysis but most employment-based cases will not centre on issues such as freedom of expression and privacy in the way these terms have so far been used in human rights' jurisprudence. Nevertheless, the potential is always there. *Cream Holdings* itself involved an ex-employee in-house accountant passing information about alleged company malpractices to a local newspaper. The employee was under a duty of confidentiality and was in breach of this by relating her stories to the newspaper. Much of the detail of this case is contained in a closed judgment owing to the nature of the information, but, since the court affirmed the granting of the injunction, we must conclude that the presence of the duty was enough to persuade the court to continue with the temporary stop to publication (together with the fact that the delay in publication would not destroy the newsworthiness of the article itself). Nor did the well-established principle that there can be no confidentiality in iniquity (i.e., the company's alleged misconduct) prove to be a major decisive factor (but contrast, for instance, Sedley LJ's comments at [87]with those of Arden LJ at [96]). The injunction did not, however, relate to disclosures made by the accountant to relevant professional and supervisory bodies under the Public Interest Disclosure Act 1998.

8.11.4 Summary of rules regarding interim applications

There are different standards to apply in justifying the granting of interim injunctions depending upon the basis for the claim.

(a) Where the issue is one of the protection of trade connexions *only* the normal *American Cyanamid* principles should apply.

(b) The merits of the case may nevertheless have to be examined where a speedy trial is not possible. This is a matter of discretion and the courts should rarely attempt to resolve complex issues of disputed fact or law: *Series 5*.

(c) Any case involving the disclosure of confidential information may bring with it human rights implications in the form of art. 10 ECHR and even, possibly, art. 8 rights. If so, the procedures described in s. 12(3) HRA 1998 must be adhered to. If not, one presumes that the *American Cyanamid/Series 5* principles continue unabated (though this is not clear and it seems safer to work on the basis that s. 12(3) is the guiding light).

(d) Although *American Cyanamid* was distinguished in *Cream Holdings*, and a different test used, in many practical ways the test under s. 12(3) is not that dissimilar to the one created by Laddie J in *Series 5* (though generated by different considerations).

8.11.5 Search orders (formerly *Anton Piller* orders)

The idea of search orders is derived from the case of *Anton Piller KG* v *Manufacturing Processes Ltd* [1976] RPC 719. They represent the final link in a chain of orders which seek to deal with physical evidence. Along with freezing orders (formerly *Mareva* injunctions) they have been described as the law's nuclear weapons. Search orders have now been placed on a statutory footing: Civil Procedure Act 1997, s. 7. They are dealt with in CPR, r. 25.1(1)(h) and by Practice Direction 25.

Search orders were developed in intellectual property actions and represent the extreme limits of such processes to regain property because they are granted on a without notice (formerly an *ex parte*) application by the claimant. There will almost invariably be other mandatory orders attached, relating to assisting in the search and preventing the destruction of material. Their effect (to varying degrees) is to allow the claimant immediate access to the defendant's premises to search for and seize documents and other evidence such as information stored on computer. The purpose behind such orders is to prevent dishonest defendants dealing with the evidence in a manner prejudicial to the case. The employer may seek a search order against an employee or former employee where the safeguarding of evidence is believed necessary, i.e., where there is a grave danger that vital evidence will be destroyed.

Circumstances have to be exceptional for a search order to be made. There must be an extremely strong *prima facie* case, the extent of possible damage must be serious, there must be clear evidence that the other party is likely to disobey any court order, and the items to form the subject of the order must be clearly identifiable. An order might be made, for instance, where an employee is secretly making 'pirate' copies of the employer's copyright work and selling them abroad. An order will not be made where the claimant is simply on a 'fishing expedition'.

Care must also be taken where the right of inspection (and consequent search) might actually reveal the other side's trade secrets, etc. An undertaking for damages will be required and the court demands that the applicant comes with 'clean hands' so that all matters even remotely relevant to the case must be disclosed. The order must be served by an independent solicitor who must explain the effect of the order to the defendant and inform the defendant of the legal right to seek legal advice before complying with the order.

An application for a search order may be refused where there is the possibility of self-incrimination regarding criminal offences on the provision of the evidence by the defendant. This privilege does not, however, extend to the possibility of physical violence being meted out to the defendant by his associates should he comply with the order (*Coca-Cola Co. & Schweppes Ltd* v *Gilbey* [1996] FSR 23).

8.12 Self-test question on Chapters 7 and 8

Your client is Phoenix Guitars of Bristol. The company manufactures guitars and guitar parts and employs 26 employees. Your Principal wishes you to provide some preliminary guidance notes on a key question: if *Phoenix Guitars Ltd* go ahead and dismiss one of their employees (Mr Setters), will they still be able to enforce the confidentiality and restraint of trade clauses against him? *The Personnel Director, Mr Burek, briefs you as follows:*

1. **The business:** *Phoenix Guitars Ltd* is a long-established company which makes and sells a range of standard handmade guitars and guitar parts to retail outlets plus custom-made guitars for individual customers (ranging from ordinary guitar players to internationally-renowned rock stars). It is located in Bristol. It has a network of sales across the UK to specialist guitar shops and general musical outlets but receives the custom-made orders directly from the public through telephone, internet or personal contact. The company derives its raw materials (various kinds of hardwood, electrical fixtures, etc) from across the world.

2. **The work undertaken by Setters:** Mr Setters is the senior (of two) product designers. Mr Setters has been with the company for five years. His contractual notice period is two months. His work involves creating new designs for sale to the retail outlets together with designing the custom-made guitars we produce for individual customers. His work is mainly factory-centred, but involves some contact with those customers who get in touch with us directly as well as with the retail outlets that stock our goods. He reports directly to the managing director. Mr Setters has access to a wide range of information which the company regards as confidential, *viz:*

   (i) Customers' (retail and personal) specific requirements, especially in the case of long-established relationships;

   (ii) Future expansion plans;

   (iii) Details of contracts with suppliers around the world, including discounts obtained.

This information is contained on held on computers (subject to passwords), paper files and customer file records. Mr Setters has been made aware, both from the clauses in his contract and from company documentation issued annually, of the importance to the company of all this information. The establishment of customer contacts is very dependent on the reputation of employees and Mr Setters was originally engaged by the company specifically because of his standing in the market. He brought with him a number of contacts at the time.

3. **Recent events:** A couple of weeks ago we held an investigation into Setter's conduct during a presentation team's visit to a potential client. At dinner one evening he informed the potential client that '*Phoenix* may be a market leader now but they are not investing enough in general research or advertising for the future'. The potential client immediately asked us to respond to this. We recalled Setters immediately and instigated disciplinary procedures. Setters has insisted that this was 'only general talk and taken out of context'. Nevertheless, we are considering dismissing him. However, we have received reliable information that Setters has already been in negotiations with a rival company (*Andrea Amati)* and that they are on the verge of offering him a contract of employment. It would also seem that Setters has been talking to his fellow designer about transferring with him to *Andrea Amati.*

4. **Competitors:** We have two main competitors within the UK: *Le Strad Ltd* (whose headquarters are in Birmingham) and *Andrea Amati (Musical Instruments) Ltd* (in London). There are, of course, numerous American, Japanese, Korean, and Mexican companies operating world-wide, including within the UK but these produce mass-market guitars and parts. Ours is a specialist operation and we do not compete directly with these the large-scale-production companies. Until now, *Andrea Amati* has concentrated on the European market (in which we have no interest). However, we have firm evidence that *Andrea Amati* is seeking to expand its share of the UK market in the near future and plans to offer new designs centred on a very competitive pricing policy. Such a development could affect our market share adversely. We do not therefore want to lose any of our key employees to any of our competitors, especially *Andrea Amati*. We believe that Mr Setters is likely to use or disclose our trade secrets in these areas if he leaves or is dismissed.

5. **Likelihood of damage to the company:** Should Setters leave and disclose our trade secrets he will cause us substantial harm in that the financial deals and design/production methods we use together constitute business processes which provide us with a competitive edge over our rivals. *Andrea Amati Ltd* is a major rival who is seeking to mirror our activities and undercut our prices. Our new business strategy has emerged after intensive analysis and is near completion. The life-span for the information in Mr Setters' possession can be conservatively calculated as three years in terms of business strategy/re-designs.

Setters has good contacts with both customers and suppliers and would undoubtedly make use of these in any new business venture. It is a fickle market; some would transfer their allegiance from us and follow him, especially if his new employer were to undercut us.

Extracts from Setter's contract of employment relating to restraint and confidentiality terms

8. CONFIDENTIALITY

8.1 The Employee acknowledges that during the course of his employment with the Company he will receive and have access to confidential information of the Company and he will also receive and have access to detailed client/customer lists and information relating to the operations and business requirements of those clients/customers.

8.2 The Employee shall not (other than in the proper performance of his duties or with the prior written consent of the Board or unless ordered by a court of competent jurisdiction) at any time either during the continuance of his employment or after its termination disclose or communicate to any person or use for his own benefit or the benefit of any person other than the Company or any Associated Company any confidential information which may come to his knowledge in the course of his employment and the Employee shall use his best endeavours to prevent the unauthorised publication or misuse of any confidential information provided that such restrictions shall cease to apply to any confidential information which may enter the public domain other than through the actions of the Employee.

8.3 For the avoidance of doubt and without prejudice to the generality of Clause 8.1 the following is a non-exhaustive list of matters which in relation to the Company are considered confidential and must be treated as such by the Employee:-

8.3.1 any secrets of the Company or any Associated Company:

8.3.2 marketing strategies and plans;

8.3.3 customer lists and details of contracts with or requirements of customers;

8.3.4 pricing strategies;

8.3.5 discount rates obtained from suppliers or given to customers and sales figures;

8.3.6 lists of suppliers;

8.3.7 any invention technical data know-how or other manufacturing or trade secrets of the Company or any Associated Company and their clients/customers.

9. **RESTRICTIONS ON ACTIVITIES FOLLOWING TERMINATION**

9.1 For a period of TWELVE MONTHS after termination of the Employment, the Employee shall not directly or indirectly (and whether on his own account or for any other person, firm, company, or organisation) deal with any person, firm, company or organisation who or which at any time during the preceding TWENTY FOUR MONTHS shall have been a customer of or in the habit of dealing with the Company, and with whom or which the Employee has had direct dealings or personal contact as part of the Employment so as to harm the goodwill of the Company or any Associated Company or so as to compete with the Company or any Associated Company.

9.2 For a period of SIX MONTHS after termination of the Employment, the Employee shall not canvass solicit or approach or cause to be canvassed, solicited or approached in relation to a business which may in any way be in competition with the Company, the custom of any person who at the date hereof or at any time during the period of TWENTY FOUR MONTHS prior to the Termination Date shall have been a client or customer of the Company or any Associated Company.

9.3 For a period of SIX MONTHS after termination of the Employment, the Employee shall not solicit or induce or endeavour to solicit or induce any person who on the Termination Date is an employee of the company with whom the Employee has had dealings during his employment to cease working for or providing services to the Company whether or not any such person would thereby commit a breach of contract.

9.4 The covenants given by the Employee in sub-clauses 9.1 to 9.3 inclusive above will not cease to apply in the event that the Employment is terminated by the Company in breach of contract.

9 Termination of the contract at common law

9.1 Introduction

A contract of employment can come to an end in a number of different ways:

(a) by agreement;
(b) by completion of a specific task;
(c) by expiry of a fixed term;
(d) by automatic termination, e.g., frustration of the contract;
(e) by dismissal;
(f) by resignation.

These forms of termination describe the basic layout of the chapter. However, we are also iterested in the consequences of any termination, so that we will adopt the following additional headings:

(g) Justifiable and wrongful dismissals.
(h) Post-termination duties.
(i) Damages and other remedies.
(j) Outline of tax considerations.

Under every heading there may be statutory as well as common law consequences. We shall concentrate on the common law consequences in this chapter, but will make cross-references to certain statutory points where there is a substantial overlap.

The points raised in **Chapters 3, 4,** and **5** should also be noted regarding the structure and operation of the contract.We saw there, for instance, that where the employer makes unilateral changes to the contract there may be a number of consequences such as wrongful dismissal claims, wrongful repudiation claims, and the granting of injunctions (see **Chapter 5** at **5.4.4**). But clearly there does not have to be an attempt at altering the contract before resignations and dismissals may occur. A termination of the contract may occur for a variety of reasons, e.g., because of the employee's misconduct or incapability, or because there is a redundancy. Before examining these consequences we need to note the other, less common forms in which a termination may occur.

9.2 Termination by agreement

The parties are free to agree at any time that the contract may terminate on the happening of certain circumstances. They might also agree at any time that if the contract comes to an end in specific or general circumstances then an agreed sum (a 'golden handshake') will be payable. This will stand as liquidated damages (enforceable if a genuine pre-estimate of loss).

Agreements simply to end the contract are not common. Usually there will be a dismissal or resignation. As a consensual termination cannot by its very nature amount to a dismissal the courts are naturally suspicious of these arrangements because, without some form of a dismissal, statutory rights such as unfair dismissal will be nullified. Indeed, ERA 1996, s. 203 forbids any *exclusions* of statutory rights. Therefore the burden of proving the presence of a genuine agreement and absence of an exclusion of rights is an onerous one. Anything that smacks of duress, fraud, or general bad faith will find disfavour and so be classed as a dismissal. The areas that have caused most problems are:

(a) *Apparent resignation.*
The employer and employee may agree to termination without notice so that the employee can take another job more easily. This is genuine and unlikely to cause problems. But where a resignation has arisen from an employer's statement along the lines of 'resign or be sacked', the courts are reluctant to accept this as a valid agreement. We shall deal with this more fully at **9.8.1**.

(b) *Employees' concessions.*
In granting extended leave of absence employers have developed a practice of asking for a written undertaking that, should the employee fail to return by a set date, the parties agree that this will automatically terminate the contract. In *Igbo v Johnson Matthey Chemicals Ltd* [1986] ICR 505, the Court of Appeal outlawed such terms; to find otherwise, it was noted, could lead to every contract containing a clause whereby the employee 'agreed' that if late to work on Monday mornings this would automatically terminate the contract.

The most common *valid* consensual terminations therefore relate to contracts for the completion of specific tasks and non-renewal of fixed-term contracts.

9.3 Termination by completion of a specific task

A termination in these circumstances used not to count as a dismissal for common law or statutory purposes, but such contracts are now classed as 'limited-term' and subject to the rules noted below: see EA 2002, sch. 2, para 3(7) and 13.

9.4 Expiry of limited-term contracts

Both contracts for the completion of a specific task and fixed-term contracts fall under the general description of 'limited-term'. 'Task' contracts will include things such as employees doing so-called 'seasonal' or 'casual' work who have contracts for a short period or task that end when the period expires or the task is completed (e.g., agricultural workers or shop assistants working specifically for Christmas or another busy period). The most commonly-occurring limited-term contract, however, is the fixed-term one. We will generally use the phrase 'limited-term' below. Where we refer to 'fixed-term' this is simply because that is the best example, but the regulations still apply to both forms of contract.

A fixed-term contract usually has clear start and finish dates. The contract may last weeks, months or years. At common law the arrival of the agreed date terminates the contract automatically and no further consequences flow from this. The contract has terminated by effluxion of time and no advance notice by either party is necessary.

It should be noted, however, that the expiry *and non-renewal* of any limited-term contract *will constitute a dismissal for statutory purposes* (see **10.3.5**) and employees on 'limited-term' contracts have also gained protection from receiving less favourable treatment under the Fixed-Term Employees (Prevention of Less Favourable Treatment) Regulations SI 2002/2034 noted above at **6.1.1.8**.

9.4.1 Limited-term contracts and notice provisions

Odd though it sounds, it is possible to have limited-term contracts which expressly allow for termination (by either party giving notice) which will take effect at an earlier date than the set finish date: *Dixon* v *BBC* [1979] ICR 281. The reasons for this are again tied in with preserving statutory rights. Do not worry about the apparent illogicality of it all.

Some fixed-term contracts will delineate the stated period but permit indefinite continuance after the final date. A notice period applicable to this second stage will then be specified. In these circumstances the parties may give notice during the fixed term to terminate the contract at the end of that period (and so before the extension has begun) or to take effect at some time during the extension: *Costigan* v *Gray Bovier Engines Ltd* (1925) 41 TLR 372.

If a limited-term contract is terminated prematurely the amount of damages will be either for the given notice period (if there is one) or else for the remainder of the term (see **9.10** below). There may also be an action for unfair dismissal or redundancy.

Where a limited-term contract is about to end employers often notify employees of this fact. There is no requirement to do so, but it does make for sound practice. However, employers should be wary of issuing any such letter in the form of 'giving notice'; such words may invite a tribunal to conclude that the dismissal occurred for reasons other than expiry of the term and may revive arguments about unfair dismissal.

9.4.2 Waiver/contracting-out clauses

Such clauses state that an employee will not be able to claim *statutory* rights such as unfair dismissal and redundancy payments on the expiry and non-renewal of the contract. Although these clauses can still be found in a number of contracts, they are of decreasing validity (see **10.3.6** below).

9.4.3 Successive terms

It has been quite common for employers to use a succession of fixed-term contracts rather than create a contract of indefinite duration. The reason for this was to add on waiver clauses and thereby seek to avoid any liability for unfair dismissal or redundancy. Under reg. 8 of the Fixed-Term Employees (Prevention of Less Favourable Treatment) Regulations SI 2002/2034, such employees will now be regarded as ordinary employees (i.e. the contract will be regarded as having no temporal restrictions) if:

(a) the employee was employed on a fixed-term contract before the start of the present contract or the current fixed-term contract has been renewed; *and*

(b) discounting any period before 10 July 2002, the employee's period of continuous employment is four years or more; *and*

(c) the employment of the employee under a fixed-term contract was not justified on objective grounds. That justification must be present either at the time of the last renewal or, where the contract has not been renewed, at the time it was entered into.

> This means that a burden is placed on the employer to justify the continuing use of fixed-term contracts. The term 'renewal' includes any extension.

Under reg. 9, an employee on a limited-term who believes they should be classed as a perman-ent employee may request a statement from the employer confirming or denying this, with reasons. If the employer does not respond, or denies permanency, an employee may also make an application to the tribunal for such a declaration (reg. 9(5)). These points may be modified by way of a collective agreement with a trade union or through a workforce agreement (see § ch. 1).

9.4.4 Probationary periods

These are devices commonly used by employers when hiring or promoting employees. They purport to offer some form of 'trial period'. In fact they are generally meaningless. Unless the wording specifies such they are *not* fixed-term contracts of any nature and dismissal can occur during the course of the probationary period: *Dalgleish* v *Kew House Farm Ltd* [1982] IRLR 251. They are a traditional warning to employees, nothing more. New employees will generally only have a claim if the employer acts in breach of the contract, e.g., by not giving adequate notice of dismissal. This is because unfair dismissal rights generally do not accrue until there has been one years' service (although note **10.3.1** below). Existing employees who are promoted and put on a 'probationary' period maintain any existing rights they have to claim unfair dismissal.

9.5 Automatic termination

9.5.1 Frustration

Frustration of a contract occurs when unforeseen circumstances, which are beyond the control of either party, make it impossible to perform the objectives of the contract. The most common examples of the doctrine of frustration applying to employment contracts are illness, death, and imprisonment. A frustrating event terminates the contract automatically, except where the event relates to the employer and the claim is for redundancy; in this case the employee's rights are preserved.

If the 'frustrating event' has been *caused* by the fault of one party, that party cannot rely on it. The burden of proof lies with the party claiming frustration of the contract.

9.5.1.1 Frustration and sickness

The application of the doctrine of frustration to employment contracts, especially where illness is the issue, should be treated with great caution. Cases like *Condor* v *Barron Knights Ltd* [1966] 1 WLR 87, where a pop group drummer was unable to 'drum' for the seven nights per week required, are rare examples of frustrating events. Guidelines on when illness will frustrate a contract have been laid down: see, for instance, *Egg Stores (Stamford Hill) Ltd* v *Leibovici* [1977] ICR 260. Thus the following factors need to be considered:

(a) What is the nature of the illness?

(b) How long has the incapacity lasted?

(c) How long is it likely to continue?

(d) What are the terms of the contract, e.g., as to sick pay?

(e) How long was the employment set to last?

(f) What was the nature of the employment, e.g., was he or she a key employee?

(g) For how long has the employee been employed?

Questions of frustration tend to arise either when there is an accident or illness which will obviously have long-term effects, or where the position with a long-term illness employee has been allowed to drift. This may seem unlikely, but it happens, e.g., an employee is off work, the sick pay scheme becomes exhausted, the employers lose contact with the employee and then maybe a year or more later someone decides to 'tidy up the books'. They then discover the employee—or 25 such workers in one case dealt with by the authors.

On the other hand, the acceptance of medical certificates and retention of the P45 does not necessarily mean the frustration *has not occured*. This is because the matter is beyond the control or the intentions of the parties—it has either happened or not happened: *Hart* v *Marshall & Sons (Bulwell) Ltd* [1977] ICR 539. The right to receive notice does not survive a frustrating event.

The key point is whether performance of the contract has now become impossible, or at least radically different from the original undertaking. The doctrine can also apply to contracts where a short period of notice is due (see *Notcutt* v *Universal Equipment Co. (London) Ltd* [1986] ICR 414); but whatever the type of contract, reliance on the doctrine is generally inadvisable—the employer would be wiser to decide whether or not to dismiss for incapacity. First, as will be seen in **Chapter 10**, the test for fairness in ill-health dismissals bears a remarkable similarity to the issues raised in frustration. Secondly, if there is the prospect of recovery then, unless there is an issue of 'key worker', this will usually mean there is no frustration.

9.5.1.2 Frustration and imprisonment

The second possibility of a frustrating event occurs when the employee is sent to prison. This makes turning up for work slightly difficult! In *Shepherd* v *Jerrom* [1986] ICR 802, the Court of Appeal decided that imprisonment is capable of frustrating the contract (here, an apprentice received a sentence of between six months' and two years' borstal training). The longer the sentence the more likely the frustration; though again one must relate this to the actual contract—status of the employee as a key worker, length of notice period, whether there is a fixed-term contract, etc. The same considerations will apply to restrictive bail conditions and being placed on custodial remand.

9.5.2 Winding up of the company

The compulsory winding up of a company will operate as a notice of dismissal. A resolution for voluntary winding up will, in most cases, also constitute such notice; at least where the business is being discontinued. An employee may then have a claim for wrongful dismissal.

9.5.3 Appointment of a receiver

The appointment of a receiver by the court or as an agent for the creditors will again constitute an automatic termination of the contracts of employment. Not so, it appears, with an appointment by the debenture holders, at least for junior employees whose positions effectively remain intact.

9.5.4 Changes in a partnership

The retirement of a partner operates as a dismissal at law. Most employees will simply be re-engaged, however, and the employees' continuity of employment is preserved under

ERA 1996, s. 218(5): *Stevens* v *Bower* [2004] EWCA Civ 496. The practical effects are therefore minimal. The dissolution of the partnership does, technically, bring about a termination. So, where re-engagement does not occur the employee may claim wrongful dismissal plus any statutory rights.

9.5.5 Transfer of the business

At common law, where the business is sold, this will operate as a termination; but the position now has to be read in the light of the Transfer of Undertakings (Protection of Employment) Regulations 1981, as discussed in **Chapter 12**, so that if there is a 'relevant transfer' under these Regulations it is most likely that the contracts of employment will simply be transferred along with the sale. Consequently there will be no dismissal and continuity of employment gained with the old employer will be deemed to have been with the new employer. The basic idea behind the Regulations is that nothing should really have changed simply because the business has been transferred.

9.6 The meaning of dismissal

The meaning of 'dismissal' is central to employment law. It ranges from 'being given the sack' through to resignations which are deemed dismissals. It is an area of technicalities which can occasionally confuse, and one which can certainly trap the unwary. The reason for all this is straightforward enough: an employee cannot claim wrongful dismissal, unfair dismissal or redundancy unless actually dismissed. This will be for the employee to prove if challenged. But the ordinary meaning of 'dismissal' is given an expanded statutory form in ERA 1996, ss. 95 and 136, which incorporate non-renewal of a fixed-term contract and resignations which are deemed dismissals.

Employees may therefore find themselves 'dismissed' (as legally defined) for the purposes of common law and statutory claims in the following circumstances:

(a) where the employee is given the sack (see **9.6.1** below);

(b) where the employer uses language which amounts to dismissal (see **9.6.1**);

(c) where the employer intimates a future dismissal (see **9.8** below);

(d) where the employer says 'resign or be sacked' (see **9.8**);

(e) where the employer repudiates the contract and the employee resigns (see **9.6.3** and **9.8**);

(f) where a fixed-term contract is not renewed. This applies only to statutory claims (see **9.4** above).

At common law the consequences of being dismissed are that if the employer has acted in breach of contract the employee will be able to sue for damages. This is known as a *wrongful dismissal action*. As we will see, the assessment of damages is governed by ordinary contractual principles. In employment contracts this generally means that an employee will be able to sue for the amount that he or she should have received as a notice of termination payment.

In **Chapters 10** and **11** we will also see that a dismissal may lead to other *statutory* forms of compensation, i.e., unfair dismissal compensation and redundancy payments.

9.6.1 Being sacked

A dismissal will normally occur when the employer terminates the contract *with or without notice*. The decision to dismiss must be *communicated*, orally or in writing, to be effective.

Where notice is given by post (which is not too clever when seen from an unfair dismissal angle) there is no debate as to 'postal rules' applying: the notice is communicated when the employee reads or could reasonably have been expected to read the letter (*Brown* v *Southall and Knight* [1980] ICR 617).

In most cases the act of dismissal will be obvious: 'you are dismissed'; 'you're sacked'; 'collect your P45 and get out'; 'I'm giving you four weeks' notice', and so on. The 'sack', by the way, comes from the days when a dismissed worker would be handed his bag of tools; the message was obvious.

Problems will arise when the words used are not clear, were meant merely as a censure or are said in anger (and perhaps regretted). The basic rule has to be: how would a reasonable person understand the words? If the reasonable man would perceive the words as amounting to a dismissal, they will constitute a dismissal; if the employee is wrong then he or she has resigned and is in breach of the contract. There is always the possibility, however, that the words (though not an overt dismissal) were such as to destroy the mutual trust and confidence in the relationship and so amount to a wrongful repudiation/constructive dismissal. Claims in the alternative are therefore advisable, i.e., the employee was dismissed on *x* date; alternatively, if the words did not amount to an overt dismissal they destroyed the mutual trust and confidence and so amounted to a repudiation.

Harsh words can therefore produce a 'dismissal' by a number of routes. A fascinating line of cases has developed on the meaning of language in industrial and commercial settings. Consider the following:

(a) 'Go, get out, get out'—not a Victorian melodrama but the case of *Stern (J & J)* v *Simpson* [1983] IRLR 52.
(b) 'You're finished with me'—*Tanner* v *Kean* [1978] IRLR 110.
(c) 'If you do not like the job, fuck off'—*Futty* v *Brekkes (D & D) Ltd* [1974] IRLR 130.

None of these utterances amounted to a dismissal *in the circumstances*. This is a key point. In *Futty* v *Brekkes*, the employee was a fish filleter on Hull docks; and, strange though it seems, such language is not abnormal on Hull docks. The case stands out in the memory not because of the language used (there are many variations on this theme), but because of the attempt to define the term as 'If you are complaining about the fish you are working on, or the quality of it, or if you do not like what, in fact, you are doing, then you can leave your work, clock off, and you will be paid up to the time when you do so. Then you can come back when you are disposed . . .'. And the same would not necessarily hold true if the characters were a bank manager and junior clerk—more so if said in front of customers.

Words spoken in anger can cause more problems. The act of dismissal can be clear but then regretted. In *Martin* v *Yeoman Aggregates Ltd* [1983] IRLR 49, a retraction within five minutes of an angry outburst was held sufficient to counter the dismissal even though the employee insisted he had been dismissed. This owes more to the promotion of good industrial relations practice than pure logic. It is a question of degree whether the words are withdrawn too late.

9.6.2 Intention

The courts have not been consistent on the status to be given to intention. If an employer intimates dismissal but does not intend this to be the case, should this make any difference?

We have seen that if the words are *ambiguous* the general test to be applied is what would reasonably be understood from the context. The same should hold true for *unambiguous* language, and this appears to be so following the Court of Appeal's decision in *Sovereign House Security Services Ltd* v *Savage* [1989] IRLR 115. However, as with words spoken in anger, an employee will be best advised to get confirmation of dismissal before taking any further action.

9.6.3 Resigning

A dismissal may also occur when the employer repudiates the contract (e.g., by some radical alteration of the terms) and the employee accepts this repudiation by resigning. Strictly this is known as *wrongful repudiation* by the employer; though when used nowadays in relation to unfair dismissal it is usually referred to as 'constructive dismissal'. Some people incorrectly refer to both common law and statutory claims under the heading of constructive dismissal; it's not the worst sin in the world.

This topic is discussed more fully in **9.8** below.

9.7 Justifiable and wrongful dismissals

The word 'justifiable' can cause some initial problems here. Remember that we are concerned only with common law rights in this chapter, so a dismissal is 'justifiable' when it is not in breach of contract. It is irrelevant for these purposes whether it was 'fair' in all the circumstances. So, if an employee is dismissed with proper notice the common law will not be bothered that the employee had been loyal to the company for 20 years and has been treated abysmally, or that the dismissal was really motivated by sex or race discrimination. These factors are irrelevancies as far as the common law is concerned.

EXAMPLE

Anna is an employee who falls ill. She has worked for the company for five years and this is the first time she has been absent from work. Unfortunately the employer has suffered a bad spate of malingerers taking time off. This has caused immense organisational problems. The employer decides to make an example of someone and dismisses Anna. The employer gives proper notice under the contract.

It would be very unlikely that this constituted a wrongful dismissal, although one would need to see the exact terms of the contract to be sure, e.g., the contract may have a mandatory disciplinary procedure. The action does, however, seem very unfair to Anna. This is not the concern of the common law. The common law does not care whether the employer might have been a central character in a Dickens novel. If there is an 'unfair dismissal' here Anna will have to take that to an employment tribunal. The tribunal will not be that concerned whether notice was given or not; it will look to how the dismissal was handled, e.g., procedures used.

9.7.1 Justifiable dismissals: notice given

Since any contract of employment can be lawfully terminated by the giving of proper notice it is irrelevant *why* the employer decides to dismiss. The only exceptions to this general power to dismiss arise (rarely) when the contract specifies that dismissal can be only for certain defined reasons or that (even more rarely) the contract lasts for life: see respectively *McLelland* v *Northern Ireland General Health Service Board* [1957] 1 WLR 534 and *Ivory* v *Palmer* [1975] ICR 340. As we noted in **Chapter 5**, however, if the contract makes certain procedures mandatory before a dismissal can occur then an injunction may be obtained to prevent dismissal until the procedures have been completed (see **5.4.4.1**).

Like most things in employment law, however, there are variations on this theme. Thus, in *Macari* v *Celtic Football and Athletic Club Ltd* [1999] IRLR 787, detailed above at **5.2.2.1(e)**, the Court of Session (Inner House) was prepared to ignore the express terms of the contract which (i) defined the circumstances and decision-making process in which dismissal would occur; (ii) gave a notice period of two years; and (iii) stated that such notice was not to be given during the first year of employment. The Court took the view that such terms supplemented rather than excluded the employer's rights and powers of dismissal under the general law of contract for material breach of contract.

9.7.1.1 Proper notice

Proper notice is determined according to the terms of the contract. A payment in lieu of notice is an acceptable way of meeting the requirements. Both forms of giving notice are subject to the minima stated in ERA 1996, s. 86, which are as follows:

Length of service	*Minimum notice entitlement*
less than one month	no notice due
after one month	1 week
after 2 years' completed service	2 weeks
after 3 years' completed service	3 weeks
after 4 years' completed service	4 weeks
for each year of completed service	one additional week's notice
after 12 years' service	12 weeks
BUT:	
after 13 years' service	still only 12 weeks
after 20 years' service	still only 12 weeks

The statutory minimum period of notice therefore has a ceiling of 12 weeks. To determine an employee's notice entitlement, therefore, one should ask:

(a) What does the contract state? Usually this is solved by examining the express terms, though occasionally one may have to resort to devices such as custom and practice to determine the period.

(b) Is this equivalent to or greater than the s. 86 notice required?

(c) If not then apply s. 86 minimum notice.

Section 86 uses the term 'not less than *[x weeks]*': the courts and tribunals do not have to award only the minimum period. It is still open to the tribunal or court to award 'reasonable notice'. However, the idea that 'reasonable notice' may be awarded often gives the impression that courts and tribunals are quite creative in assessing notice entitlement. That idea should be discarded. Where courts have turned to reasonable notice either the contract has been unclear or the facts have been extreme, e.g., an employee of senior status with 25 years' service being awarded six months' notice.

EXAMPLE

An employee has been employed for eight and a half years. When new machines are introduced on to the production line he is dismissed as surplus to requirements. His contract stipulates that he is entitled to one month's notice; the employer duly pays wages in lieu of the employee working the notice.

The payment in lieu of notice is irrelevant here. However, on these facts the notice does not meet the s. 86 minimum, which should be eight weeks. Note that portions of years are not generally counted and that any questions of 'reasonable notice' will not be admitted on these facts.

Limited-term contracts are treated no differently, *provided there is a notice clause*.

Where notice is given the date of termination must be ascertainable. There is no dismissal if all that is given is a general warning of dismissal unless the warning is so specific that it amounts to an ultimatum and therefore an anticipatory breach: *Greenaway Harrison Ltd* v *Wiles* [1994] IRLR 381.

Sections 87–91, ERA 1996 deal with rights once notice has been given. For instance, subject to the technicalities of s. 87(4) (see *Scotts Company (UK) Ltd* v *Budd* [2003] IRLR 145), if the employee falls sick during the notice period he is entitled to be paid, even if not otherwise entitled to sick pay. But, under ss. 88(2) and 89(4), any payments made to the employee by the employer (e.g., statutory sick pay) go towards meeting the employer's liability under these sections.

9.7.1.2 Waiving rights to notice

The parties are free to agree to give shorter notice than would normally be required or even to waive notice. Provided such variations are genuine there will be no breach of contract and therefore no damages payable: *Baldwin* v *British Coal Corporation* [1995] IRLR 139.

9.7.2 Justifiable dismissal: no notice given

When an employee is in serious breach of contract (e.g., commits an act of serious misconduct) the employer has a number of options available. These include:

(a) doing nothing;

(b) disciplining the employee;

(c) suing the employee for damages;

(d) dismissing the employee with notice;

(e) dismissing the employee without notice.

This is in line with ordinary contract principles that the innocent party may, in the face of a repudiation by the other party, affirm the contract as it stands or accept the repudiation. Thus a dismissal without notice (known as a *summary dismissal*) will be justified where the employee's actions show that further continuance of the relationship is impossible: *Sinclair* v *Neighbour* [1967] 2 QB 279.

It follows, therefore, that the contract of employment itself is of vital importance in assessing whether the employee's conduct justifies dismissal without notice. The contract may define terms such as 'gross misconduct', or it may lay down specific procedures for dealing with any dismissal point, e.g., that no dismissal may occur until the employee has been given an opportunity to state a case. The more technical the contractual terms become the more likely it is that the employer will be in breach by not following them. Thus it might be that, even in the face of obvious misconduct, an employer will have to adhere to the procedures laid out in the contract *if the terms specifically set out what must happen before a dismissal can occur: Dietmann* v *Brent London Borough Council* [1988] ICR 842.

This does not establish a rule that a breach of disciplinary procedures will render a dismissal wrongful, though, because:

(a) if the dismissal is with proper notice (or payment in lieu) no further damages will be payable—though there is the possibility that the employee might obtain an injunction to prevent dismissal *until* the procedures have been complied with;

(b) most procedures are drafted more loosely than the *Dietmann* example. The issue is therefore one of construction of the particular contract. We should note, however, that some tribunal chairmen are becoming keener to hold that disciplinary rules set out in a variety of company documents do have contractual effects. Phrases such as 'the totality of documentation shows that the term was intended to be incorporated' are used to justify such inclusion (see discussion above at **3.4.2.1**).

If notice is *not given* the employer will have to justify this. If it is not justified the employee will recover damages for wrongful dismissal. Justification for dismissal without notice depends solely on the employer having a sound *contractual* reason for so dismissing. This will mean that the employee must have committed a serious breach of contract (see *Laws* v *London Chronicle (Indicator Newspapers) Ltd* [1959] 1 WLR 698). *The breach may be of express or implied terms*. Examples of serious breach by an employee will include:

(a) refusal to obey a lawful order;

(b) failure to cooperate;

(c) dishonesty (in its widest sense);

(d) assault;

(e) prolonged absenteeism;

(f) disclosing confidential information;

(g) failing to disclose the misdeeds of subordinates;

(h) gross negligence;

(i) drunkenness at work;

(j) most forms of industrial action.

However, it is usually stressed by judges that each case turns on its facts. Certainly this will be true when dealing with one-off incidents. Whereas the normal approach would be that a one-off incident is not a repudiation of the contract, that clearly cannot be a universal rule. A pilot bouncing the company jet, for instance, does not deserve a second chance. But should the pilot be dismissed with or without notice? Would you say that the same result would be reached with a salesman who crashed a company car? And an accumulation of petty incidents may also amount to a serious breach: *Pepper* v *Webb* [1969] 2 All ER 216.

The more serious the breach the more likely a summary dismissal will be justified.

9.7.2.1 Contractual term

Employers sometimes attempt to set out a right to dismiss without notice on the occurrence of certain events, other than gross misconduct. This is a questionable practice in itself; but, certainly, the wording of such clauses will be construed *contra proferentem: T & K Improvements Ltd* v *Skilton* [2000] IRLR 595, CA, where a clause allowing dismissal 'with immediate effect' on failing to reach sales targets was held not to permit dismissal without notice. A similar approach to contractual terms was seen in **9.7.1** above.

9.7.3 Wrongful dismissals

9.7.3.1 Definition

A dismissal *without notice or with inadequate notice* will constitute a wrongful dismissal unless the employer was acting in response to a serious breach of the contract by the employee.

Payment in lieu of notice, unless specifically allowed for in the contract, will also constitute a technical breach of contract. For the most part this is an irrelevancy, given that

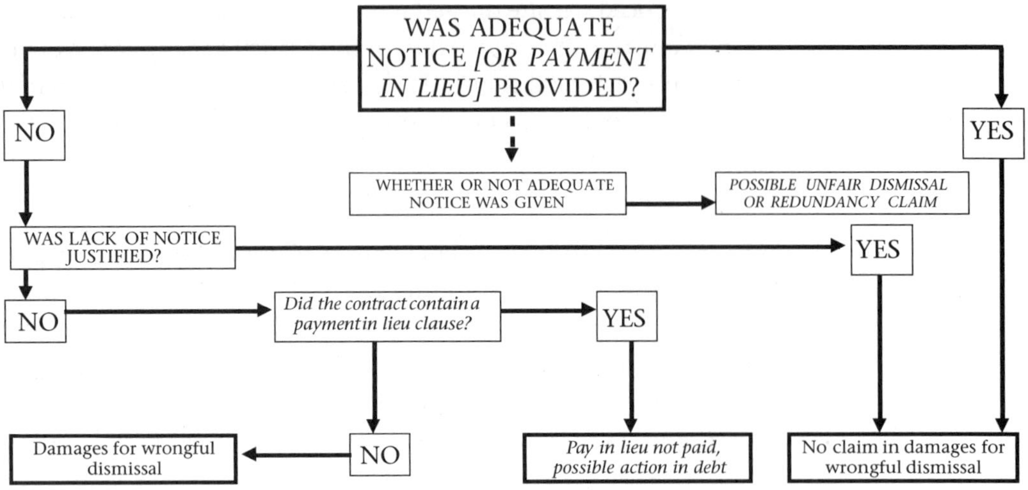

Figure 9.1 Dismissal with or without notice.

damages for wrongful dismissal would amount to the same sum, but classifying this as a technical breach may have an effect on matters such as the efficacy of restraint of trade clauses: see *Rex Stewart Jeffries Parker Ginsberg Ltd* v *Parker* [1988] IRLR 483, above at **8.9.4** and below at **9.9**.

Employers often refer to 'instant dismissal'. This is in fact a vague term and should not be taken at face value. An employee might be 'instantly dismissed' when he or she is dismissed without notice; the employee or the employer may also use the term 'instant dismissal' to describe a dismissal with payment in lieu or dismissal with notice but with no requirement to work out the notice. There can therefore be important differences between 'instant dismissals' and 'summary dismissals' and you need to be sure which you are talking about (a point missed by the employers in *Skilton* above).

Figure 9.1 illustrates the possible consequences of dismissing with or without adequate notice. The right-hand side of the diagram illustrates the fact that damages are unavailable at common law if the contract is terminated lawfully. The far left-hand side shows that the mere fact that notice has not been given does not conclude the analysis; the lack of notice may be justified. The section concerning payments in lieu of notice takes account of the decision in *Abrahams* v *Performing Rights Society* [1995] IRLR 486. We will return to discuss the significance of this decision at **9.10.3** below.

The diagram also notes the possibilities of an unfair dismissal claim flowing from either type of dismissal. This point will be taken further in **Chapter 10** but highlights the fact that there may be an unfair and wrongful dismissal, a fair but wrongful dismissal and even an unfair but lawful dismissal.

9.7.3.2 Relationship with repudiation

A wrongful dismissal is sometimes viewed as another form of repudiation of the contract. If this is so then, as in the ordinary law of contract, the repudiation does not automatically bring the contract to an end—it must be accepted by the innocent party. An unaccepted repudiation, it is said, is a thing writ in water. The innocent party has a choice whether or not to accept the repudiation. The argument is that when the employee is told to go (in breach of contract) he or she should be able to say, 'No. This is in breach and I do not accept the repudiation.' In practice this simply shows us that law and reality do not always coincide. But there can be cases where this point matters.

We have already seen some spin-off practical points that have developed from the debate. Since a repudiation does not have to be accepted by the innocent party then a breach by the employer during the currency of the contract can be met with various tactics, e.g.:

(a) It is now well-established that employees faced with a repudiation may object to the breach but remain in employment and sue for damages: *Rigby* v *Ferodo* [1988] ICR 29 (discussed in **Chapter 5** at **5.4.4.1**).

(b) We have also seen that, even when a dismissal is about to occur or has just occurred, an employee may be able to invoke the courts' help. Injunctions can be granted to restrain dismissals or declare dismissals invalid which do not comply with mandatory contractual procedures: *Dietmann* v *Brent London Borough Council* [1988] ICR 842, although this does not mean that the rules of natural justice will be imputed to contracts of employment generally.

But the question in relation to wrongful dismissal is more difficult. Assume that an employer has just told the employee that he is dismissed without notice. Does the employee have to accept this?

There has been a long-standing debate on whether an employee must simply accept this repudiation and sue for damages, or whether there is some other remedy available: see *Gunton* v *Richmond-upon-Thames London Borough Council* [1980] ICR 755, *London Transport Executive* v *Clarke* [1981] ICR 355 and comments by Lord Oliver in *Rigby* v *Ferodo*. In most cases, however, this debate is somewhat sterile since there is no practical benefit in having a right other than for damages. The employee may object but, given that specific performance will not be ordered, the objection may be futile. Thus, an employee may prevent a dismissal occurring or may have a dismissal nullified on the grounds noted above, but faced with a straightforward dismissal without notice there is nothing that most employees can do but accept the dismissal and sue for damages.

However, if the 'repudiation' argument is correct in relation to wrongful dismissal the practical effects are:

(a) the employee, by accepting the *de facto* position, will have in law accepted the wrongful repudiation by the employer. The employee will therefore, technically speaking, have resigned (see below) rather than have been overtly dismissed;

(b) there may be a difference in calculating the exact date of termination.

This question has occupied many pages of text, but does not occur frequently in practice. In the latest case the Court of Appeal reluctantly followed the *Gunton* line: *Boyo* v *Lambeth London Borough Council* [1994] ICR 727. Here the employee was suspended pending the outcome of fraud charges. When additional charges of perverting the course of justice were added the employer informed the employee that he was effectively absent without permission so that the employer considered the contract frustrated. When the employee later attempted to return to work he was prevented from doing so. The employer's actions were held to be an unlawful repudiation of the contract which the employee had not accepted. The court held that the employer's repudiation did not *automatically* terminate the contract; but damages were limited to the notice period plus (in this case) the time it would have taken to follow the disciplinary procedure properly (see also **9.10.1.1** below).

9.7.3.3 Proof of conduct

The employer will have to justify any dismissal *without notice*. Normally proof will relate to the employment record of the individual known at the time of the dismissal. However, the employer is also entitled to rely on evidence *not known to him at the time of dismissal: Boston*

Deep Sea Fishing and Ice Co. v *Ansell* (1888) 39 ChD 339. This is because the arguments are based on the fact as to whether or not there has been a breach of contract. The employer's knowledge or lack of it does not affect the materiality of the breach.

EXAMPLE

The employer summarily dismisses an employee for theft. The employer has no proof, only strong suspicions. Some weeks after the dismissal the employer discovers the proof. The employer may use this subsequently-discovered information in order to prove the employee's breach of contract, thereby justifying the dismissal without notice. The same logic applies even if the employer had *no reason* to dismiss but later discovered one.

By way of advance warning, however, the rules regarding proof in an unfair dismissal action are different. There the employer can rely only on facts known *at the time of dismissal*. Thus out of one incident of dismissal there may be different rules of proof depending on whether one is claiming for wrongful or unfair dismissal.

9.8 Resignation

An employee may resign at any time by giving proper notice under the contract. The minimum s. 86 period is one week; and this does not alter with length of service. The contract may set any notice requirement.

If an employee leaves without serving proper notice then he or she is in breach of contract. The employee will be liable for damages, though specific performance will not be ordered. The employee may, however, still be subject to a restraint of trade clause. The fact that the employer has accepted the employee's repudiation of the contract is ignored because the employee will not be allowed to profit from his or her own breach.

Once a lawful resignation has been given it cannot be withdrawn except:

(a) with the employer's permission; or
(b) where the resignation came in the heat of the moment and is retracted quickly; or
(c) where the resignation was in breach of contract and the employer has not yet obviously accepted the repudiation.

However, an employee is entitled to resign, with or without serving notice, and claim damages where the employer has repudiated the contract (see 'wrongful repudiation' below).

The discussion on 'resignation' and its effect should be read in conjunction with the topic of 'constructive dismissal' in **Chapter 10**. When this is taken into account you will see that a resignation may amount to an unfair dismissal as well as to a wrongful repudiation at common law.

9.8.1 Meaning of 'resignation'

In most cases an employee will resign to take up another job elsewhere. If the employee gives proper notice (and there is no question of restraint of trade) no further problems will occur. There can be no claim for wrongful or unfair dismissal or for redundancy payments and the employer cannot force the employee to remain in employment. The employer may indeed waive all or some of the notice because an employee who is set to leave can prove disruptive (intentionally or otherwise).

We are concerned here with *apparent* resignations which might turn out to be *dismissals*:

(a) resignations in the heat of the moment;

(b) pressure from the employer;

(c) the employer's bad faith;

(d) voluntary redundancies and early retirement.

9.8.1.1 Resignations in the heat of the moment

Employees, like employers (see **9.6.1**), are allowed some leeway with heated outbursts. If the words spoken are ambiguous there is the preliminary point as to whether they constituted a resignation at all. If the words are unambiguous the employer is entitled to take these at their face value and the employee must live with the consequences. However, an employee is allowed to retract within a reasonable time if the words were spoken in anger: *Kwik-Fit (GB) Ltd* v *Lineham* [1992] ICR 183.

An employer who refuses to allow a reasonable retraction will have dismissed the employee from that point.

9.8.1.2 Resignations under pressure

Employees who resign following an invitation to 'resign or be dismissed' may still have a claim for wrongful or unfair dismissal—were they pushed or did they jump? But advance warning of dismissal at some future time does not constitute pressure and so is not a dismissal (nor is this enough to amount to a repudiatory breach by the employer). If the employer were to indicate that the future termination will be in breach of contract, however, then this will amount to an anticipatory breach which the employee may act upon immediately.

There may be a fine line between these two points. The key aspect is whether there is to be found in the employer's words an *ascertainable future date of dismissal*; if there is then any resignation may be treated as a dismissal.

EXAMPLE

A month ago the employer told the employee that the factory would be closed down by next September, i.e., in 11 months' time. The employee has just resigned and wishes to claim a redundancy payment on the basis that he has been dismissed.

Although there is a final date when the employee's contract will seemingly come to an end this is not enough. The employee might be dismissed before then, or the redundancy may never come about. The resignation is just that: there is no further claim based on a 'dismissal' (see *International Computers Ltd* v *Kennedy* [1981] IRLR 28).

The real cases of 'resign or be sacked' therefore arise when the employee is clearly going to face some form of disciplinary procedure and is 'given the honourable choice'—a sort of industrial hara-kiri option. This may indeed be honourable, but it is also possible that it is a dismissal. It is not a dismissal simply to instigate disciplinary procedures, nor even to offer the employee a way out of the proceedings. Such conversations become dismissal when the employer threatens dismissal by other words: when the conversation is effectively, 'We are going to dismiss you come what may, go now'. One recent example arose when an employer told the employee she had a choice of either moving from full-time to part-time work or taking redundancy. She chose the latter. The employment tribunal felt this was a termination by agreement but the EAT disagreed, holding that, as she had rejected the only alternative she had been faced with a compulsory redundancy. The case was remitted to the tribunal to be heard on its merits.

9.8.1.3 Resignation generated by the employer's bad faith

This bears a close resemblance to pressurised resignations. In *Caledonian Mining* v *Bassett and Steel* [1987] ICR 425, the employers had announced the proposed closure of the workplace. No date was actually given. The employers informed the employees that they could arrange transfers to another site some distance away. Alternatively, they said that they had reached agreement with the Coal Board so that the employees could change employers, stay in the area, but take a wage cut. The employees chose this option. They then claimed redundancy pay from Caledonian Mining, who replied that the employees had resigned and so were not entitled. It was held that the employers had acted in bad faith and had inveigled the employees into resigning in order to deprive them of their statutory rights. Therefore this constituted a dismissal.

9.8.1.4 Voluntary redundancies and early retirement

In many cases where redundancies are announced the employer will first ask for volunteers. Any subsequent termination could be classed as a resignation, a dismissal, or even a consensual termination. In order to claim a redundancy payment the employee must have been dismissed.

Early retirement usually takes a considerable amount of time to work out problems with dates, pension arrangements and so on. Such cases are therefore more likely to constitute mutual agreement (provided the agreement was genuine) rather than dismissal or resignation: *Birch* v *University of Liverpool* [1985] ICR 470. An employee could not claim redundancy pay in addition to the terms of the early retirement scheme.

9.8.2 Wrongful repudiation

If the *employer* commits a *serious* breach of contract this will amount to a repudiation which the employee may accept as terminating the contract. The employee will have effectively been 'dismissed' and will be able to recover damages, which again are limited to the notice period.

The obvious question, therefore, is what constitutes a *serious breach* on the employer's part? The law on this topic owes more to the cases on unfair (constructive) dismissal than to the common law itself. The list of examples is therefore drawn from that setting. Examples would include:

(a) a failure to pay wages;
(b) harassment (including harassment by other employees);
(c) victimisation by the employer or senior staff;
(d) unilaterally changing the employee's job content or status;
(e) humiliating employees in front of others including the use by a manager of foul and abusive language, whether or not the employer argues that that is part of the 'normal working environment': *Horkulak* v *Cantor Fitzgerald International* [2003] IRLR 756;
(f) unwarranted demotion or disciplinary sanctions;
(g) falsely accusing an employee of misconduct or incapability;
(h) unilateral variation in contract terms, e.g., a change in hours or pay;
(i) requiring a substantial transfer of location (certainly if without reasonable notice);

(j) suspension without pay where the contract does not allow for this—and even *with pay* if prolonged.

A series of breaches may also fall within the definition of repudiation, though this is always more difficult to substantiate unless the employee has kept careful records.

Many of these points tend to be classified as a breach of the implied term of *mutual trust and confidence* owed by the employer to the employee. Clearly the list is not closed.

It should also be remembered from **Chapter 5** (at **5.4.4**) that an employee does not have to resign in the face of a repudiatory breach. If the contract is still capable of being performed the employee may remain and seek other remedies, e.g., suing for breach, or may simply put up with the breach.

9.8.2.1 Employer's intentions

In the commercial contract case of *Woodar Investment Development Ltd* v *Wimpey Construction (UK) Ltd* [1980] 1 WLR 277, the House of Lords held that a genuine misconstruction of the contract by one party did not constitute a repudiation because repudiation involves a subjective element. That principle was applied to employment contracts by the EAT in *Frank Wright & Co (Holdings) Ltd* v *Punch* [1980] IRLR 217 but doubted by later EAT judgments. In *Brown* v *JBD Engineering* [1993] IRLR 568, for instance, the EAT held that there was certainly no rule of law that a genuine mistake means there is no repudiation. The Court of Appeal has now commented on this and rejected any subjective approach: *Transco Plc (formerly BG Plc)* v *O'Brien* [2002] EWCA Civ 379, [2002] ICR 72. Here, the employers genuinely believed that O'Brien (who had a unique work history in the company) was not an employee and therefore not entitled to various bonuses (as had been offered to most other employees). O'Brien brought a claim for breach of contract in the tribunal. The tribunal and EAT held he was an employee and that the failure to offer him the new terms was a breach of the implied term of mutual trust and confidence. The Court of Appeal agreed: identifying the refusal to offer new terms (even when based on an erroneous decision made in good faith and even when it involved no capricious act) was a breach of contract. The employer's genuine mistake was therefore irrelevant; the Court stressing that it is the overall picture that one must examine to determine breach. Interestingly, *Woodar* was not cited and we would suggest that there may still be an argument for its application to employment in the case of anticipatory breach or cases only involving the construction of documents.

9.8.2.2 Beyond repudiation

On several occasions now the EAT has held an employer's breach to be so severe in seeking to vary the contract that it amounts to a 'withdrawal or removal of the contract' and so constitutes a dismissal. This line of reasoning began with *Hogg* v *Dover College* [1990] ICR 39. It rests on the premise (a questionable premise) that the variation is so substantial that the employees are deemed to have been dismissed and started a new contract. Where the employees have continued working through the breach *Hogg* states that they may nevertheless claim they were unfairly dismissed under the original contract. Such arguments rarely arise and leave massive problems in their wake as to appropriate levels of compensation, etc. For the most recent application see *Alcan Extrusions* v *Yates* [1996] IRLR 327.

9.9 Post-termination duties

In **Chapters 7** and **8** we noted that a breach or even a technical breach may have the effect of invalidating post-termination terms such as restraint of trade clauses: see *Rex Stewart*

Jeffries Parker Ginsberg Ltd v *Parker* [1988] IRLR 483. A wrongful dismissal will invalidate a restraint of trade clause: *General Billposting Co. Ltd* v *Atkinson* [1909] AC 118. Even a payment in lieu will invalidate a restraint clause *unless* the contract expressly allows for this form of termination.

9.10 Damages and other remedies

9.10.1 Damages

Employment contracts are no different from other contracts, in that the basis for awarding damages is to fulfil the reasonable expectations of the parties; to put the injured party in the same position as if the contract had been performed properly: *Hadley* v *Baxendale* (1854) 9 Exch 341. Damages for wrongful dismissal are therefore based on the contemplation of the parties—which means payments that would have fallen due in the notice period. The limitation period is six years (3 months if claiming in an employment tribunal).

It is also worth noting in this context that an employee may have a claim under the law of contract and under ERA 1996, Part II for any outstanding wages on termination. These are claims which are distinct from wrongful dismissal claims (see **4.4** and **5.8** above).

9.10.1.1 Employees' damages

In the abstract one could argue that when the employee is wrongfully dismissed (especially if jobs are scarce) the loss could be enormous. But at any given time and for any reason an employment contract may be lawfully terminated by one or other party giving the notice required under the contract. Thus, in assessing what has been lost one needs to know the maximum that could have been gained had the parties behaved properly in bringing the contract to an end. The maximum that could have been gained in the overwhelming majority of employment contracts is payment for the notice period. Thus damages are limited to the amount that would have been paid if notice had been properly given, or any shortfall between the payment due and that which was made.

Where an employee has resigned and successfully claims *wrongful repudiation* of the contract, the amount of damages will be equivalent to a wrongful dismissal claim and the same rules as to calculation will apply.

To the basic figure of wages one needs to add (at least in some cases) other sums which could have been gained *during that notice period*. Thus, to the basic wages figure one might add:

(a) fringe benefits, e.g., a company car, medical insurance;

(b) tips, to which the employee was contractually entitled (usually given as estimated value);

(c) commission and bonus to which the employee was contractually entitled;

(d) share options and payments under profit-sharing schemes;

(e) pension loss—at its lowest level an amount representing the employee's contributions;

(f) backpay (including holiday entitlements);

(g) interest from date of dismissal to date of hearing.

As with so many of these lists, therefore, one needs to know the terms of the contract in order to determine quantum. These additional elements, however, are given *for the length of the notice period* and not as general, life-long sums. The loss of the company car will therefore be calculated according to its value to the employee for the eight-week (or other) period of notice. Reference is made here to tables such as those compiled by the AA to determine value.

In most cases the basis of the 'notice period' calculation will be straightforward, although quantifying the exact amount of (a) to (g) above can lead to some debate. In this context, therefore, the case of *Silvey* v *Pendragon plc* [2001] EWCA Civ 784, [2001] IRLR 6 was an unusual one. Here, a long-standing employee was dismissed just short of his 55th birthday. He received a redundancy payment, a payment in lieu of notice (although the contract did not contain a payment in lieu clause) and outstanding holiday. However, if he had still been employed at his 55th birthday (or serving out his notice period), he would have hit a key date as regards his pension rights and would have been nearly £6,000 better off. As we shall see shortly (and at **10.3.1.1** below), in accepting the payment in lieu of notice his contract terminated at the summary dismissal date (and not the projected date at the end of the notice period) and so, by not being an employee at the crucial point, he lost the pension entitlement. He therefore claimed that the dismissal with payment in lieu was a technical breach of contract, and he claimed damages based on the accrued pension sum for which he now failed to qualify.

The Court of Appeal held that although Silvey was no longer an employee once he had accepted the payment in lieu, he was able to claim a sum to which he would have been entitled if not for the employer's repudiatory breach of contract. That sum would be made up of salary, bonuses, etc., and also would include any pension rights which accrued or would have accrued during that notice period. In ruling in the employee's favour the court distinguished a long-standing authority (*Dixon* v *Stenor Ltd* [1978] IRLR 28—employee dismissed just short of qualifying date not allowed to deem the contract extended by the notice period so as to gain redundancy rights) and also found that Silvey had not acted in such a positive way that his acceptance of the payment in lieu amounted to an estoppel as regards claiming further damages. One can almost hear the voice of Lord Denning in such judicial inventiveness!

9.10.1.2 Damages for more than the notice period

In some circumstances the damages for wrongful dismissal may actually be *greater* than the notice period. If, for instance, an employee has been dismissed without notice and in breach of contractually binding disciplinary rules (e.g., the procedure clearly laid down in the contract was not followed) the damages may be calculated in this way:

(a) take the date of dismissal and calculate how long it *would have taken* to comply with the contractual disciplinary scheme;

(b) add the notice due from the imaginary date of the disciplinary hearing properly conducted.

We will return to this at **9.10.6.2** below. It should be noted, however, that

- An employer must be assumed to discharge his contractual responsibilities in the manner most favourable to him: *Laverack* v *Woods* [1967] 1 QB 278, CA, e.g., by making a (contractually permissible) payment in lieu instead of serving notice. As we shall see (at **10.3.1.1** below) the EDT is usually the date that the notice period expires. However, if an employer makes a payment *in lieu* of notice, the EDT is the actual date of dismissal. Thus, an employee who has an entitlement to four weeks' notice and who is dismissed with payment *in lieu* of notice two weeks before they would otherwise qualify for unfair dismissal will not acquire the statutory right to claim unfair dismissal. If the employee had served out his or her notice period they would have done so (though note that **10.3.1.2** below deals with cases of brinkmanship in this area) so it has been the subject of some debate as to whether an employee should be able to claim damages for this 'loss of opportunity' to acquire statutory rights. In *Harper* v *Virgin Net Ltd* [2004] EWCA Civ 271, [2004] IRLR 390 the Court of Appeal finally shut the door on such arguments—though we understand this is subject to an appeal to the House of Lords.

- There is no such thing as an implied contractual term not to be unfairly dismissed: *Fosca* v *Birkett* [1996] IRLR 325.

9.10.1.3 Injured feelings and psychological injuries

Damages are not generally awarded for loss of future prospects or injured feelings: *Addis* v *Gramophone Co. Ltd* [1909] AC 488 and *Bliss* v *South East Thames Regional Health Authority* [1987] ICR 700. However, loss of reputation (stigma damages) has now been recognised as a head of damage by the House of Lords in *Malik and Mahmud* v *Bank of Credit and Commerce International SA (in compulsory liquidation)* [1997] ICR 606, emanating from breach of the implied term of mutual trust and confidence (specifically, not to run a corrupt and dishonest business so as to damage the employees' future employment prospects). This head of damages has so far been given a narrow application, so the fact that an unjustifiable, even capricious, dismissal diminishes future job prospects does not trigger *Malik* damages.

The potential for claims based on psychological injuries was first noted at **5.2.2.1(d)** above. The House of Lords addressed the issue of psychiatric illness arising from workplace stress in the landmark case of *Barber* v *Somerset County Council* [2004] UKHL 13, [2004] ICR 457. The case concerned a maths teacher who, following a restructure, had to take on extra responsibilities for the same salary. Working up to 70 hours a week he suffered a mental breakdown and sued his employer for personal injury. The Court of Appeal held against him on the grounds that an employer is entitled to believe an employee is up to the normal stresses of a job unless something different is known: the point of foreseeability was absent here. The House of Lords disagreed. Recognising that this case was 'fairly close to the borderline', as the employee's actions were not particularly helpful in themselves, their Lordships nevertheless held that the employers were in breach of their duty of care. An employer's duty is to take positive thought for the safety of the workers in the light of what the employer knows or ought to have known. The key point that emerges from *Barber* is that this is a general positive duty to take some steps to be aware of pressures on employees, not one which only applies where the employer is aware of a vulnerable employee. This is not an absolute duty, however, and where the evidence does not support the view that the employer should have known about the stress, etc, then no liability can follow.

The pre-*Barber* cases still provide us with some useful applications of the duty. There are two aspects to consider: first, the safety angle which will arise in personal injury claims and is relevant to the ordinary courts; secondly, an argument based on damages for breach of contract arising from a breach of mutual trust and confidence, which can surface in either the courts or in the employment tribunal.

(a) *The safety angle*: This was first seen in *Walker* v *Northumberland County Council* [1995] ICR 702. Here, the employers knew the employee was under stress (he had already had to take time off work) but failed to take this into account in piling on even more work. The employers were held to be liable for the resulting psychological injury suffered by the employee.

In *Page* v *Smith* [1995] 2 WLR 644, the House of Lords had held that, as a matter of general principle, physical and psychological injury are subject to the same test of foreseeability. Their Lordships explained the application of this in relation to employment in *White* v *Chief Constable of South Yorkshire Police* [1999] 2 AC 455 (the case concerning the police officers who suffered nervous shock after attending at the Hillsborough disaster) by stating that there were no special rules to be applied beyond those of ordinary tortious principles. Again, in *Rorrison* v *West Lothian College and Lothian Regional College* 2000 SCLR 245, the Court of Session drew a distinction between liability for emotional distress and psychiatric illness. Here, an employee had been victimised by her line manager to the point where she had suffered from anxiety and depression resulting in absence from work. On her return the victimisation continued and she suffered further psychological distress. Lord Reed held that she could only recover for psychiatric illness and this medical condition had not been proven on the facts; neither could the employer reasonably have foreseen that the employee was at a material risk of suffering psychiatric illness as opposed to emotional upset.

In the light of *Barber*, the Scottish case of *Fraser* v *The State Hospitals Board for Scotland* [2001] SLT 1051 is interesting. A charge nurse at a high-security hospital who possessed an exemplary employment record was disciplined following an incident involving fraternisation and the supply of alcohol to inmates. He had denied the charges and felt great humiliation and resentment at the employer's handling of the incident. He fell ill as a result. Lord Carloway held that any such psychological illness that did result was not foreseeable. Any employer knows that disciplinary action will annoy an employee; however, they had not been alerted that their actions would produce psychological harm in this case. This rather begs the question as to how an employer can discipline someone whom they do know to be 'on the edge'.

(b) *Mutual trust*: Running alongside the *safety* argument has been a debate about whether an employer's actions (which might produce psychological injury) might constitute a breach of the implied term of mutual trust and confidence. Once the case of *Malik* had extended the duty to matters such as how an employer's conduct affects an employee's reputation (see above at **9.10.1.1**), the opportunity to argue an extension of the duty of mutual trust to conduct which causes psychological harm became ever-present. The limits of *Malik* are being well and truly tested.

The first major test arose in *Johnson* v *Unisys Ltd* [2001] UKHL 13, [2001] ICR 480 where the Court of Appeal [1999] ICR 809 and then the House of Lords revisited the area in the context of a dismissed employee who claimed that his summary dismissal (based on allegations made against him) represented a breach of the term of trust and confidence leading to severe psychiatric illness and financial damages. Their Lordships held that, though *Addis* v *Gramophone Co. Ltd* might be reviewed in modern circumstances, here the position was clear: there was no need to develop the common law to overlap this remedy. Further, whereas *Malik* may be applicable to breaches of contract arising *during* the employment relationship, it was not relevant to the manner of the *termination*.

This apparently simple distinction has complications: what happens where an employer commits a breach of mutual trust (say, in terms of false allegations or bad faith disciplinary measures) and the employee is eventually dismissed or resigns? Is the breach one occurring 'during' the contract and so actionable as a common law claim under *Malik*, or one related to termination and so *not* actionable under *Johnson?*

In *Gogay* v *Hertfordshire County Council* [2000] IRLR 703, the Court of Appeal upheld an employee's claim for damages for psychological injury arising from the employer's breach of mutual trust. This case involved a female care worker employed in a children's home. When one 13-year-old girl with learning difficulties kept making (and withdrawing) claims of sexual abuse against the employee the employer suspended the care worker from the home on full pay pending an investigation under Children Act 1989, s. 47. The terms of the contract allowed for such suspension where there were suspicions of gross misconduct or where the employee's presence might hinder the investigation (though the 1992 Warner Committee's Report on Children's Homes had recommended that options other than suspension should be considered). The investigation concluded that there were no grounds for the claim of abuse and the employee was reinstated. Unfortunately, over the next two years this incident led the employee to suffer from clinical depression. The damage suffered passed the key tests of being caused by the employer's actions and of psychiatric illness being reasonably foreseeable. *Johnson* was distinguished on the grounds that that case involved a dismissal and here there was only a suspension; the significance of the suspension being that the employment relationship was still continuing.

Again, in *King* v *University Court of the University of St Andrews* [2002] IRLR 252, the Court of Session (Outer House) distinguished *Johnson* and held that it did not apply while an employer was carrying out investigative procedures which might not necessarily culminate in dismissal. During that time an employee was entitled to rely on the implied duty of trust and confidence as subsisting so that the failure by the employer to allow the employee the opportunity to reply to the charges made and cross-examine witnesses amounted to an actionable breach of confidence.

Inevitably, cases arose where a dismissal did result and the *Johnson* v *Unisys* distinction had to be tested. In the joined cases of *Eastwood and another* v *Magnox Electric plc* and *McCabe* v *Cornwall County Council and others* [2004] UKHL 35, [2004] 3 WLR 322 the House of Lords pronounced on this position. Their Lordships decided that a common law claim for psychological injury arising from a breach of the duty of mutual trust will only arise where the cause of action has accrued before dismissal. Unfortunately (as their Lordships recognised) the distinction between discipline and dismissal can become very fudged and, if dismissal does result, we shall see that injury to feelings, etc is not something which an employment tribunal can award as part of unfair dismissal compensation either: see **10.13.4.4** below.

9.10.1.4 Employers' damages

It should be noted that employers are also entitled to sue for damages where the employee has not served proper notice according to the contract (the contract is the only real issue here as the ERA 1996, s. 86 minimum for employees is fixed at one week). Employers may also counterclaim in any contractual claim brought by an employee (but not under an ERA 1996, Part II claim).

The amount of the employer's damages in these circumstances will be limited to the sum needed to find a replacement. A general clause which allow employers to deduct a sum of money from any final payment owed to an employee (e.g., outstanding pay) when the employee leaves without giving notice are not a genuine pre-estimate of loss and so likely to be classed as a penalty clause: *Giraud* v *Smith* [2000] IRLR 763. Such 'recovery' clauses can be drafted so as to amount to genuine estimations, though: see *Neil* v *Strathclyde Regional Council* [1984] IRLR 14, on recovering the costs of a training scheme. If another employer has induced the employee to break his or her contract that employer will also be liable. But these are not usually real, practical issues. If employers need to do something in these circumstances they will either seek an injunction to hold employees to their notice period ('garden leave' injunctions), or seek to enforce a restraint of trade clause (see **Chapter 8**).

9.10.2 Deductions from employees' damages

Nothing in life, so they say, is free. The employee may well have a good claim for wrongful dismissal, but deductions can be made from any award. First, the employee cannot avoid tax liabilities so the award will generally be made net of tax and National Insurance. This applies to all cases where the damages are under £30,000.

If the award exceeds £30,000 complications set in. The basic rule is that the courts must decide on the loss and then add to this figure ('gross up') an amount representing the tax which will eventually have to be paid by the employee. This grossed up figure represents the damages awarded against the employer, and the employee can then sort out the tax position with the Inland Revenue. Thus, if a court calculates that the damages come to £60,000 it may have to award £80,000 so that the employee will actually get £60,000 after the taxman has made a request the employee cannot refuse (see *Shove* v *Downs Surgical Supplies Ltd* [1984] IRLR 17).

There are different methods used for grossing up. The two main methods depend in part on the level of detailed information available to the court/employment tribunal. The *Shove* approach is the more accurate. It involves the following steps:

1. Take the value of gross salary and benefits.
2. Calculate taxable value of 1 above.
3. Calculate tax and NI payable after deduction of allowances.
4. Deduct tax and NI from gross salary and benefits.
5. Multiply this net figure of annual loss by period of damages/compensation.
6. Make any deductions for mitigation.
7. Make deductions for accelerated receipt.
8. Deduct £30,000.
9. Gross up taxable slice and add back the £30,000.

In all cases, damages may be reduced because of the 'duty' to mitigate any loss. This means that the victim of any breach must minimise the loss, not act unreasonably to increase the loss, and account for any benefits received. The burden of proving failure to mitigate lies with the employer.

Deductions from damages

Usually Deducted	Not usually deducted	Debatable
Payment in other work (including fringe benefits, commission, shares etc.)		Failure to make use of appeals procedure. The most recent EAT authority (*Lock* v *Connell Estate Agents* [1994] IRLR 444) disapproves of such a deduction being made.
Any payment in lieu received.	Payment in lieu, where the basis of the claim is a debt action: *Abrahams* v *Performing Rights Society* [1995] IRLR 486—below.	Money from temporary or short-term employment. The chain of causation may not be broken where employee finds new work and then that employment fails.

Usually Deducted	Not usually deducted	Debatable
Sum representing failure to take reasonable steps to find new employment (i.e. failure to mitigate).	No deduction for failure to mitigate where ex-employee has failed to make profits in new (self-employed) enterprise.	Offer of re-employment by employer. Always debatable, but must certainly be made or repeated **after** dismissal: *Shindler* v *Northern Raincoat* [1960] 1 WLR 1038.
Jobseekers' allowance, to the extent that this constitutes a net gain: *Westwood* v *Secretary of State for Employment* [1985] ICR 209.	Private pension payments: *Hopkins* v *Norcross* [1994] ICR 11, CA—possible with caveat that contract may disallow this.	Compensatory award for unfair dismissal: *O'Laoire* v *Jackel International Ltd* [1990] ICR 197.
Income support to the extent that this constitutes a net gain.	Statutory redundancy payment and the Basic Award element of Compensation for unfair dismissal.	Failure to make a claim for social security benefits: *Secretary of state for Employment* v *Stewart* [1996] IRLR 334.
Tax, NI and pension contributions.	Insurance moneys or charitable payments other than by employer.	Sick pay.
Accelerated receipt (usually only in cases of very long-term notice periods or remainders of fixed-term contracts), of 5–10 per cent deduction.		*Ex gratia* payments by the employer. These are certainly deductible if clearly intended to compensate employee for dismissal.

Note: Deductions in unfair dismissal cases are treated differently (see **10.13.4** below).

9.10.3 Action for debt

In *Abrahams* v *Performing Rights Society* [1995] IRLR 486 the Court of Appeal added a new gloss to this area. Here, in March 1992, the parties had failed to reach agreement concerning the extension of the employee's fixed-term contract. Instead, the employee agreed to continue working '*under the terms of his existing contract*' for two years until March 1994. That fixed-term contract had contained a clause allowing for two years' notice or payment in lieu to be given.

After only six months of the new contract the employer dismissed the employee summarily. Following considerable debate as to the exact meaning of the phrase 'under the terms of his existing contract', it was held that the employee was still entitled to two years' notice or payment in lieu (a trifling sum of £232,292). In a case full of twists and turns, the central question then became whether, on what appeared to be a straightforward wrongful dismissal, the employee had to mitigate his loss on the principles described above.

In an uncommon reversal of arguments, the *employer* contended that this was indeed a wrongful dismissal and so subject to mitigation. The employee argued that where, as in this case, the contract of employment expressly provides that the employment may be terminated by the employer on payment of a sum in lieu of notice, any summary dismissal is a *lawful* termination, not a breach of contract, and the amount unpaid constitutes a debt (which is not subject to mitigation). The court agreed with the employee:

(a) the provision in the contract for payment in lieu gave rise to a contractual entitlement and therefore created a debt; and, *obiter*,

(b) even if the notice provision were to be regarded as liquidated damages, no duty to mitigate would apply.

Amongst the many practical implications to this case we would note the following:

(a) most senior employee contracts (and many others) incorporate a payment in lieu provision, so the ramifications of this case are extensive;

(b) many of these contracts use this clause so as to take advantage of the reasoning in *Rex Stewart Jeffries Parker Ginsberg Ltd* v *Parker* and avoid any technical breach of contract (see above at **9.9**).

(c) employers and their solicitors must therefore balance the potential sums due *as a debt* against the need for restraint of trade protection when drafting the contract.

The decision in *Abrahams* has had a mixed reception, not least because of the *dicta* that earnings from new employment are not to be deducted even where the dismissal was wrongful. The courts have now begun to examine the application of the *Abrahams* case. In *Gregory* v *Wallace* [1998] IRLR 387 the Court of Appeal again held that earnings from new employment were not deductible, but stressed the unusual circumstances of the case.

In *Gregory* v *Wallace*, the employee was summarily dismissed and claimed two years' salary in lieu of notice (as set out in the contract). The contract contained an unusual clause that the employee was free to 'take other full-time employment during the notice period'. Thus the employee could at any time have earned the new salary and still have been entitled to pay in lieu. Beldam LJ confirmed that the normal rule is that an employee who is dismissed without notice must give credit for any earnings from new employment as, in normal circumstances, an employee would not be free to earn money from new employment whilst under notice, but as that was not the case here the new earnings could not be deducted from the damages.

Similar logic was employed in *Hutchings* v *Coinseed Ltd* [1998] IRLR 190 where the employee was given garden leave and took up another appointment during that time. As there was no restraint of trade clause and she was not disclosing any confidential information, the Court of Appeal held that she was entitled to reclaim the payment in lieu which has been withheld and the duty to mitigate loss did not apply.

In *Cerberus Software Ltd* v *Rowley* [2001] IRLR 160, this area lurched in another very strange way. Here the employee was summarily dismissed without good cause. He was entitled to six months' notice. Five weeks into that period he obtained new employment and the employers sought to argue that, accepting they were liable to pay damages for the due notice, this should be limited to five weeks' salary on the grounds that the employee had mitigated his loss. The employer argued that the phrase in clause 18 of the contract, 'It is agreed that the employer may make a payment in lieu to the employee', meant that the employer was merely reserving the right to give notice or its monetary equivalent. Rowley, who was unrepresented, argued that the phrase created a debt for monies due under the contract and that the employer should not be allowed to benefit from its bad faith and Rowley's diligence in finding a new (better-paid) job so quickly (which is a common argument when mitigation is raised). He argued that a debt had been created and mitigation was irrelevant.

The Tribunal and the EAT agreed with him; unfortunately, the Court of Appeal (by majority) disagreed and held that the phrase meant that if the employer chose not to give notice, he could also choose whether or not to give a payment in lieu; he was not *contractually committed* to pay the monies in lieu of notice. Therefore, any non-payment amounted to a simple breach of contract on which mitigation principles operated. *Abrahams* was distinguished on the basis that there the payment in lieu was expressly provided for in the contract so that the employer did not have the right to election. Ward LJ recognised in *Cerberus* that 'the company behaved in a deplorable manner', and stated that he understood Rowley's incredulity that the employers could behave with such bad faith and yet not pay for it, but his Lordship held in favour of the employer's interpretation.On the other hand, Sedley LJ (in the minority) commented more directly: 'If this is the law, there is something wrong with it.' Effectively, *Cerberus* turned (somewhat dubiously) on the meaning of the word *may* in clause 18 of the contract. So, if the wording of the payment in lieu clause reserves to the employer the right to decide whether to make the payment or not it is more likely that any non-payment can only be recovered in a claim for damages rather than debt.

9.10.4 Where there is no dismissal

We have so far fixed on wrongful dismissal. It may be that the employee is not dismissed and yet suffers loss. Such was the case in *Rigby* v *Ferodo* [1988] ICR 29 (discussed in **Chapter 5**), where the employees, faced with a pay cut in breach of contract, remained in employment and sued for damages representing their lost wages.

The employee may likewise always sue for any other form of breach of contract. A difficulty arises here, however. *Rigby* v *Ferodo* was an easy case because the quantum was the lost wages. If the employee is suing for a breach relating to an unlawful order, e.g., to move to another site or undertake different responsibilities, damages will be more difficult to quantify. This problem has not really been addressed by the courts.

Again, a claim under ERA 1996, Part II, Protection of Wages, should be noted here as a possibility (see **Chapter 4** at **4.4** above).

9.10.5 Limited-term contracts

We repeat in this context that damages for breach of a limited-term contract will be for the remainder of the term *unless* the contract contains a notice provision, in which case damages will be for that notice period.

Clearly, if the remainder of the term is the relevant period the employee will be claiming a large sum in many cases. Here tax implications will come into their own. However, some heed must be taken of the fact that instead of earning a £25,000 salary each year for the next, say, three years the employee will be getting this money in one fell swoop. The courts therefore take account of this *accelerated receipt* and reduce the award to reflect this. A rule of thumb deduction has been 5 per cent but recent judicial comments have indicated a willingness to equate this with the personal injury figure of 2 per cent.

9.10.6 Equitable remedies

These discretionary remedies do not have a strong foothold in employment contracts, especially if they amount to a request for an injunction for specific performance.

9.10.6.1 Declarations

An employee (or employer) may seek a declaration by the court as to the contractual position and rights of the parties. There must be a genuine grievance to pursue—the courts are not prone to giving lecture courses. A declaration is not a decision, it is an opinion. It cannot require the parties to undertake a particular act—though it would seem generally inadvisable to ignore it.

9.10.6.2 Injunctions

The courts are not keen to turn service into servitude and will therefore be loath to come to any decision which smacks of specific performance of the contract. Damages will usually suffice here as a remedy so, *unless damages are inadequate*, injunctions will not be granted. The concern of *employers* seeking injunctive relief regarding the maintenance of confidentiality, 'garden leave' clauses and restraint of trade was dealt with in **Chapter 8** (at **8.11**). Those points will not be repeated here.

An *employee* may seek an injunction in three main circumstances:

(a) to prevent a dismissal occurring which will be in breach of contractually enforceable rules of procedure;

(b) to prevent a dismissal taking place at all;

(c) to get the employee's job back.

It is unlikely that an injunction will be granted for the last point: *Marsh* v *National Autistic Society* [1993] ICR 453. Injunctions preventing dismissals in any circumstances are again a rare event. However, injunctions to hold the dismissal until procedures have been adhered to have become more common over the years. Thus, although a dismissed employee will not be able to obtain an order for specific performance to *regain* employment, it is feasible that a court would grant an interim injunction requiring the dismissal not to take effect *unless and until* the employer had complied with the contractual terms (e.g., disciplinary procedures).

The decisions are not consistent in this area but it seems that injunctions may be granted (remember it is a discretionary remedy) where:

(a) the dismissal is in breach of a mandatory contractual procedure (usually relating to disciplinary action; but this may also extend to things such as redundancy selection procedures: *Anderson* v *Pringle of Scotland Ltd* [1998] IRLR 64). Injunctions can be granted to restrain dismissals which do not comply with set contractual procedures: *Dietmann* v *Brent London Borough Council* [1988] ICR 842;

(b) trust and confidence has been maintained between the parties, i.e., the parties are still content to continue working together (judged on rational, not purely subjective, grounds: *Powell* v *Brent London Borough Council* [1988] ICR 176), or at least the contract is still 'workable'.

Injunctions come in two forms: interim (pending a full hearing of the issues) and final (granted at the conclusion of the full action). In most cases a prohibitory interim injunction will be granted or refused on the *American Cyanamid* principles (from *American Cyanamid Co.* v *Ethicon Ltd* [1975] AC 396—see **Chapter 8**).

9.10.6.3 Part 24, Civil Procedure Rules

One of the problems in this area is that if an employee fails to obtain an interim injunction preventing dismissal this will effectively decide the issue, because by the time the full action comes to trial the issue will be dead and buried except for damages.

Thus we noted in **Chapter 5** the case of *Jones* v *Gwent County Council* [1992] IRLR 521, where a novel and interesting approach to these problems was taken when RSC Ord. 14A, r. 1 was used to prevent a letter of dismissal being effective. RSC Ord. 14 and 14A have now been amalgamated into CPR, Part 24. This part covers applications by claimants or defendants for summary judgment and allows a court to determine any question of law or construction of any document at any stage in the proceedings (there must be no dispute of fact) where the question is suitable for determination *without a full trial* and that determination will decide the claim.

In *Jones* a catalogue of ineptly-handled disciplinary hearings took place until Jones eventually received a letter of dismissal. Jones sought an injunction to restrain the Council from dismissing her pursuant to the letter until full trial. Chadwick J held that, for the purposes of Ord. 14A, the status of the purported dismissal letter could be determined as easily in the current hearing as at full trial. That being so, the letter of dismissal was not a valid and effective dismissal because it did not comply with the disciplinary procedures set out in the contract. Further, it was held that under Ord. 14A the presence or absence of mutual trust *was irrelevant*. A permanent injunction was therefore issued restraining the Council from dismissing Jones *pursuant to its dismissal letter* and an interlocutory injunction was granted restraining the Council from dismissing unless proper grounds existed after carrying out the correct procedure.

Part 24, CPR could thus prove to be a very effective weapon for employees where the dispute is only about the meaning of documents, e.g., in cases of threatened demotion or dismissal which hinge on the wording of the contract. The number of cases making use of this device is steadily increasing; although use of RSC Ord. 14A in *Abrahams* v *Performing Rights Society* was the subject of some critical comment from Hutchinson LJ. Whether Part 24, CPR could be applied to confidentiality or restraint of trade cases is debatable. If there is no dispute as to fact so that 'reasonableness' is purely a point of law, there seems no reason why this should not be the case.

9.10.6.4 Judicial review

Judicial review is not relevant to employment law except in very limited circumstances. These were defined in *McLaren* v *Home Office* [1990] ICR 824 as being (i) that the decision was made by a public body; or (ii) where an employee or employer is entitled to refer disputes on the employment relationship to a disciplinary or other body established by statute.

9.11 Outline of tax considerations

This section makes no attempt to describe in detail the various schemes employed by companies to deal with taxation matters, merely to note some key points to be considered when termination is effected.

9.11.1 Normal rule

Monies paid on the termination of a contract will be subject to tax in the same way that wages are where there is a contractual obligation to make that payment and this still applies even when:

(a) the payment is expressed as being discretionary; and

(b) the contract is silent on the point but such payments constitute normal practice.

This will apply equally to express terms allowing for payment in lieu of notice (*EMI Group Electronics Ltd* v *Caldicott (Inspector of Taxes)* [1999] IRLR 630) and will apply to other benefits such as the retention of company cars. Where the contract (or practice) does not allow payment in lieu of notice employers may still, theoretically, deduct tax; but most will pay gross as the first £30,000 is not taxable in the employee's hands under ss. 401–405, Income Tax (Earnings and Pensions) Act 2003. The Inland Revenue has issued guidance notes on tax and pay *in lieu* of notice: see www.inlandrevenue.gov.uk/bulletins/tb63.pdf

9.11.2 Compensation for loss of office

Ex gratia payments (e.g., 'golden handshakes') will not be subject to the general rule provided they do not relate to services rendered and are not a contractual right. In such cases the first £30,000 is not taxable.

As *any prior agreement* may be subject to tax, various schemes have been devised to help reduce the chance of tax being charged where there is no contractual obligation but termination terms are being negotiated. Such tactics involve complicated assessments of liabilities for relevant tax years.

9.11.3 Damages for wrongful dismissal

The basic principles in this area were set out in *British Transport Commission* v *Gourley* [1955] 3 All ER 796. The employee should be placed in the same position as if the contract had been performed properly. The *Gourley* principle means that deductions must be made from any award for tax, as described in **9.10.2** above.

9.11.4 Statutory payments

Such payments are taxable, but in general are treated as exempt from tax up to £30,000.

(a) The basic award in unfair dismissal (see **Chapter 10**) is payable as a gross figure.

(b) The compensatory award in unfair dismissal is already calculated on a net pay figure (but see **10.15.1** below) so no further adjustment is necessary.

(c) The additional award in unfair dismissal is payable as a gross figure.

(d) Statutory redundancy pay (see **Chapter 11**) is payable gross.

(e) Contractual redundancy pay, strictly, should be treated as a contractual right and subject to tax. However, the Inland Revenue have issued a Statement of Practice on this (SP1/94) to the effect that if the scheme is a genuine redundancy payment no tax will be taken. The amount will still go towards the calculation of the £30,000 exemption (this point is explained further in **10.15.1** below).

10

Unfair dismissal

10.1 Introduction

This chapter is concerned with the most important (or at least the most notorious) of the statutory rights: the right to claim unfair dismissal. The sole arena for deciding these claims is the employment tribunal; unfair dismissal actions *cannot* be heard in the ordinary courts. The bulk of employment tribunals' workload is made up of unfair dismissal cases. Many are settled before going to a tribunal; most of the cases heard are decided in favour of the employer. Appeal lies to the Employment Appeal Tribunal (EAT) on 'a question of law' (a term which has been given an increasingly narrow ambit by the EAT and the Court of Appeal).

The right to claim unfair dismissal was born in the now-defunct Industrial Relations Act 1971 and is available only to *employees*. Section 94 of the ERA 1996 states that 'An employee has the right not to be unfairly dismissed by his employer'. The basic pattern to any successful claim for unfair dismissal is that:

(a) the employee has been 'dismissed';

(b) the employee qualifies for the right to claim unfair dismissal;

(c) the employer did not have a 'fair reason' for the dismissal; or

(d) if the employer did have a fair reason, that reason was not implemented fairly.

Right at the start the differences between *wrongful dismissal* actions and *unfair dismissal* actions should be noted. We have seen that wrongful dismissal is concerned with awarding damages for breach of contract. Unfair dismissal rights centre on the *reason for* the dismissal and *the manner* in which the dismissal was handled. It is quite possible to have the following combinations:

(a) a dismissal which is unfair but which is not wrongful;

(b) a dismissal which is wrongful but which is not unfair;

(c) a dismissal which is both unfair and wrongful;

(d) a dismissal which is neither unfair nor wrongful.

We will consider the topic under the following headings:

(a) Preventive measures.

(b) Qualifying for the right.

(c) The burden of proof.

(d) The meaning of dismissal.

(e) Constructive dismissal.

(f) The standard of proof.

(g) The potentially fair reasons.

(h) Fairness.
(i) Industrial action.
(j) Action short of dismissal.
(k) Other methods of dispute resolution.
(l) General principles of compensation.
(m) Overlap between unfair dismissal and wrongful dismissal.
(n) Calculating the compensation.

10.2 Preventive measures

Most employers these days are aware of the importance of being able to justify dismissal decisions and of the need to follow correct procedures. But many dismissals (especially in small companies) can result from hasty management decisions; and it is not uncommon for employers to sit on problems (e.g., an employee's incompetence) and then expect to be able to dismiss without any warning having been given to the employee, without any consultation, and immediately. Another common practice is to dismiss for the event *following* the big one, i.e., the employer misses or dodges the opportunity to dismiss for the misconduct which would have been easy to defend but, almost as a knee-jerk reaction, dismisses for an event that is not justifiable.

You may not have control over any of this because usually the parties will come to you with a *fait accompli* rather than in advance for advice. However, if you can advise your client prior to dismissal there are some general industrial relations and personnel points to note. The reasons why these pieces of advice are given here will become clear later when we look at how employment tribunals judge the fairness of dismissals.

There are two main practical categories in which the employer will wish to dismiss:

(a) *Maintaining standards.*
Employers regard it as important to maintain standards of acceptable behaviour on the part of employees, relating for example to quality of workmanship, rate of output, punctuality, attendance, and working relationships with other staff. Employees who fail to meet these standards will (or at least should) generally be warned about their shortcomings but dismissal is the final sanction that can be used.

(b) *Relationship impossible to maintain.*
The employee's actions here will include dishonesty (especially in a position of trust), sexual misconduct and harassment of other staff, and assault.

Quite often both strands are present in a single case so that the position can become muddied and the employer may need advice on analysing the reason for any dismissal. For instance, senior management may centre on the maintenance of standards whilst supervisors focus on the effect of misconduct on fellow workers. When evidence is given as to why dismissal occurred it is clearly better if everyone is in general agreement, and this is better sorted out *before the dismissal*.

Before any dismissal employers should be also advised to examine other available courses of action and to:

(a) make proper use of the statutory disciplinary procedures (if applicable) and their own company disciplinary procedures (which should comply with the guidelines laid down by ACAS);

(b) consider the effect on remaining employees in terms of future loyalty and performance (arising from leniency or excessive severity);

(c) consider the effect of any decision on supervisors, e.g., undermining their authority;

(d) consider the effect on any relationship with trade unions;

(e) consider all the alternatives if business reorganisation or redundancy is the reason for dismissal.

If dismissal is inevitable, try to control the manner of the dismissal. Your checklist should include:

(a) consider the terms of the contract;

(b) make sure that all the evidence is available and clear;

(c) make sure that the employer genuinely believes that dismissal is a reasonable course of action;

(d) make sure that all the relevant disciplinary procedures have been complied with;

(e) make sure that any hearing is properly conducted;

(f) make sure that dismissal is consistent with previous practice within the company.

10.3 Qualifying for the right

Although ERA 1996, s. 94 states that every employee has the right not to be unfairly dismissed, there are certain conditions to be met. We noted these qualification aspects in **Chapter 5** (**5.3**). So, if we assume that your employee-client has asked you for advice following a dismissal, you need to ascertain, to begin with:

(a) that your client was in fact an employee; and

(b) that your client had one year's continuous employment (although there are many exceptions to this rule, see **10.3.1.3** below); and

(c) that your client was aged below 65, or the company's 'normal retirement age' at the date of dismissal; and

(d) whether your client has fulfilled his or her part in any statutory and contractual dispute resolution procedures; and

(e) that your client is not prevented from claiming because of the application of international law; and

(f) that your client does not fall within a miscellaneous excluded category; and

(g) that your client is still within the three-month limitation period which begins at the effective date of termination (the EDT).

These points are expanded below, except for (d) which is dealt with more generally in the text.

10.3.1 Service

The length of time an employee has spent with his or her employer (the continuity of employment) has always been a vital factor in determining whether or not he or she qualifies for unfair dismissal rights. The present position is contained in the Unfair Dismissal and Statement of Reasons for Dismissal (Variation of Qualifying Period) Order 1999, SI 1999/1436, which reduced the qualifying period from two years to one year.

10.3.1.1 The effective date of termination

The period of continuity ends at the effective date of termination (EDT). The EDT is not necessarily the date when an employee is told that he or she is dismissed. *The EDT varies according to whether notice is given or not.* Any notice given begins to run on the day after notification. So the EDT is defined in ERA 1996, s. 97(1), as:

- the date the notice period expires, if the employee is given notice (whether or not all the notice is worked and whether or not the correct notice was given); or
- the date of dismissal, if the employee is summarily dismissed (i.e., dismissed without any form of notice); or
- the date of dismissal, if the employee is dismissed with payment in lieu; or
- the date a fixed-term contract expires without being renewed.

The difference between the first and third points may seem to be one of semantics; and sometimes this is true. But the basic difference is that in the first instance the employee is either given the choice of working out the notice, or the employer insists on some work, e.g., to tidy up existing jobs or to pass on operational information to other employees; payment in lieu, on the other hand, is of immediate and unchallengeable effect. The position can, however, be complicated further. The way the employer expresses (orally or in writing) the dismissal and making of the payment in lieu may also affect the EDT. If the employer makes it clear that he is dismissing the employee immediately but paying him his notice entitlement, the EDT is that date of notification (this is the usual pattern). However, if the employer gets carried away (or has no concept of the problems) and talks about dismissing with notice but giving a payment in lieu instead of asking for notice to be worked, the EDT is the date the notice would have expired (see *Adams* v *GKN Sankey Ltd* [1980] IRLR 416).

Employers frequently use the third option described above because, provided there is no contractual term guaranteeing payment in lieu, it may avoid the tax liability arising in the first point. These distinctions prove to be a common point of confusion and need to be treated very carefully. For instance, the third option may have tax advantages but also means, as we saw at **8.9**, that, if there is no contractual right to dismiss with payment in lieu, this is a technical breach of contract which will render any restraint of trade clause ineffective.

If an employee is dismissed he or she may well appeal against that decision in accordance with the statutory dispute resolution procedures or within the company's disciplinary/grievance procedure. The question then arises, if the dismissal is confirmed on appeal, whether the employee's date of dismissal was the original date of the decision or the confirmation of that decision at the culmination of the appeals procedure. In most cases, unless there is express contractual provision to the contrary, the *original date* will count: *West Midlands Co-operative Society Ltd* v *Tipton* [1986] ICR 192. Thus any summary dismissal runs from that date and any notice given runs from that date too. If, however, the employee is suspended *pending a decision to dismiss*, the time can only run from the actual decision to dismiss. The employee's case becomes even easier to argue where that suspension was on full pay: *Drage* v *Governors of Greenford High School* [2000] IRLR 314.

It is not open to the parties to agree an EDT which is different from the normal method of calculation: *Fitzgerald* v *University of Kent at Canterbury* [2004] EWCA Civ 143, [2004] ICR 737. The effective date of termination is a statutory construct which depends on what has actually taken place and not on what the parties agreed.

10.3.1.2 Extending the EDT

Under ERA 1996, s. 97(2), the EDT may be deemed extended in certain circumstances by adding on to it the s. 86 statutory minimum period of notice (see **9.7.1.1** above).

EXAMPLE

An employee is dismissed summarily after 51 weeks' service. Strictly, she does not have the requisite one year's (52 weeks) service to claim unfair dismissal. However, s. 97(2) allows the employee the fiction of adding on the s. 86 notice that should have been given (here, one week) in calculating the EDT. Thus the employee gains the one year's qualification and can claim unfair dismissal. This device lessens the opportunities for unscrupulous employers to engage in brinkmanship tactics.

Note, however, that only the s. 86 notice can be used this way. The contractual notice (which may be longer) is irrelevant. The statutory extension also applies where the employee has waived his right to notice or has received payment in lieu of notice because such matters relate only to the employee's contract and do not affect his statutory rights: *Secretary of State for Employment* v *Staffordshire County Council* [1989] ICR 664. This method of extending the EDT also applies to constructive dismissal claims (see below at **10.6**). Note, however, that if the summary dismissal was contractually justified (e.g., because the dismissal was for gross misconduct or other serious breach by the employee) then this device cannot be applied.

As well as ensuring statutory rights in borderline situations the same technique can be used to calculate years of service for compensation purposes; so a dismissal close to four years' service would normally count as three years (because only whole years are considered), but the use of the s. 86 notice might take the qualification over the line into four years' service. This might affect the quantum of an employee's entitlement to, say, redundancy pay.

10.3.1.3 Exceptions to the service qualification

Some unfair dismissals do not require a one-year qualification period. These are set out in ERA 1996, s. 108 and TULRCA 1992, s. 154. They are:

(a) Dismissals for trade union activities and membership as defined in TULRCA 1992, s. 152 (as amended by sch. 2, ERA 1999). Taking industrial action is not counted as a trade union activity.

(b) Dismissals falling within ERA 1996, s. 99 (leave for family reasons), i.e. those relating to pregnancy, childbirth, maternity, maternity leave, parental leave, or taking time off (as defined in ERA 1996, s. 57A) to care for dependants.

(c) Dismissals relating to health and safety matters falling within ERA 1996, s. 100.

(d) Dismissals of certain shop and betting workers who refuse to work on Sundays, as set out in ERA 1996, s. 101.

(e) Dismissals relating to the enforcement of the Working Time Regulations as set out in ERA 1996, s. 101A.

(f) Dismissals of occupational pension scheme trustees falling within ERA 1996, s. 102

(g) Dismissals of certain employee representatives falling within ERA 1996, s. 103.

(h) Dismissals under the Public Interest Disclosure Act 1998, as set out in ERA 1996, s. 103A—the 'Whistleblower' provisions.

(i) Dismissals relating to the assertion of statutory rights as set out in ERA 1996, s. 104

(j) Dismissals in relation to national minimum wage claims falling within ERA, s. 104A.

(k) Dismissals relating to the claiming of tax credits under the Tax Credits Act 1999 as set out in ERA 1996, s. 104B.

(l) Dismissals arising out of suspension on medical grounds as defined in ERA 1996, s. 64(2)—*the qualifying period here is one month.*

(m) Dismissal (in defined circumstances) while taking part in official industrial action (known as 'protected industrial action'): TULRCA 1992, s. 238A (as inserted by ERA 1999, s. 16 and Schedule 5).

(n) Dismissals of *employees* (not 'workers') for a defined reason (e.g., the employee seeking to influence how votes should be cast in a ballot) connected with the recognition or de-recognition of a trade union, under ERA 1999, sch. 1, paras 161 and 164.

(o) Dismissals where the worker exercised, or sought to exercise, the right to be accompanied (or accompanied another worker) under ERA 1999, s. 10.

(p) Dismissals of part-time workers under ERA 1996, s. 108(i), as inserted by para. 2(2) of the Schedule to the Part-time Workers (Prevention of Less Favourable Treatment) Regulations 2000 (SI 2000/1551). Part-time workers who have exercised or sought to exercise rights (as set out in reg. 7, paras 1 and 3, e.g., those who have brought proceedings against their employer under the Regulations) fall within this exception.

(q) Dismissals where the principal reason is that the employee has exercised or sought to exercise certain rights relating to limited-term contracts. For details see reg. 6(3) of the Fixed-Term Employees (Prevention of Less Favourable Treatment) Regulations SI 2002/2034.

(r) Dismissals relating to the performance by employees in relation to transnational information and consultation under the Transnational Information and Consultation of Employees Regulations 1999.

Two further points should also be noted. First, a *selection for redundancy* based on these exceptions is automatically unfair and requires no qualifying period (see TULRCA 1992, s. 153 and ERA 1996, s. 105). Secondly, where the dismissal is for reasons of discrimination an action may be brought for that discrimination (rather than being tied in to unfair dismissal) and, as we noted in **Chapter 6**, no qualifying period is required for that particular action. Where a tribunal finds that the dismissal is both unfair and discriminatory it will set-off the awards to avoid double recovery but, as there is no upper limit to the compensation payable for discrimination, such a claim should always be considered where appropriate.

10.3.2 Hours worked

Under ERA 1996, s. 210(4) it is no longer necessary for an employee to have worked for any set number of hours per week in order to qualify for statutory rights such as unfair dismissal, redundancy or extended maternity leave.

10.3.3 Retirement age

Employees who have reached the 'normal retirement age' for the position which they hold lose the right to claim unfair dismissal. ERA 1996, s. 109(1) states that employees *cannot* claim for unfair dismissal if, prior to the EDT:

(a) they have reached the normal retirement age for employees in that position; and

(b) in any other case, they are 65 or over.

So, some companies may have, for example, 55 as their stated retirement age; many companies will have 60 or 65. A few may even have an age greater than 65, at least for some senior employees. In each case the 'normal retirement age' needs to be established. A comparator employee is not required.

Under s. 109(2), ERA 1999, s. 12 and TULRCA 1992, s. 239 dismissals for certain reasons (the same as covered in **10.3.1.3** above) are not subject to the provisions of s. 109(1). This means that these dismissals have no upper age limit qualification. Further, s. 154 of TULRCA 1992 states that the rules as to upper age limit also do not apply to inadmissibile reasons such as dismissals on grounds related to union membership or activities (set out in s. 152, TULRCA 1992). *These provisions apply equally to men and women.*

The provisions of the former manifestation of s. 109(1) were interpreted by the House of Lords in *Northman* v *Barnet London Borough* [1979] ICR 111. That case decided that the employee had to be below the normal retirement age (if there was one) *or* 65 (if there was no normal retirement age) in order to claim. Thus, if the normal retirement age for a particular employee is 70 then unfair dismissal rights will continue until that age. If the normal retirement age is 55, unfair dismissal rights will cease at that point. Prior to this case it had been thought that the *maximum age* would be 65 in all cases (*but note*: 65 is the maximum age for statutory redundancy payments rights, see **Chapter 11**).

10.3.3.1 Determining 'normal retirement age'

This phrase has caused headaches. There may be a normal retirement age for a particular company, or even for different types of employees within that company. This is perfectly legitimate. But merely because employees *generally or commonly* retire at, say, 60, does not mean that that is the applicable 'normal retirement age'. Sections 109(1) and 235(1) of ERA 1996 provide a fairly vague definition for determining whether employees are in the same 'position' for comparison purposes; the question turning on similarity of status and terms and conditions. In *Waite* v *GCHQ* [1983] ICR 653, the House of Lords held that the normal retirement age was *prima facie* to be determined by what the contract said and not by the fact that some employees happened to be kept on past the stated age of, say, 60. However, if the employees' *reasonable expectations* were that they would work past this age then there is probably no normal retirement age so that the age of 65 is taken as the retirement age. 'Reasonable expectation' is judged at the time of dismissal.

These principles were further developed in *Brooks* v *British Telecommunications plc* [1991] IRLR 4, where the EAT held that one must:

(a) identify the undertaking in which the employee is employed (i.e., there may be different ages in a multi-site company);
(b) identify which employees hold the *particular position* also held by the employee in question (e.g., identify the specific group of computer operators);
(c) establish the normal retirement age for that group of employees.

It is therefore permissible to have different retirement ages for different groups of employees within a company (e.g., all managers retire at 60, but all welders retire at 65), provided the practice is not discriminatory. The practical problem will therefore be accurately to identify the *group of employees*. Employees sharing the same job title could still occupy different 'positions' under this test and so have different retirement ages. But at least we know one new thing about 'groups': in *Wall* v *British Compressed Air Society* [2003] EWCA Civ 1762, [2004] ICR 408 the Court of Appeal overturned a 1983 EAT decision and held that one person could have a normal retirement age if the express terms of the contract so specified (here, to work until 70). There was no need to find comparators in such a case.

In *Barclays Bank plc* v *O'Brien* [1994] IRLR 580 the Court of Appeal set out 10 guidelines on determining normal retirement age (at p. 583 per Peter Gibson LJ). In brief these are:

(a) the social policy is to secure fair treatment as between employees holding the same 'position';

(b) the contractual retirement age can be rebuttably presumed to be the normal retirement age (NRA);

(c) rebuttal can occur by evidence of employees retiring at a higher age;

(d) 'normal' does not mean 'usual';

(e) tribunals must ask: at the date of termination, what was the expectation of all employees in that position (of whatever age) regarding the NRA?;

(f) that some of those employees expect to retire at a different age for special reasons does not invalidate the NRA;

(g) the 'position' of an employee does not include employment history or age but the inclusion of different retirement ages in the contract may be taken into account in determining 'position';

(h) the test of reasonable expectation is an objective one;

(i) an NRA policy, once promulgated, will take effect unless it is a sham or is abandoned;

(j) if that policy has been abandoned (e.g., by practice) so that employees retire at a variety of ages, there will be no NRA and the statutory alternative of 65 will apply.

In *Bratko* v *Beloit Walmsley Ltd* [1995] IRLR 629 the EAT held that where an employer seeks to change retirement ages within the company a mere statement of policy is ineffective unless it is an agreed contractual variation of the retirement age.

10.3.4 Working outside Great Britain

Some employees spend some or all of their time working abroad. Jurisdiction over such contracts is now determined by the rules of international law such as the Brussels Convention on Jurisdiction and Enforcement of Judgments in Civil and Commercial Matters and the Rome Convention on the Law Applicable to Contractual Obligations (transposed respectively into our law via the Civil Jurisdiction and Judgments Act 1982 and the Contracts (Applicable Law) Act 1990). These focus on where the employee's work has some connexion with the UK. The test is essentially: during the whole of the contract's duration, where does the employee habitually carry out his work? If his habitual place of work cannot be determined, the applicable law is that in which the place of business through which he was engaged is situated unless the circumstances show that the contract is more closely connected with the law of another country.

In addition, the Posting of Workers Directive (96/71/EC) deals with the position where a person is posted temporarily abroad for a limited period (either from the UK or to the UK) and was implemented in the UK via the ERA 1999. Article 6 of the Directive provides: 'In order to enforce the right to the terms and conditions of employment guaranteed in Article 3, judicial proceedings may be instituted in the Member State in whose territory the worker is or was posted, without prejudice, where applicable, to the right, under existing international conventions on jurisdiction, to institute proceedings in another state'. In *Lawson* v *Serco* [2004] EWCA Civ 12, [2004] ICR 204 the Court of Appeal examined all the provisions noted above and held that the right not to be unfairly dismissed applied only to employment in Great Britain. Here, the claimant was employed as a security supervisor by a British company which provided support services for the RAF and police on Ascension

Island. He was domiciled in Britain, paid in sterling but did not pay UK tax. The Court placed emphasis on where the employee worked rather than where the company was based or where the employee was domiciled and decided that the tribunal did not have jurisdiction to hear the claim.

10.3.5 Contracting out

The general position is that it is not possible to contract out of statutory rights except where there is an ACAS conciliation or a compromise agreement under ERA 1996, s. 203 (see **10.12** below).

10.3.6 Limited-term contracts

We noted in **9.4.2** that, in the past, clauses commonly appeared in limited-term contracts which permitted the contracting-out (or waiver) of the employee's statutory rights to claim unfair dismissal or redundancy payments on expiry and non-renewal of the term. However, under: (i) ss. 18(1) and 44 and ERA 1999, sch. 9 a limited-term contract entered into on or after 25 October 1999 can no longer exclude rights relating to unfair dismissal; and (ii) under EA 2002, s. 45 and sch. 2, para. 3(13)–(17) and the Fixed-Term Employees (Prevention of Less Favourable Treatment) Regulations, SI 2002/2034 [para 5], the same applies to redundancy payments rights where the dismissal occurs on or after 1 October 2002. However, any waiver/contracting-out clauses entered into before these respective dates will remain valid until the term expires so you may still encounter valid waiver clauses for some time yet in the case of lengthy fixed-term contracts. One limitation on this is that such waivers cannot be included in any renewal or extension of the limited-term.

The position is summarised in the table below:

Key date	Rules on unfair dismissal	Rules on redundancy
Contract entered into before 25 October 1999	Any contracting-out regarding unfair dismissal rights is still effective (s. 197 (1) and (2))	Any contracting-out regarding redundancy payments rights is still effective (s. 197 (5) ERA 1996): the term must be for two years or more
Contract entered into before 25 October 1999 *but renewed or extended after that date*	Unfair dismissal rights *cannot* be excluded (s. 18(1) amendments to s. 197)	Redundancy payments can still be excluded in the renewed term, the proviso that the agreement must be reached after expiry of the original agreement, s. 197(5) ERA 1996 (*though it is not clear whether the extended term must be for two years or more as well)*
Contract entered into/renewed after 25 October 1999 but before 1 October 2002	Unfair dismissal rights *cannot* be excluded	Redundancy payments can still be excluded, but with provisos as above
Contract entered into after 1999 but before 1 October 2002 *and renewed or extended after 1 October 2002*	Unfair dismissal rights *cannot* be excluded	Statutory redundancy payments *cannot* be excluded (contractual schemes will be subjected to the test of objective justification)
Succession of limited-terms	Four-year maximum (without more), but this is not relevant to any part of the term occurring before 10 July 2002	Four-year maximum (without more), but this is not relevant to any part of the term occurring before 10 July 2002

10.3.7 Excluded categories

There are a number of miscellaneous categories. The most common ones are:

(a) The police force. This includes all those who have the powers or privileges of a constable.

(b) Share fishermen, i.e., masters and crews of fishing vessels who take a share in the profits of the catch.

(c) Employees working under illegal contracts.

10.3.7.1 Employees working under illegal contracts

This category deserves one or two special comments. As with the ordinary law of contract, a contract of employment which is illegal will be unenforceable. No rights, under common law or statute, will therefore flow from a dismissal. The most obvious example is a contract designed to evade tax liabilities: *Napier* v *National Business Agency Ltd* [1951] 2 All ER 264 (agreement to classify wages as expenses).

In some cases the illegal part of the contract may be severed, leaving the rest to stand. For example, an unlawful restraint of trade clause will not affect the validity of the remainder of the contract and discriminatory clauses can be ignored or modified.

If the employee is innocent of the fact of illegality it seems that he or she may still claim unfair dismissal rights. The test is subjective and relates to ignorance of the relevant facts, not ignorance of the law. Likewise, if the employee gains no advantage from the illegality (e.g., participates in a VAT evasion) it is likely that the right to claim unfair dismissal is not damaged: *Hewcastle Catering Ltd* v *Ahmed and Elkamah* [1991] IRLR 473. And a short-term illegality may have the effect only of breaking the employee's continuity of employment, which can start again after the duration of the illegality.

10.3.8 Limitation period

In general, the employee must present any claim within the three-month limitation period which begins at the EDT: ERA 1996, s. 111(2). The period begins on the EDT itself and 'month' means calendar month, so one must find the EDT, take the date of the day before the EDT and project this forward three months. Thus a dismissal on 3 October must be presented *on or before* 2 January of the following year (3 January is too late). This topic is dealt with more extensively in **Chapter 13**.

Waiting until the last possible date may therefore test your ability to use a calendar but is not usually advisable. Equally, giving lengthy detailed advice when the employee is already outside the limitation period could prove to be a waste of time (this is not uncommon). Calculation of both the EDT itself and the limitation period can be treacherous. Because of the short limitation period, therefore, solicitors are advised to determine the EDT as soon as possible in order to protect the employee's rights (see **10.3.1** above). Employment tribunals will allow claims to be made out of time in exceptional circumstances.

10.4 Burden of proof

Before turning to the detail of what is meant by fairness and unfairness, it is important to note that there are three stages in an unfair dismissal action and the burden of proof at each stage is different. Thus:

(a) the *employee* (if challenged) must prove there was a dismissal;
(b) the *employer* must show that the dismissal was for one of the accepted *fair reasons*;
(c) the burden of proving the *fairness* of the dismissal is neutral.

We will now examine what is meant by 'dismissal', 'fair reason', and 'fairness'.

10.5 The meaning of 'dismissal'

We noted in **Chapter 9** that the term 'dismissal' is a technical term which can occasionally confuse, and one which can certainly trap the unwary. Employees may therefore find themselves 'dismissed' (as legally defined) in the following circumstances:

(a) where the employee is given the sack;
(b) where the employer uses language which amounts to dismissal;
(c) where the employer intimates a future dismissal;
(d) where the employer says 'resign or be sacked';
(e) where the employer repudiates the contract and the employee resigns;
(f) where a limited-term contract is not renewed.

These points were discussed in detail in **Chapter 9** at **9.6** and **9.8**.

10.6 Constructive dismissal

10.6.1 A resignation which is deemed a dismissal

We saw in **Chapter 9** that when an employee resigns this may still constitute a dismissal for common law purposes (termed a 'wrongful repudiation'). The position is the same as regards *statutory rights* and is dealt with in ERA 1996, s. 95(1)(c). This states that a resignation will amount to a dismissal if 'the employee terminates the contract under which he is employed (with or without notice) in circumstances in which he is entitled to terminate it without notice by reason of the employer's conduct'.

In this context this is known as 'constructive dismissal'. But the definition creates a further problem: what sort of conduct by the employer *entitles* the employee to resign and claim unfair dismissal? Throughout the 1970s two views developed. One view argued that constructive dismissal arose where the employer's conduct was *unreasonable*. The other view stated that constructive dismissal could arise only where the employer committed a serious *breach of contract*.

The issue was determined by the Court of Appeal in the key case of *Western Excavating (ECC)* v *Sharp* [1978] QB 761. An employee had been suspended without pay as part of disciplinary proceedings. He was therefore short of cash and asked his employer for an advance. This was refused so he resigned (in order it seems to gain access to his holiday pay!) and claimed that the refusal was so unreasonable as to amount to a constructive dismissal. Astonishingly the employment tribunal and the EAT agreed with him. Lord Denning MR held that an employee is entitled to resign and claim unfair dismissal only if:

(a) the employer's actions are a significant breach of contract (an employer who is merely acting unreasonably is not necessarily in breach of contract, but the two can overlap substantially);

(b) the resignation is obviously related to the employer's conduct; and

(c) the employee responds quickly.

Sharp therefore lost on this analysis—as he should have done on any analysis—and the contractual analysis pattern was set. The *Western Excavating* v *Sharp* analysis held good for some twenty-six years until the implementation of EA 2002, s. 32 in October 2004 (which covers the procedures that must be followed when an employee has a grievance). All the case law which flowed from *Western Excavating* must now be read in the light of this statutory provision. Thus, points (a) and (b) of Lord Denning's analysis above will still stand true, but (c) needs further attention and we will return to this specifically at **10.6.5** below.

Note: throughout this chapter we will use the term 'overt dismissal' when we need to distinguish an ordinary employer-driven dismissal from a 'constructive dismissal' arising from a resignation. These are not statutory terms.

There may also be problems with apparent resignations which turn out to be nothing of the sort, e.g., resignations in the heat of the moment. As we saw in **Chapter 9**, employees are allowed some leeway with heated outbursts. If the words spoken are ambiguous there is the preliminary point as to whether they constitute a resignation at all. If the words are unambiguous the employer is entitled to take these at their face value and the employee must live with the consequences. This approach has been confirmed in *Hogan* v *ACP Heavy Fabrications Ltd* (1994, unreported, EAT 340/92) where the EAT held that there is no obligation on the employer formally to accept the employee's resignation where the employee has responded to a clear breach by the employer. The EAT indicated that an employer *would have to accept the resignation* if the employee simply resigned without giving proper notice; which only adds to the confusion because it means an employer effectively has to judge its own actions! However, an employee is allowed to retract within a reasonable time if the words were spoken in anger or the intellectual capability of the employee is in question: *Kwik-Fit (GB) Ltd* v *Lineham* [1992] ICR 183. An employer who refuses to allow a reasonable retraction will have *dismissed* the employee from the point.

Inviting employees to resign is often seen by employers as an honourable way of avoiding dismissing them so that, in future job applications, the employees will not have the stigma of 'dismissal' on their record. However, such invitations may in themselves constitute a breach of mutual trust and confidence if, in the context of a non-disciplinary hearing an employee is advised to consider this action (see *Billington* v *Michael Hunter and Sons* (unreported, UKEAT/578/03/DM); nor does the tag 'without prejudice' aid the case, as this may not always prevent such discussions or letters being used in litigation: *BNP Paribas* v *Mezzotero* [2004] IRLR 508 where the EAT held communications were only privileged under the 'without prejudice' rule where they were made in a situation where there was a genuine attempt to settle an extant dispute.

10.6.2 Type of conduct required

In practice it is not always easy to distinguish between *merely unreasonable* conduct and conduct which is *repudiatory. Western Excavating* v *Sharp* was easy, but later cases have shown a steady blurring of the distinction. The position has become less clear as the courts and tribunals have turned to breaches of implied terms such as mutual trust and confidence as the source of constructive dismissal claims. And even where the employer argues that there is an express term which legitimises the conduct, tribunals may declare the particular *application* of the term invalid as an abuse of the contract.

A good example of this occurred in *Cawley* v *South Wales Electricity Board* [1985] IRLR 89. The employer utilised the disciplinary procedure (technically within the contractual bounds) to demote an employee by many grades. The EAT decided nevertheless that this was an excessive use of the contractual power and found a breach of contract. In reality, many cases have to turn on a judgment call. The line between merely unreasonable conduct (which is not a constructive dismissal) and seriously unreasonable conduct (which will be) has to be a question of fact: *Brown* v *Merchant* [1998] IRLR 682. Another variation of this can occur when salespeople have their areas or range of products changed under company reorganisations. If the contract defines area, commission, etc. any change by the employer will at least technically constitute a breach. But even if the contract is unclear on these matters (yes, it does occur!) one would expect the courts to find an implied term to the effect that the company should at least come to some agreement concerning the impact on commission: *Star Newspapers Ltd* v *Jordan* (1993, unreported, EAT 709/91). Wider still, in *Woods* v *WM Service (Peterborough) Ltd* [1981] ICR 666, it was stated that employers will not, without reasonable and proper cause, conduct themselves in a manner calculated or likely to destroy or seriously damage the relationship of confidence and trust between employer and employee. The width of this statement (which looks remarkably like imposing a duty to act reasonably) has not been without its critics.

Examples of constructive dismissal actions are:

(a) harassment (including harassment by other employees);

(b) victimisation: *Gardner* v *Beresford* [1978] IRLR 63;

(c) unilaterally changing the employee's job content or status: *Coleman* v *Baldwin* [1977] IRLR 342;

(d) humiliating employees in front of others: *Isle of Wight Tourist Board* v *Coombes* [1976] IRLR 413;

(e) unwarranted demotion or disciplinary sanctions: *Cawley* v *SWEB* (above); or improper use of disciplinary sanctions such as issuing a final warning for a minor offence, as happened in *Stanley Cole (Wainfleet) Ltd* v *Sheridan* [2003] ICR 297;

(f) falsely accusing an employee of misconduct or incapability: *Robinson* v *Crompton Parkinson Ltd* [1978] IRLR 61;

(g) unilateral variation in contract terms, e.g., a change in hours or pay: *Woods* v *WM Service (Peterborough) Ltd* (above);

(h) deliberately withholding pay: *Cantor Fitzgerald International* v *Callaghan* [1999] IRLR 234.

(i) demanding that the employee undertakes a substantial transfer of location (certainly if without reasonable notice);

(j) suspension without pay where the contract does not allow for this—and even with pay if prolonged;

(k) failure to support a manager in the light of well-known operational difficulties;

(l) failure to provide a working environment which is reasonably suitable for the performance of contractual duties;

(m) failure to investigate properly the possibility of finding alternative work for an employee who is suffering from work-related stress: *Thanet District Council* v *Websper* (unreported, 2002, EAT 1090/01).

These are just examples and one would need to investigate the alleged breach very carefully. For instance, as we noted extensively in **Chapter 5**, an employee is expected to be adaptable in the operation of the contract. Therefore, what appears to be a unilateral variation of the contract may prove to be no such thing in law. Equally, the breach must be *serious* and much will depend upon the particular facts and the particular contract—though points such as harassment and victimisation will be easier to argue. What is clear, however, is that the employee must show a serious breach by the employer (whether of the express or implied terms).

Note also that:

(a) it is usually one breach that is in issue, but the idea of a 'last straw' can also apply so that a history of incidents can be drawn together: see *Lewis* v *Motorworld Garages Ltd* [1986] ICR 157. Note that there does not necessarily have to be temporal proximity between the events, but the larger the gap the weaker the case becomes. The 'last straw' does not have to be an breach itself; it is the overall picture which counts: *Omilaju* v *Walthan Forest* LBC [2004] 3 All ER, 129;

(b) the mere fact that an employee has other, additional reasons for leaving, e.g., to go to a different job, does not mean that the effective cause of the resignation has ceased to be the employer's breach. Neither does a delay of a few weeks in order to find such work damn the employee's case automatically;

(c) a constructive dismissal can arise by way of anticipatory breach;

(d) particular care should be taken where the only issue is the *construction of the contract* itself. Authorities (occasionally used in employment cases) have indicated that the employer's conduct has to show that he clearly intends not to be bound by the contract before a breach will occur. This is an uncertain and little-used area: see *Brigden* v *Lancashire County Council* [1987] IRLR 58.

10.6.3 Are all breaches repudiatory?

We have seen in *Western Excavating* v *Sharp* that a *serious* breach is required. Moreover, in *Hilton* v *Shiner* [2001] IRLR 727, the EAT confirmed and applied previous dicta to the effect that the employer's conduct must have been without reasonable and proper cause. Instigating disciplinary action against an employee would not per se be a breach of mutual trust and confidence if there appeared good grounds for doing so. A gloss was added to this by the EAT in *Morrow* v *Safeway Stores* [2002] IRLR 9 that, once a breach of mutual trust has been found, this implied term is so fundamental to the workings of the contract that its breach automatically constitutes a repudiation—a tribunal cannot conclude that there was such a breach but, on the facts, it was not that serious. Like many EAT decisions, if one starts trying to apply this to real situations these two decisions do not sit together comfortably. It is suggested that the solution seems to be that a tribunal must make a clear finding of serious breach/no breach, incorporating the *Hilton* v *Shiner* aspect and, if there is a breach, must make a finding of constructive dismissal accordingly.

10.6.4 Consequences of showing a constructive dismissal

Proving a constructive dismissal means nothing in itself. There is no statutory remedy for being constructively dismissed (though there may be a wrongful repudiation claim at common law). All that a constructive dismissal proves is that the employee was dismissed. This can be seen in **Figure 10.1** below. As you will see later in this chapter, once an employee has established a constructive dismissal the question of the fairness of that dismissal has to be decided in the normal way.

10.6.5 What should the employee do when faced with a serious breach?

We have not yet dealt with the question of how swiftly the employee must act in the face of the breach. All the case law since *Western Excavating* has stressed that, if the breach is supposedly repudiatory, the employee must act quickly and resign within a reasonable time in response to that breach. If the employee did not act quickly enough he or she was said to have *affirmed* the breach and lost the right to claim constructive dismissal.

One of the key features in the EA 2002, introduced by the Employment Act 2002 (Dispute Resolution) Regulations SI 2004/752, is that employers and employees should seek to resolve their differences within the workplace, using a mixture of statutory and contractual procedures, before going to a tribunal. As we noted at **5.3** above, if either party fails to use the new statutory procedures there are financial consequences, and in some cases a tribunal may not admit the claim at all.

10.6.5.1 Admissibility issues

Section 32, EA 2002 describes the position where an employee has a grievance and therefore this section affects how any resulting constructive dismissal claim will be dealt with. The section prevents a claimant bringing certain claims, including an unfair dismissal claim, until the statutory procedures have been complied with or treated as having been complied with. As we have commented, a constructive dismissal claim is only a prelude to an unfair dismissal. Unfair dismissal is one of the actions listed in EA 2002, schs 3 and 4, so a constructive dismissal falls within the scope of s. 32. This means that when the statutory procedures apply an employee cannot make a claim for unfair (constructive) dismissal until:

(i) he has made use of the statutory grievance procedure, setting out the grievance in writing and sending it to the employer (for details see **5.3**); and

(ii) 28 days have passed since the day that requirement was complied with (which covers the case where the employer does not respond to the grievance).

It is therefore clear that the old 'act quickly' rule now has a cooling-off period built into it.

The employee is also barred from presenting a claim if he has lodged his Step 1 statement of grievance but this occurred more than one month after the end of the limitation period for bringing the claim (three months from the EDT in the case of an unfair dismissal action). However, where the employee has tried to lodge a claim within the three-month limitation period but this has been rejected by the tribunal under s. 32(2), the time limit for bringing the claim will be automatically extended for a further three months (i.e. the time limit will now be six months from the act complained of: see reg. 15(3)). The employee who still wishes to pursue the claim must now send a Step 1 statement to the employer and wait 28 days before lodging the claim again. This extension is subject to s. 32(4) which states that: 'An employee shall not present a complaint to an employment tribunal under a jurisdiction to which this section applies if: (a) it concerns a matter in relation to which the requirement in paragraph 6 or 9 of Schedule 2 has been complied with (*Step 1 of the procedures*), and (b) the day on which the requirement was complied with was more than one month after the end of the original time limit for making the complaint.' So, if the employee lodges the Step 1 statement after four months have run from the act complained of he will lose his right to pursue the claim.

Tribunals will not admit claims which have not adhered to the statutory grievance procedures where the breach of the procedures is apparent from the information provided by the employee or the tribunal is satisfied of the breach as a result of the employer raising the issue.

10.6.5.2 Before resignation

The procedures noted above describe what should happen once the employee resigns and wishes to pursue a claim. That still leaves open the question as to how long employees can wait, when faced with a repudiatory breach by the employer, before any inaction on their part amounts to *affirmation* of the breach so that no further claim is possible. The case law to date has shown that a delay of a few days, even a month, will not usually be fatal provided the employee has objected to the conduct. If the employee then resigns in the face of the breach he or she is said to have *accepted the repudiation.* Nothing in the new legislation affects this because s. 32 only operates on issues of admissibility, not the substance of the claim.

There is one potential loophole in all this, highlighted by the authors of the *IDS Brief*: what if the employee never raises a grievance but reacts immediately to the alleged breach by the employer and resigns? This action would fulfil the requirements of *Western Excavating* and, debatably, would not fall within the auspices of s. 32 (invoking the cooling-off period) because the definition of a grievance in the Regulations is that it is a 'complaint by an employee'. The argument has been posited that, if the employee remains silent then there is no complaint *by* the employee and so the statutory procedures do not operate. This is a nice technical argument, but whether it will run before tribunals is a little more questionable.

10.6.5.3 When the statutory grievance procedures do not apply

Aside from the potential loophole noted above, there are instances where the statutory procedures do not operate or are deemed to have been complied with (detailed at **5.3.2.3** and **5.3.2.4** above). In such cases an employee may only be bound to follow the modified grievance procedure or may even not be bound by the s. 32 admissibility rules at all.

For instance, reg. 6(3) deals with the position of the application of the modified grievance procedure. This will apply where the employee has ceased to be employed by the employer, **and** either the employer was unaware of the grievance before employment ceased, or was so aware but the standard procedure had not been commenced or had not been completed before the last day of the employee's employment; **and** the parties must have agreed in writing that the modified, rather than the standard, grievance procedure shall apply. The agreement has to be specific to each case and a clause in the contract allowing for this to happen will be inoperative: reg. 6(3)(c).

Reg. 6(4) allows for the position where the employee has ceased to be employed by the employer, neither procedure has been commenced, and since the employment ended it has *ceased to be reasonably practicable* for him to issue a statement of grievance. In such a case the grievance procedures are disapplied.

In addition, reg. 11(3)(c) carries a more general exemption: where 'it is not practicable for the party to commence the procedure or comply with the subsequent requirement within a reasonable period'. The difference is that reg. 6(4) relates to the employee's circumstances and deals specifically with the case where the employee's employment has ended; reg. 11 applies to the general position which includes the position where the grievance relates to a continuing employment relationship.

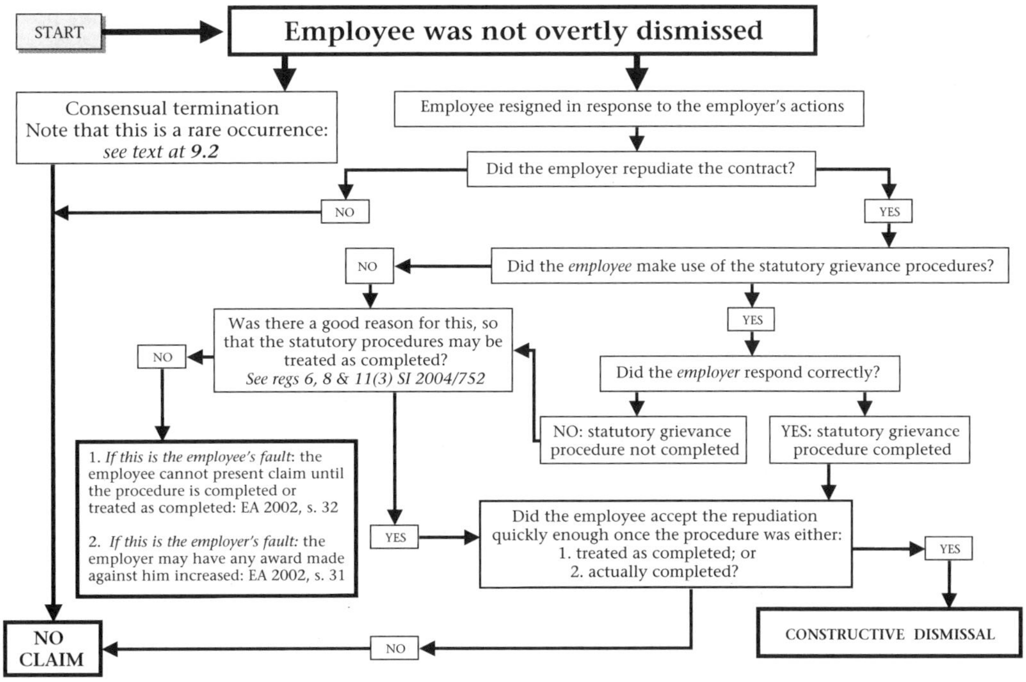

Figure 10.1 Showing a constructive dismissal.

One also needs to note here the circumstances when the grievance procedures are treated as complied with so that one or other party is excused further action. These are set out in **5.3.2.4** above and are not repeated here for reasons of space.

We summarised the requirements for a constructive dismissal action in the diagram above (**Figure 10.1**). We should stress that **Figure 10.1** does not tell the full story because once a constructive dismissal has been proven the tribunal must then consider whether that deemed dismissal was fair or unfair in the circumstances. *It is possible to have a constructive dismissal which is still fair.*

EXAMPLE

Suppose Aquitaine Ltd employs Eleanor on terms that include a mobility clause. Aquitaine asks Eleanor to move to a newly-acquired site close by. Eleanor is unhappy and raises various objections. Aquitaine does its best to meet these objections but Eleanor is quite uncooperative and refuses to move. In desperation, Aquitaine issues an instruction to Eleanor to move on a stated date, having met all the practical difficulties. Eleanor still refuses, resigns and claims unfair dismissal.

If the mobility clause is not as watertight as the company had hoped Eleanor may succeed in persuading the employment tribunal that there was a constructive dismissal, but it is unlikely that the tribunal will find that it was an unfair (constructive) dismissal because of the employer's actions. Whether this action amounts to indirect discrimination is another matter.

10.7 Standard of proof

We noted above in **10.4** where the burden of proof lay for each stage of an unfair dismissal claim. The question raised in this section relates specifically to the issues of 'fair reason' which we are about to discuss in **10.8**. If the employer says that he or she dismissed the employee for incompetence, is it enough that the employer simply *believed* the employee was incompetent, or does that belief have to be tested against some wider, objective analysis? In other words: to what standard of proof is the employer to be put?

The principal case is the House of Lords' decision in *Devis (W) & Sons Ltd* v *Atkins* [1977] AC 931. This established that the employer must *honestly believe at the time of the dismissal* that the facts disclosed a fair reason to dismiss. Provided there is an honest belief it does not matter that the employer was mistaken. Thus if an employer honestly believes that the employee has committed theft and dismisses for that reason (misconduct), it is irrelevant at this stage whether the employee did or did not commit the theft.

Most employees will not believe your advice when they are told this. They will argue that the employer has no right to dismiss them unless the offence can be proven. They will be wrong. In an unfair dismissal claim, positive proof of the offence is not required.

Practically speaking, of course, in order for the employer to show this honest belief he or she will have to show that the evidence was at least *capable* of generating the conclusion. Waking up one morning and 'honestly believing' an employee is incompetent is clearly not enough. Thus, although the employer does not have to *prove* the incompetence, the decision to dismiss must flow from an *honest belief based on reasonable grounds*. Indeed, in some cases the employer does have to show that the reason for dismissal exists and mistake is no defence, e.g., redundancy dismissals and dismissals on grounds of statutory requirements.

As the test is one of 'honest belief' it follows that the employer can only rely on evidence known to him at the date of dismissal. Any evidence which comes to light after the dismissal relating to the employee's conduct *during* the relationship cannot be relied upon as it could not have been known to the employer at the point of dismissal. So, if an employer dismisses for theft (honestly believing the employee was guilty) this will constitute a fair reason. The tribunal will then have to decide whether it was fairly handled. If, subsequent to the dismissal, the employer disovers new facts which show that the employee had committed other acts of misconduct these facts are irrelevant in judging the fairness or unfairness of the dismissal—they were not in the employer's mind at the moment of dismissal. Note the contrast here with the common law position where the employer *is entitled* to rely on evidence not known to him at the time of dismissal: *Boston Deep Sea Fishing and Ice Co.* v *Ansell* (1888) 39 ChD 339 (see **Chapter 9** at **9.7.3.3**).

An employee's arguments are also affected by what was in the employer's mind. In *St Anne's Board Mill* v *Brien* [1973] ICR 444 the employees were dismissed because, after proper investigations, the employer believed they were unreasonably refusing to obey a lawful order. The employees had refused to work with a colleague because they said he was dangerous and had caused the injury of another employee. The employer believed otherwise. Some time after the dismissal it was shown that the employees were correct. But this did not matter. The employer had acted fairly on the evidence reasonably available at the time of dismissal.

The case of *West Midlands Co-operative Society Ltd* v *Tipton* [1986] ICR 192, added an interesting angle to this. The employees here were dismissed and then were refused the right to an internal appeal under the disciplinary procedure, as granted in the contract. Part of their case was that the employer had acted unfairly in not allowing them to appeal. But any appeal must logically come after a dismissal and so, strictly, is irrelevant under *Devis* v *Atkins*. The House of Lords resolved this by treating the matter of appeals as part of the *continuing process of the dismissal*. Not necessarily logical, but good common sense.

Lastly, it should be noted that although subsequently discovered events are generally irrelevant to the fairness of the dismissal, they can be taken into account in the following situations:

(a) where the evidence relates *directly* to the reason for the dismissal and helps to substantiate that reason;

(b) in assessing the level of compensation (see **10.13.3** below);

(c) where the event occurs during the employee's notice period, e.g., the employee dismissed on grounds of ill-health recovers before the expiry of the notice or the redundancy situation is rectified. The employer should react to this change: *Williamson* v *Alcan (UK) Ltd* [1978] ICR 104.

This reasoning means that the 'reason' has to be assessed both in relation to the point at which notice is given and the termination itself. A fair redundancy selection, for instance, might become unfair if the circumstances of the business change in this period: see *Stacey* v *Babcock Power Ltd* [1986] ICR 221, *Alboni* v *Ind Coope Retail Ltd* [1998] IRLR 131 and *West Kent College* v *Richardson* [1999] ICR 511.

In *Devis* v *Atkins* the main concern of the House of Lords was to outlaw the use of *fresh reasons* by an employer to justify a dismissal. That point is still sacrosanct. Thus the order of analysis is:

(a) What was the reason for the dismissal?

(b) Was that reason a fair reason under ERA 1996, s. 98?

(c) Did the employer handle the dismissal fairly in treating that reason as a sufficient reason for dismissal?

10.8 Potentially fair reasons

As can be seen in (b) and (c) above, assessing fairness involves a two-stage process.

It cannot be over-emphasised that these stages are *separate* and will be considered in sequence by the employment tribunal. Employers frequently misunderstand the process and suppose that an outstandingly good reason (e.g., strong evidence of theft) somehow makes up for a poor handling of the situation (e.g., not giving the employee a chance to explain). Nothing can be further from the truth. If the handling is unfair the dismissal will most likely be unfair, no matter how good the reason. Indeed, if the handling breaches the statutory dispute resolution procedures the dismissal may be classed as automatically unfair or, if not this, the employer may have to pay additional compensation for this failure in procedure.

Thus, proving that the dismissal was for one of the fair reasons set out below does not mean that the employer has won. This is just the first stage. If the employer cannot show a fair reason, however, the employee will win at this stage and, as will be seen in **10.8.7**, some reasons may be classed as *automatically unfair* irrespective of how they were handled.

10.8.1 The reason or principal reason

Under ERA 1996, s. 98 the burden of proof lies with the employer to show a defence under one of the headings detailed below as the *reason or principal reason* for dismissal.

In the text below we will first note some basic rules on assessing 'reasons', then we will give the basic requirements of each potentially fair reason and then turn to the fairness of their operation in **10.9**. The five fair reasons for dismissal are:

(a) Capability (s. 98(2)(a)).

(b) Conduct (s. 98(2)(b)).

(c) Redundancy (s. 98(2)(c)).
(d) Statutory illegality (s. 98(2)(d)).
(e) Some other substantial reason (s. 98(1)(b)).

10.8.1.1 Multiple reasons

The employer may have more than one reason for the dismissal; the notion of a 'principal reason' does not mean 'a single reason'. But the section does prevent an employer relying on a 'shotgun approach' of detailing every unsatisfactory aspect of the employee's work in the hope that one will hit the target: *Smith* v *Glasgow City District Council* [1987] ICR 796. The weakness with multiple reasons (certainly those which are interdependent) is that as the structure of reasons becomes more complicated the questions of proof become more difficult to establish clearly. The most common overlaps arise:

(a) when the employer cites different incidents to justify the dismissal, e.g., various forms of misconduct; and
(b) between misconduct and incapability, e.g., a history of intermittent absences could be a case of incapability (e.g., health) or misconduct.

10.8.1.2 The label given by the employer

The employer is required to have dismissed on the grounds of 'honest belief'. The initial reasons given by the employer are therefore important, and a manufactured or unproven reason obviously cannot succeed. Thus suddenly dismissing a long-serving employee for alleged incompetence puts the employer under a heavy burden of proof; more so if a good reference is then provided for the employee citing the outstanding contributions to the business over the years.

Tribunals do not, therefore, simply have to accept an employer's stated reason. The reason can be rejected as a fraud or as a mistake. A discovered fraud—for example, dismissing an employee because of trade union activities but citing incapability—will lead to a finding of unfair dismissal at this stage. But where there is simply a genuine mistake of labelling on the employer's part at the time of dismissal the tribunal may have more sympathy if the facts relied upon by the employer as constituting the reason for the dismissal were clear to the employee at the time of termination: *Abernethy* v *Mott, Hay and Anderson* [1974] ICR 323. The key element, therefore, is that if the employer consistently relies on the same *facts* to justify the dismissal a change of *legal reasons* may not be fatal. It will nevertheless be a dangerous course of action to dismiss for one stated reason and then plead another in the tribunal.

Where employers have sought to soften the blow of dismissal by labelling it as a 'redundancy' when no redundancy actually exists they run the risk of being trapped by that stated reason.

10.8.1.3 ERA 1996, s. 92

Section 92 allows an employee to demand from the employer written reasons for the dismissal. There must be a specific request and the employer must reply within 14 days of that request. Any unreasonable refusal or lies by the employer may lead to the employer having to pay the employee two weeks' pay (whether dismissed unfairly or not). The employer's statement is admissible in any proceedings. Except for women dismissed while pregnant or on maternity leave, qualification for this right requires one year's service. There is, however, no upper age limit.

10.8.1.4 Pressure of industrial action

The ERA 1996, s. 107, states that, in assesssing the reason for dismissal, the employment tribunal must ignore pressure placed on the employer to dismiss arising from threats, etc.

of industrial action made by third parties, e.g., other employees or trade unions. Expressions of disgruntlement about the employee from third parties do not fall within this section. But if fellow employees say that they will go on strike unless an employee becomes a member of a union, that is the area covered by s. 107.

10.8.2 Capability as a fair reason

Section 98(3) of ERA 1996 defines capability as 'capability assessed by reference to skill, aptitude, health or any other physical or mental quality'. This breaks down into three sub-headings:

(a) *Qualifications.*
Cases in this area are rare. Section 98(3)(b) states that qualifications means 'any degree, diploma or other academic, technical or professional qualification relevant to the position which [the employee] held'. What amounts to qualification (as opposed to a licence or permit, for instance) has been given a narrow interpretation in *Blue Star Ship Management Ltd* v *Williams* [1978] ICR 770. The qualification must be connected substantially to the employee's job.

(b) *Incompetence.*
Employees are incompetent when they cannot perform their duties as required under the terms of the contract. It is rare for one-off incidents of incompetence to justify a dismissal, though not impossible; where, for example, bad workmanship causes the employer a massive loss. Examples of incompetence include: slow completion rates; making misjudgments or mistakes; lack of adaptability; inability to work with colleagues; and inability to deal with clients.

(c) *Ill-health.*
If an employee's absence from work (either on prolonged absence or on an intermittent but frequent basis) means that he or she is unable to do the job, an employer is entitled to rely on this as the reason for dismissal. Unjustified absence (e.g., being caught painting the house while drawing company sick pay on the pretext of back pain) will probably count as *conduct* (see **10.8.3** below). Employers who categorise ill-health absence as *capability*, on the other hand, are not necessarily doubting that the reason is perfectly genuine: the employee may simply be incapable of attending often enough to comply with the contract.

It is often thought that, if the employer's actions caused the illness or injury, the employer cannot then dismiss for reasons of incapability. Such logic was denied by the then President of the EAT in *London Fire & Civil Defence Authority* v *Betty* [1994] IRLR 384 where the employer had falsely accused the employee of racial harassment to the point where the employee suffered a nervous breakdown. It was held that the employee's remedy lay in an action for damages; the cause of the illness did not prevent it constituting a fair reason for dismissal. However, the EAT moved away from this stance in *Edwards* v *Governors of Hanson School* [2001] IRLR 733, saying that the cause of illness etc is not always irrelevant to the question of fairness (e.g., 'if the employer . . . has acted maliciously, or wilfully caused an employee's incapacity'—per Bell J) and certainly has a place in assessing what is 'just and equitable' compensation. Consistency is not always a byword of the EAT.

10.8.3 Conduct as a fair reason

The difference between conduct and capability is often that the employee can improve conduct; but capability can imply something about the employee's innate ability that cannot be changed (in the same way that the authors might improve their attendance record at an athletics club but will never run a mile in under four minutes!). Some issues, such as excessive absence or incompetence, may fall under both heads and the choice of one over the other may rest on how far the employee is believed to be at fault—doing one's best, albeit one's incompetent best, is better argued as capability for instance.

The heading therefore covers a diverse range of activities, such as:

(a) disobedience to lawful orders;
(b) gross insubordination;
(c) abusive language;
(d) theft;
(e) fraud;
(f) taking bribes;
(g) drunkenness at work;
(h) unacceptable personal appearance;
(i) disclosing confidential information;
(j) gaining unauthorised access to computer files;
(k) assault;
(l) intermittent absenteeism;
(m) persistent lateness;
(n) taking unauthorised and prolonged leave; and even
(o) conduct occurring outside the employment relationship which has a direct bearing on the contract of employment.

There is no requirement that the misconduct must have been gross. The misconduct may have been a one-off but serious incident, or the culmination of a series of incidents over which warnings have been issued.

10.8.4 Redundancy as a fair reason

To make someone redundant is to *dismiss them* for reasons of redundancy. Redundancy has its own particular rules which are dealt with in **Chapter 11**, but one may have a fair or unfair dismissal for reasons of redundancy. The meaning of 'redundancy' is given in ERA 1996, s. 139(1) and (6). This provides a highly technical definition. In general terms s. 139 states that a redundancy occurs in three situations:

(a) where there is a cessation of the business;
(b) where there is a closure of the employee's particular workplace;
(c) where there is a cessation or diminution in the requirements for employees to do work of a particular kind (i.e., there is a surplus of labour for that particular type of job).

Tribunals will rarely second-guess an employer's decision to declare a redundancy.

10.8.5 Statutory illegality as a fair reason

In rare cases it may become legally impossible to continue to employ the employee, e.g., the expiry of a work permit, or where a teacher has been declared unsuitable by the Department for Education. The ERA 1996, s. 98(2)(d), states that such occurrences provide a fair reason for dismissal where the employee 'could not continue to work in the position which he held without contravention (either on his part or on that of his employer) of a duty or restriction imposed by or under an enactment' (thus statutory instruments are included in the definition). It is for the employer to show that any continued employment would have contravened the statute, etc.

It is also now a criminal offence under s. 8 of the Asylum and Immigration Act 1996 to employ a person who does not have permission to work in the UK.

10.8.6 Some other substantial reason as a fair reason

Under ERA 1996, s. 98(1)(b), the employer can show 'some other substantial reason of a kind such as to justify the dismissal of an employee holding the position which the employee held'. This sounds like some sort of major catch-all category. It is. The words are not read *eiusdem generis* with the other fair reasons. The most common forum in which this reason is argued, however, is that of a business reorganisation falling short of redundancy, e.g., where the workload remains the same but certain employees are deemed unsuitable for the new requirements of the business or will simply not put up with the changes to their terms or status and resign.

The line between dismissal for reasons of business reorganisations and dismissal by reason of redundancy can be a fine one. However, the key point is whether the statutory definition of redundancy is fulfilled or not: put simply, did the requirement for employees to do their particular work cease or diminish? If all that has happened is that there is a reorganisation of the way existing work is performed, the fact that an employee is replaced by someone with different skills or doing a slightly different job does not mean there is a redundancy. In *Shawkat* v *Nottingham City Hospital NHS Trust (No. 2)* [2001] EWCA Civ 954; [2001] IRLR 555, the Court of Appeal held that when the hospital merged two departments so that a thoracic surgeon was required to also take on cardiac work (and refused to do so and was dismissed) there was no redundancy as there was on diminution in the employer's need for employees to carry out thoracic surgery.

Other examples of 'some other substantial reason' have been:

(a) a refusal to accept the imposition of a restraint of trade clause;

(b) a refusal to accept a change in terms relating to hours, or pay or job content;

(c) discovering that the employee had originally concealed medical problems from the employer;

(d) where an employee's epileptic attacks scared fellow employees;

(e) where heavy pressure to dismiss was brought to bear on the employer by a valued customer (though it is advisable to have a term in the contract allowing for such dismissals);

(f) a mistaken belief that continuing to employ the employee would be in breach of a statute;

(g) reasonably believing (mistakenly as it turned out) that an employee had resigned;

(h) Termination of employment as chief executive as an automatic consequence, under the express terms of the contract, of the termination of a directorship: *Cobley* v *Forward Technology Industries plc* [2003] EWCA Civ 646; [2003] ICR 1050.

This area is full of unpredictability. The temptation is to over-use it because it provides what has been described as an 'employer's charter'. This label is probably true in relation to business reorganisations, but the examples cited above should not be treated as precedents. Sometimes it is useful to plead it on behalf of the employer 'in the alternative': see **Chapter 13**.

10.8.7 Automatically unfair reasons

Certain reasons for dismissal are deemed automatically unfair. The list is the same as for the exceptions to the one-year qualifying period as set out at **10.3.1.3** above (apart from (l)—dismissal in relation to a suspension on medical grounds). There are some further reasons which still require the one-year qualification but are automatically unfair reasons:

(a) Dismissal for a conviction which is 'spent' under the Rehabilitation of Offenders Act 1974: s. 4(3)(b).

(b) Dismissals relating to a transfer of an undertaking (though oddly in some cases these may still be found to be fair, see **Chapter 12**).

(c) Dismissal relating to the employee seeking to enforce rights on flexible working detailed in ERA 1996, ss. 80F–H: see ERA 1996, s. 104C.

(d) Dismissals where the employer is at fault in not adhering to the Statutory Dismissal and Disciplinary Procedures: ERA 1996, s. 98A(1).

Note: Points (a) to (d) above still require the employee to have attained the necessary qualifications as regards length of service (one year usually) and age (below normal retirement age).

We dealt with the detailed provisions of the statutory procedures mentioned in (d) at **5.3** above and we shall return to them as regards their impact on unfair dismissal at **10.9** below. For the moment, two of the headings mentioned in the list in **10.3.1.3** (which are also automatically unfair reasons for dismissal) need further explanation.

10.8.7.1 Asserting statutory rights

Under ERA 1996, s. 104, if the employee claims that certain statutory rights have been infringed then any dismissal by the employer in response to this is automatically unfair. Thus retaliatory action by the employer now carries with it specific penalties. It does not matter that the employee's claim was wrong, nor that it was not correctly labelled, as long as it was made in good faith. The first case in this area (*Mennell* v *Newell & Wright (Transport Contractors) Ltd* [1996] ICR 607) reinforced the interpretation of the 'good faith' test as being of the 'pure heart but empty head' variety. In this case the employee was asked to agree a new contract. The new terms would have allowed the employer to recover money for training costs from the employee's final salary on leaving the company. The employee refused to agree the terms and was dismissed. He could not bring a claim for unfair dismissal as he had less than two years' service (as required at the time), so he brought a claim under what is now s. 104 of ERA 1996. The Court of Appeal rejected his claim. Their Lordships stated that:

(a) the employee must have made an allegation to his employer that a statutory right was being infringed;

(b) the allegation need not be specific, provided it has been made reasonably clear to the employer what right was claimed to have been infringed (and, *on the facts*, no such claim was made);

(c) it does not matter whether the statutory right has actually been infringed, nor need the allegation be correct as to the employee's entitlement to the right, provided the claim is made in good faith;

(d) the onus will lie on the employee to establish that he was dismissed for his assertion of a statutory right.

The term 'reasonably clear' has been given a liberal interpretation by the EAT: the employee is not required to spell out the infringement.

The 'relevant statutory rights' are set out in s. 104(4) of ERA 1996. They include:

(a) 'any right conferred by the Act for which the remedy for its infringement is by way of a complaint or reference to an employment tribunal' (e.g., minimum notice, right to receive a written statement, health and safety dismissals)—the list is extensive;

(b) rights concerning the protection of wages under ERA 1996, Part II;

(c) rights conferred under TULRCA 1992 concerning union activities.

10.8.7.2 The Public Interest Disclosure Act 1998

We noted the main provisions of this Act in **Chapter 7** (at **7.3.5**). The purpose of the Act is to permit employees to make certain disclosures about the activities of their employers without suffering any penalty for having done so. This is achieved through the insertion into ERA 1996 of two new sections: s. 47B and s. 103A.

Section 47B(1) of ERA 1996 (as inserted by PIDA 1998, s. 2) states that: 'A worker has the right not to be subjected to any detriment by any act, or any deliberate failure to act, by his employer done on the ground that the worker has made a protected disclosure.' Section 103A (as inserted by PIDA 1998, s. 5) states: 'An employee who is dismissed shall be regarded for the purposes of this Part as unfairly dismissed *if the reason (or, if more than one, the principal reason) for the dismissal is that the employee made a protected disclosure*'. Though the employee only has to show good faith in the nature of the allegations to come under the umbrella of 'protected disclosure', there must be a clear causative link between any dismissal and the protected disclosure for the automatically unfair provision to kick in: *London Borough of Harrow* v *Knight* [2003] IRLR 140. Compensation for unfair dismissals arising out of disclosures under the 1998 Act is not subject to any financial limit: ERA, s. 124(1A).

10.8.8 Automatically fair reasons

The basic premise of ERA 1996, s. 98 is that although the reason may be *fair* this does not mean that the dismissal is fair; this has yet to be decided. However, in the case of dismissal involving national security the tribunal may never get to debate the issue of fairness. Here, if there is a certificate purporting to be signed by or on behalf of a Minister of the Crown certifying that the action complained of was taken for the purposes of safeguarding national security then, except in limited cases relating to pregnancy dismissals, certain health and safety matters and employee representation, the certificate is conclusive evidence of that fact (see ETA 1996, s. 10(4)). This is not limited to civil servants.

10.9 Fairness

The question of 'fairness' is a judgment call and depends very much on the facts. Nevertheless, we can detail some general points that tribunals will look at for each 'fair reason'. In **Figure 10.2** we can see the pathway that tribunals trace in analysing an unfair dismissal case.

You can see in **Figure 10.2** that once the employee qualifies to bring the claim and shows dismissal (even though the employer has established a fair reason), the question of whether that reason was handled fairly is the determining matter.

What is meant by 'fairness' tends to be something of a mixture of fact and law. The 'fact' part relates to investigating the way in which the employer relied on the cited fair reason; the 'law' relates to general guiding principles that have been established over the years. The best way to describe fairness, therefore, is by recounting some general principles used by tribunals and then relating them to the particular fair reasons.

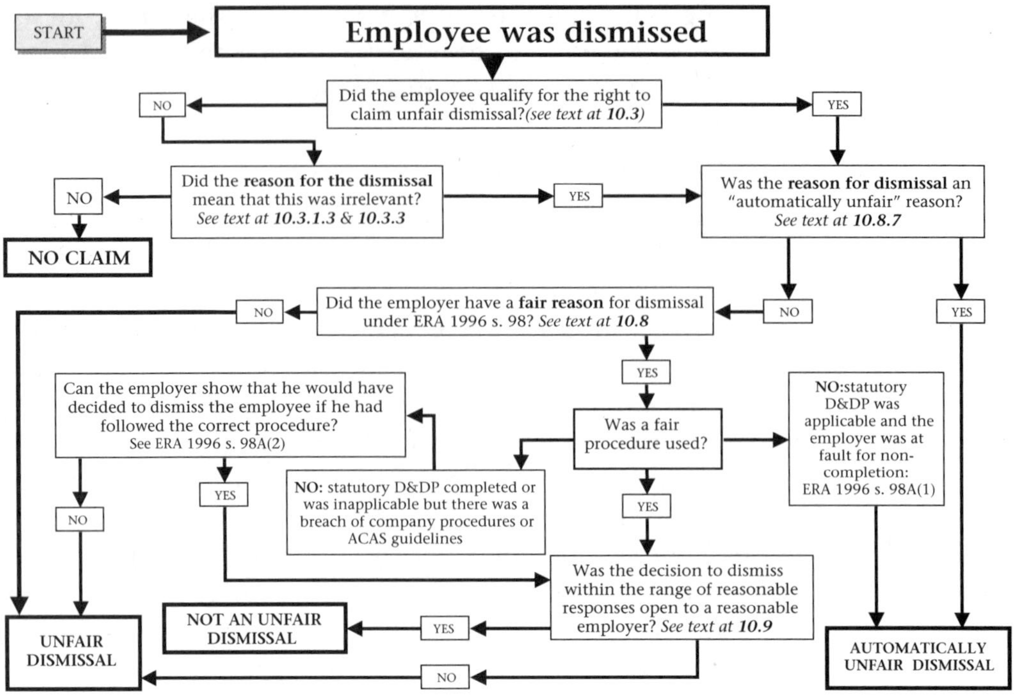

Figure 10.2 Determining fairness.

10.9.1 General principles of fairness

The ERA 1996, s. 98(4) states:

... the determination of the question whether the dismissal is fair or unfair (having regard to the reason shown by the employer)—

(a) depends on whether in the circumstances (including the size and administrative resources of the employer's undertaking) the employer acted reasonably or unreasonably in treating it as a sufficient reason for dismissing the employee, and

(b) hall be determined in accordance with equity and the substantial merits of the case.

This may be broken down into *two* pervasive questions:

(a) Did the employer utilise a *fair procedure*?

(b) Did the employer's decision to dismiss fall within the *range of reasonable responses* open to a reasonable employer?

The burden of proof regarding *fairness*, it will be remembered, is *neutral*. But all this really means is that the employer does not bear the burden when the facts are doubtful or in dispute. The reality is that, since the employer made the decision and generally has the greater access to information, the tribunal effectively expects the employer to show *why* the decision was made and *how* it was reasonable.

The impact of the Human Rights Act 1998 on unfair dismissal was considered by the Court of Appeal in *X* v *Y* [2004] EWCA Civ 662. Although no breach of human rights was found in this case (which centred on art. 8 ECHR—'privacy') Mummery LJ set out some suggestions on dealing with human rights points, especially as regards actions taken against private employers. The statement must be *obiter* but it is nevertheless extremely useful. His Lordship suggested the following framework of questions at [64]:

(1) Do the circumstances of the dismissal fall within the ambit of one or more of the articles of the Convention? If they do not, the Convention right is not engaged and need not be considered.

(2) If they do, does the state have a positive obligation to secure enjoyment of the relevant Convention right between private persons? If it does not, the Convention right is unlikely to affect the outcome of an unfair dismissal claim against a private employer.

(3) If it does, is the interference with the employee's Convention right by dismissal justified? If it is, proceed to (5) below.
(4) If it is not, was there a permissible reason for the dismissal under the ERA, which does not involve unjustified interference with a Convention right? If there was not, the dismissal will be unfair for the absence of a permissible reason to justify it.
(5) If there was, is the dismissal fair, tested by the provisions of s98 of the ERA, reading and giving effect to them under s3 of the HRA so as to be compatible with the Convention right?'

10.9.2 First general aspect of fairness: fair procedure

In previous editions of this book the point we made at this stage was a relatively simple one: for a dismissal to be fair the employer must have followed a fair procedure. The importance of this aspect of fairness has now been heightened with the introduction of the statutory dispute resolution procedures (detailed in **5.3** above). Now, an employer contemplating a dismissal must be aware of the significance of:

- the statutory procedures;
- the ACAS Guidelines; and
- the employer's contractual procedures.

10.9.2.1 The statutory dispute resolution procedures

The Employment Act 2002 (Dispute Resolution) Regulations SI 2004/752 and The Employment Act 2002 (Commencement No. 6 and Transitional Provision) Order SI 2004/1717 brought into operation the key features on dispute resolution in the Employment Act 2002 and introduced a new section in the Employment Rights Act 1996, namely s. 98A. As noted in **5.3**, the new procedures relate to a wide range of disputes and claims but here we are only concerned with their impact on unfair dismissal claims. For reasons of space we have not repeated all the procedures in this chapter. We should note, however, that the Standard Dismissal and Disciplinary Procedures (referred to here as 'D&DPs') apply to all cases where the employer is contemplating dismissing the employee (**for any reason**) or taking 'relevant disciplinary action' against the employee. A 'relevant disciplinary action' is defined in SI 2004/752, reg. 2(1) as an 'action, short of dismissal, which the employer asserts to be based wholly or mainly on the employee's conduct or capability, other than suspension on full pay or the issuing of warnings (whether oral or written)'. The procedures do not apply in cases such as 'collective dismissals' and those tainted by threats of violence (see **5.3.1.4** above for details). Section 98A (1) ERA 1996 was introduced by EA 2002, s. 34. It states:

An employee who is dismissed shall be regarded for the purposes of this Part as unfairly dismissed if—
(a) one of the procedures set out in Part 1 of Schedule 2 to the Employment Act 2002 (dismissal and disciplinary procedures) applies in relation to the dismissal,
(b) the procedure has not been completed, and
(c) the non-completion of the procedures is wholly or mainly attributable to failure by the employer to comply with its requirements.

This means that if the employer is at fault for the collapse of the procedures any dismissal is **automatically unfair**. Indeed, even if the procedures are completed but the employer has infringed, say, one of the 'general requirements' along the way (see **5.3.1.1**, e.g., there has been an unreasonable delay at some stage) then the dismissal will still be automatically unfair. Further, even if the employer has complied with all the requirements of the D&DPs that in itself does not mean the dismissal was fair. The statutory D&DPs only create a minimum standard; the tribunal is entitled to compare what took place with the ACAS Guidelines and the company's own procedures.

10.9.2.2 The ACAS Guidelines

Under TULRCA 1992, s. 199 ACAS may issue codes of behaviour. The latest code on dismissal and disciplinary action came into effect by order of the Secretary of State on 1 October 2004. Although a failure to follow any part of this Code does not, in itself, make a person or organisation liable to proceedings, employment tribunals will take the Code into account when considering relevant cases. Similarly, arbitrators appointed by ACAS (see **10.12.2** below) to determine relevant cases under the ACAS Arbitration Scheme will take the Code into account. The Code represents a common sense approach to industrial relations matters (e.g., informing employees as to the procedure, not dismissing for the first offence). Here is an extract:

Operating disciplinary procedures

- Establish facts before taking action (Paragraph 8).
- Deal with cases of minor misconduct or unsatisfactory performance informally (Paragraphs 11-12).
- For more serious cases, follow formal procedures, including informing the employee of the alleged misconduct or unsatisfactory performance (Paragraph 13).
- Invite the employee to a meeting and inform them of the right to be accompanied (Paragraph 14-16).
- Where performance is unsatisfactory explain to the employee the improvement required, the support that will be given and when and how performance will be reviewed (Paragraphs 19-20).
- If giving a warning, tell the employee why and how they need to change, the consequences of failing to improve and that they have a right to appeal (Paragraphs 21-22).
- If dismissing an employee, tell them why, when their contract will end and that they can appeal (Paragraph 25).
- Before dismissing or taking disciplinary action other than issuing a warning, always follow the statutory dismissal and disciplinary procedure (Paragraphs 26-32).
- When dealing with absences from work, find out the reasons for the absence before deciding on what action to take. (Paragraph 37).

The Code generally recommends the use of informal action to resolve matters followed by formal action (such as a first warning, second, and final warning). It sets out procedures designed to help the employee correct the behaviour. For instance, in dealing with unsatisfactory performance it recommends that, 'Following the meeting, an employee who is found to be performing unsatisfactorily should be given a written note setting out: the performance problem; the improvement that is required; the timescale for achieving this improvement; a review date; and any support the employer will provide to assist the employee.' It therefore goes beyond the minimum set out in the statutory D&DPs. The full Code can be accessed through http://www.acas.org.uk/publications/.

10.9.2.3 Contractual procedures

The tribunal will also be concerned with the contractual procedures and whether these have been adhered to. The more elaborate these are the more complications set in when the employer finds he cannot comply with them. The risks are obvious. Thus, in one case the authors once dealt with a Cornish company had, as its final appeal, the involvement of the parent-company chairman. He was in Switzerland and did not speak English. When this procedure was tested it was found wanting and came under severe criticism.

Company disciplinary codes often spell out what is meant by 'gross misconduct' or 'gross breach of duty'. If these clauses pretend to give *exhaustive* definitions they lose the possibility of flexibility in the face of the unexpected and employers may be caught by their own wording. Some provisions should also be made in the contract for determining when a warning becomes 'stale', e.g., three or six months for an oral warning, six months for a written warning, and 12 months for a final warning. No tribunal will allow reference to be made to a warning given five years previously as proof of compliance with the disciplinary code (though these earlier incidents might be referred to in the hearing as evidence of the employment history).

If the employer wishes to impose suspension without pay as a penalty this must be spelt out in the contract; otherwise it will be a breach which may, in itself, lead to claims for contractual damages, or even constructive dismissal.

10.9.2.4 Failure to operate the contractual procedures properly

Throughout the 1980s there existed a rule devised by the Court of Appeal called the 'it makes no difference' test. This held that where the employer had not followed the correct procedure but, had he done so, it would have been reasonable to dismiss the employee anyway then that dismissal could still be fair. This approach was laid to rest by the House of Lords in *Polkey* v *A.E. Dayton Service Ltd* [1987] AC 344. However, like Arnold Schwarzenegger in the 'Terminator' series, it is back. Section 98A(2) ERA 1996 states:

> Subject to subsection (1), failure by an employer to follow a procedure in relation to the dismissal of an employee shall not be regarded for the purposes of section 98(4)(a) as by itself making the employer's action unreasonable if he shows that he would have decided to dismiss the employee if he had followed the procedure.

The reference to subsection (1) means that this 'get out of jail' clause **does not apply** to breaches of the statutory D&DPs. Thus, under s. 98A(2), where employers have complied with the D&DPs—or they do not apply at all—but have not adhered to part of the contractual procedure, they may now argue that *had* the procedures been followed, on the balance of probabilities, they would have decided to dismiss anyway and that this would have been reasonable in all the circumstances. This might arise where, for example, the employer may not have conducted the investigation of the allegation according to the terms of the contract or where the stated selection criteria for a redundancy of more than 20 employees have not been applied correctly. This is illustrated in **Figure 10.2**. The box which poses the question, 'Was a fair procedure used?' has a 'yes' consequence which leads us to the text in **10.9.3** below, but there are two 'no' boxes: one which takes us to the 'automatically unfair dismissal' box via a breach of the D&DPs as discussed in **10.9.2.1**; the other leading us to the issues raised by s. 98A. Here we ask whether, given all the above, the decision to dismiss was one which a reasonable employer would have made.

10.9.2.5 Relevance of appeals' procedures

In *West Midlands Co-operative Society* v *Tipton* (see above at **10.7** above) the House of Lords held that the appeals' procedure was an integral part of deciding the question of fair procedure. Indeed, a properly-conducted appeal can remedy some procedural deficiencies in the original hearing. Where the statutory D&DPs apply, however, 'getting it right eventually' will no longer be an option.

10.9.2.6 A fair hearing

In misconduct dismissals especially, but also with incapability and 'some other substantial reason', the employee should have a chance to state a case. In *Clark* v *Civil Aviation Authority* [1991] IRLR 412, the EAT stated that a hearing should adopt the following pattern:

(a) Explain the purpose of the meeting.
(b) Identify those present.
(c) If appropriate, arrange representation.
(d) Inform the employee of the allegations.
(e) Indicate the evidence—in writing or by calling witnesses.
(f) Allow the employee to ask questions (though there is no legal obligation to allow the employee to cross-examine witnesses: *Santamera* v *Express Cargo Forwarding* [2003] IRLR 273).

(g) Allow the employee to call witnesses.

(h) Listen to the arguments raised.

To this we would add that the hearing needs to be seen to be fair, so that staff who were involved in earlier stages which generated this hearing should not also act as judge and jury. In particular, an appeal should not (wherever possible) be heard by the same panel which decided to dismiss.

10.9.2.7 Right to be accompanied

Under ERA 1999, s. 10 a *worker* (defined in s. 13) is entitled to be accompanied at a disciplinary or grievance hearing by a single companion where the hearing 'could result in . . . the administration of a formal warning . . .'. The label attached to any disciplinary hearing ('informal' or 'formal') is irrelevant and this right is not limited to the statutory dispute resolution procedures; the right is triggered where the warning will become part of the employee's disciplinary record: *London Underground Ltd* v *Ferenc-Batchelor* [2003] IRLR 252. It is not that common these days for an employer to issue oral informal warnings and keep no record at all, so this decision widens the right substantially. The person accompanying the worker must be either a trade union official or another of the employer's workers. If the employer fails to comply with this the worker may present a complaint to an employment tribunal under s. 11, the maximum compensation being two weeks' pay. Under s. 12, a worker dismissed as a consequence of seeking to exercise these rights or for making a complaint to an employment tribunal will be regarded as automatically unfairly dismissed.

10.9.3 Second general aspect of fairness: range of reasonable responses

In this part the tribunal sets what has happened against the actions of the 'reasonable employer' (a figure drawn from the extensive experience of employment tribunal panels). This part of the assessment is derived from *British Leyland (UK) Ltd* v *Swift* [1981] IRLR 91 (and *Iceland Frozen Foods* v *Jones* [1983] ICR 17). The question posed will be: Is it possible that a reasonable employer, faced with these facts, would have dismissed? For instance, let us imagine that an employee has committed theft. The employer has investigated the matter thoroughly and has to decide whether to dismiss. The range of options open to the employer could include:

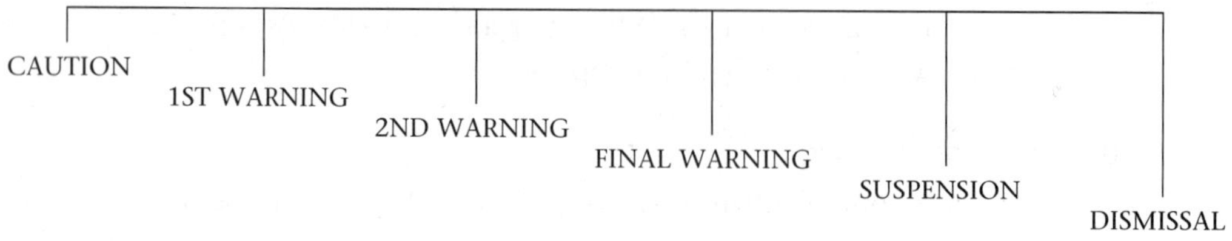

Some employers may not have dismissed in these circumstances; they may have gone to a final warning instead: but if the decision to dismiss falls within *the band of reasonableness* then this will show fairness. The theft example would satisfy this test, even though with a long-serving employee *some* employers might stop short of dismissal (for example, because of the employee's disciplinary record: see *Strouthos* v *London Underground* [2004] EWCA 402, [2004] IRLR 636). With questions of frequent lateness, absenteeism, incapability, or refusal to obey an order the debate opens out a little. However, what the tribunal should not do is to substitute its own standard of reasonableness—the test is whether the employer acted as a reasonable employer, having regard to the size and administrative resources available. Thus, the employer's beliefs that the grounds for dismissal justified the action have to be weighed against the tribunal's *perception* of reasonable practice based on its experience of industrial practice. The decision to dismiss may be one the employer would always follow, but the key question is whether the rest of industry would be so like-minded.

Where an employee has already been subject to various stages of the disciplinary process it is not too difficult to justify the final decision to dismiss. Most problems will arise when stages are by-passed or, in the case of gross misconduct, omitted. There the tribunal has to be clear that a reasonable employer could have dismissed in the circumstances. After some debate at the end of the century the Court of Appeal confirmed the range test in *Foley* v *Post Office; HSBC (Formerly Midland Bank)* v *Madden* [2000] IRLR 827: the role of employment tribunals is not to impose their own standards of reasonableness, but to test the employer's actions against those of a reasonable employer.

The introduction of the statutory D&DPs and s. 98A provisions concerning the 'it makes no difference' test do not affect the analysis above. As was stated in *Sainsburys Supermarkets Ltd* v *Hill* [2002] EWCA Civ 1588; [2003] ICR 111, the 'range of reasonable responses' test applies equally to the procedures used as to the penalty being imposed (the dismissal). Nothing in the EA 2002 has changed that.

10.9.4 Capability and qualifications: fairness

Where an underlying reason could have been classed as conduct *or* capability, we noted in **10.8.3** above that *conduct* may be more appropriate where the employee is easily able to improve with a little effort; *capability* is more appropriate if it is accepted by the employer that the employee either is or has become incapable of meeting the requirements (perhaps because the job has changed). With *conduct* the emphasis on handling the dismissal fairly is one of giving a chance for improvement; with *capability*, on compassionate treatment over such things as investigating alternative and more suitable work.

In the text below we consider the special requirements affecting capability dismissals other than the procedures required under the statutory D&DPs. To avoid constant repetition, these requirements are taken as either having been complied with or not applicable as any failure by the employer as regards D&DPs will have led us already to an automatically unfair dismissal.

The points noted below are the areas in which an employer may now be able to rely on the application of ERA 1996, s. 98A. You will see, however, that most of these points relate to nothing more than good practice and decent behaviour, so an employer who pleads the 'it makes no difference' line here still has a long way to go to persuade a tribunal that it was fair to omit these key considerations.

10.9.4.1 Qualifications

We noted above that the qualification must be connected substantially to the employee's job. So, if an employee loses his or her driving licence this will merit dismissal only if the licence was vital to the job and the employer has considered other alternative jobs within the company. A requirement for an employee to pass a key examination or aptitude test would fall within this category: *Blackman* v *Post Office* [1974] ICR 151 (a salutary point perhaps!).

10.9.4.2 Competence

If an employer claims that an employee was fairly dismissed for incapability the employment tribunal will expect clear evidence, not just some vague subjective assessment that the employee 'couldn't cut it'. As a basic checklist, therefore, the following matters should be considered:

(a) How good is the evidence of incompetence? Is it objectively proven, e.g., after a proper investigation?
(b) Was there a proper appraisal system in operation, or at least some formal way in which the employee could know of the defective performance?
(c) Were warnings given? In particular, was it made clear what would be the consequences for failure to improve?
(d) Were the warnings/objectives impossible to meet? For instance, an instruction that unless the company obtains a market share of 80 per cent by the end of the year the employee-manager will be dismissed may or may not be pure fantasy.
(e) Were any opportunities for training or retraining given?
(f) What form of supervision was operative?
(g) Were alternatives considered?
(h) What consideration was taken of the employee's status, length of service and past performance?
(i) Have incompetent employees been dismissed in similar circumstances in the past?

The relevance of some of these factors will depend upon the size of the company. For instance, a small, backstreet engineering company will not have the facility to look at many (if any) alternative jobs.

With incompetence dismissals emphasis has to be placed here on giving an opportunity to the employee to improve and listening to the employee's opinion, e.g., are the demands impossible to fulfil? Equally, if the employee challenges the employer's assessment it would be advisable to allow the employee (if feasible) the chance to demonstrate his or her case: *Morgan* v *Electrolux* [1991] IRLR 89. In that case the employee was found to have overbooked piece-work. In explaining her activities she asked to demonstrate her work speed. This request was refused. The Court of Appeal held that the employers had not acted reasonably in denying her this opportunity.

As with gross misconduct, there may also be gross incompetence which will justify dismissal without previous warnings, but greater care needs to be taken with incompetence. Indeed, if a single incident is that important it often involves an overlap between incompetence and misconduct, e.g., *Alidair Ltd* v *Taylor* [1978] ICR 445, where a pilot 'bounced' the company jet.

10.9.4.3 Ill-health

Dismissals on the grounds of ill-health have always been treated more cautiously by employment tribunals than any other potentially fair reason. Two forms of absence for ill-health may arise: intermittent absences and those lasting for prolonged periods. In the latter case it may be that the contract is frustrated (though for reasons noted in **Chapter 9** at **9.5.1** reliance on this should be avoided). General guidelines on dealing with sickness dismissals have been proffered in a number of cases, e.g., *Spencer* v *Paragon Wallpapers Ltd* [1977] ICR 301 and *East Lindsey District Council* v *Daubney* [1977] ICR 566. From these cases we can draw up a list of actions expected of the employer.

When dealing with long-term absence there is a duty on the employer to ascertain the true position, to discuss the future with the employee (and possibly his or her doctor), and to look for alternative work. When dealing with intermittent absences the employer needs to make the employee aware of the standard required, giving the employee time to meet this and perhaps attempting to resolve the issue via medical investigations and analysing the possibility of alternative work. Thus, the employer should:

(a) investigate the nature of the illness;

(b) investigate the likely length of absence;

(c) assess the impact on the business (i.e., does that employee hold a key position?). The more important the employee is to the business the more the absence cannot be tolerated for any great length of time. It is therefore perhaps ironic that the more valued employee might have to be dismissed sooner than the lesser employee in order to find a replacement. Temporary replacements provide an answer, but not realistically in key positions for few recruits would be found on this basis;

(d) assess the impact the absence will have on other employees, i.e., the increase in *their* workload or the effect on their pay if part of a team working on commission or bonuses;

(e) take account of available medical evidence. This will often mean that the employer will have to obtain appropriate medical reports. In such situations, the Data Protection Act 1998 may be relevant;

(f) take notice of the employee's length of service and any contractual sick pay scheme;

(g) consider alternative work;

(h) consult the employee over the issues noted above (warning an employee to get better is somewhat futile, but an employer may have to indicate at some time that the position cannot go on forever).

There are three points that need some elaboration:

(a) *Obtaining proper evidence.*
The aspect of discussion and consultation is useful not only to keep the employee informed of developments, but also to ascertain exactly what the position is at any time. Dismissing shortly before the employee is set to return does not, for instance, exemplify good management. Equally, if the employer needs medical evidence in order to make a decision the employee's assistance is needed; more so under the provisions of the Access to Medical Reports Act 1988 and the Data Protection Act 1998 (see **Chapter 7** at **7.9.3**). In all cases tribunals must decide (i) as a matter of fact, what level of consultation was necessary or desirable; and (ii) whether the process employed was adequate in the circumstances.
A failure to seek medical advice damages the employer's argument of fairness. The employee's own GP, or possibly a specialist, is the obvious source to provide independent medical assessments (especially if there is a conflict of medical opinion). However, unless there is an express contractual power to request the employee to undergo a medical examination the employer cannot force the employee to do so. Any such *demand* would constitute a repudiatory breach: *Bliss* v *South East Thames Regional Health Authority* [1987] ICR 700 (request for a psychological examination). But if the employee does refuse to cooperate the employer is entitled to make a decision on the facts available.

(b) *Intermittent absences.*
These pose a different kind of problem. The employer's tolerance of such situations does not have to be infinite. Warnings following consultation may be more appropriate here because of both the disruptive effect of short-term but frequent absence and also the possibility that there is a question of misconduct as well as or instead of incapability. Medical evidence may prove useful here too, though if an

employee has been diagnosed as suffering from, say, back trouble which flares up periodically this evidence does not actually resolve the problem.

(c) *Relationship with contractual sick pay scheme.*
Most companies operate a sick pay scheme (as noted at **5.2.2.1** above) and a frequently asked question is: can an employer dismiss someone who is still on sick leave? The usual advice is, yes, but with great caution. If the employee commits an act of gross misconduct during the sick leave or fails to cooperate with the reasonable requests of the employer whilst on sick leave that will justify dismissal: *Briscoe* v *Lubrizol Ltd* [2002] EWCA Civ 508, [2002] IRLR 607); likewise if the employer has to make people redundant, being ill is no safeguard against selection: *Hill* v *General Accident Fire & Life Assurance Corporation plc* [1998] IRLR 641.

But the real problem comes where the employer wishes to dismiss *because* of the employee's absence owing to illness. Tribunals have long accepted that an employer may have to dismiss someone, despite the presence of a clause which seems to 'guarantee' an employee a period of sick leave, if genuine business needs drive them that way e.g., in the case of a key employee. The question is then whether the dismissal is handled fairly.

At **5.2.2.1** we noted that a conflict has developed (as it often does in employment) between the form of analysis used by the ordinary courts and that used by employment tribunals in dealing with dismissals of employees who are on contractual sick leave. We saw that a recent run of cases has, by reliance on express or implied terms, concluded that an employee can only be dismissed *for cause* (e.g., redundancy) whilst on sick leave, especially if the dismissal would adversely affect any healthy insurance entitlements. The ordinary courts are concerned only with the contractual analysis. Thus, in *Hill* v *General Accident*, Lord Hamilton (in the court of Session, Outer House—the equivalent to the High Court) stated that: 'Where provision is, as here, made in the contract for payment of salary or other benefit during sickness, the employer cannot, solely with a view to relieving himself of the obligation to make such payment, by dismissal bring that sick employee's contract to an end.'

There is now the basis for an argument that, by a sidewind almost, these contractual arguments have overridden the generally accepted industrial reality argument that, whatever the contract says, an employee's absence cannot be tolerated forever. Perhaps the message to employers (and those drafting employment contracts) is to make the terms of the sick leave provisions clear as to dismissal rights. Otherwise, as Lord Hamilton says, such provisions will be treated as enforceable contractual rights, not some form of charity on the part of the employer.

10.9.4.4 Overlap with disability discrimination

In **Chapter 6** (at **6.9**) we noted the main provisions of the Disability Discrimination Act 1995 regarding direct discrimination and victimisation in relation to recruitment, terms, promotion opportunities, etc. The Act also has relevance as regards any dismissal based on a person's disability. Section 4(2)(d) states that 'It is unlawful for an employer to discriminate against a disabled person whom he employs . . . by dismissing him, or subjecting him to any other detriment'. The term 'dismissal' in DDA 1995 is likely to include the non-renewal of limited-term contracts and constructive dismissal, although there is no definition given in the Act.

Thus a disabled person who has been dismissed has two main statutory claims:

(a) a discrimination action under DDA 1995; and

(b) an unfair dismissal action under ERA 1996.

There can be considerable overlap in the substantive analysis of these claims.

(a) *Action under DDA 1995.*

For an employee to claim successfully under DDA 1995 the following points will be relevant:

(i) The employee must be a 'disabled person' as defined in s. 1(1) of DDA 1995. A disability is 'a physical or mental impairment which has a substantial and long-term adverse effect on [the person's] ability to carry out normal day-to-day activities'. In turn, this definition is expanded upon in sch. 1, para. 4(1) of the Act, the Disability Discrimination (Meaning of Disability) Regulations 1996 and the guidance notes. We commented on this definition in **6.9.1.2** above.

(ii) There must have been a dismissal.

(iii) The dismissal must have been discriminatory, i.e., 'for a reason which relates to the disabled person's disability' (s. 5(1)(a)) or because the employer has been discriminatory in failing 'to comply with a section 6 duty [duty to make reasonable adjustments] imposed on him in relation to the disabled person' (s. 5(2)(a)).

(iv) The employer must not be able to show that the treatment in question was justified. The reason given for justification must be both material to the circumstances of the particular case and substantial: s. 5(3).

(b) *Alternative action.*

There is nothing in DDA 1995 to prevent an employee from also claiming unfair dismissal under ERA 1996 either exclusively or in the alternative. For example, a disabled person may be dismissed owing to absenteeism. A claim of unfair dismissal might be defended on the grounds of capability or even misconduct (if the employer believes the absenteeism was deliberate). The employee might also make a claim under DDA 1995 if it is thought that the reason for dismissal was discriminatory. But even if the dismissal was not discriminatory for the purposes of DDA 1995 the requirements of good practice which have emanated from the Act, the guidance notes, etc. will have an impact on how employers treat disabled employees, and therefore the ambit of unfair dismissal.

(c) *Unfair dismissal action.*

Dismissal of a 'disabled person' is not automatically unfair. Neither does DDA 1995 specifically alter the general provisions of s. 98 of ERA 1996. However, if an employee falls within the provisions of DDA 1995 it is highly unlikely that it will be sufficient for an employer merely to show that the disabled employee was incapable under s. 98(2)(a) in order to defend an unfair dismissal claim. Effectively, where a 'disabled person' is dismissed or subjected to any other detriment then, in any unfair dismissal action defended on the grounds of capability, the tribunal will have to take into account the requirements laid out in DDA 1995 as evidence of good practice and, as seen in the House of Lords' disability discrimination case of *Archibald* v *Fife Council* [2004] UKHL 32; [2004] IRLR 651 this may mean making extensive arrangements for transferring jobs, etc as part of the duty to make 'reasonable adjustments'.

The safest advice for all employers must therefore be that an employer must have in mind, when dealing with an employee who is ill or who has absences from work (or who might be made redundant), the requirements of DDA 1995.

(d) *Choice of claim.*

There are advantages to pursuing a claim directly under DDA 1995, e.g., no age limit; no qualifying period of employment; the specific inclusion of 'injury to feelings' as a head of compensation; and no limit on the amount of compensation that may be awarded. However, to succeed in a claim under DDA 1995 the employee must have been the subject of direct discrimination or victimisation. This might be difficult to establish in any given case. An unfair dismissal claim, although initially less attractive, might still prove to be the better course of action.

It is possible for there to be an unfair dismissal under s. 98 of ERA 1996 but for a disability discrimination claim to fail where the employee may not be able to establish all elements for the latter claim (e.g., the employer's actions were justified) but in assessing the overall reasonableness of the employer's actions in an unfair dismissal claim they are found wanting. The converse is less likely.

10.9.5 Misconduct: fairness

In the text below we consider the special requirements affecting conduct dismissals other than the procedures required under the statutory D&DPs. As with capability dismissals (above), to avoid constant repetition these requirements are taken as either having been complied with or not applicable as any failure by the employer as regards D&DPs will have led us already to an automatically unfair dismissal. The forms of misconduct can be legion. However, standard methods of dealing with misconduct dismissals emerge from the cases. The employer needs to show:

(a) an honest belief that the employee was guilty of the offence;

(b) that there were reasonable grounds for holding that belief; and

(c) that these came from a reasonable investigation of the incident(s).

This is not an immutable checklist and, given that the burden of proof as to fairness is neutral, minor failures under these principles will not inevitably damn an employer's case: *Boys' and Girls' Welfare Society* v *McDonald* [1996] IRLR 129.

These principles were first clearly stated in relation to dishonesty dismissals in *British Home Stores* v *Burchell* [1980] ICR 303, and have been approved on wider grounds since then. They are often referred to as the '*Burchell* principles'. They demonstrate that *conclusive proof is not necessary*. So the employer is required to formulate an opinion and then to decide whether, on that evidence, a dismissal is justified. The tribunal must therefore examine the basis for the belief and then go on to determine whether a reasonable employer would have dismissed in those circumstances.

There is no requirement to find some form of *mens rea* in the employee's actions. The test is simpler than this: did the employee commit the act complained of? For example, say an employee has assaulted another employee. The employee claims that the other employee provoked him by teasing him about his inability to carry out a temporary task. The employee also says that he cannot remember hitting the other person; that he 'blacked out'. Provided the dismissal is dealt with fairly (see below) the employer is not expected to launch into criminal law in order to establish the state of the employee's mind. Equally, an employer does not have to cogitate on whether there is a line to be drawn between intent and commission where the employee has been discovered, about to commit an act, e.g., a theft: *British Railways Board* v *Jackson* [1994] IRLR 235.

A general checklist for misconduct dismissals would therefore be:

(a) The employer must adhere to the spirit of the *Burchell* principles, or the evidence must be so obvious (or there is a confession) that it fulfils the same function.

(a) e'er must adhere to the spirit of the Burchell principles, or the evidence must be so obvious that it fulfils the same function.
(b) The employer must adhere to the procedures set out in the statutory D&DPs.
(c) The employer must have conducted a proper hearing.
(d) The employer should review the status of previous warnings.
(e) The employer should note the employee's disciplinary record.
(f) The employer should take note of the employee's length of service.
(g) The employer's policy of dealing with misconduct should show consistency.
(h) Alternatives to dismissal should be considered.
(i) The terms of the contract should be adhered to.
(j) The relevance of criminal proceedings, or acquittals or convictions should be considered.

Some of these matters, such as the conduct of a fair hearing, have been noted above. One or two deserve further elaboration. A misconduct dismissal does not have to be for gross misconduct. A series of lesser incidents might bring about a fair dismissal if proper procedures have been followed. Gross misconduct will more easily justify moving straight to dismissal, without going through warnings, but otherwise all forms of misconduct fall under the same general guidelines.

There is an obvious question here: what is 'gross' misconduct? Many contracts define what is regarded as gross misconduct. If they are so tightly drawn that they provide an exhaustive list it will be difficult to add to this. But most contracts merely give the primary examples. These would include: dishonesty (usually whatever the amount and whatever the form), fighting at work and assault, disclosure of confidential information, setting up in a competing business (at least as regards senior employees), and gross insubordination. The list will vary from industry to industry though. Thus, 'fighting' might take various forms. A snowball fight in a foundry, where pieces of metal, etc. may be on the floor, could prove dangerous and an employee could fairly be dismissed for participating. Equally, an offence may be serious without being gross misconduct, e.g., where an employee incompetently fails to deal with invoices and so loses the company money. He or she may have committed a serious offence but, if the amount is small, this will hardly be gross negligence. In the end, the definition of 'gross misconduct' is relevant only:

(a) to show why the employer by-passed the warnings stage and went straight to dismissal;
(b) in relation to *wrongful dismissal*, to show why summary dismissal was chosen.

10.9.5.1 The employee's disciplinary and service history

The point of emphasis here is that in each case the employer is dealing with an individual, therefore that individual's history in the company is a major component of any decision to dismiss. This is especially true where the dismissal relates to conduct which is not gross misconduct.

As a rule of thumb, employers will treat long-serving employees with a little more leniency because of the loyalty factor. Thus, although this does not afford complete protection, a reasonable employer will at least take service into account in deciding whether to dismiss or impose some lesser penalty. But if the employment record shows a history of disciplinary problems, this can equally damn the employee. In one unusual case the EAT even allowed an employer to carry forward warnings from one fixed-term contract to another: *Stolt Offshore Ltd* v *Fraser* (2003, unreported, EAT 0041/02)—here, an employee on a succession of two 12-month fixed-term contracts received a final warning during the first contract. The warning had a 'lifespan' of 24 months so when there was another act of misconduct during the second contract the employer was able to go straight to dismissal rather than start the whole process over again.

If warnings for other matters are still operative this will have a major influence on the decision to dismiss. Normally one would expect an employer to issue the next warning. If some stages are to be omitted the employer will need to justify this.

10.9.5.2 Consistency of treatment

There are two matters here. There should be consistency in dealing with employees involved in the same incident, e.g., a fight. But, wider than this, there should be some consistency across the years in dealing with types of offence. This may apply even when the management personnel has changed over the years: *Proctor* v *British Gypsum Ltd* [1991] IRLR 7. Here the EAT stated three points on consistency of treatment:

(a) An otherwise fair dismissal might be classified as unfair in the light of inconsistency of treatment.

(b) Though ERA 1996, s. 98 demands consideration of the *individual's* case, comparisons may be valid if they reveal a pattern that it is understood in the company that such conduct will be overlooked, that the comparisons reveal that the reason given for dismissal is not genuine, or that the cases are analogous.

(c) Changes in circumstances, e.g., an increase in theft, might well justify changes in policy (though some form of prior notification would be necessary). In such cases, acting severely as a deterrent to others may be acceptable.

The Court of Appeal has issued further guidance on 'consistency' in *Paul* v *East Surrey District Health Authority* [1995] IRLR 305. Whilst not overturning any of the above, there is a recognition that similar incidents are not that common across the years when examined carefully and employers do have some flexibility. Thus, an employer may take account of mitigating personal circumstances (or aggravating circumstances), how contrite the employee is, and the levels of seriousness of the offences involved. Points (a) and (b) above also received specific approval. Nevertheless, the quite common cry of the employer that 'We will make an example of this one' is therefore prone to attack.

Linked with this is the problematic area of suspected theft when the employer can pinpoint a group of employees but cannot identify the guilty individual or individuals specifically. Should the employer dismiss one, some, all or none? The cases reveal that, provided the employer's investigations are reasonable and all other factors have been taken into account, dismissing *all* of the group will be a fair method of dealing with the problem: *Monie* v *Coral Racing Ltd* [1981] ICR 109. The employer must be convinced on 'solid and sensible grounds' that one or more *of that group* has committed the act. The employer does not, however, *have* to dismiss all the members of the group (this is where the other factors may be relevant, e.g., past disciplinary record). This principle has been extended to other situations where it is impossible directly to apportion blame to a group, e.g., for faulty workmanship.

10.9.5.3 The relevance of criminal proceedings

Employers are not required to await the outcome of criminal proceedings before deciding on dismissal. Equally, employers cannot dismiss simply because an employee has been charged with an offence. First, the mere fact of being charged is irrelevant and, secondly, the offence will ultimately have to have some bearing on the employment relationship to justify the dismissal: *Singh* v *London Country Bus Services Ltd* [1976] IRLR 176.

This means that employers will have to conduct their own investigations before any decision to dismiss is likely to be fair: *Lovie Ltd* v *Anderson* [1999] IRLR 164. All this is quite awkward in practice because the employee (unless confessing) is hardly liable to prove cooperative! Indeed, the Court of Session in Scotland and the English EAT have disagreed over the appropriateness of employer investigations. Perhaps the key point is that the employer, on the evidence available, has to be sure that dismissal is the right course; any doubts may mean having to wait.

A conviction does not absolve the employer from some investigation of the matter, but this relates more to matters such as mitigation; an employer is certainly entitled to treat a conviction as proof of guilt: *P* v *Nottinghamshire County Council* [1992] ICR 706. But neither will an eventual acquittal turn an existing properly-conducted dismissal into an unfair dismissal. Further, if the employer does await the outcome of the trial a dismissal following acquittal may still be fair because the standards of proof are different and other matters may have come out at the trial. Employers who state that *they will be bound* by the outcome of the trial are in a difficult position: any subsequent dismissal will most likely be unfair.

10.9.5.4 Concluding points on misconduct

Because the forms of misconduct are so various, all that can be given here are the general guidelines. These will hold true in each case, but the considerations for absentee dismissals, dismissals for fraud, fighting, disobedience and so on will each have their variations in terms of appropriate forms of procedure and investigation. Most importantly, the employer must be able to demonstrate, as regards whichever type of misconduct is pertinent, that the decision to dismiss that particular employee for that particular offence was warranted.

One further point worth emphasising arises where the employee is dismissed for misconduct in refusing to obey an order from the employer. Most employees believe that if the order was unlawful (i.e., in breach of the contract) they cannot be dismissed fairly for refusing to obey it. In many cases the lawfulness of the order will indeed affect the fairness of any dismissal, but it is only a factor in the equation. If the employer has, for instance, given ample warning of any change being implemented, consulted sufficiently and acted reasonably any resulting dismissal in the face of the employee 'sticking to the contract' may not be unfair (for further discussion see below at **10.9.6.1**).

10.9.6 Redundancy: fairness

With redundancy dismissals, where there is a collective redundancy of 20 or more employees and a duty to consult and inform representatives arises the statutory D&DPs do not apply (see SI 2004/752, reg. 4) but where there are redundancies affecting fewer than 20 employees, or where the redundancies will take effect in a period longer than 90 days, the statutory procedures will still apply.

With a redundancy dismissal the tribunal will be concerned to discover whether the redundancy was implemented fairly. It is rare for a tribunal to question the need for redundancy; that is a business decision for the employer to make (unless there is bad faith): *James W. Cook & Co. (Wivenhoe) Ltd* v *Tipper* [1990] ICR 716. Instead, the area most rife for debate is that of *selection* for redundancy. Thus if selections for redundancy are badly handled and the selection criteria are not objectively justifiable, there may be an unfair dismissal for reason of redundancy (a full discussion of these points occurs in **Chapter 11** generally, and specifically at **11.5**).

Indeed, certain dismissals for redundancy will be automatically unfair as described above at **10.8.7**.

The burden of proving that any of the above reasons apply lies with the employee. Thus the fact that trade unionists are selected does not in itself breach any provisions: the selections have to be *because* the employees were trade unionists, or had asserted a statutory right, etc.

In ordinary cases the employer may still have acted unfairly. Thus an employer must also:

(a) ensure that the selection criteria were objectively justifiable and applied fairly;

(b) undertake proper individual and/or collective consultation; and

(c) ascertain whether suitable alternative employment is available.

Hence the selection process and the procedure for decision-making and implementation will be called into question in deciding fairness.

Selection for redundancy because of a person's disability is not automatically unfair but will have to be justified, and that justification must be both material to the circumstances of the particular case and substantial: s. 5(3) of DDA 1995.

10.9.7 Statutory illegality: fairness

Again, under SI 2004/752, reg. 4, where it has become illegal for the employee to continue in his job the D&DPs do not apply.

We have already noted that it is for the employer to show as a fact that any continued employment would have contravened the statutory rule in question in order to claim this as a fair reason for dismissal. As with other 'fair reasons', the citing of an enactment does not absolve the employer from showing that the dismissal was handled fairly. The problem of the illegality, for instance, might only have a short life-span and so might easily be corrected, or the illegality might affect only part of the employee's duties so that alternative work or a change in duties could be looked at. In other words, if the situation can be remedied the employer would be unwise to dismiss before checking this.

10.9.8 Some other substantial reason: fairness

In the text below we consider the special requirements affecting 'some other substantial reason' dismissals other than the procedures required under the statutory D&DPs. The D&DPs are taken as either having been complied with or not applicable.

The tag of 'miscellaneous categories' applies to this area, dragging along with it all the lack of definition inherent in the phrase. Thus if the dismissal does not fall within any of the other four fair reasons it *might* come within this heading. Equally, many employers will plead this 'catch all' in the alternative, e.g., if the dismissal was not for redundancy it was for 'some other substantial reason, etc.' such as a business reorganisation; or if the employer was mistaken about the effect of a statutory rule and dismissed for statutory illegality, the honest belief might be pleaded as 'some other substantial reason'.

The most common form of 'some other substantial reason' is that of business reorganisations. We noted in **Chapter 5** that where an employer effects a change to the employee's terms and conditions a range of alternative consequences is possible at common law, e.g.:

(a) the change may be lawful via the express or implied terms of the contract;

(b) the employee might simply accept the change (reluctantly or otherwise);

(c) the employee might object and seek an injunction or damages;

(d) the employee might refuse to accept the change and be dismissed, in which case there may be a claim for wrongful dismissal;

(e) the employee might resign and claim wrongful repudiation.

To this we have added, in the earlier stages of this chapter, that:

(f) the employee might refuse to accept the change and be dismissed, in which case there may be a claim for unfair dismissal; or

(g) the employee might resign and claim constructive unfair dismissal.

Whichever way the unfair dismissal claim comes about, the employer can argue that the fair reason was 'some other substantial reason' under ERA 1996, s. 98. How will this be analysed by the employment tribunal?

10.9.8.1 Business reorganisations

Employers frequently wish to reorganise parts of a business in order to increase efficiency. Often this will simply involve a change in working patterns or methods, and, as seen in *Cresswell* v *Board of Inland Revenue* [1984] ICR 508 in **Chapter 5**, this may not involve any variation of the employment contract at all. An employee who refuses to cooperate and who resigns in the face of such changes will have no claim for wrongful repudation at common law or for unfair dismissal because there will have been no dismissal. If the employee refuses to cooperate and is dismissed there may be a claim for wrongful or unfair dismissal; but from the unfair dismissal perspective the fair reason could be incapability or misconduct (and fairness would be decided accordingly).

If the change does constitute a breach of contract the employer may still argue that the dismissal was not unfair because of the business reorganisation. The tribunal is not allowed to second-guess the employer's business decision, so the employer can establish the 'fair reason' quite easily, e.g., insisting on the insertion of restraint of trade clauses because of recent problems with ex-employees joining competitors: *RS Components* v *Irwin* [1973] ICR 353. The test was once quite stringent: was there a 'pressing business need' for the change? However, greater leniency is now evident so that all that is needed is a 'sound business reason' (*see Hollister* v *National Farmers' Union* [1979] ICR 542), or even merely that the change was beneficial to the operation of the company. A mere assertion that there is a business reason is not enough, but employers are only expected to show the factual *evidence* as the basis for making their business decision.

The question of fairness still has to be decided, however. As with any unfair dismissal claim, the manner in which the employer handled the dismissal is still important. The tribunal is therefore seeking to find out whether the reorganisation was effected in a reasonable way. One of the difficulties that crops up here is that just because the employer is acting reasonably in seeking to implement the change it does not automatically follow that the employee is acting unreasonably in refusing to accept it. All manner of reasons may be relevant, e.g., family commitments or travel arrangements and, again, one must also consider the question of indirect discrimination arising from any reorganisation (see, for instance, *London Underground Ltd* v *Edwards (No. 2)*, at **5.4.2.3** above).

The tribunal will therefore need to look at:

(a) whether the employer consulted with the employee and any employee representatives;

(b) whether the employer considered alternative courses of action;

(c) whether the terms were those which a reasonable employer would offer;

(d) what is the balance of advantages and disadvantages to both parties;

(e) whether the majority of employees have accepted the change.

No one factor is given greater weight than another and the whole context of the reorganisation needs to be examined: *St John of God (Care Services) Ltd* v *Brooks* [1992] IRLR 546. Again, however, one needs to be aware of the possible impact of DDA 1995. For instance, employers must now look at making reasonable adjustments to working arrangements and physical features of premises in relation to disabled employees. These adjustments include such matters as altering working hours, modifying equipment, assigning a different place of work (s. 6). Thus, these matters must be taken into account in effecting a business reorganisation otherwise there is a likelihood that the change in terms, etc. will be seen as unreasonable.

10.9.9 Constructive dismissal and fairness

It is a common assumption that a constructive dismissal is automatically unfair. This view is wrong. All that a finding of constructive dismissal does is to show that the employee (despite having resigned) was in fact *dismissed*.

The question of fairness is a separate matter. Constructive dismissal asks whether the employer's conduct was repudiatory. It is a contractual test and, as with any other dismissal, the employer's breach of the contract is not what the idea of 'fairness' centres on. *Thus there may be fair or unfair constructive dismissals*. If you look back at **Figure 10.1** you will see that it only dealt with the analysis of whether or not there had been a constructive dismissal; it said nothing about fairness. It only told half the story because, once a constructive dismissal has been found the tribunal's attention then shifts to the analysis in **Figure 10.2**—as with any other unfair dismissal action.

Having said all this, in many cases it will be quite unusual for an employment tribunal to be convinced that a constructive dismissal was nevertheless fair in all the circumstances. For instance, in *Cawley* v *South Wales Electricity Board* [1985] IRLR 89, an employee had been seen (by a member of the public) urinating out of the back of a SWEB van as it travelled down a main street. Apparently the employee had bladder trouble and the whole incident arose out of a practical joke being played by his workmates. The employee was at first dismissed but on appeal this was turned into a heavy demotion. He complained that, although the demotion was allowed for in the contract, its implementation was an abuse of power. He resigned and claimed that he was (unfairly) constructively dismissed. The tribunal found constructive dismissal and never really directed its mind to the question of fairness. However, on appeal the two points were found to be so closely intertwined that the general points had been covered. So it will be with most misconduct constructive dismissals.

The major exception to all this arises with constructive dismissals based on business reorganisations. Here the two questions of serious breach and fairness are quite distinct. Let us say, for example, that an employer decides unilaterally to change the terms of the contract for good economic reasons. The employees object. The employer insists, and eventually your employee-client resigns and claims unfair (constructive) dismissal. There is probably very little difficulty in showing a serious breach of contract by the employer here (though one cannot be sure of this without considering such factors as implied terms and employee adaptability: see **Chapter 5** at **5.5.3**). But, assuming that a serious breach can be shown, there is a constructive dismissal. We are also assuming that the employee qualifies to bring a claim for unfair dismissal in the first place, otherwise all we are left with is a common law claim for wrongful repudiation.

Now, the next question is: was this dismissal unfair? The employer may claim business reorganisation as 'some other substantial reason' and this is not the most difficult hurdle to overcome. Thus it is quite likely that, although the change was a repudiation of the contract, and although the employee was contractually entitled to refuse to accept the alteration, any resulting dismissal may well not be unfair.

Your employee-client may well have difficulty accepting this point (along with some of the others noted above). Your employer-client may be equally surprised.

10.10 Industrial action

Under ERA 1996, s. 16 and sch. 5 the relevant provisions in TULRCA 1992, i.e., ss. 238–239, were amended and a new section (s. 238A) inserted. The dismissal of an employee *because* he or she is taking part in *official* (otherwise called 'protected') industrial action will be *automatically unfair* if:

(a) the dismissal takes place within the period of eight weeks beginning with the day the employee started to take industrial action; or

(b) it takes place after the end of that period and the employee had stopped taking industrial action before the end of that period; or

(c) it takes place after the period, and though the employee had not stopped industrial action, the employer had not taken defined procedural steps (defined in s. 238A (6)) to resolve the dispute.

10.10.1 What is industrial action?

Industrial action may take many forms, including a strike, a work-to-rule, a go-slow, or an overtime ban. The question of what is and what is not industrial action in any particular set of circumstances is *a question of fact* for the employment tribunal. Different tribunals may reach different conclusions on similar (or even on the same) facts. The action does not need to be in breach of contract: *Power Packing Casemakers Ltd* v *Faust* [1983] ICR 292. In this case the employees refused to work non-contractual overtime (so there could hardly be a breach) as part of wage bargaining tactics. What was present in *Faust*, however (and is generally required), is some pressure, some disruption of the employer's business for industrial relations reasons, e.g., pay demands.

Although there is no statutory definition of 'industrial action', 'strike' is defined in ERA 1996, s. 235(5) as '(a) the cessation of work by a body of employed persons acting in combination, or (b) a concerted refusal, or a refusal under a common understanding, of any number of employed persons to continue to work for an employer in consequence of a dispute . . .'. This must be done to compel the employer to accept the employees' view on bargaining positions or for showing sympathy with other workers. This definition has, however, been limited to determining continuity of employment; so essentially the definition of strike is also a question of fact.

Traditionally more than one person was needed to take a strike or other forms of industrial action—those persons acting in concert. But in *Britton* v *E. Mason & Sons* [1994] IRLR 4 the EAT stated that there was no reason why an individual could not take industrial action. We would respectfully disagree with the EAT here. Finally, a *threat* of industrial action is not enough; there must be some acts which are designed to exert pressure beyond threats or the holding of meetings: *Midland Plastics* v *Till* [1983] ICR 118.

10.10.2 What is 'taking part'?

This has proved to be a problem area as regards employees who are on holiday or sick when the action occurs, or who feel unable to go into work because they are afraid to cross picket lines.

It is vital to know who is 'taking part' because the employer must be careful (at least with official action once the protected period seen in **10.10** has passed) to treat all those taking part, at the moment that one participant is dismissed, in the same way. Thus an employer does not want later to discover that an employee was not dismissed along with others taking part in an official action, because this would mean that the employees who were dismissed would once again be able to claim unfair dismissal. The employer's ignorance is no defence and the employee's motives are also irrelevant: *Coates & Venables* v *Modern Methods & Materials Ltd* [1982] ICR 763. Again, participation is a question of fact.

The employer therefore has to be sure, before dismissing anyone, *which* employees are taking part. For to dismiss the relevant employees *but miss one* will be a fatal error; and to dismiss someone who *is not taking part* will mean that that individual will have a good claim for unfair dismissal. The burden lies on the employer. As regards those employees who are absent from the company (e.g., those on sick leave), the employer needs to ascertain by reasonable investigation whether they are *associated* with the action: *Hindle Gears Ltd* v *McGinty* [1985] ICR 111. But if an employee originally took part in the industrial action and returned to work before any dismissals occurred, he or she is not participating at the relevant time.

10.10.3 Rules vary according to the type of action

Industrial action can be classed in a number of ways depending on whether a trade union has sanctioned the action. Thus, if a trade union supports the action it is referred to as '*official action*' and the employee gains certain protection from this tag. If a trade union does not support the action this is called '*unofficial action*' and the industrial action is not protected. Industrial action will be unofficial *unless*:

(a) the employee is a union member and the action has been authorised or endorsed by the union; or

(b) although the employee is not a union member, some of those taking part are and the action has been authorised or endorsed by the union (see TULRCA 1992, s. 237).

An employee who is dismissed whilst taking part in *unofficial action* has no right to complain of unfair dismissal even if others are not dismissed: TULRCA 1992, s. 237 (but note s. 238A: there is a day's grace allowed if the action was official and then was repudiated by the union).

Where none of the participants is a union member the action is sometimes called '*not unofficial action*'. This means that it is not protected action within s. 238A, but is covered by s. 238 which, broadly, allows the employee to claim unfair dismissal if all those taking part were not treated the same by the employer.

10.11 Action short of dismissal

Before we turn to the remedies for unfair dismissal we should note that, in certain cases where an employee has action taken against him short of dismissal he will gain rights to obtain a declaration against the employer or compensation. The aim here is that where an employee has sought to enforce rights under the contract and is then subjected to a detriment by the employer as a result of this but is not dismissed, he should have some right of recourse against the employer. We will not cover all the detailed provisions here, but, in outline, the grounds contained in Part V, ERA 1996 (ss. 44–49) are:

(a) cases where the employer has carried out activities in connexion with health and safety matters (s. 44);

(b) cases where the employee has refused to work on Sundays (s. 45);

(c) cases involving the working time regulations (s. 45A);
(d) cases concerning the actions of trustee of occupational pension schemes (s. 46);
(e) cases concerning employees acting as employee representatives under TULRCA 1992 (s. 47);
(f) cases where employees have sought to enforce rights relating to trade union activities or membership (TULRCA 1992, s. 146 as amended);
(g) cases involving employees who have sought time off in certain defined circumstances (s. 47A);
(h) cases where employees have made protected disclosures (s. 47B);
(i) cases where employees have sought leave for family and domestic reasons (s. 47C);
(j) cases involving employees seeking to enforce tax credits rights (s. 47D); and
(k) cases involving applications for flexible working (s. 47E).

The remedies for such actions are set out in ERA 1996, s. 49. Awards may be made which include a sum for injury to feelings (akin to discrimination claims and using the *Vento* guidelines applied in such cases—see **6.6.3** above): *Virgo Fidelis Senior School* v *Boyle* [2004] IRLR 268 (a case of disciplinary action being taken by the school against a teacher following a protected disclosure).

10.12 Other methods of dispute resolution

10.12.1 Settlements and conciliation

Many cases are settled before the hearing. Any settlement concluded through an ACAS officer, reached orally or in writing, is binding on the parties. An ACAS officer is always given the employee's ET 1 (the equivalent to a statement of claim) and the employer's ET 3 (the defence). The officer will then seek to conclude a settlement between the parties. A settlement can be reached at any stage in the proceedings. Settlements through ACAS are usually put down in writing on a form known as a COT 3.

For years this was the only way to ensure that a settlement was binding on the parties. However, under ERA 1996, s. 203(2)(f) and (3) the parties may now reach their own binding compromise agreement. In outline:

(a) the agreement must be in writing;
(b) it must relate to the particular complaint;
(c) the employee must have received advice from a relevant independent adviser; and
(d) the employee's adviser must be insured or have indemnity provided for members of a profession or professional body.

The issue of settlements and the considerations involved are dealt with more fully in **Chapter 13**.

10.12.2 ACAS arbitration scheme

In May 2001, a voluntary arbitration scheme was introduced under the auspices of ACAS as an alternative to going to an employment tribunal for dealing with simple unfair dismissal disputes. It was designed to relieve some of the workload of tribunals. The scheme is limited in its form, e.g., the scheme excludes other (even related or overlapping) claims such as discrimination issues, jurisdictional problems such as continuity of employment, contractual disputes and transfer of undertakings issues. ACAS also strongly recommends that questions of EC Law are left to employment tribunals. Both parties must agree, in writing, to go to arbitration and this agreement contains certain waivers, e.g., a very limited right of appeal against the arbitrator's decision. The ACAS arbitrator may conduct proceedings anywhere (e.g., at the workplace), those proceedings are held in private, no oath is administered, the arbitrator will take a strong inquisitorial role, and the matter will be decided on general grounds of fairness, not the rules developed under unfair dismissal case law (e.g., the range of reasonable responses test). The statutory procedures are relevant here though ACAS has issued guidelines for the scheme (see http://www.acas.org.uk/). The Arbitration Act 1996 does not apply to this scheme.

10.13 General principles of compensation

10.13.1 What remedies are available?

10.13.1.1 Reinstatement

Reinstatement means to be put back in the same job with compensation for loss between dismissal and reinstatement. If reinstatement is requested by the employee the employer can refuse to reinstate only where it is reasonable to do so, e.g., where the mutual trust and confidence has been shattered. The employee is not obliged to request reinstatement, nor is the tribunal bound by any request. Indeed, the employee can have a change of mind at any time. However, tactically some employees request reinstatement (although they do not really want it) because a refusal *may* increase the amount of compensation. This tactic can also backfire.

An unreasonable refusal by the employer to reinstate where it would have been practicable to do so may lead to an *additional award* being given in addition to the *basic award* and the *compensatory award* (see below). Though reinstatement is the primary remedy (as emphasised in *Polkey* v *A. E. Dayton Services Ltd* [1987] AC 344), it has traditionally occurred in less than 2 per cent of cases.

10.13.1.2 Re-engagement

This consists of returning the employee to a similar job or to a job with an associated employer. Re-engagement is subject to the same tests as reinstatement.

10.13.1.3 Compensation

The two main elements are the basic award and compensatory award. They are assessed on quite different grounds which are discussed in detail below. The figures which form the basis for calculating these awards are now changed annually according to the Retail Price Index changes for September of each year (see ERA 1999, s. 34) and brought into effect in the following February. The principles for assessing compensation are set out in ERA 1996, ss. 118–126 (as amended).

The figures given here, therefore, are only valid for dismissals occurring before 1st February 2005.

10.13.1.4 Interim Relief

Under ERA 1996, s. 128, employees who have been dismissed may apply for 'interim relief' in a limited number of cases. The claim must be presented before the end of the period of seven days immediately following the EDT. Where the tribunal finds that it is likely that on final determination the tribunal will find that the reason for dismissal falls within:

- s. 100(1)(a) or (b) ERA 1996—health and safety-related dismissal;
- s. 101A(d)—working time-related dismissal;
- s. 102(1)—occupational pension scheme trustee-related dismissal;
- s. 103—employee representative-related dismissal;
- s. 103A—protected disclosure-related dismissal; or
- Para 161(2) sch. A1, TULRCA 1992—trade union membership and activities-related dismissal.

it may order continuance of the contract or, ultimately, award compensation. Interim relief actions are not common.

10.13.2 Assessing the basic award

This is calculated on length of service. It is a fixed formula which looks far more daunting than it really is. When a client asks how much he or she will get or have to pay in an unfair dismissal case, this is the one figure that provides some level of certainty. The formulation is set out in ERA 1996, s. 119(2). It is almost identical to the redundancy entitlement.

CALCULATION:	[AGE factor] × [SERVICE] × [WEEK'S PAY]
AGE:	For any service where the employee was 41 or over the factor is 1.5
	For any service between the ages of 22 and 41 the factor is 1
	For any service below the age of 22 the factor is 0.5
SERVICE:	Subject to a maximum of 20 years
WEEK'S PAY:	Subject to a maximum of £270 per week

The maximum basic award is therefore £8,100, i.e., 1.5 × 20 × 270.

Note: Where the EDT is beyond the employee's 64th birthday the basic award is reduced by $\frac{1}{12}$th for every completed calendar month after that birthday. Thus the basic award ceases to be payable when the employee reaches 65.

The method of calculating this can be seen in the following examples.

EXAMPLE 1

An employee is aged 56 at the time of dismissal and has 10 years' service with the company (only complete years can count). He earns £300 per week. To calculate the basic award you must take the length of service as at the EDT and count back from the employee's present age to see how many years of service fall into each age bracket. This tells you that here all the years of service fall within the age bracket of 'over 41'. Therefore the factor for each of these years will be 1.5. As the employee earns more than the maximum 'week's pay' he is limited to the £270. Thus 1.5 × 10 years × £270 gives a figure of £4,050 (i.e., 15 × £270).

EXAMPLE 2

Where the employee's years of service straddle two of the age brackets the computation becomes more difficult. If we take the same employee but change his age to 46 the method of calculation becomes: (1.5 × 5 years) plus (1 × 5 years) × £270 giving a figure of £3,375 (i.e., 12.5 × £270). This is because five years of his service fall within the age bracket of '41 or over' and are given a multiple of 1.5, but the remainder fall within the age bracket '22–41' and are only given a multiple of 1.

It is comforting to know that the DTI publishes a booklet (PL 808) which provides a 'ready reckoner' for calculating these figures. There you can read off the length of service against the present age and obtain a factor (e.g., **12.5**) which can be multiplied with the week's pay.

Note: *If the employee earns less than £270 per week it is that lower figure that will be used in the calculation*, subject to the National Minimum Wage rate as described in **4.2.3** above: *Pagetti* v *Cobb* [2002] Emp LR 651.

10.13.2.1 Minimum Basic Award

Under ERA 1996, s. 120(1) a minimum Basic Award of £3,600 will be made where the reason for dismissal is one specified in ERA 1996, ss. 100(1)(a) and (b), 101A(d), 102(1) and 103 (see **10.13.1.4** on which types of dismissals these sections refer to).

10.13.2.2 Minimum Basic Award and the statutory dispute resolution procedures

Where an employee is automatically unfairly dismissed under s. 98A because of the employer's non-compliance with the relevant procedures and the basic award (before deductions) would be less than four weeks' pay, the tribunal shall award four weeks' pay unless this is not just and equitable (ERA 1996, s. 120 (IA)).

10.13.2.3 Minimum Basic Award and certain redundancy cases

In some cases (detailed in ERA 1996, ss. 138 and 141) an employee may be made redundant but be offered re-engagement immediately or soon after dismissal. There are detailed rules as to whether a refusal by the employee to be re-engaged destroys his right to claim redundancy pay. Section 121 ERA 1996 sets out an employee's rights to a minimum basic award in such instances.

10.13.2.4 Reductions in the Basic Award

The situations where a tribunal may reduce the basic award are listed in **10.13.6** below and are dealt with in ERA 1996, s. 122.

10.13.3 Assessing the compensatory award

The method of calculation is set out in ERA 1996, s. 123. Compensation is based on what is 'just and equitable in all the circumstances having regard to the loss sustained by the complainant in consequence of the dismissal' and the tribunal must be satisfied that there was a causal link between the dismissal and the loss suffered: *Simrad Ltd* v *Scott* [1997] IRLR 147. It is calculated on *nett* payments. Unlike the basic award, the compensatory award is payable even though the employee has reached or passed 65 if still below the normal retirement age.

The maximum Compensatory Award is £55,000 (see ERA 1996, s. 124).

Tribunals have long used one leading case as the basis for calculating the Compensatory Award: *Norton Tool Co. Ltd* v *Tewson* [1973] 1 All ER 183.

We have noted above that discrimination claims (e.g. sex or race) are not subject to any 'capping' of compensation. Section 37, ERA 1999, lists the following reasons for an unfair dismissal as also not being subject to any cap:

- A dismissal falling under the 'whistleblower' provisions of the Public Interest Disclosure Act 1998 and ERA 1996 s. 103A.
- A dismissal falling under ERA 1996, ss. 100 and 105(3) (automatically unfair dismissal where the reason relates to health and safety).

10.13.4 The Norton Tool principles

Under the principles enunciated in *Norton Tool*, certain general principles for calculating loss have been laid down. These include the following headings:

10.13.4.1 Immediate loss of wages

This heading deals with loss dating from the EDT to the date of hearing. This normally is an easy calculation. If notice or payment in lieu of notice has been given, the employee's loss will date from the expiry of that period worked or the period covered by the payment. The corollary to this is that, if notice has not been given, loss flows from the date of dismissal (in effect compensating the employee for not receiving a notice payment).

Payments received during the period from EDT to hearing will normally be offset against any compensation because the tribunal is concerned with real loss. In other words, the tribunal will apply general contractual principles of mitigation of loss. Where the employee has remained unemployed throughout this time there is no probem with this calculation. Equally, where the employee has gained a new job at a lower rate of pay than before, the amount received may be taken into account in reducing the overall award.

Real problems arise where the employee has obtained a new job before the hearing which pays **better** than the old one. There has been some debate about how to take this into account: (i) calculate loss from EDT to hearing and take away all new payments—which might actually wipe out the award; or (ii) calculate actual loss if any from EDT to the date of new employment. In *Whelan* v *Richardson* [1998] IRLR 114 the EAT has come down in favour of method (ii) as most favouring the interests of justice.

Strangely, after 30 years since *Norton Tool*, there is still some debate on how the mitigation rules relate to an employee's notice period when the employee has not been given all (or sometimes any) of his due notice. Is the notice period (at least the statutory minimum) to be regarded as a debt and so not subject to mitigation, or damages, and subject to the normal rules?

Section 123(1) ERA 1996 uses the phrase '**loss** sustained by the complainant' in describing the general principles of compensation. Section 123(4) states that, in assessing this loss, 'the tribunal shall apply the same rule concerning the duty of a person to mitigate his loss as applies to damages recoverable under the common law . . . '. Wrongful dismissal damages always include a duty to mitigate (see **9.10.2** and **9.10.3** above) and this applies to both contractual notice and the ERA 1996, s. 86 minimum period.

Norton Tool suggested that where an employee has not received due notice or payment in lieu no mitigation should be applied to that period (or at least to the now s. 86 minimum). This was confirmed by the Court of Appeal in *Addision* v *Babcock FATA Ltd* [1987] ICR 805. But *Norton Tool* was not followed by the EAT in *Isleworth Studios Ltd* v *Rickard* [1988] IRLR 137 where an employee was dismissed with 29 weeks left on his fixed-term contract. He set up his own business immediately and made greater profits from this than if he had remained in employment. The EAT here decided that he had suffered no loss.

In *Abrahams* v *Performing Rights Society* [1995] IRLR 486 the Court of Appeal held (in a wrongful dismissal action) that a failure to pay a contractually-specified payment in lieu created a debt, not damages, thus avoiding the mitigation principles (see **9.10.3** above). Since then, however, the Court of Appeal has pulled back from this analysis somewhat in the case of *Cerberus Software Ltd* v *Rowley* [2001] EWCA Civ 497, [2001] IRLR 160 in holding that a notice entitlement was not a debt where the wording of the payment in lieu clause allowed the employer the right to choose whether or not to make the payment. Thus, by this stage it should be clear that it was not clear whether to treat the notice period as creating debt or damages in any given situation.

These points were considered in *Hardy* v *Polk* [2004] IRLR 420 by the EAT, which decided that *Norton Tool* and *Addison* were effectively *per incuriam* decisions and need not be followed, and that the *Cerberus* approach should be followed. The EAT held that a notice entitlement does not create a debt and is subject to mitigation. This is unlikely to be the end of the matter—which is why we have explained this in full—and this decision certainly provides something of an incentive to employers to not give notice and see what happens as a result (though there are consequences as regards restraint clauses here).

In general, therefore, payments received must be accounted for. This has been extended to cover various social security benefits. Thus, if the employee has received social security benefits (other than income support and housing benefit) the tribunal will order this part of the compensatory award to be withheld until the Department for Work and Pensions has determined what amount it is reclaiming under the Employment Protection (Recoupment of Jobseeker's Allowance and Income Support) Regulations 1996 (SI 1996/2349). The loss for the period between dismissal and hearing (after any deductions have been made) must be noted formally by the tribunal in its judgments; this figure is known as '*the prescribed element*'.

10.13.4.2 Future loss of wages

This involves a degree of industrial guess-work. The tribunal will need to establish how long the applicant is likely to be unemployed, what are the employee's attributes, skills, the market for such skills, and whether he or she might have been dismissed for redundancy anyway in the near future. The tribunal will therefore seek to make an award relating to the employee *as an individual*, so that similarly-aged employees dismissed at the same time might still receive different compensations. The award is discretionary.

If the employee has already found another job which is better paid there will probably be no loss under this heading; if less well paid, the tribunal will have to judge when (if at all) the equivalent payment will be reached. These general statements are subject to the points made at (a) above in *Whelan* v *Richardson*, and also to those made by the Court of Appeal in *Dench* v *Flynn & Partners* [1998] IRLR 653. Here, an employee had been dismissed, had lodged a claim for unfair dismissal and then taken up new permanent employment; but within a two months of starting had then terminated that employment. The question was whether, once the employee took up the (eventually aborted) permanent position, that marked the end of the period for which she could claim compensation from her original employer. The Court of Appeal said that the question for the tribunal is whether the unfair dismissal can be regarded as a continuing course of loss when the employee is subsequently dismissed by her new employer with no right to compensation after a month or two in her new employment. They held that it could be: tribunals must assess what is a just and equitable compensation; in doing so, they must determine *why* the new employment did not last. If there was good reason why it did not last, its presence does not in itself break the chain of causation between dismissal and loss.

Such cases illustrate the important point that the employee can only recover the financial loss which is attributable to the employer's unfair dismissal. We saw this above in point (a) in cases where an employee gains a new job quite quickly after dismissal; it is only *actual* loss that is compensated for, and even this is subject to the duty to mitigate that loss.

Cases such as *Leonard* v *Strathclyde Buses Ltd* [1998] IRLR 693 have made it clear that the test for causation should be one of applying common sense—what are the natural and direct consequences of the dismissal?—rather than intricate legal arguments on remoteness. Nevertheless, the reasonableness of the dismissed employee's actions subsequent to dismissal will come under much greater scrutiny than has previously been the case. Thus, for instance, what should be the position where an employee's response to dismissal is to set up in business (which will have a major lead-in period before profits can be made) or decides to go to university to increase his or her market-ability. Should the immediate financial loss which results from these decisions still be attributable to the employer's actions? The latter example was seen in *Khanum* v *IBC Vehicles Ltd* (2000, unreported) where an obviously progressive employer dismissed Khanum for attending an open day at a university. She had great difficulty in finding another job—there was evidence she had been blacklisted—and, after ten months, enrolled on a university degree course. It was accepted in evidence that, given the job market, this was a reasonable course of action and the chain of causation remained unbroken (unlike the earlier case of *Simrad Ltd* v *Scott* [1997] IRLR 147 where a decision to retrain was a matter of choice rather than need).

In the joined cases of *Kingston upon Hull City Council* v *Dunnachie (No. 3)* and *HSBC Bank plc* v *Drage* [2004] ICR 227 the EAT discouraged the use of 'Ogden Tables' (used extensively in personal injury cases) to calculate unfair dismissal compensation for future loss (other than pension loss). They may be appropriate where it can be shown that the employee's loss will last for the rest of his career, but this will be rare.

10.13.4.3 Loss of fringe benefits

For example, company cars or accommodation or even the difference in value between shares sold back to the company by the employee on termination (at the then market value) and the new market value of those shares at the date of the hearing.

10.13.4.4 The manner of dismissal

In *Johnson* v *Unysis Ltd* [2001] UKHL 13, [2001] ICR 480 the House of Lords rejected a claim in contract for damages for injury to feeling arising *from the manner of dismissal*. In doing so, Lord Hoffmann contemplated (unfortunately, out loud) whether, instead, an employment tribunal might be able to compensate for injury to feelings in an unfair dismissal action. This was news to employment lawyers but sparked a raft of cases where this was pleaded. In turn this led to the House of Lords (including Lord Hoffmann) holding that Lord Hoffmann's words were *obiter: Dunnachie* v *Kingston upon Hull City Council* [2004] UKHL 36, [2004] 3 WLR 310. Further, the natural meaning of the word 'loss' in s.123 ERA 1996 did not admit damages for injury to feelings or psychiatric injury as part of unfair dismissal compensation.

We should note three things here:

- first, that compensation in discrimination actions can include an award for injury to feelings;
- secondly, that an award for injury to feelings can be made in relation to an action short of dismissal (see *Virgo Fidelis Senior School* v *Boyle* above);
- thirdly, that damages can be awarded for injury to feelings where the **cause of action accrues before dismissal** (see the joined cases of *Eastwood* v *Magnox Electric plc* and *McCabe* v *Cornwall County Council* [2004] UKHL 35, [2004] 3 W.L.R. 322 above at **9.10.1.3**—which consisted of the same House of Lords' panel as in *Dunnachie)*.
  The combination of *Dunnachie* and *Eastwood* will inevitably lead to a great deal of confusion as to when an act relates to dismissal or events prior to dismissal, with resultant protracted legal argument on this distinction.

10.13.4.5 Loss of statutory employment protection rights

When an employee starts a new job he or she will generally have to work for one year before any unfair dismissal rights accrue. This heading provides some compensation for that loss, although the figure is nominal (usually about £250). Tribunals may also award compensation for loss of ERA 1996, s. 86 statutory notice rights (usually assessed at half the employee's statutory entitlement, e.g., four weeks for eight years' service).

10.13.4.6 Loss of pension rights

This is a potentially horrendous area which needs specialist advice. There are various methods of calculating pension rights losses, e.g., those published by the Government's Actuary Department: *Employment Tribunals: compensation for loss of pension rights*. Tribunals will usually follow these guidelines, but they are not bound to do so. With the increase in the maximum compensatory award, pension loss is set to become a major factor and source of argument in tribunal hearings. This is not an area for the amateur; reference should be made to specialist books and the Guidelines noted above on this matter.

Thus the tribunal sets out to do two things. First, it must assess the loss from the EDT to the date of hearing. This can be calculated quite easily. Secondly, the tribunal must assess the future loss. Even using the *Norton Tool* guidelines, this will always involve an estimation. The two figures together form the compensatory award. When added to the basic award this gives a maximum figure of £63,100.

10.13.5 Increased compensation

When the statutory dismissal and disciplinary procedures or the statutory grievance procedures have not be complied with and the fault lies with the employer then, as well as any dismissal being automatically unfair, the award made against the employer may be adjusted. This principle was introduced by EA 2002, s. 31 and, though we are only concerned with unfair dismissal here, we should note that s. 31 applies to any of the jurisdictions listed in EA 2002, sch. 3 (e.g., discrimination claims or equal pay claims—for the full list see **5.3.1.6**). The rules on allocation of blame for non-completion of the procedures can be found in SI 2004/752, reg. 12.

Section 31 provides that a tribunal may increase an award where:

(a) the claim falls within EA 2002, sch. 3;

(b) the claim concerns a matter to which a statutory D&DP or grievance procedure applies and this was not completed before the proceedings were begun; and

(c) the non-completion is wholly or mainly attributable to the employer.

Section 31(3) states that the 'tribunal *must* increase any award to the employee by 10 per cent and *may*, if it considers it just and equitable in all the circumstances to do so, increase it by a further amount, but not so as to make a total increase of more than 50 per cent' *(emphasis added).*

Section 31(4), however, modifies this slightly so that the duty, 'to make a reduction or increase of 10 per cent does not apply if there are *exceptional* circumstances which would make a reduction or increase of that percentage unjust or inequitable, in which case the tribunal may make no reduction or increase or a reduction or increase of such lesser percentage as it considers just and equitable in all the circumstances'. *(emphasis added).* With the use of the word 'exceptional' we would suggest that this provision is not likely to apply in many instances.

A new ERA 1996, s. 124A, inserted by EA 2002, s. 39, states that, where an award of compensation for unfair dismissal falls to be increased under s. 31, or increased under s. 38 (failure to give statement of employment particulars), the adjustment shall be in the amount awarded under ERA 1996, s. 118(1)(b) (the compensatory award) and shall be applied immediately before any reduction under s. 123(6) or (7) (contributory fault on the part of the employee).

10.13.6 Deductions from the overall award

Deductions may be made from both the basic award and compensatory award figures. These deductions are generally at the discretion of the tribunal. In the summary chart below you will see that there are a number of reasons why deductions can be made. One deserves special mention, namely deductions concerning the statutory dispute resolution procedures.

When the statutory dismissal and disciplinary procedures or the statutory grievance procedures have not be complied with and the fault lies with the employee then any award may be reduced. This is the corollary to **10.13.5** above and the comments on s. 31 apply here too. Again, see SI 2004/752, reg. 12 for the rules on allocation of blame for non-completion of the procedures.

Section 31(2) states that where the employee has not complied with the procedure or exercised a right of appeal under it the 'tribunal *must* reduce any award to the employee by 10 per cent and *may*, if it considers it just and equitable in all the circumstances to do so, reduce it by a further amount, but not so as to make a total reduction of more than 50 percent' *(emphasis added).* Interestingly, there is no requirement in the statutory dispute resolution procedures for an employee to appeal; only an obligation for the employer to inform the employee of the right. Section 31(2), however, imposes a potential penalty where the employee does not appeal; therefore it must follow that the statutory procedures are not in fact 'completed' until an appeal has been pursued. Otherwise s. 31(2), regarding appeals, could never be enforced as the statutory procedures would have been completed and therefore the s. 31 trigger could not operate.

Section 31(4) again modifies this slightly in the case of *exceptional* circumstances. Section 124A ERA 1996 states that, where an award of compensation for unfair dismissal falls to be reduced the adjustment shall be in the amount awarded under ERA 1996 s. 118(1)(b) (the compensatory award) and shall be applied immediately before any reduction under s. 123(6) or (7) (contributory fault on the part of the employee).

DEDUCTIONS FROM THE BASIC AWARD

(i) Any amount for an unreasonable refusal on the employee's part to be reinstated.

(ii) Any amount for conduct before dismissal whenever discovered. There need be no causal link with the dismissal.

(iii) Any amount for contributory fault.

(iv) Any statutory redundancy payments already made, but only if the dismissal is for redundancy.

(v) A non-discretionary reduction to reflect the employee's age at EDT and his proximity to retirement (see first note to **10.13.2** above).

DEDUCTIONS FROM THE COMPENSATORY AWARD

(i) Recoupment of benefits including some part of sickness and invalidity benefits.

(ii) Mitigation, as with ordinary contractual principles.

(iii) Any contractual redundancy payments which are in excess of the statutory scheme.

(iv) Any *ex gratia* payments.

(v) Any contributory fault.

(vi) An amount falling within s. 31 EA 2002.

(vii) An amount representing the likelihood that the employee would have been dismissed sometime in the future anyway (e.g., for redundancy).

The basic award is not reduced for a failure to mitigate loss, even where the employee has not actually suffered any financial loss (e.g., on getting a new and better paid job immediately). Also, it should be noted that, even where the tribunal has made a finding of contributory fault on the part of the employee and reduced the compensatory award by a discretionary percentage, it still has a discretion whether to reduce the basic award as well, and may (because the two awards rest on different principles) legitimately decline to do so: *Optikinetics Ltd* v *Whooley* [1999] ICR 984.

Where an employer has reached a settlement on compensation with the employee, or has made an *ex gratia* payment, it is advisable that the ambit of either payment is made clear. If the payment or settlement is not expressed to cover the basic award as well as the compensatory award, there is a danger that the employee will still be entitled to the full basic award (see *Chelsea Football Club and Athletic Co. Ltd* v *Heath* [1981] ICR 323).

10.13.6.1 Order of making deductions

The basic award calculation is relatively straightforward, even when deductions are involved. With compensatory award calculations, however, tribunals have to estimate the employee's actual loss and attempt to award a 'just and equitable sum' on the facts. The exercise of discretion thus brings with it obvious problems. What is not so obvious at first glance is the importance of deciding in which order to make any deductions.

The order in which one applies percentage reductions (e.g., for contributory fault or failure to mitigate) may mean that vastly different figures are reached depending upon that order. For instance, say an employee is earning £20,000 per annum and is dismissed. The statutory D&DPs have been complied with but the tribunal finds an element of contributory fault to the extent that the employee was 50 per cent to blame for the dismissal. The employee has mitigated his loss by immediately finding a new job but it only pays £10,000. Ignoring Basic Award etc, what is the loss? If you apply the percentage reduction first, the figures are: £20,000 × 50% = £10,000, minus the mitigation of the new job (£10,000) = no loss. If you deduct the mitigation amount first, this leaves £10,000; apply the 50 per cent reduction and you have £5,000 per annum loss.

The cases in this area have been all over the place because the tribunals and courts have been in disagreement as to what elements go to calculating *the actual loss suffered as a result of the dismissal* and what factors go to *reducing loss*, e.g., if an employer makes an *ex gratia* payment to the dismissed employee, does that reduce the actual loss suffered or should you calculate loss and then take away the *ex gratia* payment made? As with the simple example above, the answer can make a big difference.

The conflict in the case law has thankfully now been simplified by the decision of the Court of Session in *Heggie* v *Uniroyal Englebert Tyres Ltd* [1999] IRLR 802. Taken together, the cases illustrate that the order of deduction is slightly different where there is an ordinary case of unfair dismissal from one which also involves a redundancy in which the employer has already made a contractual redundancy payment in excess of the statutory entitlement. A word of warning based on experience: tribunals in different regions often apply their own methods of calculating the order of deductions!

The order of deductions and increases takes this pattern:

(a) Deduct all kinds of payments made on termination by the employer, other than any contractual redundancy payment which is in excess of the statutory entitlement.

(b) Make appropriate deductions for mitigation or failure to mitigate.

(c) Apply EA 2002, s. 31 reductions or increases.

(d) Apply any deduction for contributory fault—inserted at this level on the basis of *Rao* v *Civil Aviation Authority* [1994] ICR 495.

(e) Apply the statutory maximum. The only problem here is that, where the case involves a contractual redundancy payment in excess of the statutory entitlement the case of *Digital Equipment* v *Clements* [1998] ICR 258, CA states that one should apply the statutory maximum (i.e., cap the award) and then deduct any excess contractual redundancy payment. *Leonard* v *Strathclyde Buses* [1998] IRLR 693 (Ct. Sess., Inner House-equivalent to the Court of Appeal) reverses this order.

Note: It is possible in making this calculation for the EA 2002, s. 31 adjustment in (c) to take the figure over the statutory maximum. Where this happens the effect of EA 2002 s. 39 is that the statutory maximum (the 'cap') is still applied. Thus, an employee who is awarded £50,000 and then awarded a s. 31 increase of 50 per cent will still get no more than the statutory maximum.

10.13.7 The Additional Award

Where a tribunal has ordered reinstatement or re-engagement (generally referred to here as re-employment) and the employer has not complied with this the tribunal must make an additional award, unless the tribunal is satisfied that it was not practicable to comply with the order. Where the employer has unreasonably refused to re-employ the employee an Additional Award of 26–52 weeks' pay on top of the Basic and Compensatory Awards can be ordered by the employment tribunal (ERA 1996, s. 117(3)(b) as amended by ERA 1999, s. 33(2)).

10.14 The overlap between unfair dismissal and wrongful dismissal

We noted at the start of this chapter that it is quite possible to have the following combinations:

(a) a dismissal which is unfair but which is not wrongful;

(b) a dismissal which is wrongful but which is not unfair;

(c) a dismissal which is both unfair and wrongful;

(d) a dismissal which is neither unfair nor wrongful.

This overlap often causes confusion to those new to the area. The following points are therefore repeated by way of guidance.

10.14.1 Jurisdiction overlap

In **Figure 1.1** above we noted that:

(a) Employment tribunals have sole jurisdiction to deal with statutory rights such as unfair dismissal and redundancy pay claims.

(b) In cases such as wrongful dismissal and wrongful repudiation an applicant may now choose whether to pursue these claims in the ordinary courts or in an employment tribunal under ETA 1996, s. 3. Employees may pursue actions for wrongful dismissal, etc. in a tribunal even though they are not claiming unfair dismissal or redundancy payments.

In the ordinary courts there is no limit to a claim for breach of contract. By contrast, any claim for contractual damages in a tribunal is limited to a maximum of £25,000—even where there are a number of claims involved. The limitation period for such claims is the same as for unfair dismissal (three months from the EDT). Further, tribunals are still restrained from deciding upon contractual points *during* the currency of the employment relationship (e.g., whether an employee's contract has a mobility clause) as well as all matters such as personal injury claims and restraint of trade disputes.

10.14.2 The substantive overlap

Wrongful dismissal and wrongful repudiation claims are concerned only with whether the employee received adequate notice according to the contract and ERA 1996, s. 86 statutory minima (plus the fringe benefits relating to that notice and minus any deductions). Unfair dismissal claims are concerned with the *reason why* and the *manner in which* an employee was dismissed. Whether or not an employee was dismissed with adequate notice is irrelevant to an unfair dismissal claim. Thus:

EXAMPLE 1

An employee has worked for a company for 10 years. He is dismissed without notice for absenteeism.

(a) He might have a claim for wrongful dismissal in the ordinary courts or in an employment tribunal if his employer cannot justify the summary dismissal. Justification depends upon whether or not the employee's actions constituted a repudiation of contract which the employer was accepting by dismissing him.

(b) He might (at the same time) have a claim for unfair dismissal in an employment tribunal, *whether or not he was wrongfully dismissed*.

(c) He has no claim for redundancy pay as there is no redundancy situation here.

EXAMPLE 2

An employee (of 10 years' service) is dismissed owing to a surplus of labour because the company's sales have been hit by a recession.

(a) He might have a claim for wrongful dismissal if he does not receive adequate notice (here, at least 10 weeks).

(b) He appears to have a claim for redundancy pay. Likely as not the employer will simply pay the statutory (and perhaps contractual) amount due. There would be no need to go to a tribunal on this aspect.

(c) He may still have a claim for unfair dismissal on the grounds that:

   (i) the redundancy was conducted unfairly (e.g., selection procedure); or

   (ii) there was no redundancy situation—it was a sham; or

   (iii) the employer correctly claims there was a business reorganisation and not a redundancy situation.

EXAMPLE 3

An employee is told that major changes will be made to her terms and conditions of employment (e.g., pay levels). She refuses to accept these and resigns.

(a) She may have a claim for wrongful repudiation in the ordinary courts or in an employment tribunal. She will claim that she has accepted the employer's repudiation of the contract by resigning. Her claim will be for her notice period.

(b) She may have a claim for unfair dismissal, but first she will have to prove she was constructively dismissed.

(c) She may have a claim for redundancy pay, in that she might prove she was constructively dismissed but the employer shows that this was for reasons of redundancy and was fair in all the circumstances.
(d) In addition she may also have a claim based on discrimination (direct or indirect).

In all the examples above, where the action is taken in the employment tribunal any award may be increased or reduced where the statutory D&DPs have not been complied with. The statutory D&DPs do not relate to any actions in the county court or High Court.

10.14.3 The financial overlap

It has long been established that an employee should not benefit from 'double recovery'. Thus any payments, or awards, made for the notice period should be accounted for when assessing loss from date of dismissal to date of hearing. With the introduction of limited contractual jurisdiction for employment tribunals it has been much easier to assess the relevant loss (including therefore both wrongful and unfair dismissal awards) in one fell swoop. In assessing unfair dismissal claims tribunals:

(a) first assess the loss relating to the basic award;
(b) then assess the compensatory award, which in turn is split into the two elements of:
  (i) loss between the EDT and the date of hearing—the prescribed element; and
  (ii) future loss.

In most cases, if there is a wrongful dismissal claim standing alongside the unfair dismissal claim then the wrongful dismissal damages will be covered by the assessment of loss from date of dismissal to hearing.

If notice has been given then the EDT will occur at the end of the notice period: thus *actual loss* can date only from that time (the same applies where notice is given but there is no requirement to work it).

If payment has been given in lieu of notice then, although the EDT will be the date of leaving, the employee has received a sum of money to cover 'loss' from date of leaving to the end of the notice period due to him. Thus the tribunal will ignore this period. Provided payment has been made for the notice period by one means or another, the notice period and some or all of the existing loss cancel each other out.

However, if no actual notice or no payment in lieu has been given, the EDT will be the date of leaving, so loss dates from that time and effectively the tribunal awards an amount covering the same period as would have been covered by the notice period, plus an amount up to the date of the hearing. As noted above (**10.13.3(a)**) principles of mitigation must be applied here.

Thus, under the principle preventing 'double recovery', it would be impossible now to ask for that loss to be made good again. One way round this problem, at least when an award is made which goes beyond the statutory 'cap', is for the tribunal to *first* award damages for wrongful dismissal and then make the compensatory award, this time running from the end of the notice period For example, say the tribunal calculates the compensatory award at £80,000. Say also that this includes a figure of £20,000 for non-payment of notice. If a simple compensatory award is made it will be capped at £55,000, but if damages are first awarded as a separate contractual item for the notice period, this leaves £60,000 relating to the other heads of the compensatory award. True, in this example it will still be capped, but the difference in the actual amount awarded is marked. There seems nothing in principle to prevent this.

In the unlikely event that an employee has succeeded in a separate county court action for wrongful dismissal claim *before* having the tribunal hearing, the tribunal can still make the normal award but will not give compensation for loss covered by the notice period.

Note: The basic award remains unaffected by all this. That is due to the employee irrespective of any wrongful dismissal claim or proper notice payment because it is equivalent to a redundancy pay claim.

10.15 Calculating the compensation

10.15.1 Tax implications

The raising of the unfair dismissal compensation 'cap' to £55,000 has brought with it a need to examine whether tax might be payable on the award. There are two elements to be borne in mind.

- The first is that tribunals have traditionally assessed the compensatory award on the basis of net pay (though this is not strictly a requirement) because that figure represents the actual loss an employee suffers. This equates with how wrongful dismissal damages are assessed (see *British Transport Commission* v *Gourley* [1956] AC 185, HL). In most cases, therefore, there will be no further tax implications on any award made because problems only arise where £30,000 or more is awarded.
- The second element arises where the £30,000 threshold is exceeded. Here, the compensatory award may count as employment income under s. 62 and Chapter 3 of Part 6, Income Tax (Earnings and Pensions) Act 2003 and so be subject to tax. Section 401(1) states that 'This Chapter applies to payments and other benefits which are received directly or indirectly in consideration or in consequence of, or otherwise in connection with: (a) the termination of a person's employment. . . . ' Section 403(1) states that 'The amount of a payment or benefit to which this Chapter applies counts as employment income of the employee or former employee for the relevant tax year if and to the extent that it exceeds the £30,000 threshold.'

The effect of all this is that, on any tribunal award of £30,000 or greater, the employee will receive a tax demand on the amount over £30,000. Therefore, for the employee to gain the actual amount assessed by the tribunal, some 'grossing up' (as described at **9.10.2**) is necessary so that the employee will have the correct amount net after payment of tax (i.e., in order for the employee to actually receive, after all tax is paid, say £35,000, the tribunal may have to award £40,000).

This begs the further question: can tribunals award more than the £55,000 cap as a grossed up figure so that, when tax is later paid under s. 401, an employee will have actually received the £55,000? On the wording of ERA 1996, s. 124 (inserted by ss. 33 and 37 ERA 1999) this appears unlikely as it says 'The amount . . . of the compensatory award . . . shall not exceed [£55,000]'.

It should also be noted that payments made for wrongful dismissal, payments in lieu of notice, the Basic Award, the Compensatory Award, *ex gratia* payments, and statutory or contractual redundancy payments will all have their own rules as to tax, but they all go to the calculation of the £30,000 trigger point.

The assessment point for tax will be the tax year in which *payment is received*. This may matter where the dismissal and hearing do not fall within the same tax year and the employee is unemployed at the time of hearing.

EXAMPLE

An employee who is awarded £60,000 (by a combination of the awards/damages noted above) will have this reduced to £55,000 by the capping restriction. Any tax due would then be calculated on the £55,000 figure. No grossing up would be available because the tribunal has reached its limit. Thus, instead of the £60,000 (or even the £55,500) which the employee has been awarded, there will be a subsequent tax bill on the excess of the award over £30,000. For instance, the employee would at some future date receive a bill from the Inland Revenue assessed on, say, 40 per cent of the excess (here 40% × £25,000 = £10,000). This obviously means that out of the original tribunal assesment of £60,000 the employee only ends up with £45,000 (£55,000 – £10,000).

10.15.2 The calculation

On the basis of all that we have discussed above we may now consider a fairly simple worked example. In this case, John Collins, aged 40, was employed at Hall & Lee Ltd for the past 10½ years. He was dismissed on the grounds of frequent absenteeism. His appeal within the disciplinary procedure failed. He earned £400 per week gross. He was given 10 weeks' pay in lieu of notice and has remained unemployed since his dismissal some 20 weeks ago (the present date being the date of the hearing). You represent the company and, on the facts, you had previously advised reaching a settlement. The company had offered £2,000; you could not persuade them to go higher and their offer was rejected. You will argue that the dismissal was not unfair but, on the facts, you are not optimistic. Thus, you also intend to argue that the applicant contributed to his dismissal owing, amongst other things, to his aggressive attitude at the disciplinary hearing. You have already advised that the company are likely to lose because although Hall & Lee went through the statutory D&DPs, they did not adhere strictly to their own procedures and really dismissed Collins in order to set an example for the workforce. Further, you have grave doubts over some of the company's witnesses. You have calculated that the compensation figure is likely to top £6,000.

The employment tribunal has now made a finding of unfair dismissal. All your fears were realised, except that you think you may have convinced the tribunal that Collins contributed to his dismissal. You are hoping for a 50 per cent reduction.

The tribunal must now assess the level of compensation due. Fortunately for you and the tribunal (and the authors), there is no loss of pension calculation to be made here. The 'recoupment of benefits' figure is calculated at £1,000.

We must consider three basic steps and then make a final calculation. These steps are laid out in **Figures 10.3** to **10.6**.

N.B.: In all these tables the figures apply to dismissals occurring in 2004–2005. The proposed annual increase (see 10.13.1.3 above) is usually laid before Parliament in January of each year to be implemented in February.

Calculating the Basic Award

STEPS TO BE TAKEN	*AMOUNT*	*NOTES ON MAKING THE CALCULATION*	*RUNNING TOTAL*
STEP 1: CALCULATE *GROSS* WEEKLY PAY (INCLUDING VALUE OF FRINGE BENEFITS)	£400	*EQUIVALENT TO APPROX. £20,800 PER ANNUM*	*n/a*
STEP 2: IMPOSE CEILING OF MAXIMUM WEEKLY AMOUNT ALLOWED UNDER BASIC AWARD	£270	*EQUIVALENT TO APPROX. £14,000 PER ANNUM*	*n/a*
STEP 3: CALCULATE WEEKLY PAY FIGURE FOR PURPOSES OF BASIC AWARD	£270	*NO REAL CALCULATION IS THEREFORE NECESSARY WHERE THE APPLICANT IS EARNING MORE THAN £14,000 PER ANNUM* *IF APPLICANT IS EARNING LESS THAN £14,000, THAT ACTUAL FIGURE WILL BE TAKEN, e.g., £10,000 per annum EQUALS approx. £192 per week*	*n/a*
STEP 4: MAKE INITIAL CALCULATION OF BASIC AWARD *(applicant has 10 years' service)*	£270 × 10 = £2,700	THE CALCULATION DEPENDS UPON TAKING LENGTH OF SERVICE × AGE FACTOR × WEEKLY PAY. IT IS SUBJECT TO A MAXIMUM OF *£8,100 (see **10.13.2** above)*	£2,700
STEP 5: MAKE NECESSARY DEDUCTIONS	£2,700 − £675 = £2025	*DEDUCTIONS MAY BE MADE FOR THE REASONS SET OUT IN **10.13.4** ABOVE* *HERE A SUM OF £675 HAS BEEN DEDUCTED FOR CONTRIBUTORY FAULT (REPRESENTING A FINDING OF 25% CONTRIBUTION)*	£2,025
STEP 6: NOTE CALCULATION OF BASIC AWARD	£2,025	*THIS FIGURE WILL BE CARRIED FORWARD TO THE FINAL CALCULATION IN FIGURE 10.6 BELOW*	

Figure 10.3 Method of calculating the Basic Award.

CALCULATING THE COMPENSATORY AWARD

1: *Calculating The 'Prescribed Element'*			
STEPS TO BE TAKEN	*AMOUNT*	*NOTES ON MAKING THE CALCULATION*	*RUNNING TOTAL*
STEP 1: CALCULATE WEEKLY PAY (INCLUDING VALUE OF FRINGE BENEFITS)	£272	*THIS TIME THE NET FIGURE MUST BE TAKEN AFTER DEDUCTING TAX AND NATIONAL INSURANCE.* **THE £270 CEILING DOES NOT APPLY HERE**	*n/a*
STEP 2: CALCULATE LOSS FROM DATE OF DISMISSAL TO DATE OF HEARING	£272 × 20 = £5,440	*THIS ASSUMES A 20 WEEK GAP BETWEEN DISMISSAL AND HEARING. THE ACTUAL GAP MAY BE GREATER OR LESS, DEPENDING ON THE COMPLEXITIES OF PREPARING THE CASE AND TRIBUNAL HEARING DATE PRESSURES.*	£5,440
STEP 3: DEDUCT ANY SUM IN RELATION TO EARNINGS FOR THIS PERIOD OR NOTICE/ PAYMENT IN LIEU OF NOTICE RECEIVED	£272 × 10 = £2,720 £5,440 − £2,720 = £2,720	*THE APPLICANT RECEIVED 10 WEEKS' PAY IN LIEU AS PER THE MINIMUM STATUTORY ENTITLEMENT (S. 86 ERA). THIS HAS TO BE ACCOUNTED FOR. THE SUM HERE IS THE NET PAYMENT [NOTE: SOME EMPLOYERS PAY THE GROSS SALARY—IN WHICH CASE IT WOULD BE THAT GROSS SUM WHICH WOULD BE DEDUCTED].*	£2,720
STEP 4: MAKE ANY NECESSARY FURTHER DEDUCTIONS	£2,720 − £680 = £2,040	*DEDUCTIONS MAY BE MADE FOR A NUMBER OF REASONS (SEE* ***10.13.4*** *ABOVE)* *HERE A SUM OF £680 HAS BEEN DEDUCTED FROM THE £2,720 CALCULATION FOR CONTRIBUTORY FAULT (REPRESENTING A FINDING OF 25% CONTRIBUTION)*	£2,040
STEP 5: NOTE THE CALCULATION OF THE PRESCRIBED *ELEMENT*	£2,040	*THIS SUM WILL NOT BE PAID OVER TO THE EMPLOYEE IMMEDIATELY. THE EMPLOYER MUST WAIT FOR NOTIFICATION OF DEDUCTIBLE SOCIAL SECURITY BENEFITS AND ONLY THEN PAY OVER THE REMAINDER.* **THIS FIGURE WILL BE CARRIED FORWARD TO THE FINAL CALCULATION IN FIGURE 10.6 BELOW**	

Figure 10.4 Method of calculating the Prescribed Element in the Compensatory Award.

CALCULATING THE COMPENSATORY AWARD

2: Calculating Other/Future Loss

STEPS TO BE TAKEN	*AMOUNT*	*NOTES ON MAKING THE CALCULATION*	*RUNNING TOTAL*
STEP 1: ASSESS LOSS FROM DATE OF HEARING TO FUTURE POINT	£ 272 × 15 = £4,080 *PLUS* £400 = £4,480	*THE TRIBUNAL WILL REFER TO THE* NORTON TOOL *V* TEWSON *PRINCIPLES (SEE ABOVE AT* ***10.13.3****).* *A KEY PART OF THIS CALCULATION IS THE FACT THAT THE TRIBUNAL MUST ASSESS FOR HOW LONG THE APPLICANT WILL REMAIN UNEMPLOYED OR SUFFER OTHER LOSS (E.G., IF IN EMPLOYMENT AT LOWER WAGE). HERE WE HAVE TAKEN AN ESTIMATE OF 15 WEEKS AT THE NETT WEEKLY SUM. WE HAVE THEN ADDED A FIGURE FOR THE REMAINING HEADS UNDER* NORTON TOOL	£4,480
STEP 2: MAKE ANY NECESSARY FURTHER DEDUCTIONS	£4,480 – £1,120 = £3,360	*DEDUCTIONS MAY BE MADE FOR A NUMBER OF REASONS (SEE* ***10.13.4*** *ABOVE). HERE A SUM OF £1,120 HAS BEEN DEDUCTED FOR CONTRIBUTORY FAULT (REPRESENTING A FINDING OF 25% CONTRIBUTION).* **NB***: AS WITH THE PRESCRIBED ELEMENT WE HAVE TAKEN THE POSITION HERE THAT THE TRIBUNAL IS SATISFIED THE APPLICANT HAS NOT RECEIVED ANY PAYMENTS WHICH MITIGATE HIS LOSS, NOR HAS THERE BEEN ANY FAILURE TO FIND SUITABLE WORK.*	£3,360
STEP 3: NOTE THE CALCULATION OF OTHER/ FUTURE LOSS	£3,360	***THIS FIGURE WILL BE CARRIED FORWARD TO THE FINAL CALCULATION IN FIGURE 10.6 BELOW***	

Figure 10.5 Method of calculating other/future loss in the Compensatory Award.

To obtain the final figure payable to the employee we need to make the following calculations:

Take Net Basic Award *(from Figure 10.3 above)*		£2,025
Add any Additional Award	*n/a here*	
Add Net Compensatory Award *(The Prescribed Element—taken from Figure 10.4 above)*	£2,040	
Add Net Compensatory Award *(This is the other/future loss—taken from Figure 10.5 above)*	£3,360	
Monetary Award (Compensatory Award plus any Additional Award)	£5,400	£5,400
Adding together the Basic Award plus Monetary Award gives the total award, though this is still subject to any recoupment figure	£2,025 + £5,400 £7,425	£7,425
Deduct recoupment figure		(£1,000)
Final Figure		£6,425

Figure 10.6 Making the final calculation.

11

Redundancy

11.1 Introduction

This chapter examines the meaning of redundancy, the obligations of the employer and the circumstances in which the law may give a redundant employee some redress. Rights to a redundancy payment first arose in 1965 and are now found in ERA 1996.

First and foremost, it needs to be stressed that *redundancy is merely a particular reason for dismissal*. Clients—both employers and employees—often miss that obvious point and use 'make redundant' instead of 'dismiss' in the belief it sounds less harsh. Indeed, the really trendy now use a range of euphemisms from 'downsizing' to allowing jobs to 'fall away'. Lawyers need to be more precise. So we shall refer to 'dismissal for redundancy'.

Why, then, is dismissal for redundancy any different from dismissal for anything else? The answer is that the dismissed employee may have any of four claims against the former employer, three of which are peculiar to this reason for dismissal:

(a) A complaint of wrongful dismissal. This is the one possible claim that is the same as for any other dismissal.

(b) A claim for a statutory redundancy payment.

(c) A complaint of unfair dismissal. Redundancy is one of the potentially fair reasons for dismissal.

(d) A claim for a higher level of severance payment based on some alleged contractual entitlement.

We shall return to those four possible claims in **11.5**. Meanwhile, though, we need to ask two important preliminary questions in *every* individual case:

(a) Has there been a dismissal?

This is dealt with in **11.2** below. The definition of dismissal for the purpose of entitlement to a redundancy payment is slightly broader than for the other purposes.

(b) Was that dismissal for redundancy?

This is dealt with in **11.3** below. The essence of redundancy is that the employee's job must have disappeared, possibly along with the jobs of other employees.

After looking at those preliminary questions we shall consider in **11.4** a list of steps an employer needs to work through in handling a redundancy fairly, a list drawn mostly from decided cases on unfair dismissal. That will bring us back to the employee's point of view in **11.5**.

The chapter will therefore be set out in the following four sections:

(a) The definition of dismissal.

(b) The definition of redundancy.

(c) Duties of the employer in carrying out a redundancy.

(d) Remedies for the redundant employee.

There is one final introductory comment to make. In general this book deals only with individual employment law: the law involving the employer and the employee. It does not attempt to cover collective employment law involving employers and trade unions, or other employee representatives. In the present chapter some blurring of that rule is necessary. For instance, if an employer failed to comply with a duty to consult employee representatives about which employees were selected for dismissal, that may appear to have little to do with the individual employees. However, the solicitor representing one of them will want to argue that proper consultation might have led to a different method of selection and to the dismissal of someone else instead of the client. Possibilities like that mean that we must mention in outline some of these collective matters at various points in the text.

11.2 The definition of dismissal

As we have seen, redundancy is a particular *reason* for dismissal. It is not something alternative to dismissal. So whether a particular set of circumstances constitutes a dismissal has to be measured against the tests that we considered in **Chapters 9** and **10**. In **Chapter 9** we noted that at common law a contract can end in various ways: resignation by the employee, dismissal by the employer, operation of law, and termination by mutual consent. As with unfair dismissal, dismissal is defined for purposes of redundancy payments more broadly than that. Indeed the two definitions in ERA 1996, s. 95 and s. 136 are almost the same, and we shall concentrate here on specific points relating only to redundancy payments. In both matters doubt can arise whether particular events do actually constitute a dismissal.

11.2.1 Uncertain dismissals

In practice the most common circumstance in which doubt arises as to whether there has been a dismissal is the giving by an employer of advance warning of redundancy. As we shall see shortly, employers are required to consult employees before issuing formal notices and such advance warnings are common. Sometimes the distinction between a warning and notice is a fine one.

The basic rule is that for a dismissal to be effective it must enable a precise date of termination to be ascertained: *Morton Sundour Fabrics Limited* v *Shaw* (1967) 2 ITR 84.

In *ICL* v *Kennedy* [1981] IRLR 28, the employer announced on 12 October 1979 that a factory was to be closed by the end of September 1980. K resigned so that her employment ended on 2 November 1979 and, *inter alia*, claimed that she was under notice of dismissal. The EAT held there was no dismissal. A general statement about closure did not permit precise ascertainment in October 1979 of *when* the particular employee would be dismissed.

11.2.2 Constructive dismissals

As we noted in **Chapter 10**, an employee is entitled to resign without notice if the employer has committed a serious or 'fundamental' breach of the contract of employment. Such a resignation is called a constructive dismissal, and under s. 95(1)(c) of ERA 1996 it qualifies as a dismissal for purposes of unfair dismissal law. By s. 136(1)(c) of ERA

1996 it similarly qualifies for purposes of entitlement to a redundancy payment. The statutory language is almost identical and the cases set out in **Chapter 10** therefore also apply here.

A constructive dismissal for redundancy might arise in circumstances like these. The production director in a company retires and is not to be replaced, at least for the time being. His secretary is told to go to work for the production manager. She refuses on the grounds it is a more junior post and resigns. If the secretary's contract was specifically as secretary to the production director, this is probably a constructive dismissal for redundancy. There will be no constructive dismissal for redundancy or anything else if her contract required her to perform whatever secretarial duties the employer requires. In that case she has been given an instruction within the terms of the contract.

11.2.3 Dismissals for redundancy payment purposes

There are three sets of circumstances set out in ERA 1996 which might not obviously seem to constitute a dismissal by the employer but which nevertheless qualify as such for purposes of entitlement to a redundancy payment:

(a) rejection of an alternative job during or after a trial period;

(b) anticipation of the employer's notice;

(c) resignation because of lay-off or short-time.

Case (c) rarely occurs. An employee who has been kept on short-time for a defined period may resign and serve notice on the employer that the resignation is a dismissal under s. 148 of ERA 1996. Cases (a) and (b) occur more often, however, and require further attention.

11.2.3.1 Trial periods for alternative jobs

An employer can escape the obligation to make a redundancy payment by offering a different job as an alternative to dismissal. The employee must be given a trial period in the new job—see **11.4.7** below. Rejection of the alternative job during the trial period is treated as a dismissal, but entitlement to a redundancy payment will depend on the reasons for rejection—see **11.4.7.1**.

11.2.3.2 Anticipation of the employer's notice

It often happens that the employer gives the employee notice of dismissal for redundancy and, during the notice period, the employee manages to find another job which it is necessary to start as soon as possible. Can the employee leave early and still claim a redundancy payment?

Such a resignation is regarded as a dismissal for redundancy and a redundancy payment is due provided the requirements of s. 136(3) of ERA 1996 have been met:

(a) The employee must be under actual notice of dismissal and not merely have received some vague or preliminary warning.

(b) The employee must give written notice of resignation. It must be submitted to the employer close enough to the original termination date that the outstanding period is less than the employee's contractual notice.

(c) The employer must not have served on the employee a counter-notice requiring the employee to remain in employment until the original termination date. If that is done, entitlement to a redundancy payment depends on an assessment by the employment tribunal of whether it would be just and equitable to award all or part of it in the light of the employer's reasons. See ERA 1996, s. 142.

There is a way of avoiding these requirements, established in *CPS Recruitment* v *Bowen* [1982] IRLR 54. B resigned in advance of the obligatory period, but it was held that the circumstances constituted a *consensual variation* of the date of termination set by the employer. That was sufficient to qualify as a dismissal by the employer, and a redundancy payment was due.

11.2.4 Volunteers for redundancy

An employer wishing to reduce the size of the workforce will often invite employees to volunteer to leave, perhaps offering some enhanced severance payment as an inducement, and/or giving the opportunity to those approaching retirement age to retire early with some augmentation of pension.

The question arises whether such circumstances constitute a dismissal for any purpose. There is no general answer: everything depends on the facts. Sometimes the termination of employment will be by mutual consent and there will be no dismissal by the employer: *Birch* v *University of Liverpool* [1985] ICR 470. Most *early retirements* are likely to be of this kind. In other cases, however, the employee may merely have intended to enquire what the severance payment might be, and in the absence of any clear mutual consent any termination is likely to be a dismissal.

11.3 The definition of redundancy

The essence of a dismissal for redundancy is that the employer requires fewer people. Redundancy can be contrasted with capability, conduct or the other reasons contemplated in s. 98(1) and (2) of ERA 1996, in that those other reasons imply some criticism of the employee, whose job then needs to be filled by someone else. Redundancy involves no criticism and no need to replace. Employees dismissed for redundancy may have been brilliant performers at their job; they lose their jobs solely because the employer is affected by circumstances often (if inelegantly) described as a redundancy situation.

11.3.1 The statutory definition

The statutory definition of redundancy is contained in s. 139(1) of ERA 1996:

> **139.**—(1) For the purposes of this Act an employee who is dismissed shall be taken to be dismissed by reason of redundancy if the dismissal is wholly or mainly attributable to—
>
> (a) the fact that his employer has ceased or intends to cease—
>
> (i) to carry on the business for the purposes of which the employee was employed by him, or
>
> (ii) to carry on that business in the place where the employee was so employed, or
>
> (b) the fact that the requirements of that business—
>
> (i) for employees to carry out work of a particular kind, or
>
> (ii) for employees to carry out work of a particular kind in the place where the employee was employed by the employer,
>
> have ceased or diminished or are expected to cease or diminish.

That definition is a good example of a statutory provision that is at first sight unintelligible and yet which uses precise words that practitioners will need to borrow when drafting documents. It will be found to envisage four possible sets of circumstances, each of which we shall consider further below:

(a) The employer is shutting down the business entirely. (The business disappears.)
(b) The employer is shutting down the business in the place where the employee works. (The place of work disappears.)
(c) The employer eliminates the work the employee does, either generally or in the particular place of work. (The job disappears in its entirety.)
(d) The number of people doing that job is to be reduced but not eliminated. (Fewer people are required in the job.)

Before we proceed any further, it is worth spotting two key omissions from the definition in s. 139(1):

(a) Nothing is said about the reasons why the employer's requirement ceases or diminishes. Indeed, s. 139(6) reinforces that point and states that the reduction may be permanent or temporary and for whatever reason. So a reduction in the workforce because of a loss of orders and a reduction because of a wish to increase profits are both covered: *Cook* v *Tipper* [1990] ICR 716.
(b) There is no suggestion of any objective test of the needs of the business. An employment tribunal will not normally go behind the employer's assessment of what the requirement was, at least in relation to examining whether the definition of redundancy is satisfied. (The question of whether the employer acted reasonably is another matter: see **11.4.1** below.)

11.3.2 The business disappears

If the employer ceases business, there is rarely in practice any dispute that the ending of employees' employment was by reason of redundancy. The only complication arises when the employer ceases business but someone else takes over. In many such cases there is no dismissal and no redundancy because employment is automatically taken over by the new owner—see **Chapter 12**.

11.3.3 The business survives but the job disappears

The other three cases—paragraphs (a)(i) and (b)(i) and (ii) in the statutory definition—are not quite so straightforward. Until recently there was much argument about the correct construction of the statutory language. With luck, the uncertainty has now been removed by the decision of the House of Lords in a Northern Irish case, *Murray* v *Foyle Meats Ltd* [1999] ICR 827. Before returning to that case it may help to explain the problem.

As a solicitor in practice you will find that private clients often misunderstand completely the legal notion of redundancy. They complain that the employer has described their dismissal as for redundancy but it cannot be so: their work remains to be done and it is in fact being shared out among other former colleagues. A friend-of-a-friend has told them that it is always jobs and not people who are redundant; on that reasoning their job clearly remains in existence. You will need to take the client back to the statutory language and explain that it is the *requirement of the business* for employees that matters. So the friend-of-a-friend is making a meaningless distinction. Yet you may still find that the statutory language causes problems.

Sometimes the uncertainty relates to the *work of a particular kind* that the employee was employed to do. In *Cowen* v *Haden* [1983] ICR 1, for example, Mr Cowen had been employed as a divisional contracts surveyor, having previously been a regional surveyor, until a heart attack made it difficult for him to travel and he was promoted to a more static job. He argued that the work he actually did was as a surveyor and that, when the employers decided to eliminate the particular job of divisional contracts surveyor, they should not simply have dismissed C as the holder of that post but rather should have made a selection from all surveyors. In the jargon that has since become widely used, the employee interpreted his work in that case by reference to a *function test*; the employer had used a *contract test*. The Court of Appeal held that it was the terms of the contract that mattered and the case became authority for the contract test.

In other cases an analogous question arises in a different form and relates to the place where the employee was employed. Lots of employees nowadays have some sort of mobility clause in their contracts, entitling the employer to move them, perhaps in defined circumstances or with defined notice, to other sites. If there is a surplus of employees at one site but not at another, it becomes important whether the place of work is to be defined by the terms of the contract including the mobility clause (a *contract test* again) or by reference to what actually happens and where the employee in fact works (the *factual* or *geographical* test)?

The preference of the authorities for the contract test in both cases was never popular with the employment tribunals, where lay members sometimes resented having to ignore practical reality in favour of outdated scraps of paper. Indeed some remarkably imaginative reasoning can be found in certain decisions.

In *Safeway Stores plc* v *Burrell* [1997] ICR 523, the EAT adopted a radical new approach which supposedly reverted to the language of the statute and resolved the conflict between the two tests. Mr Burrell was employed as petrol station manager at a supermarket. There was to be a major reorganisation of the management structure and B was invited to apply for a more junior job as petrol filling station controller. His duties as controller would be less than those set out in his contract as manager, but substantially the same as the work he actually performed. The two lay members of the employment tribunal applied the function test and concluded B was not redundant; the chairman felt bound by the *Cowen* v *Haden* authority to find that he was indeed redundant. The EAT held that both the contract test and the function test were predicated on a misreading of the statute and suggested that the correct approach was similar to the sequence of questions we set out at the start of the Chapter:

(a) Was the employee dismissed?

(b) If so, had the requirements of the employer's business for employees to carry out work of a particular kind ceased or diminished, or were they expected to cease or diminish?

(c) If so, was the dismissal of the employee caused wholly or mainly by the state of affairs identified at (b)?

A little later, the Court of Appeal, dealing with the issue of the place of work, took the opportunity of also going back to the statutory language in preference to either test in *High Table* v *Horst* [1998] ICR 409. The employees in that case were waitresses employed by an agency under a contract which provided for mobility, but they had in fact worked throughout their employment at one particular canteen. The Court of Appeal rejected the employers' contention that there was no 'redundancy situation' because of the mobility clause. They did so on the basis of a pragmatic consideration of all the factual circumstances, and related that to the statutory language in a way that depended more on the geographical test than the strict terms of the contract.

The saga was not yet over. In *Church* v *West Lancashire NHS Trust* [1998] ICR 423, a different division of the EAT, including the President, cast doubt on some aspects of the *Safeway* decision. Furthermore the *Cowen* v *Haden* decision had never been overruled by any court with the authority to do so.

That is the background against which the House of Lords decided *Murray* v *Foyle Meats Ltd* [1999] ICR 827. Murray was employed in a slaughterhouse and was described like everyone else as a 'meat plant operative'. In fact he worked exclusively in the slaughter hall. The employer decided to reduce the number of 'killing lines' from two to one and to reduce the number of staff accordingly. The industrial tribunal (Northern Ireland has not changed the name) had to address the question we have been discussing, applied in this case to the equivalent Northern Irish statutory wording: should they regard the work as that specified in the contract (the contract test) or should they consider what Murray actually did (the function test)? The tribunal and the Northern Ireland Court of Appeal both found that dismissal was for redundancy and the applicants appealed against that decision.

Their Lordships rejected the appeal. They described the statutory language as 'simplicity itself' and regarded both the contract test and the function test as 'missing the point'. They expressly approved the reasoning of the EAT in *Safeway Stores* that we summarised earlier. First a tribunal must ask whether there exists in a particular case one of the sets of economic circumstances described in s. 139 of ERA 1996, and secondly they must ask whether the dismissal was *attributable* to those circumstances. This pragmatic approach based on the statutory language must now be regarded as authoritative, but many practitioners have not found it easy to accept that 30-plus years of authorities are quite so instantly made obsolete. Furthermore, the new approach seems to make the statutory words *work of a particular kind* superfluous and there just may be some scope for further consideration in due course.

The *Murray* decision is so dismissive of most of the earlier cases that it is probably now unwise to rely on any of them. Indeed many reflect history and not the current state of the law. Early cases about redundancy were brought under the Redundancy Payments Act 1965, now consolidated into ERA 1996, and it suited the employee to argue that dismissal was for redundancy so as to claim a redundancy payment. It was the employer who argued otherwise. The arrival of unfair dismissal in 1972 meant that the tables were turned. Now the employer often argues redundancy as a potentially fair reason for dismissal, and it is the employee who resists that, suggesting that there was no valid reason for dismissal within ERA 1996, s. 98.

In *Shawkat* v *Nottingham City Hospital Trust (No. 2)* [2001] EWCA Civ 954; [2001] IRLR 555, the Court of Appeal used the *Murray* principle to rule that the question whether a business reorganisation did or not amount to a redundancy was a question of fact for the employment tribunal to decide.

11.4 Duties of the employer in carrying out a redundancy

A succession of statutes, beginning with the Redundancy Payments Act 1965, and a vast body of case law has now created an extensive list of duties for the employer to fulfil when reducing the size of the workforce. Failure to follow the steps the law expects may make resulting dismissals unfair. We shall therefore now proceed to examine the topic from the employer's standpoint. A solicitor advising a company how to handle a redundancy will need to cover the nine interlinking steps in **Figure 11.1**:

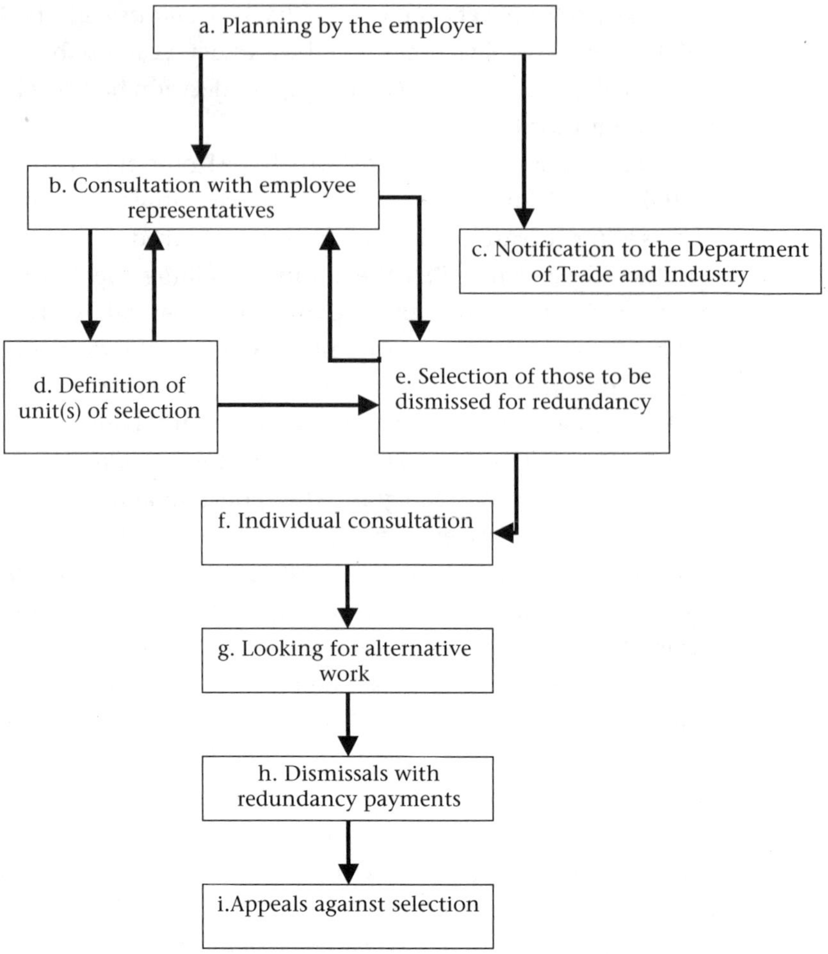

Figure 11.1 Scheme for handling a redundancy.

As the steps are drawn mostly from decided cases about unfair dismissal, this is also a useful checklist for a solicitor advising *either* party about such a complaint. Although the steps are set out in sequence, they interrelate closely and the list must also be viewed as a whole.

Although some of the steps may sound like common sense, some such organised approach by the employer is essential to avoid missing something important. The employment tribunals seem recently to have exposed dismissals for redundancy to particularly close scrutiny. Perhaps it is out of concern that, because employers tend to select for retention the best workers and to dismiss the poorest performers, an unscrupulous employer can use a redundancy to lose those who contribute least but are not so bad as ever to have been warned under a disciplinary procedure. A systematic approach is good evidence that the employer is behaving compassionately and fairly. In practice employers are most often found at fault in tribunal hearings about unfair dismissal in connection with steps (e), (f), and (g).

11.4.1 Planning the redundancy

The employer's wish to reduce numbers employed normally reflects some kind of business planning and employers often reach fairly clear decisions about what they wish to do. We shall see shortly that an essential part of the proper handling of a redundancy is consultation of employees and possibly also their representatives—see **11.4.2** and

11.4.6 below. It is therefore important that the solicitor contributes to the planning process while redundancies remain a *proposal* and before a firm *decision* to dismiss has been made.

11.4.1.1 The needs of the business

The employer needs to identify clearly why the redundancy is necessary at all. In due course the reason may have to be disclosed to employee representatives and the Department of Trade and Industry. The form HR 1 which can be used for notification to the Department suggests the following reasons: the employer may find that more than one is appropriate, or that other reasons beyond those on the list are involved:

(a) Lower demand for products or services.

(b) Completion of all or part of contract.

(c) Transfer of work to another site or employer.

(d) Introduction of new technology/plant/machinery.

(e) Changes in work methods or organisation.

The reason or reasons for the redundancy may dictate in whole or in part the way the employer then has to handle it. In particular, the selection of those to be dismissed will depend very much on the business plan, and especially on the question of what activities (and therefore what jobs) are to remain in the new, smaller organisation.

11.4.1.2 A programme of action

After being guided through all the steps in handling the redundancy, the employer will need to draw up a detailed programme setting out target dates for the various steps we are now considering. There are minimum periods for the collective consultation described in the next section and time will be required for other steps in the sequence.

11.4.1.3 Examining alternatives to redundancy

Except where the employer manages to achieve the required reduction in a workforce by volunteers, redundancy always involves the dismissal of people through no fault of their own and with likely consequent hardship in many cases. The tribunals expect employers to recognise the human cost of redundancy and to regard dismissal as a last resort in reducing costs. Other options should be explored, such as the reduction of overtime, or ceasing sub-contract work.

The point is reflected in a leading case on the handling of redundancies by an employer: *Williams* v *Compair Maxam* [1982] ICR 156. In the course of its decision the EAT set out five principles to be followed by the employer—see later at **11.4.5.2** for the full list. The first reads as follows.

> 1. The employer will seek to give as much warning as possible of impending redundancies so as to enable the union and employees who may be affected to take early steps to inform themselves of the relevant facts, consider possible alternative solutions and, if necessary, find alternative employment in the undertaking or elsewhere.

As with so many of these duties on the employer, the important point for the tribunal is not whether the employer has actually adopted any of these alternatives to dismissal, but rather that there is evidence that they were considered seriously. The employer must seek to reach agreement with the employee representatives about ways of avoiding or minimising dismissals for redundancy—see **11.4.2** below.

11.4.1.4 Fixing the number of dismissals

As we have seen, the statutory definition of redundancy speaks of the employer's *requirement* for people to do work. The implication is important. It is not some objectively determined requirement of the business but the *employer's* requirement, and in practice the tribunals almost always accept that it is the employer's responsibility to decide how many people the business needs.

Sometimes it is tempting to challenge the 'need for' redundancy on behalf of the dismissed employee on the basis that the employer could perfectly well have kept the employee in employment. This may be worth trying if the employer has failed to consider alternatives, or if it appears that the so-called redundancy is in truth a cover for dismissal for some other reason. Experience suggests it will rarely do much for the dismissed employee to argue in effect that the employer should have run the business in some other way. The employment tribunals will not 'second-guess' the employer and speculate what they might have done in the employer's shoes. See, for example, *Watling* v *Richardson* [1978] ICR 1048.

11.4.2 Consultation

11.4.2.1 The duty to consult employee representatives

Whenever 20 or more people are to be dismissed for redundancy, the employer is required to consult employee representatives. This is part of collective employment law and beyond the scope of the book, but any failure by the employer to consult collectively as the law requires may tend to make individual dismissals unfair and this topic cannot be ignored.

The duty appears in TULRCA 1992, s. 188. A solicitor advising a private client may find the following points of help in deciding whether it is worth exploring further. Anyone wanting to know more about this topic should refer to one of the standard works on collective issues or on redundancy.

(a) The statutory duty to consult arises if 20 or more dismissals are proposed. Minimum periods (of 30 or 90 days) are specified depending on the number involved.

(b) Where the employer normally negotiates terms and conditions of employment with a trade union, consultation must be with union representatives. In those circumstances the tribunals will probably expect the employer to discuss all redundancies with the union, even where less than 20 are involved. In cases of 20 or more where there is no union recognition, representatives must be elected.

(c) Amongst the matters about which the employer will need to consult are means of avoiding dismissals altogether, reducing the numbers to be dismissed and mitigating the consequences and also the proposed method of selection—see **11.4.4** and **11.4.5** below.

(d) 'Consultation' is defined by the statute as an attempt to reach agreement with the representatives.

(e) A claim that the employer has failed to consult as required may be presented to the employment tribunal by the trade union or other employee representatives, or (subject to some restrictions) by any of the employees who have been dismissed as redundant.

(f) This collective consultation about proposed redundancy is quite separate from the individual consultation about selection for dismissal—see **11.4.6** below. Neither replaces the other.

(g) The law does not forbid the issue of individual notices of dismissal during the consultation process so that notice and consultation run concurrently. However, notices must not be issued so early in the consultation period as effectively to make consultation a sham: *NUT* v *Avon County Council* [1978] ICR 626. For example, it would undermine consultation if the employer identified individuals for dismissal or issued notices while the topics at (c) above were still under active discussion—see *Middlesbrough Borough Council* v *TGWU* [2002] IRLR 332.

11.4.2.2 Remedy for failure to consult

If a claim has been presented to the employment tribunal that the employer has not consulted as required and the claim is established, the tribunal has a mandatory duty under TULRCA 1992, s. 189(2) to make a declaration to that effect. It has a discretion to make a protective award. This is effectively an order to the employer to keep the redundant employees in employment, or at least to pay their wages, for a defined protected period.

Since amendments of the rules in 1999, the maximum possible protective award is 90 days, which can be a significant extra cost for the employer. There may however be an even greater consequence. A serious procedural failing like inadequate collective consultation (especially if of sufficient culpability as to have caused the employment tribunal to have exercised its discretion to make a protective award) may well lead to a finding of unfair dismissal since the decision of the House of Lords in *Polkey* v *A. E. Dayton Services* [1988] ICR 142—see **11.4.6**, below. An award of compensation is not automatic but could well follow if it can be shown that better consultation might have changed the final result.

Where a solicitor acting for a private client suspects that collective consultation was required but has been inadequate or absent, it is always worth investigating whether anyone has made a claim about that failing. If so, a copy of the decision should be obtained, or, if the other case remains to be decided, an application should be made to the employment tribunal to delay listing of the individual claim until after the collective claim has been decided.

If no claim has been presented, an attempt should be made to find out why not: for example, a trade union may have consented to a curtailment of the consultation process in order to obtain some other benefit (like notice to be paid in lieu in order to escape tax) for its members and any criticism of the employer in such circumstances could be counterproductive.

11.4.3 Notification to the Department of Trade and Industry

An employer proposing to dismiss as redundant between 20 and 99 employees must notify the Department of Trade and Industry 30 days before the first dismissal takes effect. If 100 or more employees are to be dismissed the period is 90 days. The precise details are set out in TULRCA 1992, s. 193.

Although the statute speaks of notifying the Secretary of State, in practice the duty is easily met by completing the standard form HR 1, obtainable from the Department of Trade and Industry. A copy of the form must also be given to employee representatives.

The form HR 1 is reproduced on pages 322 and 323.

11.4.4 Definition of the unit of selection

We noticed in **11.3** above that the definition in s. 139(1) of ERA 1996 allowed four kinds of redundancy:

(a) The business disappears.

(b) The place of work disappears.

(c) The job disappears in its entirety.

(d) Fewer people are required in the job.

Department of Trade and Industry | Trade Union and Labour Relations (Consolidation) Act 1992

Advance notification of redundancies

0390/1

What you are required to do

As an employer, you are required by law to notify a **proposal to make redundant 20 or more employees within a 90 day period.**

- If 20 to 99 redundancies may occur at one establishment, ***you must notify us at least 30 days before the first dismissal.***
- If 100 or more redundancies may occur at one establishment, ***you must notify us at least 90 days before the first dismissal.***
- The date on which we receive your completed form is ***the date of notification.***

How to complete this form

- Use a separate form for each establishment where 20 or more redundancies may occur within a 90 day period.
- Write your answers in CAPITALS, as this will make it easier for us to read.
- Where tick boxes appear, please tick those that apply.
- If there is not enough space for your answers, please use a separate sheet of paper and attach it to this form.
- Please return the completed form to:
  Department of Trade and Industry
  Redundancy Payments Office
  Hagley House
  83-85 Hagley Road
  Birmingham B16 8QG
- You must send a copy of this notification to the representatives of the employees being consulted.
- If the circumstances outlined in this form change, please notify us immediately.

Data Protection Act 1998

We will store the information you give us in a computer system, which will help us deal with it more efficiently.

- We may give it to selected government agencies and Training and Enterprise Councils/Local Enterprise Companies and Careers Services, who may offer to help you deal with proposed redundancies.
- We will ***not*** give it to any other agencies or organisations without first obtaining your consent.

Further Information

- A more detailed explanation of this subject can be found in our booklet PL833 "Redundancy consultation and notification".
- You can get booklet PL833 from any Jobcentre

1 Employer's Details

Name

Address

Post Code

Telephone number

2 Employer's Contact

Name

Address *(if different to that given at 1)*

Post Code

Telephone number *(if different to that given at 1)*

3 Establishment where redundancies proposed

Address given at **1** ☐

Address given at **2** ☐

Address different to that given at **1** or **2** ☐ ▶ ***please give address below***

Post Code

Nature of main business

HR1 (Rev1) — **over ▶**

4 Reasons for redundancies

Please tick one or more boxes to show the main reason(s) for the proposed redundancies:

- lower demand for products or services ☐ **A**
- completion of all or part of contract ☐ **B**
- transfer of work to another site or employer ☐ **C**
- introduction of new technology/plant/machinery ☐ **D**
- changes in work methods or organisation ☐ **E**
- another reason ▶ ***please give brief details below*** ☐ **F**

5 Staff numbers/redundancies at this establishment

Occupational group	Number of employees	Number of possible redundancies
Manual		
Clerical		
Professional		
Managerial/technical		
Other		
Totals		
Number of long-term trainees included in above who may be made redundant		
Number of long-term trainees under 20 years of age included in above who may be made redundant		

6 Closure of establishment

Do you propose to close the establishment?

Yes ☐

No ☐

7 Timing of redundancies

Date of first proposed redundancy

Date of last proposed redundancy

8 Method of selection for redundancy

Please give brief details of how you will choose the employees to be made redundant

9 Consultation

Are any of the groups employees, who may be made redundant, represented by a recognised trade union?

Yes ☐ ▶ ***please list these trade unions below***

No ☐

Have you consulted any of the trade unions listed above?

Yes ☐ ▶ ***Date consultation started***

No ☐

Have you consulted elected representatives of the employees?

Yes ☐ ▶ ***Date consultation started***

No ☐

Declaration

I certify that the information given on this form is, so far as I know, correct and complete.

Signed

Date

Position held

For our use

6/98 Guilbert Niceday 29885

Case (d) is different from the other three: not everyone doing the particular job is to be dismissed, but only one or more out of several. Which employees will the employer choose to dismiss and which to retain? This is the very important question of selection, to which we shall return shortly in **11.4.5**.

First, though, there is an important preliminary point: what exactly is 'the job' in which fewer people are required? If that sounds like a non-issue, it is certainly not in practice. For example, many modern methods of production demand considerable versatility from a workforce. So a particular person may operate this machine today, that machine tomorrow and have been doing something else entirely yesterday. To say that the redundancy affects work on one machine in particular reduces selection to a game of musical chairs in which the music stops whenever the employer happens to make the selection. The group from which a selection is made is known as the 'unit of selection'.

This issue is not at all easy for the employer. If the unit of selection is defined too narrowly, employees who are selected will complain that a wider group should have been considered, in which case they themselves might well have kept their jobs. If the unit of selection is drawn too broadly, there will be some employees who argue that the work they were doing remains wholly unaffected by the redundancy, so that their dismissal was not really for redundancy at all. In some circumstances different people could pursue the two arguments about the same selection.

Until recently, it seemed that the second group might well have a good argument. In *Church* v *West Lancashire NHS Trust* [1998] ICR 423, Mr Church was employed in computer services. The hospital trust, like a good many employers nowadays, wanted completely to reorganise that department. Every available job was 'up for grabs' and C, like other employees, was assessed for his suitability. He was unsuccessful, but his own job remained in existence. Could he be said to be dismissed for redundancy when he had in fact been dismissed to make way for someone else, and it was another person's job that had disappeared? In *Safeway Stores plc* v *Burrell* [1997] ICR 523, the EAT had held that such a *bumped redundancy* (as the jargon has it) was indeed a redundancy. In *Church* the EAT noted that that part of the *Safeway* decision was *obiter*, went back to the statutory language and held that *bumping* was not redundancy.

Now we have to review both the *Safeway* and *Church* decisions by the EAT in the light of the House of Lords decision in *Murray* v *Foyle Meats Ltd* [1999] ICR 827 (see **11.3.3** above), which specifically approved the reasoning of the EAT in *Safeway*. Their Lordships held that a tribunal must first ask whether there exists in a particular case one of the sets of economic circumstances described in s. 139 of ERA 1996, and secondly whether the dismissal was attributable to those circumstances. Under that pragmatic approach, which takes an overall view of the employer's requirements, it seems inevitable that *Church* would now be decided differently. Bumping may now fall within the definition of redundancy.

Those cases guide the employment tribunal in the view it should take if the employer *chooses* to adopt an approach of bumping. There is no clear rule of law that tells the employer how to define a unit of selection. Provided regard is had to the principles in *Safeway*, the employer is usually free to define the job in whichever way best suits the business. Sometimes, though, the choice is limited. In the example we considered of the versatile machine operators, it is almost inevitable that the unit of selection must include all machine operators.

Cases where the employer will need to take particular care in defining the unit of selection include the following:

(a) where there is some versatility or flexibility amongst employees affected by the redundancy (as above);

(b) where people with similar skills or doing a similar job are employed in several departments or functions: should the employer take each such group separately or together?

(c) where people doing similar but not identical work are employed on different grades or their equivalent, reflecting different degrees of skill: is it appropriate to divide the function into several units or to take it all together, and (if the latter) how does the employer ensure a result giving the right balance of 'chiefs and Indians'?

In all these instances, the important point is that the employer should have considered the choice of the unit of selection with some care and be able to justify the result logically to an employment tribunal. There are no general rules of law as to which answer should be given. So the solicitor acting for a dismissed employee will usually achieve more by showing that the employer failed to address the point than by arguing that a particular choice lay outside the band of reasonableness.

So far this question of the unit of selection has been examined only in relation to the fourth kind of redundancy, that where the job is not to be eliminated but numbers are just to be reduced. Perhaps it is already obvious that the point is in fact of somewhat wider application. When in case (c) we speak of the job as *disappearing*, exactly the same consideration needs to be given to what may be the job. It is not good enough for the employer to treat a particular employee as redundant on the basis that that individual's job has disappeared if one of the examples described above raises doubt about the definition of that job. Similarly in case (b), an employee who is required to be mobile between several places of work may be unfairly selected for redundancy if that is done solely on the basis of his or her happening to be working at a particular site that is being closed on the day the selection is carried out—see **11.3.3** above.

This issue of the choice of the unit of selection is one that ought to be included in collective consultation about the redundancy. Sometimes, even where employee representatives are unwilling to agree with the employer a method of selection for dismissal from within the unit, it is still possible for the two sides to reach agreement about the definition of the unit. The employer will need to consider properly any suggestions put forward by employee representatives: hence the arrows in both directions in **Figure 11.1**.

11.4.5 Selection

We now need to turn to the aspect of the employer's handling of the redundancy which is perhaps more likely than any other to lead to a claim in the employment tribunal of unfair dismissal—the selection of which employee or employees in the unit are to be dismissed and which retained. More tribunal applications are concerned with alleged unfair selection than with any other aspect, and the parties probably have radically different outlooks.

Employees and trade unions often prefer the employer to select for dismissal on the basis of length of service alone, arguing that this is impartial, well understood by those affected and consequently generally accepted as fair. The practice of 'last-in-first-out' is widely referred to by its initials: LIFO.

The employer probably has quite a different view. If the workforce is being drastically reduced, it is extremely important to the employer that the business retains those key skills that are essential to its survival. Some process of evaluating employees' skills and suitability is therefore required.

At one stage there was widespread public belief that LIFO was the normal way to select for redundancy, and it is possible to detect something close to a legal presumption to that effect in some early cases: *International Paint* v *Cameron* [1979] ICR 429. By 1987, however,

LIFO had been described as outdated: *Suflex* v *Thomas* [1987] IRLR 435. Meanwhile some form of evaluation of employees had become common, and in 1982 the EAT laid down some important guidelines about the way it should be done: *Williams* v *Compair Maxam* [1982] ICR 156. Those guidelines still make *Compair Maxam* the leading case on selection, but various others have followed since.

We need to consider two main kinds of case—those where some method of selection has been established on a previous occasion, and those where, because no such precedent exists, a method has to be designed from scratch.

11.4.5.1 Use of established criteria, customary or agreed

Until 1994 there was an important rule that the selection of an individual employee for dismissal on the ground of redundancy would be *automatically unfair* if it was in breach of a customary arrangement or agreed procedure. There was an exception if special reasons could be shown to justify departure from the customary arrangement or agreed procedure, but the cases gave a very narrow interpretation to those terms.

The rule caused employers great difficulty. There were many cases where an agreement had been reached during an earlier redundancy, for example, providing for selection by LIFO. Now that numbers were already much reduced, it was impossible for the employer to continue to operate LIFO without risking the loss of employees with skills vital to the survival of the business. The Draconian effect of a rule providing automatically unfair dismissal made it difficult to know how to cope with this practical problem.

The Deregulation and Contracting Out Act 1994 repealed the rule of *automatically* unfair dismissal. It does not give employers a free hand to ignore all past practice or to break existing agreements. Any such action by the employer is now assessed alongside any other consideration of reasonable behaviour under ERA 1996, s. 98(4).

It should not of course be assumed that all past practices are necessarily bad or in need of changing. Many employers who recognise trade unions have reached an agreement on a method of selection for redundancy that can be operated whenever the need arises and is regarded as satisfactory by all concerned.

11.4.5.2 Design of a method of selection

We now need to consider what should happen if there is no satisfactory past practice to rely on. How should the employer select who is to go and who to stay?

There is no single right answer to the question. Nowadays, though, the most common solution by far is to choose a set of criteria and to mark each employee under each of them, to add up the resulting scores, and to select for dismissal those whose total is lowest. We shall look further at this method shortly. It is not the only possibility, however.

Occasionally employers are still content to select on the basis of LIFO despite all its shortcomings.

Sometimes the decision rests on a single criterion. For example, if a company has a European sales force of two, one of whom speaks French and the other French and German, it is probable that the second will need to stay and the first to be dismissed, irrespective of their relative sales abilities. The only alternative choice would limit the sales territory available to the company.

Occasionally, the needs of the business can be set out in a sequence of decreasing priorities, so that they can be applied as a series of criteria. So, for example, if there is a problem of an ageing workforce, the employer may decide that the needs of the business are best served by choosing first for dismissal those close to retirement age. Other criteria may then follow to choose a second and third group.

EXEMPLARY MANAGEMENT LIMITED
ASSESSMENT FOR REDUNDANCY SELECTION – JANUARY 2005

Employee's Name .... Department .... Clock No ....

Job .... Date of start .... Date of birth ....

	D **1 point**	C **2 points**	B **3 points**	A **4 points**	**Factor**	**Score**
1 Length of service as at 31 December 2004	Less than 2 years	2 years but less than 5	5 years but less than 10	10 years or more	X2	
2 Attendance record **a) Days absent during 2003-04**	More than 20	20 or less but more than 10	10 or less but more than 5	5 or less	X1	
b) Number of absences	11 or more	6-10	3-5	0-2	X1	
3 Quantity of work	Requires supervision to achieve acceptable level.	Average worker for the grade, normally achieves expectations without frequent supervision.	Always achieves targets and often exceeds them.	An exceptionally good worker, consistently exceeding targets by a substantial amount	X3	
4 Quality of work	Correction of errors is often necessary; work needs to be checked.	Occasionally makes errors requiring correction, but quality usually acceptable.	Seldom makes errors. Usually reliable.	Almost never makes mistakes. Consistently reliable.	X3	
5 Versatility	Limited to skills of own job.	Can carry out tasks closely related to usual job.	Can undertake a broad range of work within department or discipline.	Capable of a wide range of work within the discipline and outside it.	X4	
6 Adaptability	Tends to resist change	Adapts to change slowly	Generally accepts change and adapts well to new ideas	Shows a positive attitude to change and adapts on own initiative.	X3	

Total

Assessment performed by .... Date..................................

Approved by .... Date..................................

Checked by Personnel Department.................................. Date..................................

More often, the various factors all have some part to play and it is better to apply them simultaneously. This brings us back to the score-sheet approach we have already mentioned as the most common, certainly amongst large employers. An example of a score-sheet, or 'matrix' as it is often described, is shown at **Figure 11.1**. It is quite common to attach different weighting factors to the different criteria and to have some predetermined tie-break arrangement to distinguish those with equal totals. The tie-break may well be length of service.

Because the matrix approach is so common, much of the guidance to be drawn from the cases is actually expressed in those terms. Indeed the leading case on methods of selection—*Williams* v *Compair Maxam* [1982] ICR 156—is based on that approach. We have already encountered the first of five principles set out by the EAT in that decision. It is now necessary to set out the remainder.

(1. The employer will take steps in collaboration with any trade union to avoid dismissals altogether.)

2. The employer will consult the union as to the best means by which the desired management result can be achieved fairly and with as little hardship to the employees as possible. In particular, the employer will seek to agree with the union the criteria to be applied in selecting the employees to be made redundant. When a selection has been made, the employer will consider with the union whether the selection has been made in accordance with those criteria.
3. Whether or not an agreement as to the criteria to be adopted has been agreed with the union, the employer will seek to establish criteria for selection which so far as possible do not depend solely upon the opinion of the person making the selection but can be objectively checked against such things as attendance record, efficiency at the job, experience, or length of service.
4. The employer will seek to ensure that the selection is made fairly in accordance with these criteria and will consider any representations the union may make as to such selection.
5. The employer will seek to see whether instead of dismissing an employee he could offer him alternative employment.

Since those five principles were first set out in 1982 there has been some criticism of the EAT for adopting the approach in that and several other cases of setting out guidelines for future reference as if they were a statute or a code of practice. Nevertheless, the principles have never been overturned and remain valid. Indeed subsequent cases have tended to enlarge them. We can therefore set out some advice for employers in designing a matrix:

(a) Discuss it with trade unions or employee representatives and 'seek to agree . . . criteria': *Williams* v *Compair Maxam*.

(b) Include some factors on the list that are capable of objective measurement and are not solely subjective opinion: *Williams* v *Compair Maxam*. Subjective judgments can be given a greater objectivity if two or more people are involved.

(c) Ensure that enough guidance is given to those doing the marking that they clearly understand what they are to do: *Rolls Royce Motors* v *Dewhurst* [1985] ICR 869. In practice, however, a competent manager or supervisor is unlikely to experience much difficulty if the categories are clearly defined.

(d) Be careful of vague factors like attitude which appear to give excessive scope for personal prejudice, but do not necessarily exclude them if relevant: *Graham* v *ABF* [1986] IRLR 90.

(e) It is best to include length of service as a factor, although there is no definite authority that its omission is wrong. Using it merely as a tie-break is probably not enough: *Westland Helicopters* v *Nott* (1989, unreported, EAT/342/88).

(f) Avoid any selection criterion which is directly or indirectly discriminatory on grounds of sex, race, or trade union membership or activities. See **Chapter 6** about sex and race; **11.4.5.3** below about trade union membership.

(g) Exercise particular care when a factor such as rate of work, quality of output or attendance record may be influenced by the employee's disability: see **6.9** above about disability discrimination.

(h) Ensure that the assessments are made accurately and fairly according to the criteria: *Williams* v *Compair Maxam*. Although this sounds like common sense, simple errors often occur in practice, e.g., misreading a sickness record or making a mistake of arithmetic.

(i) Give some thought to whether employees selected for dismissal will be permitted to see the marks scored by other employees in the unit of selection—during individual consultation, on appeal, only during employment tribunal proceedings (see **13.8.3** below), or never. This is a difficult issue: most employers do not wish to risk demotivating those who, unbeknown to themselves, were 'near misses' for selection.

The example of a matrix in **Figure 11.1** attempts to reflect that advice. In an example at the end of the chapter we shall look at one that does not. The authors' anecdotal experience suggests that the employment tribunals are exposing selection methods to closer scrutiny than before. Employers sometimes appear to use redundancy as an opportunity to get rid of those who may have been poor performers but who have never been so bad as to suffer any disciplinary action. While tribunals are unwilling to fault an employer's method of selection simply on the basis that they might have done differently—see, for example, *British Aerospace Plc* v *Green* [1995] ICR 1006—many established methods are very susceptible to challenge, especially on the grounds of disability discrimination.

11.4.5.3 Selection related to trade union membership or activities

Under s. 153 of TULRCA 1992, a selection for redundancy is automatically unfair if the reason for it is the employee's trade union membership or activities.

Selection based on trade union membership or activities does not have to be deliberate. An evaluation influenced by trade union activity, perhaps because a shop steward was unable to achieve as high an output as some others because of the amount of time spent on trade union business, may well be caught by this rule.

11.4.6 Individual consultation

After the process of selection, the employer will have decided who is to stay and who to go but the employees concerned do not yet know. The next step is to inform them.

The law makes it very clear that this step involves much more than merely conveying information. Redundant employees have the right to be consulted individually about their redundancy before notice of dismissal is given. The leading case on this individual consultation is the House of Lords' decision in *Polkey* v *A. E. Dayton Services* [1988] ICR 142. It is important and well worth reading. As this requirement forms part of the concept of reasonableness in unfair dismissal it has been possible to argue that consultation is inappropriate or superfluous in particular cases, although the circumstances in which the tribunals have been prepared to accept such an argument have become fewer as a consultative approach to employment relations generally has become more established. In *Mugford* v *Midland Bank* [1997] ICR 399, for example, it was suggested that the employer would have to show that consultation would have been an utterly futile exercise.

Now the requirement has acquired statutory backing from 1 October 2004. The statutory dismissal and disciplinary procedures under EA 2002 (see **10.9.2** above) apply to all dismissals as well as disciplinary action, including dismissals for redundancy. So the three stages apply: employers must set out the grounds for dismissal in writing, inviting the employee to a meeting; employers must hold such a meeting before dismissal; employers must provide a right of appeal. Strictly speaking the statutory right of the employee to be accompanied under ERA 1999, s. 10 (see **5.3.1** above) does not apply to such meetings as they are not disciplinary hearings, but normal standards of reasonableness may still require it to be provided. Under ERA, s. 98A(2) as now inserted from 1 October 2004 it is possible for the employer to argue that dismissal should still be fair if failure to follow the statutory dismissal procedure made no difference to the decision to dismiss, a limited restoration of a possibility that seemed to have been closed in 1988 by the *Polkey* decision. The extent to which the tribunals are now willing to accept such an argument remains to be seen in the cases, but it seems unlikely to be widespread.

What is the employer actually obliged to do? This question is not precisely answered by the *Polkey* decision, although *Rowell* v *Hubbard Group Services* [1995] IRLR 195 gives useful guidance on the need for consultation to be proper and genuine. The authors offer the following as an indication of the approach of the tribunals:

(a) Do not rush the process. Encourage the employee to be accompanied by a colleague. Recognise that the employee may be in a state of some shock from the announcement, and allow time for a response.

(b) Explain to the individual why the particular job is affected by redundancy at all.

(c) Explain why this particular employee is at risk of selection for redundancy, but do nothing at this stage that could be interpreted as giving notice of dismissal. If an assessment matrix has been used, show it to the employee and explain the marks given.

(d) Give the employee and/or the representative a few days to express any views about (b) or (c) and consider them properly and genuinely. In particular, examine any representation which suggests that the assessment may have been performed incorrectly.

(e) Discuss whether there is any possibility of alternative work—see **11.4.7** below—or any other alternative solution.

(f) Do not finalise the redundancy list or issue any notices of dismissal until the process of individual consultation has been completed. Alterations may be required.

(g) Hold a second interview to confirm the selection if no alternative solution has been found. Issue notice of dismissal only at this stage.

The processes of collective consultation with employee representatives and individual consultation are not alternative processes. However extensive the first, the second is necessary too: see *Rolls Royce Motors* v *Price* [1993] IRLR 203. The required scope of individual consultation may well be reduced in practice by collective consultation, especially if the trade union or other employee representatives have agreed some aspects of the redundancy. See *Mugford* v *Midland Bank plc* [1997] ICR 399. In cases where there has been no collective consultation, individual consultation needs to be especially thorough and to include at least some elements of the topics considered at **11.4.2.1** above.

Solicitors advising smaller employers may well find that these requirements are not well understood. There are still employers without previous experience of handling a redundancy who believe that the whole process can be completed effortlessly in a couple of hours. Thus, whilst selection of individuals may be the most common issue in tribunal applications concerning large companies, lack of consultation is very common amongst smaller ones.

11.4.7 Alternative work

The employer will next want to consider the possibility of alternative work for a redundant employee. Curiously this step arises for two quite different reasons. First, the employer, by making an offer of suitable alternative work, may escape the liability of making a redundancy payment if the employee unreasonably refuses it: ERA 1996, s. 141. Secondly, and quite unconnected with that express statutory provision, there is the general requirement on the employer as part of acting reasonably to seek alternative solutions to whatever problem caused the redundancy, including looking for alternative work for the employee who might otherwise be dismissed. Without that step dismissal may be unfair. We shall look at both aspects in turn.

11.4.7.1 Alternative work as an alternative to a redundancy payment

The rule in s. 141 of ERA 1996 permits two possible kinds of offer by the employer as a means of avoiding a redundancy payment: an offer of employment which is identical to the old job in all respects, and an offer of some different job which is suitable for the employee. The first is unusual in practice and generally arises only if the employer, having dismissed the employee, then finds that the dismissal was a mistake and that the business now has a continuing requirement for that employee after all. In either case, though, the entitlement to a redundancy payment is lost only if the employee unreasonably refuses the offer. In the more common case of a different job, the two elements of a *suitable* job and an *unreasonable* refusal must be considered separately.

The question whether the offer is of suitable employment is primarily a matter of objective fact for the tribunal to assess: *Cambridge and District Co-op* v *Ruse* [1993] IRLR 156. All aspects of the job can be taken into account, including, for example, the level of skill involved and not only the pay and conditions: *Standard Telephones and Cables* v *Yates* [1981] IRLR 21.

The question whether the employee has refused the offer unreasonably often requires consideration of broadly the same matters, but viewed this time from the subjective standpoint of the individual employee: *Carron* v *Robertson* (1967) 2 ITR 484. It is not necessary to imagine the viewpoint of a notional reasonable employee nor to take account of the views of other people who may have been made the same offer: *Everest's Executors* v *Cox* [1980] ICR 415 and *Fowler (John) (Don Foundry)* v *Parkin* [1975] IRLR 89. Thus, for example, if the employer closes one factory and offers alternative jobs at another a few miles away, some employees who have farther to travel to work in consequence may be found to have refused reasonably, whilst others living close to the new jobs may have refused unreasonably.

It is not entirely clear from the cases how far reasons for a reasonable refusal have to be related to the job. The better view seems to be that there must be some connection. Refusal for a wholly extraneous reason like the wish to take another job would almost certainly be unreasonable.

11.4.7.2 The timing of such an offer

For an offer of alternative work to be effective in denying an employee a redundancy payment the new job must start no later than four weeks after the ending of the old job: ERA 1996, s. 141(1). The offer must be made before the old job ends.

In every case where the employee accepts different, alternative work the first four weeks of performing the new job are to form a trial period, unless the parties expressly agree a longer period for purposes of retraining. At any time during that period or at the end of it, the employee can reject the new job and elect to be treated as dismissed for the purposes of receiving a redundancy payment: ERA 1996, s. 138.

11.4.7.3 Alternative work as part of reasonableness

The cases such as *Williams* v *Compair Maxam* [1982] ICR 156—and in particular the first of the five principles we set out at **11.4.1.3**—as well as the codes of practice make it clear that the employer should always try to avoid dismissals for redundancy if possible. In almost every case that requirement will oblige the employer to take the trouble to look on behalf of every redundant employee for possibilities of continuing employment in the same company or in 'associated' companies, i.e., other companies within the same group of companies: *Vokes* v *Bear* [1974] ICR 1.

In some groups of companies where there are many plants scattered over a wide area, the requirement in *Vokes* v *Bear* is demanding. More recent cases such as *Quinton Hazell* v *Earl* [1976] ICR 296, make it clear that the duty of the employer is to take reasonable steps to look, but not to conduct an exhaustive search. The employer is not permitted to eliminate some possibilities because of an assumption that the employee will not be interested, perhaps because the alternative job is of a lower status: *Avonmouth Construction Co.* v *Shipway* [1979] IRLR 14. The employee should be given the chance to decide, and this is one of the purposes of the individual consultation we considered at **11.4.6** above (see also *Huddersfield Parcels* v *Sykes* [1981] IRLR 115).

11.4.7.4 'Bumping'

Sometimes a redundant employee A is capable of doing other jobs in an organisation and would like to take B's job thereby displacing B who is dismissed instead, a process often referred to as *bumping* (discussed at **11.4.4** above). Maybe B is of much shorter service. The general rule is that the employer is not required to accede to A's wish. Most employers refuse to do so, reflecting the view of the EAT in *Elliott Turbomachinery* v *Bates* [1981] ICR 218 that bumping, a term they described as 'singularly inelegant and esoteric,' was a recipe for industrial unrest amounting to chaotic proportions if applied wholesalely and indiscriminately. (Note that, since the House of Lords decision in *Murray* v *Foyle Meats Ltd* [1999] ICR 827 mentioned at **11.4.4**, employers can no longer safely resist bumping by arguing that B's dismissal falls outside the definition of redundancy.) However A may sometimes be able to present the same case in a different way, by arguing that A and B are doing such similar jobs that they should have been considered together and the unit of selection was in fact too narrowly defined (again see **11.4.4**).

11.4.8 Redundancy payments

The original reason for a separate legal category of dismissal for redundancy was that it qualified the employee for a redundancy payment, subject to certain rules. So the next duty for the employer is to see what redundancy payment is due to each of the dismissed employees. There are two matters to consider: statutory redundancy payments and contractual severance terms. In addition, of course, there is an entitlement to notice or pay in lieu. The position sometimes appears complicated by the way contractual payments are expressed, so as to include both a statutory payment and pay in lieu of notice. It is, however, convenient for us to look at each in turn.

11.4.8.1 Statutory redundancy payments

In essence the statutory scheme of payments is very simple. As the calculation of the amount (unlike possible entitlement) is scarcely ever in issue, we shall do no more than to sketch the rules in outline. Under ERA 1996, s. 162, the redundant employee is entitled to a number of weeks' pay, depending on both age and service. There is no entitlement whatever below two years' service, and this rule remains unchanged despite the reduction in qualifying service to claim unfair dismissal.

The definition of 'service' is the same as for other statutory purposes: see ERA 1996, ss. 210–219 and also **5.4**, except that service under the age of 18 does not count—s. 211(2). If a redundancy payment was made at some earlier point in the employee's service, continuity of service runs only from that date—see s. 214.

A week's pay is similarly the same as for other statutory purposes: the normal pay for the normal hours if pay does not fluctuate; the average of the previous 12 weeks if it does; and subject in all cases to the statutory maximum of £270, apparently now also subject to the national minimum wage—see **10.13.2**. above. See ERA 1996, ss. 220–229 for the detailed rules. The right always ends at normal retirement age or at the age of 65, whichever is earlier, as confirmed by the EAT in *Secretary of State for Trade and Industry* v *Rutherford* (*No. 2*) [2004] IRLR 858.

The Department of Trade and Industry booklet on redundancy payments contains a convenient ready-reckoner on the entitlement in weeks for all possible combinations of age and service. The calculation is almost the same as for a basic award of compensation for unfair dismissal as set out in **10.13.2** above:

CALCULATION:	[AGE factor] × [SERVICE] × [WEEK'S PAY]
AGE:	For any service where the employee was 41 or over the factor is 1.5
	For any service between the ages of 22 and 41 the factor is 1
	For any service between the ages of 18 and 22 the factor is 0.5
SERVICE:	Subject to a maximum of 20 years
WEEK'S PAY:	Subject to a maximum of £270 per week

The maximum statutory redundancy payment is therefore £8,100, i.e., 1.5 × 20 × 270. (These are the figures from 1 February 2004.)

Note: Where the relevant date is beyond the employee's 64th birthday the payment is reduced by 1/12th for every completed calendar month after that birthday. Thus statutory redundancy pay ceases to be payable when the employee reaches 65.

If the employee was dismissed with less than the minimum statutory notice appropriate to length of service and thereby failed to meet the minimum of two years' service, or just missed the anniversary of starting so as to obtain one more year's service, it is possible to read forward the date of termination of employment accordingly.

11.4.8.2 Contractual severance payments

There are many employers, especially large companies and those that were or still are publicly owned, which have set up their own schemes of redundancy or severance payments (sometimes known by some other name) in excess of the statutory scale. We have used the term 'severance payment' in this book to distinguish such contractual payments from statutory redundancy payments, but that terminology is not standard and it should not be assumed to apply elsewhere.

The important question, when employees are then dismissed for redundancy, is whether the better scheme has become a contractual entitlement or not. The tests are no different in this matter from any other examination of contractual status discussed in **Chapter 3**. Particular attention will be paid to the circumstances in which the scheme was first introduced and the apparent beliefs of the parties at the time: see, for example, *Lee* v *GEC Plessey Telecommunications* [1993] IRLR 383.

Many employers, aware of the danger of establishing a contractual entitlement that might be a financial embarrassment on a future occasion, take care to explain that better terms are specific to a particular redundancy.

It should not be assumed that any superior set of terms automatically becomes a contractual entitlement because used once or more in the past: it will be necessary to produce some evidence to turn mere practice into a contractual term. The question of whether mere past practice has been turned into a contractual entitlement depends on a detailed examination of all the surrounding circumstances as listed in *Albion Automotive Ltd* v *Walker* [2002] EWCA Civ 946.

11.4.8.3 Cancellation of contractual arrangements

Most of the cases that have reached the courts have concerned employers who have established (intentionally or not) some contractual scheme of enhanced severance payments and who have then wanted to abandon it. A company of some 500 employees and a severance payment scheme that yields an average of £20,000 per employee has a potential liability of £10 million. This is likely to exceed the total value of the business if it is put up for sale, and the consequence of such schemes is often serious for the future of the business concerned.

In such circumstances some employers have sought to bring such schemes to an end and to replace them with something poorer, or even with nothing at all except the statutory scheme. The mechanism for doing so is the same as for introducing any other change in the terms of employment as discussed in **Chapter 5**. Employees or their representatives may agree to the abandonment of the severance scheme, but this is obviously rather unlikely when the employer has no significant inducement to offer. More likely the employer will have to terminate the employment of all the employees on the existing terms of employment and then offer re-engagement on terms that are identical in all respects except for the loss of the severance scheme: see **5.5.4.5**.

Such a mass ending of employees' contracts of employment is, of course, a dismissal and the people concerned will be able to bring complaints of unfair dismissal. The employment tribunal will still have jurisdiction to hear those complaints even though the employees may have accepted the new jobs under protest: see *Hogg* v *Dover College* [1990] ICR 39. The employer will classify the dismissals as for a substantial reason, and the question whether the employer acted reasonably in so dismissing the employees will enable the employment tribunal to examine the importance of ending the severance payment scheme.

The employer will need to consult employee representatives about this mass dismissal under the provisions discussed at **11.4.2** above. This is not because the employees are truly redundant under the definition we have been considering throughout the chapter; clearly they are not. It is because there is a special definition of redundancy for the purposes of collective consultation, introduced to comply with the European Directive on multiple dismissals. Collective consultation is required about all dismissals not related to the individual employee. The employer may therefore find that the very act of seeking to end generous severance payments is argued by employees to constitute a redundancy, and to give rise to an entitlement to the payments! However it is unlikely that any scheme of contractual severance payments will in fact depend on such a definition.

11.4.9 Appeals

Most employers who operate some formal mechanism for selecting employees for dismissal for redundancy then provide an opportunity for those selected to appeal against that decision. This is usually separate from and subsequent to the individual consultation we considered at **11.4.6**. There has been no clear authority requiring such a stage: indeed, in *Robinson* v *Ulster Carpet Mills* [1991] IRLR 348, the Northern Ireland Court of Appeal expressly found that it was not necessary.

Now that individual consultation about redundancy is subject to the rules about dismissal procedures under EA 2002 as we discussed at **11.4.6**, we must assume that those rules require provision of an opportunity to appeal. The rules and the accompanying code make clear that an appeal must comply with the rules of natural justice. In particular the person hearing it must not be in a position of bias by having been involved in the decision to dismiss. So employers need to ensure that selection is made low enough in a management hierarchy to leave someone more senior to hear the appeal.

11.5 Remedies for the redundant employee

So far, this chapter has looked at redundancy from the point of view of giving advice to the employer before dismissals have taken place. Now it is necessary to look at the other side of that coin and to consider the redress available to an employee who has been dismissed. The principles apply equally, of course, whether the solicitor acts for the dismissed employee or for the ex-employer. As we noted at the start of the chapter, any redress at all depends on establishing that there has been a dismissal, but there are then four possibilities that we shall need to consider in turn:

(a) A complaint of wrongful dismissal, i.e., a claim for notice or pay in lieu of notice.

(b) A claim for a statutory redundancy payment.

(c) A complaint of unfair dismissal, seeking reinstatement, re-engagement or compensation.

(d) A claim for a contractual severance payment.

11.5.1 Wrongful dismissal

The same rules about the employee's right to notice apply to a dismissal for redundancy as to any other dismissal. If the employee appears not to have been given due notice or pay in lieu, you should refer to **9.10**.

There is just one special point that is probably peculiar to dismissal for redundancy. Some severance payment schemes provide a total sum including pay in lieu, a statutory redundancy payment and an additional payment, without any specific identification of the amount of the component parts. At one stage there was a benefit to be gained from this device but the loop-hole has now been blocked. Nevertheless the approach remains in some severance payment schemes and it is worth checking that an individual client who seems not to have received pay in lieu of notice is not in fact covered by a scheme of this kind.

In one Scottish case, *Anderson* v *Pringle of Scotland Ltd* [1998] IRLR 64, the Court of Session held that selection on the basis of LIFO had become an incorporated term of the contract and they granted interdict (equivalent to an injunction) restraining the employer from selecting for redundancy on any other basis. Use of the injunction effectively to require specific performance of a contract of personal service is of course contrary to conventional principles of equity, and the case is exceptional.

11.5.2 Statutory redundancy payments

We have already considered the method of calculating a statutory redundancy payment at **11.4.8.1** above.

An employee with more than two years' service is entitled to a statutory redundancy payment and can present a claim of non-payment or insufficient payment to the employment tribunal. In practice most employers are aware of the need to pay redundancy payments and such cases are nowadays rare, except where there is a dispute as to whether the dismissal was for redundancy.

A typical case where redundancy may be in dispute as the reason for dismissal is provided by the example of constructive dismissal for redundancy we considered at **11.2.2** above. The employer gives the employee (the production director's secretary) an instruction to change job (to be secretary to someone else), regarding it as a lawful instruction within the existing contract. The employee regards the proposed job as of lesser status and outside the terms of the contract, refuses to move and resigns in protest. The employee's entitlement to a redundancy payment will depend upon the true construction of the contract, and that may be a matter for the employment tribunal.

11.5.3 Unfair dismissal

Of the four possible remedies, the one most often adopted is a claim to the employment tribunal of unfair dismissal. We have seen in **Chapter 10** that there are four potentially fair reasons for dismissal (plus the catch-all fifth of 'some other substantial reason') and that redundancy is one of them. Under ERA 1996, s. 98(4), the employer must act reasonably in dismissing for the stated reason. The advice to employers we have been considering in **11.4** above is distilled from cases of alleged unfair dismissal, and therefore reflects the tribunals' view of what constitutes reasonableness when the reason is redundancy. So a solicitor acting for either party will need to establish the facts and then to match them against the nine stages in **Figure 11.1**.

Before we return to that sequence there are two preliminary questions worth asking:

(a) Was the dismissal truly for redundancy?

(b) Is the dismissal automatically unfair?

11.5.3.1 Was the dismissal truly for redundancy?

The dismissed employee may have received a dismissal letter which refers to a redundancy, but the solicitor acting for the dismissed employee doubts whether that is really an accurate description. It is worth examining the facts against the definition of redundancy we considered at **11.3** above.

Sometimes an employer will describe as a redundancy the dismissal of an employee, perhaps quite a senior person, who is not considered to have been performing very well but whom the employer does not wish to retain while going through the disciplinary procedure. The redundancy in such circumstances may be rather obviously false: perhaps steps are already being taken to recruit a replacement, thereby demonstrating that the employer's requirement for people to do work of that kind has neither ceased nor diminished. Since the burden of proof as regards the *reason* for dismissal rests with the employer (unlike the burden of proof as regards *reasonableness* which is neutral), the employer who has wrongly described a dismissal in this way will find it difficult to satisfy that burden and the dismissal will be unfair.

The employee may well be unclear whether dismissal in the context of a business reorganisation is for redundancy or not. We have already discussed the topic in relation to dismissal for some other substantial reason at **10.8.6** above. As we noted at **11.3.3**, the question whether there is a redundancy depends on application of the statutory definition as required by *Murray* v *Foyle Meats Ltd* [1999] ICR 827, and that is a matter of fact for the employment tribunal to decide: *Shawkat* v *Nottingham City Hospital NHS Trust (No. 2)* [2001] EWCA Civ 954; [2001] IRLR 555.

11.5.3.2 Is the dismissal automatically unfair?

As was noted at **11.4.5.3** above, an employment tribunal is *bound* to find a selection for redundancy unfair under TULRCA 1992, s. 153 if it was based intentionally or otherwise on trade union membership or activities. This finding is mandatory and does not depend on any question of reasonableness under ERA 1996, s. 98(4). The solicitor representing the employee has only to show that the reason for dismissal was redundancy, that other similar employees were not dismissed and that the reason for selection of this employee reflected trade union membership or activities, whether the employer discriminated deliberately or not. This right covers trade union representatives, safety representatives and those functioning as employee representatives for the purposes of consultation about the redundancy.

Recent cases suggest that this kind of challenge to a selection for redundancy may be becoming increasingly common. Employees selected for dismissal often have a difficult task in challenging the method of selection adopted by the employer and dicta in *British Aerospace plc* v *Green* [1995] ICR 1006 imply that the task will become no easier. It is suggested in that case that it is sufficient for the employer to show a good system of selection and that it was fairly administered, and that ordinarily there is no need for the employer to justify all the assessments on which the selection for redundancy was based. Against that background, challenge under s. 153 becomes an attractively safe mechanism for attacking the employer's selection. Perhaps, though, as we mentioned at **11.4.5.2**, there are now more other opportunities than there were before the Disability Discrimination Act 1995 came into force.

There is no parallel provision of automatic unfairness if the selection can be shown to be discriminatory on grounds of race, sex or disability, but the effect is similar. Such a complaint could, of course, be brought either under the relevant anti-discrimination statute or under unfair dismissal law, or indeed under both. If discrimination is involved, compensation is potentially unlimited. If an employee is disabled and has been selected for dismissal as a result of assessment according to a matrix like that described at **11.4.5.2**, it is often possible to show that one or more of the marks obtained may adversely have been affected by the disability.

11.5.3.3 Unreasonableness

Unless the employee's case can be brought within the special rule we have just described, and if the stated reason of dismissal for redundancy seems genuine, we must return to the issue of reasonableness under s. 98(4) of ERA 1996. Each of the nine stages of the employer's checklist (except perhaps notification and redundancy payments) is worth examining for possible objections. The most likely stages for finding material failings may well be:

(a) Selection (perhaps unit of selection).

(b) Individual consultation.

(c) Failure to look for alternative work.

The employment tribunal will examine those three key aspects of the employer's handling of the redundancy, whether or not they are expressly pleaded in the claim to the tribunal: see *Langston* v *Cranfield University* [1998] IRLR 172.

11.5.3.4 Remedies for unfair dismissal for redundancy

We noted in **Chapter 10** that the remedies for a successful claim of unfair dismissal were to be considered in sequence by the employment tribunal: reinstatement, re-engagement (if the employee so wished) and compensation. That rule applies in exactly the same way to a dismissal for redundancy as to any other reason.

In practice, except for cases like those at **11.5.3.2** above, orders for reinstatement are very uncommon where the reason for dismissal is redundancy. The employer would need to find someone else to dismiss if ordered to reinstate the employee, although occasionally re-engagement in a different job or at a different place of work may be feasible. The more common remedy where there has been a finding of unfair dismissal on grounds of redundancy is compensation.

11.5.3.5 Compensation in redundancy cases

In principle the rules applying to other unfair dismissals also apply to compensation where dismissal was for redundancy but has been found unfair. However, the following points occur:

(a) A statutory redundancy payment and a basic award of compensation for unfair dismissal are normally exactly the same figure. By s. 122(4) of ERA 1996 the redundancy payment is offset against the basic award. This will normally exactly extinguish it entirely, except where the basic award has already been reduced for some other reason. The scope of this rule is unclear, since deduction by reason of the employee's contributory conduct is expressly excluded where the reason for dismissal is redundancy: s. 122(3).

(b) Any redundancy payment in excess of the basic award is to be offset against the compensatory award: ERA 1996, s. 123(7). This rule includes any contractual or *ex gratia* severance payment but not pay in lieu of notice: *Rushton* v *Harcros Timber* [1993] ICR 230. However, this offset, like other calculations affecting a compensatory award, is performed before application of the statutory maximum, so that the employer paying a substantial non-statutory severance payment may still have to pay the maximum compensatory award in addition if the employee's loss is considerable: *McCarthy* v *BICC* [1985] IRLR 94.

(c) There is provision in s. 123(3) of ERA 1996, apparently very little used, that in assessing the appropriate amount of a compensatory award the employment tribunal can include the excess of any redundancy payment (or, as we have been calling it, a severance payment) above the statutory payment if the employee had a potential entitlement to such a payment, or even an expectation of it. This last element of an expectation being sufficient makes the lack of use of the rule surprising. It appears to permit an employee whose dismissal for redundancy is found to be unfair to enforce against the employer a voluntary severance scheme even where that scheme has no contractual basis, provided the employee had some expectation, presumably reasonably founded, of being paid.

(d) The important decision of the House of Lords in *Polkey* v *A. E. Dayton Services* [1988] ICR 142, which we have already mentioned in connection with individual consultation, also resolved a long-running argument about the effect of a finding that some procedural failing in fact made no difference to a final decision to dismiss. *Polkey* v *Dayton* determined that a procedural failing that truly made no difference to the result should be reflected in the amount of compensation awarded. Since then the tribunals have very often adopted an approach of trying to assess the chances, usually on the basis of a percentage probability (rather than the horse-racing equivalent of odds), that a correct approach might have led to a different result. This is particularly relevant to a dismissal for redundancy. If the dismissed employee was one of a unit of selection of three of whom one was to be dismissed for redundancy, and it is found that the method of selection was unfair, then it can be said that there was a 33 per cent chance the same result would have ensued if a correct method had been followed (unless of course there is evidence that the three were not in fact equally at risk). So, having assessed compensation on the basis of actual gross loss, the tribunal then reduces it by one-third to take account of that probability. Further guidance was given by the EAT in *Cox* v *London Borough of Camden* [1996] IRLR 389, and this case now sets out the correct sequence of calculations. We do not expect that the 2004 amendment partially restoring the pre-*Polkey* rule (see **11.4.6**) will make much difference to these cases.

(e) Sometimes where the employer has failed properly to consult the individual it is found under the *Polkey* reasoning that consultation would have made no difference to the result. In such cases, compensation is normally limited to wages for a period that the tribunal estimates proper consultation might have lasted—usually about two weeks as in *Mining Supplies (Longwall) Ltd* v *Baker* [1988] ICR 676. Where it can be shown that the lack of consultation had a greater effect, compensation may be greater, as in *Elkouil* v *Coney Island Ltd* [2002] IRLR 174, where the employee was disadvantaged in looking for another job because the employer concealed the likelihood of redundancy for ten weeks.

11.5.4 Civil action to recover a contractual severance payment

We have already noted when considering the matter from the employer's standpoint that there may be a contractual scheme of redundancy or severance payments higher than the statutory scheme. We also noted that employers (especially successor employers following a change of ownership) sometimes try to avoid meeting contractual duties, especially if the business is now less profitable than when the contractual scheme was first introduced.

Until recently, employees seeking to enforce a contractual entitlement to a superior severance payment could not do so in the employment tribunals. Proceedings could only be brought in the county court or High Court. As we noted at **5.7.4** above, dismissed employees can now bring proceedings for breach of contract in the employment tribunals and claim up to £25,000. Larger amounts will still have to be sought in the courts.

As we mentioned at item (c) in the list at **11.5.3.5**, it may be possible for an employee who can show unfair dismissal as well as redundancy to include the *expectation* of a superior severance payment as a head of compensation, even where the entitlement was not strictly contractual.

11.6 Self-test questions

1. Which of the following examples involves a dismissal for redundancy and why?

   (a) The employer's business makes and packs foodstuffs for several supermarket and other outlets. One of the largest customers moves its contract elsewhere and the employer declares a redundancy of a quarter of the production workers.

(b) The circumstances are the same as (a) except that there is no loss of a contract. The employer has decided to reduce costs in order to boost profits and that the factory is currently over-staffed. About a quarter of the workers will lose their jobs. The trade union objects strongly that there is no reduction in work and therefore no redundancy: such chasing of excessive profits is immoral.

(c) The production supervisor has not been performing well. The managing director tells him that the post is being eliminated and he is redundant. The supervisor then learns that a production director is being appointed, with substantially the same duties but a bit more responsibility, including a seat on the local board of management.

(d) The site in Bristol is being closed and the work is being transferred to another factory in Clevedon, about 13 miles away. The employer says there is no redundancy because work is available for everyone in Clevedon.

(e) In the context of the reduction in numbers at (a) one of the quality control inspectors is to lose her job. She objects. She has never been involved in any of the work under the contract that is being cancelled; the work she does remains exactly as before and she cannot therefore be redundant.

2. Mr Vijay Patel comes to your office while you are out to talk about his recent dismissal for redundancy by St Werburgh's Electrical Apparatus Testing Shop Limited. Your secretary has arranged for him to come to see you tomorrow and meanwhile he has left for you to study beforehand a copy of his assessment form—**Figure 11.3**. You will note he scored 31 points; he was obviously close to retention as a colleague who scored 33 kept his job. Try to compile a list of all the possible grounds to argue unfair dismissal so that you can explore the evidence tomorrow.

ST WERBURGH'S ELECTRICAL APPARATUS TESTING SHOP LIMITED
ASSESSMENT FOR REDUNDANCY SELECTION – JANUARY 2005

Employee's Name V PATEL Department Main stores Clock No 789

Job Storekeeper Date of start 2.7.84 Date of birth 31.1.47

	Poor 1 point	Satisfactory 2 points	Good 3 points	Excellent 4 points	Factor	Score
1. Absenteeism	16 days plus X	6 – 15 days	2 – 5 days	0 – 1 days	X4	4
2. Output of work	Fails to meet targets X	Meets targets if constantly supervised ~~X~~	Output above average	Always meets or exceeds targets; actively works to increase productivity	X3	~~6~~ 3
3. Initiative and judgment	Judgment suspect; needs help in organising	Organises work fairly well and judgment usually sound X	Uses initiative when required. Uses common sense to advantage	A lot of initiative; a good organiser.	X4	8
4. Attitude	Unco-operative	Prefers the status quo but will change if forced to X	Keen to try new ideas and responds well to requests for change	Exceptionally co-operative with any request	X6	12
5. Potential	Will not progress further X	Limited promotability; more likely to remain in present job	Will be promotable with greater experience and/or training	Could undertake more senior job now	X5	5
					Total	31

Total

Assessed by J Brown Stores Foreman

Date 13.12.04

12

Takeovers and transfers of undertakings

12.1 Introduction

In this chapter we examine the consequences for employees and their contracts of employment when the ownership of a business changes. It is convenient to add the implications for employment of an employer's insolvency or death.

Why, it might be asked, is there a problem at all? If employer B buys employer A's business as a going concern, does the sale not include the employees as well as the premises, plant, equipment and work-in-progress?

One answer might be that slavery was abolished in this country rather a long time ago. The common law rule of privity of contract requires that every contract, of employment or anything else, is a private relationship between two contracting parties, neither of whom has any unilateral right to assign its rights or obligations to anyone else: *Dunlop* v *Selfridge* [1915] AC 847. Applying that common law rule to the example above, we find that on ceasing the business that is being sold, A will no longer have anything for the employees previously involved in it to do. So they must all be dismissed, and the reason is redundancy within the definition we considered in **11.3**. If B wishes to recruit some or all of A's former employees, it will be necessary to enter into new contracts with them as with A's former customers and suppliers. There will be no continuity of service.

Rather obviously, a rule under which any change in the ownership of a business results in the wholesale redundancy of all those employed by it is incompatible with modern legal principles of employment protection that we have been considering in this book. So there are various statutory rules to give some continuity of employment and to reverse the common law rule in five broad categories of change of ownership. Simple continuity is provided by ERA 1996, s. 218, but there are other matters we shall need to consider:

(a) The employer is a limited company and the ownership of shares in that company changes through some takeover or sale of shares. We shall look at this further in **12.2**.

(b) One legally constituted employer transfers a business activity to another such employer. This kind of change brings in a European Directive as well as the Transfer of Undertakings (Protection of Employment) Regulations 1981 (TUPE). We shall look further at the regulations in **12.3**, and at the Directive in **12.4**. In **12.5** we shall examine which transfers the regulations cover, and in **12.6** the practical effects when they apply.

(c) There is a transfer between associated companies: see **12.7**.

(d) The employer becomes insolvent and a business activity is available for acquisition from the receiver, liquidator or administrator. The various possible kinds of insolvency will be examined briefly in **12.8**.

(e) The employer dies: see **12.9**.

12.2 Share transfers

We need to remind ourselves of the principle of company law that regards a limited company (both plc and Ltd) as a legal person. The company can sue and be sued in its own name, it can own property, and it can enter into contracts. All of those external activities are unaffected by changes in the shareholders' identities or ownership of shares.

Thus, since employees of a limited company look to the company as the legal employer and are not directly interested in what individuals or corporate persons own the shares of the company, it follows that a change in share ownership has no consequence for the position of the employees. Their rights and obligations relate to the legal person that employs them, and that has not changed. This principle applies equally to a small-scale sale of a few shares in a personal shareholding as to a change in the controlling interest, majority shareholding or even wholly-owned status of a limited company.

This principle is of great importance. In the United Kingdom (as contrasted with some of the rest of Europe) most changes in ownership of a business are in fact executed by a transfer of shares. The legal entity that employs employees therefore does not change, and neither do any of the conditions of employment.

Since the next kind of change in ownership that we shall have to deal with is much more complicated, it is always worth checking before embarking on any detailed consideration of the application of TUPE 1981 to a particular case that it is not in fact merely a share transfer. Clients often ask questions about TUPE 1981 which on closer examination prove to be about share sales where those regulations have no impact.

12.3 The Transfer of Undertakings (Protection of Employment) Regulations 1981

Before we proceed to look in more detail at the operation of the regulations, it is useful to summarise their effect.

Where there is a *relevant transfer*:

(a) employment is *automatically transferred* (unless the employee objects) with full continuity of service;

(b) the transferred employment is on the *same conditions*—including trade union recognition but excluding pensions;

(c) any dismissal because of the transfer is *automatically unfair* (unless in narrowly defined circumstances);

(d) employee representatives of both transferor and transferee must be *consulted*.

Those five elements, beginning with the definition of a 'relevant transfer', need to be examined in turn. First, it may help to give an example. Suppose an engineering company makes and sells both agricultural equipment and garden machinery. Its business is organised in two separate divisions for the two sets of products, with the first rather larger and more profitable than the second. It receives an offer for the garden machinery business from another garden machinery manufacturer which believes it could run the division more profitably, perhaps by some economies of scale through combining some parts with its existing business. If the sale goes ahead, TUPE 1981 operate to protect the continuity of employment of the employees in the garden machinery division with unchanged conditions of employment. If the two activities were organised as subsidiary companies

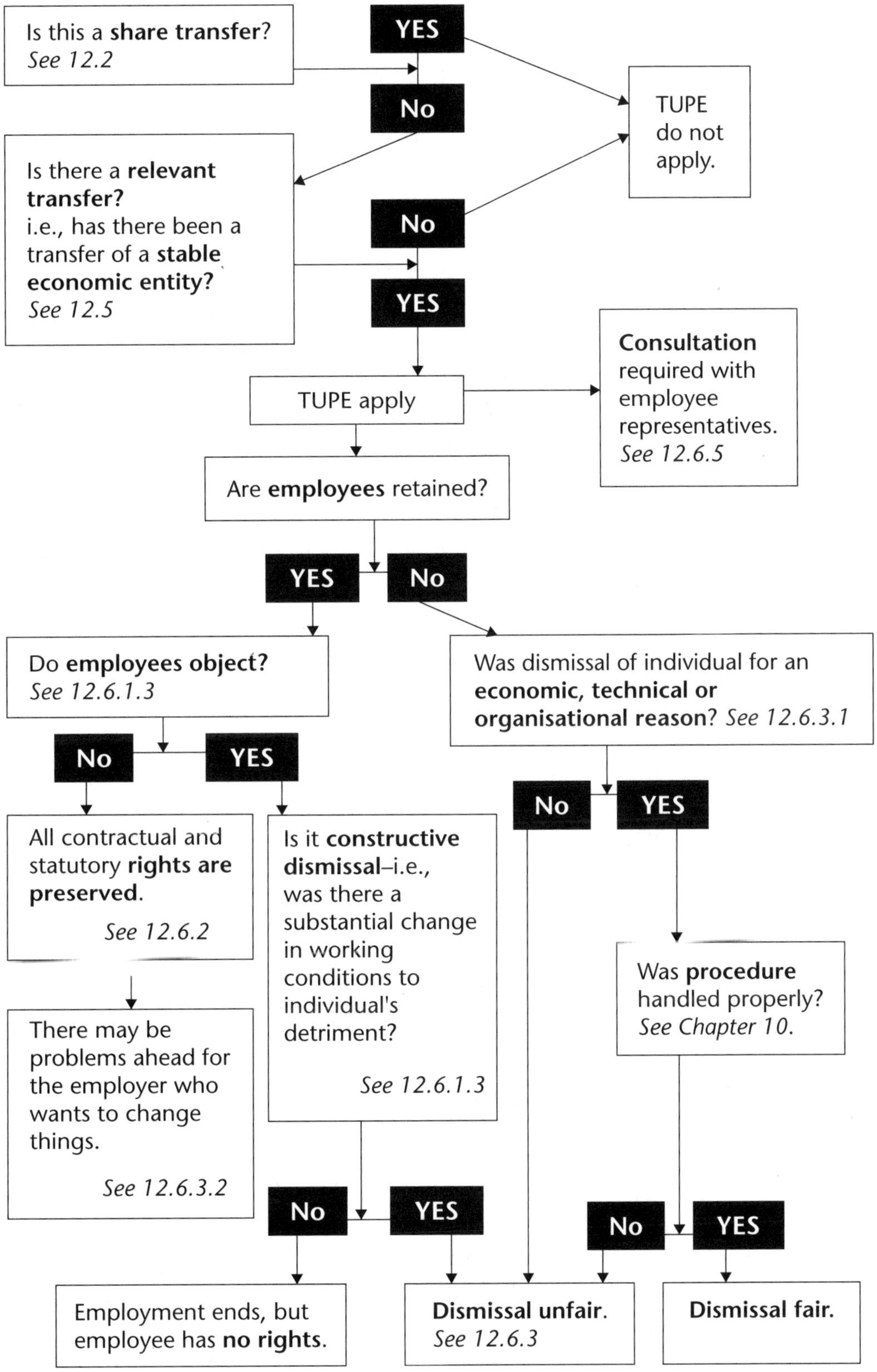

Figure 12.1 Effect of the Regulations.

rather than as divisions of one company, then a sale of the shares involves no change in the legal identity of the employer and continuity of employment is preserved in any event.

Some people find it easier to follow such a sequence if it is set out in the form of a diagram, and we hope that **Figure 12.1** may help. It may be useful to keep it in mind for the remainder of this part of the chapter.

We need to note that the 1981 TUPE Regulations in the United Kingdom resulted from a European Directive, the Acquired Rights Directive 77/187/EEC. There are several aspects of the operation of TUPE 1981 where we shall find that the courts in the United Kingdom have been influenced in their interpretation of the statutory instrument by the Directive, or where decisions of the ECJ have affected interpretation in this country.

The 1977 Directive was subsequently amended and has now been repealed and replaced by another Directive 2001/23/EC as we shall note shortly. As amending regulations have not yet been made and TUPE 1981 remain in force, it is convenient to begin by tracing their relationship with the original 1977 Directive.

12.4 The Acquired Rights Directives (77/187/EEC and 2001/23/EC)

Most readers reaching this point in their legal training will already be familiar with the basic principles of the law of the European Union. Indeed you may well remember that many of the leading cases you had to remember were about the Acquired Rights Directive.

For the rest, or any whose memory is getting a little rusty, a quick reminder may help.

A European Directive is an instruction from the Council of the EU (after completion of the appropriate procedures) addressed to the Member States and requiring them to legislate within a defined time-scale so as to achieve specified results. Thus the Acquired Rights Directive was adopted by the Council on 14 February 1977 and required legislation in the Member States within two years of that date. Like most Directives it set general objectives and not precise rules. It contained only ten articles and had the simple aim of preserving continuity of employment when a business changes hands. This simplicity creates some difficulty in Member States like the UK that are accustomed to very precisely drawn statutes, especially since (for reasons we shall consider very shortly) the terms of the Directive may come to be construed in the British courts. To be on the safe side, governments of Member States sometimes 'copy out' parts of a Directive so as to ensure that their own statute complies with the Directive but does not go beyond its terms. The problem arises when such 'Eurojargon' is itself incomprehensible. 'Economic, technical and organisational reasons' are a good example: see **12.6.3** below.

As we noted, a Directive is addressed to the Member States. Of itself it does not establish rights that can be enforced by one person in a Member State (e.g., an employee) against another (e.g., an employer). As the jargon has it, there is no *horizontal direct effect*. A Treaty obligation like art. 141 (previously art. 119) that we considered in **Chapter 6** is different: it has horizontal direct effect. A Directive has *vertical* direct effect, i.e., it can be enforced by an individual against the state, and this includes the case where the state (or an 'emanation of the state') is the employer. It may also give the individual rights against the state if the state has failed to implement the Directive, according to the rule first set out in *Francovich* v *Italian Republic* [1995] ICR 722. See **1.5.3** above for further explanation of all of this, but it is not of much relevance to the Acquired Rights Directive. Of much greater relevance here are the circumstances in which a Directive may have *indirect* effect in this country. There are two aspects to consider.

(a) *Purposive construction*

It is now well established that, if a British court is required to construe a British statute or statutory instrument like TUPE 1981 that is intended to implement a European Directive, it must do so in such a way as will as far as possible give effect to the terms of the Directive. One of the leading cases in this rule of *purposive construction* is *Litster* v *Forth Dry Dock* [1989] ICR 341 that we shall return to at **12.6.1** below.

(b) *References for preliminary rulings*

Under art. 234 of the Treaty of Rome (previously art. 177) any court in a Member State may refer to the ECJ any question of interpretation of a Directive that is relevant to a case it is handling. Often this arises where a purposive construction is being given to a domestic statute or equivalent. The procedure, known as a reference for a *preliminary ruling*, has been used by the full range of courts from employment tribunals to the House of Lords. The courts of the other Member States also use it and, although the ECJ does not operate any strict rule of binding precedents, decisions relating to other states frequently establish interpretations that then have to be followed here. This explains why the authorities cited in **12.5.3.1** to **12.5.3.3** below, for example, are such a mixture of British and foreign cases.

The history of TUPE 1981 and its interrelationship with the Directive might provide a good topic for an academic thesis. Here, though, our aim here is to be rather more practical. Nevertheless we have included a little of the history in the sections that follow because it is often important in explaining to clients some of the continuing uncertainties about TUPE 1981.

Few would disagree that the scope of the Directive has been broadened by decisions of the ECJ beyond anything that was in the mind of those drafting it in 1977. We shall encounter in **12.5.3.1** below the case of *Schmidt* v *Spar- und Leihkasse der Früheren Ämter Bordesholm, Kiel und Cronshagen* (Case C-392/92) [1995] ICR 237, where it was held to protect the job of a single office cleaner when a bank 'privatised' its cleaning operations. The British courts have then been required to give a purposive construction to TUPE 1981 so as to reflect all these ECJ decisions.

In the light of the widening interpretation of the Directive from the ECJ, the original form of TUPE 1981 was found to be an inadequate implementation. The Commission started infraction proceedings against the British Government in October 1992. For example, the 1981 version excluded any transfer of a business that was not in the nature of a commercial venture, an exception that did not appear in the Directive.

The result was a set of amendments to TUPE 1981 in 1993 which we shall mention at the appropriate points in the text. The amendments have helped to clarify the law and have lessened the difficulty in advising clients about very uncertain requirements.

The 1977 Directive was amended in June 1998 by Directive 98/50/EC and the deadline for member states to pass domestic legislation was 17 July 2001. The Department of Trade and Industry issued a consultation document about revisions to TUPE 1981, but no amending regulations in fact resulted by March 2001, when the latest Directive 2001/23/EC was adopted. It seems the Government then decided to have one set of amending regulations rather than two. Since then there have been various consultations about revisions and rumours of new regulations, but no change has actually happened. The latest as we go to press is that a further consultation document is expected in October 2004. It may be that the Secretary of State will use her power to make regulations under ERA 1999, s. 38, so that she will not be restricted to mere implementation of the Directive as would be the case under the European Communities Act 1972.

12.5 Relevant transfers

Having looked at the source of TUPE 1981 in a European Directive, we must now return to the five key elements we noted earlier. The various consequences we set out at **12.3** above follow if (but only if) the events that occurred fall within the definition of a 'relevant transfer' in reg. 3 of TUPE 1981. There are two key elements of that definition:

(a) Some business activity must pass *from one legal person*, the transferor, *to another*, the transferee. See **12.5.2**.

(b) That which is transferred must be a *business or an identifiable part* of a business. See **12.5.3**.

12.5.1 Some exclusions

Before we look further at each of those two points, it is of help in understanding the broad scope of the definition to notice some omissions:

(a) It does not matter *how* the transfer occurs. The business may be sold, but equally it may be transferred in other ways. Many of the recent important cases concern employers who have 'contracted out' services like a canteen, security or office cleaning that were previously provided in-house by the employer's own employees. Privatisation of some local government services like refuse collection is of the same kind. There is no sale in these cases.

(b) Since amendments in 1993, there is no longer any requirement that the business should be 'in the nature of a *commercial venture*'.

(c) Also as a result of the 1993 amendments, there is no requirement that what passes from transferor to transferee consists of real or personal *property*, nor that either is legal *owner* of anything involved.

(d) As a third item from the 1993 amendments, it is not necessary to be able to point to a single transaction that effected the transfer: there can be a series.

12.5.2 Transfer from transferor to transferee

We have already reminded ourselves in **12.2** that company law operates to provide continuity of employment where a business changes hands through a change in share ownership and that there is no need for any special statutory protection. Regulation 3(1) defines a relevant transfer in terms of the transfer of the business from one legal person to another, and this means that share transfers are in fact completely excluded from the scope of TUPE 1981.

12.5.3 A business or identifiable part of a business

We need first to ask what it is that must be transferred to constitute a relevant transfer. Several landmark cases in the ECJ have made radical changes in our understanding of the Directive.

We shall look first at the general scope of the definition and then at two categories of case that have attracted particular recent attention—non-profit making organisations and the contracting out of services. We shall then return to see where this leaves us in terms of trying to advise clients in such an uncertain branch of the law.

12.5.3.1 The general scope of the definition

The definition of a relevant transfer in TUPE 1981, reg. 3(1) is imprecise. It states that the regulations apply to any transfer from one person to another of the whole or part of an undertaking situated in the United Kingdom. The regulation goes on to include various transactions that might possibly otherwise be excluded. But the only indication of what constitutes an undertaking is the definition in reg. 2(1) that it includes any trade or business or, in reg. 2(2), any part that is transferred as a business.

The problem is that the use of terms like 'trade' and 'business' implies that the undertaking must be transferred as a going concern. In relation to the garden machinery business we used as an example at **12.3** above there is no problem: it is clearly run by the transferor as a going concern and will be continued as such by the transferee. But what of something less easily defined like the sales activity, or something like office cleaning which is run by the transferor as a service but not a business? Can either of those be a trade or business? Although the terms appear in the English version of the Directive, the ECJ has pointed out in *Schmidt* v *Spar- und Leihkasse der Früheren Ämter Bordesholm, Kiel und Cronshagen* (Case C-392/92) [1995] ICR 237 that there are significant differences in the terminology of the different languages of the Directive. Most use a term better translated as 'economic entity' than 'business'.

Recent decisions in the British courts have generally interpreted TUPE 1981 as if the term 'economic entity' appeared there. A good starting point is to consider the two key questions identified by ECJ in the leading case of *Spijkers* v *Gebroeders Benedik Abattoir CV* [1986] 2 CMLR 296: first, can we identify a stable economic entity before and after the transfer; and, secondly, has it retained its identity as a result of the transfer? In that case the transferor's business of running a slaughterhouse had ceased entirely. After a break in time the transferee took over all the employees except Mr Spijkers, but none of the customers. Advocate-General Sir Gordon Slynn recommended 'a realistic and robust view' that involved considering all the facts. In the particular case the ECJ held that there had indeed been a transfer within the Directive despite the break and the lack of transfer of goodwill. The new slaughterhouse business was sufficiently similar to the old one to say that there was a stable economic entity that had retained its identity. No one factor alone is decisive. It is necessary to look at everything—the function, assets, and employees before, the possible transfer and the function, assets and employees afterwards.

A category of cases where the *Spijkers* principles have often come to be applied concerns activities ancillary to the main business, like cleaning, security, or canteens. These are looked at in more detail at **12.5.3.3** below. Some later cases, both domestic and in the ECJ, especially *Süzen* v *Zehnacker Gebäudereinigung GmbH Krankenhausservice* [1997] ICR 662, seem to involve a step back from the very broad interpretation in *Spijkers*, and as can be seen later, it is possible to discern some conflict in the cases. From time to time the courts have attempted to clarify the confusion by setting out new lists of factors to consider and it may still be useful sometimes to refer to a list from the EAT in *Cheesman* v *R Brewer Contracts Ltd* [2001] IRLR 144. A recent case, however, *RCO Support Services Ltd* v *UNISON* [2002] EWCA Civ 464, [2002] ICR 751 confirms that the authority remains *Spijkers* and that as no one factor alone is decisive it is necessary to look at the total answer to the underlying two key questions.

12.5.3.2 Non-profit making organisations

Until the 1993 amendments, charitable activities were held to be not in the nature of a commercial venture and therefore outside the scope of TUPE 1981. So in *Woodcock* v *Committee for the Time Being of the Friends School, Wigton* [1987] IRLR 98, several teachers were held by the Court of Appeal to be unable to claim the protection of TUPE 1981 against unfair dismissal because the school was a charitable body. Then, however, the ECJ held differently in a Dutch case, *Dr Sophie Redmond Stichting* v *Bartol* [1992] IRLR 366. The ECJ found that the Directive *did* apply to employees of a charitable drug-rehabilitation foundation who lost their jobs when local authority funding was withdrawn. Under the rule of purposive construction that we mentioned at **12.4** above, the British courts now follow *Bartol* in preference to *Woodcock*, even in relation to transfers that occurred prior to 1993.

12.5.3.3 Activities ancillary to the main business

As mentioned at **12.5.1** above, an aspect of the coverage of TUPE 1981 that has recently attracted much attention is the 'contracting-out' of services, both by private employers and by public authorities. This is a real and very topical issue. For example, many manufacturing companies used to run their own canteens, intending them to be a service for the employees and not expecting to make a profit. In *Expro Services* v *Smith* [1991] ICR 577, the EAT held that such an activity was not a commercial venture, and therefore incapable of being a relevant transfer. In that case the main employer was in fact the Ministry of Defence, the 'canteen' was an officers' mess and the catering was privatised by transferring it to a contract caterer.

Then, in a Danish case, *Rask and Christensen* v *ISS Kantineservice* [1993] IRLR 133, the ECJ held that the Directive *did* apply to the contracting-out of the Philips works canteen, even though the sub-contractor was to be paid a flat fee by Philips and had no opportunity to run the canteen as a normal commercial undertaking.

The 1993 amendments of TUPE 1981 now clearly establish that any similar case in the UK involving a transfer after 30 August 1993 would be decided following *Rask* and not *Expro Services*. The principle applies equally to office cleaning, factory security or any other contracted-out service which is an identifiable business. Although the economic entity in such cases may not have been run commercially by the transferor, it is usually the transferee's intention to make a profit of some kind.

An important outstanding question is this. What happens if the employer originally awards the contract to sub-contractor A, but then becomes dissatisfied with the service provided by A, and awards the contract to another contractor, B? If the original sub-contracting was a relevant transfer, is the shift from A to B not equally within the definition?

The question demonstrates the practical difficulty of applying to actual examples the apparently straightforward tests that we discussed at **12.5.3.1**. The problem is that people tend to try to focus on one or more of the factors (inevitably one that suits the answer they would like to obtain) and to regard it as decisive. The cases now make it clear that *all* the factors must be taken into account simultaneously.

An early decision on the reallocation of contracts was that of the Court of Appeal in *Dines* v *(1) Initial Health Care Services and (2) Pall Mall Services Group* [1995] ICR 11. The contract for cleaning a National Health Service hospital was reallocated from the first to the second respondent. The Court of Appeal analysed the event as a transfer in two stages: the hospital first took the economic entity back from Initial and in a second stage handed it to Pall Mall. Taken together the two stages constituted a relevant transfer.

There was then a shock decision from the ECJ in *Süzen* v *Zehnacker Gebäudereinigung GmbH Krankenhausservice* [1997] ICR 662. Mrs Süzen was dismissed by a school cleaning contractor after the cleaning contract was reallocated from another contractor. The ECJ applied the *Spijkers* tests and found it impossible to identify a stable economic entity that had retained its identity. The second contractor took over from the first no significant assets and no major part of the relevant workforce. A little later the Court of Appeal followed *Süzen* rather than *Dines* in *Betts* v *Brintel Helicopters* [1997] ICR 792. The case concerned the reallocation of a contract to operate helicopter services to the North Sea for Shell. The second contractor took over none of the first contractor's employees, used different helicopters and operated out of a different airport. There was no relevant transfer. The trouble now was that employers appeared to be able to circumvent TUPE under this view of the rule from *Süzen* by ensuring that the transferee took over none of the transferor's employees. It was a circular argument and a logical nonsense.

In *ECM (Vehicle Delivery Service) Ltd* v *Cox* [1999] IRLR 559 the Court of Appeal decided that there *was* a relevant transfer in the reallocation of a contract for delivery of imported vehicles for Audi and Volkswagen. Similarly, the ECJ decided that both a reallocation of a subcontract and a resumption of a subcontracted cleaning activity by the main undertaking fell within the Directive. See *Francisco Hernández Vidal SA* v *Gómez Pérez* [1999] IRLR 132 and *Sánchez Hidalgo* v *Asociación de Servicios Aser* [1999] IRLR 136. Slightly unhelpfully the ECJ put some emphasis in its decision in *Abler* v *Sodexho MM Catering GmbH* (Case C-340/01), [2004] ICR 168—that reallocation of a hospital catering contract constituted a transfer within the Directive—on the reasoning that the new caterer took over a lot of catering equipment. The reasoning must be viewed in the light of the requirement explained above to consider all the surrounding circumstances and it should not be taken to indicate that a different conclusion would be drawn simply from the absence of any handing over of equipment.

If you reach this point somewhat confused as to where the law now stands, take heart! The Court of Appeal felt similarly in *ADI (UK) Ltd* v *Willer* [2001] EWCA Civ 971, [2001] IRLR 542. They helpfully confirmed a rule from *ECM* that, if the transferee's reason for not taking on the transferor's employees was to avoid TUPE 1981, then that fact cannot be relied on to argue that there was no transfer. However, May LJ criticised the unsatisfactory state of the authorities and Simon Brown LJ in the minority thought it impossible to reconcile *ECM* with the ruling ECJ jurisprudence! Just possibly there is some hope to be drawn from the emphasis placed on the two key *Spijkers* questions in *RCO Support Services Ltd* v *UNISON* [2002] EWCA Civ 464, [2002] ICR 751, mentioned in **12.5.3.1** above.

12.5.3.4 The practitioner's dilemma

The confusion must not be exaggerated. In most cases that a solicitor will encounter in practice it is fairly clear whether TUPE 1981 apply or not. Suppose you decide on the way home to buy a packet of cornflakes from Sainsburys when you normally shop at Safeway. Not even a particularly argumentative law student after an exceptionally difficult day at college would want to argue that supply of your breakfast constitutes a stable economic entity. On the other hand, any client running a factory who wants to subcontract security or cleaning is almost bound to be involved in a relevant transfer. The problems arise, as always, at the margins. There is still quite a lot of uncertainty to be resolved and, for example, as most of the leading cases concern services, there is much scope for speculation as to whether TUPE 1961 can ever apply to the manufacture or supply of goods (apart from your cornflakes).

All of this is fascinating stuff for the academic lawyer, and a pain in the neck for the solicitor in practice whose clients expect straight answers to simple questions. A logical approach of identifying the economic entity and comparing it before and after the transfer always helps.

Imagine a business undertaking which has a canteen on the premises in which food is prepared, cooked and served to employees. If the main employer subcontracts the running of the canteen, so that the employer of the canteen staff changes, there is likely to be a relevant transfer provided that the entity before and after the change continues to prepare, cook and serve food. However, it would probably be different if the main employer decided to close the canteen and to replace it (as has happened in some factories) with a delivery service in which food is prepared and cooked in a central kitchen by a subcontractor and then delivered to the premises for sale in vending machines on the premises with microwave cookers available for reheating. In that case, the economic entity probably *has* changed its identity, and there is no relevant transfer.

An interesting example of a case where the ECJ found there was no transfer within the meaning of the Directive occurred in *Ledernes Hovedorganisation* v *Dansk Arbejdsgiverforening* [1996] ICR 333 (*Rygaard's* case). Here the supposed economic entity being transferred consisted of a part of the work under one specific building contract, transferred with a view to its completion. It was held that the item transferred, consisting of two apprentices and one employee together with some materials, lacked the stability to constitute an economic entity. The Directive did not apply.

While the uncertainty persists, competing subcontractors use it to their advantage. Those tendering for a contract often claim to know 'ways round' TUPE 1981, while those already in position and seeking to deter competitors threaten them with dire consequences regarding conditions of employment because of the clear existence of a relevant transfer. Practitioners will find that the result is that many contracts for the sale of businesses now contain indemnity clauses about the effect of TUPE 1981 should they be found to apply.

In the public sector the question may now be academic, since public sector contracts are normally now drawn up on the assumption that TUPE 1981 apply, following a 'Statement of Practice on Staff Transfers in the Public Sector' issued by the Government in January 2000. The rules cover all contracting-out in the public sector (which includes Government departments and agencies and the National Health Service), any return of such a contract to the public sector, and any reallocation of such a contract from one subcontractor to another. Occupational pensions must be protected, notwithstanding their exclusion from TUPE 1981, and staff must be given protection similar to TUPE 1981 on transfers within the public sector, even if TUPE do not strictly apply. Under the rules, tenders for Government work are invited on the basis that TUPE apply and that existing staff are transferred, save only in 'genuinely exceptional circumstances', examples of which are given in the Statement.

12.6 The consequences

We have already noted that if a transfer of a business falls within the statutory definition of a relevant transfer there are four consequences, that we now need to examine in detail.

12.6.1 Automatic continuity of employment

Wherever there is a relevant transfer, TUPE 1981, reg. 5 provides that the transferor's responsibilities under contracts of employment pass automatically to the transferee. The rule is expressed as applying to all those employed *immediately before* the transfer *in the undertaking* transferred and unless *the employee objects*. Each of those elements emphasised requires further examination.

12.6.1.1 'Immediately before'

Not surprisingly, the expression has been exposed to some scrutiny in the cases and an argument as to how short a time constituted employment immediately before a transfer was finally resolved in *Secretary of State for Employment* v *Spence* [1986] ICR 651. The Court of Appeal held in that case that it was to be taken quite literally. A gap of even an hour or two was sufficient to break continuity.

An important qualification of that rule was introduced by the House of Lords in *Litster* v *Forth Dry Dock* [1989] ICR 341, however. In that case, the use of a purposive interpretation led to the imaginary insertion of additional words into TUPE 1981 so as to include both those employed immediately before the relevant transfer and also those who would have been so employed if they had not been unfairly dismissed in the circumstances described by reg. 8(1), which we shall consider at **12.6.3** below. See also **12.6.3.2** for an important question left unanswered by *Litster*.

It was noted at **12.5.1** above, that a relevant transfer did not have to occur in a single transaction but could result from a series of events, as in fact happened in *Astley* v *Celtec Ltd* [2002] EWCA Civ 1035, [2002] IRLR 629, where the date of the transfer became important. The Court of Appeal held it was a matter of fact for the employment tribunal to decide and it was possible for the transfer to take place over a period of several years.

12.6.1.2 Which employees are transferred?

In some cases it is obvious what it is that constitutes the undertaking or part transferred. In other cases it is not so clear, and there may be people who work both in the part of the transferor's business that is transferred to the transferee and in the part that the transferor retains. For example, in the two-division agricultural equipment and garden machinery company that we described earlier in the chapter, there may be departments such as buying or finance that support both divisions. It is important to know whether such employees are transferred or not.

The test was set by the ECJ in *Botzen* v *Rotterdamsche Droogdok Maatschappij* [1985] ECR 519. The critical question is whether a particular employee has been *assigned to* the part transferred, and that is essentially a matter of the employee's function rather than of the terms of the contract. Thus a mobility clause in the contract that is not in fact operated is irrelevant: *Securicor Guarding Ltd* v *Fraser Security Services Ltd* [1996] IRLR 552. Employees who are assigned to the part of the undertaking transferred become employees of the transferee under TUPE 1981, reg. 5.

The application of the test of assignment or allocation to the part of the undertaking transferred does not require the employee to work *exclusively* for that part: *Buchanan-Smith* v *Schleicher & Co. International Ltd* [1996] ICR 547. It is a matter of fact for the employment tribunal to decide, as in *CPL Distribution Ltd* v *Todd* [2002] EWCA Civ 1481, [2003] IRLR 28.

12.6.1.3 The employee's objection

Until a 1993 addition to TUPE 1981, reg. 5, the transfer of employment of the employee from transferor to transferee was entirely *automatic*. In effect none of the three parties involved had any choice in the matter. Now the employee is given a statutory right to object, but in a strange form. The amendment provides that an objection to being transferred has the effect of ending the contract but that it is not for any purpose to be regarded as a dismissal. An objection must consist of an actual refusal to be transferred, and not merely an expression of concern or unwillingness: *Hay* v *George Hanson (Building Contractors) Ltd* [1996] ICR 427.

Regulation 5(5) preserves the employee's right to resign and to claim constructive dismissal if some substantial change is made in working conditions which is to the employee's detriment. Thus in *University of Oxford* v *(1) Humphreys and (2) Associated Examining Board* [2000] IRLR 183 the employee successfully claimed damages for wrongful constructive dismissal against the transferor when his terms of employment were altered to his detriment. The same rules apply here as under domestic unfair dismissal law—see **10.6** above. In *Rossiter* v *Pendragon plc* [2002] EWCA Civ 745, [2002] ICR 1063, the Court of Appeal overturned an earlier EAT decision that the rules were different under reg. 5(5). The transferee employer's revision of a commission scheme was not a breach of a salesman's contract, entitling him to resign, and, in any event, he had affirmed the contract by working under it for 16 months. The provisions of reg. 5(5) specifically exclude a change consisting merely of a change in the identity of the employer, unless the employee can show it to be significant and detrimental in the particular case. Perhaps a conscientious objection to being associated with a particular industry might fall within the definition.

12.6.2 Maintenance of terms and conditions of employment

All employees whose continuity of employment is preserved on a relevant transfer take with them their existing terms and conditions of employment, entirely unchanged except for one matter we shall consider at **12.6.2.3** below.

12.6.2.1 Individual and collective matters

In this country contractual relationships between employer and employee are considered to be individual, even where employees are treated as a group for some purposes. The European origin of TUPE 1981 means that this rule extends to some collective matters as well as individual terms. So all collective agreements are maintained, and this includes trade union recognition.

12.6.2.2 New recruits

The continuity of terms and conditions applies to those transferred at the time of the transfer. Those subsequently recruited into employment cannot claim the same terms: *Landsorganisation i Danmark* v *Ny Mølle Kro* [1989] ICR 33.

12.6.2.3 The exception of pensions

TUPE 1981, reg. 7 excludes from the automatic transfer of terms and conditions anything to do with occupational pension schemes. One of the 1993 amendments defines this as restricted to provisions concerned with old age, invalidity or survivors' benefits, a clarification apparently designed to ensure that superior redundancy payment schemes linked to early retirement were not included and to bring British law into compliance with the decision of the ECJ in *Katsikas* v *Konstantinidis* [1993] IRLR 179. In *Beckmann* v *Dynamco Whicheloe Macfarlane Ltd* (Case C-164/00) [2002] IRLR 578, the ECJ held that even a pension paid early under an early retirement arrangement in a redundancy was not covered by the exception, as it was not an old-age benefit.

The result of this exception is that an employee whose employment is transferred on a relevant transfer seems to have no redress if the pension provision in the new employment is inferior to that with the transferor. See *Walden Engineering* v *Warrener* [1993] IRLR 420 for an example where the EAT declined to do more than operate the strict rule of TUPE 1981. The lack of protection under TUPE for occupational pension rights has been one of the matters of greatest practical concern to employees affected by transfers and the 2001 Directive also requires that some protection should be introduced. It now exists under the Pensions Act 2004, where s. 204 will require employers to continue to make certain contributions to pension schemes.

12.6.2.4 The maintenance of terms: for how long?

TUPE 1981, reg. 5(2) preserves the employee's contract of employment so that the terms of employment with the transferee after the transfer are exactly the same (except perhaps for pensions) as those with the transferor beforehand.

Let us return to the earlier example in **12.3** above. The engineering company wanted to sell the garden machinery business because it was not sufficiently profitable. The transferee wanted to buy it because it hoped to make it more profitable. The difference in profitability will not be achieved by magic. The new owner will need to cut costs by integrating the undertaking transferred into the existing garden machinery business. Employees will need to be interchangeable between old and new businesses, but this may well be unrealistic if conditions of employment are sufficiently different as to cause resentment between the two groups of employees. Very often one group will have a better condition under one head and a poorer condition under another. The employer may well be able to obtain the agreement of individuals or their trade union to some programme of harmonisation. The question is whether that is permitted under TUPE 1981 and we shall return to it at **12.6.3.2** below.

It is not only benefits to the employee that may be in issue. In *Crédit Suisse First Boston (Europe) Ltd* v *Lister* [1999] ICR 794, the Court of Appeal had to consider a case in which the transferee had given employees additional benefits in return for a post-termination restraint. The transferee now tried to enforce the latter. The Court held that the change in terms and conditions was by reason of the transfer, and therefore void under reg. 5.

12.6.3 Automatically unfair dismissal

By reg. 8 of TUPE 1981, any dismissal of an employee by transferor or transferee *because* of the transfer is automatically unfair, unless it can be shown to be for an 'economic, technical or organisational reason entailing changes in the workforce'. This is a strict rule. If it applies and the case does not fall within the exception, dismissal is always *automatically unfair*. If the exception applies, this is deemed to be an additional fair reason besides those provided in s. 98(2) of ERA 1996 and the tribunal will proceed to consider whether the employer acted reasonably. The requirement for qualifying service of one year applies as for other complaints of unfair dismissal: see **Chapter 10**.

In *Morris* v *John Grose Group Ltd* [1998] ICR 655 the EAT was required to consider a dismissal by receivers *before* any transfer had been arranged. They rejected the contention that reg. 8 presupposed the existence of a particular transfer and held that it still applied if dismissal was because of a transfer still to be arranged.

12.6.3.1 Economic, technical, and organisational reasons

The words 'economic, technical or organisational' ('eto') are taken literally from the Directive and it is not immediately clear what they are intended to mean in the law of this country. Each of them must also involve changes in the workforce. Some Government guidance on the application of TUPE 1981 to privatisations in the public sector gives three examples:

(a) An *economic* reason might arise where demand for the employer's output has fallen to such an extent that profitability could not be sustained unless staff were dismissed.

(b) A *technical* reason might arise where the transferee wishes to use new technology and the transferor's employees do not have the necessary skills.

(c) An *organisational* reason might arise where the transferee operates at a different location from the transferor and it is not practical to relocate the staff.

For the exception to have any effect it must be shown that the 'eto' reason entailing changes in the workforce was indeed the actual reason for dismissal in a particular case. In *Berriman* v *Delabole Slate* [1985] ICR 546, the transferee sought to standardise conditions of employment for newly transferred and existing employees and Berriman resigned, claiming constructive dismissal. The Court of Appeal held that the actual reason for dismissal was not one entailing changes in the workforce. See also *Crawford* v *Swinton Insurance* [1990] ICR 85.

We noted in **Chapter 10** that under the general law of unfair dismissal the tests of fairness and of a constructive dismissal were different so that not every constructive dismissal is unfair. We must ask whether the same can be true here, given the different definition of constructive dismissal we considered at **12.6.1.3** above. Can the employer who has altered terms of employment to the employee's detriment then claim an 'eto' reason for doing so? In theory it has to be possible, but the *Berriman* decision suggests it is so unlikely that we have not allowed for it in the algorithm at **Figure 12.1**.

In many actual examples there is a conflict between two very practical sets of considerations. The transferor wants to dispose of the undertaking because it is not sufficiently profitable. The transferee sees a prospect of making it profitable by combining it with an existing business and achieving some economies of scale, in other words by employing fewer people in the combined business.

To put too strict a test on the employer would discourage transfers and improved efficiency in business; to put too easy a test would undermine the whole purpose of TUPE 1981 and the Directive. The compromise the tribunals seem to have evolved puts a fairly broad interpretation on an 'eto' *reason* but then investigates quite thoroughly whether the employer behaved *reasonably*. This happened in *Meikle* v *McPhail* [1983] IRLR 351, where the business was a public house and its small size was held to be a relevant factor in determining reasonableness in dismissing a barmaid.

The Court of Appeal has examined the scope of economic reasons within the 'eto' exception. In *Warner* v *Adnet Ltd* [1998] ICR 1056 they confirmed that 'eto' cases form an exception to the general rule of automatic unfairness and that consequently reg. 8(1) and reg. 8(2) are not mutually exclusive. The dismissal of an accountant in that case was for redundancy, and was held to be fair (despite a lack of consultation) because of the urgency of the transferor's financial problems. In *Whitehouse* v *Chas A. Blatchford & Sons Ltd* [1999] IRLR 492, the dismissal of one employee among 18 was also held to be fair, because it was essential to the conduct of the business under the transferee's ownership. This contrasts with an opposite finding by the EAT in *Wheeler* v *Patel* [1987] ICR 631, where the employee's dismissal was held to fall outside the 'eto' exception. In the earlier case the evidence had been that the transferor had dismissed her in order to comply with a prospective purchaser's wishes, and was not related to the future conduct of the business.

12.6.3.2 Variation of contractual terms

We must now return to the question we left unanswered at the end of **12.6.2.4** above. The leading authority is the House of Lords decision in the joined cases of *British Fuels Ltd* v *Baxendale*; *Wilson* v *St Helens Borough Council* [1998] IRLR 706.

Mr Wilson and some others were employed by Lancashire County Council at a children's home. The council gave notice that they would cease to run the home and St Helens Council agreed to take it over, but on condition that it would not be a charge on their resources. As a result of negotiations between the transferor and a trade union, it was agreed that some staff would be redeployed to other jobs and others (including W) would be dismissed for redundancy by the transferor and re-engaged by the transferee on different terms and conditions. Subsequently, W argued that TUPE 1981 operated to preserve continuity of employment on identical terms and complained of unlawful deductions from wages by the transferee. The EAT found in his favour on the basis that the reason for the variation was the transfer of the undertaking. It therefore offended reg. 5 despite the passage of time. That decision suggested that employers would have considerable difficulty in rationalising conditions of employment in circumstances such as were set out above.

The Court of Appeal noted that W had been dismissed by the transferor and that the employment tribunal had expressly found that the dismissal was not automatically unfair under reg. 8(1). It was not merely because of the transfer, but for an 'eto' reason entailing changes in the workforce. His argument of continuity of employment therefore failed, because it depended on the rule in *Litster* (see **12.6.1.1** above), which only applied to those automatically unfairly dismissed under reg. 8(1) before the transfer.

Mr Meade had been employed as a plant operator by National Fuel Distributors Ltd who had then merged with another company in circumstances that constituted a relevant transfer to form British Fuels Ltd. M was dismissed by the transferor, given a redundancy payment and was re-engaged by the transferee on less favourable terms. Here there was no evidence to bring M's dismissal within the exceptional cases of reg. 8. The evidence suggested it was *because of* the transfer. The Court of Appeal found that he could therefore claim the benefit of the rule in *Litster* which gave continuity of employment with the transferee on unchanged conditions of employment. Mr Baxendale's case raised similar issues although the employment tribunal found that he had not been dismissed at all, at the relevant time.

The Court of Appeal decision brought out into the open a difficult question that had remained unresolved since the decision in *Litster* v *Forth Dry Dock* [1989] ICR 341. Where an employee is dismissed shortly before a transfer by the transferor, does reg. 8 operate to give the employee a remedy against the transferor for unfair dismissal, or does the rule in *Litster* make the dismissal a nullity, so that automatic transfer of employment occurs under reg. 5(1), and any remedy is then against the transferee?

The usual rule of law in this country is of course that there is no specific performance of contracts of personal service. Thus while employment tribunals are entitled to order reinstatement or re-engagement as a remedy in unfair dismissal cases, the description of these as 'orders' is something of a misnomer, since the employer always has the option of refusing to comply and of paying additional compensation instead.

There had been an interesting difference of approach between the EAT (which seemed concerned to maintain the common law rule) and the Court of Appeal (which was willing to be more radical and to accept that reg. 8(1) could indeed nullify some pre-transfer dismissals). Practitioners were confused, especially when the EAT adhered to its view and subsequently described the concept of nullifying a dismissal as having 'unsatisfactory practical consequences' in *Cornwall County Care Ltd* v *Brightman* [1998] ICR 529. Furthermore the ECJ suggested in *Jules Déthier Équipement S.A.* v *Dassy* [1998] ICR 541 that art. 4 of both the 1997 and 2001 Directives (on which reg. 8 is based) required only that a dismissal might be declared unlawful in the sense of giving a right to compensation but not necessarily of being declared a nullity.

Now the House of Lords has given a clear answer to the unresolved question. Reviewing the history of ECJ decisions, referring in particular to *Déthier* and also quoting with some approval from the EAT in *Brightman*, they rule that reg. 8 gives a right to compensation but does not provide for a dismissal to be nullified. They analyse in some detail the speeches of the Law Lords in *Litster* and hold that they should be construed as deeming the contract of employment to be kept alive only for the purpose of enforcing rights for breach of it or enforcing statutory rights dependent on it. A dismissal that offends reg. 8 is *unfair* but nevertheless *legally effective*.

Although the House of Lords has very helpfully given a clear answer to the question whether a pre-transfer dismissal is at risk of being nullified, they have not disposed so finally of the question we posed at **12.6.2.4**: when can the employer safely change terms and conditions after a relevant transfer?

The question was of course raised by the cases of each of the three applicants in *British Fuels* but it became irrelevant in relation to Wilson and Meade because of the decision on the first point that their dismissals were not a nullity and in relation to Baxendale because of a finding of fact by the employment tribunal that he had accepted a variation of conditions.

Comments on the issue of when conditions can lawfully be varied were therefore *obiter*. Lord Slynn of Hadley (with whom the other Law Lords agreed) rejected the argument that the automatic preservation of rights and duties under reg. 5 was restricted to the time of the transfer. A purported variation would still be invalid if *due to the transfer and for no other reason even if it came later*. He accepted that there must come a time when the link with the transfer could be said to be broken, but said that, if the appeal turned on that point, he would refer it to the ECJ under art. 234. He did not venture any further guidance on it.

In practice the question remains a very real one in circumstances such as we discussed earlier. In most examples, the transferor wants to dispose of some business undertaking because it is not sufficiently profitable. The transferee is prepared to take it over in order to put into effect some rationalisation plan that will improve efficiency. The rationalisation does not necessarily involve dismissing anyone. It sometimes will, but it may also involve harmonisation of conditions of employment, especially if the transferee wants to amalgamate the transferred undertaking with an existing enterprise. The solicitor will be asked when it is safe to take such steps. After *British Fuels* it seems that the answer has to be a pragmatic one based on commonsense. If the variation is *due to* the transfer and for *no other reason* it is invalid according to Lord Slynn's dictum. If it is for an 'eto' reason involving changes in the workforce, it is possible to read across the languge of reg. 10 into reg. 5 and the variation will not be due solely to the transfer. The more time has passed since the transfer, the more difficult it will be for an applicant to show that the variation was due solely to the transfer. That was the approach adopted by the EAT in *Solectron Scotland Ltd* v *Roper* [2004] IRLR 4 which traces the authority for it right back to the ECJ decision in *Foreningen af Arbejdsledere i Danmark* v *Daddy's Dance Hall A/S* (324/86) [1988] IRLR 315.

12.6.4 Joint and several liability

It is possible under art. 3.1 of both the 1977 and 2001 Directives for member states to legislate that transferor and transferee share joint and several liability for obligations to employees. There is no such provision in TUPE 1981, where reg. 5(2) provides simply that all rights, powers, duties and liabilities pass from transferor to transferee on the transfer. Indeed in *Bernadone* v *Pall Mall Services Group* [2000] IRLR 487, the Court of Appeal held that the rule even extended to liability (and consequently an insurance indemnity) in respect of a personal injury, because it was 'in connection with' the contract of employment.

In *Allan* v *Stirling District Council* [1995] ICR 1082 employees sought to enforce rights against the transferor on the basis of the Directive. The Scottish Court of Session overruled the EAT and held that the power given to member states by the Directive was permissive and not mandatory, and could not therefore contradict the clear provision of reg. 5(2). Once the transfer has taken place, the transferor no longer has any rights or duties under the employees' contracts of employment.

12.6.5 Consultation of employee representatives

The employers—both transferor and transferee—are required to consult employee representatives about the forthcoming transfer. This duty is not unlike the requirement to consult representatives about proposed dismissals for redundancy (see **11.4.2.1** above) but no minimum time periods are defined. The main practical problem is that commercial negotiations often need to remain confidential, and it is consequently almost impossible for either employer to inform anyone until the deal has reached a point at which consultation is unlikely to change the result. If no trade union is recognised, the employer must arrange for employee representatives to be elected.

12.6.6 'Hiving down'

There is a special case provided for under reg. 4 of TUPE 1981 which we have not yet mentioned. It arises on the insolvency of a company. For this purpose it does not make any difference whether the insolvency is through receivership, administration, or voluntary liquidation, and we shall use the term 'specialist' to include receivers, administrators, and liquidators.

Quite often the specialist finds that, although the company as a whole is insolvent, there is a part or parts of it that is/are quite capable of being run profitably if separated from the rest. The specialist therefore sets up a subsidiary company to run the profitable part of the business independently, and this is known as 'hiving down'. The hived-down subsidiary can then be sold to help raise funds for the liquidation of the rest.

According to the definitions we have considered so far, the act of hiving down is a relevant transfer of an identifiable part of the business to a different legal person. By contrast, the subsequent sale is probably of shares and is therefore not a relevant transfer. Regulation 4 operates to reverse that result so that all the duties associated with a relevant transfer arise on the sale by the specialist and not on hiving down.

12.7 Transfer between associated employers

Within large groups of companies, reorganisations of company structure are common, and in some cases frequent. There may be tax advantages or some administrative benefit in shifting responsibilities from a parent company to a subsidiary or vice versa, or between subsidiaries. Sometimes the company is organised into divisions or different establishments of the same limited company. There is no legal significance at all in a shift of administrative responsibility within one limited company; but technically any transfer of employees from one limited company to another is probably covered by TUPE 1981, even if the companies are associated.

Few employers properly comply in such circumstances with the TUPE 1981 requirements, although it is probably only the duty to consult recognised trade unions that has any practical significance. Most regard it as purely administrative. Even so, there is a duty on them to inform employees of any change in the identity of the employer within one month of its happening: ERA 1996, s. 4.

Whenever any employee's employment moves from one company to another associated company, continuity of employment is preserved: ERA 1996, s. 218(6). This rule applies irrespective of the circumstances. So an employee of one company in a group who happens to get a job in another group company will have continuity of employment preserved, even if the move resulted from an advertisement on the open market and was not in the usual sense a transfer initiated by the group.

12.8 Insolvency

One of the circumstances where the ownership of a business certainly undergoes some change is when the employer becomes insolvent. Insolvency is, of course, a very complex aspect of company law and we shall not attempt to deal with it in any detail here. We are concerned only with the position of the employees when an insolvency occurs, and there are two questions we shall want to answer:

(a) Does the employment of the employees come to an end on insolvency, or is it possible for them to continue to be employed—and, if so, by whom and on what conditions?

(b) What rights have the employees against the assets of an insolvent business for arrears of pay, outstanding holiday pay and other debts owing to them, especially in comparison with other creditors?

Before we proceed to address those questions it is convenient to put them in context by describing the various kinds of insolvency that now exist.

12.8.1 Kinds of insolvency

There are four main kinds of insolvency that we shall need to consider in outline:

12.8.1.1 Bankruptcy

This applies only to individual traders and to partnerships. It is less important for our purposes than the kinds of insolvency affecting companies.

12.8.1.2 Administration

This is the newest of the procedures, having been introduced in the Insolvency Act 1986. The intention is to provide a temporary means by which companies in difficulty but capable of being rescued can indeed be saved. The issue of an administration order requires a reference to the court leading to the appointment of an administrator, who has extensive powers to run the business and is deemed to act as an agent of the company.

12.8.1.3 Receivership

A receiver is appointed to receive the income of a company, to realise its assets and to meet its debts in a statutorily-defined sequence of priorities. There are various ways that the receiver can be appointed, some leading to a receiver who is deemed to be an officer of the court and some as an agent of the company. In practice it is now very rare to find anyone other than an *administrative receiver*, a category introduced by the Insolvency Act 1986 and given the power to continue to run the business. An administrative receiver is not the same as an administrator, the first being an open-ended appointment and the second normally requiring a conclusion within three months.

12.8.1.4 Liquidation or winding up

This is the final ending of the existence of the company and may be set in train by court order (compulsory winding up) or through a voluntary winding up if the directors believe the company can pay its debts.

12.8.2 The effect on contracts of employment

If the employer is an individual or a partnership that becomes bankrupt, the employment comes to an end.

The reason why the basis of appointment of the administrator, receiver or liquidator (the 'specialist') is important is that appointment by the court leads, under a long-standing rule, to the automatic termination of employment of the employees: *Reid* v *Explosives Co. Ltd* (1887) 19 QBD 264 and *Golding and Howard* v *Fire Auto and Marine Insurance (in liquidation)*

(1968) 4 ITR 372. The reason for dismissal is redundancy; but the employee's right to a redundancy payment will depend on having the necessary two years' service, and the ability to obtain it will depend on the matters we discuss in **12.8.3** below.

In all other cases the specialist's appointment as agent of the company has no effect on the employees' contracts of employment: *Re Foster Clark's Indenture Trusts* [1966] 2 All ER 403.

The Insolvency Act 1986 expressly provides that an administrative receiver is personally liable in relation to any contract of employment 'adopted' in connection with performing his functions. Adoption cannot occur within 14 days of the administrative receiver's appointment but is otherwise not defined. Until recently it had been unclear whether some specific act of adoption was required or whether mere continuance beyond 14 days was sufficient. As there was some authority for the second possibility, administrative receivers usually issued a disclaimer to prevent adoption. However, in *Powdrill* v *Watson* [1995] ICR 1100, the House of Lords held that adoption is a matter of fact if employees are continued in employment for more than 14 days. A full or partial disclaimer was ineffective.

Very often the specialist dismisses some at least of the employees in an effort to reduce the outgoings of the business. This is normally a redundancy. Employees have the same rights to notice and to statutory redundancy payments that we discussed in earlier Chapters. Although it is usually the rule that legal proceedings cannot be brought against an insolvent company without the leave of the court, it appears that this does not prevent a dismissed employee from complaining to the employment tribunal, except in connection with a compulsory liquidation. For example, the employee may wish to complain of unfair selection for redundancy—see **Chapter 11.**

Although one of the specialist's main objectives is to get the insolvent company into such a state that it can be sold as a going concern, it is dangerous to dismiss employees solely for this purpose because of the effect of TUPE 1981: *Litster* v *Forth Dry Dock* [1989] ICR 341.

12.8.3 Rights of employees to outstanding debts

When the employer becomes insolvent, various creditors may be competing for the assets. The rights of the employees can be considered in two parts:

(a) rights against the assets of the insolvent employer; and

(b) rights to claim from the National Insurance Fund.

12.8.3.1 Rights of employees against assets of the insolvent employer

In any insolvency there is a strict order of priority in which the specialist must seek to meet the claims of outstanding creditors. In outline the sequence is as follows:

(a) The costs of realising the assets.

(b) Other costs and remuneration of the specialist.

(c) Claims from holders of fixed charges.

(d) Preferential claims.

(e) Claims from holders of floating charges.

(f) Unsecured claims.

Each item in that list must be met in full before the next item is considered at all. If there is insufficient in the assets to meet the whole of an item it must be met in proportion to the amount that is available. So, for example, if there is enough on liquidation to meet the first three items but then only half the amount required for preferential claims, they will be satisfied only as to half their full amount and holders of floating charges and unsecured creditors will receive nothing at all.

Under sch. 6 of the Insolvency Act 1986, certain debts due to employees count as preferential debts for the purposes of that sequence:

(a) remuneration (defined to include wages and salary and various other items) in respect of the period of up to four months prior to the appointment of the receiver or liquidator, subject to the statutory maximum of £800;

(b) accrued holiday pay.

Any claim from an employee in addition to those amounts can still be pursued, but will rank as an unsecured claim and will be amongst the lowest priorities.

12.8.3.2 Rights against the National Insurance Fund

Very often the assets of an insolvent employer are insufficient to meet the debts due to preferential creditors, including employees. Even where that is not the problem, the process of liquidation is often so slow as to leave some employees in financial difficulty because of the absence of immediate income.

Some help is provided by s. 182 of ERA 1996, which provides some limited immediate payment to the employee from the National Insurance Fund, which then stands in the employee's shoes in seeking redress from the insolvent employer. Insolvency is defined for this purpose as meaning bankruptcy or any of the corporate states of insolvency defined at **12.8.1** above, but not merely that the employer cannot meet debts. This provision meets the requirements of European Directive 80/987/EEC.

Payments available from the National Insurance Fund are in all cases limited to the statutory maximum week's pay of £270 which we have encountered elsewhere, and are as follows:

(a) arrears of pay for up to eight weeks;

(b) minimum statutory notice as in s. 86 of ERA 1996;

(c) holiday pay for up to six weeks;

(d) a basic award for unfair dismissal;

(e) statutory redundancy pay: ERA 1996, s. 166;

(f) certain unpaid pensions contributions—those due from the employer and those employee's contributions already deducted but not paid over by the employer;

(g) statutory maternity pay.

12.9 Death of the employer

The rights of the employee when the employer dies are set out in s. 206 of ERA 1996. The rights of personal representatives of a deceased employee are covered in s. 207.

The death of an employer obviously changes the status of the employee only if the employer was acting as a sole individual. If the employer was a partnership, the usual rule of survivorship provides that the remaining partners become the new employer; if the employer traded as a limited company, the death of a major shareholder does not affect the continuing existence of the company.

The essence of the statutory rules is that rights enjoyed by the employee against the employer can be maintained against the personal representatives. This includes employment tribunal proceedings, subject only to the rule that in a case of unfair dismissal, reinstatement or re-engagement cannot be ordered against personal representatives.

If the death of the employer results in the ending of the employment, that is to be treated as a dismissal for redundancy: ERA 1996, s. 136(5). This will usually apply to domestic servants and the like. However, if the employment is a business the personal representatives are more likely to want to keep it going to maximise its resale value, and there is continuity of employment in such cases. The liability of the personal representatives to make a redundancy payment can be avoided if the employee unreasonably refuses an offer of suitable continuing employment. However, the employment will not be continued by default: there needs to be some agreement between the employee and the personal representatives to continue: *Ranger* v *Brown* [1978] ICR 608.

12.10 Self-test questions

1. Is there any single test you can apply when a business (or part of one) changes hands to decide whether there has been a relevant transfer within the meaning of TUPE 1981?

2. A client comes to you wanting to discuss his proposed purchase for a very favourable price of an unprofitable part of an existing business, in the hope of amalgamating it with his current business and making it profitable through economies of scale. Your detailed enquiries indicate quite clearly that the purchase will be a relevant transfer within the meaning of TUPE 1981. What key employment law consequences would you bring to the client's notice as a result of that conclusion?

13

Employment tribunal procedure

13.1 Introduction

The feature that links most of the rights of employees set out in this book is that the remedy for infringement is a complaint to the employment tribunal. There are, of course, a few items where this is not the case—mostly matters involving alleged breach of contract, including wrongful dismissal. The procedure there is to be found in any standard work on civil procedure and the key points have been noted in **Chapters 5** and **9**, but the employment tribunals are unique to employment law and we need in this chapter to describe their operation and procedure.

In this edition of our book the authors have something of a problem. New procedural rules for the tribunals came into effect on 1 October 2004, which is the date we have set to state the law, but they only fully apply to claims started (or at least responded to) after that date. So, as we go to press we have no experience at all of the practical operation of the new rules because all the cases that are currently underway started (and therefore in some respects continue) under the rules from 2001. Yet by the time those reading this chapter come to put any of it into effect, the new rules will be the norm. We have therefore presented the chapter using the new terminology and as if the new rules were in full operation. We shall indicate where we believe our comments involve some speculation.

For our purposes the claimant presenting a claim to the tribunal is always the employee (or, in appropriate cases, the applicant for a job, the 'worker', or the ex-employee) and the employer is the respondent. Except for the rare case mentioned at **6.8** above, there are no circumstances in which an employer can make a claim to the employment tribunal. Employers have other remedies: dismissal, or very occasionally civil litigation, perhaps, for example, in order to seek an injunction restraining an ex-employee from disclosing trade secrets. If the ex-employee brings a claim for breach of contract in a tribunal, the employer may counterclaim, but the employer cannot initiate proceedings.

There are a few jurisdictions in which an employee can bring proceedings in the employment tribunal against a trade union or a trade union against the employer, but the number of such cases in practice is so small that we shall ignore both possibilities.

The solicitor is most likely to become involved on behalf of either side once something has already gone wrong in the employment relationship. As in any other branch of the law, litigation is the last resort and clients should be advised not to ignore obvious and less formal solutions. We have always regarded it as good practice to suggest that the employee could complain personally to the boss or use the trade union to pursue a grievance. Now, however, the claimant who comes to the tribunal with a claim other than dismissal without having used the employer's grievance procedure will be required in the claim form to explain why not, and will suffer a penalty if the explanation is not good enough. Similarly, as we saw in **Chapter 10**, a claimant who successfully complains of unfair dismissal will find compensation reduced if there is no good explanation for not having used the employer's appeal procedure. Both sides, though, will need to take care to ensure that discussions held 'without prejudice' do not adversely affect them if tribunal proceedings follow. The 'without prejudice' rule only applies once a dispute can be said to exist and in any case does not protect from disclosure any remark that involves unlawful discrimination—*BNP Paribas* v *Mezzotero* [2004] IRLR 508.

If those informal steps fail, an application to the tribunal becomes inevitable and we shall set out the procedure to be followed in the remainder of the chapter, which takes the following form:

(a) The constitution and workload of the employment tribunals.
(b) Bringing a claim.
(c) Presentation of the claim on time.
(d) Acceptance of the claim.
(e) The response.
(f) Acceptance of the response and default hearings.
(g) Case management.
(h) Pre-hearing reviews.
(i) Conciliation and the role of ACAS.
(j) The hearing.
(k) The tribunal decision.
(l) Costs and preparation time orders.
(m) The remedies available to the tribunal.
(n) Challenge of an employment tribunal decision.
(o) A summary of main jurisdictions, time limits, and awards.

In trying to understand how the procedures work it will be helpful to use four imaginary examples, three of them complaints of unfair dismissal: Anastasia was dismissed for redundancy and Basil for alleged dishonesty; Catherine claims constructive unfair dismissal. Dmitri complains of disability discrimination. The detailed facts will emerge as we introduce and develop the cases.

13.2 Constitution and workload of the employment tribunals

13.2.1 History

The current workload of the employment tribunals is broad, but their origin is surprisingly narrow. From humble beginnings in 1964 their workload has burgeoned.

As we explained at the start of the book, the employment tribunals were known as industrial tribunals until 31 July 1998. The Employment Rights (Dispute Resolution) Act (ERDRA) 1998, s. 1, provides that from 1 August 1998, every reference to an industrial tribunal in earlier statues and elsewhere should be deemed to be a reference to an employment tribunal. We have followed that rule throughout this book, even when referring to decisions in old cases.

Since 1 October 2004 the operation of the employment tribunals has been governed by the Employment Tribunals (Constitution and Rules of Procedure) Regulations 2004 (the

ET Regs 2004), which contain in sch. 1 the Employment Tribunal Rules of Procedure (ET Rules 2004). We shall not concern ourselves with the special rules for certain specific jurisdictions that are contained in sch. 2 to 6, sch. 6 being a subsequent addition to ET Regs 2004 that covers claims of equal pay for work of equal value—see **6.7.3** above for a very brief summary. Those familiar with the previous regulations and rules from 2001 will notice many differences, not least that the new provisions apply to the whole of Great Britain, whereas there were previously separate sets for England and Wales and for Scotland.

13.2.2 The composition of the tribunals

The employment tribunal system is an executive agency. Its judicial side is headed by the President and the administration by a chief executive who is based in London. The Central Office of Employment Tribunals where the central records are maintained is at Bury St Edmunds in Suffolk.

The system in England and Wales is organised into 21 offices, 14 of which have the status of regions, each headed by a Regional Chairman. In each region there are several full-time chairmen, and a number of part-time chairmen who can be called on to help when the workload is heavy. By reg. 8 of the ET Regs 2004, the chairman of an employment tribunal must be a barrister or solicitor of seven years' standing. The part-time chairmen in fact consist of some practising lawyers and some retired, former full-time chairmen. Tribunal chairmen of both sexes have been content to use that title; some have reacted rather forcibly to being addressed as a chair, despite the now widespread use of the term in some walks of life.

When the tribunal sits it must be chaired by the President or another chairman, who normally is accompanied by one person from each of two lists (or 'panels') of people representative of employers' organisations and of employed people's organisations. In interlocutory matters and uncontested cases the chairman sits alone. There has been increasing use of the provision under ETA 1996, s. 4(2) as amended by ERDRA 1998, s. 3, whereby chairmen sit alone in other matters and that is now normal practice in relation to protection of wages and breach of contract questions. It is possible for chairmen to sit alone if parties consent in other matters including unfair dismissal. Chairmen sometimes sit with one other member, usually where the third member has become indisposed or is forced to withdraw for some reason.

13.2.3 Procedure at the tribunals

The employment tribunals were originally intended to provide a means of resolving employment disputes that was informal, speedy, and cheap. To an extent they still do, but the informality is more apparent to lawyers who compare them with the courts than to the general public who often find them daunting. Under ET Regs 2004, reg. 3, their overriding objective is to deal with cases justly.

Until now there has been no equivalent in the tribunals to the Woolf reforms in the courts. In practice this has often not made much difference as the rules gave tribunals a wide power to determine their own procedure. Many chairmen adopted Woolf-type practices in order to clarify the issues in advance of any hearing, and such action has been justified by reference to the overriding objective. The problem for practitioners has been that individual chairmen have different preferences, and it has been difficult to know how cases will be handled in an unfamiliar region. Thus, for example, there have been widely differing practices among regions and even among individual chairmen in some regions regarding the use of written witness statements (see **13.8.10** below). Clients often express dislike of tighter procedural management, which they see as adding to formality in the tribunals and causing cases to be won or lost on technicalities rather than the merits.

The new ET Regs 2004 now change tribunal procedure considerably to make it more similar to the courts, with increased emphasis on case management by the tribunals. As in the courts, terminology is changed to make it less arcane, and, for example, interlocutory proceedings now become interim hearings. A claim (previously an originating application) is presented by the claimant (applicant), usually using form ET 1 (IT 1) and the respondent (no change) replies in a response, form ET3 (notice of appearance, IT 3).

Under reg. 13 of ET Regs 2004 the President has the power to make practice directions. We expected that the power would be used very soon after the new rules came into effect on 1 October 2004 so as to start to standardise practice across the country, especially in matters like the use of witness statements. In fact nothing has been issued. We understand that the President prefers to write informally to Regional Chairmen commending examples of good practice rather than to be prescriptive by issuing practice directions. It remains to be seen how far this 'softly softly' approach succeeds in removing those regional variations that most practitioners dislike.

We shall note the most important aspects of the tribunals' procedure as we work through the progress of a case in the following sections.

13.2.4 Jurisdictions

Although, as we have noted, there is a wide range of jurisdictions for the employment tribunals, the largest part of their workload is concentrated on relatively few issues.

During the fiscal year 2002-3 the tribunals in Great Britain received a total of 115,042 applications, which contained 197,365 complaints, as shown in **Table 13.1**.

13.2.5 Appeals

An appeal from a decision of the employment tribunal lies on a point of law only to the EAT, and thereafter in the usual way to the Court of Appeal and the House of Lords. We shall consider briefly the mechanism for appealing to the EAT in **13.15.2** below.

13.2.6 Scotland

The substantive statute law that we have been considering throughout this book applies equally to Scotland as to England and Wales. There are, of course, a few differences as to the common law.

Table 13.1 Workload of the employment tribunals in 2003–4

Unfair dismissal	47,376	24%
Redundancy pay	9,087	5%
Deductions from wages	42,524	$21\frac{1}{2}$%
Discrimination: race, sex, equal pay, disability, part-time etc.	32,114	16%
Breach of contract	29,661	15%
Working Time Regulations	16,869	$8\frac{1}{2}$%
All other jurisdictions, i.e., miscellaneous employment rights, and trade union issues	19,734	10%
Total	197,365	100%

Source: *Employment Tribunal Service Annual Report, 2003–4.*

Although, as we noted at **13.2.1** above, ET Regs 2004 apply equally to Scotland as to England and Wales, the Scottish structure of employment tribunals is separate, with its own Central Office in Glasgow and its own President. Appeals lie to a Scottish division of the EAT, then to the Court of Session and finally to the House of Lords. In a statement arising out of *Davidson* v *City Electrical Factors Ltd* [1998] ICR 443, however, the President of EAT has explained that there is one EAT and not two, so that a judgment of EAT wherever it sits has an equal effect in law in Scotland and in England and Wales. We should refer to 'the EAT sitting in Scotland' and not to a 'Scottish EAT'.

Practitioners may occasionally find themselves called upon by clients in England and Wales to deal with cases in Scotland. For example, a company with its only premises in the south of England that dismisses a service engineer who used his home in Edinburgh as a base for work in that area will find an employment tribunal claim sent to a Scottish tribunal (see **13.3** for the reasons why). We expect that the few remaining differences in practice in Scotland will become less significant under the common rules of procedure, but practitioners straying north of the border must expect any reference they make to documents, costs or staying proceedings to be corrected to 'productions', 'expenses' and 'sisting' proceedings.

13.3 Bringing a claim

The means of bringing an action in the employment tribunal is to present a claim to the appropriate local office of the tribunals, determined by reference to the postcode of the place of work or former place of work. Very clear guidance for claimants can be found at the employment tribunal website www.employmenttribunals.gov.uk, which is worth visiting. It includes the standard form ET1 which replaces the old version IT1 that was current until 30 September 2004. At the time we go to press, ET Rules 2004 specify the information to be included in any claim, but use of the form is not mandatory, although in practice almost everyone uses it. Under r. 1(3) it will become mandatory to use the five-page form ET1 on 6 April 2005 and a copy is to be found below, reprinted here by kind permission of the Employment Tribunal Service.

The new form is much longer than the old version and contains sections specific to particular kinds of claim. It is designed to be user-friendly and straightforward, and we shall comment only on a few aspects.

13.3.1 How much information is required?

Hitherto, although the old version of the rules provided that certain matters should be included in any claim to the tribunal, the authorities seemed to ignore the rule and held that particulars of the grounds of a claim were not essential: *Burns International* v *Butt* [1983] ICR 547. The only statutory requirement as to form was that an application was in writing. Such flexibility of approach seems out of keeping with the stricter requirement of r. 1(4) of ET Rules 2004, listing matters to be covered in a claim, and we do not expect it to survive, especially after 6 April 2005, when use of form ET 1 becomes mandatory.

A significant difference between ET Rules 2004 (and form ET 1) and the previous versions is that express provision is now made for multiple claims against the same employer. Names and addresses must be given for each claimant.

Claim to an Employment Tribunal

Please read the **guidance notes** and the notes on this page carefully **before** filling in this form.

By law, you **must** provide the information marked with ✻ and, if it is relevant, the information marked with ● (see guidance on Pre-acceptance procedure).

You may find it helpful to take advice **before** filling in the form, particularly if your claim involves discrimination.

How to fill in this form

All claimants **must** fill in **sections 1, 2 and 3**. You then only need to fill in those sections of the form that apply to your case. For example:

For **unpaid wages**, fill in **sections 4 and 8**.

For **unfair dismissal**, fill in **sections 4 and 5**.

For **discrimination**, fill in **sections 4 and 6**.

For a **redundancy payment**, fill in **sections 4 and 7**.

For **unfair dismissal** and **discrimination**, fill in **sections 4, 5 and 6**.

For **unfair dismissal** and **unpaid wages**, fill in **sections 4, 5 and 8**.

Fill in **section 10** only if there is some information you wish to draw to the tribunal's attention and **section 11** only if you have appointed a representative to act on your behalf in dealing with your claim.

If this form sets out a claim by more than one claimant arising from the same set of facts, please give the names and addresses of additional claimants on a separate sheet or sheets of paper.

Please make sure that all the information you give is as accurate as possible.

Where there are tick boxes, please tick the one that applies.

If you fax the form, do not send a copy in the post.

ET1

1 Your details

1.1 Title: Mr ☐ Mrs ☐ Miss ☐ Ms ☐ Other

1.2* First name (or names):

1.3* Surname or family name:

1.4 Date of birth (date/month/year): / / Are you: male? ☐ female? ☐

1.5* Address:

Postcode

You do not need to answer 1.6 and 1.7 if you have appointed a representative (see section 11).

1.6 Phone number **(where we can contact you during normal working hours):**

1.7 How would you prefer us to communicate with you? Post ☐ Fax ☐ E-mail ☐

Fax:

E-mail address:

2 Respondent's details

2.1* Give the name of your employer or the organisation or person you are complaining about (the respondent).

2.2* Address:

Postcode

2.3 If you worked at an address different from the one you have given at 2.2, please give the full address.

Postcode

2.4● If your complaint is against more than one respondent please give the names, addresses and postcodes of additional respondents.

3 Action before making a claim

3.1* Are you, or were you, an employee of the respondent? Yes ☐ No ☐
If 'Yes', please now go straight to section 3.3.

3.2 Are you, or were you, a worker providing services to the respondent? Yes ☐ No ☐
If 'Yes', please now go straight to section 4.
If 'No', please now go straight to section 6.

3.3● Is your claim, or part of it, about a dismissal by the respondent? Yes ☐ No ☐
If 'No', please now go straight to section 3.5.

3.4● Is your claim about anything else, in addition to the dismissal? Yes ☐ No ☐
If 'No', please now go straight to section 4.
If 'Yes', please answer questions 3.5 to 3.7 about the non-dismissal aspects of your claim.

3.5● Have you put your complaint in writing to the respondent?

Yes ☐ Please give the date you put it to them in writing. / /
No ☐

If 'No', please now go straight to section 3.7.

3.6● Did you allow at least 28 days between the date you put your complaint to the respondent and the date you sent us this claim? Yes ☐ No ☐
If 'Yes', please now go straight to section 4.

3.7● Please explain why you did not put your complaint in writing to the respondent or, if you did, why you did not allow at least 28 days before sending us your claim.
(In most cases, it is a legal requirement to take these procedural steps. Your claim will not be accepted unless you give a valid reason why you did not have to meet the requirement in your case. If you are not sure, you may want to get legal advice.)

4 Employment details

4.1 Please give the following dates if possible.

When your employment started: / /

When your employment ended or will end: / /

Is your employment continuing? Yes ☐ No ☐

4.2 Please say what job you do or did.

4.3 How many hours do or did you work each week? ....hours each week

4.4 How much are or were you paid?

Pay before tax: £ each

Normal take-home pay (including overtime, commission, bonuses and so on): £ each

4.5 If your employment has ended, did you work (or were you paid for) a period of notice? Yes ☐ No ☐

If 'Yes', how many weeks or months did you work or were you paid for? ....weeks ....months

5 Unfair dismissal or constructive dismissal

Please fill in this section only if you believe you have been unfairly or constructively dismissed.

5.1 ● If you were dismissed by your employer, you should explain why you think your dismissal was unfair. If you resigned because of something your employer did or failed to do which made you feel you could no longer continue to work for them (constructive dismissal) you should explain what happened.

5 Unfair dismissal or constructive dismissal continued

5.1 continued

5.2 Were you in your employer's pension scheme? Yes ☐ No ☐

5.3 If you received any other benefits from your employer, please give details.

5.4 Since leaving your employment have you got another job? Yes ☐ No ☐
If 'No', please now go straight to section 5.7.

5.5 Please say when you started (or will start) work.

5.6 Please say how much you are now earning (or will earn). £ each

5.7 Please tick the box to say what you want if your case is successful:

a To get your old job back and compensation (reinstatement) ☐

b To get another job with the same employer and compensation (re-engagement) ☐

c Compensation only ☐

6 Discrimination

Please fill in this section only if you believe you have been discriminated against.

6.1 ● Please tick the box or boxes to indicate what discrimination (including victimisation) you are complaining about:

Sex (including equal pay) ☐

Disability ☐

Sexual orientation ☐

Race ☐

Religion or belief ☐

6.2 ● Please describe the incidents which you believe amounted to discrimination, the dates of these incidents and the people involved.

7 Redundancy payments

Please fill in this section only if you believe you are owed a redundancy payment.

7.1 ● Please explain why you believe you are entitled to this payment and set out the steps you have taken to get it.

8 Other payments you are owed

Please fill in this section only if you believe you are owed other payments.

8.1 ● Please tick the box or boxes to indicate that money is owed to you for:

unpaid wages? ☐
holiday pay? ☐
notice pay? ☐
other unpaid amounts? ☐

8.2 How much are you claiming?

Is this: before tax? ☐ after tax? ☐

8.3 ● Please explain why you believe you are entitled to this payment. If you have specified an amount, please set out how you have worked this out.

9 Other complaints

Please fill in this section only if you believe you have a complaint that is not covered elsewhere.

9.1 ● Please explain what you are complaining about and why.
Please include any relevant dates.

10 Other information

10.1 Please do not send a covering letter with this form.
You should add any extra information you want us to know here.

11 Your representative

Please fill in this section only if you have appointed a representative. If you do fill this section in, we will in future only send correspondence to your representative and not to you.

11.1 Representative's name:

11.2 Name of the representative's organisation:

11.3 Address:

Postcode

11.4 Phone number:

11.5 Reference:

11.6 How would they prefer us to communicate with them?

Post ☐ Fax ☐ E-mail ☐

Fax:

E-mail address:

Please sign and date here

Signature: Date: / /

Data Protection Act 1998. We will send a copy of this form to the respondent(s) and Acas. We will put some of the information you give us on this form onto a computer. This helps us to monitor progress and produce statistics.

13.3.2 Representation (box 11)

At item 11 the claimant is asked to name a representative if one exists. The ET Rules 2004 do not specify who may appear in the employment tribunals, but in practice representatives include counsel and solicitors, representatives of trade unions, employers' associations, and Citizens' Advice Bureaux and various personnel consultancies. Contingency-based fees are common.

As legal aid is not available in the tribunals and costs have rarely been awarded (see **13.13** below), many claimants choose to appear in person, being reluctant to incur the cost of instructing lawyers. Employers sometimes do so too. It will be found in practice that chairmen have always aimed to meet the objective of ET Regs 2004, reg 3(2) (a) to ensure that the parties are on an equal footing and try to compensate for any disadvantage suffered by an unrepresented party, especially a claimant. The procedural rules are applied less strictly than to any professional representative. However, in *Mensah* v *East Hertfordshire NHS Trust* [1998] IRLR 531, the Court of Appeal (unlike the EAT) refused to allow a claimant to re-open a ground of complaint merely because the employment tribunal had allegedly not been astute in ensuring that she covered during the hearing all matters contained in the claim form.

13.3.3 The remedy being sought (box 5.7)

At item 5.7 on the form ET 1 the claimant is asked to state in relation to claims of unfair dismissal what remedy is being sought: reinstatement, re-engagement or compensation. It is perhaps strange that such a question should be asked at this early stage, and indeed the form makes clear that the claimant is not bound by the answer given here but may ask for something else at the end of tribunal proceedings.

There is, of course, a tactical advantage to the claimant in asking for reinstatement or re-engagement, even if not having any real wish to go back to work for the same employer. As we noted in **Chapter 10**, the amounts of compensation awarded if the employer has failed to carry out an order for reinstatement or re-engagement are substantially increased. So such a request at this stage may assist in the negotiation of an out-of-tribunal settlement—see **13.10** below.

13.3.4 Particulars of the claim

Each of the main sections of form ET 1 contains a box for details of the claim—box 5.1, 6.2, 7.1, 8.3, or 9.1, depending on the subject of the claim. The question then arises of how much detail is required.

The new rules may possibly lead to a requirement for greater detail than previously but until we find otherwise we shall assume that the answer is still that the documents exchanged between the parties in relation to tribunal proceedings are not subject to the strict rules or terminology that you will have learned in civil procedure. It is necessary to set out sufficient detail that the other side cannot claim to be taken by surprise by any aspect of the claim. It will be found in practice that lawyers appearing in the tribunals are expected to meet usual professional standards in this regard even if lay-people are given greater latitude. The balance between too much and too little detail is difficult to describe in the abstract and an example may help.

EXAMPLE

Consider the following entry by Anastasia at box 5.1 on her ET 1 when her claim is solely of unfair dismissal:

I was called into my manager's office in the afternoon of Friday, 26 November and was told that I was being dismissed as redundant. I was told to collect my personal belongings at once and to leave the premises before the end of the afternoon. I do not accept that I was fairly selected. There was no individual consultation before notice was given to me. At the time of my dismissal there were sub-contractors working in the design office in jobs that I could easily have filled. My employment ended on 3 December.

This is a good statement. It succinctly sets out the essential facts of the case and clearly identifies the items that the claimant is putting in issue. By implication at least it therefore also identifies those that are not being challenged. Yet it does not disclose more of the claimant's case in advance than is helpful. The items put in issue are three:

(a) unfair selection;

(b) lack of individual consultation;

(c) failure to look for alternative work.

The statement does not challenge matters such as the following:

(a) that the dismissal was not truly for redundancy (although, as we noted at **10.8.1** above, the burden of proof of a reason for dismissal always rests with the employer and the tribunal may always require the employer to prove it);

(b) that the claimant's selection was automatically unfair by being based on trade union activities;

(c) that Anastasia's selection involved any discrimination on grounds of race, sex, or disability, all of these being arguments that if successful could lead to unlimited compensation.

A solicitor representing a claimant like Anastasia may not be permitted to raise such arguments at the hearing without warning. The respondent will be unprepared to defend them and will object. If the arguments are allowed at all, the hearing may then be adjourned until another day. Whilst costs are not normally awarded in the employment tribunals, extra costs resulting from such an adjournment may well have to be borne by the party responsible for it.

Note that while the statement clearly defines the issues for an eventual tribunal hearing, it does not disclose the arguments in advance. For example, it may be that the manager who selected the claimant for dismissal was biased, or did not properly research the records, or failed to take proper account of a reason for recent poor attendance like an industrial accident. The claimant's solicitor will wish to challenge the manager about these points in cross-examination and has wisely decided that there is no need to disclose such valuable bits of information before the hearing. The employer who protests at being taken by surprise by such matters scores an own-goal: these are all matters that plainly should have been in the manager's knowledge when making the decision. By contrast, the employer is entitled to advance warning of *specific* points that might reasonably be outside the manager's knowledge, such as an argument that another, named employee was treated differently a year or two ago.

It is usually a good idea to avoid statements that leave the reader unclear what exactly it is you are talking about. References to 'certain shortcomings', for example, merely invite the other side to apply for additional information (see **13.8.3** below) about precisely what shortcomings you mean. In the above example it is possible to argue that the reference to sub-contractors is unclear in this way, and that might be a criticism. In practice, though, the employer is probably well aware of exactly who is meant, as there are unlikely to be many people fitting the description.

As with most other forms of legal drafting, there is no single right or wrong way to complete employment tribunal documents and different practitioners have different preferences, especially in relation to how much detail to include at an early stage and how much to keep until the hearing. Nevertheless, we can summarise points that emerge from the example like this:

(a) Be as succinct as possible. As a rule of thumb, it should not usually be necessary to expand beyond the space provided on the ET 1, although an increasing number of representatives now do so.

(b) Ensure that nothing so important is omitted as to entitle the other side to complain of being taken by surprise.

(c) Do not disclose unnecessarily facts that would more effectively be used with some surprise value in cross-examination.

(d) Avoid loose ends which almost invite the other side to apply for additional information. For example, the passive voice 'The claimant was told' invites the question, 'Who told her?'. Unless the answer is obvious or well-known to the other side, it is better to use the active voice from the outset: 'The manager told the claimant.'

13.4 Presentation of the claim on time

It is important that the claim is presented on time. 'Presentation' consists of delivering the originating application to the tribunal office, by hand, through the post or by fax. In the case of the post it is the time of arrival and not the time of posting that counts.

If we look at the first ten jurisdictions of the tribunals set out in **Table 13.1**, which together account for 90 per cent of the workload, we find that each has its own rule and we need to look at them in turn.

13.4.1 The various time limits

13.4.1.1 Unfair dismissal

A claim can be presented on or after the date notice is given, even if that is before the employment terminates. It must be presented to the tribunal office within *three months* beginning with the effective date of termination, or such further period as the tribunal considers reasonable if presentation within three months was *not reasonably practicable:* ERA 1996, s. 111(2).

13.4.1.2 A claim for a redundancy payment

A claim must be made within *six months* beginning with the relevant date, or within a further six months if the tribunal considers it *just and equitable*. A 'claim' in this context is widely defined: it includes a demand directly of the employer, a claim in the tribunal for a redundancy payment or a complaint to the tribunal of unfair dismissal: ERA 1996, s. 164.

13.4.1.3 Protection of wages

A claim about a deduction from wages must be presented within *three months* beginning with the most recent date of payment of wages from which the unlawful deduction was allegedly made, or such further period as the tribunal considers reasonable if satisfied that it was *not reasonably practicable* for the claim to be presented within the three months: ERA 1996, s. 23.

13.4.1.4 Racial discrimination

A claim must be presented to the tribunal within *three months* of the allegedly discriminatory act, or such further period as the tribunal considers *just and equitable*: RRA 1976, s. 68(1) and (6). If the discrimination was continuous over a period, time runs from the most recent occurrence: *Barclays Bank* v *Kapur* [1991] ICR 208.

13.4.1.5 Sex discrimination

A claim must be presented to the tribunal within *three months* of the allegedly discriminatory act, or such further period as the tribunal considers *just and equitable*, an exactly similar rule to that relating to racial discrimination: SDA 1975, s. 76. The *Barclays Bank* rule about repeated discrimination applies here too. If discrimination occurs through the employer's refusal of a request by the employee, time starts to run again *every* time the employer reconsiders the request and refuses again: *Cast* v *Croydon College* [1998] ICR 500.

That rule relates to proceedings brought under the SDA 1975. There is *no time limit* in relation to proceedings brought directly under the European Treaty or a European Directive, but the ECJ normally regards such procedural matters as appropriate for determination by the Member States.

A particular problem has arisen in relation to the time limit within which claims must be brought when decisions of the ECJ or domestic courts in effect create new rights, e.g., the right to equality in pensions schemes following *Barber* v *Guardian Royal Exchange Assurance Group* [1990] ICR 616 (see **6.4.3** above). The approach seems to be one of regarding time as running from the point when the claimant ought to have been aware that a right existed (see *Biggs* v *Somerset County Council* [1996] ICR 364, and **13.4.4** below).

13.4.1.6 Disability discrimination

The DDA 1995, sch. 3 sets the same rules as RRA 1976 and SDA 1975, of a claim within *three months* beginning when the act complained of took place, and allows extension if the tribunal considers it *just and equitable*.

13.4.1.7 Discrimination against part-time workers

The same rule of a claim within *three months* (or, in this case, *six months* if concerning a member of the armed forces) and extension if the tribunal considers it *just and equitable* exists under PTW Regs 2000 as for the other categories of discrimination.

13.4.1.8 Equal pay

A claim may be presented at any time during the continuation of employment. As regards arrears, see **6.8** above. A claim must be presented within *six months* of the termination of the employment. There is *no extension* of this period: Equal Pay Act 1970, s. 2.

13.4.1.9 Breach of contract

The rule here is the same as for unfair dismissal. See **13.6.3** below for the time limit regarding any counterclaim by the employer.

13.4.1.10 Claims under the Working Time Regulations 1998

Under reg. 30(2) a claim must be presented within *three months* (or *six months* for the armed forces) of the alleged start of infringement, with a possibility of extension if it was *not reasonably practical* to present before the end of that period.

13.4.2 Interrelation with the statutory grievance procedure

We have already encountered at **5.3.2** the statutory grievance procedures (SGP), which came into effect on 1 October 2004. Their coverage fairly obviously includes grievances that employees may have about any of the above jurisdictions except the first, but in fact the first is included too in relation to constructive dismissal. An employee who claims constructive unfair dismissal on the basis of any act or omission by the employer is expected to raise the dissatisfaction through the SGP prior to bringing a claim to the tribunal. Claims under any of the jurisdictions where the SGP applies but where it has not been used can result in an increase or a decrease in any award of compensation depending whether the fault lies with respondent employer or claimant respectively.

The time limit for presenting a claim to the tribunal can be extended for three months in either of two cases. First, if at the time of presenting within the time limit a claim to the tribunal the employee has not yet used the SGP or has raised a grievance only within the last 28 days, there can be a three-month extension to put in a claim in the light of use of the SGP, provided that the grievance is raised within one month of the normal time limit. Secondly, there can also be a three-month extension if the employee has sent a statement of grievance to the employer within the normal time limit but it has not completed the SGP when the time limit expires.

Solicitors are unlikely generally to become involved in proceedings under SGPs concerning individual employers, so that compliance with these requirements will most often rest with client claimants. Clients will need to be warned of the importance of meeting the time limits.

13.4.3 Presentation within time and the possibility of extension

As we noted at the start of this section, the rule about presentation in time is important. The reason is that it has been held to be a rule about *jurisdiction* and not merely *procedure*: see *Rogers* v *Bodfari (Transport) Ltd* [1973] ICR 325 and *Dedman* v *British Building and Engineering Supplies Ltd* [1974] ICR 53. If it were procedural, the tribunal could refuse to let a respondent employer use the time limit as a defence if it felt that the lateness was wholly or partly the respondent's fault or that the respondent's conduct had ignored the time limit. As the rule is jurisdictional there is no such flexibility and it must be applied strictly. Nevertheless, the effective date of termination in an unfair dismissal application is a matter of fact, not law, and an agreement about that was binding on the parties in *Lambert* v *Croydon College* [1999] ICR 409.

There are two aspects to the operation of the time limit and we shall consider each in turn:

(a) whether the claim was presented in time; and, if not,

(b) whether time should be extended in the circumstances.

Where a time limit is expressed as beginning on a particular date, it has been held to mean precisely that: see *University of Cambridge* v *Murray* [1993] ICR 460 for confirmation. Thus, if the employee was dismissed on 3 April and wishes to complain of unfair dismissal, a claim must be presented at the tribunal on or before 2 July. Presentation on 3 July is one day after the end of the three-month period *beginning on* 3 April, and a claim received then would be out of time. It is calendar months that count, notwithstanding variations in their length. So, for example, periods of three months beginning with an effective date of termination between 29 November and 1 December will all end on 28 February (in a non-leap year). The rule about statutory periods of time starting *on* a date is different from that under ET Regs 2004, reg. 15, which provides that any period defined under ET Rules 2004 or in a tribunal decision *excludes* the start date.

The rules about the application of time limits when a claim is presented by post were reviewed in *Consignia plc* v *Sealy* [2002] EWCA Civ 878, [2002] ICR 1193. It is now to be assumed as in Civil Procedure Rule 6.7 that first-class post arrives on the second day after it is posted, excluding Sundays, bank holidays, Christmas Day and Good Friday. So a claim due to be received on a Saturday or Sunday will be in time if it is posted first class no later than the previous Thursday, even if the tribunal office does not open it until the Monday or it is unexpectedly delayed even longer. For this reason the tribunals retain the envelopes in which claims arrive.

The detailed time limits we considered at **13.4.1** contained two broad definitions of an exception:

(a) the 'just and equitable' rule in relation to redundancy payments, racial discrimination and sex discrimination; and

(b) the 'not reasonably practicable' rule in relation to unfair dismissal, the protection of wages, breach of contract and claims under WT Regs 1998.

Those two rules are of very different severity and we shall consider each in turn.

13.4.4 The 'just and equitable' rule

In relation to claims for redundancy payments and claims of discrimination, the relevant time limit can be extended if the tribunal considers it *just and equitable* to do so.

The discretion allowed to the tribunal by this formula is very broad: *Hutchinson* v *Westward Television* [1977] ICR 279. Furthermore, there can be circumstances in which the extension may be lengthy, so that cases considerably out-of-time can still be heard. In *Southwark London Borough Council* v *Afolabi* [2003] EWCA Civ 15, [2003] ICR 800, the claimant was allowed to present a claim of racial discrimination almost nine years late because the facts only came to light when he inspected his personal file. In *Chohan* v *Derby Law Centre* [2004] IRLR 685 the EAT accepted a late claim under this rule where delay was due to bad advice the claimant had received from her legal adviser.

Despite the new rules about extensions of time while a statutory grievance procedure is completed that we mentioned at **13.4.2**, it still seems unlikely that a claimant could use the 'just and equitable' rule to justify any other delay while a grievance or internal appeal was pursued under the employer's own arrangements. We still regard as authoritative the decision of the Court of Appeal in *Apelogun-Gabriels* v *London Borough of Lambeth* [2001] EWCA Civ 1853, [2002] ICR 713: pursuit of a domestic grievance or appeal was not normally sufficient ground for delaying an application to the tribunal, but it may be one factor for the employment tribunal to take into account.

13.4.5 The 'not reasonably practicable' rule

By contrast with the rule in those three jurisdictions, the rule in relation to claims of unfair dismissal, of unlawful deductions from wages under ERA 1996, Part II, or of breach of contract or WT Regs 1998 is much stricter. An extension of time is permitted only if:

(a) it was *not reasonably practicable* to present in time; *and*

(b) the length of the extension is *reasonable*.

The meaning of 'not reasonably practicable' has been exposed to much scrutiny in the cases over a long period of time. An early example was *Dedman* v *British Building* [1974] ICR 53, in which Lord Denning MR held that when a claimant, through no fault of his own, was ignorant of the time limit for presentation, that was enough to make it not reasonably practicable for him to meet it. Fault therefore became an important criterion. If the claimant's lateness was not his fault he might well get through; if he or his advisers were in some way at fault that would usually be fatal.

The authorities were reviewed by the EAT in *Trevelyans (Birmingham)* v *Norton* [1991] ICR 488. Wood J suggested that as time passed it would become more difficult than it was in 1974 to persuade employment tribunals that claimants did not know of the time limit. He also set out some important principles, reaffirming the rule that any fault by claimants or their advisers is to be attributed to claimants in deciding whether it was reasonably practicable to present in time.

The rule has further been reviewed by the Court of Appeal in *London Underground Ltd* v *Noel* [1999] IRLR 621. In that case an offer of alternative employment had been accepted by the claimant who therefore did not present a claim of unfair dismissal within the three-month period. The employer subsequently withdrew the offer. The Court of Appeal held that it would nevertheless have been reasonably practicable for her to have presented the claim within the period. The case seems to impose a rather stricter test than that adopted by the same Court only three months before in *Schultz* v *Esso Petroleum Co. Ltd* [1999] IRLR 488. In that case the claimant suffered from depression during the latter part of the three-month period but had been fit and capable of presenting a claim in the first part. It was held that attention had to be focussed on the latter part of the period, and that the claimant had established that presentation within the period was not reasonably practicable.

The second half of the statutory discretion is also important. If it is established that presentation within the statutory period is not reasonably practicable, the period should be extended only by as much as is *reasonable*. The claimant must act without delay once presentation becomes reasonably practicable: *James W. Cook (Wivenhoe)* v *Tipper* [1990] IRLR 386. So, for example, a claimant who claims ignorance of the time limit must act as quickly as possible on learning of it.

A particularly difficult category of case for exercise of either statutory discretion occurs where a decision of the ECJ or one of the higher courts in this country effectively establishes a new jurisdiction. So, for example, until the decision of the House of Lords in *R* v *Secretary of State for Employment, ex parte Equal Opportunities Commission* [1994] ICR 317, it was generally believed that most part-time employees did not have the right to present a claim of unfair dismissal. In *Biggs* v *Somerset County Council* [1996] ICR 364 an employee who was dismissed in August 1976 argued that her complaint of unfair dismissal was in time because, as a part-time teacher working 14 hours per week, her right to claim only ran from the date of the House of Lords decision on 1 June 1994 and her claim was presented within three months of that date. Her claim was brought under art. 141 of the EC Treaty, and therefore did not need to wait for UK legislation about part-time workers. The Court of Appeal held that time ran from her dismissal in 1976 and the 'not reasonably practicable' rule could not be stretched to the extent she suggested. A different result occurred with the 'just and equitable' rule: *Director of Public Prosecutions* v *Marshall* [1998] ICR 518.

13.5 Acceptance by the tribunal office of the claim

Under rr. 2 and 3 of ET Rules 2004 a new step is added to the tribunal procedure. Hitherto, receipt of the claim (then known as the originating application) involved the tribunal office merely in the administrative tasks of stamping it with the date, giving it a reference number and a code indicating the nature of the complaint, and notifying the employer accordingly. Now the office is given a duty to examine the content of the claim and to consider whether it can be accepted.

Any administrative decision within the tribunal office not to accept a claim must be referred to a chairman who makes the final decision. The grounds for refusing to accept are set out in r. 3:

(a) the claim is not made on the prescribed form (from 6 April 2005);

(b) it does not include the relevant information;

(c) the tribunal has no jurisdiction to consider it; or

(d) the claim is not in accordance with the provisions of EA 2002, s. 32 regarding the pursuance of grievances.

If rejection is on ground (a), the claimant is told the reason and sent a copy of the form. We do not expect this new element in the procedure to have any massive effect. Although employers have sometimes complained that it is too easy for disgruntled employees to bring cases to the tribunal that stand no prospect of success, it appears that this provision allows tribunals to reject claims only because of formal failings and not because they lack merit.

13.6 The response

If the claim is accepted, the tribunal office stamps it with the date, gives it a reference number and sends a copy with a covering letter ET 2 to the employer named on the form together with a blank response form ET 3 and an explanatory booklet.

As with form ET 1, the use of form ET 3 for the response is not mandatory as we go to press but it will become mandatory under r. 4(2) from 6 April 2005. However, the use of the form is already almost standard and it is usually a convenient means of supplying the necessary information, so that personal experience suggests the tribunals already tend not to recognise a response made in any other way. With permission from the Employment Tribunal Service we reproduce the form below.

The response must be presented to the tribunal office within 28 days of the date the copy of the claim was sent to the employer—r. 4(1). The employer may apply for an extension of time to present a response but must do so within the 28-day period and give an explanation—r. 4(4). Unlike earlier versions of the rules, there is no discretion allowed to the tribunals to validate late responses where no such application has been made, except following a default judgment, as we shall see at **13.7.2**. This may well cause problems in practice. Employers have sometimes failed to recognise the importance or urgency of tribunal communications and in some large companies internal post often seems to take a long time to get papers to the right individual. Papers sometimes sit waiting for the right person to return from holiday. Solicitors instructed to act for client employers when only a very short time is left to draft a response will wish to emphasise to the client the importance of acting more speedily next time.

13.6.1 The use of form ET 3

Completion of form ET 3 is as straightforward as that of ET 1. There are, however, a few points worthy of note:

At box 1.1 it is necessary to enter the employer's name and at 1.2 the address. The name and address to which the notices have been sent will be those the claimant has given on

Response to an Employment Tribunal claim

IN THE CLAIM OF:

Case number:
(please quote this in all correspondence)

This requires your immediate attention. If you want to resist the claim made against you, your completed form must reach the tribunal office within 28 days of the date of the attached letter. If you do not return the form by __/__/__ you may not be able to take part in the proceedings and a default judgment may be entered against you.

Please read the **guidance notes** and the notes on this page carefully **before** filling in this form.

By law, you **must** provide the information marked with ✻ and, if it is relevant, the information marked with ● (see guidance on Pre-acceptance procedure).

Please make sure that all the information you give is as accurate as possible.

Where there are tick boxes, please tick the one that applies.

If you fax the form, do not send a copy in the post.

ET3

1 Your details

1.1* Name of your organisation:	
Contact name:	
1.2* Address:	Postcode

You do not need to answer 1.3 and 1.4 if you have appointed a representative (see section 7).

1.3 Phone number:	
1.4 How would you prefer us to communicate with you?	Post ☐ Fax ☐ E-mail ☐ Fax: E-mail address:

2 Action before a claim

2.1 Is, or was, the claimant an employee? Yes ☐ No ☐
If 'Yes', please now go straight to section 2.3.

2.2 Is, or was, the claimant a worker providing services to you? Yes ☐ No ☐
If 'Yes', please now go straight to section 3.
If 'No', please now go straight to section 5.

2.3 If the claim, or part of it, is about a dismissal, do you agree that the claimant was dismissed? Yes ☐ No ☐
If 'Yes', please now go straight to section 2.6.

2.4 If the claim includes something **other than** dismissal, does it relate to an action you took on grounds of the claimant's conduct or capability? Yes ☐ No ☐
If 'Yes', please now go straight to section 2.6.

2.5 Has the substance of this claim been raised by the claimant in writing under a grievance procedure? Yes ☐ No ☐

2.6 If 'Yes', please explain below what stage you have reached in the dismissal and disciplinary procedure or grievance procedure (whichever is applicable).
If 'No' and the claimant says they have raised a grievance with you in writing, please say whether you received it and explain why you did not accept this as a grievance.

3 Employment details

3.1 Are the dates of employment given by the claimant correct? Yes ☐ No ☐
If 'Yes', please now go straight to section 3.3.

3.2 If 'No', please give dates and say why you disagree with the dates given by the claimant.

When their employment started / /

When their employment ended or will end / /

Is their employment continuing? Yes ☐ No ☐

I disagree with the dates for the following reasons.

3.3 Is the claimant's description of their job or job title correct? Yes ☐ No ☐
If 'Yes', please now go straight to section 3.5.

3.4 If 'No', please give the details you believe to be correct below.

3.5 Is the information given by the claimant correct about being paid for, or working, a period of notice? Yes ☐ No ☐
If 'Yes', please now go straight to section 3.7.

3.6 If 'No', please give the details you believe to be correct below. If you gave them no notice or didn't pay them instead of letting them work their notice, please explain what happened and why.

3.7 Are the claimant's hours of work correct? Yes ☐ No ☐
If 'Yes', please now go straight to section 3.9.

3.8 If 'No', please enter the details you believe to be correct. hours each week

3.9 Are the earnings details given by the claimant correct? Yes ☐ No ☐
If 'Yes', please now go straight to section 4.

3.10 If 'No', please give the details you believe to be correct below.

Pay before tax £ each

Normal take-home pay (including overtime, commission, bonuses and so on) £ each

4 Unfair dismissal or constructive dismissal

4.1 Are the details about pension and other benefits given by the claimant correct? Yes ☐ No ☐
If 'Yes', please now go straight to section 5.

4.2 If 'No', please give the details you believe to be correct below.

5 Response

5.1* Do you resist the claim? Yes ☐ No ☐
If 'No', please now go straight to section 6.

5.2● If 'Yes', please set out in full the grounds on which you resist the claim.

6 Other information

6.1 Please do not send a covering letter with this form. You should add any extra information you want us to know here.

7 Your representative

If you have a representative, please fill in the following.

7.1 Representative's name:

7.2 Name of the representative's organisation:

7.3 Address:

Postcode

7.4 Phone number:

7.5 Reference:

7.6 How would they prefer us to communicate with them?

Post ☐ Fax ☐ E-mail ☐

Fax:

E-mail address:

Please sign and date here

Signature: Date: / /

Data Protection Act 1998. We will send a copy of this form to the claimant and Acas. We will put some of the information you give us on this form onto a computer. This helps us to monitor progress and produce statistics.

the ET 1 and may be incorrect. Claimants sometimes give a trading name that has no standing to defend litigation. This is the opportunity to make any corrections. Solicitors will find that some large companies reorganise themselves remarkably often, and it may take some effort to get proper instructions about the identity of the employer, ending with 'Limited' or 'plc,' but it is better to do the investigation now than to suffer the indignity at a tribunal hearing of being unable to identify your client properly.

In cases where the claim depends on a dismissal, the respondent must answer at box 2.3 whether dismissal is admitted. The practical significance of the answer to this question is that if the claimant claims to have been dismissed and the employer denies it, the claimant will have to prove dismissal and will have to open the case at the hearing: see **13.11.3** below. If the employer admits dismissal, the employer begins in order to prove the reason for dismissal. The employer will usually wish to deny dismissal if:

(a) challenging a claim of constructive dismissal;

(b) the employee resigned voluntarily or there was a termination by mutual consent;

(c) the contract ended through frustration;

(d) the claimant is regarded by the employer as still employed.

At box 5.1 the employer must answer whether the claim is resisted. Under ET Rules 2004 it appears that any case where the employer's response fails to indicate resistance will proceed to a default hearing.

The next box, 5.2, is the one where the employer is required to set out the grounds of resistance and this requires rather more consideration.

13.6.2 Grounds of resistance—box 5.2

The general remarks at the end of **13.3.4** about completion of a claim apply equally to the response, and especially to the descriptive part. Parties are not expected to meet High Court standards, but, especially where lawyers are acting for the employer, tribunals will expect the points at issue to be identified clearly. This still leaves considerable scope for individual practitioners to follow their own preferences.

We shall discuss technique by reference to our first three examples: Anastasia whose ET 1 we thought at **13.3.4** was well drafted, and two others, Basil and Catherine, where the ET 1 is badly drafted. Basil's is too long; Catherine's is too brief.

13.6.2.1 An ET 3 for Anastasia

Consider the following as a response to the ET 1 we have already examined at **13.3.4**:

> The Respondent company suffered a severe loss of business as a result of the cancellation of a large order by a major customer in September 2004 and was forced with much regret to reduce the size of its workforce by approximately 10 per cent.
>
> The Applicant's dismissal on 3 December was for redundancy. It was essential if the company was to remain in business and was not unfair.

This response is inadequate. While some practitioners prefer to leave as many of their options open as possible, brevity to this extreme is disliked by the tribunals. It deals with the *reason* for dismissal, perhaps in more detail than is necessary, but makes no attempt to show that the employer *acted reasonably* in dismissing for that reason. The tribunal would probably react by asking for additional information (see **13.8.3** below) of *how* it is alleged the employer acted reasonably. This may include questions that the employer might have preferred to leave to be answered at the hearing.

It is therefore better to prepare a fuller response which deals with those matters in the way the employer chooses. The ET 3 should show that the employer knew how to handle a redundancy reasonably and aimed to do so, especially in relation to the matters put in issue by the ET 1. Consider the following second attempt:

On 15 November 2004 the Respondent company announced a redundancy of 20 people because of the cancellation of an important order and started consultation with the recognised trade unions. The unions declined to agree a method of selecting who was to be dismissed, but urged the Respondent to select speedily and to allow those selected to leave as soon as possible immediately after interview on 26 November so as to maximise the value to them of severance payments by avoiding tax.

The Claimant was employed as a design engineer and the Respondent decided to reduce the number so employed from eight to seven. All eight were marked for their length of service, attendance record, quality and quantity of work and their versatility. The Claimant scored the lowest total mark and was therefore selected for dismissal.

She was called to an interview on 26 November. She declined the offer of being accompanied by another employee. The reason for the redundancy and the selection method were explained to her. She was told she was at risk of redundancy and did not need to attend at work during a consultation period. She had the right to appeal against selection, and to remain in employment while the appeal was heard. She did not appeal, or raise any other questions and, in the absense of any alternative, her dismissal was confirmed on 3 December.

At the time of the claimant's dismissal, two sub-contract design engineers were working in the design office. They were engaged in the final stages of a specific project which was expected to last only two more weeks and which in fact ended at the Christmas holiday. The claimant would have required training to undertake that work and it could not have been completed in the available time.

In all the circumstances the claimant's dismissal for redundancy was not unfair.

This is much better. Unlike a High Court defence it does not follow exactly the same sequence as the ET 1 it is answering and admit or deny each element one by one. Indeed, it appears to tell a remarkably different story. Yet it demonstrates that the employer was aware of some at least of the legal requirements of handling redundancy reasonably and attempted to satisfy them. It states clearly the employer's point of view about the key contentions we spotted in the ET 1 but does not waste time asserting things that are not in issue in any event. Nor does it gratuitously expose the weaknesses the solicitor has uncovered in the respondents' case. We shall see later that it will probably prompt Anastasia's solicitor to ask for inspection of documents, but, apart from that, the case is now ready for hearing.

It is a good test of a well-drafted ET 1 and ET 3 that, taken together, they clearly establish the points at issue.

13.6.2.2 An ET 3 for Basil

Basil was dismissed for theft of company products. The employer understood the requirements of *British Home Stores* v *Burchell* [1980] ICR 303, and aimed to comply with them.

Basil, by contrast, has never heard of *BHS* v *Burchell* and is simply aggrieved that he has lost his livelihood in circumstances where the police say there is insufficient evidence to press criminal charges. He submits an ET 1 claiming unfair dismissal. His entry in box 5.2, completed in a spidery handwriting, runs on beyond the form itself on to two more sheets of lined A5 paper. The following is a considerable précis:

He stresses his long and hitherto unblemished record of employment with this company and earlier employers going back thirty years. He was a willing and cooperative worker and the quality of his workmanship has never been questioned. The evidence against him is scanty. In any event, dismissal is an excessive penalty for petty pilfering. Minor theft and other corrupt practices are widespread in the workplace and he threatens to reveal misconduct by senior people. No disciplinary action has been taken against anyone else. Perhaps he was set up.

Dealing with long and rambling claims like this is often difficult. Basil's statement is so wide-ranging that it is impossible to discern his real complaint. He does not expressly deny theft, but it would be unfair to assume that such an omission by an unrepresented claimant was deliberate. One device is to ask for additional information, specifying precisely what are the grounds for complaining of unfair dismissal, perhaps even seeking leave to delay completion of the ET 3 until it is supplied. In other cases it is better tactically to ignore irrelevant grouses. The claimant may well have been upset by the dismissal and have included in the ET 1 various things written in the heat of the moment that will not in fact be pursued.

Basil's case is probably more of the second kind than the first. The employer will probably want to refute the allegations of widespread dishonesty, more for the record than for this case. (If Basil did not mention such allegations at disciplinary interviews or any appeal hearing, the usual rule that fairness is to be judged by reference to the employer's knowledge *at the time of dismissal* will mean that he gains little by raising them for the first time here.) If there is a serious prospect of accusations being made at the hearing that could take the employer by surprise, it may be necessary to ask later for information: see **13.8.1** below.

Applying the above reasoning, Basil's employer's solicitor may decide to produce an ET 3 which denies general dishonesty in the workplace but otherwise concentrates entirely on showing that the employer tried to comply with the *BHS* v *Burchell* tests and followed a correct procedure:

The Respondent company manufactures small domestic electrical appliances. Because of its susceptibility to petty theft, random security checks are undertaken from time to time.

On 3 November such a random search found the Claimant leaving the works with a machine, in its sales carton, in his bag. He was suspended on full pay while his departmental manager obtained written statements from the security officer and others involved and checked computerised stock records. The statements were sent to the Claimant.

The Claimant was called to a disciplinary interview on 8 November which he attended with his shop steward. His manager invited his comments. He said he did not know the item was in his bag and could not explain how it got there.

During an adjournment the manager and a colleague considered the Claimant's explanation and decided they did not believe it. On resumption the manager told the Claimant they concluded he was trying to steal the machine and he was summarily dismissed.

The Claimant exercised his right of appeal but was unsuccessful.

It is not admitted that dishonesty is widespread or tolerated in the works as alleged or at all.

13.6.2.3 An ET 3 for Catherine

The third of our examples concerns an ET 1 which, by contrast with Basil's, is extremely brief and really gives the employer little indication of Catherine's complaint. Her ET 1 reads like this:

Box 3.5
No.

Box 3.7
Because I have complained informally so many times without anything being done that I needed to react firmly at the time described at 5.1 below.

Box 5.2
Since Mike Jones became my manager two years ago he keeps picking on me for all the unpleasant jobs that the other girls do not want to do. Obviously he does not like me and prefers the younger, prettier ones. I have complained about this treatment on several occasions but nothing is ever done. On 5 November he told me to change jobs. This was the last straw and I resigned.

The employer cannot proceed to the tribunal hearing with a claim as vague as this. At some stage it will be necessary to establish answers to three questions:

(a) What exactly is Mike Jones supposed to have done?

(b) When, how, and to whom were the complaints made?

(c) Is the implied complaint of sex discrimination going to be pursued? (Under old versions of the ET 1 form the category of claim was less clear than now and complaints like this could sometimes be pursued. The new form is clearer and in theory Catherine should not be allowed to pursue such a claim if section 6 of the ET 1 is left blank; as we go to press we do not know whether the tribunals will in fact be so strict.)

The mechanism for dealing with such vagueness is through a request for additional information: see **13.8.3** below.

Meanwhile, it is a question of tactics whether or not the employer prefers to delay completion of the ET 3 until that information is supplied. It is of course the claimant's responsibility to show that she was dismissed, and not the employer's to show that she was not. In view of that burden, a blanket denial by the employer may seem to be enough:

It is not admitted that any act or omission by the Respondent employer entitled the Claimant to resign without notice as alleged or at all.

Note the addition of 'as alleged or at all'. This is a standard device in any drafting, and avoids a trap called the *pregnant negative*. If the employee alleges in the ET 1 that something was done to her by a named person on a Friday afternoon in the office, and the ET 3 denies it in precisely the same terms, someone reading the statement may conclude that the event did indeed take place, but the claimant has made some minor error of detail, perhaps with the date, or time or place.

At one stage, when tribunal proceedings were much more informal and hearings more exploratory, such a brief response would probably have been accepted. Now, with the emphasis on case management and clarification of issues in advance of hearing, a tribunal office might well not accept it (see **13.7** below) and insist on more information. In any event an employer who knows the background to Catherine's complaint would probably wish to demonstrate a coherent and reasonable approach to her and think it tactically better to produce a fuller version:

The Claimant was employed as a machine operator and it was a term of her employment that she could be moved at any time from one machine to another and from one shift to another. Whilst the departmental manager usually tries to accommodate the personal preferences of the operators in terms of allocation to machines, this is not always possible and the terms of the contract sometimes have to be adhered to.

During October the Claimant repeatedly declined requests to move to a particular stapling machine. The manager realised that this refusal was causing ill-feeling amongst other operators and told the Claimant she would have to move. He offered to try to resolve any particular difficulties the Claimant might have in complying with such a request but she raised none and persisted in her refusal. The Respondent has a well-used grievance procedure which requires any grievance to be sent in writing to the human resources department but the Claimant has never registered any complaint under it; nor has she made use of the statutory grievance procedures.

On 5 November the manager therefore instructed the Claimant to move.

The said instruction was within the terms of the Claimant's contract of employment. Neither that instruction nor any other act or omission by the Respondent entitled the Claimant to resign without notice.

If, which is not admitted, the said instruction constituted a dismissal, it was for the substantial reason of needing to share out unpopular work and was not unfair.

The final paragraph of that revised version may be important. As we emphasised in **Chapter 10**, a constructive dismissal is not necessarily unfair. Sometimes, in cases of alleged constructive dismissal, it is therefore necessary to plead '*in the alternative*' so that the defence about fairness is in place lest the issue of whether there was a dismissal is lost.

Occasionally, if the employer omits to do this, the tribunal office will write asking whether it is wished to do so. Note the reference to the SGP (see **10.6.5.1** for consequences).

13.6.3 Breach of contract counterclaim by the employer

As we noted in **Chapter 5**, the provision that has now become ETA 1996, s. 3 was brought into effect by the Employment Tribunals Extension of Jurisdiction (England and Wales) Order 1994. Employees can now bring a claim of breach of contract *in the employment tribunal*, rather than only in the courts as previously.

The novel feature of the breach of contract jurisdiction is that the employer is permitted to make a counterclaim against the employee, but only if the employee's claim alleges breach of contract, and not (for example) if the ET 1 is about unfair dismissal alone. Counterclaims are covered by ET Rules 2004 in r. 7, which requires very little except that the counterclaim should be in writing and permits the President to make a practice direction about counterclaims. The requirement as to timing seems not to have been changed from the 1994 Regulations, so that it must be presented by the employer to the tribunal office within six weeks of the date that the employer *received* the copy of the claim. (Those familiar with the old rules will recognise this timing from receipt of the copy of the claim; generally under ET Rules 2004 timing is from the date the copy is *sent*.) The counterclaim cannot relate to the topics listed at **5.7.4**, which remain actionable in the courts alone, especially:

(a) intellectual property;
(b) restrictive covenants.

13.7 Acceptance and non-acceptance of the response

We have already noted at **13.5** a new provision under ET Rules 2004 for the tribunal to accept the claimant's claim. There is an equivalent provision in r. 5 for the tribunal to accept the respondent's response.

13.7.1 The acceptance procedure

The procedure for acceptance of the response is parallel to that for acceptance of the claim, and there are three grounds for the tribunal office to decline to accept:

(a) the response is not on the prescribed form (from 6 April 2005);
(b) it does not include all the required information; or
(c) it was not presented within the time limit.

As with acceptance of the claim, acceptance of the response does not depend on the merits of the case. If it is rejected on ground (a) above, the employer is told the reason and sent a copy of the appropriate form.

13.7.2 Default judgments

Under ET Rules 2004, r. 8 any claim where a response has not been presented within time or where a response has not been accepted may be referred to a chairman for a default judgment, which may deal with liability alone or liability and remedy. The employer (who technically has not even become a respondent) will not be heard. The judgment will be reached without a hearing on the basis of information available to the chairman, which presumably means the information contained in the ET 1, although it is also possible under r. 10 for the tribunal itself to ask the claimant for additional information.

The only opportunity for the employer subject to a default judgment to be heard about the case is by applying for a review of the default judgment under r. 33. The application must be in writing and be presented within 14 days of the date the default judgment was sent to the parties. It must include a response to the claim, an application of an extension of time to present it and an explanation of why it was not presented within time.

Those accustomed to representation of employers under the old rules may find these provisions draconian. At one stage all late responses by employers were automatically deemed to include a request for an extension of time and extensions were granted as a matter of course. More recently employers have faced a possible order for costs if responding late, but extensions have still not been difficult to obtain. The leniency accorded to employers perhaps seems unfair compared with the strict approach that has always been taken to claimants' presentation of the ET 1 on time, and the new rules redress that imbalance. It remains to be seen how strict tribunals are in allowing review of default judgments, but we imagine that employers will still have no problem if the failure to present the ET 3 on time is not their fault—perhaps because of exceptional postal delays or because wrong identification of the employer on the ET 1 has resulted in delay in reaching the right respondent.

An aspect of the rule regarding default judgments that does not seem to be covered in ET Rules 2004 is the interrelationship with employers' counterclaims. As the time limit for an employer to present a counterclaim is just over two weeks longer than the time to present a response to the claim, it seems to be possible for a claim to have entered the default judgment procedure in the absence of a response, but for a valid counterclaim still to be raised. Maybe we shall see in due course how that is handled.

13.8 Case management

We have already noted in the imaginary cases we have been considering that the ET 1 and the ET 3 do not always adequately define the issues that need to be explored at a hearing to decide a case. Often the parties need to communicate with one another, or in default of agreement the tribunal must ensure that a case is properly prepared. In rr. 10–13 of ET Rules 2004 under the title 'Case Management' we find grouped together a number of powers given to tribunal chairmen to make orders for the efficient handling of cases. Although some of the terminology is new, most of these powers are based on earlier rules. A list of orders is set out in r. 10(2), but it expressly states that the items listed are examples and the full range envisaged by s. 10(1) could therefore be even more extensive. Orders can be made by a chairman on consideration of the papers or at a case management discussion. The list of possible orders is comprehensive and includes the manner in which proceedings are to be conducted including setting time limits, linking together of cases and separation of issues in a case to be dealt with separately. Particular matters that we need to consider further are these:

(a) case management discussions;

(b) provision of additional information;

(c) witness orders ('attendance of any person to give evidence');

(d) disclosure of documents;

(e) supply of written answers to questions;

(f) dealing with part of the proceedings separately;

(g) pre-hearing reviews;

(h) leave to amend claim or response;

(i) witness statements; and

(j) penalties for non-compliance.

In many regions such as Southampton some simpler categories of cases by-pass this procedure entirely. Straightforward claims of unlawful deduction from wages or breach of contract, for example, are put into a 'fast-track' system whereby they are simply listed for hearing and some regions set aside time on a fixed day each week to deal with a large number of such cases. In one example the date for this fast-track hearing has been sent to the employer with the copy of the ET 1, but we do not know whether that practice will survive the new rules, especially the provisions about fixed periods for conciliation that we shall consider at **13.10.1**.

13.8.1 Cooperation between the parties

Before we start to look at the list from the standpoint of orders made by the tribunal it is worth repeating that in practice these steps often start, especially if the parties are legally represented, with an exchange between parties or representatives.

We have already observed, for example, that Catherine's ET 1 was so lacking in detail that the respondent employer was having difficulty in filling in the ET 3. The respondent requires more information, and we shall see shortly in **13.8.3** and **13.8.6** how the tribunal can be asked to order its disclosure. However, the tribunal chairman will expect, especially if the parties are represented, that, before the respondent seeks an order, the claimant will have been asked to comply voluntarily. The chairman will want to know what was in the request and in the reply to it, and any order may cross-refer to the request.

13.8.2 Case management discussions

A case management discussion (CMD) is a hearing to consider making any of the orders we have been discussing or any other orders about the handling of a case. Such hearings have in fact been held for some time, often known until now as hearings for directions, but the express provision for them in ET Rules 2004, r. 17(1) is new. They may be instigated by the tribunal or they may be requested by the parties, provided the requirements of r. 11 concerning all applications for orders are satisfied.

(a) An application for any order must be made at least ten days before the hearing at which it is to be considered.

(b) It must be in writing, be sent to the tribunal office and include the reference number and the reasons for the request.

(c) An application for a CMD must identify what orders will be sought at it.

(d) An application for an order must explain how it will assist the tribunal in dealing with proceedings efficiently and fairly.

(e) Legal representatives must notify other parties of any application for an order (except a witness order) with the reasons for it and notify them of their right to object within seven days.

A CMD is held by a chairman alone, it may be in private and it cannot determine the rights of a case. That last rule has not prevented chairmen in some regions from expressing an opinion about the merits of a case with a view to encouraging settlement, not necessarily having regard to all the complexities of that matter described in **13.10.3**. There is provision in r. 15(1) for a CMD to be held using electronic communications and this rule will permit continuation of the recent practice whereby they are usually in the form of conference telephone calls.

At one stage CMDs were held only exceptionally, reflecting the cost to the parties of attending a hearing in person at the tribunal office and the time requirement for the chairman. There was even a worry in some regions that the use of telephone conferences offended the requirement to hold hearings in public, but that was resolved and they are now used extensively in all cases of any complexity.

As an example of the usefulness of a CMD it is time to introduce our fourth claimant. Dmitri is a salesman in a furniture shop who has applied several times for promotion to supervisor but has been unsuccessful. He alleges in the ET 1 that his departmental manager told him that he was rejected because of his high level of sickness absence since he developed a serious intestinal disorder, and he claims discrimination on grounds of disability contrary to DDA 1995. The ET 3 says that Dmitri was turned down on his merits and denies that the manager ever made such a statement; it also denies that Dmitri is a disabled person within the meaning of DDA 1995. In cases like this it is very common for the tribunal to take the initiative in calling a CMD at which the chairman will check that the employer continues to deny that Dmitri is disabled and a timetable will then be set to deal with that issue. Dmitri's solicitor will be instructed to serve the necessary medical evidence on the employer by a defined date and the employer will be given a deadline to respond, conceding disability or not. (Tribunals are urged by ET Regs 2004, reg. 15(4) to set calendar dates rather than time limits where possible.) The employer may be warned about an order for costs if a challenge to Dmitri's status is regarded as unreasonable. The chairman may then decide to hear the question of Dmitri's disabled status and the merits of the discrimination case as separate issues and will require the parties to estimate the time needed for both hearings in the case. Dates will be set for hearings, for agreeing documents and for exchange of witness statements (see later) and the chairman will ask whether there are any other orders required by the parties. The tribunal will then be very reluctant to change any of these agreed arrangements unless one party can show an extremely good reason for doing so.

It will be seen from the example that solicitors taking part in a CMD need to be well-prepared. Chairmen usually expect to end a CMD by fixing a date for a hearing, which requires the solicitor to have established the availability of witnesses, and that in turn requires the solicitor to know enough about the case to have decided which witnesses need to give evidence. Sometimes such case management seems to add to the costs of cases that may well not in the end proceed to a hearing.

13.8.3 The provision of additional information

The authors hope that the tribunals may be patient with those of a certain age who have had such long exposure to asking for further and better particulars of the other party's contentions that it proves difficult to remember henceforth to refer to additional information. Or maybe some tribunal chairmen may have the occasional lapse too. In any event that is what this provision is all about. The tribunal will order a party to provide further information if the ET 1 or ET 3 does not give the other side sufficient to prepare for the hearing. Hitherto 'particulars' necessarily involved some kind of development of something already contained in either ET 1 or ET 3; the new name seems likely to allow much broader requests to be made, and the older fine distinctions no longer matter.

In our examples there is plainly a need for the employer to request additional information in Catherine's case. This is done either in the body of a letter or more formally. In either case the request itself will look something like this:

REQUEST FOR ADDITIONAL INFORMATION
ABOUT THE CLAIM

Under Item 5.1

Of 'I resigned' describing precisely with dates and the names of persons involved each and every act or omission by the Respondent employer which allegedly entitled the Claimant to resign her employment without notice.

Of 'I have complained about this treatment on several occasions' specifying the subject matter of the complaints, when and to whom they were made, whether orally or in writing and what was the result in each case.

We have deliberately not requested any additional information to establish whether Catherine is in fact pursuing the implied claim of sex discrimination. The likelihood is that the discrepancy between the implication at box 5.2 on the ET 1 and the blank in box 6 may be sufficient to prompt a chairman to call a CMD at which it will be explored. If she says she wishes to pursue the point her representative may in effect be invited to apply to amend the ET 1 accordingly—see **13.8.9** below. If she does not do so, she will not be permitted to raise it without warning at a hearing. So there is no benefit to the respondent in seeking information about it.

We noted above that one of the objectives of making such a request direct of the other party is to prepare the ground to ask for an order if the other party does not comply voluntarily. Such a request can be made during any CMD or as a written application to the tribunal office that complies with the requirements of r. 11 set out at **13.8.2.**

13.8.4 Witness orders

The employment tribunal can issue witness orders against witnesses, usually those who are not willing to attend a hearing voluntarily. The difference between this order and the other orders we are considering is that this is not issued against the other party but directly to the witness. The party applying for the order is not required by r. 11 to notify the other party. Thus the employer may find that witness orders have been issued to several members of staff on the claimant's application and without the employer having any opportunity to express a view.

Basil's case provides two examples of the kind of instance where this rule may be used.

Basil has alleged that dishonesty is widespread in the workplace. If he wishes to proceed with this contention, he may well want to call as witnesses other employees who would not wish to attend voluntarily. A witness order forces them to attend, to give evidence and (if the order so provides) to bring documents with them.

The employer may also find it necessary to apply for a witness order. Perhaps a shop steward of the trade union would admit that dishonesty is not widespread or would give evidence against Basil's conduct during the disciplinary procedure. The shop steward might well feel it was wrong to give evidence voluntarily against a union member, but would respond favourably if a witness order was issued.

An application to set aside a witness order must be made by the individual to whom it is issued. In practice, however, there is no problem if an employer coordinates applications from an excessive number of staff called to give evidence.

13.8.5 Disclosure of documents

As in the county court, each party in the employment tribunal is entitled to know what documents the other party has in its possession that are relevant to the case and, subject to very limited safeguards, to inspect them. In practice parties almost always comply by supplying the other with photocopies. If disclosure is not given voluntarily, it can be ordered by the tribunal. This rule often causes practical problems: employers frequently regard documents as confidential and resist disclosure, while the tribunals take a different view.

For example, Anastasia was selected for dismissal for redundancy because her score on an assessment was less than that of seven colleagues. She will naturally want to see how the other seven were marked. The employer, on the other hand, will regard the other forms as confidential to the seven individuals and will resist disclosure. This disagreement has been explored in the cases.

Under the rules that have existed until now, the tribunals will order disclosure only of documents that actually exist and a party cannot be required to produce documents or statistics specially: *Carrington* v *Helix Lighting* [1990] IRLR 6. Under ET Rules 2004, that distinction is less important as the tribunal can now order disclosure of documents *or information*, and we shall se at **13.8.6** that they can also order a party to answer questions.

The rule is to be used for documents that can be identified and not for 'fishing': *Clwyd County Council* v *Leverton* [1985] IRLR 197. Thus it is for the parties to make specific requests and usually disclosure depends on the initiative of the party wanting to see a document. There is an increasing tendency, however, especially in some regions, towards the practice in the courts of requiring parties to disclose to each other all relevant documents in their power, possession or control. In *Scott* v *Commissioners of Inland Revenue* [2004] EWCA Civ 400, [2004] IRLR 713 the employer was criticised for not disclosing a revised retirement policy that had an effect on the claimant's expected future working life before retirement and therefore on compensation.

There is no immunity for confidential documents, although sometimes the tribunal will inspect them before ordering disclosure: *Science Research Council* v *Nassé* [1979] ICR 921. If the names of other people in documents are not necessary, they can be obliterated: *Oxford* v *DHSS* [1977] ICR 884. Documents may be anonymised or redacted to protect the confidence of informants if the principles set out in *Linfood Cash & Carry Ltd* v *Thomson* [1989] ICR 518 are observed, and, for example, the employer was not required to disclose the identity of witnesses in *Asda Stores Ltd* v *Thompson* [2002] IRLR 245, where dismissals resulted from the alleged use of hard drugs. Whilst documents passing between a client and the lawyer in connection with litigation are *privileged* and cannot be included in an order for inspection, this rule is restricted in the tribunals to lawyers and does not apply to other representatives: *New Victoria Hospital* v *Ryan* [1993] ICR 201.

Anastasia's care raises an issue about disclosure of documents that is common in cases of dismissal for redundancy: can she insist on seeing the assessment forms for the others in her unit of selection? She will argue that such information is essential to the preparation of her case, while the employer may feel that disclosure breaks the confidence owed to the other employees. In *British Aerospace plc* v *Green* [1995] ICR 1006 the employer sought to avoid disclosure of other forms. The Court of Appeal declined to support the tribunal chairman's order for disclosure of the forms. The tribunal was concerned only with the question of whether an assessment system was properly applied, and should not scrutinise its workings officiously; disclosure of the forms of those retained in employment was unnecessary for this purpose. Despite that authority, many tribunals seem in practice to have found reasons to distinguish *Green* and have continued to order disclosure. Thus, for example, in *John Brown Engineering Ltd* v *Brown* [1997] IRLR 90, the EAT in Scotland supported an employment tribunal finding that withholding other employees' marks rendered the appeal procedure 'a sham'. If disclosure is required for an internal appeal, it is difficult to see how it could be refused for tribunal proceedings. A middle course that the tribunals sometimes adopt is to order disclosure of forms with names and other personal details obliterated. Obviously Anastasia is bound to respect the confidentiality of any documents she receives and will expose herself to action if she discloses them outside the tribunal case.

13.8.6 Supply of written answers to questions

The tribunal may order either party to answer questions posed by the tribunal. In practice, the tribunal may require the applicant to produce a schedule of losses (which quantifies the claim) but most other questions are prepared and posed by the other party. Quite often the dividing line between questions and additional information becomes blurred, and requests are made that fall somewhere between the two.

In some kinds of case it is useful to be able to serve questions that could not possibly be described as additional to ET 1 or ET 3. A solicitor acting for Dmitri may well want to exploit this provision, perhaps asking for statistical information about numbers of disabled and non-disabled people who have been promoted. As we noted at **6.6.1** above, the employer cannot be forced to reply to the statutory questionnaire in a discrimination case. However, if Dmitri asks some of the same questions under this provision, the tribunal can require the employer to answer. There are also occasions when the rule can be used to agree non-contentious matters of fact between the parties, thus reducing the evidence that needs to be given at the eventual tribunal hearing and possibly saving a lot of time. Solicitors will generally resist answering questions that really amount to cross-examination in advance.

13.8.7 Dealing with part of the proceedings separately

We have already encountered this possibility in the context of the CMD we discussed for our fourth imaginary example at **13.8.2** above. Dmitri claims to be a disabled person within the meaning of DDA 1995, and the employer challenges that claim. The issue whether he falls within the statutory definition is clearly a matter of some importance; if he does not, the whole of the remainder of his claim fails and there is no point in the parties wasting time preparing for a hearing about the merits or of course in the tribunal's holding such a hearing. So that point is decided first as a separate matter, and (although the term does not appear in ET Rules 2004) this is usually called a preliminary hearing.

Preliminary hearings have often taken place about issues of jurisdiction, such as whether a claim was presented in time or whether a claimant has sufficient service to make a particular claim. Under ET Rules 2004 we may find that some of those issues are considered by the tribunal when deciding whether to accept a claim, and the only hearing would then be on an application to review a decision not to accept.

A preliminary hearing is a full hearing of the tribunal, but it can often be heard by a chairman sitting alone, especially since the widening of that power by ERDRA 1998, s. 3. The EAT held in *Sutcliffe* v *Big C's Marine* [1998] ICR 913 that chairmen should not sit alone if contentious issues of fact are involved, apparently overruling their earlier decision to the contrary in *Tsangacos* v *Amalgamated Chemicals Ltd* [1997] ICR 154.

13.8.8 Pre-hearing reviews

One of the case management orders available to a tribunal is an order to hold a pre-hearing review (PHR). There are special provisions about PHRs in ET Rules 2004 rr. 18–19 and we shall consider them separately at **13.9** below.

13.8.9 Leave to amend a claim or response

Among the case management orders listed at ET Rules 2004, r. 10(2) is (q) the giving of leave to amend a claim or response. At a time when tribunals were more informal, such amendments were unimportant; new arguments were often raised at a hearing. Now, it would be inconsistent with the modern style of case management for parties to be taken by surprise, and it is necessary to apply to amend a claim or response if in the course of preparation for a hearing you find that the original version inadequately covers the case you wish to make. This often happens if the client drafted a claim or response and sent it in to the tribunal before you were instructed.

Sometimes it can be difficult to know whether the omission is important enough to matter, or whether it puts you at a tactical disadvantage to seek leave, or even looks incompetent to your client unless done carefully. Catherine's case is a good example where amendment is undoubtedly necessary, as we noted at **13.8.3**. If she is serious about her allegation of sex discrimination, section 6 of her ET 1 must be completed. The employer will want if possible to resist the broadening of her claim in this way. So we must ask what grounds there are to object, and how the tribunal decides the matter.

The authority on this matter is *Selkent Bus Company Ltd* v *Moore* [1996] ICR 836 and the tribunal will not allow an amendment that has the effect of circumventing the usual rules about time limits. So, if a claimant completes an ET 1 about one jurisdiction and is then out of time to present a claim about something different, the tribunal will not allow an amendment to the first so as to bring in the second by the back door. It is different if the first is so expressed as to include the second, so that the second claim is in fact merely a tidying-up of the legal process. Catherine's case is of this latter kind: the reference in the ET 1 that we examined at **13.6.2.3** contains sufficient to put the respondent on notice that there is an element of sex discrimination in her allegation and leave to amend the ET 1 will not be refused.

13.8.10 Written witness statements

There is an express reference in the list at r. 10(2)(s) to an order for the preparation or exchange of a witness statement. In some tribunal regions it is now almost invariable practice with all cases except those put into the 'fast-track' (see **13.8** above) to issue an order requiring agreement between the parties about a bundle of documents for the hearing and the exchange of witness statements. Occasionally the parties are ordered to prepare a schedule of agreed facts or events in the case. Dates are set for all these steps to be completed.

Recent practice has varied considerably among regions and we had expected that a practice direction issued by the President under ET Regs 2004, reg. 13 might introduce some standardisation. No practice direction has been issued and we do not expect that the letter to Regional Chairmen commending good practice will remove the differences. So solicitors must for the time being read such orders carefully. In the Leeds and Bedford regions, for example, the order has often required a bundle to be agreed four weeks after presentation of the ET 3 and witness statements to be exchanged two weeks later. In Bristol and Birmingham the bundle must be agreed 14 days before the hearing and witness statements must be exchanged seven days before hearing. In Cardiff no such orders are usually made at all.

We shall return to both bundles of documents and written witness statements when we discuss preparation for the hearing in **13.11** below.

13.8.11 Penalties for non-compliance with an order

The penalties for failing to comply with any of these orders are laid down in ET Rules 2004, r. 13 and there are three possibilities open to a chairman or tribunal.

(a) Costs may be awarded.

(b) After notice is given to the defaulting party, the whole or part of the claim or response may be struck out, but this can only be done at a hearing or PHR.

(c) If the order itself provides that failure to comply will lead to striking out, then the claim or response can be struck out on the date of non-compliance without further ado.

In practice striking out for failure to comply with an order has been very rare indeed and costs have usually been considered the appropriate penalty.

13.9 Pre-hearing reviews

The provisions regarding the holding of a PHR are now to be found in ET Rules 2004, r. 18. The idea is to discourage parties from pursuing hopeless cases.

Either party can apply for a PHR, or the tribunal can take the initiative itself. In practice very few claimants apply. The tribunals have in the past seldom instigated PHRs themselves and in many regions have been reluctant to grant respondents' applications. Recently they have been used more extensively. In Bristol, for example, where PHRs are often held as telephone conferences, the tribunal has indicated it will hold them as a normal course in claims of unfair dismissal involving the rule in *British Home Stores* v *Burchell* [1980] ICR 303, where the facts seem largely agreed. So Basil's case would probably proceed to a PHR if his employment was in that region.

Under r. 18, a PHR is an interim hearing and is to be conducted by a chairman alone, unless one party makes a written request ten days beforehand for a hearing by a full tribunal or the chairman decides that substantive issues of fact have to be decided and that a tribunal is desirable. A PHR is to be held in public but it can use electronic communications. So the chairman must conduct any telephone conference from a room to which the public has access.

The purpose of a PHR is to carry out a preliminary consideration of the proceedings. Under the old rules of procedure this was confined to the ET 1, the ET 3 and written representations and/or oral argument, with a view to identifying contentions that stood no reasonable prospect of success and warning the appropriate party accordingly. The provision under ET Rules 2004 is less narrow and allows the chairman or tribunal to look at evidence and to reach a broader set of conclusions:

(a) to determine interim or preliminary matters;

(b) to perform any of the functions of a CMD;

(c) to require a party to pay a deposit as a condition of proceeding with a contention that has little reasonable prospect of success; and/or

(d) after giving due notice, to strike out all or part of a claim or response which is scandalous, vexatious or has no reasonable prospect of success, or has been conducted scandalously, unreasonably or vexatiously, or which has not been actively pursued (see r. 18(7)).

The deposit that the chairman or tribunal can order is up to £500, subject to enquiry about the party's ability to pay, and it has to be paid within 21 days of the date the decision is sent to the parties in writing. If the deposit is not paid, the claim, response or part concerned is struck out. Most such orders are made against the claimant and it is unusual for the deposit to be paid, so that the claim is struck out, but if the deposit is paid and the case proceeds to a hearing where that contention fails, the party concerned may lose the deposit as a contribution to costs.

If a PHR considers the possibility of requiring a deposit, whether or not such an order is made, no chairman or member of the tribunal who heard the PHR may then sit at the full hearing of the case.

The most radical of the above provisions is (d), the right to strike out various categories of case, including those with no reasonable prospect of success. At this stage it is impossible to predict how much it may be used, but we suspect most chairmen will be reluctant to strike out any but the very obviously hopeless cases.

13.10 Conciliation and the role of ACAS

13.10.1 How ACAS becomes involved

Under all the jurisdictions of the employment tribunals we have been considering in this chapter there is a standard procedure under ETA 1996, s. 18 that a copy of every claim to the tribunal is sent by the tribunal office to ACAS. It is the job of the ACAS conciliation officer to seek to reach an agreement between the parties to settle the complaint without its being determined by the employment tribunal. Conciliation was extended to cover claims to redundancy payments as well as all the other jurisdictions by ERDRA 1998, s. 11.

The conciliation officer makes contact as a matter of course with both parties, usually telephoning professional representatives and arranging to meet unrepresented parties. This initiative avoids either party creating the appearance of lack of confidence in their case. The role of the conciliation officer is to try to promote a settlement and not to adjudicate on the merits of the case. In practice this is often too fine a distinction to draw and some debate on the merits takes place.

A new element is introduced into the conciliation process by ET Rules 2004, r. 22. Except for claims that include any complaint of discrimination or claim of equal pay (even if among other jurisdictions), there is now to be a fixed period for conciliation, during which no full hearing is permitted to take place, although a CMD or PHR may take place and dates can be fixed. Claims concerning breach of contract or deductions from wages and claims for a statutory redundancy payment are subject (unless a chairman directs otherwise) to the *short conciliation period of seven weeks* beginning with the date the copy of the ET 1 is sent to the respondent. The other categories of claim we have been considering in this chapter (unfair dismissal and claims under the Working Time Regulations 1998) and claims from the first group where a chairman so directs are subject to the *standard conciliation period of 13 weeks*, beginning on the same date, with the possibility of extension by two weeks if everyone agrees.

Although the conciliation period is described as 'fixed,' this is in the sense that a full tribunal hearing may not happen during that period. We understand that ACAS will nevertheless continue to make its services available if required after the period is over.

The ACAS officers use a number of standard forms, often referred to by their initials. Form COT 1 is the office record for ACAS, but the others may be seen by the parties:

COT 2 is the form used to record reinstatement or re-engagement of the claimant.

COT 3 is used to record terms of a settlement, usually involving some payment of money, but sometimes other matters like the provision of a reference (either in addition to money or instead of it) or confidentiality as to the terms.

COT 4 is used to record a withdrawal by the claimant.

As soon as the conciliation officer reaches some settlement of the claim, the tribunal office is notified and the case is held in abeyance pending receipt of the appropriate form, signed as necessary by one or both of the parties.

13.10.2 Binding settlements

Most of the statutory rights we have been considering in this book are subject to the rule that the parties cannot contract out of them. For example, the right to complain of unfair dismissal is protected by s. 203 of ERA 1996. Exceptions, where they exist at all, are closely defined.

Because of the breadth of that rule, even an agreement between the parties to settle terms of dismissal will not preclude a later change of mind by the ex-employee who can then start tribunal proceedings. There are two exceptions, where settlements are binding. The first is in relation to agreements reached with the involvement of ACAS. However, ACAS has become unwilling to act merely as a 'rubber stamp' in giving its formal blessing to agreements already concluded between the parties and declines to prepare a COT 3 settlement in relation to negotiations it has not led, partly because of worries about the resulting workload and partly because to do so might exceed its statutory powers. This has caused practical problems where both sides have wanted a COT 3 settlement and ACAS has felt unable to help.

The second exception is contained in ERA 1996, s. 203(2)(f) which provides that a 'compromise agreement' is binding if reached with the advice of the applicant's *relevant independent adviser*. The adviser concerned must be covered by insurance, and the agreement itself must be in a form that complies with each of the requirements of s. 203(3). Under amendments introduced by ERDRA 1998 into s. 203(3A) and (3B), advisers covered by this rule include not only lawyers (as hitherto) but also trade union officials and workers in advice centres, except in relation to their own employees. There is sometimes a problem under either method when such representatives purport to have the authority to settle on their members' behalf, but have not properly obtained it—see *Gloystarne & Co. Ltd* v *Martin* [2001] IRLR 15.

13.10.3 Considerations for the parties about whether to settle

The decision whether to fight a case in the employment tribunal or to seek to settle before the hearing may be a complex one for both parties.

In the simplest cases the matter is merely one of the amount of money involved. Suppose, for example, that the claim is of unfair dismissal, and both sides are considering the possibility of settlement through the involvement of ACAS.

The claimant may consider that the likely award of compensation from the tribunal if the claim is successful may be £5,000, but that the chances of success are only fifty-fifty. Maybe, therefore, a definite promise of £2,500 is as good as taking a chance on £5,000. However, the costs of contesting the case in the tribunal may be £1,000 more than has already been incurred. This suggests that settlement at anything in excess of £1,500 may be worthwhile.

The employer's estimate of the likely award may be lower (perhaps £4,000) and the estimate of the chances of losing rather higher (say three to one). So applying the odds of one-in-four to the likely award suggests a settlement of £1,000. The employer may also be likely to incur additional costs by contesting the case, perhaps £1,000. So the employer will be attracted by the prospect of settling at anything below £2,000.

The conciliation officer has a relatively easy task in such a case. Where the parties eventually come together in the range between £1,500 and £2,000 will obviously reflect their respective skills as negotiators.

Cases in real life are rarely quite so simple. Both parties have a much more complicated agenda and will look to their solicitors for advice. The issues involved in such a decision may be significantly different from those in most civil litigation, and the solicitor may wish to encourage the client to try to analyse some of the factors involved. **Table 13.2** provides a model for use in complaints of unfair dismissal; cases like Dmitri's where it is necessary to preserve a continuing relationship between the parties raise even more complex issues.

Table 13.2 Issues for both sides in deciding whether to settle a tribunal claim

Issues for the claimant	*Issues for the employer*
How much will be awarded if I win?	How much is at stake if we lose, including any special or additional awards or orders for reinstatement or re-engagement?
What are my chances of winning?	What are the chances of losing?
What are the legal costs of continuing the fight?	What are the legal costs of fighting?
What are the costs or disadvantages of losing a day or more in the hearing, especially in a new job?	What is the cost in management time?
What is the effect of the Recoupment Regulations (see **13.12.1**)?	
How much might the other side offer?	How much will the claimant accept?
Will the publicity of a tribunal hearing, probably reported in the local press, adversely affect my chances of future employment or my security in my present job?	Will publicity be damaging in the local labour market, with customers or with the boss at group headquarters?
Can I and any witnesses face the personal strain of a tribunal hearing?	Might fighting the case require us to call witnesses we would rather not use, e.g., the fellow-employee who originally brought dishonesty to our notice or to disclose confidential documents?
Has the employer more to lose than I have by going to the tribunal?	What precedents are set by being seen to have settled out of court for any future cases where employees will expect like treatment?
	Will the manager who originally made the decision to dismiss feel that his or her authority has been compromised?
	Shall we lose the opportunity of training supervisors in the importance of following procedures by avoiding a tribunal hearing?
	Does settlement compromise the integrity of our disciplinary procedure or damage the motivation of other employees?
Is my former employer likely to be offended by my refusal to settle in a way that may prejudice any future reference? (Victimisation is in theory forbidden but is difficult to prove.)	

13.10.3.1 Other issues

In assisting clients to analyse issues like those listed above, solicitors will wish to discourage reliance on irrelevant reasoning:

(a) Claimants such as Basil (**13.5.3.2**) sometimes want to go ahead to clear their names, especially against implications of dishonesty. Such logic displays a widespread but erroneous view of the role of the tribunals. The solicitor will have to try to explain the principles of *British Home Stores* v *Burchell* [1980] ICR 303. However, it is difficult for claimants to understand that tribunals are concerned only to assess the *reasonableness* of the employer's belief and not its objective proof to a criminal standard.

(b) Both parties often see the issue for the tribunal as one of principle and are keen to get their own back on the other side. It needs to be explained that this too is not the role of the tribunals. As time passes, however, both sides probably become more pragmatic and less concerned about the supposed principles.

13.10.4 Drafting a settlement

A compromise agreement must meet the requirements of ERA 1996, s. 232(3) as to its format. In particular it must be in writing, identify the adviser, and state that the conditions regulating compromise agreements have been satisfied. A model can be found in books of precedents.

A solicitor preparing such an agreement or the wording for a COT 3 must give some thought to the question of what it should cover. In relation to a dismissal, for example, an employer will want any payment to settle all claims (whether or not yet made) for unfair dismissal, wrongful dismissal, discrimination of any kind, and any contractual or similar claim that may be outstanding on the termination of employment. Employees, on the other hand, will wish to ensure that any such broad definition does not preclude them from enforcing their future pension rights or from litigation about some future industrial disease or personal injury. Many solicitors acting for employees and also ACAS conciliation officers ask for these matters to be excluded expressly. The precaution may in fact be unnecessary.

It is unlikely, whatever words are used, that a settlement will preclude a party from pursuing an action which was not known about and could not be known about at the date of the agreement. See, for example, the House of Lords decision in *Bank of Credit and Commerce International* v *Ali* [2001] ICR 337. Former employees were permitted to pursue a claim for damages for disadvantage on the labour market caused by widespread publicity about corruption and dishonesty at the bank, despite accepting terms 'in full and final settlement'. When signing the agreement neither party could realistically have supposed that such a claim was a possibility. In *Royal National Orthopaedic Hospital Trust* v *Howard* [2002] IRLR 849, the EAT left open the possibility that 'extremely clear words' could compromise claims that have not yet arisen, but we know of no examples. In practice the wording used in compromise agreements has been given more searching scrutiny than that on forms COT 3.

13.10.5 The arbitration alternative

In May 2001, there was brought into force a scheme of arbitration in unfair dismissal applications provided for under s. 7 of ERDRA 1998 as an alternative to tribunal proceedings. See ACAS Arbitration Scheme (England and Wales) Order 2001, SI 2001/1185. It was mentioned at **10.12.2** above. The parties may agree, through the ACAS conciliation officer, to submit a dispute about unfair dismissal to binding arbitration, which ACAS will then arrange but not itself conduct. The scheme took a long while to develop because of worries that the denial of a fair trial, albeit by agreement, might breach the HRA 1998, and the result is consequently somewhat cumbersome. It has been very little used: the ACAS report for the year 2002-3 records 23 cases in total during the year.

13.10.6 Withdrawal

Claimants can withdraw their claims at any time, and frequently do so, whether on their own initiative or as a result of the involvement of ACAS. It is in theory possible for the respondent to claim costs, but this almost never happens, and costs have rarely been awarded: see **13.11.2** below. In *Ako* v *Rothschild Asset Management Ltd* [2002] EWCA Civ 236, [2002] ICR 899, the Court of Appeal advises a tribunal to ask an applicant about the circumstances of withdrawal, as a cause of action estoppel will arise if the application was dismissed judicially on the applicant's withdrawal, but not if it was merely discontinued. Now, under ET Rules 2004, r. 25 dismissal of the claim no longer follows automatically on the claimant's withdrawal, but requires an application from the respondent.

Care should however be taken in relation to complaints of breach of contract. In *Patel* v *RCMS Ltd* [1999] IRLR 161, the EAT held that the employer's counterclaim survived the employee's withdrawal. Obviously a settlement providing for mutual withdrawal would have been a safer option for the applicant than unilateral action.

13.11 The hearing

If the efforts of ACAS prove unsuccessful the claim now proceeds to a hearing in the employment tribunal. If the ET 1 and ET 3 are reasonably well drafted and the case management procedures have been used properly, it should by this stage be fairly clear what the issues for the tribunal are going to be.

For example, in Anastasia's case (**13.5.3.1**), a key issue is whether the assessment that led to her selection for redundancy was fairly and properly carried out. The employer will presumably call as a witness the person or people who performed it; Anastasia herself, and possibly other witnesses, will want to challenge its fairness, partly by their own evidence and partly by challenging the employer's evidence. Both sides may wish to produce documents to support their contentions.

We now need to examine how that all happens in practice. We shall do so by reference to the main hearing (denoted Hearing by ET Rules 2004, r. 26) of the merits of a claim, but we have already noted at **13.8.7** that the tribunal can order under r. 10(2) that part of the proceedings should be dealt with separately. Each part, like any CMD or PHR, then qualities as a hearing under r. 14(1) and the following remarks apply to each part.

13.11.1 Preparations

By the ET Rules 2004, r. 14(4), the tribunal office is required to give the parties 14 days notice of a hearing except a CMD, unless the parties agree to shorter notice. Many dates of hearing are fixed in the course of a CMD, so that the parties have already agreed their availability, but some are notified by post or e-mail. If the parties have not been consulted about a date, the tribunal office is normally very amenable to granting one postponement, although some regions have been known to require detailed justification for such a request. The request is more likely to be granted if the party making it has consulted the other parties and is able to write as soon as possible after the notification, proposing an alternative date or dates. The tribunal offices are much less willing to grant late requests, and will require detailed justification for any request to postpone an agreed date, including evidence of the illness or other non-availability of a witness. No postponement will usually be granted, for example, if a witness has booked a holiday *after* the tribunal date was fixed.

Increasingly notices of hearing include the chairman's estimate of the likely length of hearing and it is for the parties to say so if they disagree for any reason. Many chairmen are already limiting cross-examination and speeches to ensure that cases are completed in the time allocated.

Hearings are normally public and the press are admitted. Under r. 16(1) of ET Rules 2004 hearings may be in private in tightly defined and exceptional circumstances. Under r. 50 hearings may be subject to restricted reporting orders where allegations of sexual misconduct are involved. In *X* v *Commissioner of Police of the Metropolis* [2003] ICR 1031 the EAT held that this provision should be used to ensure applicants were not deterred from bringing such cases, a protection required by art. 6 of the European Equal Treatment Directive 76/207/EEC.

We noted when discussing the operation of a CMD at **13.8.2** above that it was important for a solicitor acting for either party to have given careful thought at a very early stage to the presentation of the client's case at an eventual tribunal hearing. So as we come now to consider how it should be done, we hope you are not looking at this part of the chapter for the first time once the hearing is fixed.

Appearing for a client at a tribunal hearing is all about *persuasion*. You have to persuade the chairman or a tribunal of three, none of whom has any personal interest in the outcome, to adopt your client's version of the facts and your interpretation of the law rather than your opponent's. You have three tools available to you: the documents, the evidence of witnesses, and the authorities. Without compromising your personal integrity you have to decide how to use each of them most effectively in support of your case.

13.11.2 Documents

We have already discussed at **13.8.10** the orders that tribunals often issue for parties to agree a joint bundle of documents. In practice it is not usually difficult to reach agreement when both parties are represented, as both accept that the other has the right to put in whatever is required, but occasionally unrepresented parties require an unreasonable number of documents. In such a case it may be desirable to write suggesting fewer, so that it is plain where the fault lies if the tribunal later objects to an excessively large bundle. The tribunals are less strict than the courts in operating the 'best evidence' rule, and photocopies of documents are usually sufficient, but it is a wise precaution to take originals to the hearing in case any issue of authenticity arises.

Sometimes certain documents are obviously required. Thus in Basil's case the employer's disciplinary procedure, any rules stipulating what conduct may lead to summary dismissal and the notes of disciplinary meetings will probably be required by both parties. Irrelevant material should be left out—both because the tribunals dislike needlessly large bundles and because the persuasive power of anything good is reduced if it is buried in a lot of paper. So if, for example, the procedure and rules are contained in an employee handbook, it is a good idea to take a copy of the handbook to the hearing in case anyone wants to see the whole, but only the relevant parts should go into the bundle.

Contemporaneous documents have much greater persuasive power than anything written up after the event. So working documents concerned with Anastasia's selection may be very helpful in showing how carefully the employer approached the task. Any manuscript notes taken by either side during the crucial meeting with the departmental manager in Dmitri's case will far outweigh typed notes prepared subsequently.

Documents should be assembled in a folder, in chronological order, with an index at the front and with the pages (rather than the documents) numbered in sequence. It will be found that this makes reference during the hearing as simple as possible.

13.11.3 The order of proceeding and burden of proof

Under ET Rules 2004, r. 14(4) it is provided that either party may send in to the tribunal written representations as an alternative to attending in person. They must be lodged at the tribunal office at least seven days before the hearing. In practice this is a very unsatisfactory alternative and should be used with great reluctance.

Apart from that possibility, the parties turn up on the day appointed to give their own evidence, to cross-examine witnesses for the other side and to address the tribunal. Although the tribunal is given wide powers under the rules to determine its own procedure, that power is in practice much circumscribed by custom and by cases such as *Aberdeen Steak Houses* v *Ibrahim* [1988] ICR 550, which sets out some general principles.

In practice the order of proceeding is standardised. Generally speaking it is for the party on whom the burden of proof rests to start the proceedings. Thus, in relation to deductions from wages, discrimination and equal pay it is for the *claimant* to start by making out a case. In dismissal cases (unfair dismissal and claims for redundancy payments), it is for the *claimant* to go first if it is necessary to prove dismissal, i.e., if the employer denies dismissal. If the employer admits dismissal, the *employer* goes first to prove the reason for dismissal. This rule is of long standing (*Gill* v *Harold Sheepbridge* [1974] ICR 294) and pre-dates the present statutory provision about burden of proof.

13.11.4 Opening statement

In the past the party opening proceedings often made an opening statement, as in the county court. Occasionally chairmen still permit that to happen and it can be helpful in identifying the real issues in a case. Increasingly, though, and especially where witness statements and the bundle are handed in to the tribunal in advance, chairmen regard opening statements as superfluous and prefer to get on with the evidence. Solicitors may sometimes be permitted to draw the attention of the tribunal to key parts of the bundle before the evidence starts.

13.11.5 Evidence-in-chief

The two sides will need to decide what facts they need to prove in order to establish their cases and to decide what witnesses need to be called. As in the courts, this evidence given on behalf of the party calling the witness is called evidence-in-chief.

13.11.5.1 The rules of evidence

The rules of evidence followed in the employment tribunals are based on those in the county courts, but are less rigid. The rule against hearsay is not strictly followed, and evidence is often permitted that would be forbidden in the courts. Indeed, the definition of hearsay is complicated by the slightly special nature of the issues the tribunals often need to investigate. If a manager decided to dismiss a claimant because of a report made to him by a subordinate about the claimant's behaviour, the content of the report may sometimes be direct evidence of the manager's reasoning in deciding to dismiss, rather than hearsay evidence of the claimant's behaviour.

During evidence-in-chief, the solicitor should follow the normal rule of not asking leading questions, except when presenting background evidence about non-contentious aspects of the case. Even then it is courteous to ask the tribunal's permission before leading a witness.

13.11.5.2 Written witness statements

At one stage the tribunals required all evidence to be given through oral examination. The chairman was required to write down the salient points and, if the case went to appeal, could be required by EAT to produce a transcript of the notes. From 1991 onwards the tribunals in several regions experimented with systems of written witness statements as a means of saving time at the hearing. Most regions now impose some such requirement but there is considerable variation.

It must be stressed that the saving of time is of tribunal hearing time and not in preparation. A solicitor preparing written statements of witnesses' evidence needs to be meticulous in achieving complete accuracy. If a proof of evidence for the use of counsel contains a minor inaccuracy (e.g., the colour of a car), it will be corrected during examination-in-chief. If a witness statement contains such an inaccuracy, it will cast doubt on the reliability of more important elements. So the additional work in preparing such statements is in fact considerable. Each statement should end with a statement of truth signed by the witness.

Most regions order witness statements to be exchanged between the parties who may be required to arrive early and to hand in copies of the bundle and of the witness statements so that members of the tribunal can read them before the start of the hearing. The tribunal may then require witnesses to read the statements aloud under oath or, increasingly, they take the statements as read and move straight on to cross-examination. Representatives are sometimes not permitted to ask additional questions by way of examination-in-chief without leave of the tribunal, although such leave is usually given in relation to points raised by the other side's statements. Such procedures do not add much to informality in the tribunals.

The variation in procedure causes problems for solicitors and other representatives. The style of a witness statement prepared for reading aloud may be rather different from one prepared for the tribunal to read for itself. It is always a good idea to try to find out local practice before appearing before any tribunal for the first time.

13.11.6 Cross-examination

The art of cross-examination cannot be learned from a book but only by practice. The rules are the same as in the courts and it is important that key elements in your case are 'put to' the witnesses of the other side so that they have a chance to refute them. With an unrepresented claimant the tribunal will sometimes permit recall of the witness for the purpose, as the claimant may not have understood the requirement, but solicitors may not be given that flexibility.

13.11.7 Questions from the tribunal and re-examination

The final stage of evidence from each witness is for the party calling that witness to tidy up loose ends resulting from cross-examination. This gives the representative the chance to give the full story of any matter raised during cross-examination in a way that tells only half a story. It is not permitted to raise completely new material at this late stage. While the tribunal may permit an unrepresented claimant to do so, and then give the other side a chance of further cross-examination, a solicitor will not normally be allowed to make this mistake.

At some stage the chairman and members of the tribunal will wish to ask questions of the witness. Practice varies considerably. Some chairmen interrupt continuously during evidence-in-chief; others wait until the end. The lay-members are not usually given their chance until the end. There is no uniform practice as to whether re-examination or questions from the tribunal come first.

13.11.8 Closing addresses

When all the evidence has been presented, the two parties or their representatives each have the chance to address the tribunal. This gives them the opportunity both to review the evidence and to refer to any statute and to relevant authorities. Recent practice in the tribunals has been to discourage excessive dependence on the authorities and to concentrate on the statutory provisions. It is therefore unwise to encumber a closing address with references to the very well-known cases like *British Home Stores* v *Burchell* or *Williams* v *Compair Maxam*. The tribunals dislike being treated like imbeciles! It is also unnecessary to waste time on authorities where a decision really rests entirely on the facts. Some chairmen limit the time allowed. Skeleton arguments are not normally submitted in writing, but their use has become more common than it was. Even if a skeleton argument is not prepared it is worth trying to give a closing address a clear structure, especially if you wish to present alternative lines of reasoning that need to be considered in a particular sequence. It is also important to ensure that you cover all the factual matters from the evidence that are essential to your case.

It is usual for the party that went first at the beginning of the hearing also to have the last word by giving the second closing address. This practice is not invariable, however, and some chairmen prefer to reverse it, especially in Scotland.

13.12 The tribunal decision

We have been used to calling the final result of a tribunal hearing the decision, but that term is not used in ET Rules 2004. Instead in r. 28(1) we find definitions of judgments and orders. The first represents a final determination of the whole or part of a claim and may include an award of compensation, a declaration or a recommendation, while the second is an interim decision, most often resulting from a CMD or PHR.

Under r. 28, the tribunal may issue its judgment or order orally at the end of the hearing (almost always after an adjournment to consider it), or it may reserve its decision and issue the judgment or order in writing later. Judgments must always be recorded in writing, and reasons must be given, but there is no longer any requirement for the reasons for an oral judgment to be recorded in writing unless one party so requests either at the hearing or within 14 days, or the EAT so orders. There is no obligation on the tribunal to give reasons for an order unless a request for reasons is made at the hearing.

A judgment may simply be on the merits of the case, so that the tribunal announces whether it finds for the claimant or dismisses the case, or (if it finds for the claimant) it may go on to announce a remedy. A subsequent hearing is sometimes arranged as to remedy, leaving the parties time meanwhile to try to negotiate a settlement.

The tribunal may reach a unanimous decision, or it can decide by a majority. Chairmen usually work hard to try to achieve unanimity. Where a tribunal is reduced to a chairman and one other, the chairman has a second, casting vote.

Where reasons are given, the rule until now has been that they must contain enough detail to allow the parties to see how the decision was reached, but need not necessarily address each and every contention advanced at a hearing: *Meek* v *City of Birmingham District Council* [1987] IRLR 250. We cannot be certain that the authority survives the change in procedural rules.

The tribunal may correct clerical errors in a decision but is otherwise *functus officio* having given its decision and may not change it.

13.13 Costs and preparation time orders

13.13.1 The new rules in 2004

There is now a new regime about the award of costs in the employment tribunals and much has been written elsewhere about the changes. Part comes from the new s. 13 and s. 13A inserted into ETA 1996 by EA 2002 (with effect from July 2004) and part from ET Rules 2004 (with effect from October 2004). As we go to press it is impossible to predict how significant the changes will really prove to be. Recent experience suggests a long-running battle between the legislators (who see costs as a good way of discouraging hopeless cases and thereby reducing the massively increased public expenditure on the employment tribunal service) and most tribunal chairmen, especially those who support widespread access to justice, who have been reluctant in practice to award costs unless parties behave outrageously. So everything hinges on the question whether the new rules are applied more often in practice than their predecessors. We therefore propose to restrict ourselves to a fairly brief section on this topic.

13.13.2 The meaning of costs and preparation time

Costs are defined in r. 38(3) to mean fees, charges, disbursements or expenses incurred in relation to tribunal proceedings and a tribunal may make a costs order only in favour of a party which is legally represented. A costs order can be made up to £10,000 without detailed assessment under the Civil Procedure Rules, more with such assessment.

A preparation time order can be made in favour of a party which is not legally represented, but not in addition to a costs order in favour of the same party in the same case. Preparation time is time spent by the party or its employees or advisers in preparation for a hearing but not at the hearing itself—r. 42(3). A preparation time order has to be calculated by multiplying the number of hours actually spent by £25 (£26 from 6 April 2005), subject to a maximum of £10,000.

13.13.3 When costs are awarded

Despite other changes to the rules, there has been no major change in the general provision as to when costs (or equally, a preparation time order) may be awarded. Costs *must* now be awarded against an employer if postponement or adjournment of a hearing was because the employer failed without a special reason to provide evidence about availability of the job in a case of unfair dismissal where the claimant sought reinstatement or re-engagement. Costs *may* (much as before) be awarded against a party or representative who has acted vexatiously, abusively, disruptively or otherwise unreasonably or if the bringing or conducting of proceedings has been misconceived—r. 40(3) for costs and r. 44(3) for preparation time. See *Stein* v *Associated Dairies* [1982] IRLR 447 for an example where the EAT sitting in Scotland approved a tribunal award of costs under a similar rule.

A new provision allows for the award of wasted costs *against a representative* and not the party in the event of any improper, unreasonable, or negligent act or omission by the representative. It remains to be seen whether the new rules make any difference to the practice.

13.13.4 Applying for costs

Under ET Rules 2004, r. 38(7) or r. 42(5) respectively, an application for costs or a preparation time order can be made during proceedings, at the end of a hearing or in writing to the tribunal office within 28 days from the issue of the judgment.

Past experience suggests that the highest chance of success in an application arises when the tribunal has held a PHR and the other side has been ordered to pay a deposit, has paid it and has then lost the case on the grounds predicted. It doesn't happen often but it is a pleasant dream.

More often the threat of an application for costs on the ground that the other side has been pursuing the case unreasonably has been much more significant in practice, especially where you are having difficulty in getting the other side to negotiate seriously about a settlement.

In the courts, where the possibility exists of paying money into court, this procedure involves the writing of a formal letter threatening an application for costs if the offer is rejected, as in *Calderbank* v *Calderbank* [1976] Fam 93. In *Kopel* v *Safeway Stores plc* [2003] IRLR 753, the EAT suggested that this procedure cannot be copied in the tribunals where there is no system of paying money into the tribunal, but in fact a similar procedure to the *Calderbank* letter is sometimes operated.

In *Beynon* v *Scadden* [1999] IRLR 700, the claimants' trade union, Unison, supported them in a complaint of a breach of the consultation requirements under TUPE (see **12.6.5** above). The case was in fact hopeless because the transfer of the business was achieved by a share transfer and was not covered by TUPE. The employment tribunal had found as a fact that the reason Unison pursued the case was the collateral purpose of achieving recognition. That finding was enough for the EAT to support an award of costs, based on vexatious conduct by the claimants or their representatives. In *Kovacs* v *Queen Mary & Westfield College* [2002] EWCA 352, [2002] ICR 919, the Court of Appeal approved the reasoning in *Beynon* and held that an award of costs did not require the tribunal to assess a party's ability to pay, something that is now permitted by r. 41(2) and r. 45(3) but is not mandatory.

13.14 The remedies for the tribunal

We have already considered the appropriate remedies relevant to the various jurisdictions in earlier chapters, but several points remain to be made here.

13.14.1 Recoupment of benefits

Under the Employment Protection (Recoupment of Jobseeker's Allowance and Income Support) Regulations 1996, the full amount of a monetary award of compensation may not be payable to a claimant who succeeds in a claim of unfair dismissal. The tribunal is required to assess the approximate amount of jobseeker's allowance and income support benefit the claimant has received between the date of dismissal and the date of hearing. This figure is called the 'prescribed element'.

The compensatory award is assessed without regard to any benefits the claimant may have received during that period. Only the excess of the compensatory award over the prescribed element is payable immediately to the claimant at the end of the hearing. The Department of Social Security then sends the employer a demand in respect of benefits actually paid to the claimant, an amount that may not exceed the prescribed element. The employer pays that amount to the DSS, and any surplus remaining to the claimant.

Since the Recoupment Regulations apply to tribunal awards and not to conciliated settlements, it is an inducement to both sides to settle and to avoid their effect.

13.14.2 Payment of interest

Under the Employment Tribunals (Interest) Order 1990, interest is payable on tribunal awards still outstanding on a date 42 days after a decision is issued to the parties. The rate of interest is as laid down for other similar purposes in relation to court awards and varies from time to time.

13.14.3 Remedy hearings

In October 1999 there was a very large increase from £12,000 to £50,000 in the maximum amount of the compensatory award that can be made in cases of unfair dismissal, now raised further to £55,000. We speculated that the increase might result in a more rigorous approach from the tribunals to the assessment of compensation, but there does not seem to have been any significant change. Although a few cases result in very large awards, the average amount actually awarded in 2003–4 was £7,275. The tribunals often require a claimant to prepare at an early stage of preparation a schedule of loss. Calculation at the hearing is speeded up because the relevant facts have already been ascertained.

In discrimination cases unlimited compensation has been available since 1993. In *Buxton* v *Equinox Design Ltd* [1999] ICR 269 (which we encountered at **6.9.5** above), the EAT stressed the need for proper management by the tribunal of the assessment of compensation in a disability discrimination case. It was not good enough to assess future unemployment on the basis of 'guestimate'; some medical evidence was required about the claimant's employability, given his multiple sclerosis.

A tribunal decision about remedy has usually required additional evidence beyond that used at the hearing on the merits of the case. Is reinstatement or re-engagement feasible? If not, and the tribunal moves on to the assessment of compensation, what was the state of the employment market locally and how much did the claimant do to mitigate loss? Now, as a stricter approach starts to be taken, even more evidence may be required in some cases. For example, if the employer loses in Basil's case, the evidence called about the alleged theft at the hearing on the merits will have concentrated on the reasonableness of the employer's belief. In assessing contributory fault, the issue is one of fact: did Basil steal or not? That may require different witnesses whom neither side needed to call at the first hearing.

The availability of a much higher limit may also give rise to some new heads of compensation. In *Sheriff* v *Klyne Tugs (Lowestoft) Ltd* [1999] IRLR 481, the Court of Appeal held that compensation for psychiatric damage as well as injury to feelings fell within the jurisdiction of an employment tribunal in a case concerning racial discrimination.

13.14.4 The effect of tax

At **10.15** above we dealt with the general principles of taxation of compensation awarded by the tribunals in cases of unfair dismissal. It is still relatively unusual for these rules to apply in practice: most awards are well below £30,000 and therefore are not taxable in the applicant's hands. Reference should be made to the earlier chapter if there is a need to consider 'grossing up' to compensate for the effect of tax.

13.15 Challenge of a tribunal decision

There are two ways a tribunal judgment or decision can be challenged after it is given: it can be reviewed by the tribunal, or an appeal can be taken to the EAT.

13.15.1 Application for review

The power for a tribunal to review a decision is contained in r. 34 of the ET Rules 2004. The application must be made in writing within 14 days of the issue of a decision. The application must be on one or more of the following grounds:

(a) an administrative error has occurred;

(b) a party did not receive notice of proceedings;

(c) the decision was made in the absence of a party;

(d) new evidence, not reasonably foreseeable, has come to light;

(e) the interests of justice require a review.

This is the correct way to remedy minor slips discovered shortly after the hearing: *British Midland Airways* v *Lewis* [1978] ICR 782. It is not an alternative to an appeal. Any challenge to the reasoning that led to the decision must go to the EAT: *Trimle* v *Supertravel* [1982] ICR 440.

Whilst other applications for review can be considered and refused without a hearing, an application for review of a default judgment must always be considered at a public hearing—r. 33. See **13.7.2** above for the rules regarding information that must be included in applications for this special kind of review.

13.15.2 Appeal to EAT

If the decision of an employment tribunal contains an error of law, an appeal lies to the EAT. As we go to press the EAT is still producing a final version of new rules of procedure which will adopt similar changes to those we have been discussing for the employment tribunals. Until now, appeals to the EAT had always to be based on the full written judgment of the employment tribunal. This is likely to change to take account of the new tribunal practice on issuing written judgments and the fact that the EAT, of its own volition, may demand to see the written decision. Appeals will have to be entered within 42 days of the date the employment tribunal gives judgment. Employment tribunal judgments are usually sent to the parties with an accompanying leaflet explaining how standard forms can be obtained from the EAT at Victoria Embankment in London.

Parties often express a wish to appeal on the basis that they do not like the judgment of the employment tribunal and wish for a second opinion. It has to be explained to them that this is not the function of the EAT, which will not interfere with a properly-reached judgment of the employment tribunal on the facts of the case. It is also almost always impossible to raise at the EAT new points of law that were not raised at the employment tribunal: *Jones* v *Governing Body of Burdett Coutts School* [1998] IRLR 521.

13.16 A summary chart of the main jurisdictions

Jurisdiction	Source	Service condition	Time limit for IT application	Extension of time	ACAS involvement	Maximum award*
Unfair dismissal	ERA 1996, s. 94	1 year	3 months from EDT	'not reasonably practicable'	Yes 13 weeks	£63,100 unless re-employment ordered
Redundancy payment	ERA 1996, s. 135	2 years	6 months from RD	'just and equitable'	Yes 13 weeks	£8,100
Deductions from wages	ERA 1996, Part II	Nil	3 months from payday	'not reasonably practicable'	Yes 7 weeks	Unlimited
Racial discrimination	RRA 1976	Nil	3 months from act complained of	'just and equitable'	Yes – no fixed period	Unlimited
Sex discrimination	SDA 1975	Nil	3 months from act complained of	'just and equitable'	Yes – no fixed period	Unlimited
Equal pay	Equal Pay Act 1970	Nil	6 months after termination	None	Yes – no fixed period	Unlimited
Disability discrimination	DDA 1995	Nil	3 months from act complained of	'just and equitable'	Yes – no fixed period	Unlimited
Breach of contract	ITA 1996, s. 3 and 1994 Order	Nil	3 months from EDT	'not reasonably practicable'	Yes 7 weeks	£25,000
Working time	WT Regs 1998	Nil	3 months from infringement	'not reasonably practicable'	Yes 13 weeks	No general limit

* These are the figures from 1 February 2004 and are likely to change from 1 February 2005

SUGGESTED ANSWERS TO SELF-TEST QUESTIONS

Chapter 4

1. First let us look at the position under WTRegs 1998. It is only in relation to adolescent workers that employers are required to take account of time spent in other jobs. So, while your friend's daily rest over Friday night is less than 11 hours, he is an adult and the shopkeeper is not required to take account of time spent working in the bar. There is no breach of reg. 10. Similarly, as an adult worker, not an adolescent, he is not entitled to a rest break under reg. 12 until his working time exceeds six hours. The shop manager is wrong, however, to deny him paid holidays. Reg. 13 gives all workers a right to paid annual leave irrespective of hours of work and indeed we shall see later in **6.5.8** that it is unlawful discrimination to treat part-time workers less favourably than those on full time.

The position regarding NMW is not quite clear from the information you are given. If his rate of pay is stated either as £30 for the morning or as £6 per hour, he is paid more than the £4.10 appropriate for his age of 19, and the shop manager is within the regulations. If, however, there is anything, preferably in writing, to confirm his entitlement to time-and-a-half, the portion of his pay (half of NMW) that represents a premium for working at a particular time must be disregarded under reg. 31(1)(c)—see **4.2.2** above—and the remainder is less than the minimum of £4.10 he is entitled to receive. He is short by 15 p per hour.

2. Yes. The question is about jurisdiction and the case does not fall into any of the exceptions from s. 27(2) that we set out at **4.4.1** above. So the missing quarter (the difference between time-and-a-half and time-and-a-quarter) can certainly be presented as a deduction, thereby bringing the matter within ERA 1996, s. 23. The example is very similar in that sense to the case we discussed at **4.4.4** above. Note, however, that this issue is a grievance, and neither the trade union nor individual employees should be making a tribunal application without first using the statutory grievance procedure—see **Chapter 5**, especially **5.2.4** and **5.3.2.5**.

The case will then raise some interesting and difficult contractual issues. When is acquiescence deemed to be consent to a variation? Has a contractual change taken effect? What is the precise evidence about the employees' question and the supervisor's reply? (For example it would be different from the report of evasiveness if the supervisor's story is of having said that the notified change would take effect, but that anyone dissatisfied could raise this as a grievance later.) Is there an argument, since each employee has the option of working overtime when requested or of declining, that each occasion of working overtime is a separate contract? All these matters will need to be considered, but, on the limited evidence we have, none of them seems to be a contention with no reasonable prospect of success, and their complexity does not detract from the answer about jurisdiction.

Chapter 6

1. After trying to answer this question, have a look at the analysis of the issues by the EAT at [2004] IRLR 348. The employment tribunal had found unlawful discrimination because women were given greater choice than men, but the EAT ruled that they had asked the wrong question. The correct question was whether on contemporary standards the required smartness for men could be achieved otherwise; if so (but by implication only if so) men had received less favourable treatment. The cases they cited seem generally to accept that some detailed differences of rule about dress or appearance between men and women are permitted if they reflect normally accepted contemporary standards. This case was remitted to a different employment tribunal.

2. Refer to **6.9.1.2** above and DDA 1995, s.1. The key elements are that the person must have

(a) a physical or mental impairment

(b) which has a substantial [adverse effect] and

(c) [a] long-term adverse effect

(d) on his ability to carry out normal day-to-day activities.

Chapters 7 and 8

This question requires an assessment of:

(i) if any dismissal proved to be a wrongful dismissal would this invalidate the restraint—no matter how well-drafted it is—and (more arguably) the confidentiality duties, implied or express? (see **7.5.1** and **8.3**)

(ii) the distinction between trade secrets/confidentiality and "employee know-how", as developed through examining the supposed secrets identified in Setters' statement and the contract. (see **7.5.3, 7.5.4** and **7.6.4**); and

(iii) the drafting of the express term on confidentiality (if found relevant under the *Faccenda* tests) and the **quality** of the clauses regarding restraint of trade as it applies to the **individual employee**. (see, in particular, **8.6**)

In a question such as this, you cannot be expected to have mastered all the intricacies of a new industry without a lot more information and without interviewing the client. It is therefore difficult to reach any firm decision here on whether a practice or a secret is really protectable. What you should be aware of, therefore, is how what details you would need to acquire and how they fit in to the general pattern of the law.

The specific question: if *Phoenix Guitars Ltd* go ahead and dismiss Setters, will they still be able to enforce the confidentiality and restraint of trade clauses against him?

On the evidence from Mr Burek it may well be that Mr Setters is going to leave anyway. If this is so, there is the practical point of giving the employer as much time as possible to obtain a replacement (and dismissing Setters immediately will not do this). There is also the practical/legal point that, in dismissing Setters, the company jeopardises the confidentiality and restraint clauses which they say are so important to them. You therefore need to consider the following points:

(a) Effect of any dismissal
We have seen that, if the dismissal is wrongful this will constitute a breach of contract so that the restraints (and arguably the confidentiality clause) will be invalid in any case: *General Billposting* v *Atkinson*. Your client needs to be aware of this. For you to be able to make a decision on whether any dismissal would be wrongful you will need to read **Chapter 9**. However, we can say here that the basic question is whether *Phoenix* can dismiss without notice in the face of the gross misconduct on Setter's part. If *Phoenix* dismiss with proper notice they cannot have committed a wrongful dismissal. One might also note:

(i) the irrelevance of any unfair dismissal claim;
(ii) the possible impact of the *Rock Refrigeration* analysis, especially as developed through *Campbell* v *Frisbee* and
(iii) the relevance of the *Rex Stewart* case—that even where the employer makes a payment in lieu of notice this may still bring *General Billposting* into play.

Further information would also be required on the apparent 'throwaway' line in section 3 of Mr Burek's statement that Setters has already been in negotiation with a rival company. If Setters is already in breach of contract (see *Laughton* v *Bapp)* there is the possibility that, whatever the state of the express terms on confidentiality and restraint, the springboard doctrine might apply (see **7.3.4**). However, this is dangerous ground and should not be relied upon alone.

(b) Confidentiality
First, consider the relevance of the implied term of good faith. If the information Setter's possesses can be classed as a trade secret then it automatically receives protection under the continuing implied term. The express wording of the contract (good or bad) will not be needed. So, which of the 'secrets' identified in the contract might be classed as trade secrets, or at least as highly-confidential? How convinced are you that any of these could be defended in court?

This requires a discussion of the effects of *Faccenda Chicken* and should involve some discussion of the later cases (such as *Lansing Linde)* which have developed the meaning of 'trade secrets' as opposed to confidential information. You should also be aware of the major battle-ground of distinguishing between trade secrets (or 'confidential information' generally) and the employee's know-how. Recent cases, such as *FSS Travel* v *Johnson* show just how difficult it may be for an employer to demonstrate clearly *what* secrets require protection and why they are distinguishable from the employee's know-how. In particular, you need to try to apply your understanding of 'trade secrets', 'know-how', etc directly to the matters identified in the contract and in Burek's statement at para. 2(c). The *Series 5* case demonstrates that the burden is on the employer to clearly identify the material which it is claimed amounts to a trade secret (rather than merely state it so).

If the information is not a trade secret it may not be protectable at all. If protection is going to be given it must be based on the effectiveness of the express confidentiality clause (clause 8). *Faccenda* would have us believe that an express confidentiality term is of no use anyway, so this could be a major stumbling-block. But even if the clause is valid, its wording is loose. It has no 'lifespan' built into it and one might question whether the confidential information may have a shorter lifespan than the unlimited period given in clause 8 (given Mr Burek's own assessment). Clause 8 may not be defendable on its wording anyway.

(c) Restraint of trade
It should be noted that:

- You need to find a 'legitimate interest' and be aware of the presumption that any restraint will be void unless reasonable.
- It may be difficult to base any restraint argument on confidentiality as:
  - (i) this could only apply to trade secrets, and we have decided this issue one way or the other already;
  - (ii) the restraint clause (9) seems to have inappropriate time scales in it as regards confidentiality, given the evidence;
  - (iii) the efficacy of the restraints therefore depends on the question of customer contacts/reputation as Setters also has (limited) access to some of these people.
- You should have identified the *types* of clauses involved (non-dealing in 9.1, non-solicitation in 9.2 and non-poaching in 9.3—*there is no non-competition clause so the company cannot prevent Setters working for their rivals as such*) and their relevance to the case in hand.
- You should consider the reasonableness of clause 9 based on 'time, geography and market setting'. For instance:
  - (i) the clauses have very long 'relation back' periods, which would be difficult to defend in terms of establishing reasonableness;
  - (ii) the non-poaching clause (9.3) is badly drafted as it does not define the employees affected in terms of seniority. It is unlikely to be enforceable.

One might also consider the practical issue as to the procedures involved. Enforcement will have to be through an application for injunctive relief. This demands an understanding of the requirements of *American Cyanamid*. These principles apply both to applications regarding the protection of confidential information and restraint of trade: *Johnson and Bloy* v *Wolstenholme Rink and Fallon*.

Chapter 11

1. The key quotation from ERA 1996 that must be applied to all these examples is that redundancy means that the requirement of the employer's business for people to do work of a particular kind ceases or diminishes—either generally or at a particular place.

   (a) This case is a straightforward example of a reduction in the employer's requirement for people to do work of a particular kind. It is a classic redundancy.

   (b) The practical consequences of the employer's decision here are exactly the same as in (a). The statutory test of redundancy is a reduction in the employer's requirement, and the reason behind that reduction is immaterial. This case is as much a redundancy as (a). Whether dismissals are unfair may be another matter, although tribunals generally avoid 'second-guessing' the employer's decision about how many people are required by a business.

(c) This does not sound like a redundancy. An unsatisfactory employee is being replaced by someone else the employer likes better. There is no indication of any reduction in any requirement for people to do work of a particular kind. We cannot give a definitive view without hearing the employer's argument, which may be that the jobs of supervisor and director are genuinely different, so that there is a reduction in the requirement for supervisors. That sounds a difficult case for the employer to make sound convincing!

(d) The statutory definition allows for the possibility that the reduction in the employer's requirement is at a particular place. So this too is a redundancy. The employer's denial may make defence of any claims of unfair dismissal difficult: if the reason for dismissal is not redundancy, which else of the permitted fair reasons can apply? If, on the other hand, the employer admits redundancy there is the possibility of arguing that the Bristol employees, or some of them, unreasonably refused an offer of suitable alternative employment in Clevedon and are not due any redundancy payment—see **11.4.7.1**.

(e) It is difficult not to sympathise with the an employee in a position like this, but her argument rests on a much narrower view of the employer's requirement than the tribunals adopt. On a broader view the employer's requirement for people to do work like hers has diminished and she is therefore redundant. There may be scope for her to argue about the basis of her selection.

2. Some possible points to explore could include the following:

(1) Was there a customary arrangement or agreed procedure (e.g., LIFO) that has been broken by this method of selection? That no longer leads to automatic unfairness but is still a relevant question.

(2) Mr Patel may be from an ethnic minority. If his selection depends on racial discrimination (even if inadvertant, perhaps because his English is limited), it may be unlawful by the Race Relations Act 1976 as well as unfair by unfair dismissal law.

(3) Mr Patel has scored particularly badly at lines 1 and 2, which could well be exactly the factors affected by some disability. Make a note to investigate whether he is disabled.

(4) The unit of selection may be wrong or unreasonable.

(5) The form is defective in giving no recognition at all to service.

(6) The form has been marked by only one person: is the result too subjective? Worse still, is there any evidence of personal antagonism from the assessor towards VP?

(7) What steps were taken to check consistency if others in the unit of selection were marked by someone else?

(8) There is a remarkable precision implied by the range of weighting factors. Can it be justified?

(9) Line 1 should accord with some factual record. Is it accurate?

(10) There is no definition of the period considered for line 1. Was a fixed period taken, is it reasonable and has it been applied consistently?

(11) There is no stated scope for examination of reasons behind line 1. Was VP's absence for any extenuating reason and, if unlikely to recur, should some allowance have been made?

(12) What rule was applied where someone's absence fell between two definitions in line **1**, e.g., 5 days as a result of being sent home in the middle of a working day? Was it applied consistently?

(13) Establish whether SWEAT-Shop operates any regular appraisal of employees and, if so, obtain recent appraisals of VP with a view to exploring any marked discrepancy between the appraisal and lines 2 to 5 of the assessment, which may measure the same qualities.

(14) In line 2 the definition of 'poor' which VP scored implies some unsatisfactory behaviour. Has he ever been warned?

(15) Why is there an alteration here? Has someone adjusted the marking to give a pre-determined result?

(16) In line 3, the definitions are quite ill-defined. Why has VP been given 2 points rather than 3 when the difference is so vague? What more would have been required of him to get the higher mark?

(17) In line 4, 'attitude' is always a vague and highly subjective quality. Yet it is here given the highest weighting of all. What evidence can SWEAT-Shop adduce to show that VP's low mark is factually justified?

(18) Why is line 5 included at all? If VP's job remains to be done, why penalise him for being likely to stick at it?

(19) The score is added up wrongly. It should be 32. Is such carelessness indicative of a cavalier attitude to the whole process? (Do not suppose this is fanciful: it derives from the authors'experience.)

Chapter 12

1. Helpfully or not, the correct answer is Yes and No! Yes, in that the key test is the two-stage question from *Spijkers* that we introduced at **12.5.3.1**: can we identify a *stable economic entity that retains its identity* before and after the transfer? No, in that the decision in that case and all the others that have developed from it since emphasise that the answer depends on all aspects—function, assets (which includes premises, plant and machinery, goodwill, work-in-progress, stocks and so on), employees, etc.—and that no one factor is ever decisive.

2. There are at least five important points to make.

(a) The client will automatically acquire with the transferred undertaking all its current employees—unless any object, which is unlikely to happen.

(b) Their transfer will be on their existing terms and conditions of employment, which may present the client with a significant practical problem if his existing staff are materially different.

(c) Dismissal of anyone because of the transfer is automatically unfair. If the client's wish to achieve economies of scale means reducing the number employed, he can only avoid that automatic result by ensuring that any dismissals fall within the statutory exception of being for an economic, technical, or organisational reason entailing changes in the workforce. It will then be necessary to proceed as for a redundancy—see **Chapter 11**.

(d) The client must consult representatives of his existing employees about the proposed transfer and supply the transferor with information sufficient to enable the transferor to consult employees there too.

(e) The client should ensure that those negotiating the purchase on his behalf are aware of these employment matters so that necessary indemnities can be included in the terms of sale.

Index

U

V

W

Z